797,885 Books
are available to read at

Forgotten Books

www.ForgottenBooks.com

Forgotten Books' App
Available for mobile, tablet & eReader

ISBN 978-1-333-63389-9
PIBN 10528948

This book is a reproduction of an important historical work. Forgotten Books uses state-of-the-art technology to digitally reconstruct the work, preserving the original format whilst repairing imperfections present in the aged copy. In rare cases, an imperfection in the original, such as a blemish or missing page, may be replicated in our edition. We do, however, repair the vast majority of imperfections successfully; any imperfections that remain are intentionally left to preserve the state of such historical works.

Forgotten Books is a registered trademark of FB &c Ltd.
Copyright © 2015 FB &c Ltd.
FB &c Ltd, Dalton House, 60 Windsor Avenue, London, SW19 2RR.
Company number 08720141. Registered in England and Wales.

For support please visit www.forgottenbooks.com

1 MONTH OF FREE READING

at

www.ForgottenBooks.com

By purchasing this book you are eligible for one month membership to ForgottenBooks.com, giving you unlimited access to our entire collection of over 700,000 titles via our web site and mobile apps.

To claim your free month visit:

www.forgottenbooks.com/free528948

* Offer is valid for 45 days from date of purchase. Terms and conditions apply.

English
Français
Deutsche
Italiano
Español
Português

www.forgottenbooks.com

Mythology Photography **Fiction** Fishing Christianity **Art** Cooking Essays Buddhism Freemasonry Medicine **Biology** Music **Ancient Egypt** Evolution Carpentry Physics Dance Geology **Mathematics** Fitness Shakespeare **Folklore** Yoga Marketing **Confidence** Immortality Biographies Poetry **Psychology** Witchcraft Electronics Chemistry History **Law** Accounting **Philosophy** Anthropology Alchemy Drama Quantum Mechanics Atheism Sexual Health **Ancient History Entrepreneurship** Languages Sport Paleontology Needlework Islam **Metaphysics** Investment Archaeology Parenting Statistics Criminology **Motivational**

Cultures and Institutions of Natural History

Essays in the History and Philosophy of Science

Edited by

Michael T. Ghiselin
and
Alan E. Leviton

California Academy of Sciences
San Francisco, California
2000

Copyright ©2000 by the California Academy of Sciences

Published by the California Academy of Sciences
Golden Gate Park, San Francisco, California 94118, USA
Memoirs of the California Academy of Sciences No. 25

ISBN 0-940228-48-3
Library of Congress Card Catalog Number 00-131784

This book has been composed in Adobe Systems Times Roman
Typeset in the United States of American by the California Academy of Sciences
 in Ventura Professional Publisher®; camera-ready copy produced on a
 Lexmark Optra R^{+8} laser printer.

Printed in the United States of America by
 Norcal Printers, San Francisco, California

This is the first of a series of volumes that will be issued
to commemorate the Sesquicentennial of the
California Academy of Sciences
1853–2003

All rights reserved. No part of this publication may be reproduced or
transmitted in any form or by any means, electronic or mechanical,
including photocopying, recording, or any information storage or
retrieval system, without permission in writing from the publisher.

TABLE OF CONTENTS

Introduction, by *Michael T. Ghiselin* and *Alan E. Leviton* (San Francisco, California) . . . .

18th and 19th Centuries

The Museum and the Academy: Geology and Paleontology in the Academia dei Fisiocritici
of Siena During the 18th Century, by *Ezio Vaccari* (Genova, Italy) . . . .

Considerations of Certain Pecularities in Scientific Institutions in Central Europe in the
Eighteenth Century, by *Agnese Visconti* (Pavia, Italy) 27

The Founders of Morphology as Alchemists, by *Michael T. Ghiselin* (San Francisco, California) 39

India: A Case Study of Natural History in a Colonial Setting, by *Alan E. Leviton* and
Michele L. Aldrich (San Francisco, California and Ithaca, New York) 51

The Museums and the Construction of Natural Sciences in Brazil in the 19th Century, by
Maria Margaret Lopes (Campinas, São Paulo, Brazil) 81

Spencer Baird's Dream: A U.S. National Museum, by *Pamela M. Henson* (Washington, DC) 101

Paleontology in Washington DC: A Brief History of Institutional Change or the Waxing
and Waning of Two Disparate Organizations, by *Ellis L. Yochelson* (Washington, DC) 127

Samurai at the Smithsonian: First Japanese Visitors to a Western-Style Museum in the U.S.,
by *Kae Takarabe* (Nagoya, Japan) 161

West & East: The California Academy of Sciences and the Smithsonian Institution,
by *Michele L. Aldrich* and *Alan E. Leviton* (Ithaca, New York and San Francisco, California) 183

People, Plants, and Politics: The Development of Institution-Based Botany in California,
1853–1906, by *Barbara Ertter* (Berkeley, California) 203

Agassiz's Notions of a Museum: The Vision and the Myth, by *Mary Pickard Winsor*
(Toronto, Canada) 249

A Bioeconomic Perspective on the Organization of the Naples Marine Station, by
Michael T. Ghiselin and *Christiane Groeben* (San Francisco, California, and Naples, Italy) 273

The Institutions of Natural History versus Herbert Spencer, 1890–1895,
by *Daniel Becquemont* (Lille, France) 287

20th Century

The Awkward Embrace, by *Léo F. LaPorte* (Redwood City, California) 301

An Essay on the History of the Biosystematists of the San Francisco Bay Area,
by *William Z. Lidicker, Jr.* (Berkeley, California) 315

Scientific Research versus Public Exhibits: A Schizophrenic Aspect of Natural History
Museums, by *Giovanni Pinna* (Milan, Italy) 329

A Philosophy for Natural History Museums, by *Giovanni Pinna* (Milan, Italy) 333

The Ranks and the Names of Species and Higher Taxa, or a Dangerous Inertia of the
Language of Natural History, by *Alessandro Minelli* (Padova, Italy) 339

INDEX 353

Cultures and Institutions of Natural History
Essays in the History and Philosophy of Science

INTRODUCTION

This volume consists mainly of papers delivered at two meetings cosponsored by the Museo Civico di Storia Naturale in Milan and the California Academy of Sciences in San Francisco. The first, on the Culture of Natural History, was held in Milan, November 14–16, 1996. The second, on Institutions of Natural History, was held in San Francisco, October 5–7, 1998. They followed two earlier conferences on Biology as History (Pinna and Ghiselin 1996; Ghiselin and Pinna 1996) likewise held in Milan and San Francisco. We intend to continue the series of meetings and have publications based on them in commemoration of the Academy's sesquicentennial in 2003.

The emphasis here is mainly upon natural history museums and the kind of science that goes on in them. Although the essays were originally written to stand by themselves, when arranged in chronological order they suggest a common theme. To paraphrase Darwin, the culture and institutions of natural history have been, and are being, evolved. They have adapted to local circumstances, diversified, and sometimes even progressed. We may hope that the future holds more than just retrogression and extinction in store.

Read as case studies the essays provide valuable insights into not just how, but why, the institutions have come into being and subsequently been transformed. Previous generations had quite different ideas than we do about how a collection of naturalia is supposed to function and how it should be organized. And there were conflicting goals and serious disputes about policy, much as there are today. Often, though not always, the institutions turn out to be very different from what had been envisioned by their founders.

Although it was not deliberate, we have given our Italian colleagues both the first word and the last. Obviously Italy has a long history. We should not be surprised at Italians being concerned about the future as well. Essays about what happened on the East Coast of the United States tend to precede those about what happened in California. The traditional historiography of biology has proceeded as if everything important happened within a few miles of Boston, or for those with more of a laboratory orientation, Baltimore. Materials that help to correct the imbalance are included, and in this case it was deliberate. A few other parts of the world that have been neglected are considered here as well.

Ezio Vaccari begins with a discussion on a very old geological and paleontological institution in Italy. Agnese Visconti shows how scientific academies in central Europe have been organized on the basis of quite different philosophies, and with important effects upon the scientific quality of the research. Michael Ghiselin argues that alchemy has had important, but virtually neglected, influences upon some branches of biology. Next there are two essays on natural history museums in parts of the world far distant from Europe. Alan Leviton and Michele Aldrich consider India as an example of colonial science and argue that contrary to the views of some historiographers, colonial science was neither done by lesser minds nor was it subservient to the special interest of the stay-at-home European savants. Maria Lopes treats museums of nineteenth century Brazil. Then come four essays having to do with museums in Washington D.C. The early history of the Smithsonian is treated in some detail by Pamela Henson. The disciplines of geology and paleontology engaged the attention of two separate organizations in that city, the Smithsonian Institution and the U.S. Geological Survey, and Ellis Yochelson considers among other things some of the consequences of that. Kae Takarabe recounts the mid-19th century visit of some Japanese dignitaries, who obviously had very different values than those of their hosts. Michele Aldrich and Alan Leviton next discuss the relationships between the Smithsonian Institution and the California Academy of Sciences, and the focus shifts to the West Coast. Barbara Ertter examines botany in California, considering several institutions, some highly significant personalities and their personal likes and dislikes, often for one another, and the shift from free-standing museum to university-based research. Returning to the East, Mary P. Winsor's study of the organization of the Museum of Comparative Zoology reveals how the rationale was linked to the conduct of research in a manner that had not been previously understood. Rounding out the treatment of the nineteenth century, we have essays on Anton Dohrn and Herbert Spencer. Michael Ghiselin and Christiane Groeben explain the success of Dohrn's marine laboratory in Naples, Italy, in terms of bioeconomic theory. By contrast, Daniel Becquemont shows how Herbert Spencer became marginalized as the professional evolutionary biologists developed their own laboratories and journals. Léo Laporte examines the life of one of the giants of twentieth century paleontology, George Gaylord Simpson, explaining the difficulties he had with his employers and his colleagues in museum settings. William Lidicker considers an old and venerable club of scientists, the Bay Area Biosystematists, which attracted both experimentalists and museum specialists, thus helping to flesh out our account of natural history in California. To bring this volume to a close, two essays by Giovanni Pinna deal with the philosophy of natural history museums and his perspective on the relationship between research and public exhibits. And, lastly, Alessandro Minelli addresses some possible changes in the manner in which scientific names are bestowed upon groups of organisms, a matter, that, in one guise or another, has been of concern to museum-based scientists for more than two centuries.

If there is one thread that clearly connects all of the essays in this volume, it is that the science which engages the attention of museum scientists, from its earliest days, changes along with its sponsoring institutions. The essays in the volume show that change is not only not a stranger to those associated with museums, but that museum scientists often play leading roles in initiating the very changes to which they and their institutions must then adapt.

At this point, we want to express our appreciation to the many people who in one way or another participated in the development of this volume. We already noted that many of those who contributed papers to the volume also took part in one or more of the workshops at which they gave oral presentations. We must add that several of the papers the editors chose to include came by invitation; these include the paper by Pamela Henson and two additional contributions she recommended, one by Maria Margaret Lopes and a second by Kae Takarabe. Also, William Lidicker's essay on the Bay Area Biosystematists, originally submitted for publication in another Academy series, was transferred to this volume because the editors felt it contained material germane to their central theme. And then, there is the long list of reviewers who pored through each of the papers with fine-toothed combs. We want to take this opportunity to acknowledge the work they did and to thank them for taking on what is ofttimes a not-too-pleasant job. In addition to the contributors, several of whom were asked to review one or more of the papers, other than their own, we are appreciative of the work done by Steve Anderson (University of the Pacific), Kennard Bork (Denison University), William Brice (University of Pittsburgh at Johnstown), Thomas Daniel (California Academy of Sciences), Robert Drewes (California Academy of Sciences), J. Thomas Dutro, Jr. (U.S. Geological Survey, Washington, DC), Terrence Gosliner (California Academy of Sciences), Mikael Härlin (University of Växjö), James Griesemer (University of California, Davis), Nina Jablonski (California Academy of Sciences), Patrick Kociolek (California Academy of Sciences), Ernst Mayr (Harvard University), Nancy Slack (Russell Sage College), Alberto Simonetta (University of Florence), Joseph Slowinski (California Academy of Sciences), and Betty Smocovitis (University of Florida). Lastly, we are pleased to acknowledge Michele Aldrich who not only helped in the ordinary review process but then read the entire work with an eagle eye, saving both the editors and authors from countless embarrassments.

INTRODUCTION

DEDICATION

About the time of 1996 meeting of our informal group of essayists, our friend and colleague Giovanni Pinna retired as director of the Museo Civico di Storia Naturale. Subsequently, he has played a leading role in the formulation of museum policy as well as being a prolific author. Given the role he played in establishing our collaboration and given his ongoing commitment to the continuation of the biannual meetings of the group, we take great pleasure in dedicating this volume to Professor Pinna. We and our friends and associates who have participated in these programs look forward to many more years of productive collaboration with Giovanni Pinna.

Michael T. Ghiselin and Alan E. Leviton
San Francisco, California
31 July 2000

Giovanni Pinna
At the California Academy of Sciences, San Francisco,
for the fourth international meeting of the consortium
on Cultures and Institutions of Natural History in the
Biological and Earth Sciences, November 6, 1998

The Museum and the Academy
Geology and Paleontology in the Accademia dei Fisiocritici of Siena during the 18th Century

EZIO VACCARI
Centro di Studio sulla Storia della Tecnica, C.N.R.
via Balbi 6, 16126 Genova, Italy
tel. +39 0102465459 fax +39 0102099826
E-mail: ezio.vaccari@lettere.unige.it

This paper analyzes the role of an early geological and paleontological museum within an 18th century scientific academy, the *Accademia dei Fisiocritici* of Siena in Italy. Starting as a small cabinet, it developed gradually as a more articulated natural history museum during the 19th century. The case of Siena was not isolated in Italy because, for example, the importance of the paleontological collection of Giuseppe Monti (*Museum Diluvianum*) in the Institute of Science of Bologna at the beginning of the century can also be cited. The establishment of a 'specialized' museum at the Fisiocritici confirms the fundamental 18th century links among geological fieldwork, production of scientific writings, collection, classification and display of naturalistic specimens. Thanks to the scientific activity of the Fisiocritici, today Siena has a museum of natural history linked to the University and created within an Academy as a significant expression of the 18th century Italian science.

Riassunto

Questo studio ricostruisce la formazione ed il ruolo di un museo geologico e paleontologico all'interno di un'accademia scientifica settecentesca, l'Accademia dei Fisiocritici di Siena. Le prime collezioni di fossili, rocce e minerali furono infatti il punto di partenza per la costituzione ed il graduale ampliamento di un articolato museo di storia naturale nel corso dell'Ottocento. Il caso senese non fu unico nell'Italia del Settecento, poiché basta ricordare, ad esempio, l'importanza della collezione paleontologica *(Museum Diluvianum)* costituita da Giuseppe Monti nell'Istituto delle Scienze di Bologna all'inizio del secolo. La creazione di un primo museo 'specializzato' all'interno dell'Accademia dei Fisiocritici conferma quindi il fondamentale rapporto settecentesco tra ricerca geologica sul campo, produzione di scritti scientifici, raccolta, classificazione ed esposizione di campioni fossili, rocciosi e minerali. Grazie all'attività scientifica dei Fisiocritici oggi Siena dispone di un museo di storia naturale collegato all'Università e formatosi all'interno di un'accademia che rappresenta un'espressione significativa dello sviluppo della scienza italiana nel Settecento.

The role of the scientific academies and the meaning of their naturalistic museums are significant topics, though still too little studied, within the rich context of the Italian natural sciences in the 18th century. During the last decades, historians have undertaken fascinating studies of naturalistic collecting in the 16th and in the 17th centuries, as recently shown by the detailed works of Giuseppe Olmi (1992) and Paula Findlen (1994), as well as by several interdisciplinary studies on the "Cabinet of Curiosities" and "Wunderkammern" (Lugli, 1983; Impey and MacGregor, 1985). However, if in the 16th and 17th centuries the collections and museums of natural history — together with the botanical gardens — can be considered alternative and complementary to the culture of universities and academies (Maccagni, 1981), in the 18th century this relationship started to change. Naturalistic collections were still mainly assembled and owned by individuals who were not always linked to institutions, but gradually some of these collections became part of the scientific academies, which also established new museums in their premises.

This turning-point took place in particular, but not exclusively, within State-supported institutions, such as major national academies, which "were more likely to possess well-equipped astronomical observatories, botanical gardens, laboratories, and cabinets of natural history or experimental physics" (McClellan, 1985:16). The Italian academicians began to contribute to the building of these museums of "natural curiosities" while collecting specimens for their own private cabinets: in some significant cases, distinguished naturalists were directly involved in the curation of the academic museums and vouched for their quality and authenticity. Consequently, from the late 18th century, academic museums were regularly visited by foreign travellers and were enriched by donations of private collections from the members of a local scientific community.

General Considerations

This paper intends to stress a relevant aspect for the study of the scientific academies and for the historical development of a culture of natural history in Italy. The subject is the making and the function of an early specialized naturalistic museum. The example studied is based on the geological and paleontological collections within the *Accademia delle Scienze detta de' Fisiocritici* of Siena in Tuscany, one of the major Italian scientific academies of the second half of the 18th century.

This case-study involves some significant issues:

(1) First of all, it confirms the general 18th century redefinition of natural history, which led to a redefinition of the naturalistic museum itself. The main goal was no longer to assemble "Cabinets of Curiosities" and "Wunderkammern," as in the two previous centuries, but a "more systematic and normative approach to collecting" (Findlen, 1994:399), which determined the creation of the first specialized museums. These collections started to be 'disciplinary oriented' — especially toward zoology, botany, and paleontology — for example the paleontological *Museum Diluvianum* in the *Istituto delle Scienze* of Bologna (Institute of Science, later Academy of Science). This impressive collection was assembled by Giuseppe Monti (1682–1760), probably during the 1710s, and was initially located in his own house (Sarti, 1988, 1992). In 1720, Monti became assistant to the director of the Museum of Natural History of the Institute of Science of Bologna. During the following years he travelled extensively in the Bolognese hills and in the northern Apennines to collect specimens to enrich his *Museum Diluvianum*.

(2) Moreover, the case of the Fisiocritici shows the process of gradual opening to the public of an institution originally conceived as a closed elitarian group. This was determined in part by its transformation to a State-supported official academy in 1759. A contributing factor was also the early links with the University of Siena, which became particularly strong during the 19th century and determined the present state of symbiosis betweeen the two institutions. Consequently the 'use' of the naturalistic museum within the Academy gradually moved from the original function of a systematic and illustrative support of researches of academicians toward display and didactic purposes.

(3) Finally, the early naturalistic museum at the Fisiocritici was strongly linked to fieldwork in surrounding localities. In fact the geological and paleontological collections assembled during the 18th and 19th centuries largely represented the results of several detailed researches in the Tuscan territory; but to historians they also show the conscious attempt of a community of scientists to reconstruct a geological history based on a regional scale. Within this context, the making of an

academic museum was not the aim which determined the fieldwork, rather it was the consequence of that typical exploring attitude of the 18th-century Tuscan naturalists, so well described in the writings of Francesco Rodolico (1945; 1963).

Italian scientific academies in the 18th century were essentially centers for presentation and discussion of individual researches, which were later officially diffused through printed transactions — such as *Atti, Commentarii, Memorie* or *Mémoires* — though often without a regular periodicity. McClellan (1985:99–104; 127–133) has provided a short overview of the activity of the Italian scientific academies, mainly based on secondary literature. A modern comparative historical study, which analyzes in depth the socio-political context and the scientific production of these societies, is still needed. Such a study could start from the excellent work undertaken in recent years by several historians on the history of the Academy of Sciences of Bologna (Università degli Studi di Bologna, 1979; Tega, 1986; Tega, 1987; Cavazza, 1990; Angelini, 1993).

In spite of the lively context of activities of the 18th-century Tuscan academies, which attracted the interest of the skillful historian Eric W. Cochrane (1953; 1961), the Academy of Fisiocritici is probably one of the most neglected of the Italian scientific societies. The only works available on its early history are the old writings by Carlo Sanquirico (1891), Michele Maylender (1929) and Francesco Spirito (1934), the booklet by Carlo Ricci (1972) and some papers on the history of science in Siena (Baccetti et al., 1985), which also treat particular aspects of the scientific activities of the Fisiocritici. Most of these works are based on the same manuscript source, compiled by Massimiliano Ricca in 1818 (Ricci, 1985a), which deals with the early history of the Fisiocritici. This unsatisfactory historiographical situation is not due to lack of primary sources: in fact, the richness of the archives of the Senese academy recently has been described in detail in the printed catalogue of its oldest materials, such as manuscripts, letters and documents of the 17th and 18th centuries (Bacci, Parrini and Vannozzi, 1994). Furthermore, the existence of manuscripts and correspondence related to the early years of the Academy, kept in the Public Library (Biblioteca Comunale) of Siena, was also well known to historians (Maylender, 1929:25–26; Ricci, 1972:37–49).

Early History of the Fisiocritici

The Fisiocritici Academy of Siena, one of the oldest Italian scientific academies, was founded in 1691 by Pirro Maria Gabbrielli (1643–1705), a Senese professor of theoretical medicine and botany, together with twenty other scholars (Fig. 1). Its establishment as "accademia fisico medica" was probably inspired by the Florentine *Accademia del Cimento* (Academy of Experiment, 1657–1667). In fact, the first article of its academic constitution stated that the work of the Senese academy had to be based on "nuove esperienze" (new experiments). The early years of Fisiocritici's activity, until the death of Gabbrielli, were devoted mainly to physical experiments and medical lectures, as shown by the content of two manuscript volumes of unpublished academic dissertations dating from 1691 to 1731 (Fisiocritici. Dissertazioni, 1691–1731). During this period,

FIGURE 1. Shield adopted in 1692 by the Academy of Fisiocritici, with the motto "Veris quod possit vincere Falsa" (from Lucretius *De rerum natura*) and the Lapis Lidius, the stone for testing the authenticity of gold and silver.

the Fisiocritici organized several private and public meetings in the library of the Senese main Hospital ("Spedale grande"), where Gabbrielli usually gave his lectures in medicine. Later, thanks to the influential protection of the Medici family — in particular Cardinal Francesco Maria Medici, brother of the Granduke Cosimo III — the Academy enlarged its activities, and in 1694 it obtained a new residence within the University of Siena.

The academicians gathered periodically in a room called "Sala della Sapienza" (Fig. 2) for all the meetings, which were carefully recorded in the minute-books (Fisiocritici. Verbali, 1691–1768). In the private meetings, the new members and officers were nominated and various decisions about internal rules were taken. In each public meeting, four lectures were given and also physical experiments were displayed to different kinds of audience. For this reason, some instruments were kept in the academic room: the "heliometro fisiocritico," the sundial or meridian line made by Gabbrielli in 1703-04 (Gabbrielli, 1705), and the so called "antlia pneumatica" or "pneumatic horizontal machine of Boyle," which was often used in public demonstrations between April 1701 and December 1704 (Fisiocritici. Verbali, 1691–1768). The latter was an early 18th-century modification of the air-pump, originally conceived as a vertical instrument by the Anglo-Irish scholar Robert Boyle (1627–1691), that was constructed by his assistant Robert Hooke (1635–1702) and first described in 1660 (Shapin, 1985). The air-pump kept at the Fisiocritici had been constructed by Gabbrielli (De Gregorio, 1992:170). It was used to perform several experiments, including impressive demonstrations of the power of the vacuum pressure of the air, different observations on the behaviour of air, both compressed and expanded, and also the fact that both life and combustion were impossible in the vacuum. According to Cochrane (1961:127), the Fisiocritici also constructed "a 'Torricellian tube,' or mercury barometer, upon which they based their discussion of weight, gravity, and the density of the atmosphere."

FIGURE 2. "Sala della Sapienza," the meeting room of the Academy of Fisiocritici (plate published in Gabbrielli, 1705).

Therefore, it is evident that at the beginning of its history the Academy of Fisiocritici housed some physical instruments, but still no naturalistic specimens. There is no mention of a possible establishment of a museum in the first constitution of the Academy (Fisiocritici. Dissertazioni, 1691–1731:cc. 3–4). In particular, the unpublished dissertations and the minute-books from 1691 to 1750 show only occasional interest for subjects relating to the Earth sciences, apart from some lectures on earthquakes, which were a frequent phenomenon in the Senese area, and an isolated but significantly timely presentation of the book by Carl Nicolaus Lang (1670–1741), *Historia Lapidum Figuratorum Helvetiae* (1708), where the Swiss fossils were considered as formed by dust borne germs of living species (Fisiocritici. Verbali, 1691–1768:17 giugno 1708).

Giuseppe Baldassarri and the Natural History Collection

A few years after the death of Gabrielli, from about 1710, the Fisiocritici went through a long period of crisis, which ended in 1759 when the Tuscan regency government of Francis of Lorraine assumed both financial and management control of the Academy (Pasta, 1992; De Gregorio, 1992). The central figure of this process of reopening, which took place after about 15 years during which time no meetings or academic activities were held, was the powerful minister Pompeo Neri (1706–1776). In November 1759, Neri promoted the establishment of an annual state fund for the Fisiocritici to cover expenses arising from the experiments and for the purchase of new physical instruments (De Gregorio, 1992:169–171). Meanwhile, again under the direction of Neri, the Academy reinforced its links with the University, initially admitting all the professors as members (Fisiocritici. Verbali, 1691–1768:11 dicembre 1759), and shortly thereafter acquired new thermometers, hygrometers, barometers and siphons for public experiments (Fisiocritici. Verbali, 1691–1768:15 aprile 1760).

In these first years of renewed academic activity, Pompeo Neri also promoted the formation of a naturalistic collection at the Fisiocritici: he encouraged the interest in natural history shown by some academicians and used his political power to convince several Senese nobles to donate specimens from their private collections to the new "piccolo museo di cose naturali" (De Gregorio, 1992:183; Cochrane, 1961:57, footnote 51). According to the botanist Giovanni Campani (1860:21), who was director of the Fisiocritici Museum of Natural History in the late 19th century, the museum itself was founded in 1759 by Giuseppe Baldassarri (1705–1785), one of the most active members of the Fisiocritici. This statement was confirmed by the secretary Emidio Selvani (1865), who also pointed out the lack of an academic room suitable for the specimens during these early years. In reality, although Baldassarri had started to assemble in his own private collection some rocks and fossils, which he collected on frequent fieldtrips in the Senese region during the 1750s, his official appointment as curator of the newly established small naturalistic museum at the Fisiocritici was ordered by Pompeo Neri only in the summer of 1766 (Fisiocritici. Epistole, 1692–1799, n. 276, 277; De Gregorio, 1992:183, 205).

Giuseppe Baldassarri had already been secretary of the Fisiocritici from 1729 to 1732. In 1759 he had been nominated professor of natural history at the University of Siena, with the duty of conducting some experiments at the academic meetings (De Gregorio, 1992:170). His position as "Soprintendente" (curator) of the natural history collection, of the sundial and of the physical instruments kept at the "Sala della Sapienza," is officially stated by the archival sources on the 29th of March 1768, when the Fisiocritici applied to the Granduke Peter Leopold for renewal of Baldassarri's appointment as permanent (Fisiocritici. Verbali, 1768–1812:30 aprile 1768).

Baldassarri was already well known among the 18th century Italian naturalists, especially after the publication of his first works on the clay strata (1750) and on the most remarkable spring of mineral waters in the Senese region (1756). In these writings, the Tuscan naturalist paid particular attention to the geological investigation of the territory. He also clearly stated the importance of a regional collection of "produzioni naturali" (natural products), compiling and publishing together with his work the catalogue of the naturalistic museum of the Senese noble Giovanni Venturi Gallerani (Baldassarri, 1750). This catalogue was divided in two sections, the first listing minerals, rocks and earths, the second, invertebrate fossils ("Testacei Fossili"). The 167 specimens of rocks, minerals and fossils were analyzed in relation to their nature and provenance, and were also described in detail with the help of the available specialized literature. The absence of the records and our inability to recognize in the present museum most of the original naturalistic collection assembled by Baldassarri — due to the lack of an 18th century catalogue and of original labels — does not allow us to know if the Venturi Gallerani collection was later included in the museum of the Fisiocritici (Guasparri, 1992:69). In 1772, these two cabinets were still separate, as reported by the Swedish mineralogist and traveller Johann Jakob Ferber (1743–1790), who visited the academic museum of the Fisiocritici, but regretted not having seen the Venturi Gallerani collection (Ferber, 1776:247–248).

The formation of the early naturalistic collection of the Academy of Fisiocritici during the last forty years of the 18th century was not exclusively the result of the work of Baldassarri, although his contribution was certainly fundamental for enlargement of the museum in the late 1760s. In fact, Baldassarri was not alone in studying the rocks, minerals and fossils of the Senese territory. The contents of the first seven volumes of the academic transactions *Atti dell'Accademia delle Scienze di Siena detta de' Fisiocritici* (Bacci, 1981) and the handwritten dissertations read in the public meetings (Fisiocritici. Memorie, 1759–1798), which were not always published in the *Atti*, show an articulated interest by a small but active group of academicians in various geological and paleontological subjects.

The first volume of the *Atti*, published in 1761, was a special medical issue on the question of the inoculation of smallpox (Fadda, 1983); it was followed during the rest of the century by six more volumes printed in 1763, 1767, 1771, 1774, 1781 and 1794. The significant variety of the scientific subjects treated in this first series of transactions, rich in papers also from non-Senese scholars, has been well emphasized (Pasta, 1992; De Gregorio and Landi, 1992:172–174); the writings on medical topics, the most consistent group of articles published in the *Atti* during the 18th century, has been analyzed in detail by Francesca Vannozzi (Bacci, Parrini and Vannozzi, 1994:203–245); the precise extent of the significant contributions devoted to the earth sciences in the Academy of Fisiocritici will be the subject of a later study. At this time, however, it is possible to provide the following quantitative data: from 1763 to 1794 the *Atti* published 43 articles on medicine, 25 on mathematics, 20 on physics, 15 on earth sciences, 11 on astronomy, 11 on chemistry (of which 8 papers were on the analysis of mineral waters), 7 on botany, 5 on hydraulics, 4 on zoology, 3 on civil engineering, 3 on meteorology, 2 on veterinary medicine, and 2 on agronomy.

In spite of evident interest for the earth sciences, which, in the *Atti*, was second only to the predominant medical and physical-mathematical sciences, the existence of an organized working-group, which systematically contributed to the building of a specialized museum at the Fisiocritici, is not proved. Nevertheless, the common attitude of many scholars at the time was to explore in detail the Senese territory, describe its "produzioni naturali" (rocks, fossils, minerals, and also plants), and collect specimens, which went to increase both their private collection and the academic museum.

Consequently, these local academicians, sometimes stimulated by different scientific targets, soon produced a mosaic of data which gave shape to a sort of 'naturalistic map' of the Senese area. In this work, the influence of the great Florentine scientist Giovanni Targioni Tozzetti (1712–1783) was more than evident (Targioni Tozzetti, 1751–1754). The importance of the naturalistic travel, the accuracy of the observations in the field, the process of collecting specimens, the cataloguing of them in a published paper, and finally classifying and displaying them in a museum, were all elements of a growing new sense of the natural history within this small but lively scientific community.

Giuseppe Baldassarri, as curator of the museum and later president of the Academy from 1772 to 1785 (year of his death), played a central role in stimulating the geological studies of the Fisiocritici in the 1760s and in the early 1770s. In his works of those years (Baldassarri, 1763a; 1763b; 1767; 1771a; 1771b), the collecting of rock and fossil specimens was strictly linked to his interpretations of the origin and the formation of strata which he observed in the Senese territory. According to Baldassarri (1750:6–7; 1756:23–24), the sea had covered all the Tuscan region for a very long time and had determined in successive times the deposition of several kinds of rock strata, which included different groups of fossils of the same species, well separated and distinct from each other, as the distinguished naturalist AntonioVallisneri had already noticed in his book *De' Corpi Marini* (1721).

The regular distribution of these fossils and the evidences of a series of gradual different lithological sedimentations, suggested to Baldassarri (1756:25–26) an interpretation which today can be defined as "uniformitarian." It was expressed by the statement that the natural phenomena — mainly of sedimentation and erosion — visible in the present sea also quietly and regularly occurred "nella maniera stessa" (in the same way) in the ancient sea which had entirely covered Tuscany. This interpretation clearly rejected the idea of a major catastrophic event, such as the Deluge, for explaining the geological changes which had occurred in the Senese territory.

On the other hand, some years later Baldassarri realized that the theorized uniformity, based on the constant action of the sea waters, could not explain why some groups of fossils were found completely mixed, broken, squashed and confused. Moreover, these fossil remains seemed to be related to exotic species not living in the Mediterranean sea. This interpretation was also supported by the finding of fossil bones of so called "elephants" in different European regions, including Italy.

When Baldassarri published his paper on the description of an extraordinary fossil jaw found in the Senese territory (1767), he was conscious that the Earth's surface had undergone many "strani cangiamenti" (strange changes) during a long and complex geological history. The problem now was to find and demonstrate the causes of these changes, which could be also of a catastrophic nature ("gravi rovesci"). However, the firm rejection of the geological role of the Deluge, not considered adequate in explaining all the geological and paleontological features observed in the Senese area, also determined Baldassarri's scepticism toward the theory of a big flood, which could have moved to Europe the remains of the exotic animals and plants, later to be fossilized. On the other hand, he seemed to accept the hypothesis that a much warmer ancient European climate had provided the right environment for the life of those species. Nevertheless, he concluded, the real proof of this hypothesis was not yet available and too many doubts ("tante incertezze") did not allow him to understand the real cause of the Earth's changes. According to Baldassarri, the research-work of the scientists had not yet accumulated a sufficient quantity of "materiali" (material data) for solving this geological question. His words expressed properly the meaning given to the museum at the Fisiocritici, which had just been entrusted to the Senese professor of natural history and was to become the collecting place of these "materiali" (Baldassarri, 1767:243–248).

In fact, in the second part of his paper, Baldassarri described and figured new and important specimens which had contributed to the enlargement of his reflections on the complexity of the history of the Earth (Fig. 3). The specimens included two parts of a fossil jaw, now identified as being from a Pliocene mastodon, *Anancus arvernensis* (Fig. 4), which are still kept in the present paleontological collection of the Academy of Fisiocritici in Siena (Guasparri, 1992:84, 87–88). Despite of his knowledge of the findings of various fossil bones of "Elefanti" (elephants), Baldassarri did not relate

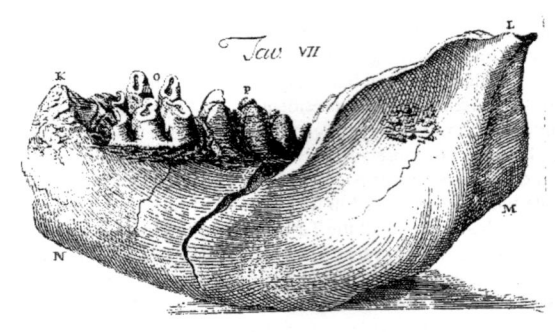

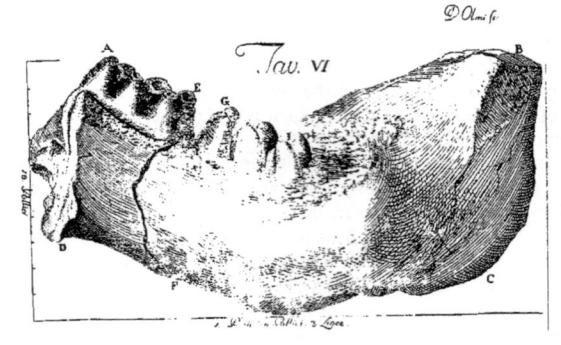

FIGURE 3. Fossil jaw described by Giuseppe Baldassarri (1767: plates 6 and 7).

his specimens to a possible large mammal: according to him, the animal to whom those bones had belonged was still unknown, but probably was neither a big fish nor a "mostro marino," such as a whale (Baldassarri, 1767:249–253).

Baldassarri's paleontological paper was not an isolated contribution within the scientific researches carried out by the Fisiocritici in the 1760s. Again, in the third volume of the *Atti*, Francesco Caluri, later professor of logic and practical medicine at the University of Siena and president of the Fisiocritici from 1785 to 1789, published a detailed description of some fossil shells found in the Senese hills (Caluri, 1767). One of these shells was of a Pliocene gastropod ("porporite"), very similar to a specimen of *Hexaplex conglobatus* that is to this day kept in the Museum of Fisiocritici (Guasparri, 1992:74). The gastropod described by Caluri contained an unknown little shell (eventually named "crepidula parasitica") and he tried to identify

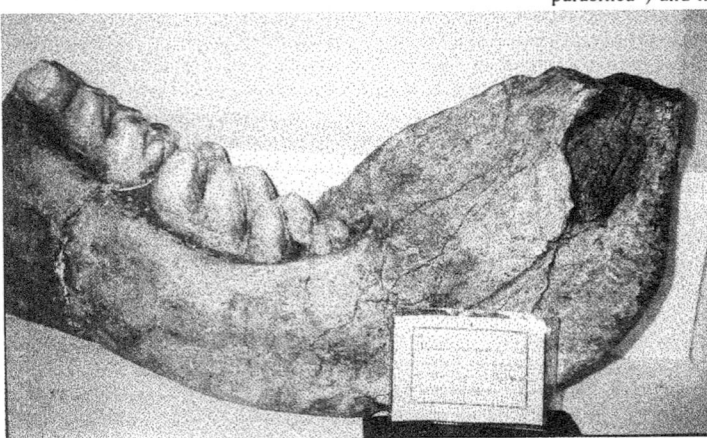

FIGURE 4. Fossil jaw of the Pliocene mastodon *Anancus arvernensis*, collected and described by Giuseppe Baldassarri in 1767, as presently displayed in the museum of the Academy of Fisiocritici, Paleontological Collections (photo by E. Vaccari).

both of them using the available contemporary literature. It is interesting to note that in the plate at the end of the paper (Fig. 5), the fossil specimens found in the Senese territory (numbered 1–4) were compared with a similar living species of the Tyrrhenian Sea (numbered 5–7). Caluri undertook his paleontological fieldwork under the influence of Baldassarri's research, and the two scientists were constantly in contact. In September 1765 Baldassarri explored the area where Caluri had found the fossil shells and then communicated his observations to his colleague, who was preparing the lecture to read at the Fisiocritici in November of the same year (Caluri, 1767:265–266, note *b*). Likewise, Caluri entirely adopted Baldassarri's geological "uniformitarianism," based on the idea that an ancient sea had covered the Tuscan territory for a very long time and later had gradually retreated from it ("appoco appoco ritirato"). Also, the catastrophic results of the Deluge could not be accepted by Caluri for explaining the perfect state of preservation of fossil molluscs with extremely fragile shells like the ones described in his paper (Caluri, 1767:262–264).

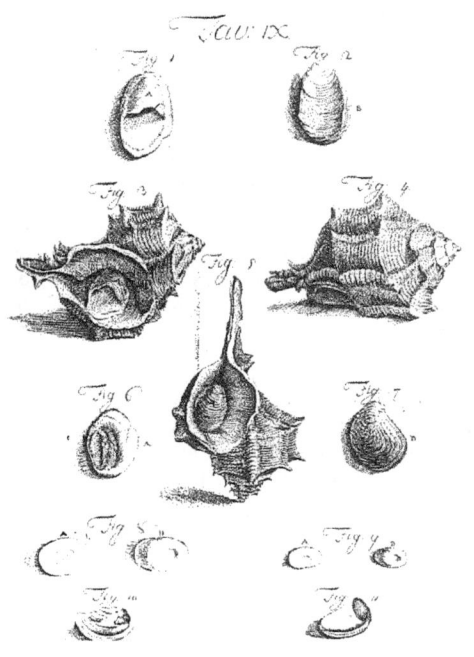

FIGURE 5. "Porporite" and "Crepidula parasitica" described by Francesco Caluri (1767: plate 9).

It is not clear if all the specimens (fossils, but also rocks, minerals and plants) described in the papers published in the *Atti* during the second half of the 18th century were given to the academic museum of natural history. Caluri, like Baldassarri, had his own private collection of "natural products," which included many varieties of fossil molluscs from the Senese area (Caluri, 1767:274, note *a*). In any case, different kinds of primary sources can still provide new pieces of information about the early collections of the museum of the Fisiocritici, in particular the numerous 18th century writings on the Tuscan territory not directly published by the Senese academy or apparently related to it. Of course, this research requires a long and detailed survey which at the present must be considered still in progress, though it has already produced some significant results. For example, Annibale Bastiani, doctor of medicine, naturalist and member of the Academy since 1739, in his book on the analysis of the mineral waters of San Casciano (between Florence and Siena) reported collecting of more than 20 species of fossil molluscs, mainly cephalopods (Bastiani, 1770:8). The specimens were immediately sent to the Academy of Fisiocritici in separate boxes which included a full series of different sizes for every species. This episode demonstrates that the museum of the Fisiocritici was gradually becoming a reference point for an increasing number of Tuscan naturalists. It did not substitute for the private collections, still assembled by most of these scientists, but it could be a possible and highly considered alternative.

Expansion, Reputation, and Continuance

In 1772, the newly elected president, Giuseppe Baldassarri, and all the academicians obtained permission from the Granduke to admit the university students and other non-members to the private meetings of the Academy (Fisiocritici. Verbali, 1768–1812:26 marzo 1772). In this way the Fisiocritici acquired an institutional dimension which reinforced their links with the University of Siena. At the same time, the Academy enlarged its European reputation by nominating new, distinguished members from other Italian and European states. Some prominent non-Senese scientists — such as Giovanni Arduino, Pietro Arduino, Leonardo Ximenes, Felice Fontana, Giovanni Bianchi and Paolo Frisi — had become academicians during the 1760s, but in the following decade Alessandro Volta, the Swiss naturalist Charles Bonnet, and the English scholar John Symonds were also elected Fisiocritici. The geologist Giovanni Arduino (1714–1795), one of the first new members nominated after the academic reopening of 1759, in 1773 promoted the affiliation of the famed botanist Linnaeus and of three distinguished mineralogists from Austria, Saxony and Sweden, respectively Ignaz von Born, Johann Friedrich Wilhelm Charpentier, and Johann Jakob Ferber (Fisiocritici. Verbali, 1768–1812:16 giugno 1773, 15 dicembre 1773).

Ferber had visited Siena and the Academy of Fisiocritici between April and May 1772, during his long mineralogical travel through Italy. He noted that "the University has several learned and celebrated Professors, which are members of the Academy of Sciences, established in former times; but of late revived under the name of *Accademia de' Fisiocritici*. The library, and the cabinet of Natural curiosities, is common to the University and the Academy. The latter has got a great celebrity by the four volumes of its transactions. The cabinet was, some years ago, bequeathed to the Academy by its president, the Professor of Natural History Dr. Giuseppe Baldassarri, who collected it, and has still under his inspection" (Ferber, 1776:247). This last statement seems to confirm that the most relevant part of the original museum of the Fisiocritici, promoted in the middle 1760s by Pompeo Neri, was formed by a large donation from Baldassarri's private collection. Still, Ferber recalled in 1772 the existence in Siena of other two naturalistic cabinets separated from the academic museum and owned by Baldassarri and Francesco Caluri. Ferber's brief description of the most remarkable specimens kept in these three collections (see Appendix at the end of this paper) today represents the best primary source about the content of the museum of the Fisiocritici in the 18th century, which later was probably enriched by the private collections of Baldassarri and Caluri (Ferber, 1776:248–254).

After his nomination as a member of the Fisiocritici, Ferber immediately wrote from his residence in Bohemia to the secretary, Domenico Bartaloni, promising future contributions to the *Atti* and the possible shipment of Swedish minerals for the academic cabinet of "natural curiosities" (Fisiocritici. Epistole, 1692–1799:n. 440). Indeed, Ferber published a geo-mineralogical dissertation in the fifth volume of the Senese transactions (Ferber, 1774), but it is not known if any specimens from Sweden were ever sent to the Fisiocritici.

During the last two decades of the 18th century and at the beginning of the 19th century, the scientific heritage of Baldassarri was continued by his assistant Biagio Bartalini (1750–1822) and by the naturalist Ambrogio Soldani (1736–1808), one of the most remarkable Italian scientists of the late 18th century. These two scholars contributed greatly to the improvement of a detailed knowledge of the physical characteristics of the Tuscan region, following the footsteps of Giovanni Targioni Tozzetti.

Bartalini was professor at the University of Siena, where he took over the chair of Baldassarri in 1780. Two years later he became curator of the naturalistic museum of the Fisiocritici and director of the attached botanical garden in 1783 (Ferri and Miraldi, 1993). From 1805 to 1812, he was also secretary and, from 1815 to 1822, president of the Academy. Bartalini's writings, published in the *Atti*, show the results of intense research activity undertaken for illustrating and analyzing the "natural products" of the Senese territory, with particular attention to botany (Bacci, 1981:108). The impressive amount of fieldwork resulted in a considerable naturalistic collection of about 6000 specimens (including many minerals); this was further enriched by the acquisition of the private cabinet of Baldassarri in the middle 1780s (Pasta, 1992:230, footnote 34), which was finally purchased by the Academy of Fisiocritici in 1826, two years after the death of its former president (Guasparri, 1992:103).

The frequent naturalistic travels carried out by Bartalini in the Senese area allowed him to study in particular the geological and mineralogical features of the territory (1781) and some paleontological specimens (1800), as well as the "prodotti naturali" (geological and botanical), which could be observed within the city and surroundings of Siena (1808). In his paper, published in volume eight of the *Atti*, Bartalini described and figured in five plates several fossil specimens, which he attempted to identify as marine flora (Fig. 6). These and other fossils of "straniere produzioni marine" (foreign marine products), which may be found in the Tuscan region, together with many bones of exotic animals, in particular "Elefanti", could not be explained by geological agents such as the volcanic activity and the meteoric waters (Bartalini, 1800:224–227). Nevertheless, Bartalini carefully avoided indicating the possible real cause of these paleontological findings; the 'cause' was considered different ("cagione diversa") from those mentioned, but the reader was left free to formulate his own hypothesis.

The naturalistic tradition in the field established within the Fisiocritici by the works of Baldassarri, Caluri, and later Bartalini also stimulated the early research of the young Paolo Mascagni (1755–1815), a future prominent member of the Senese academy, who became renowned for his advanced anatomical studies, published posthumously between 1823 and 1831 (Ricci, 1985b; Vannozzi, 1996). At the beginning of 1779, Mascagni explored the territory between Siena and Volterra, examining the geological

FIGURE 6. Fossil specimens of marine flora, according to Biagio Bartalini (1800: Plate 8).

and chemical features of the natural pools called "lagoni" that were edged by boric saline incrustations that had formed in conjunction with rock fractures from which gas and saturated steam was escaping into shallow waters. (Burgassi and Donati, 1995). He presented the journal of his observations in a dissertation read at the Fisiocritici in March (Ricci, 1985c); later he analyzed in detail the phenomenon of the "lagoni" in a book published in September of the same year (Mascagni, 1779). It is interesting to note that during his lecture, Mascagni illustrated several lithological and mineralogical specimens collected in the field that later may have been given to the museum of the Fisiocritici.

Ambrogio Soldani, who was secretary of the Fisiocritici from 1802 to 1805, worked extensively on the descriptions of microfossils, in particular Foraminifera (Ricca, 1810; Manasse, 1908; Lipparini, 1987). He was also an excellent field geologist who carefully observed the strata. He distinguished them according to their lithological and fossiliferous contents (clay hills with microfossils / limestone strata with ammonoids) and considered the difference of causes (sea-waters or volcanic fire) and the times of their formation. In his first work, the *Saggio Orittografico* (1780), Soldani analyzed in detail a great number of fossils collected in the field, which were mostly cephalopods related to the clay strata, the so called "terre ammonitiche e nautiliche della Toscana." At the same time he began to assemble an impressive collection of microfossils, which he described in his seminal contribution to micropaleontology, the *Testaceographiae ac Zoophytographiae parvae et microscopicae* (Soldani, 1789–98), well illustrated by a wonderful atlas with 179 plates (Fig. 7).

The micropaleontological collection of Soldani was definitively housed in the natural history museum of the Fisiocritici between 1808 and 1810, in accordance with his last will and testament (Campani, 1860:11). For this reason, it was not damaged by the great earthquake of 1798, which ruined the historical residence of the Fisiocritici at the "Sala della Sapienza," partially destroying the collection of scientific instruments and the original museum (Soldani, 1798). Thus, today, it is possible to admire Soldani'$_s$ micropaleontological collection in its original structure and display, as it represents the most important section of the modern museum of the Academy of Fisiocritici in Siena (Guasparri, 1992:51–55). The 311 specimens of microfossils are contained in small jars with labelled covers, called "vasa." Some specimens are incapsulated between two slides for microscopes (Fig. 8): the numbers of these "vasa" correspond to the groups of specimens listed, described and figured by Soldani in the *Testaceographiae* (Fig. 9–10), which actually can be used as a catalogue of the collection itself.

Rebuilding

After the Napoleonic period, in 1814 the museum of the Academy of Fisiocritici was re-established in the former monastery called "Convento della Rosa" and this is still the present academic residence (Ricci, 1985a:259). Here the naturalistic collections were reorganized under the di-

FIGURE 7. Title page of the second volume of the *Testaceographiae ac Zoophytographiae parvae et microscopicae* of Ambrogio Soldani (1789–1798).

FIGURE 8. Specimens of microfossils from the collection of Ambrogio Soldani, in their original glass jars ("vasa") and slides for microscopes, as presently displayed in the museum of the Academy of Fisiocritici, "Sala Soldani" (photo E. Vaccari).

rection of the president, Biagio Bartalini, and Massimiliano Ricca (1761–1835), the latter an eclectic naturalist interested in geology and paleontology, who was also professor of mathematics and physics at the University of Siena (Selvani, 1865). Around 1829, Ricca provided the first specimens of stuffed animals, especially birds, for the future zoological cabinet. This cabinet was gradually increased by new animals prepared by Francesco Baldacconi, employed as "preparatore del Gabinetto," with an annual budget established by the Academy for the care of the zoological collection (Ricca, 1985b:230–231). In the years following, Gaspero Mazzi, professor of zoology and anatomy, was nominated curator of the museum and contributed personally to the paleontological and mineralogical collections, in particular several Pliocene molluscs and brachiopods, which are still preserved to this day in their original display (Guasparri, 1992:24).

FIGURE 9. Example of cover of a glass jar ("vas") from the micropaleontological collection of Ambrogio Soldani. The "vas" is numbered 226 and its content is described as "Orthocer:³".

The first official report on the state of the Imperial and Royal Museum of Natural History of the Fisiocritici Academy was published in 1841. It presented only the catalogue of the ornithological collection, because the other zoological collections and the cabinet of mineralogy and paleontology were still being reorganized by Mazzi. However, the report stated that the academic collection of fossil and non-fossil shells, which included, of course, all the microfossils of Soldani, had already reached 20,000 specimens (Museo Fisiocritici, 1841).

In the same year, Granduke Leopold II ordered that the Academy was to be regarded as an university-based institution ("stabilimento universitario"). Consequently, its administration and its staff, including the newly appointed curator, Baldacconi, were put under control of the Provost of the

University of Siena (Ricci, 1985a:264). This administrative fusion did not modify the autonomous constitutions of the Fisiocritici, but changed decidedly its relationship with the University. During the years of the Italian wars of independence, from 1848 to 1860, scientific activities were reduced. As a further result of this disruption the publication of the *Atti* was suspended after the tenth volume of the first series (1841) and the second series was started twenty years later. When Tuscany became part of the newly established Kingdom of Italy, the Fisiocritici renewed their constitution (1862) and later gave about half of their rooms to the University's scientific institutes of zoology, botany, anatomy and mineralogy. Meanwhile, the academic museum began to be used by the University for public teaching (Selvani, 1865; Ricci, 1972:27).

After the inventory compiled by Giovanni Campani in 1853, which determined a partial reorganization a few years later (Fisiocritici. Documenti, 1853; Campani, 1860), the description of the Natural History Museum of the Academy was regularly updated in other reports published in the 1860s and 1870s. These documents

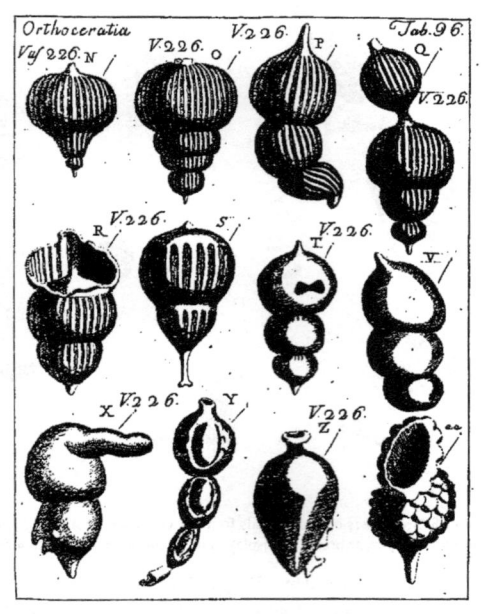

FIGURE 10. Different shapes of microfossils, called "Orthoceratia", contained in the "vas" 226 (Fig. 9) and described by Ambrogio Soldani (1789–1798, plate 96).

showed the constant increase in size of the museum's collections due to frequent donations, in particular of geological, mineralogical and paleontological specimens (Tassi, 1862; Bernardi and Casuccini, 1868; Pantanelli A., 1869, 1873; Pantanelli D., 1876, 1877). In 1862, Pellegrino Bertini and G. Tarduzzi enriched the mineralogical cabinet with 117 specimens of Senese marbles and ornamental stones, while the mining engineer Theodor Haupt left to the Academy 41 minerals from the copper mines near Massa Marittima (Cataloghi, 1905). Among other 19th century donors must be mentioned Francesco Bernardi, who sent a valuable collection of shells, Francesco Valenti Serini, who donated his rich herbarium and his mycological collections (both of which are still partially housed in the Academy), and Baron Bettino Ricasoli, a distinguished figure of Italian politics, who also contributed specimens to enrich the museum of Fisiocritici (Guasparri, 1992:13–14, 31–32 69–71).

Modern Collections and Historical Specimens

In general, within the present museum, identifying the specimens collected and displayed during the 18th century will likely never be possible, apart from the micropaleontological collection assembled by Soldani and the fossil jaw collected by Giuseppe Baldassarri (Guasparri, 1992; Farsi and Guasparri, 1997). The lack of documentation is aggravated by the results of the several reorganizations of the museum that occurred during the 19th century, when the adoption of new schemes of classification led to new arrangements of displays and the elimination of the old labels. Moreover, the curators discarded even old specimens, when a more recently collected and nicer mineral, rock or fossil of the same kind was available. Many duplicates were also probably used for exchanges with other museums or institutions and this contributed to the dispersion of the historical material.

Within this context, it is not easy to reconstruct through primary sources related to the naturalistic museum the debates on the classification of the specimens, because in most cases new labels simply replaced and cancelled the old ones. To date, it seems likely that Giovanni Campani, director of the Natural History Museum of the Fisiocritici, adopted the mineralogical classification established by the French geologist François-Sulpice Beudant (1787–1850) in 1824, later republished in several editions and also translated into Italian (Beudant, 1846). This system was used for arranging the specimens of the mineralogical cabinet of the Fisiocritici around 1867 (Fisiocritici. Documenti, 1867).

Further research works on the 19th century sources will certainly allow us to obtain a better knowledge of these possible scientific discussions among the academicians, as well as to acquire more elements on the history of the Academy of Fisiocritici.

ACKNOWLEDGMENTS

The research for this paper was made possible by a fellowship awarded in 1994–95 by the "Seminario di Storia della Scienza" at the University of Siena. I would like to thank Prof. Paolo Freguglia, Prof. Giulio Barsanti and Dr. Mario De Gregorio for their support and suggestions; Dr. Chiara Bratto, Dr. Anita Bacci and Dr. Ferruccio Farsi for their precious help and assistance during my researches in the library, archive and museum of the Academy of Fisiocritici. Finally, the comments and suggestions provided by Dr. Alan Leviton and Dr. Ellis Yochelson greatly improved the final version of the manuscript.

BIBLIOGRAPHY

ANGELINI, ANNARITA. 1993. *Anatomie Accademiche. 3. L'Istituto delle Scienze e l'Accademia.* Il Mulino Bologna. 573 pp.

BACCETTI, BACCIO, et al. 1985. *Documenti per una storia della scienza senese.* Accademia delle Scienze di Siena detta dei Fisiocritici, Siena. 393 pp. [Memorie, n. 2]

BACCI, ANITA. 1981. Indici della prima serie degli Atti dell'Accademia dei Fisiocritici (1761–1841). *Atti dell'Accademia dei Fisiocritici* ser. 14, 13:105–139.

BACCI, ANITA, DONATELLA PARRINI, and FRANCESCA VANNOZZI. 1994. *I documenti dell'Accademia. 1: Verbali. memorie, epistole ed atti dalla fondazione al secolo XVIII.* Accademia delle Scienze di Siena detta dei Fisiocritici, Siena. 261 pp. [Memorie, n. 5]

BALDASSARRI, GIUSEPPE. 1750. *Osservazioni sopra il sale della creta, con un Saggio di produzioni naturali dello Stato Sanese che si ritrovano nel Museo del Nobil Signor Giovanni Venturi-Gallerani.* F. Rossi, Siena. 36 + 32 pp.

BALDASSARRI, GIUSEPPE. 1756. *Delle acque minerali di Chianciano. Relazione.* A. Bindi, Siena. 273 + 58 pp.

BALDASSARRI, GIUSEPPE. 1763a. Saggio di osservazioni intorno ad alcuni prodotti naturali fatte a Prata ed in altri luoghi della Maremma di Siena. *Atti dell'Accademia delle Scienze di Siena, detta de' Fisiocritici* 2: 1–43.

BALDASSARRI, GIUSEPPE. 1763b. Analisi fisico chimica di un acqua minerale, che scaturisce in vicinanza di Siena chiamata l'Acqua Borra. *Atti dell'Accademia delle Scienze di Siena, detta de' Fisiocritici* 2:44–78.

BALDASSARRI, GIUSEPPE. 1767. Descrizione di una mascella fossile straordinaria trovata nel territorio Sanese. *Atti dell'Accademia delle Scienze di Siena, detta de' Fisiocritici* 3:243–254.

BALDASSARRI, GIUSEPPE. 1771a. Descrizione di un sale neutro deliquescente che si trova nel tufo intorno alla città di Siena. *Atti dell'Accademia delle Scienze di Siena, detta de' Fisiocritici* 4:1–14.
BALDASSARRI, GIUSEPPE. 1771b. Considerazioni sopra i principj costitutivi della pietra amianto per i quali resiste questa alla violenza dei fuochi ordinarj, e si rende atta ad essere filata. *Atti dell'Accademia delle Scienze di Siena, detta de' Fisiocritici* 4:217–232.
BARTALINI, BIAGIO. 1781. Osservazioni di Storia Naturale fatte in alcuni luoghi dello Stato di Siena, ed attorno ai Lagoni di Castel Nuovo di Valdicecina presso Volterra. *Atti dell'Accademia delle Scienze di Siena detta de' Fisiocritici* 6:330–352.
BARTALINI, BIAGIO. 1800. Ragguaglio di alcune produzioni naturali dell'Agro Sanese scritto ad un Amico. *Atti dell'Accademia delle Scienze di Siena detta de' Fisiocritici* 8:224–230.
BARTALINI, BIAGIO. 1808. Lettera ad un Amico o sia succinto ragguaglio della situazione della Città di Siena, e dei prodotti naturali, che dentro alla medesima si ritrovano. *Atti dell'Accademia delle Scienze di Siena detta de' Fisiocritici* 9:213–219.
BASTIANI, ANNIBALE. 1770. Analisi delle acque minerali di San Casciano de' bagni, e dell'uso di esse nella medicina. G. Cambiagi, Firenze. 126 pp.
BERNARDI, FRANCESCO, and P. CASUCCINI. 1868. Sui miglioramenti operati nell'anno 1866 nel Museo di Storia Naturale della R. Accademia dei Fisiocritici di Siena. *Atti della Regia Accademia dei Fisiocritici* ser. 2, 4:95–101
BEUDANT, FRANÇOIS-SULPICE. 1846. *Mineralogia — Geologia*. Edizione Italiana per cura del dott. Giusti Arpesani. F. Vallardi, Milano. 589 pp.
BURGASSI PIER DOMENICO, and C. DONATI. 1995. Contribution to knowledge of the geothermic phenomenon: the historical analysis of geological research in the geothermic region of Tuscany until the beginning of the twentieth century. Pages 51–66 *in* G. Giglia, C. Maccagni and N. Morello eds., *Rocks, Fossils and History*. Proceedings of the 13th INHIGEO Symposium Pisa — Padova (Italy), 24 September–1 October 1987. Festina Lente, Firenze.
CALURI, FRANCESCO. 1767. Conghietture ed osservazioni sopra una cochiglia marina fossile non alterata, creduta di un nuovo genere, ritrovata dentro un altra cochiglia fossile non alterata della campagna Sanese. *Atti dell'Accademia delle Scienze di Siena, detta de' Fisiocritici* 3:262–275.
CAMPANI, GIOVANNI. 1860. Su i miglioramenti operati nel Museo di Storia Naturale della R. Accademia dei Fisiocritici di Siena nel 1859. Rapporto letto nella pubblica adunanza del 15 aprile 1860. Porri, Siena. 22 pp.
CATALOGHI. 1905. *R. Accademia dei Fisiocritici di Siena. Museo Mineralogico, Geologico e Paleontologico. Cataloghi*. Tip. Cooperativa, Siena. 9 pp.
CAVAZZA, MARTA. 1990. *Settecento inquieto. Alle origini dell'Istituto delle Scienze di Bologna*. Il Mulino Bologna. 281 pp.
COCHRANE, ERIC W. 1953. Le relazioni delle accademie toscane del Settecento con la cultura europea. *Archivio Storico Italiano* 111:78–108.
COCHRANE, ERIC W. 1961. *Tradition and enlightement in the Tuscan academies, 1690–1800*. University of Chicago Press, Chicago. 286 pp.
DE GREGORIO, MARIO. 1992. Un "gran commis" al servizio delle scienze: Pompeo Neri e l'Accademia dei Fisiocritici. Pages 161–216 *in* A. Fratoianni, and M. Verga, eds., *Pompeo Neri*. Atti del Colloquio di Studi. Società Storica della Valdelsa, Castelfiorentino.
DE GREGORIO, MARIO, and SANDRO LANDI. 1992. I torchi del Granduca. Editoria e opinione pubblica a Siena nell'età delle riforme. *Bullettino Senese di Storia Patria* 99:163–192.
FADDA, BIANCA. 1983. *L'innesto del vaiolo. Un dibattito scientifico e culturale nell'Italia del Settecento*. Franco Angeli, Milano. 212 pp.
FARSI, FERRUCCIO, and GIOVANNI GUASPARRI. 1997. La catalogazione informatica delle collezioni di minerali e rocce del Museo dell'Accademia dei Fisiocritici. *Atti dell'Accademia dei Fisiocritici* ser. 15, 16:23–36.
FERBER, JOHANN JAKOB. 1774. Memorie epistolari di osservazioni Mineralogiche e Orittografiche [. . .] scritte dalla Boemia al chiarissimo Signor Giovanni Arduino. *Atti dell'Accademia delle Scienze di Siena detta de' Fisiocritici* 5:203–227.

FERBER, JOHANN JAKOB. 1776. *Travels throught Italy in the Years 1771 and 1772 described in a series of letters to Baron Born, on the Natural History particularly the Mountains and Volcanoes of that Country*. Translated from the German, with explanatory notes, and a preface on the present state and future improvement of mineralogy. By Rudolf Erich Raspe. L. Davies, London. 377 pp. [First edition, in German: Prague, 1773].
FERRI, S., and E. MIRALDI. 1993. Biagio Bartalini (1750–1822) e l'Erbario conservato all'Accademia dei Fisiocritici di Siena. *Webbia* 48:397–408.
FINDLEN, PAULA. 1994. *Possessing nature: museums, collecting, and scientific culture in early modern Italy*. University of California Press, Berkeley. 449 pp.
FISIOCRITICI. DISSERTAZIONI. 1691–1731. *Composizioni dottrinali recitate nell'Accademia dei Fisiocritici. Volume I, dall'anno 1691 sino al 1696; Volume II, dall'anno 1696 al 1731.* Biblioteca Comunale, Siena, mss. L.III.1–2:393 + 345 cc.
FISIOCRITICI. DOCUMENTI. 1853. *Nota generale di Cataloghi ed Inventari relativi al Museo spettante alla Accademia dei Fisiocritici di Siena, consegnati in due volte al Sig. Giovanni Campani direttore del Museo stesso, per servirgli nel riordinamento scientifico e materiale di quello stabilimento* [20 maggio 1853]. Archivio Accademia dei Fisiocritici, Siena, Documenti, vol. 5, mss.
FISIOCRITICI. DOCUMENTI. 1867. *R. Accademia dei Fisiocritici di Siena. Catalogo della Collezione di Mineralogia ordinato secondo il metodo di Beudant dall'Ill.mo Sig. Cav. Prof. Giovanni Campani (catalogo di 24 fogli). Aprile 1867 A. Pantanelli. Scaffali dall'1° al 10°*. Archivio Accademia dei Fisiocritici, Siena, Documenti, vol. 5, mss.
FISIOCRITICI. EPISTOLE. 1692–1799. *Lettere in arrivo*. Cartelle I & II. Archivio Accademia dei Fisiocritici, Siena, mss. (529 letters).
FISIOCRITICI. MEMORIE. 1759–1798. *Fondo Memorie. II:1759–1770; III:1771–1787; IV:1788–1798*. Archivio Accademia dei Fisiocritici, Siena, mss.:842 + 895 + 593 cc.
FISIOCRITICI. VERBALI. 1691–1768. *Verbali delle sedute accademiche*. Volume I. Archivio Accademia dei Fisiocritici, Siena, mss.:259 + 13 + 19 cc.
FISIOCRITICI. VERBALI. 1768–1812. *Verbali delle sedute accademiche*. Volume II. Archivio Accademia dei Fisiocritici, Siena, mss.:230 + 56 cc.
GABBRIELLI, PIRRO MARIA. 1705. *L'Heliometro Fisiocritico, o vero, la Meridiana Sanese*. Bonetti, Siena. 144 pp.
GUASPARRI, GIOVANNI. 1992. *L'Accademia dei Fisiocritici di Siena. Guida ai Musei*. Editoriale Donchisciotte, Siena. 166 pp.
IMPEY, OLIVER, and ARTHUR MACGREGOR, eds. 1985. *The origins of museums. The Cabinet of Curiosities in sixteenth- and seventeenth-century Europe*. Clarendon Press, Oxford. 335 pp.
LANG, CARL NICOLAUS. 1708. *Historia Lapidum Figuratorum Helvetiae, ejusque viciniae, in qua non solum enarrantur omnia eorum genera, species et vires aeneisque tabulis repraesentatur, sed insuper adducuntur eorum loca nativa, in quibus reperiri solent, ut cuilibet facile sit eos colligere modo adducta loca adire libeat*. J. Tomasini, Venetiis. 80 pp.
LIPPARINI, TINO. 1987. J. B. Beccari e P. A. Soldani fondatori della micropaleontologia. *Atti dell'Accademia dei Fisiocritici* ser.15, 6:133–137.
LUGLI, ADALGISA. 1983. *Naturalia et Mirabilia. Il collezionismo enciclopedico nelle Wunderkammern d'Europa*. Mazzotta, Milano. 262 pp.
MACCAGNI, CARLO. 1981. Le raccolte e i musei di storia naturale e gli orti botanici come istituzioni alternative e complementari rispetto alla cultura delle Università e delle Accademie. Pages 283–310 *in* L. Boehm and E. Raimondi, eds., *Università, Accademie e Società scientifiche in Italia ed in Germania dal Cinquecento al Settecento*. Il Mulino, Bologna.
MANASSE, ERNESTO. 1908. Commemorazione di Ambrogio Soldani. *Atti dell'Accademia dei Fisiocritici* ser. 4, 20:365–376.
MASCAGNI, PAOLO. 1779. *Dei Lagoni del Senese e del Volterrano*. V. Pazzini Carli, Siena. 87 pp.
MAYLENDER, MICHELE. 1929. "Accademia Fisiocritica — colonia arcadica — Siena" and "Accademia dei Fisiocritici — Siena". Pages 18–26 *in* M. Maylender, *Storia delle Accademie d'Italia*. Cappelli, Bologna, vol. 3.

McClellan, James E. 1985. *Science reorganized. Scientific societies In the eighteenth century.* Columbia University Press, New York. 413 pp.
Museo Fisiocritici. 1841. Stato attuale dell'I. e R. Museo di Storia Naturale dell'Accademia Fisiocritica. *Atti dell'Accademia delle Scienze di Siena detta de' Fisiocritici* 10:255–259.
Olmi, Giuseppe. 1992. *L'inventario del mondo. Catalogazione della natura e luoghi del sapere nella prima età moderna.* Il Mulino, Bologna. 457 pp.
Pantanelli, Antonio. 1869. Relazione annuale del Museo Mineralogico. *Atti della Regia Accademia dei Fisiocritici* ser. 2, 5:55–59.
Pantanelli, Antonio. 1873. Relazione del Museo Mineralogico per l'anno 1871. Relazione del Museo Mineralogico per l'anno 1872. *Atti della Regia Accademia dei Fisiocritici* ser. 3, 1:38–42, 87–90.
Pantanelli, Dante. 1876. Regia Accademia dei Fisiocritici. Direzione del Museo di Mineralogia e Geologia. Rapporto annuale 1875. *Atti della Regia Accademia dei Fisiocritici* ser. 3, 1 (4):193–203.
Pantanelli, Dante. 1877. Regia Accademia dei Fisiocritici. Direzione del Museo di Mineralogia e Geologia. Rapporto annuale 1876. *Atti della Regia Accademia dei Fisiocritici* ser. 3, 1 (7):259–265.
Pasta, Renato. 1992. Istituzionalizzazione della scienza e controllo del sapere: il contributo di Pompeo Neri alla rinascita dei Fisiocritici. Pages 217–238 *in* A. Fratoianni and M. Verga, eds., *Pompeo Neri.* Atti del Colloquio di Studi. Società Storica della Valdelsa, Castelfiorentino.
Ricca, Massimiliano. 1810. *Discorso sopra le opere del p. Ambrogio Soldani.* Porri, Siena. 23 pp.
Ricci, Carlo. 1972. *L'Accademia dei Fisiocritici in Siena, 1691–1971.* Accademia dei Fisiocritici, Siena. 54 pp.
Ricci, Carlo. 1985a. Breve storia dell'Accademia dei Fisiocritici in un inedito di Massimiliano Ricca del 1818. Pages 259–273 *in* Baccetti et al. 1985.
Ricci, Carlo. 1985b. Università, Accademia dei Fisiocritici e Grande Anatomia di Paolo Mascagni. Pages 221–239 *in* Baccetti et al. 1985.
Ricci, Carlo. 1985c. Un inedito di Paolo Mascagni: le sue osservazioni sui lagoni presentate all'Accademia dei Fisiocritici il 16 marzo 1779. Pages 185–194 *In* Baccetti et al. 1985.
Rodolico, Francesco. 1945. *La Toscana descritta dai naturalisti del Settecento. Pagine di storia del pensiero scientifico.* Le Monnier, Firenze. 351 pp.
Rodolico, Francesco. 1963. *L'esplorazione naturalistica dell'Appennino.* Le Monnier, Firenze. 433 pp.
Sanquirico, Carlo. 1891. *Vicende dell'Accademia dei Fisiocritici.* Tip. San Bernardino, Siena. 19 pp.
Sarti, Carlo. 1988. *I fossili e il Diluvio Universale. Le collezioni settecentesche del Museo di Geologia e Paleontologia dell'Università di Bologna.* Pitagora, Bologna. 189 pp.
Sarti, Carlo. 1992. Giuseppe Monti and palaeontology in the eighteenth century Bologna. *Nuncius. Annali di Storia della Scienza* 8:443–455.
Selvani, Emidio. 1865. Risposta al Foglio del li 25 Marzo del Ministero dell'Istruzione Pubblica Div. II. Oggetto: Storia Accademica. Pages 272–273, *in* Ricci 1985a.
Shapin, Stephen. 1985. *Leviathan and the air-pump: Hobbes, Boyle, and the experimental life*: including a translation of Thomas Hobbes, Dialogus physicus de natura aeris by S. Schaffer. Princeton University Press, Princeton. 440 pp.
Soldani, Ambrogio. 1780. *Saggio Orittografico ovvero Osservazioni sopra le terre nautiliche ed ammonitiche della Toscana, con Appendice o Indice Latino Ragionato de' piccoli Testacei, e d'altri Fossili d'origini marina per schiarimento dell'Opera.* V. Pazzini Carli, Siena. 146 pp. + 25 plates.
Soldani, Ambrogio. 1789–1798. *Testaceographiae ac Zoophytographiae parvae et microscopicae.* F. Rossi, Siena. 2 vol. + 1 atlas.
Soldani, Ambrogio. 1798. *Relazione del terremoto accaduto in Siena il dì 26 maggio 1798.* V. Pazzini, Siena. 98 pp.
Spirito, Francesco. 1934. Vicende storiche della R. Accademia dei Fisiocritici in Siena. *Atti dell'Accademia dei Fisiocritici* ser. 9, 2:185–190.
Targioni Tozzetti, Giovanni. 1751–1754. *Relazioni d'alcuni viaggi fatti in diverse parti della Toscana per osservare le produzioni naturali e gli antichi monumenti di essa.* Stamperia Imperiale, Firenze. 6 vol.

TASSI, [prof.]. 1862. Relazione del Direttore del Museo de' Fisiocritici. *Atti della Regia Accademia dei Fisiocritici* ser. 2, 1:156–161.
TEGA, WALTER, ed. 1986. *Anatomie Accademiche. 1. I Commentari dell'Accademia delle Scienze di Bologna.* Il Mulino, Bologna. 513 pp.
TEGA, WALTER, ed. 1987. *Anatomie Accademiche. 2. L'Enciclopedia scientifica dell'Accademia delle Scienze di Bologna.* Il Mulino, Bologna. 351 pp.
UNIVERSITÀ DEGLI STUDI DI BOLOGNA. 1979. *I Materiali dell'Istituto delle Scienze.* Clueb, Bologna. 264 pp.
VALLISNERI, ANTONIO. 1721. *De' corpi marini che su' monti si trovano, della loro origine, e dello stato del mondo davanti il Diluvio, nel Diluvio e dopo il Diluvio. Lettere critiche.* D. Lovisa, Venezia. 254 pp.
VANNOZZI, FRANCESCA, ed. 1996. *La scienza illuminata. Paolo Mascagni e il suo tempo (1755–1815).* Nuova Immagine Editrice, Siena. 254 pp.

APPENDIX

The Museum of the Academy of Fisiocritici and the private collections of Giuseppe Baldassarri and Francesco Caluri in 1772
(Ferber, 1776:248–254)

"The following articles seemed to me the most remarkable in the Academical-cabinet.

1. Coals, either bituminous wood or true coals, and argillaceous slate, impregnated with petroleum, lie in flats or beds under the clay and marl-hills in several parts of Toscana.

2. A jaw, with the teeth on an unknown animal, found in a marl-hill in Toscana, and described by Mr. Baldassarri in the Academical Transactions – agrees with an American jaw described by Mr. Guettard in his Memoirs.

3. A blunted limestone, worm-eaten by pholades, found in a marl-hill in the Sanese.

4. Yellow sand-stone, with a petrified sea-star or asteria; from a hill near Giusuri, a mile distant from Siena.

5. Black quartz-crystallizations; either pitch-black throughout, or only tinged in the surface; having eight triangular faces, or rather the form and bigness of rough diamonds; from *monte Pulciano*.

6. Native yellow sulphur in cubic crystallizations, inclosed with pyramidical calcareous spar in grey limestone; from *S. Agatha di monte Feltro in Ducato d'Urbino, in Romagna*. This native sulphur resembles a yellow knotty blende; but yelds a yellow sulphur powder as soon as scraped with the nail.

The private cabinet of Dr. *Baldassarri*, which is to be delivered after his death to the Academy, contains several remarkable curiosities. I notice,

1. Native sulphur, in a large yellow, transparent crystal, half an inch diameter, nearly of sherl or columnar form; from *S. Agatha di Monte Feltro*. A scarce and precious piece indeed!

2. White and black quartz-crystallizations, pyramidical on both ends; (*Iris nigra Aldrovandi, lapis Dichonus Mercati in Metallotheca, Ingemmamenti crystallini appuntati in ambe le parti di Ferrante Imperato*); found loose and detached in the surface of the earth in many places of the Sanese; such as *Leceto, ai bagni di S. Filippo, di Cianciano, a Belriguardo*, &c.

3. Dark-green quartz crystallizations in and on dark-green *soslag*, or *asbestus fibris abruptis et conglutinatis (Cronst. Mineral. § 105),* which seems to have dyed or tinged them. Mr. *Baldassarri* did not remember positively, whether this rare curiosity came from *monte Christo,* or from *Giglio,* two small islands in the Tuscan sea.

4. Blue quartz-crystallization, from a copper mine in the Sanese.

[5.] Shells petrified into agate, in a yellow fine tophaceous sand-stone, found in a sand-hill at the Florentine gate at Siena.

6. White and transparent petrified turbinites in a similar sand-stone; the turbinites hollow.

7. Native copper in quartz, with crysocolla, from a new-discovered mine at *Paris*, in the Sanese, twenty-three miles distant from Siena, close to the *Via consularis* to *Grossetto*.

8. Grey antimony in large and long crystals, covered with crystallized native sulphur and farinaceous auripigment, from an antimony-mine, near *Pereta nella Maremma Sanese*.

9. *Granite*; the substance of some hills in the Sanese.

10. Argillaceous slate, from Montagnuola and Prata, in the beginning of the *Maremma Sanese*, where it is in large hills covered with calcareous; described by Mr. *Baldassarri* in the eleventh volume of the Sanese Transactions, or in his Sketch of a Natural History of Prata.

11. Argillaceous slate, with white marble veins, without any quartz; different from the proceeding species on account of its antiquity and position as being not inferior to the calcareous strata; but stratified in the calcareous hills near Gerfalco, between that place and Prata. The micaceous stripes in the Greek *Cipollino*-marble are, perhaps, owing to a similar position.

12. Micaceous slate with dendrites, from *Montagnuola presso la villa Cettenati*, eight Italian miles distant from Siena.

13. Sand-stone from *Belriguardo*, three miles distant from Siena.

14. Travertino, from *Rapolano* in the Sanese; produced there by the sediments of hot waters. *Rapolano* is situated at the entrance of the valley, called *La Valle di Chiana*, twelve Italian miles from Siena; celebrated on account of its baths which incrustated like the *Bagni di S. Filippo*, whatever is valid into them.

15. *Serpentino* or *Gabbro*, green and black spotted, from Vallerano in the Sanese; called by the stone-cutters *Marmo di Vallerano*.

16. *Serpentino* or *Gabbro* from *Prata*, is green and black, or red spotted; commonly called *Verde di Prato*.

17. White scaly marble, as beautiful and saline as that from Carrara, from *Montagnuola* in the Sanese; the whole mountain being commonly grey, it is found but in small blocks or lumps.

18. *Brocatello di Siena*, a yellow marble with black veins; the ground sometimes purple; but burning makes the whole red coloured; dug at *Montarenti* in *Montagnuola*, in the Sanese; eight Italian miles distant from Siena; generally known, and much employed in Italy.

19. *Marmo tigrato di Vall' di Rati*, a fine spotted marble.

20. White handsome alabaster, and *alabastro fiorito*, dug at *Castel nuovo dell'Abbate*, in the Sanese.

Dr. *Calluri*, professor of physic at Siena, has a small but choice collection of Natural History. I noticed the following pieces.

1. A petrified shell in a flint (*sylex pyromachus*), from *S. Chianciano de Bagni. S. Casciano de Bagni*, in the Sanese, is different from the precedent place; and described in the *Analisi delle acque minerali di S. Casciano de' Bagni, &c. di Annibale Bastiani*. Firenze, 1770, 8vo.

2. Microscopical shells, as described and drawn by *Janus Plancus*; common in several sand-mixed clay-hills, two miles distant from Siena, on the road to Florence.

3. A petrified wendel-trapp (*turbo-scalaris*), a scarce and precious shell, found in an argillaceous sand hill near *monte Algino* in *Toscana*.

4. Several univalves, compressed and crushed by the pressure of superior beds; petrified from the hills near *monte Algino*.

5. White fullers earth, dug at *Personatina* near *Cettinale*, seven miles distant from Siena.

6. *Nummi diabolici Mercati*, round and flat pyrite-lamellae, from *Cuna*, six miles distant from Siena, on the road to Rome.

7. Magnesia, form *S. Casciano de' Bagni*.

8. Quartz-crystallizations, with an air bladder and inclosed water, from the Sanese.

9. Lamellated quartz-crystal, from the Sanese. The same frequently found in Christina-shaft, at Shemnitz, in Lower Hungary.

10. Oblique rhomboidal transparent gyps-crystals, four inches long, two inches large, called *Specchio d'Asino*, found near *Villa di Cettenali nella Montagnuola*. Some are said to double the objects.

11. Large black and columnar sherl, from *Monte Christo*, a small island near *Isola di Gighi*, on the coast of Toscana.

12. Some copper ores and malachites, from the mines near *Massa di Maremma*, in the Sanese.

13. Agates, amethysts, and quartz-crystallizations, from *Maremma*, some miles distant from the copper mines of *Massa*.

14. Slate, with pyrite-cubes of marcasites, from *Rocca Strada*, near *Massa di Maremma*.

15. Great white argillaceous and sulphureous bullets, some of the bigness of a man's head, from *Monte Antico*, three Italian miles distant from the baths of *Petriulo* in the Sanese; described by *Pinelli* in his *Lettera de' Bagni di Petriulo*. Roma, 1716. 4to."

Considerations of Certain Peculiarities in Scientific Institutions in Central Europe in the Eighteenth Century

AGNESE VISCONTI
Facoltà di Scienze Politiche
Università degli Studi di Pavia
Strada Nuova 65
27100 Pavia, Italy

The purpose of the work is to bring out, starting from the analysis of the statutes of two Lombard scientific Societies founded during the Austrian domination (1706–1796), a few differences, which I found significant and which to my knowledge have not been dealt with before, between the constituent principles of the Royal Society of London and the Académie des Sciences of Paris on the one hand, and the principles of scientific associations in Central Europe and Lombardy on the other. Among these differences, particularly relevant is the adherence of the Central European scientific associations to concepts relating to God, national pride and well-being. So we have in France and England, on the basis of the principles set out by Francis Bacon, a concept of science as an institution which is free to establish relationships with the outside non-scientific world (i.e., economic, political, manufacturing) and in Central Europe, following the German philosopher Gottfried Wilhel Leibniz, a concept of science as an institution which is subject to the economic and political choices imposed by a central power.

CONSIDERAZIONI SU ALCUNE SPECIFICITÀ DELLE ISTITUZIONI SCIENTI-FICHE DELL'EUROPA CENTRALE NEL DICOTTESIMO SECOLO. Il lavoro si propone di mettere in evidenza, sulla base dell'analisi degli statuti di due Società scientifiche lombarde fondate durante la dominazione austriaca (1706–1796), alcune differenze, che mi sono parse di qualche rilievo e che non sono state considerate in precedenza, tra i principi costitutivi della Royal Society di Londra e dell'Académie des Sciences di Parigi da un lato, e quelli delle associazioni scientifiche dell'Europa Centrale e della Lombardia dall'altro. Tra queste differenze emerge in modo particolare la presenza nelle associazioni dell'Europa centrale di riferimenti a Dio, al benessere della patria e al prestigio dello stato. Ne conseguono due diversi concetti di scienza. In Francia e Inghilterra, sulla base dei principi dettati da Bacone, la scienza è una forma di attività libera di stabilire relazioni con il mondo extra-scientifico (economico, politico produttivo), mentre in Europa Centrale, seguendo le idee di Gottfried Wilhelm Leibniz, essa rimane rigidamente sottoposta alle scelte politiche ed economiche imposte dal potere centrale.

It is well known that the first two modern (Rossi, 1977:19) scientific associations were the Royal Society of London and l'Académie Royale des Sciences of Paris, founded in 1662 and 1666 respectively. The former was created as an independent association, lacking any relationship with the government; the latter was the outcome of an agreement between scientists and statesmen. The result of such an agreement was that sciences obtained great prestige and were to some extent identified with the political power. These two associations, founded, as is well known, on the concept of science as expounded by the English philosopher Francis Bacon, represent the model upon which the principal 18th century scientific institutions were based in northern Europe and in the United States: the Societas Literaria et Scientiarum of Uppsala, created in 1710 and officially inaugurated in 1728 (not to be confused with the Svenska Vetenskaps-Akademie of Stockholm, founded in 1739); the Kongelige Danske Videnskabernes Selskab (Royal Danish Academy of Sciences and Letters) of Copenhagen, established in 1742; the Academia Scientiarum Imperialis Petropolitana (Imperial Academy of Sciences of Petersburg), founded in 1726 by Catherine I; the Königliche Preussiche Akademie der Wissenschaften, created by Frederick II in 1744; the American Philosophical Society of Philadelphia 1769 by Benjamin Franklin; and the American Academy of Arts and Sciences of Boston, founded in 1780 on the initiative of John Adams.

It is in my opinion interesting to note the differences between these types of scientific associations and those which were established in the 18th century in Central Europe. The first clue in this analysis of the elements which distinguish the two categories of scientific research comes from a close analysis of the statutes of two specific scientific institutions, including their purposes and the members' socio-economic origins. These institutions were established in Lombardy during the Austrian domination (1706–1796) and were namely, the Accademia di Scienze, Lettere e Arti (Academy of Science, Literature and Arts) of Mantua (Baldi, 1979), founded in 1767 by empress Mary Theresa with the aim of "qualifying itself to serve the prince and the state" and to seek "those truths that can more easily lead to public welfare" (Carnevali, 1885–1887:34); and the Società Patriotica per l'incremento dell'Agricoltura, delle Arti e delle Manifatture (Patriotic Society for the Development of Agriculture, Arts and Manufacture) of Milan, founded in 1776 (Molla Losito, 1982) (Fig. 1), with the aim of "more easily paving the way to those minds that are willing to make themselves useful to

FIGURE 1. The Brera Building (Palazzo di Brera), Milan, where the Società Patriotica had its seat. Courtesy Civica Raccolta Stampe Achille Bertarelli, Milan.

the state" (Circolare, 1777) and "to concur in the prosperity of these provinces of ours" (Dispaccio, 1776).

The goals of these Lombard societies were not identical to the aims of the Royal Society of London or to those of the Paris Académie des Sciences. A review of their respective statutes reveals that the Royal Society was aimed at gathering groups of scholars — on the basis of the principles set out by Bacon — to lead them to work together in order to "improve the knowledge of natural things and all useful arts, manufactures, mechanic practices, engines and inventions by experiments" (Mathias, 1972:61); and the Académie des Sciences — also firmly based on Bacon's beliefs — was aimed at "banning all prejudices, by basing everything on experiments, in order to find something certain, to dispel all chimeras and to pave the way to truth for those who are willing to follow this practice" (Hahn, 1971:15–16).

Therefore, on the one hand, in Lombardy we find a vision of science as an instrument in the service of the State's economic and political objectives, while, on the other hand, in England and France, science is viewed as a means to increase man's knowledge, both in theory and in practice, and to reveal the truth. In the light of these differences, which are by no means insignificant, two questions arise, namely, (1) where did the aims of the two Lombard institutions come from, and (2) what is the reason for the difference between their goals and those of the two most important European academies? In seeking to answer these questions, a useful starting point is to consider the political and economic situation in Lombardy at the time. In 1760 the central Hapsburg power, because of a conceived lack of solid local scientific traditions (Visconti, 1997), created a large number of scientific institutions, aimed at including the sciences among the cognitive instruments it was gradually bringing together in order to strengthen and extend its hold on new spheres of interest and activity. These new scientific institutions included the above-mentioned Accademia of Mantua and the Società Patriotica of Milan; the Museo di Storia Naturale (Museum of Natural History) founded at the University of Pavia in 1770 (Spallanzani, 1985) (Fig. 2); the Orto Bontanico (Botanical Garden) of the same University, which was completely renovated between 1771 and 1773; the chair of Natural History of the Palatine Schools of Milan and the annexed St. Alexander's Mineralogical Museum inaugurated in 1772 (Boffito, 1933:179); and, finally the Orto Botanico (Botanical Garden) of Brera, started in 1774 (Liva, 1989).

The Hapsburg's policy was not limited to the foundation of the necessary structures in order to support the development of research into the natural sciences, it also extended its ambit to include the nomination of the academics who would be responsible for the direction and working management of these structures. This decision, which was justified by the need to overcome the intellectual poverty of the local educated classes who were not capable of setting up new institutions, was the root cause of the arrival in Lombardy of various notable academics, hailing from other parts of the Empire or the peninsula: among them Giovanni Antonio Scopoli from Trento and Lazzaro Spallanzani from Reggio, who respectively obtained the chair of Natural History and that of Botany at the University of Pavia (Jucci, 1961); the Bavarian abbot Fulgenzio Vitman, from Vallombrosa (Ciferri, 1961; Jucci, 1961; Pichi Sermolli, 1999:131–140), who directed the Botanical Garden of the University of Pavia and then the Botanical Garden of Brera in Milan (Liva, 1989); Francesco Griselini from Venice, who directed the Società Patriotica since 1776 (Torcellan, 1965); Carlo Amoretti from Liguria, who in 1781 succeeded Griselini (Visconti, 1997).

Having thus established the foundations for the study of nature and natural products, the Hapsburg government decided to expand the scope of its sphere of influence to include the control over the criteria used, terms adopted and subject-matter of the research being carried out by the academics that were supposed to be overseeing the creation of the new institutions. An example of

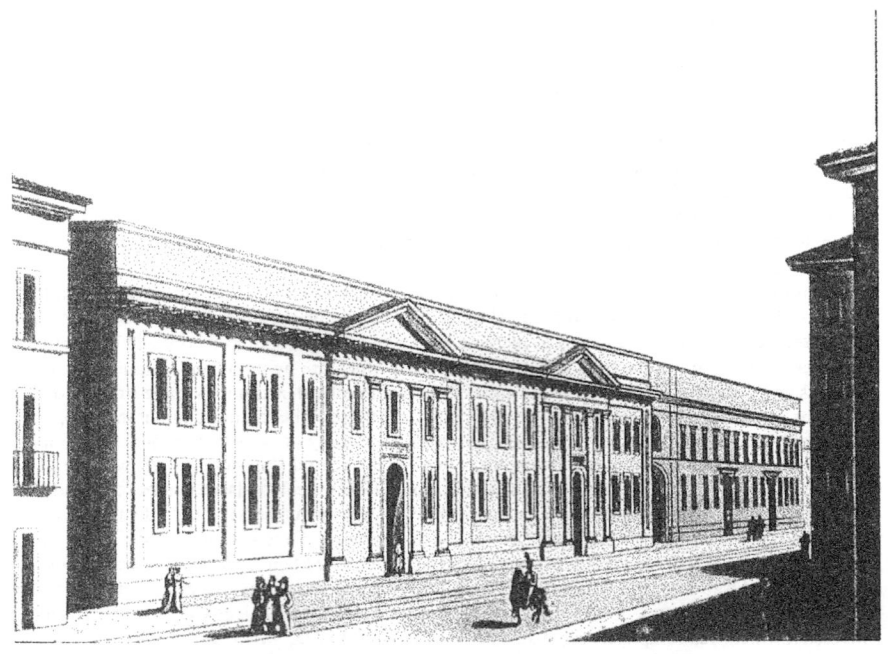

FIGURE 2. The University of Pavia, reorganized in the 18th century by the Austrian Empire.
Courtesy Civica Raccolta Stampe Achille Bertarelli, Milan.

this interference can be seen in the following governmental order received by Spallanzani: "the best way to organise series is to set out only those parts of the plant that have medicinal properties, i.e. wood, roots, bark, flowers" (Spallanzani, La collezione naturalistica, 1985:117). Similar directives were received by Scopoli, Vitman and others (Visconti, 1997).

These directives and pretensions, which found no counterpart either in France or England (where men of science used their social status to maintain their autonomy in their relations with the central power), were the result of the political power's policy to use the scientific research, in order to provide itself with solid support for its ultimate political and economic goals, which included the general welfare of the people living within its domain, the increased prosperity of the state, and the benefit of motherland (Rassem, 1992). The object was therefore not to examine, study and analyse nature for the sake of knowledge. In other words, the aim was not "the knowledge of causes, and secret motions of things; and the enlarging of the bounds of human empire, to the effecting of all things possible" (Bacon, 1952:210), according to which philosophy, scientific knowledge was perceived as a form of universal wisdom aimed at understanding nature and resulting in the expansion of all mankind's power to new spheres of interest and action (Boas Hall, 1975). The intent, instead, was to subordinate the sciences to the political power and its purposes, that is to deny their autonomy according to a concept which, by placing the state's welfare ahead of the formulation of nature's laws, was aimed at integrating scientists within the state bureaucracy and at turning them into submissive officials in charge of contributing, through technological improvement, to the achievement of the economic and manufacturing objectives set by the central power authority (De Maddalena, 1975:687; Schiera, 1975:414).

After having thus reviewed the Lombard political and economic situation, it was thought useful to expand the field of study to include the provinces of the Austrian Empire in order to verify whether similar institutions existed there. We then realised there were several associations whose scientific research was likewise aimed at carrying out the economic and financial directives of the governing power. A series of scientific-manufacturing institutions were founded around the 1760s, when the implementation of the fundamental reforms of the Austrian State created a set of conditions that allowed the central power to start trying to bridge the economic gap with more advanced European countries (Schindler and Bonss, 1980). The Austrian government, in fact, decided to consider the possibility of integrating technical and scientific knowledge into the stream of its mercantilist economic strategy and, more specifically, to use this knowledge to favour the agricultural and manufacturing development of the Empire's most advanced regions. Chancellor Wenzel Anton Kaunitz, in charge of Hapsburg foreign policy, was the main promoter of this financial and economic plan. In a letter to the Austrian Ambassador in Bavaria dated 30 October 1764, Kaunitz supported the foundation in Austria of societies which, "like the Munich society, contribute also in our provinces to the acquisition and growth of the taste for useful sciences" (Hammermayer, 1983:15). Counsellor Fremaut's suggestions added to these convictions. During his trips, made in the same year, through the territories of the Empire, he decided that the provinces of Carintia, Tyrol, Styria and Carniola were the most suited to the creation of a first series of technical-scientific institutes aimed at carrying out the economic objectives established by the State (Hammermayer, 1983:4) in the agricultural sector (relating to the choice of cultivation, fertilizer, livestock, wood type) and in the manufacturing sector (Dinklage, 1965:149, 152, 157). On this basis, between 1765 and 1767 the following societies were founded: Klagenfurt, Innsbruck, Graz, Laibach, Linz and Görz, followed by the foundation of other societies starting in 1768: Vienna, Hermannstadt, Brunn, Freiburg, and Prague (Dinklage, 1965, 1966:149–170; Kraus, 1977:139; Schindler and Bonss, 1980; Hammermayer, 1983:5–12).

The Munich society Kaunitz mentioned in his letter is the Churbayerische Akademie der Wissenschaften (Bavarian Academy of Sciences), created in 1759 by will of Georg Lori, with a view to "dedicating sciences and arts to the increase in the benefits and honour of the motherland [. . .] and in the state welfare" (Hermann and Sang, 1992:32), and to "most efficiently affecting economy and general prosperity" (Hermann and Sang, 1992:33). Thanks to these objectives, which were purely economic in nature, the Academy managed to obtain from the elector Maximilian II of Bavaria the necessary funds for the creation of an Astronomical Observatory and the Chemical and Physical Laboratories, and for the publication of its *Abhandlungen* and *Neue Abhandlungen* published in German in order to create a link with the country's technical knowledge and applications (Hermann and Sang, 1992:33).

It is clear that the founding principles of the two Lombard institutions, upon which our interest is based, are the same as those of the Austrian technical-scientific-economic societies, which were modelled on the Munich Academy. Both the Lombard and the Austrian organisations viewed the academic as an official subject to the economic objectives of the state and not as an independent entity free to enter into an agreement with the governing power. The question then arose as to what was the model for the Academy in Berlin? The statutes of the German associations refer back to two scientific institutions which briefly preceded the foundation of the Academy of Munich and which inspired the foundation of the same, the Königlch Societät der Wissenschaften (Royal Society of Sciences) in Goettingen, founded in 1752 by the Minister of the Principality of Hannover, Adolf von Münchhausen, which gave as its fundamental principle the conviction that "the creation of an academy of good and useful sciences would be honourable, and sciences themselves would contribute to increase the country's wealth and happiness" (Hermann and Sang, 1992:35), and the Erfurt Akademie gemeinütziger Wissenschaften (Erfurt Academy of Useful Sciences) founded on 19 July 1754, which had similar goals. As a matter of fact, the latter's economic and productive objectives were so sharp and clearly stated that the Mainz elector said that he was willing to invest a substantial amount of money to support the implementation of its programs, especially in view of the "savings of costs, that is the advantages for citizens that this society of scholars would have brought in the field of metallurgy, chemistry, mechanics, economy or other fields" (Hermann and Sang, 1992:37).

But does a single model exist on which all of these scientific-technical-economic associations are based? We believe that a convincing answer can be gleaned from the founding principles of the Societas Regia Scientiarum, created in Berlin in 1700 by Frederick III of Brandenburg (Frederick I of Prussia) on the suggestion of Gottfried Wilhelm Leibniz (Fig. 3). These societies did not express concern for questions of truth, or the investigation into physical phenomena, they were instead based on the belief that, "in order to spread wide God's glory, to maintain and develop true fear of God, sound morals and the general welfare of all classes, it was necessary for men's inclinations to be illuminated by a good science and useful studies, and to be urged in order to acknowledge and admire God's works, thus leading to love and fear of God, the only source of every good thing" (Brather, 1993:94–97). Their coming into being was therefore in order to develop the "useful" sciences, to praise God and to improve the wellbeing of the German country.

The vision of science's role stated by the German philosopher was dominated by principles relating to God and the wealth and patrimony of the German state. These principles had been expounded by Leibniz in various proposals prepared for the creation of a German scientific society. These principles were set out in particular

FIGURE 3. Gottfried Wilhelm Leibniz, on whose conception of science the Lombard scientific and technical institutions of the 18th century were based. Portrait courtesy Civica Raccolta Stampe Achille Bertarelli, Milan.

in his *Grundriss eines Bedenckens von Aufrichtung einer Societät in Teutschland zu aufnehmen der Künste und Wissenshaften von 1671*, where he argued that, in his view, the role of the scientific association was to "amare bonum publicum, vel, quod idem est, gloriam Dei intelligere et quantum in se est facere maiorem" (Foucher de Careil, 1859:xviii–xix), and its task had to be the search for the necessary means for the implementation of "common usefulness, of the motherland's prestige, of the sustenance and preservation of many men, of God's glory and the discovery of His wonders" (Hammerstein, 1981) through actions aimed at "increasing and improving arts and sciences, at urging the Germans' intelligence so that they are not despoiled by the other nations in the commercial field, nor fall behind them as far as science is concerned" (Krafft, 1981). He also claimed that scholars should not be "led by mere curiosity or thirst for knowledge, nor pay attention to useless experiments, or be content with the simple invention of useful things that cannot be applied and installed, as it already happened in Paris, London and Florence, where the aim of sciences of reality — that is to gain benefits for the nation — had not been reached in any way." (Krafft, 1981) He stated that "since the beginning they had to seek usefulness and think only about those specimens from which the glory of the king and the whole community have reason to expect certain common advantages" (Krafft, 1981). Leibniz expressed similar remarks a few years later, in a fragmentary manuscript written after the death of the great elector Frederick William, in 1688 (Mathieu, 1951:315), where he stated he was "even convinced that under his (Frederick III of Brandenburg and I of Prussia) auspices it would be easy to overcome what in France and England was started and planned:because there, even though they worked well, they were far away from the best path. In fact surveys carried out by French and English academies paid much more attention to appearance and prestige than to practical usefulness, which is better cultivated by Germans" (Mathieu, 1951:322). On the basis of these remarks it appeared that the ultimate goal of scientific associations had to be "combining theory to practice, thus developing not only arts and sciences, but also the country and the population, agriculture, manufacturing and trade; in a word, all means of sustenance" (Krafft, 1981).

What is crystal clear from these words is Leibniz's conviction that the realisation of the great scientific discoveries of the era could not be left directly in the hands of the common people who lacked the organisational skills for such a task, instead, it was a task for a wise and well-intentioned sovereign, in his capacity as God's vessel on earth and sole protector of his subjects' well-being (Mathieu, 1951:28–30).

The Berlin society never reached its full potential. Weighed down by financial problems and the interference of Court officials and administrators, it led a marginal existence and did not achieve any scientific results. It even became universally known as "the anonymous society" (Harnack, 1900:176–241; McClellan III, 1985:71–72). It was completely revamped by Frederick II of Prussia, who came to the throne in 1740, and who had taken the decision to substitute Leibniz's concepts relating God, country, and the nation's well-being, with more cosmopolitan principles, closer to the model of the Académie des Sciences in Paris. Thus was born the new Königliche Preussiche Akademie der Wissenschaften in Berlin in 1744, firmly based on the separation of scientific objectives from political objectives; the Academy was, in fact, solely preoccupied with the search for truth, leaving to the State the task of gradually putting such truth into practice and transposing it to public life (Müller, 1975:33). The Academy chose to publish its memoirs in French thus blocking any possibility of there being a direct relationship between science and the artisan and economic world of the country (Müller, 1975:33). Pierre-Louis Moreau de Maupertuis, one-time Academy president (Hammermayer, 1983:27), played an important role in the drawing up of the organisation's constitution and in the choice of objectives. Similarly, Joseph-Louis Lagrange and Leonhard Euler contributed significantly, as did Samuel Formey, who was named secretary (Visconti, 1997).

The brainchild of Leibniz, the Berlin society was not too successful, and this was also true of the other scientific associations created in its image.

The Goettigen Royal Society distinguished itself by its objectives which were purely scientific, whilst it remained under the control of the physician and naturalist Albrecht von Haller, but after his death in 1753, the Society rapidly lost its scientific character and turned into an unassuming economic-technical-agricultural association, based on cameralistic principles (Kraus, 1977:141; McClellan III, 1985:116).

The Erfurt Academy of Useful Sciences, which mainly dealt with economic issues and awarded many prizes in such fields, lost all executive power from the moment its activities came under the control of private promoters (Kraus, 1977). The Seven Years' War (1756–1763) saw its near dissolution. But it was refounded on a sound basis in 1776, and from that moment onwards it found itself in a position to carry out various research projects in the field of natural history (Müller, 1975:37; McClellan III, 1985:117), which were published in its *Acta* until 1807.

The same can be said for the Academy of Sciences of Munich. Although it, too, disappeared with the Seven Years' War, it was restored in 1777 by the palatine elector Charles Theodore, who linked it to the Mannheim Academy, which had been modelled after the Académie de Sciences of Paris, and which developed on a cosmopolitan rather than national basis (McClellan III, 1985:118).

As far as the Austrian societies are concerned, they did not produce any scientific results and all were short lived: the Prague society closed in 1773, the Brunn society in 1775, the Innsbruck society in 1777, the Vienna society in 1783, the Graz and the Laibach societies in 1787, and the Görz society in 1790 (Dinklage, 1965; Im Hof, 1982:268; Schindler and Bonns, 1980).

Such failures have been ascribed by most recent historiographers to the structural conflict that opposed the unification process started by the central power to the resolute resistance of the representatives of local classes. The absolutist policy tried to overcome this conflict by integrating the feudal needs of noble and religious land owners into the rationalising current of administrative reformations. More specifically, the monarchical power ran against a dual limit: on the one hand the need to resort to the contribution and support of old aristocracy in order to carry out any economic development programme; on the other hand the contempt old aristocracy felt for any kind of technical-productive innovation. It was indeed because of the lack of knowledgeable, competent and expert interlocutors that the Hapsburg state was forced to assign the direction of technical-economic societies to local land owners, representing the old social order and therefore lacking an economic vision based on modern and rational bases (Schindler and Bonss, 1980).

We might add the following observation to these motives: the suffocation of growth and development of Austrian technical-scientific societies was due, paradoxically, to the continuous and insistent requests of the State that, by aiming exclusively at reaching economic and productive goals, in the end inhibited the birth of presuppositions necessary to carry out any research activity, discovery or interpretation of nature and its laws. We believe, therefore, that there was a sort of incompatibility between mercantilist demands and scientific requests.

The life and activity of the Società Patriotica of Milan did not differ very much from those of the Austrian patriotic societies. As already mentioned, it was founded in 1776, when the Austrian societies had already shown their scientific inertia. At the central power's request, it carried out a series of researches and efforts aimed at solving Lombardy's economic and financial problems, as shown by the balance-sheets of the region's payments to foreign countries (Caizzi, 1968:48–55, 217–221, 234–237). A strong tie therefore linked the studies carried out by the Società Patriotica to the financial needs of the Hapsburg State, which dictated the working subjects, times and methods of the Milanese association's scholars, on the basis of those balance-sheet's liabilities that were more strictly connected to the sciences of nature. Within the framework of such policies, researches carried out in the botanical field in order to improve textile production played a particularly important role (Visconti, 1998). They were aimed at solving the manufacturing process' weaknesses, that is dyeing and spinning, by carrying out experiments on acclimatisation in Lombardy of imported dyeing and oil-producing substances in view of the possibility of increasing their cultivation. Important experiments and research were carried out in the Botanical Garden by the Società Patriotica under the auspices of the Austrian Government, relating to *Indigofera tinctoria, Isatis tinctoria, Rubia tinctorum, Oldenlandia umbellata* (=*Hedyotis umbellata*), *Morus tinctoria* (=*Maclura tinctoria*), *Genista tinctoria, Alnus glutinosa, Cornus sanguinea, Raphanus sativus, Brassica napus,* and *Carthamus tinctorius* (Visconti, 1998).These botanical studies were supplemented by mineralogical studies, aimed at decreasing iron's passivity, which was not due to the lack of raw material, but rather to defective processing of the metal and lack of fuel. The overcoming of these obstacles was the aim of investigations on energy sources (wood, peat and coal); such investigations proved to be of paramount importance also for silk manufacturing (Visconti, 1997). The central power also ascribed importance to research on suitable leather and fur processing techniques, which represented a liability of about one million liras in the foreign balance-sheet (Caizzi, 1968:55).

The research and efforts carried out by the Società Patriotica's scholars reached a quite high standard, especially during the association's last years of activity, from the point of view of work efficiency and organisation. In certain cases they even produced a few small, short-lived economic benefits. Particularly as far as iron is concerned, the balance-sheet liability decreased by about eight hundred thousand liras between 1782 and 1791, thanks to the tireless activity of the partner Ermenegildo Pini, in charge of starting a rationalisation of Lombard iron production (Pini, 1791).

But the scientific success was rather meagre, not only for the Società Patriotica, but also for all institutions founded by the central power. Except for a few remarkable names, such as Alessandro Volta and Lazzaro Spallanzani — whose merits were not directly linked to the Austrian policy but, for the former, to his links with the Accademia delle Scienze of Bologna and, for the latter, to his close relationships with the scientific communities of Turin and Paris — the framework so zealously built in Vienna actually turned out to be full of eager and insignificant officials, more willing to grant the Court's wishes than to try and follow the path of autonomy and independence.

In the light of this situation, we might say that also for the Società Patriotica of Milan, as well as for the Austrian societies, the full and absolute subordination of scientific research to goals relating only to the general happiness and welfare of the populus — stubbornly pursued by unceasingly trying to compensate the foreign balance-sheet's deficit — represented a hindrance to the development of autonomous and independent forms of cognitive investigation.

It seems also quite clear that the Leibnizian principle, based on the belief that technical progress could become part of a known and pre-arranged social order — that is the belief that a group of experts led by a well-intentioned king would be able to define the public's needs and therefore direct, by means of technical and scientific improvement, the agricultural, manufacturing and trading development — not only wasn't able to encourage any research, discovery or transformation, but on the contrary turned any form of investigation and study into a jumble of simple suggestions, descriptions, opinions and proposals. For example, the descriptions of Lombardy by Carlo Amoretti and the observations on flax, wheat and bees by Gaetano Harasti; the experiments with olive trees and vineyards of Eraclio Landi; the works of Antonio Lecchi on Lombard rivers and canals; the observations about silk by Luigi Petazzi; the studies on Lombard grass fields of Giosuè Scannagatta; the descriptions of the natural riches of Lombardy by Domenico Vandelli; the observations on woodlands of Ermenegildo Pini (Visconti, 1997).

The result of such political choice was that Austria and Lombardy long remained totally alien and unconcerned about those new scientific concepts which, at that same moment, led to gas-studying techniques and cleared up the concept of element in France and England (Abbri, 1978:26–28). This situation represented the prelude of the fundamental role that the chemical revolution was about to play for the solution of the same economic problems that the Hapsburg power's mercantilist guidelines tried to solve by uselessly lavishing all their zeal and thoughtfulness.

ACKNOWLEDGMENTS

I am very grateful to Michael Ghiselin and Giovanni Pinna for giving me the opportunity to participate in their symposium. Elvira Cantarella and Marco Meriggi offered valuable comments on the manuscript; Stefano Bellucci helped me with the translation; and Oliver Vigo discussed with me the reading of the German texts; and Alan E. Leviton edited with careful attention the whole work.

LITERATURE CITED

ABBRI, FERDINANDO. 1978. *La chimica del 700.* Loescher, Torino. 223 pp.
BACON, FRANCIS. 1952. New Atlantis. In: *Advancement of learning Novum Organum New Atlantis.* Benton, Chicago, London, Toronto. vi + 214 pp.
BALDI, MARIALUISA. 1979. *Filosofia e cultura a Mantova nella seconda metà del Settecento I manoscritti economici dell'Accademia virgiliana.* La Nuova Italia, Firenze. 234 pp.
BOAS HALL, MARIE. 1975. La scienza agli inizi della Royal Society. Pages 69–95 *in* Maurice P. Crosland, ed., *L'affermazione della scienza moderna in Europa.* Il Mulino, Bologna.
BOEHM, LAETITIA, and EZIO RAIMONDI, eds. 1981. *Università, Accademie e Società scientifiche in Italia e in Germania dal Cinquecento al Settecento.* Il Mulino, Bologna. 460 pp.
BOFFITO, GIUSEPPE. 1933. *Scrittori barnabiti o della Congregazione dei chierici regolari di San Paolo (1533–1933),* vol. 3. Olscki, Firenze. 580 pp.
BRATHER, HANS-STEPHAN, ed. 1993. *Leibniz und seine Akademie.* Akademie Verlag, Berlin. xliv + 471 pp.
CAIZZI, BRUNO. 1968. *Industria, commercio e banca in Lombardia nel XVIII secolo.* Banca Commerciale Italiana, Milano. 286 pp.
CARNEVALI, LUIGI. 1885–1887. Cenni storici sull'Accademia Virgiliana. *Atti e Memorie della Regia Accademia Virgiliana di Mantova* 24–63.
CASTELLANI, CARLO, ed. 1978. *Opere scelte di Lazzaro Spallanzani.* Utet, Torino. 1126 pp.
CIFERRI, RAFFAELE. 1961. Dal lettorato dei semplici all'Istituto e Orto Botanico ed istituti annessi. Pages 153–170 *in* Luigi De Caro, ed., *Discipline e maestri dell'Ateneo pavese.* Mondadori, Milano.
CIRCOLARE, 1777, 18 gennaio. Archivio di Stato di Milano, Studi p.a., 16.
DE MADDALENA, A. 1975. Il mercantilismo. Pages 637–704 *in* Luigi Firpo, ed., *Storia delle idee politiche economiche e sociali,* vol. 4, t. 1. Utet, Torino.
DINKLAGE, KARL. 1965. Gründung und Aufbau der theresianischen Ackerbaugesellschaften. *Zeitschrift für Agrargeschichte und Agrarsoziologie* 13:200–211.
DINKLAGE, KARL. 1966. *Geschichte der Kärntner Landwirtschaft.* Heyn, Klagenfurt. 674 pp.
DISPACCIO, 1776, 2 dicembre. 1783. *Atti della Società Patriotica di Milano* 1 (1):7–10.
FOUCHER DE CAREIL, ALEXANDRE, ed. 1875. *Oeuvres de Leibniz,* vol.7. Firmin Didot et Frères, Paris. xxxvi + 652 pp.
HAHN, ROGER. 1971. *The Anatomy of a Scientific Institution The Paris Academy of Sciences, 1666–1803.* University of California Press, Berkeley, Los Angeles, London. xiv + 433 pp.
HALL, RUPERT A. 1976. *La rivoluzione scientifica 1500–1800.* Feltrinelli, Milano. 372 pp.
HAMMERMAYER, LUDWIG. 1983.*Geschichte der bayerischen Akademie der Wissenschaften 1759–1807,* vol. 1. C. H. Beck, München. xxiv + 387 pp.
HAMMERSTEIN, NOTKER. 1981. Accademie, società scientifiche in Leibniz. Pages 395–419 *in* Laetitia Boehm and Ezio Raimondi, eds., *Università, Accademie e Società scientifiche in Italia e in Germania dal Cinquecento al Settecento.* Il Mulino, Bologna.
HARNACK, ADOLF. 1900. *Geschichte der Königlich-Preussichen Akademie der Wissenschaften zu Berlin,* vol. 1. Olms, Hildesheim, New York. 492 pp.
HERMANN, ARMIN, and HANS-PETER SANG, eds. 1992. *Technik und Staat.* Vdi Verlag, Düsseldorf. xxvi+513 pp.
IM HOF, ULRICH. 1982. *Das gesellige Jahrhundert.* C.H. Beck, München. 263 pp.
JUCCI, CARLO. 1961. Contributi dell'Università di Pavia al progresso della Biologia naturalistica. Pages 111–127 *in* Luigi De Caro, ed., *Discipline e maestri dell'Ateneo pavese.* Mondadori, Milano.
KRAFFT, FRITZ. 1981. Luoghi della ricerca naturale. Pages 421–460 *in* Laetitia Boehm and Ezio Raimondi, eds., *Università, Accademie e Società scientifiche in Italia e in Germania dal Cinquecento al Settecento.* Il Mulino, Bologna.
KRAUS, ANDREAS. 1977. Die Bedeutung der deutschen Akademien des 18. Jahrhundert für die historische und

wissenschaftliche Forschung. Pages 139–170 *in* Fritz Hartmann and Rudolf Vierhaus, eds., *Der Akademie Gedanke im 17. und 18 Jahrhundert*. Jacobiverlag, Bremen und Wolfenbüttel.

LIVA, GIOVANNI. 1986. L'istruzione superiore e universitaria e i principali istituti culturali milanesi dall'età teresiana al periodo cisalpino. Pages 59–96 *in* Raffaele De Grada, Vita Firenza and Dario Generali, eds., *La cultura a Milano tra riformismo illuminato e rivoluzione*. Vangelista, Milano.

MATHIAS, PETER. 1972. Who unbound Prometeus? Pages 54–80 *in* Peter Mathias, ed., *Science and Society 1600–1900*. Cambridge Univesity Press, Cambridge, London, New York.

MATHIEU, VITTORIO, ed. 1951. *Scritti politici e di diritto naturale di Gottfried Wilhelm Leibniz*. Utet, Torino. 541 pp.

MCCLELLAN III, JAMES E. 1985. *Science reorganized. Scientific Societies in the XVIII Century*. Columbia University Press, New York. xxix + 413 pp.

MOLLA LOSITO, VALERIA. 1982. La Società Patriottica di Milano (1776–1796) Pages 1039–1055 *in* Aldo De Maddalena, Ettore Rotelli, Gennaro Barbarisi, eds., *Economia, istituzioni, cultura in Lombardia nell'età di Maria Teresa*, vol. 3. Il Mulino, Bologna.

MÜLLER, HANS-HEINRICH. 1975. *Akademie und Wirtschaft im 18. Jahrhundert*. Akademie Verlag, Berlin. 427 pp.

OLMI, GIUSEPPE. 1978. Alle origini della politica culturale dello Stato moderno:dal collezionismo privato al cabinet du roy. *La cultura* 4:471–484.

PICHI SERMOLLI, RODOLFO. 1999. Contributo alla Storia della Botanica in Toscana I precursori dell'esplorazione floristica delle Alpi Apuane. *Museologia scientifica*, suppl. a 2, 15:v + 289.

PINI, ERMENEGILDO. 1791, 20 maggio. Relazione al Magistrato Camerale. Archivio di Stato di Milano, Commercio p.a., 205.

RASSEM, MOHAMMED. 1992. Wohlfahrt, Wohltat, Wohlttigkeit, Caritas. Pages 595–636 *in* Otto Brunner, Werner Conze, and Reinhart Koselleck, eds., *Geschichtliche Grundbegriffe*, vol. 7. Klett-Cotta, Stuttgart.

ROSSI, PAOLO. 1977. *Immagini della scienza*. Editori Riuniti, Roma. 326 pp.

SCHIERA, PIERANGELO. 1975. La concezione amministrativa dello Stato in Germania (1560–1750). Pages 363–442 *in* Luigi-Firpo, ed., *Storia delle idee politiche economiche e sociali*, vol. 4, t. 2. Utet, Torino.

SCHINDLER, NORBERT, and WOLFGANG BONSS. 1980. Praktische Aufklärung — Ökonomische Soziätaten in Suddeutschland und Österreich im 18. Jahrhundert. Pages 255–353 *in* Rudolf Vierhaus, ed., *Deutsche patriotische und gemeintzige Gesellschaften*. Kraus International Publications, München.

SCHNEIDERS, WERNER. 1977. Gottesreich und gelehrte Gesellschaft. Zwei politische Modelle bei G. W. Leibniz. Pages 47–62 *in* Fritz Hartman and Rudolf Vierhaus, eds., *Die Akademiegedanke im 17. und 18 Jahrhundert*. Jacobiverlag, Bremen und Wolfenbüttel.

SPALLANZANI, MARIA FRANCA. 1985. *La collezione naturalistica di Lazzaro Spallanzani:i modi e i tempi della sua formazione*. Comune di Reggio Emilia Civici Musei, Reggio Emilia. 147 pp.

TORCELLAN, GIANFRANCO. 1965 Francesco Griselini. Pages 93–192 *in* Giuseppe Giarrizzo, Gianfranco Torcellan and Franco Venturi, eds., *Illuministi italiani*, Tomo VII, Ricciardi Editore, Milano-Napoli.

VISCONTI, AGNESE. 1997. Il ruolo dell'assolutismo asburgico per l'avvio dello studio della natura in Lombardia. Pages 349–365 *in* Maria Luisa Betri, and Alessandro Pastore, eds., *Avvocati, medici, ingegneri alle origini delle professioni moderne*. Clueb, Bologna.

VISCONTI, AGNESE. 1998. Il Giardino Botanico della Società Patriotica di Milano (1776–1796). *Museologia scientifica* 14 (1):263–269.

Copyright ©2000 by the California Academy of Sciences
Golden Gate Park, San Francisco, California 94118, USA.
All rights reserved.

The Founders of Morphology as Alchemists

MICHAEL T. GHISELIN
Center for the History and Philosophy of Science
California Academy of Sciences, Golden Gate Park
San Francisco, California 94118 U.S.A.
E-mail: 110640.3011@compuserve.com

Historians of systematic biology have acknowledged the influence of numerology upon that science, notably in the case of Quinarianism. However, they have paid remarkably little attention to other pseudosciences. Alchemy is a particularly interesting example, because physicists and historians of physics had a hard time admitting that alchemical research was a major activity on the part of Newton.

Germany's greatest poet, Goethe, is said to have introduced the term "morphology" and is generally given much of the credit and blame for establishing the "idealistic" approach to the subject. Literary historians have provided convincing evidence not only that Goethe was a practicing alchemist, but also that his so-called biological writings were actually alchemical treatises. If biologists and historians of biology have not altogether ignored this connection, they certainly have glossed it over.

Lorenz Oken is widely known for his priority dispute with Goethe with respect to the vertebral theory of the skull. He is also known as one of the most notorious advocates of *Naturphilosophie*. The realization that Oken was an alchemist allows one to make a great deal more sense out of his writings, which generally have been condemned without an effort to understand them.

Such connections make one wonder whether more alchemical thinking was incorporated into the morphological tradition than meets the eye. The works of Richard Owen and Ernst Haeckel are more than just suggestive that some such linkage exists, but what the influence was is difficult to establish. At any rate, those authors who deny that Owen was a Platonist have been asking the wrong questions.

The "superorganism" theory of the ecosystem and "self-organization" in various areas of biology have historical roots in the alchemical tradition. To what extent the advocates of such notions have been aware of the connections, and what inferences might legitimately be drawn from them, are problems that deserve further attention but may prove largely insoluble.

For the past thirty years the primary focus of my research has been the problem of what happened to comparative anatomy as a consequence of the Darwinian Revolution. Very few of my results have thus far appeared in print, and not just because of other interests having provided distractions. Rather, comparative anatomy is a vast and difficult topic, one that is not mastered over night.

The present essay was in large measure evoked by some reflections upon the philosophy of systematics (Ghiselin, 1997). We now appreciate the point that the species and clades of modern systematics are not kinds of organisms. Rather, they are supraorganismal wholes, or "individuals" in an ontological sense. We also recognize that modern evolutionary theory, including that of Darwin, makes no sense unless we presuppose the individuality of such taxa. There could be no historical biogeography were it not for the fact that species and lineages have a definite location in space and time. If species were (abstract) classes rather than (concrete) particulars, they could not speciate or undergo any other evolutionary process. What to us is explicit, was implicit in the work of Darwin. Thanks to him, biology became a truly historical science, with "how actually" scenarios, rather than merely "how possibly" speculations about what might have happened in the past. There is a profound difference, for example, between what Darwin says about the barnacles having evolved sessility on the one hand and what Lamarck says about webbed toes in birds on the other.

Darwin's predecessors were still trying to treat taxa as if they were natural kinds, the products of laws of nature, perhaps divinely ordained, but nonetheless sharing common attributes for some fundamentally non-historical reason. It seems to me that the difference between Darwin and his predecessors is so fundamental that few if any of them deserve to be called "evolutionists." (But for qualifications see Sloan, 1986.) The fact that so many of them are called evolutionists rather than, say, protoevolutionists only serves to underscore the problem with the traditional historiography.

On the one hand we have what one might wish to call "Whig" historians of evolutionary biology, to use a standard term in perhaps a slightly idiosyncratic sense. According to this view, there were a lot of precursors of Darwin who were trying to become modern evolutionists but hadn't yet hit upon the mechanism that would make it plausible. Along came the Darwinian revolution and such persons were vindicated. On the other hand we might actually coin a new term for an alternative position, that of "Tory" historians. According to this view, the Darwinian revolution never happened, and furthermore it was a bad thing, so the precursors play the role of showing that no fundamental changes really took place. The picture of course is vastly more complicated than such a travesty suggests. Among other things the notion that nothing really happened in 1859 is very convenient for those who want to argue that it should have happened but did not happen until Mendel, or Mayr, or Watson and Crick, or perhaps even Ghiselin. Everybody agrees that natural selection was not accepted as readily as evolution, but taking the position that the Darwinian revolution was a myth (Bowler, 1988) is hyperbolic to say the least.

In the standard literature, at least, we find frequent mention of something called *Naturphilosophie* that flourished in the early nineteenth century. Supposedly it had something to do with Herder, Schelling and other Romantics (see Jardine, 1996). *Naturphilosophie* is widely condemned for its absurdities and speculative excess. It is also widely praised for somehow being concerned with development and change: supposedly it was a precursor of evolutionary thinking (Lenoir, 1982). But we are not really told what these persons believed about biology, or why. Herein I propose to address precisely that question.

The popularity of certain pseudosciences in pre-Darwinian biology is generally recognized. Quinarianism is a case in point (Winsor, 1976; Rehbock, 1983). Various biologists tried to arrange their materials in circular patterns, usually with groups of five, though other mystic numbers such as three and seven were deemed perfectly reasonable; it was a matter of empirical research to decide which number was correct. Circles are of course the perfect geometrical figure. For quinarians it was profoundly significant that there were correspondences between the groups thus arranged. Among these correspondences was "iconism": tigers would have their equivalent in tiger beetles. There would be five races of man, five biogeographical provinces, five temperaments, and they all would correspond to, and symbolize, one another (Swainson, 1835). This all makes sense. Mathematics is the language of the perfect Being, and the task of a systematist is to attain knowledge of His mind through a kind of mystical insight.

Such mystical correspondences are by no means peculiar to quinarianism. They are a common theme among belief systems that are now dismissed as pseudoscientific. Likewise it is more or less common knowledge that the pseudosciences and what we, from our perspective, consider the real thing have only gradually become differentiated. I shall not dwell upon the difference between a belief system and a corpus of scientific knowledge. Suffice it to mention the provisional character of scientific theories and their meta-theoretical premises and the crucial role of efforts to refute, or at least to modify, hypotheses. As to mysticism, it has generally been discredited as a source of scientific, though not of religious, knowledge. Its ultimately private character is but one reason for this.

Professional intellectuals do tend to forget that the pseudosciences are still widely practiced. If you have any doubt just look at the astrology columns in the daily paper. And although we acknowledge the importance of astrology in the behavior of politicians such as Adolf Hitler and Mrs. Reagan, we hesitate to face up to the enthusiasm of practicing scientists for what is often called "occult metaphysics." (Not to be confused with the sort of metaphysics that is still a respectable branch of philosophy.) For example, the historian of physics Betty Jo Dobbs had enormous difficulties convincing her colleagues that Sir Isaac Newton was an alchemist and that his alchemical work was very important to him. Fortunately for her, there were plenty of documents to support her thesis (Dobbs, 1991). But once that thesis got accepted, it was much easier to discover and understand the alchemical work of one of the founders of modern chemistry, Robert Boyle (Principe, 1998).

The historical connection between alchemy and chemistry is common knowledge, and is considered routinely in works on the history of that science (e.g., Brock, 1993). The two gradually separated and from the point of view of the present essay it helps to understand how that separation took place. From the outset there were two aspects to it, a practical one that involved manipulation of substances, and a spiritual one that involved the enlightenment of the alchemist himself. In either case the goal was the attainment of a higher state of existence. The transformation of other minerals into gold by means of the "philosopher's stone" had its parallels in the spiritual transformation of the alchemist himself. The two aspects gradually became dissociated. The practical work, which had traditionally involved much experimentation, gave rise to chemistry. The spiritual endeavor however, persisted in the form of Rosicrucianism and various other enterprises.

It is generally believed that alchemy had been discredited and replaced by chemistry by the middle of the eighteenth century. However, it survived as occult metaphysics, and that occult metaphysics would seem to have influenced the thinking of biologists for some time after the chemists had pretty much abandoned it. The obvious link between chemistry and alchemy on the one hand, and the various branches of biology on the other, is through medicine including materia medica and pharmacology. Given that the teaching of natural history was so closely connected with medicine some kind of influence upon systematic biology would hardly be surprising. And in fact Isidore Geoffroy Saint-Hilaire (1859) discusses the influence of alchemy on early taxonomists. But the connection is not widely recognized or considered important.

Here I shall consider the connection between alchemy and what is called "morphology." The term "morphology" is very loosely used these days: generally it means anatomy and embryology, maybe with histology and all sorts of other things thrown in. Strictly speaking, however, morphology is the study of form. Physiology is the study of function. There is a long tradition of separating the two, so that "functional morphology" is a sort of oxymoron. There is also a long tradition of discussing the "form-function problem" in terms of Platonic Idealism on the one hand and Aristotelian teleology on the other. Anything but face up to the metaphysical revolution that was initiated by Darwin. I am by no means alone in criticizing this particular historiographical tradition (Asma,1996). It is a serious obstacle to our understanding of the documents whether ones interests are those of an historian, a working biologist, or both.

Goethe

Although there is some question as to who first used it in print, there is at least a tradition that the term "morphology" was coined by Germany's greatest poet, Johann Wolfgang von Goethe

(1749–1832). Anybody who has read *Faust* knows that Goethe was interested in alchemy, but it is very easy to treat the alchemy as little more than a literary ornament, rather like the Greek Gods in Baroque paintings. As to Goethe's novel *Die Wahlverwandtschaften* (*The Elective Affinities*), it is a very boring effort to use a later version of chemistry as a literary theme. However, literary historians have in fact attended to the older, alchemical background to this work (see Adler, 1987, 1990).

Be this as it may, it is clear from his autobiography that Goethe was a serious student of alchemy, and, indeed, a practicing alchemist. But to find out that his so-called scientific publications, including the "biological" works were alchemical treatises, one has to go to the literary historians, notably Gray (1952). Or one may turn to the work of Jung (1968, 1970) on the psychology of alchemy in which it is made clear that Goethe's *Weltanschauung* was permeated by it. And, indeed, if one reads his publications from that perspective, Goethe's stance on how science ought to be pursued becomes much less of a puzzle.

One does not get such an impression of Goethe out of the standard histories of biology, from his biographies (e.g., Magnus, 1949) or from the writings of his devoted followers among scientists, such as Agnes Arber (1946). The alchemical connection is briefly mentioned in passing by historians of science, but they do not pay much attention to it (Fink, 1991). To be sure, I may have missed something: there is a vast literature. But the impression is what really matters here. The vast tradition of idealistic morphology that has long flourished, especially in Germany, and is immensely influential even today, has precisely those roots. We must of course watch out for the genetic fallacy here. It would be wrong to try to discredit contemporary science on the grounds that it can be traced back to precursors that now seem disreputable. It is, however, legitimate to ask whether we are perhaps making the same old mistakes. Furthermore scientific traditions tend to get deracinated. It is all too easy to overlook the basic assumptions and premises when knowledge is passed on from generation to generation and nobody bothers to go back and read the old texts.

Oken

Lorenz Oken (1779–1851) (Figure 1) is largely remembered because of his priority dispute with Goethe over the vertebral theory of the skull (Ecker, 1880; Pfannensteil 1951a, 1959b). Oken was for some time a Professor at Jena — i.e., what might colloquially be called "Weimar U." — and much of the historical literature on him relates to his having been fired because of his political activities, with Goethe somehow involved in that episode as an advisor to the government. Also remembered is his invention of the modern scientific meeting as an institution (Degen, 1972). Finally, Oken is widely recognized as either the best example, or, depending upon one's sympathies, the worst example, of *Naturphilosophie* (Mullen, 1977; Wenig, 1985, 1988). Again, I may have missed something, but the most I find with respect to alchemy is passing mention of some similarities (e.g., Güttler, 1884, Raikov, 1969). In general, Oken is treated as having derived his views from his friend Schelling, and that does it. But Oken was the son of a pharmacist, and later became very widely read in the older medical literature, in which alchemical ideas were widely discussed (Strohl, 1935). And in his publications he occasionally discusses the views of alchemists explicitly (e.g., Oken 1808:26).

Oken's numerology is so patently obvious that nobody who even flips the pages of his *Lehrbuch* can miss it. But this numerology is superimposed upon, or at least coexists with, a system of mystical correspondences among the various components of the Universe. And many of the details are easily recognized as traditional components of alchemical cosmic schemes. The existence of correspondences among bodily parts is a phenomenon that biologists have long and rightly treated as a fact in search of an explanation. We need look no farther than the correspondences between the bones of the left and right fore-limb or between, say humerus and femur. And similar correspondences between the parts of different organisms in different branches of the phylogenetic nexus are crucial to evolutionary comparative anatomy. The correspondences take on the character of occult metaphysics when the parts are thought to symbolize one another as components of a vast cosmic scheme.

According to the vertebral theory of the skull, which even today can still be treated as a perfectly legitimate (albeit long-rejected) scientific hypothesis, the skull is made up of vertebrae that can be treated as a kind of "module" or metamere. If one grants that the head is made up of a certain number of serially-repeated units, one might try to answer the question of how many such units it contains, and try to identify and count them. Oken had a more elegant technique: he derived the number four from basic principles (Oken, 1840). There are five senses: touch, taste, smell, hearing and vision. Of these, four are localized in the head, and it stands to reason that there must be one vertebra for each!

FIGURE 1. Lorenz Oken (1779–1851).

Likewise he was able to derive a scheme for the classification of animals. Each taxonomic group symbolizes one of the five senses. So just to take human races as an example (there must be five of them) I don't even have to tell you which symbolizes touch and which vision. And it all makes sense because each and every object in the world is symbolic of the others and of the whole, which is coextensive with God. Indeed, the whole world following Plato's *Timaeus* is an organism: the *Weltorganismus*. Such taxonomic schemes are hardly evolutionary, or even protoevolutionary: they are part of a tradition that the alchemists derived from early Neoplatonism. There are some other notions in the writings of Oken that are thought of as evolutionary, and wrongly. The primordial ooze or *Urschleim* that is generally interpreted as some kind of ancestor really ought to be treated as the expression of a kind of hylozoism: the notion that matter is alive. A typically alchemical theme is that matter has the capacity to assemble itself spontaneously into organized beings by a process like crystallization. The achievement of a higher state of being may be accomplished by a kind of purification: physical or spiritual.

However, there are other ways of achieving a higher state of being, among which the conjunction of polar opposites. Figure 2 reproduces an illustration from a book on generation by Oken (1805) entitled *Die Zeugung*. It shows a scheme of polarities with the male and female, salt and sulfur and the like arranged in a rather idiosyncratic scheme, but with a triangular structure that is nonetheless typical of the alchemical literature. Like other alchemists, Oken was very interested in hermaphroditism, because it symbolizes the union of male and female, completeness, and perfection.

Oken (1805:55, 91) actually cites alchemical sources such as the writings of Athanasius Kircher. Furthermore he frequently uses alchemical symbolism. To give perhaps the most striking example, Figure 3 reproduces on the title page of *Die Zeugung*. Here Oken depicts a pair of snakes, each with the other's tail in its mouth: it is a somewhat idiosyncratic Uroboros. One commentator remarks that the Uroboros is an ancient symbol of eternity (Raikov, 1969). This need hardly be contested but it

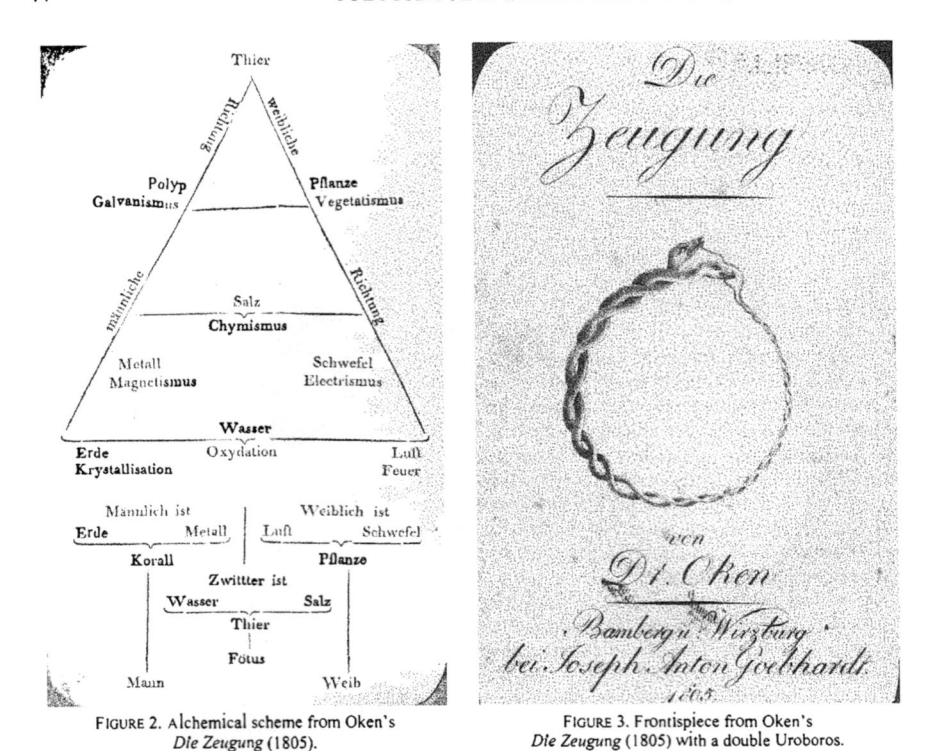

FIGURE 2. Alchemical scheme from Oken's
Die Zeugung (1805).

FIGURE 3. Frontispiece from Oken's
Die Zeugung (1805) with a double Uroboros.

completely misses the intended message. Symbols are powerful because they can convey all sorts of things at the same time. For alchemists, the Uroboros is a symbol of alchemical truth, the *aqua divina*, and the philosopher's stone (Jung, 1970). We should emphasize that the primary goal of alchemy was not the transmutation of base metals into gold, but the attainment of a kind of knowledge that such a procedure symbolizes.

Owen

Richard Owen (1804–1892) is largely remembered as a bitter opponent of Darwin, and especially of Huxley. After the *Origin of Species* was published, he claimed to have been an evolutionist all along, rather to Darwin's surprise. Lately, what I like to call Tory historians have attempted to refurbish Owen's reputation and to treat him as a kind of evolutionist. If all one means by an "evolutionist" is someone who thinks that there are successions of ancestors and descendants that become cumulatively different in one sense or another, then one can make a case for such an interpretation. But somebody who has begrudged the world such a minimal concession can easily go on to defend a position that is at once creationist, and profoundly anti-evolutionary (Ghiselin, 1997).

Owen was one of the outstanding idealistic morphologists, and in his book on the meaning of limbs, he explicitly refers to the "Archetypal World in the Platonic cosmogony...." (Owen, 1849:1).

Although Owen was sometimes called the "British Cuvier," he makes a much better British Oken. The connections between Owen and Oken are quite clear. They were personally acquainted. Owen was a strong supporter of the vertebral theory of the skull, and at the Natural History Museum in London, Owen's personal copy of Oken's basic publication on that theory is still preserved (Oken, 1807). Owen (1858) wrote an encyclopedia article on Oken, defending his priority for the vertebral theory of the skull against Goethe. Furthermore, Owen was instrumental in arranging for the publication of an English translation of Oken's *Lehrbuch der Naturgeschichte* (Oken, 1847). Around that time Charles Darwin paid a lot of attention to Owen's publications on the principles of comparative anatomy, and his personal copies of these are heavily annotated. Although Darwin's reading list says that he read the translation of Oken's *Lehrbuch* in September of 1847, he would seem not to have annotated his personal copy; nor does he discuss it in his published correspondence. He does mention Oken as one of his predecessors in the "Historical Sketch" that was inserted in later editions of *The Origin of Species*.

Among the works of Owen that Darwin paid most attention to was the *Archetype and Homologies of the Vertebrate Skeleton* (Owen, 1848). Darwin was much intrigued by Owen's notion of an archetype, but did not like the idealistic connotations and used the term as roughly equivalent to a common ancestor (as is clear from his annotations and correspondence). Owen's archetype looks very much like a fish, which is perfectly reasonable even if one reinterprets it as representing a stage in our own ancestry. Nonetheless if we look at Owen's (1849:86) quasi-evolutionary comments upon the Archetype in his *Nature of Limbs*, the following suggests the kind of metaphysics that was involved:

> To what natural laws or secondary causes the orderly succession and progression of such organic phenomena may have been committed we as yet are ignorant. But if, without derogation of the Divine power, we may conceive the existence of such ministers, and personify them by the term 'Nature,' we learn from the past history of our globe that she has advanced with slow and stately steps, guided by the archetypal light, amidst the wreck of worlds, from the first embodiment of the Vertebrate idea under its old Ichthyic vestment, until it became arrayed in the glorious garb of the Human form.

"Archetypal light" is jargon for God, and this all sounds very Platonic. One historian has flatly denied that Owen was a Platonist (Rupke, 1993) on the grounds that Owen's views were quite different from those of Plato himself. To be sure, for somebody like Plato a human being would make much more sense as an ideal vertebrate than would a fish. But to treat Owen as if he were a philosopher who derived his ideas from philosophical texts places his writings in the wrong literary context. Granted that Owen was a follower of Oken, and at least influenced by alchemy, it follows that he was a kind of Neoplatonist operating in the "hermetic tradition" and perhaps under the influence of the Cabala (Yates, 1964; Simonetta, 1995). Furthermore, as a mystic, he would have been perfectly free to pick and choose from any of a variety of notions, and mystics often revel in contradictions.

If one brings in Christianity, the fish makes a fine symbol of both Man and the Son of Man, and vertebrate anatomy thereby becomes transformed into a sort of allegory. But whether he had that in mind is just an intriguing possibility. At the very least, we ought to be sensitive to the profound difference between such an interpretation of anatomy and what somebody like Darwin was up to. Design on the installment plan is by no means what we mean by evolution: the change in question is superficial, insofar as everything was ordained from the Beginning and nothing really new has come into being.

Haeckel

Ernst Haeckel (1834–1919) is generally considered to have been Darwin's outstanding advocate among the Germans. Yet Haeckel's views were most peculiar, quite different from those of Darwin or of real advocates of Darwin's views such as Fritz Müller. Haeckel was strongly influenced by *Naturphilosophie* and his opponents sometimes made a big point of that. Elias Metschnikoff for example railed against him in both his German and his Russian publications (see Ghiselin and Groeben, 1997). Traces of Goethean mysticism in Haeckel have been noted by its advocates and opponents alike (Himleben, 1965). If we treat him as a follower of Goethe and Oken, much of Haeckel's behavior makes a lot more sense. For one thing, Haeckel (1882) claimed that both Goethe and Oken were evolutionists. For another, Haeckel advocated Hylozoism: the notion that all matter is alive. His last book in fact was entitled *The Souls of Crystals* (Haeckel, 1917). His peculiar science of "promorphology" that provided an arrangement of types of symmetry was obviously derived from Oken, perhaps through some intermediate source. His notion of protoplasm has sometimes been compared to the Okenian "*Urschleim.*"

Some Later Vestiges of Alchemy

Outside of biology, we have the interesting case of the German philosopher and psychologist Gustav Theodor Fechner (1801–1887), whose debt to Oken has lately been well documented by Michael Heidelberger (1993). Indeed Heidelberger maintains that the popularity of so-called Darwinism in Germany is unintelligible without an understanding of Oken. Like Oken, Fechner was a hylozoist and he believed that soul is in everything and that the world is God's body. The notion of self-organization, of course an important theme in alchemy, was derived by Prigogine and Glansdorf from Fechner, who in turn derived it from Oken.

The notion of a *Weltorganismus* which Oken evidently derived either directly or indirectly from Plato has been a pervasive theme in various disciplines. I discussed this theme in sociology and ecology at some length in my book on the economy of nature (Ghiselin, 1974). The present form of this superstition is of course what is called the Gaia hypothesis.

That however, may have been a sort of rediscovery. It is interesting to find that the "transformed cladists" in rejecting evolution as a basis for systematics realized that they were rediscovering the views of the so-called rational morphologists. Simonetta (1995) is quite blunt in comparing the advocates of hologenesis and like notions to cabalistic thinking. Persons of such persuasion have treated Owen as a kind of anti-hero. But when we talk about "rediscovery" it becomes problematic as to how the older tradition may have influenced much later work, perhaps unconsciously.

DISCUSSION

One might want to put in a good word for *Naturphilosophie* and even for its alchemical aspects. Finding analogies, or far-fetched resemblances, can be a most useful source of new ideas in the sciences. The problem, however, is what one makes of such analogies. The alchemist, rather than finding causal relationships among appearances, seeks a pattern of symbolic correspondences that give him a sense of communing with a world that lies beyond appearances. As it turns out, the effort to read God's mind leads to a projection of one's inner self. So what gets revealed is a subjective construct, rather than an objective discovery.

When we realize what has gone on at perhaps an unconscious level it is easy to see why morphology, at least as practiced in the tradition of Oken and Goethe, has been so formalistic and sterile. And also why it has so often been a bastion of anti-evolutionism and a focus of opposition to the theory of natural selection. When somebody is seeking that kind of order, it is obviously not the kind of order that is of interest to an evolutionist in the modern sense of that term. In comparing Oken to Darwin, some historians have suggested that what made the difference was Darwin's empirical approach. This altogether misses the point. The alchemists had their laboratories and their experiments. They interacted with nature.

It is one thing to study organisms with the goal of finding an order that lies "beyond" the organized beings themselves and their place in the material universe. It is another to treat the organisms as populations of organized beings that become reorganized through successive generations by virtue of how they interact with one another and with the rest of the material universe. If some of the answers look superficially similar, the questions were fundamentally different. We seek in vain among the advocates of *Naturphilosophie* for evidence of a research program in which the history of life is documented and that history is important in allowing us to understand the organisms themselves.

In science, the mysticism did not drop out instantaneously, and indeed it is still with us. It has gone from explicit to implicit, and then perhaps even become unconscious. Likewise it has become marginalized, moved out of the intellectual mainstream to become part of superstition, folklore, literary ornament, and religious apologetics. But in such cases it becomes very hard for the historian to deal with it. When alchemy separated from chemistry, its mystical tradition continued as the Rosicrucian movement. Cain (1992) suspected that Linnaeus was a Rosicrucian; but all that he was able to show for sure was an interest in the occult.

There are serious problems when we encounter what look like "survivals" of older ways of thinking. On the one hand, the historical connection might have little if anything to do with real content: self-organization is a real phenomenon and it needn't be approached from a mystical point of view. And things change, so that the mysticism might simply get dropped out. On the other hand just about everybody seems to posses the capacity to invent mystical notions, and these may arise without any historical connection to apparent historical predecessors. This is, broadly speaking, what Jung proposed: the human brain has a certain structure, the product of evolution, and we inherit a proclivity to behave like alchemists. So for Jung alchemy was interesting as a clue to the unconscious.

But how do we get at those aspects of scientific thinking of which scientists themselves are largely unaware? To understand the culture of natural history we may therefore need some insights from psychology. There is nothing particularly anti- scientific about that. Scientists realize that there are frequencies of sound that bats can hear but we cannot; and likewise that there are frequencies of light that bees can see but we cannot. The limitations of our senses have not kept such matters beyond our grasp.

REFERENCES

ADLER, JEREMY. 1987. *«Eine fast magische Anziehungskraft»: Goethe's «Wahlverwandtschaften» und die Chemie seiner Zeit.* Verlag von C. H. Beck, München. 260 pp.
ADLER, JEREMY. 1990. Goethe's use of chemical theory in his *Elective Affinities*. Pages 263–279 *in* A. Cunningham and N. Jardine, eds., *Romanticism and the Sciences*. Cambridge University Press, Cambridge.
ARBER, AGNES. 1946. Goethe's botany. *Chronica Botanica* 10:67–124.
ASMA, STEPHEN T. 1996. *Following Form and Function: a Philosophical Archaeology of Life Science.* Northwestern University Press, Evanston. xiii + 232 pp.
BOWLER, PETER J. 1988. *The Non-Darwinian Revolution: Reinterpreting a Historical Myth.* The Johns Hopkins University Press, Baltimore. x + 238 pp.
BROCK, WILLIAM H. 1993. *The Norton History of Chemistry.* W. W. Norton & Co., New York. xvii + 744 pp.

CAIN, A. J. 1992. Was Linnaeus a Rosicrucian? *Linnean* 8:23–44.
DEGEN, HEINZ. 1972. München als Tagungsort der Gesellschaft Deutscher Naturforscher und Ärzte. *Naturwissenschaftliche Rundschau* 25:367–382.
DOBBS, BETTY JO TEETER. 1991. *The Janus Face of Genius: the Role of Alchemy in Newton's Thought.* Cambridge University Press, Cambridge. xii + 359 pp.
ECKER, ALEXANDER. 1880. *Lorenz Oken. Eine biographische Skizze.* E. Schweizerbart'sche Verlagshandlung, Stuttgart. vi + 220 pp.
FINK, KARL J. 1991. *Goethe's History of Science.* Cambridge University Press, Cambridge. xii + 242 pp.
GEOFFROY SAINT-HILAIRE, ISIDORE. 1859. *Histoire Naturelle Générale des Règnes Organiques, Principalement Étudiée chez l'Homme et les Animaux,* vol. 2. Victor Masson et fils, Paris. 523 pp.
GHISELIN, MICHAEL T. 1974. *The Economy of Nature and the Evolution of Sex.* University of California Press, Berkeléy. xii + 364 pp.
GHISELIN, MICHAEL T. 1997. *Metaphysics and the Origin of Species.* State University of New York Press, Albany. xi + 377 pp.
GHISELIN, MICHAEL T., and CHRISTIANE GROEBEN. 1997. Elias Metschnikoff, Anton Dohrn, and the metazoan common ancestor. *Journal of the History of Biology* 30:211–228.
GRAY, RONALD D. 1952. *Goethe the Alchemist: a Study of the Alchemical Symbolism in Goethe's Literary and Scientific Works.* Cambridge University Press, Cambridge. x + 312 pp.
GÜTTLER, C. 1884. *Lorenz Oken und sein Verhältniss zur modernen Entwickelungslehre. Ein Beitrag zur Geschichte der Naturphilosophie.* Verlag von E. Bidder, Leipzig. iv + 150 pp.
HAECKEL, ERNST. 1882. *Die Naturanschauung von Darwin, Goethe und Lamarck.* Verlag von Gustav Fischer, Jena. viii + 64 pp.
HAECKEL, ERNST. 1917. *Kristallseelen. Studien über das anorganische Leben.* Alfred Kröner Verlag, Leipzig. viii + 152 pp.
HEIDELBERGER, MICHAEL. 1993. *Der innere Seite der Natur. Gustav Theodor Fechners wissenschaftlich-philosophische Weltauffassung.* Vittorio Klostermann, Frankfurt am Main. 457 pp.
HIMLEBEN, JOHANNES. 1965. *Rudolf Steiner und Ernst Haeckel.* Verlag Freies Geistesleben, Stuttgart. 175 pp.
JARDINE, NICHOLAS. 1996. Naturphilosophie and the kingdoms of nature. Pages 230–245 *in* N. Jardine, J. A. Secord, and E. C. Spary, eds., *Cultures of Natural History.* Cambridge University Press, Cambridge.
JUNG, CARL GUSTAV. 1968. *Psychology and Alchemy,* 2nd edition. Princeton University Press, Princeton. xxxvi + 571 pp.
JUNG, CARL GUSTAV. 1970. *Mysterium Conjunctionis: an Inquiry into the Separation and Synthesis of Psychic Opposites in Alchemy,* 2nd edition. Princeton University Press, Princeton. xix + 702 pp.
LENOIR, TIMOTHY J. 1982. *The Strategy of Life: Teleology and Mechanics in Nineteenth-Century German Biology.* University of Chicago Press, Chicago. xii + 314 pp.
MAGNUS, RUDOLF. 1949. *Goethe as a Scientist.* Foreword by Günther Schmid; Translated by Heinz Norden. Henry Schumann, New York. xxi + 259 pp.
MULLEN, PIERCE C. 1977. The Romantic as Scientist: Lorenz Oken. *Studies in Romanticism* 16:381–399.
OKEN, LORENZ. 1805. *Die Zeugung.* Joseph Anton Goebhardt, Bamberg. viii + 216 pp.
OKEN, LORENZ. 1807. *Über die Bedeutung der Schädelknochen.* J. a. Göbhardt, Bamberg & Würzburg. 18 pp.
OKEN, LORENZ. 1808. *Über das Universum als Fortsetzung des Sinnensystems. Ein pythagoräisches Fragment.* Friedrich Frommann, Jena. 46 pp.
OKEN, LORENZ. 1840. Idées sur la classification des Animaux. *Annales des Sciences Naturelles, Zoologie* 14:247–268.
OKEN, LORENZ. 1847. *Elements of Physiophilosophy.* Translated by Alfred Tulk. Ray Society, London. xxx + 665 pp. (Translation of 1831 ed.)
OWEN, RICHARD. 1849. *On the Nature of Limbs. A Discourse Delivered on Friday, February 9, at an Evening Meeting of the Royal Institution of Great Britain.* John van Voorst, London. ii + 119 pp., 2 Plates.
OWEN, RICHARD. 1858. Oken. Pages 498-503 *in Encyclopaedia Britannica,* 8th edition, vol. 16.
PFANNENSTEIL, MAX. 1951a. Lorenz Oken. *In* Max Pfannensteil, ed., Oken-Heft. *Berichten der Naturforschenden Gesellschaft zu Freiburg im Breisgau* 41(1):7–20.

PFANNENSTEIL, MAX. 1951b. Die Wirbelmetmorphose OKENS an Hand neuer Dokumente. *In* Max Pfannensteil, ed., Oken-Heft. *Berichten der Naturforschenden Gesellschaft zu Freiburg im Breisgau* 41(1):75–100.
PRINCIPE, LAWRENCE M. 1998. *The Aspiring Adept: Robert Boyle and his Alchemical Quest.* Princeton University Press, Princeton. xiv + 339 pp.
RAIKOV, BORIS E. 1969. *German Biologists – Evolutionists before Darwin: Lorenz Oken, Karl Friedrich Burdach, Martin Henrich Rathke.* Izdatelstvo Nayka, Leningrad. 232 pp. (In Russian.)
REHBOCK, PHILIP F. 1983. *The Philosophical Naturalists: Themes in Early Nineteenth-Century British Biology.* University of Wisconsin Press, Madison. xv + 281 pp.
RUPKE, NICOLAAS A. 1993. Richard Owen's vertebrate archetype. *Isis* 84:231–251.
SIMONETTA, ALBERTO M. 1995. Some remarks on the influence of historical bias in our approach to systematics and the so called «species problem». *Bollettino di Zoologia* 62:37–44.
SLOAN, PHILIP R. 1986. From logical universals to historical individuals: Buffon's idea of biological species. Pages 101–140 *in* Anonymous, ed., *Histoire du Concept d'Espèce dans les Sciences de la Vie.* Fondation Singer-Polignac, Paris.
STROHL, Johannes. 1935. Okens Stellung zu Paracelsus und zur Geschichte der Naturwissenschaften überhaupt. *Verhandlungen der Schweitzerische Naturforschenden Gesellschaft* 1035:395–397.
SWAINSON, WILLIAM. 1835. *A Treatise on the Geography and Classification of Animals.* Longman, Rees, Orme, Brown, Green and Longman, London. viii + 367 pp.
WENIG, KLAUS. 1985. Zur Bedeutung des naturphilosophischen Entwicklungsmodells von L. Oken in der Geschichte des Entwicklungsdenkens. Pages 226–234 *in* E. Lange, ed., *Philosophie und Natur. Beiträge zur Naturphilosophie der deutschen Klassik.* Hermann, Bölhaus Nachfolger, Weimar.
WENIG, KLAUS. 1988. Lorenz Oken - Naturphilosoph und spiritus rector der Wissenschaftsentwicklung anfangs des 19. Jahrhunderts in Deutschland. *Wissenschaftliche Zeitschrift Friedrich-Schiller-Universität Jena*, ser. Naturwiss. Reihe, 37(2):217–222.
WINSOR, MARY P. 1976. *Starfish, Jellyfish, and the Order of Life: Issues in 19th-Century Science.* Yale University Press, New Haven. x + 228 pp.
YATES, FRANCES A. 1964. *Giordano Bruno and the Hermetic Tradition.* University of Chicago Press, Chicago. xiv + 466 pp.

India: A Case Study of Natural History in a Colonial Setting

ALAN E. LEVITON[1] and MICHELE L. ALDRICH[2]
1 California Academy of Sciences, Golden Gate Park, San Francisco, California 94118
E-mail: aleviton@calacademy.org
[2] Science and Technology Studies, Cornell University, Ithaca, New York 14853
and Research Associate, California Academy of Sciences, San Francisco, California 94118
E-mail: 73061.2420@compuserve.com

In southern and southwestern Asia, 18th- and 19th-century natural history exploration, collection building, and the founding of museums, were closely tied to the geopolitics of the time. As observed by Anderson (1999:15), the early period of natural history studies by Europeans in India and neighboring countries coincided with expansionist activities most notably of Britain and France, the Ottoman Turks, and Russia. Anderson (*loc. cit.*) argued that the first two, particularly, saw the independent states and khanates of Southwest Asia as buffers between their domains of territorial hegemony, as each moved to increase trade and economic influence within its realms. He noted that each sought more, especially raw materials for expanding manufacturing industries back home, spices, teas and other exotic food stuffs, and outlets abroad for the products of their factories. Britain also found that it offered opportunity to relocate undesirables as well as provide opportunity for some of the burgeoning population at home.

Given the initial demands of colonization, the naturalists who accompanied military expeditions, boundary commissions, railway, trigonometric, and telegraph surveys, and diplomatic missions during the 18th and 19th centuries were mostly military officers and physicians attached to army units. Early in the second half of the 19th century, however, a new breed of naturalists, drawn from the ranks of professionally-trained geologists, surveyors, foresters, meteorologists, and the like began to replace the "gentlemen" explorers and soldier- and physician-naturalists of the earlier day. And some of these were seconded to military units for the purpose of conducting reconnaissance explorations along routes of march. Even so, at best natural history exploration during this period was nearly always practiced avocationally, political and military exigencies permitting. Nonetheless, large collections were amassed and journals filled with observations, maps, and sketches of animals, plants, and terrain, and these engaged the attention of many, both in the colonies and back home.

In this paper, we focus on a narrow range of activities of the colonial enterprise, those closely tied to the establishment of a scientific natural history undertaking. We examine their implications for the development of museums, botanic gardens, and government-sponsored surveys as research centers, with their associated collections, and along the way cite some of the more notable research done by the "colonials."

Several of India's extant natural history institutions have venerable histories. For some, that history dates back to the late 18th and early 19th centuries. In the limited space available, we cannot possibly chronicle the emergence of the many such institutions that today dot the subcontinent, such as the Asiatic Society of Bengal, founded in 1784, and its museum in 1814, or that of the Madras Literary Society, whose small collections formed the nucleus of the Central or Madras Government Museum in 1851, the Victoria Museum in Karachi, also in 1851, the Victoria and Albert Museum in Bombay (1857), Government [Napier] Museum in Trivandrum (1857), Central Museum in Nagpur (1863), and museums in Lucknow (1863), Bangalore (1865), Calcutta (1866), Fyzabad (1871), and elsewhere. Rather, we shall follow those events that led to the establishment of museums in general, and, most importantly, the Indian Museum in Calcutta, which to this day houses the largest, most diverse zoological, botanical and ethnological collections in India. In its one guise or another, the Indian Museum has participated in the most far-reaching programs of research and public displays of the many museums founded throughout Asia during the 19th century. In doing this, we would like to test whether these events fit the schemes of colonial science advanced by Basalla (1967), that emphasize the explorative and applied rather than theoretical, his "corporate" view downplaying the individual, and Fleming's (1964) description of colonial scientists as preferring a subservient role because "it saved them from the more perilous enterprise of theoretical constructions." While there may be a grain of truth to these assertions, we find their generalizations too sweeping, obfuscating as they do much of the exceptional science that took place in colonial settings, most notably in India, from which setting emerged such important theoretical constructs as isostasy, Permo-Carboniferous glaciation, and Gondwanaland, to name but three. We are drawn to Deepak Kumar's recent writing, *Science and the Raj*, in which he argues that science in the colonial/imperial settings of the "Raj" takes on a uniqueness of its own and is much influenced by the geography and social and political climate in which it takes place. We are also mindful that too many historians who deal with science in the 19th century, even those focusing on colonial science, look to the models of Western European science, and concentrate all too narrowly on laboratory-based physics, chemistry, microscopical biology, and physiology, with little appreciation of the impact of the field-based sciences, such as natural history and geology, with an allowance, of course, for Darwin. We contend that, on balance, historians deal poorly with the historical sciences, geology, biogeography, and faunistics and floristics, and with the influence colonial scientists had on European thought. Even MacLeod's vision of "Imperial Science," we believe is too constraining with respect to mid-19th century India, although he allows for the emergence of new "metropoles," new centers of intellectual ferment, beyond those already well established in Europe and North America. We recognize, but do not agree with, the almost universal appeal of the notion, as pointed out by MacLeod (1987:221) that "*Colonial science*

to those at home, recognizing their dominion over palm and pine, . . . meant derivative science, done by lesser minds working on problems set by savants in Europe. It was, looked at from the metropolis, 'low science,' identified with fact gathering." Thus, we, like Kumar, take exception to these too narrow perspectives, and we intend to show why.

If our comments that follow seem to focus too narrowly on geology, plants, fishes, and reptiles, allow that these engaged the attention of many 19th century scientists, professional and amateur alike. Moreover, they serve well as *exempli gratia* of the points we wish to make. Lastly, we are well aware of the close relationship between the founding of many of the provincial museums in India, with their emphasis on zoology, and the rise of teaching universities. We certainly believe that this is a subject that should court notice, but we do not pursue it here because even though started in the mid-19th century with several small specialized museums, such as the medical museum at Grant Medical College, Bombay in 1845, and museums at Calcutta University and in Bombay and Madras in the 1850s (see Markham, 1936:13–18 for additional listings), most of the activity took place early in the 20th century, and thus falls outside our purview.

The Early Years

Let us now set the clock back to December 31, 1600, to that moment in history that set "England" (and here we use the eponym in both its Elizabethan and 19th century Victorian context, which was decidedly non-European) on the path of imperial domain. On that day, Elizabeth put the Great Seal on the charter of the East India Company (Fig. 1), thereby giving royal consent to a select group of London merchants to conduct business in the "East Indies" in direct competition with Portuguese and Dutch traders. The Court of Directors of the newly founded company responded immediately and placed Sir James Lancaster (d. 1618[3]) in command of its first venture. He was ordered to sail to the East Indies, establish a "factory," a mercantile trading post, on Sumatra and purchase spices, teas, indigo, camphor, and other products for direct import to England. Until 1579, Dutch merchants had handled most of northern Europe's spice trade. They had gotten their supplies from the Portuguese in Lisbon, but that was before 1580 when Spain annexed Portugal. With the earlier defeat of their Spanish overlords and the establishment of an independent Dutch republic in 1579, Spain closed all of its ports to Dutch shipping. Cut off from their source of supplies, the Dutch saw their lucrative spice trade severely curtailed and a meteoric increase in the cost of what spices they could obtain. Northern Europe, including Britain, were of course, affected. This prompted the Dutch, in 1595, to open their own sea routes to the East Indies "in open defiance of the Portuguese monopoly, and open trade with the ports of Java and Bali" (Whitfield, 1998:105); shortly thereafter, England followed suit. Thus, with £30,000 in gold, silver coin, and other metals as barter, Lancaster set sail in 1601 with five small vessels under his command. Two years later he returned with more than a million pounds-sterling worth of spices, assuredly a successful voyage by any standard. Lancaster also left several merchants behind to set up a mercantile station, but rather than doing so on Sumatra, they moved to Bantam on the island of Java. Dealings proved difficult, however, because English goods, especially heavy English broadcloth, were not of interest to local traders. Mostly, the local merchants sought cloth made of fine Indian cotton, so when the Company decided to send out a third expedition, its destination was India.

FIGURE 1. Seal of the East India Company.

In 1608, the Company elected to set up a station on the west coast of India; Captain William Hawkins (possibly the son of Capt. Williams Hawkins [Hawkyns; d. 1589] by his first wife) was placed in command of the new undertaking. Surat, about 170 miles north of Bombay, was selected as the site for a trading post. Surat was already well known as an important merchandising center, and, perhaps even more compelling, it was not under Portuguese control. On his arrival, although politely received by the local authorities, Hawkins was told that permission to establish a mercantile "factory" had to come from the Nawab (governor), in Cambay, and the Mughal Emperor, in Agra. Hawkins negotiated and succeeded on both accounts, first because he spoke Turkish, the language of the Mughal court, and second, because he impressed both Nawab and Emperor by defeating the Portuguese in a minor skirmish off the Surat coast in 1612, much to the dismay of local Jesuit missionaries and Portuguese. Permission was granted in 1613.

The Company, once firmly established in Surat, began its relentless expansion (Fig. 2). This brought it into further conflict, first with the Portuguese, and then the French, who earlier had set up

---

[3] In providing birth and death dates for the cast of characters, we have made every effort to provide accurate dates. However, we relied exclusively on secondary sources for these data and discovered occasional conflicts among the sources consulted. For instance, Robert Kyd (*q.v.*), founder of the Royal Botanical Gardens in Calcutta, is said to have died on 26 May 1793 according to a biographical sketch that appeared in the *Dictionary of National Biography* (vol. 11, p. 348) but in 1825 in the *Catalogue of the Books . . . of the British Museum* (*Natural History*) (vol. 2, E–K, p. 1038). In the latter, Kyd's date of birth is given as 1746, but no mention is made of this in the DNB article, written by Henry Manners Chichester. Based on other sources, we believe his correct dates are 1746–1793.

FIGURE 2. British India, 1802.
From a map in the possession of the authors.

a trading center at Pondicherry, south of Madras on India's southeast coast. In time, and with the expanding commerce, the Company established additional trading centers at Fort St. George in Madras, at Bombay, at Fort St. David at Cuddalore on the Coromandel Coast, and most importantly, at Calcutta in Bengal. The Company also began to invest time, money, and people to conduct surveys of the territories under its widening influence because it needed to know more about commercially available resources, particularly the plants and coal.

Although our main concern is the elaboration of developments in natural history studies and the evolution of collection-oriented research museums in India during the 19th century, we must explore those earlier events that set the stage for these later developments. Thus, only a few European scientists touched on India during the latter part of the 17th and first half of the 18th centuries, and those that did were in the employ of the Dutch East India Company, mostly as medical officers. Paul Hermann (1646–1695), for example, went to Ceylon (Sri Lanka) about 1670 as a medical officer and while there made extensive collections of plants. These he brought back to Halle when he returned in 1677, and they formed the bases of at least two published catalogs. In 1744, Hermann's herbarium came into the possession of Copenhagen apothecary August Günther, who sent the collections to Linnaeus for naming. Georg Eberhard Rumphius (1628–1702) and Johannes Burmannus (1706–1779) are best known for their joint editorship of *Herbarii Amboinensis Auctuarium*, which appeared in 1705, three years after Rumphius' death, and Burmann's lone editorship of *Herbarium Amboinense* (1741) and *Thesaurus Zeylanicus* (1737). By the end of the third quarter of the 18th century, Jacob Klein and Christopher Samuel John, two members of the Danish mission at Tranquebar, a small trading post south of Madras, founded the "United Brothers," as a botanical society for the purpose of collecting plants and preparing herbarium specimens (Jain 1982:116). The "Brothers" was not a scientific society as understood in the 20th century. Rather it was a collegial group, and between 1768 and 1792 it attracted several of the East India Company's Medical Services employees, notably Johann Gerhard Koenig (in 1768) and William Roxburgh (in 1776), who joined the fellowship and became instrumental in making the Indian flora more widely known to European botanists. Others, not associated with the "United Brothers," such as Linnaeus' student, Carl Pehr Thunberg (1743–1828), made botanical collections in Ceylon (Sri Lanka), whereas French collectors, including the zoologist Pierre Sonnerat (1748–1814), made botanical and zoological collections in the vicinity of the French trading center at Pondicherry, as well as to the north of Madras, and in Ceylon (Sri Lanka). These collections made their way to Europe, mainly Uppsala, Paris, and London.

Of those mentioned above, Johann Gerhard Koenig [Kønig] and William Roxburgh deserve more attention. Johann Gerhard Koenig (1728–1785) (Fig. 3) had studied with Linnaeus before taking a post with the East India Company in India. He arrived in India in 1768, joined the "United Brothers," and immediately launched an ambitious program for building a herbarium of local plants, many specimens of which he sent to his mentor in Uppsala. In 1778, the Madras Government appointed him "The Hon'ble Company's Natural Historian" for the purpose of introducing plants of economic importance from Malacca and Siam (Thailand) into India. As an aside, he also introduced Linnaeus' binomial nomenclature system into India (Jain, 1982:116). Koenig held the Madras post until his premature death in 1785, at which time the Company donated his collections and manuscripts to Britain's most distinguished botanist of the day, Joseph Banks.

William Roxburgh (1751–1815) (Fig. 4) served as an army surgeon for the East India Company. On his arrival in Madras in 1776, he, too, joined the Tranquebar group. In 1793, he replaced Robert Kyd (Fig. 5), founder of the Calcutta Botanic Gardens, as its superintendent. The appointment was made in recognition of his earlier work in establishing an experimental plantation to grow cardamom, pepper, indigo and other trees of potential commercial significance to the Company. But, Roxburgh

FIGURE 3. Johann Gerhard Koenig [Kønig].
Courtesy Hunt Institute for Botanical Documentation,
Carnegie-Mellon University.

FIGURE 4. William Roxburgh.
Courtesy Hunt Institute for Botanical Documentation
Carnegie-Mellon University.

FIGURE 5. Robert Kyd.
Courtesy Hunt Institute for Botanical Documentation,
Carnegie-Mellon University.

had broader botanical interests, and these interests brought him into conflict with Company Directors, who were concerned only with those aspects of botany likely to yield a profit. Over the years, Roxburgh put together a portfolio of drawings of more than 2,500 plant species; he published several volumes on plants, including the *Flora Indica,* in 1832; and he encouraged other newly arriving Company employees to come to the Garden, giving them an "institutional" setting to pursue their avocational and professional interests. Roxburgh's botanical notes, drawings and collections ended up in the hands of Sir Joseph Dalton Hooker (1817–1911), who used them extensively in preparing his own monumental *Flora of British India* (1875–1896) (Jain, 1982:117).

The Botanic Garden

The establishment of the Royal Botanic Garden in Calcutta was the first of several landmark events that profoundly affected the development of natural history studies in India, the growth of scientific collections and, ultimately, the establishment of museums organized for the purpose of housing, displaying, and fostering research on them.

The garden was proposed to the East India Company Directors in a letter dated 1 June 1786 by Lieut.-Col. Robert Kyd (1746–1793, but see footnote 3), the Company's military secretary in Calcutta, for the purpose of "establishing a stock for disseminating such articles as may prove beneficial to the inhabitants as well as to the natives of Great Britain, and which ultimately may tend to the extension of the national commerce and riches" (Chatterjee, 1948:362). Kyd's proposal was accepted 31 July 1787 with the proviso that an effort should be made to cultivate the cinnamon tree in Bengal, which already grew abundantly in Ceylon (Sri Lanka), because "we foresee a great source of wealth to the Company of population and opulence to the provinces under your administration" (Chatterjee, 1948:362). Kyd, who died in March 1793, was not successful in his ambitious plans for the garden. He was succeeded by William Roxburgh, who became the garden's first salaried superintendent. As an indication of the importance the Company still placed on the project, Roxburgh was given funds with which to build suitable living quarters for himself (the house still stands and serves as home to the garden's superintendent).

The Court of Directors of the East India Company supported the employment of persons as natural historians, geographers and surveyors, and geologists, but it was not done out of altruism or as patrons of the sciences, but because they thought it could make money (see excellent discussion by Kumar, 1995, concerning attitudes of Europeans as they related to the emerging scientific enterprise in India). Not all, however, adhered to the Company's pragmatic guidelines. Roxburgh, for instance, instituted a scientific study of plants that strained the patience of Company Directors. But changes were already in the wind, and these worked to Roxburgh's benefit, and in the long run, to the growth of natural history studies and collections during the 19th century. Because of hard economic times the Company sought help from the Government in London. Relief was forthcoming, but at a cost; the Company had to give up much of the nearly absolute authority it exercised in its Indian domains, practiced through having secured control of the military and criminal justice systems from the Nawab of Bengal and the power to collect revenue and administer civil justice from the Mughal Emperor. Following the abolishment of the Maratha Confederacy (1817–1818), the Company seemed to exercise nearly indisputable control from the Bay of Bengal to the Arabian Sea (Sen, 1966:115), but it did so largely through the authority of the Crown's on-site representative, the Governor-General, Earl of Moira (later known as Marquess of [Lord] Hastings [1754–1836; Governor-General, 1813–1823]). Thus, the Governor-General was but one of several constraints on the free-wheeling exercise of power formerly enjoyed by the Company in India. Nearly 40 years earlier, during Pitt's administration as Prime Minister, Parliament passed the India Act in 1784, which authorized a Board of Control to serve "as an instrument for better overseeing the actions of the East India Company in the interests of the British State." (Gascoigne, 1998:61.) Even though the Act allowed for Company control of local administration and patronage, it did so at the expense of political power. The Act also held the Company responsible for the welfare of the people, held it accountable to Parliament for its behavior, and held that its Indian representatives could not engage in any aggressive military activities without prior consent of Company Directors in London. According to Percival Spear (1961:253), by the middle of the 19th century, the Company "was in fact a subordinate agency of the British Government in London." Although the relationship between British Government and Company was complex, especially as the British Crown expanded its control over the civil, financial, and military affairs of the country, both Company and Government held in common a concern for the commercial success of their Indian venture. Thus, the Company did not hesitate to enlarge its efforts to apply science to "ensure the military, administrative and economic control of the sub-continent." (Sen, 1966:115).

During the first half of the 19th Century, botanically-oriented, Calcutta-based, Company naturalists gravitated to the Botanic Gardens. Several of those botanists are of special interest in the context of this paper because they also made significant collections and published useful papers in zoology, geology and anthropology.

Although Francis Buchanan (1762–1829) and John McClelland (1805–1875) are best known of the Calcutta group, there were other naturalists who worked in isolation, at least away from centers such as Calcutta and Madras. Victor Jacquemont (1801–1832), for instance, though best remembered for his botanical investigations, collected many animals which he sent to Paris. In 1844, the Atlas, or volume 2, of his *Voyage dans l'Inde*, was published. It contained 179 plates, of which 10 were of reptiles and fishes, the rest of birds, mammals, and other organisms; the promised volume of text never appeared. And, there was Brian Hodgson, about whom more will be said shortly, who was stationed in Katmandu, Nepal, and in time became one of the most respected British scholars and naturalists resident in India.

Returning to the Calcutta corps, among the earliest and most prolific was Francis Buchanan (later Buchanan-Hamilton, and finally Hamilton). Born in 1762, Buchanan took his M.D. at Edinburgh in 1783 and joined the East India's Company service in 1794. While in India, he was seconded to various botanical, zoological, and statistical inquiries in Chittagong, Tippera, Mysore, Canara, Malabar, Nepal, and, following a trip to England in 1805 as Lord Wellesley's physician, Bengal and Assam. He served a brief stint as Superintendent of the Calcutta Botanical Gardens (1814 to 1815), but returned to Scotland in 1815, succeeding to his brother's and mother's estates and properties. It was at this time that he added his mother's family name, Hamilton, to his own (i.e., Buchanan-Hamilton) and became Chief of the Clan Buchanan (to 1826) even though he had by 1820 dropped Buchanan from his family name (Moore, 1982:402).

During his years in India, Buchanan prepared numerous illustrations of plants, fishes, some reptiles, and other animals. Buchanan's ichthyological contributions, apart from his notes and illustrations, include his *Fishes of the River Ganges* (1822), and *The Fishes and Fisheries of Bengal*, edited by Francis Day (1877). Buchanan kept voluminous notes on his observations, and prepared numerous, fine colored illustrations. Some of his journals and drawings were deposited at the Company's India House in London, but some remained in India. For nearly ten years after his death in 1829, most of his unpublished portfolio of illustrations and notes lay forgotten in cabinets in London and Calcutta. When, in 1838, John McClelland visited the Botanical Gardens in London, he discovered two folio volumes of drawings, while John Edward Gray (1800–1875), then Keeper of the Natural History Museum in London, recovered some from the India House collection for reproduction in his and Hardwicke's *Illustrations of Indian Zoology*. The odd distribution of Buchanan's journals and colored drawings attracted the attention of E. W. Gudger (1924:121–136) who, in the course of his delvings into Buchanan's life, uncovered a contentious squabble between Buchanan and the Marquis of Hastings, then Governor General of India, regarding the disposition of his notes and illustrations. This is recommended reading for those who want to get the inside story on the politics of working for the Company during the early part of the 19th century (see also Edney, 1997).

John McClelland, a member of the East India Company's Bengal Medical Service, with a keen interest in botany, worked closely with Danish botanist Nathaniel Wallich (1786–1854) (Fig. 7), Roxburgh's replacement as Superintendent of the Calcutta Gardens. Unlike Roxburgh, who wanted to build an important herbarium in Calcutta, Wallich, on his retirement, removed the herbarium to England where he presented it to the Court of Directors of the East India Company for distribution among the principal herbaria and botanists of Europe, but none to Calcutta. McClelland had broad interests, and early on we find him in the field collecting amphibians, reptiles, fishes, and other animals. His first assignment was in Assam, where he and Wallich studied the conditions under which tea plants grew, with the intent of establishing tea plantations there, also in the Northwest Himalayas, and in the Nilgris, thus marking the beginning of India's tea industry. McClelland, who also wrote about Assam fishes, reptiles, and birds, including a lengthy 250-page paper on Indian Cyprinidae (1838), later served as Secretary of the Company's Coal Committee from 1836 to 1846, as Curator of the Asiatic Society's Museum from 1839–1841, as founder and editor of Calcutta's *Journal of Natural History* (1841–1847), as Superintendent of the Royal Botanic Garden at Sibpur from 1845 to 1848, and as director of the as yet informally constituted Geological Survey of India following the death of D. H. Williams, Geological Surveyor of the East India Company, in 1848.

East India Company Naturalists

Another late-18th-century milestone in the evolution of the natural sciences in India was the founding of the Asiatic Society of Bengal, Calcutta, in 1784 by Sir William Jones (1746–1794). Jones, an Oriental scholar with broad interests in the arts and sciences, also served as a Company judge of the Calcutta High Court. *Asiatic Researches*, the Society's first periodical, appeared in 1788, and provided the earliest Asian-based outlet for publications on natural history, ethnology, art, and literature. Twenty-six years later, in 1814, with the help of Nathaniel Wallich (1786–1854), the Society established a museum (Fig. 6) to house articles to illustrate "Oriental manners or history, art and nature." Its two sections encompassed a broad cross-section of disciplines, one devoted to zoology and geology, another to ethnology, archaeology, and technology. Although financial difficulties plagued the museum from the outset, its success as a center for the accumulation of objects of nature encouraged the founding of local societies and display cabinets elsewhere in India: Madras (1851), Bombay (1857), Trivandrum (1857) and others, as previously mentioned (Lamba, 1963:185).

FIGURE 6. Museum of the Asiatic Society of Bengal in Calcutta. The museum building was built in 1814. From Anon., 1914.

Because the society found itself perpetually short of funds, in 1836 it asked the Government of

India for financial assistance. The request was forwarded to the East India Company's Court of Directors in London because the Indian government was itself already saddled with the cost of maintaining the India House museum and library in London, that had been established in 1801 under the direction of Sir Charles Wilkins (1750–1836) (Moore, 1982:399). In 1839, London acceded to the request, and the society received a grant of about 20 pounds-sterling per month for the museum. Two years later Edward Blyth (1810–1873) was appointed its first salaried curator. In 1838, the Bengal Government, because of the success of the Raniganj coal mines, authorized a Museum of Economic Geology, which was to share rooms with the Asiatic Society's museum (which it did until 1856, when it was moved to new quarters under the administration of the Geological Survey of India). At the time it authorized the geological museum, the Bengal government offered to assume responsibility for the geological collections then owned by the Asiatic Society, but the offer was declined. By 1856, the Society, having neither the physical space nor the financial resources to maintain its museum, petitioned the government to establish an Imperial Museum in Calcutta with the understanding that it would hand over all its all of collections, but not its library. The Sepoy uprising of 1857 led to the postponement of most non-military decisions, but the Society persisted, and in 1862 the government of India agreed to act. In 1866, the Indian Museum Act passed, and John Anderson was hired to superintend the collections and plan the construction of new quarters, which were not to be built for another 9 years (Leviton and Aldrich, 1984:vi–viii). However, once finished, in 1875, the Museum of the Asiatic Society, at that time popularly known as the 'Jadu Ghar,' the "House of Mysteries," transferred its collections to the new museum building. Other collections, including those of the Geological Survey of India and the Botanic Gardens, were transferred about the same time.

Returning to the waning years of the 18th century, two other company employees deserve mention. Though neither was responsible for amassing large collections, both are emblematic of the dedicated amateur naturalists employed by the Company in its military units or to superintend its economic botanical interests: Patrick Russell (sometimes spelt Russel) (6 Feb. 17[26–27]–1805) (Fig. 8) and Thomas Hardwicke. Russell was born in Edinburgh, attended the University of Edinburgh, where he obtained his M.D. He succeeded his elder half-brother Alexander as physician at an English "factory" at Aleppo (= Halab, in northwestern Syria) from 1750 to 1771, after which he returned to London (1772). In 1781, at the age of 55, he left England for India, arriving in Vizagapatam later that year. From 1785 to 1789, he served as the East India Company's botanist in the Carnatic (Karnataka) region of southeastern India. One of a few late 18th-century Indian naturalists interested in animals as well as plants, he took special note of Indian snakes and fishes of the Coromandel Coast. Russell conducted the first systematic study of Indian snakes, clearly distinguishing between venomous and non-venomous species. He also conducted many experiments with snake venoms. Russell published several treatises, notably a *Treatise on the Plague* (1791), an *Account of Indian Serpents Collected on the Coast of Coromandel,* with 46 plates, in 1796, followed in 1801[–1809] by a continuation volume with 45 plates (see Zhao and Adler, 1993:396–397, for comments on the dates of printing of the sections contained in the continuation volume), and descriptions and figures of about 200 species of fishes collected at Vizagapatam (1803, 2 vols.). Russell used local vernacular names for his illustrations and, thus, his works, though well known, are infrequently referenced save as one or more of the illustrations stand as types for Linnaean binomina given by Shaw (1801), Gray (1827), or others.

Thomas Hardwicke (1756–1835) (Fig. 9), Major-General of the East India Company's Bengal Artillery, also made collections of plants and animals. Like Russell, he, too, is best remembered for his portfolio of animal illustrations. These were published in London by John Edward Gray, then Keeper of Zoology at the British Museum (Natural History), under the title, *Illustrations of Indian Zoology* (1830–1835), which, as noted earlier, included some of Francis Buchanan's plates as well.

FIGURE 7. Nathaniel Wallich.
Courtesy Hunt Institute for Botanical Documentation,
Carnegie-Mellon University.

FIGURE 8. Patrick Russell.
Frontispiece portrait in Russell's 1802 volume
Indian Serpents of the Coromandal Coast.

FIGURE 9. Thomas Hardwicke.
Courtesy Smithsonian Institution Archives
(RU 95, Neg. #SA–645).

During the second quarter of the 19th century, the East India Company or the British Government employed a number of people whose avocational interests resulted in large collections and many publications laying out the fauna and flora of India. Already mentioned in connection with the Asiatic Society of Bengal's museum, Edward Blyth (1810–1873) (Fig. 10), acclaimed by John Gould as "one of the first zoologists of his time, and the founder of the study of that science in India," (Gould, 1853:41) was born in London on 23 December 1810, the eldest of four children. He showed an early interest in natural history, so much so that he was as a frequent truant at Dr. Fennell's school in Wimbleton, usually disappearing on excursions to the nearby woods. His early efforts at studying chemistry and a brief flirtation with a druggist's business ended in failure. He spent much of his time reading at the British Museum and collecting in the field, mainly butterflies and birds. He wrote many natural history articles between 1833 and 1841, edited an edition of the Rev. Gilbert White's *The Natural History and Antiquities of Selbourne*, and in 1849 and again in 1851 translated and annotated a one-volume edition of the mammal, bird, and reptile sections of Cuvier's *Le Règne Animal*. Blyth's reputation won him an offer from the East India Company as ill-paid Curator of the Asiatic Society of Bengal's museum, one of the first of a growing number to go to India as professional scientists (Larwood, 1961:85). He arrived in Calcutta in September 1841 and began collecting animals and writing articles on Indian natural history, which he continued to do for the next 21 years. Because of failing health, he returned to England in 1862 where he continued writing short papers on a variety of topics, including a work in preparation at the time of his death in 1873, *The Origination of Species*. Blyth was an early supporter of Darwin, having anticipated Darwin's work by more than 20 years when "he published in 1835 [Blyth, 1835:40-53] the first of two articles that discuss variation, the struggle for existence, sexual selection, and natural selection in terms that have a Darwinian sound.

[However, while] Blyth no doubt provided Darwin with many insights . . . it was Darwin's *On the Origin of Species* which seems to have revolutionized Blyth's ideas about species, and not vice versa." (McKinney, 1970:206.)

Brian Houghton Hodgson (1800–1894) (Fig. 11) stands out as the most impressive scholar of the Company's employees. Hodgson went to India at the age of 18 and attended the College of Fort William in Calcutta. After a brief stay in Kumaon as Assistant Commissioner (1818–1820), he took up residence in Katmandu, Nepal, where he served as Assistant Resident and then Resident from 1820 to 1844. Precipitously removed from office by Lord Ellenborough, even though he had performed crucial service by keeping Nepal quiet during the first Afghan war (1839–1841), Hodgson went to Darjeeling, in Sikkim, where he remained for some years. In 1858, he left India and returned to England; he died in London in May 1894. During his years in Nepal, Hodgson studied the language, literature, and religion of both Nepal and Tibet, translated Sanskrit and Tibetan manuscripts, and otherwise gathered a massive quantity of ethnographic, natural history, and geographic information about the country. He published several papers on Nepalese vertebrates, especially birds and reptiles, but his principal contributions in natural history, apart from geography, lay in the collections he sent to London. His literary attainments led to many honors including election as a Fellow of the Royal Society, corresponding member of the French Institute, and a chevalier of the Legion of Honor.

Paleontology was not neglected during this period, and there is much that could be said about it. For the moment, we will mention only the works of three. First, and perhaps foremost, there was Dr. Hugh Falconer (1808–1865) who, during the years 1831–1859, revealed the rich fossil fauna of India's now-famed upper Tertiary Siwalik Hills beds. Falconer was an assistant surgeon in the Bengal Establishment in 1830, and then superintendent of the Botanical Gardens at Sharanpur from 1832 to 1841 (Moore, 1982:404). Much of his paleontological work was done in collaboration with Sir Proby Thomas Cautley (1802–1871), then Capt. Cantley of the Bengal Artillery. The bulk of their collections

FIGURE 10. Edward Blyth.
Courtesy Kraig Adler, Cornell University.

FIGURE 11. Brian Hodgson.
Courtesy Hunt Institute for Botanical Documentation
Carnegie-Mellon University.

FIGURE 12. Thomas Claverhill Jerdon.
Courtesy Kraig Adler,
Cornell University.

was sent to London, where it was distributed among the India and British Museums, and to museums in Bombay and Calcutta as well as to the Science and Art Museum in Dublin (Moore, 1982:404). Both Falconer and Cautley did publish short papers on their discoveries, but no monographic treatments.

Paralleling the work of Falconer and Cantley was Andrew Fleming (1822–1901), who entered the employ of the East India Company in 1844 and then, in 1849, was assigned to the post of surgeon in the 4th Punjab Cavalry. While stationed in Punjab, he became interested in the Salt Range and soon was on detached duty to the Geological Survey of the Punjab. Fleming's collections were dispatched to Edinburgh, although some did end up in the British Museum in London. (Moore, 1982:405–407.) Like Fleming and Caultey, he, too did not produce any monographic works, though a few papers dealing with the fossil vertebrates did flow from his pen.

Lastly, of the naturalists of whom we wish to take note and who plied their avocational interests on the subcontinent largely during the years before the founding of the Geological Survey of India in 1851, was Thomas Claverhill Jerdon (1811–1872) (Fig. 12), who joined the Company's medical service in 1835 in Madras as surgeon and retired in 1864. Jerdon is best known for his contributions in ornithology and mammalogy, which include *Illustrations of Indian Ornithology* (1847), *The Birds of India* . . . (1862–64) in 3 octavo volumes, and *The Mammals of India,* published in 1868, and for the collections relating to these works. He also published a *Catalogue of Reptiles Inhabiting Southern India* and *Manual of Vertebrata of India*. He made small collections of fishes, amphibians and reptiles, deposited some in the Government Museum in Madras and the Indian Museum, but sent most to the British Museum (Natural History) in London.

Around the turn of the century, the need to evaluate the commercial potential of the natural resources had led the East India Company to take the first steps toward professionalizing science in India. Although it did this by hiring people to do specific jobs that required specialized training to conduct geological reconnaissances, trigonometric surveys, and botany, it was the founding of the Geological Survey of India in 1851 that solidified the trend toward the professionalization of science in India, not unlike, and at about the same time, the role played by the founding of the Geological Survey of Canada in 1852 and several state geological surveys in the United States. It also inaugurated the hiring of non-colonials and provided training to prepare them to enter the professional ranks.

Geological Survey of India

Thus, we come to the third milestone in the history of studies of natural history, collection building and museums in India, the founding of the Geological Survey of India in 1851. This followed more than two decades of Company-sponsored studies of the coal fields, especially those of Raniganj, in western Bengal, to determine the extent of undeveloped resources there and in other parts of the country. This was not, however, the first effort at geological investigations by the East India Company. As early as 1817, Lord Hastings, Governor-General of India, had geologists appointed to the newly established Great Trigonometrical Survey as well as to other survey parties, mostly military, such as those commanded by Bengal Infantry Captains William Webb (1784–1865; survey activities, 1815–1821), Frederick Dangerfield (1789–1828; survey activities, 1818–1821), and James Dowling Herbert (1791–1835; survey activities, 1816–1821, 1824–1828). Of the three, James Herbert remained active in the field the longest and in 1821 was appointed Assistant Surveyor General, in 1829, Deputy Surveyor General (Edney, 1997:296, 344). He was also accorded the rather "pleasant [even if unofficial] title of 'Geological Surveyor of the Hymalya [*sic*] Mountain'" (Anon., 1951:2). Initially, Webb and Herbert conducted surveys in the western Himalayas, Dangerfield in southern Uttar

Pradesh in the vicinity of Malwa. As for geologists, Alexander Laidlaw (d. 1836), was employed as assistant geologist on the Webb survey (Edney, 1997:296), while Henry Westley Voysey (d. 1824), a surgeon with the HM 59th, 46th and 1st Foot (Edney, 1997:347), was assigned as surgeon and naturalist to the Great Trigonometric Survey. It was Voysey who prepared India's geological map (1820), of the Hyderabad region, and for this he is sometimes referred to as the "Father of Indian Geology" (Anon., 1951:2). But, one must not lose sight of the fact that, as Edney (*op. cit.*) rightly emphasized, the "company's official geological investigations were explicitly for economic purposes," as it recognized the need for good regional maps to secure military and civilian control over the populous, to establish a tax revenue base, and to locate economically valuable resources, minerals, copper, iron, and coal.

After two decades of relatively uncoordinated geological survey activities, in 1843, the Company secured the services of David Hiram Williams (d. 1848) to do a careful survey of the coal resources of Bengal. Williams had worked on the coal beds in Wales and elsewhere in western England for the Geological Survey of Great Britain under the direction of Henry Thomas de la Beche (1796–1855). Unfortunately, Williams died in early November of 1848, and one of his two assistants, J. R. Jones, died of fever very shortly thereafter. The Company, unable to find a permanent replacement, asked John McClelland to take temporary charge. McClelland served until March 1851 when the Company hired Thomas Oldham (1816–1878) (Fig. 13), at the time in charge of the Ireland branch of the Geological Survey of Great Britain, as its Geological Surveyor and immediately placed him at the disposal of the Bengal Government. Oldham was also authorized to hire additional geologists and, before the end of the decade, he had an impressive array of talent in the field: John G. and Henry B. Medlicott (1829–1905), William T. (1832–1905) and Henry F. (1834–1893) Blanford, William Theobald 1829–1908), Ferdinand Stoliczka (1838–1874), Frederic Richard Mallet (1841–1921), Valentine Ball (1843–1895), and shortly thereafter, Ottokar Feistmantel (1848–1891) (Leviton and Aldrich, in prep.) (Figs. 14–15). Thus was inaugurated the Geological Survey of India.

FIGURE 13. Thomas Oldham. (From Geikie, 1895.)

When the Blanfords came on the scene in 1856, they were assigned to the Talchir coal fields in Orissa, about 400 km southwest of Calcutta, and later the Raniganj coal fields in western Bengal. Under Oldham's directions, the Blanfords and John G. Medlicott mapped the Talchir rocks, which Oldham and the two Blanfords named the lower Talchir and upper Mahadeva (later renamed Lower and Upper Damuda beds). These included silt and boulder and coal beds. The division proved the key to establishing the Gondwana System in India. William Blanford was intrigued by the interbedded fine silts and large boulder deposits and argued that the area had been extensively glaciated during early Gondwana time. This was the first suggestion of Permian glaciation, a radical idea for its time, all the more so because he posited that it had occurred in what is now a tropical, humid climate. Thus was born the germ of an idea, the vast supercontinent, Gondwanaland. Somewhat later, and based on fossil plants of the genus *Glossopteris* found both in the Talchir and Raniganj coal beds, Blanford also argued that the Gondwana rocks of India correlated with the Newcastle sequence of Australia

FIGURE 14. Geological Survey of India (several staff not in photo), ca. 1866. (Left to right): (standing) M. H. Ormsby, William T. Blanford, Valentine Ball, Francis Fedden; (sitting) Thomas Oldham, Henry B. Medlicott C. A. Hacket, Ambrose Tween. From Geological Survey of India, 1988.

FIGURE 15. Geological Survey of India (several staff not in photo), ca. 1875. (Left to right): (standing) Ferdinand Stoliczka, Robert Bruce Foote, William Theobald, Frederic R. Mallet, Valentine Ball, Wilhelm Waagen, Walter Lindsay Willson; (sitting): Ambrose Tween, William King, Thomas Oldham, Henry B. Medlicott, C. A. Hacket. From Somasekar, 1964.

and similar rocks in South Africa and that the Gondwana rocks of India were Permo-Carboniferous in age. Ottokar Feistmantel, the survey's paleobotanist, disagreed, believing that the plants more closely matched the mid-Mesozoic flora of Europe. Following several nasty exchanges in print, Feistmantel was won over to Blanford's views. In a daring extension of his long-range correlations, and following an earlier presentation (1869) by his brother Henry, who posited a southern landmass connecting India and Australia, William Blanford allowed for the existence of a great southern continent during Gondwana time that encompassed southern Africa, India, and Australia, thus predating Eduard Suess' Gondwana-Land by several years. It is clear from remarks made by both Henry and William in their several papers, the two talked about these matters at length and they must be given equal credit. As an aside, in the 1860s and 70s, William Blanford also correctly dated the Deccan volcanics (Blanford, 1869) and made additional and valuable contributions to the interpretation of arid-land geomorphology based on his geological field work in Cutch (1869), Bombay (1872), the "Great Desert" of India between Sind and Rájpútana (1876), Sind (1876, 1878), as well as elsewhere in India, and his travels in Abyssinia [Ethiopia] ([travel, 1867] 1870) and Persia [Iran] ([travel, 1872] 1876).

Both William (Fig. 16) and Henry Blanford (Fig. 17) had attended Henry de la Beche's Royal School of Mines before leaving for India in the summer of 1855. Thus, they, like others hired by Oldham, had professional training for the work they were to undertake. In 1865, Henry Blanford left the Survey to become government meteorologist and member of the faculty of Presidency College in Calcutta, but his interest in geology continued unabated, as evidenced by his post-survey publications (e.g., H. Blanford, 1875). William remained with the Survey as Deputy Superintendent until his retirement in 1882. He undertook important new geological investigations, in Sind, in Orissa, in Sikkim, in Burma (at the time, a province of India; today the independent country Myanmar), and elsewhere, and he provided additional new data to support the idea of a large southern continental mass during the Permian and early Mesozoic. William Blanford had a penchant for zoology, especially mollusks, birds, and reptiles, and collected whenever possible. He worked up the collections he made and published many reports on them and on specimens brought in by his survey colleagues, especially Ferdinand Stoliczka, whose important collections from the Second Yarkand Mission were reported on by Blanford in 1878 after Stoliczka's death. Blanford's collections were deposited in the British Museum, and following the arrival of John Anderson in 1865, the Indian Museum. In 1867, Blanford took part in General Napier's Abyssinia Expedition to relieve the British Residency in Magdala, and he wrote a book-length report covering the geology and natural history of the country along the route of march from Annesy Bay along the backbone of the Ethiopian highlands (Blanford, 1870). In 1872, he, Major Oliver St. John, and a native collector from John Anderson's Indian Museum staff traveled from Gwadar, in Baluchistan, to Shiraz, Isfahan, and Tehran, in Iran, collecting birds, mammals, reptiles and amphibians, all the while making geological observations enroute. Two years earlier, St. John had traveled a similar route, also in company with a native collector from the Indian Museum, and it was these two collections that formed the basis of Blanford's 1876 seminal report on the zoology and geology of Eastern Persia.

Ferdinand Stoliczka (1838–1874) (Fig. 18) died at the age of 36 while returning from field work in northern Pakistan and Yarkand (extreme western China just south of the Takla-Makan). A paleontologist whose early work focused on Tertiary invertebrates in central Czechoslovakia (1861-62), Stoliczka joined the Indian Geological Survey and worked in India, Pakistan, Burma (Myanmar), Malaysia, Andaman and Nicobar Islands, and Tibet. His principal contributions during his brief years with the survey were the three large volumes on the Cretaceous fauna of southern India. However, he also made small but valuable collections of reptiles and amphibians wherever he went, and these

FIGURE 16. William Thomas Blanford.
Courtesy Kraig Adler, Cornell University.

FIGURE 17. Henry Francis Blanford.
GS Myers/AE Leviton Portrait File in Natural
History, California Academy of Sciences.

FIGURE 18. Ferdinand Stoliczka.
From Somasekar (1964).

FIGURE 19. William Theobald.
(Enlargement from group photograph [fig. 15])

were reported on by him (e.g., Stoliczka, 1870, 1872a, 1872b) as well as by William Blanford and William Theobald, among others. Perhaps the most critical were the collections he made during the Second Yarkand Mission to Kashgar and the Pamir Steppe; these were deposited in the Indian Museum. He also collected in Kashmir, Ladak, and eastern Turkestan, and these collections went to the Indian and "Kurrachee" (= Karachi) Municipal Museums and were later reported on by James Murray in 1878 in *The Vertebrate Zoology of Sind*. Earlier, Stoliczka had sent specimens to Franz Steindachner in Vienna that Steindachner included in his *Novara* reports (1867).

William Theobald (1829–1908) (Fig. 19), previously employed by the Punjab Geological Survey for two years (1851–1853), joined the Geological Survey of India in 1853. He worked with the Blanfords in the survey of the Talchir coal fields in Orissa that resulted in the "first systematic study of Indian Geology to be published by the Indian Geological Survey" (Ghosh, 1951:308). While employed by the Survey, Theobald prepared the first complete *Descriptive Catalogue of the Reptiles of British India* (1876) to "meet a want which at present blocks the way to the general study of Herpetology in India . . . ." Two hundred and thirty-eight pages are devoted to taxonomy and descriptions, followed by 38 pages of synoptic keys and a 132-page appendix "On the means of discriminating between poisonous and harmless snakes and the treatment of snake bite." Like other survey personnel who collected natural history specimens, most of Theobald's collections went to the Indian Museum.

Before leaving the Geological Survey of India, it must be said that the Survey is also noteworthy for initiating the process of incorporating native talent into its structure. It may strike modern readers as an example of 'better late than never,' that in 1874, shortly before his retirement, Thomas Oldham appointed native-born Ram Singh as an apprentice on the Survey's geological staff. The Survey thus became a training ground in geology for Indians, whose local university-level schools lacked such preparation. Also in 1874, Oldham brought on board Kishan Singh and Hira Lal. Both were assigned to take courses in the physical sciences at Presidency College in Calcutta. Lastly, there was Pramatha Nath Bose, who had gone to London in 1874 on a scholarship to study geology at the University of London and Royal School of Mines. Bose would have preferred to stay in London, but because he was an outspoken critic of the government, he was eased out by the India Office and sent back to Calcutta, where he was appointed to a "graded post" (Kumar, 1995:215) on the Survey's staff in 1880. With these hirings began the "Indianization" of the Survey which, by the time of independence in 1947, was one of the few government agencies, along with the Zoological Survey of India, nearly fully staffed by native rather than colonial officers.

The Indian Museum

With the authorization of a national museum in Calcutta (Fig 20) a near *fait accompli* (the Indian Museum Act passed in 1866), the government hired its first superintendent, John Anderson (1833–1900) (Fig. 21), in 1865. When Anderson arrived in Calcutta, he found that the promised collections were scattered about the city, some housed at the Botanic Gardens, some in the Asiatic Society Museum, some in the Geological Survey's Museum of Economic Geology. It fell to Anderson, then, to plan the new Museum both to house these collections and for the development of appropriate public displays. Thus, Anderson's arrival in Calcutta and the construction of the Indian Museum signals the fourth milestone in the history of Indian natural history surveys, collection building, and museums. It must be remembered that to that time collections went mostly to European museums, especially the British Museum of Natural History in London, where John Edward Gray (1800–1875) (Fig. 22), Albert Günther (1830–1914) (Fig. 23), and George Albert Boulenger (1858–1937) (Fig. 24) produced

FIGURE 20. The Indian Museum, Calcutta (1906). From Anon. (1914).

a steady stream of publications describing the exotic animals they received. Some early collections always remained in India, mostly in Calcutta (Asiatic Society Museum, founded 1814), and to a lesser extent in Madras (Government Museum, originally named the Central Museum, founded 1851), Karachi (Municipal Museum, renamed the Victoria Museum, founded 1851), and Colombo (Colombo Museum, founded 1873, which received collections from Ceylon Branch of Asiatic Society). For Anderson, the Indian Museum was the country's national museum. At its inception, he organized it in three sections: Zoological, Archaeological, and Geological. He then went to great lengths to develop in each of these areas appropriate public exhibits, adequate support staff, and permanent research collections. In line with the latter, Anderson ceased sending major collections to London. Rather, he began horse-trading for specimens, especially with Albert Günther at the British Museum (see Leviton and Aldrich, 1984 for details) and Boulenger. Anderson himself took part in two major expeditions to Yunnan as surgeon-naturalist. On both expeditions, he made important collections of mammals, reptiles, and birds. These he kept in Calcutta, with the exception of hedgehogs, which he sent to Albert Günther in London because of the latter's special interest in the animals. Anderson also encouraged a network of amateur collectors, particularly army medical officers, to send specimens to the museum; thus, over the years, the museum received a steady stream of small collections from throughout the country. Notable among the contributors were Col. R. H. Beddome and W. M. Daly (South India), W. Theobald (Burma), Capt. J. Butler, S. E. Peal and J. H. Bourne (Assam), and F. Stoliczka, W. T. Blanford, and T. Jerdon. In 1887, an Economic and Art Section, formerly sponsored as a separate institution by the Government of Bengal, was incorporated into the museum (Prashad, 1931:35).

Apart from Bombay, which did not play a major role in the growth of natural history collections until after the founding of the Bombay Natural History Society in 1883, Madras and Karachi had government-sponsored museums, both founded in 1851, that supported small zoological collections. Of the two, Karachi is the more important largely because of James Murray's 13-year tenure as curator of the museum. Murray (1865–1914) explored the province of Sind (now part of Pakistan), receiving

FIGURE 21 John Anderson.
Courtesy Natural History Museum, London.

FIGURES 22–24. (Left to right) John Edward Gray, Albert Carl Ludwig Gotthilf Günther, George Albert Boulenger (Left to right) Gray — Courtesy Kraig Adler, Cornell University; Günther and Boulenger — Courtesy G.S. Myers/A.E. Leviton Portrait File in Natural History, California Academy of Sciences.

much help and many specimens from F. Gleadow, Deputy Conservator of Forests, and from officers assigned to army units stationed in the province and neighboring Afghanistan, especially Lieut. E. Y. Watson and Capt. F. B. Piele. Based on these collections, Murray published two important works on the fauna of Sind, *The Vertebrate Zoology of Sind* (1884), which dealt with the mammals, birds and reptiles, and *The Reptiles of Sind* (1886), the latter being largely a reprint of the reptile section that appeared in the earlier publication but with some new material. As a general naturalist, Murray also published on plants, authoring *A Hand-Book to the Geology, Botany, and Zoology of Sind,* and an account of the indigenous flora of Sind, with comments on the use of local plant products in commerce, medicine, and the arts, *The Plants and Drugs of Sind* (1881).

In South India, Richard Henry Beddome (1830–1911), entered the Indian Army in 1848 and in 1857 became chief assistant to the conservator of the Madras Forestry Service, whom he succeeded ten years later. He retired from the service in 1882 and returned to England where he continued his interest in horticulture. During his years in India, Beddome published several seminal works on the ferns of both southern India and India as a whole, as well as several other major botanical works on the flora of southern India. He also published more than a dozen short articles on the snakes of southern India, mostly in the *Madras Quarterly and Monthly Journal of Medical Science,* and one longer paper, *An Account of the Earth-snakes of the Peninsula India and Ceylon*. Beddome's specimens went to London and to Anderson in Calcutta.

Francis Day (1829–1889) was perhaps the most prolific and next to Buchanan-Hamilton probably the best-known 19th-century student of Indian fishes (see Whitehead and Talwar, 1976). Like many of his predecessors interested in Indian natural history, Day was employed by the East India Company Medical Service. Initially stationed in Cochin, he served in the Burmese war of 1852-54 (the aftermath of which was the annexation of Burma to India), but then was transferred to Madras where he served as Surgeon-Major in the Company's Madras Army from 1872 until his retirement in 1876, when he was promoted to Deputy Surgeon-General. In the early 60s, knowing of his interest in fishes, the government put Day to good use by assigning him to survey the condition of Indian fisheries. This enabled Day to travel widely and make large collections in nearly every important river system on the subcontinent. His *Fishes of Malabar* (1863), *Report on the Fresh-Water Fish and Fisheries of India and Burma* (1873), and the monumental work, the *Fishes of India* (1878), which contains descriptions of more than 1300 species (and drew heavily on Buchanan's notes and portfolio of illustrations), and "Fishes" in the *Fauna of British India* series (1889), are too well known to students of Asian fishes to need further introduction. Day's Indian collections ended up in Calcutta, in Madras, and in London. On his return to England, Day undertook new studies of fishes, which resulted in two important works, *The Fishes of Great Britain and Ireland* (1885) and *British and Irish Salmonidae* (1887). Day died in July 1889 at the age of 60.

A contemporary of Day's, but with a penchant for snakes rather than fish, Joseph Fayrer, M.D. (1824–1907) (Fig. 25), entered the East India Company's Medical Service in Bengal and rose to the rank of Surgeon-General. Like Day, he served in the first Burmese war. He was Residency Surgeon in Lucknow during the Sepoy uprising and siege of the city. Fayrer accompanied both the Duke of Edinburgh and the Prince of Wales on their respective tours of India, in 1869–70 and 1875–76. He published many works on tropical diseases, for which he received honors including a baronetcy, in 1896, and in 1901, appointment as honorary physician to the Queen and Prince of Wales. In natural history, Fayrer is best remembered for the admirably illustrated folio volume, *The Thanatophidia of India: Being a Description of the Venomous Snakes of India with An Account of the Influence of their Poison on Life . . .* (1878).

In 1875, John Anderson allowed the transfer of collections to the Indian Museum building which was still under construction (it was not completed until 1877). Fifteen years later, W. L. Sclater, Anderson's Deputy Superintendent, took stock of some of the collections. For instance, he reported that the collections included 3001 snakes and 30 holotypes representing 350 species (Sclater, 1891:iii). Of amphibians, Sclater reported 2045 specimens and 21 holotypes representing 180 species, of which 103 were Indian and 77 exotic (Sclater, 1892:iii). We have no comparable numbers for lizards or other groups of animals, but based on proportions of snakes to lizard specimens in other collections, it is probably safe to assume at least an equal number of specimens, if not more. Therefore, the Indian museum, by 1891, had probably more than 8,000 specimens of amphibians and reptiles, and probably around 75 holotypes. For that time, this was certainly one of the world's major collections. It was not as large as the major European collections, those at London, Paris, Vienna, Senckenberg, Basel, and Berlin, or the Smithsonian's in Washington, D.C., but was larger than most collections elsewhere.

FIGURE 25. Joseph Fayrer. From *The Lancet* (1907).

We do not have an estimate of the size of the fish collections at the close of the 19th century. Most of the fishes collected by the 19th-century naturalists went to the British Museum, though some especially important segments of Day's collections, ended up in Calcutta. We also know that all the collections from the Royal Indian Marine Survey went to Calcutta. But, we suspect that the main growth of ichthyological collections occurred after 1900, and was particularly influenced by founding of the Zoological Survey of India and the appointment of its first director, Nelson Annandale, in 1916. Both it and the Botanical Survey of India, organized in 1890, were based in Calcutta, and the directors of the principal existing research centers, the Botanic Garden and the Indian Museum, became directors of the surveys. Their responsibility was that of coordinating natural history surveys throughout the country and the development of centralized research facilities in Calcutta and several regional centers. This then brings us into the 20th century and a new chapter in the history of natural history investigations in India.

In closing, we have several comments we think germane to the topic at hand. First, certainly in the United States, many think of Spencer Fullerton Baird as the architect of collector networks, that is of collectors he contacted and encouraged to send their specimens, birds, mammals, amphibians, reptiles, fishes, plants, and other natural history objects, often won with great hardship, to a central repository, in this case, to the Smithsonian Institution. Once there, Baird immediately acknowledged receipt of the collection by letter, followed not long after by a short paper prepared for rapid publication. Baird, however, was not alone in encouraging this behavior. In England, Gray, Günther, and Boulenger were certainly as effective, as was Linnaeus in Sweden more than a century earlier. And in India, one need only note William Theobald's acknowledgments in his 1876 paper, *A Descriptive Catalogue of the Reptiles of British India*, to realize the extent to which such networks existed elsewhere and how much they paralleled Baird's network of travelers, military personnel, and local amateur naturalists in the United States.

Second, one is struck by the close association of natural science and military expeditions in India and in the United States. To date, no book has been written on India equivalent to William Goetzmann's *Army Exploration of the American West*, but such a tome is badly needed. The military seemed to perform many of the same functions in both countries, but a detailed investigation may show significant differences. Certainly in both India and the United States, geographical discovery and scientific endeavor were linked through the institution of military expeditions.

Whereas comparison to the United States is instructive, much about the history of collecting in India was unique. The Royal Botanical Garden had no counterpart in America that served the same function, although individual botanists sometimes collected animals as well as plants. The United States also had no equivalent to the East India Company, which put a special spin on the development of Indian natural science. These and other special features of the Indian scene make us wary of the sweeping generalizations about colonial science contained in the works of such widely referenced historians such as George Basalla (1967) and Susan Sheets-Pyenson (1989) who assume uniformity, homogeneity, and linearity where none exists. We are struck by how quickly new "metropoles," as shown by MacLeod, of scientific activity develop as soon as a threshold of permanent resident colonists are in place. The founding of the Royal Asiatic Society of Bengal is a prime example, as is Calcutta as a metropole. Thus, we believe one should consult Deepak Kumar's *Science and the Raj* (1995), which we take to be more insightful in that it deals directly with India and the curious set of circumstances that affected scientific endeavors in that unusual colonial setting.

Museums as centers of research and public education emerged in response largely to provide (1) a safe haven for the scientific collections being amassed by survey personnel, individual travelers, and those with a special interest in rocks and minerals, and animals and plants; (2) a place where these people and others could study the collections, that is centers for scientific investigation; and lastly, (3) places where the public could see on display the wonders of nature. The latter was not always done altruistically, however, but to meet the obligations of caring for the public and justifying appropriations, at least some of which support the scientific enterprise. Although this point has been clearly articulated with respect to American museums by Joel Orosz, nonetheless we take issue with Orosz who, in his 1990 book, *Curators and Culture: The Museum Movement in America, 1740–1870*, contends that the melding of public education and professionalism in museums in the second half of the 19th century was a distinctly "American Compromise." True, in the United States, it happened because the of egalitarian movement, which was spawned by the rejection of aristocracy and privilege, and, most notably, in the revival of the Jacksonian democratization movement in the 1850s (but see also Stroud [1997:229] who points out that shortly after its founding in 1812, the Academy of Natural Sciences of Philadelphia opened its doors to public membership and initiated biweekly members lectures to which each member could bring one woman, who did not have to be a member and who could attend free; regular members had to pay an initial fee of $10). And equally true, the raising funds for museums through popular subscription was a distinctively American solution to a problem. But, when Orosz argues that the modern museum, in effect, evolved in the United States, and was later transported elsewhere to replace elitist cabinets and museums, one need only point out that the melding of public education with professional scientific endeavours, that is, the development of the modern "research museum" occurred elsewhere, in Europe (see, for instance, Vaccari, this volume), in Asia, in Australia (e.g., Queensland Museum [Mather et al., 1986]) at about the same time and for much the same reason, financial considerations. In India, for instance, economic necessity drove the Asiatic Society of Bengal to seek government aid, and the government, in due course, responded, but there were conditions, notably that the museum had to be open to the public. In 1780, the British Parliament passed the India Act which, among other things, required that the East India Company show concern for the "welfare of the people." So, when in 1866 the act establishing the Indian Museum was passed, it should have come as no surprise that public education through the development of display halls, was given equal footing with the need to provide space for the storage and study of collections of natural history objects. Although, as Orosz correctly notes, European cabinets started off and remained for a long time the prerogative of the nobility and wealthy, the rapid escalation of collections resulting from geographic exploration, made it nearly impossible for any one individual, however wealthy, to maintain collections for their personal pleasure. The death blow to this came in the latter 1800s when even the Rothschilds, namely Walter Rothschild, had to transfer his interests in his personal museum at Tring, with its vast holdings of natural history objects, to the British Museum (Natural History) (Rothschild, 1983).

In closing, we take issue with H. J. C. Larwood (1961:83) who argued that much of the scientific work done in India during the 19th century was "humble work." Larwood then rather gratuitously says, "but it had to be done, and it was in keeping with the times. As the biological sciences advanced during the nineteenth century, it was only within the firmly fixed areas of comparative morphology and classification that the modest worker in India could be expected to move . . ." We find this assessment by Larwood neglectful of the fact that much European and North American science was similarly directed. Like many historians of mid- and late-19th-century science, he looked on the emerging laboratory sciences of physics, chemistry, and laboratory biology as truly representative of scientific progress. Unfortunately, they are unmindful of the fact that it is the observational field-oriented sciences, geology and natural history/ecology, that have given us many fundamental propositions in evolution, isostasy, continental drift, and plate tectonics, to name a few. We cannot leave without taking note that William Blanford, for instance, during his career in India as a geologist with the Geological Survey of India, was twice elected Vice-President of International Congresses of Geology; that he and his coworkers, Henry B. Medlicott and Thomas Oldham, received many honors, including election as Fellows of the leading scientific societies of the day, and that their theoretical contributions not only rivaled, but in several critical instances preceded or superseded those advanced by their European counterparts. At least in India, the colonial scientists do not fit the mold cast by Fleming (1964), MacLeod (1987), or Larwood, and it is surely not right to say that colonial science was "derivative science, done by lesser minds . . . ."

ACKNOWLEDGMENTS

The authors wish to express their appreciation to those who either listened to or read the manuscript version of this paper and commented on the contents and interpretations therein. We especially acknowledge the constructive advice received from the reviewers, Drs. Kennard Bork (Denison University), Patrick Kociolek (California Academy of Sciences), Léo Laporte (University of California, Santa Cruz), and Steven C. Anderson (University of the Pacific). Dr. Carl Ferrari, (Department of Ichthyology, California Academy of Sciences) called our attention to the interesting work by John McClelland on Indian cyprinid fishes and shared information he had garnered about Victor Jacquemont and the publication of Jacquemont's *Atlas* of illustrations of Indian natural history. We are indebted to Ms. Anita Karg, Hunt Institute for Botanical Documentation, Carnegie-Mellon University, for providing us with portraits of several early 19th-century naturalists who were active in India at the time. In a like manner, we also appreciate the assistance of the Smithsonian Institution Archives and the Library of the Natural History Museum, London for access to several additional portraits of interest to us. It seems that we are perpetually in debt to Dr. Kraig Adler (Cornell University) who not only allowed us to examine a number of 18th- and 19th-century publications in his personal library that were germane to this paper and were not otherwise available to us, but he also provided additional portraits of several key figures in our story. To the librarians in the Science Reference Section of the Library of Congress, especially Miss Constance Carter and Stephanie Marcus, we want to express our sincerest appreciation for the help they have given us over quite a period of time and across several projects, not only in locating obscure references for us but for guidance on search techniques that have made the library infinitely easier to use. In a like manner, we are also indebted to Larry Currie, California Academy of Sciences Library. Lastly, we wish to acknowledge the splendid contribution of Drs. Michael Ghiselin (California Academy of Sciences) and Giovanni Pinna (Museo Civico di Storia Naturale, Milan). Several years ago, they inaugurated a biennial colloquium for the purpose of exploring the philosophy and history behind the establishment of natural history museums, marine research stations and academies of natural science, and how their unique brand of scientific inquiry influenced biological thought.

BIBLIOGRAPHY

ADAS, MICHAEL. 1997. A field matures: Technology, science and western colonialism. [A review of two books: *Science and the Raj*, by Deepak Kumar [1995] and *Technology and the Raj* . . ., edited by R. MacLeod and D. Kumar.] *Technology and Culture* 38(2):478–487.

ALLIBONE, SAMUEL AUSTIN. 1902. Buchanan, Francis. Pages 274–275 in *A Critical Dictionary of English Literature and British and American Authors*, vol. 1. J. B. Lippincott, Philadelphia and London.

ANDERSON, STEVEN CLEMENT. 1999. *The Lizards of Iran*. Society for the Study of Amphibians and Reptiles, St. Louis, Missouri. 442 pp. (but see pp. 15–41).

ANONYMOUS. 1907. Obituary. Sir Joseph Fayrer. *The Lancet* (June 1):1530–1534, portrait.

ANONYMOUS (signed L.B.). 1908. Sir Joseph Fayrer, 1824–1907. *Proc. Royal Soc. London*, ser. B, 80:lxvi-lxx.

ANONYMOUS. 1914. The Indian Museum, 1814–1914. Trustees of the Indian Museum (printed by the Baptist Mission Press, Calcutta, India. xii + 136 + i–lxxxvii, 11 pls. (unnumbered). (Chapters unsigned, contributed by different members of the staff and Trustees.)

ANONYMOUS. 1951. *Centenary of the Geological Survey of India, 1851–1951: A Short History of the First Hundred Years*. Geological Survey of India, Calcutta, India. iii + 122, illus.

ANONYMOUS. 1964. Development of the Zoological Survey of India. *Science & Culture* 29(10):465–466.

BASAK, R. K. 1983. *BSI [Botanical Survey of India]: An Account of its Establishment, Development and Activities*. Botanical Survey of India, Howrah, India. viii + 300 pp.

BASALLA, GEORGE. 1967. Spread of western science. *Science* 156:611–622.

BAUCHOT, MARIE-LOUISE, JACQUES DAGET, and ROLAND BAUCHOT. 1990. L'ichtyologie en France au début du XIXe siècle. L'Histoire naturelle des Poissons de Cuvier et Valenciennes. *Bulletin du Muséum national d'Histoire naturelle, Paris*, sér. 4, 12[Sect. A:Zoologie: Biologie et Écologie animales](1, Supplément):3–142, figs. 1–9.

BETTANY, GEORGE THOMAS. 1917. Blyth, Edward. Pages 738–739 in Leslie Stephen and Sidney Lee, eds., *The Dictionary of National Biography*, Vol. 2. Oxford University Press, London.

BLANFORD, HENRY FRANCIS. 1875. On the age and correlations of the plant-bearing series of India, and the former existence of an Indo-oceanic continent. *Quart. Jour. Geol. Soc. London* 31:519–542, pl. 25 [map].

BLANFORD, WILLIAM THOMAS. 1869. On the geology of a portion of Cutch. *Mem. Geol. Surv. India* 6(2):17–32.

BLANFORD, WILLIAM THOMAS. 1869. On the traps and intertrappean beds of Western and Central India. *Mem. Geol. Surv. India* 6(5):137–162.

BLANFORD, WILLIAM THOMAS. 1870. *Observations on the Geology and Zoology of Abyssinia, Made during the Progress of the British Expedition to that Country in 1867-68*. MacMillan and Co., London. xii + 487 pp., pls. 1–8, 1–7. map.

BLANFORD, WILLIAM THOMAS. 1872. Sketch of the geology of the Bombay Presidency. *Rec. Geol. Surv. India* 5(3):82–102.

BLANFORD, WILLIAM THOMAS. 1876. On the physical geography of the Great Indian Desert with special reference to the former existence of the sea in the Indus Valley; and on the origin and mode of formation of the Sand-Hills. *Jour. Asiatic Soc. Bengal*, pt. 2 (Phys. Sci.), (2):86–103.

BLANFORD, WILLIAM THOMAS. 1876. On the geology of Sind. Rec. Geol. Surv. India 9(1):8–22.

BLANFORD, WILLIAM THOMAS. 1876. *The Zoology and Geology*. In: *Eastern Persia: An Account of the Journeys*

of the Persian Boundary Commission 1870–71–72, vol. II. MacMillan and Co., London. viii + 516 pp., 19 pls.
BLANFORD, WILLIAM THOMAS. 1878. On the geology of Sind (2nd notice). *Rec. Geol. Surv. India* 11(2):161–173.
BLANFORD, WILLIAM THOMAS. 1878. *Reptilia and Amphibia.* In: *Scientific Results of the Second Yarkand Mission: Based Upon the Collections and Notes of the Late Ferdinand Stoliczka, Ph.D.* Superintendent Gov't Print., Calcutta, India. 26 pp., 2 pls.
BLYTH, EDWARD. 1835. An attempt to classify the "varieties" of animals, with observations on the marked seasonal and other changes which naturally take place in various British species, and which do not constitute varieties. *Mag. Nat. Hist.* 8:40–53.
BLYTH, EDWARD. 1851. Mammals, birds, and reptiles. Pages 38–288 *in* [English translation of] Baron Georges Cuvier, *The Animal Kingdom...*, translated and adapted to the present state of science. Wm. S. Orr, London. [v]–vii + 718 pp., col. front., illus., pls. (This is an abridged translation in one volume with the sections on mammals, birds, and reptiles done by Blyth, as follows: pp. 38–153 [Mammals], 154–266 [Birds], 267–288 [Reptilia {including amphibians}], and figs. 1–132, pls. 1–30.)
BOSE, D. M. 1963. Asiatic Society's contribution to science studies in India. *Science & Culture* 29(5):219– 224.
BUCHANAN (-HAMILTON), FRANCIS. 1822. *An Account of the Fishes of the River Ganges and its Branches.* Archibald Constable, Edinburgh, Scotland. vii + 405 pp., (Atlas) 39 pls.
BUCHANAN (-HAMILTON), FRANCIS. 1877. *The Fishes and Fisheries of Bengal* (posthumously edited by Francis Day). Pages 1–120 *in* William Wilson Hunter, ed., *A Statistical Account of Bengal,* vol. 20. London, UK. (Not seen.)
BUCKLAND, CHARLES EDWARD. 1906. Alcock, Alfred William (pp. 9–10); Buchanan-Hamilton, Francis (p. 58); Day, Francis (p. 113); Fayrer, Sir Joseph (p. 144); Hodgson, Brian Houghton (p. 203); Jerdon, Thomas Claverhill (p. 222); Russell, Patrick (p. 369); Stoliczka, Ferdinand (p. 406). In: *Dictionary of Indian Biography.* Swan Sonnenschein & Co., London. (Republished in 1968 by Gale Research Co., Detroit, Michigan.)
BURMANNUS, JOHANNES. 1737. *Thesaurus Zeylanicus, Exhibens Plantas in Insula Zeylana Nascentes... Cura & Studio Joannis Burmanni.* Janssonio-Waesbergios..., Amstelaedami. 8 + 235 + [15] + 33 + [1] pp., 110 pls.
CHAUDHURI, B. L. 1918. [History of Indian ichthyology.] Presidential address, Section of Zoology and Ethnography, Fifth Indian Science Congress, Lahore, Jan. 1918. *Proc. Trans. Asiatic Soc. Bengal* 14: cxxxviii–cl.
CHATTERJEE, D. 1948. Early history of the Royal Botanic Garden, Calcutta. *Nature* 161(4088); Mar. 6):362–364.
CHOLMELEY, HENRY PATRICK. 1912. Fayrer, Joseph. Pages 15–17 *in* Sidney Lee, ed., *The Dictionary of National Biography, Supplement January 1901–December 1911,* Vol. II. Faed-Muybridge, Oxford University Press, London.
CUVIER, GEORGES. 1851. *The Animal Kingdom...* London (see Edward Blyth, above).
DAVIES, GORDON L. H. 1995. *North from The Hook.* Geological Survey of Ireland, Dublin. xi + 342 pp., illus.
DAY, FRANCIS. 1865. *Fishes of Malabar.* Bernard Quaritch, London. xxxii + 293 pp., 20 col. pls.
DAY, FRANCIS. 1873. *Report on the Fresh-Water Fish and Fisheries of India and Burma.* Office of the Superintendent of Government Printing, Calcutta. cccvii +118 pages.
DAY, FRANCIS. 1878. *The Fishes of India, being a Natural History of the Fishes Known to Inhabit the Seas and Fresh Waters of India, Burma, and Ceylon.* Vol. 1 (text), xx + 816 pp., Vol. 2 (Atlas), pls. 1–198. Bernard Quaritch, London.
DAY, FRANCIS. 1880–1884["1885"]. *The Fishes of Great Britain and Ireland.* Vol. 1 (text), cxii + 336 pp; Vol. 2 (text), 1–388 pp., Vol. 1 (plates), 1–93 pls., Vol. 2 (plates), 94–179 pp. Williams and Norgate, London, UK. 2 vols. 180 pls.
DAY, FRANCIS. 1887. *British and Irish Salmonidae.* Williams and Northgate, London, UK. iii + 298 + [2] pp., illus., xii pl. [part col.].
DAY, FRANCIS. 1889. *Fauna of British India, Fishes,* Vols. 1–2. Taylor and Francis, London, UK.
DEY, SUBHAS C. 1984. Ichthyological developments in Assam during (the) nineteenth century. *Indian Jour. Hist. Sci.* 19(4):297–313.

EDNEY, MATTHEW H. 1997. *Mapping an Empire. The Geographical Construction of British India, 1765–1843.* University of Chicago Press, Chicago, IL. xxi + 458 pp., 33 figs.

FERMOR, LEWIS. 1951. Geological Survey of India: Centennial Celebration. *Nature* 167:10–12.

FLEMING, DONALD. 1964. Science in Australia, Canada and the United States: Some comparative remarks. Pages 180–181 *in Proc. X Internat'l Congr. Hist. Sci.*, Ithaca, NY.

GASCOIGNE, JOHN. 1998. *Science in the Service of Empire: Joseph Banks, the British State and the Uses of Science in the Age of Revolution.* Cambridge University Press, Cambridge, UK. vii + 247 pp., illus.

GEOLOGICAL SURVEY OF INDIA. 1988. The Geological Survey of India: The early years. Geol. Surv. India News 19(2-3):1-9, 3 figs.

GHOSH, A. K. 1951. Geological Survey of India (1851–1951). *Science & Culture* 16(7):307–313.

GEIKIE, ARCHIBALD. 1895. *Memoir of Sir Andrew Crombie Ramsay.* London. xii + 397, 13 port.

GOETZMANN, WILLIAM H. 1959. *Army Exploration In the American West, 1803–1863.* Yale University Press, New Haven. xx + 509 pp., illus., maps (third printing, 1965, xx + 489 pp. plus illus. and maps).

GOETZMANN, WILLIAM H. 1966. *Exploration and Empire.* Knopf, New York. xiii + 656 + xviii pp., illus., maps.

GOULD, JOHN. 1853. *The Birds of Asia*, vol. 3, pt. 26, p. 41. London, UK.

GRAY, JOHN EDWARD and THOMAS HARDWICKE. 1830–1834[–1835]. *Illustrations of Indian Zoology; Chiefly Selected from the Collection of Major-General Hardwicke, F.R.S., L.S., M.R.A.S, M.R.I.A., &c., &c.* Volumes I–II. Treuttel, Wurtz, Treuttel Junior, and Richter; Parbury, Allen, both of London.

GUDGER, E. W. 1924. The sources of the material for Hamilton-Buchanan's Fishes of the Ganges, the fate of his collections, drawings and notes, and the use made of his data. *Jour. Asiatic Soc. Bengal (NS),* 19:121–136.

GUPTA, RAJ KUMAR. 1966. Botanical explorations of Victor Jacquemont (1801–1832). *Indian Jour. Hist. Sci.* 1(2):150–157.

HOOKER, JOSEPH DALTON (SIR). 1875–1897. *The Flora of British India.* 24 vols. L. Reeve, London, UK.

JACQUEMONT, VICTOR. 1844. *Voyage dans l'Inde, par Victor Jacquemont, pendant les années 1828 à 1832 publié sous les auspices de M. Guizot, Ministre de l'Instruction Publique,* Vol. 2. Atlas. Institut de France, Paris. 179 pls.

JAIN, B. L. 1982. Development of life sciences in India in the eighteenth-nineteenth century. *Indian Jour. Hist. Sci.* 17(1)114–131.

JERDON, THOMAS CLAVERHILL. 1847. *Illustrations of Indian Ornithology.* Madras, India. 166 pp., 50 pls. (Several editions were published concurrently, at least two 4to and one 8vo.)

JERDON, THOMAS CLAVERHILL. 1862–1864. *The Birds of India.* 2 vols. in 3. Calcutta, India. (Volume 2 is in two continuously paged parts, of which pt. 2 is also styled vol. 3.) Volume I, pp. (18) + xlv + 535. Volume 2, pp. (8) + 439. Volume 3, pp. 441–876 + xxxii. [*fide* Wood, Casey A. 1931. *q.v.*].)

KIRK, JOHN FOSTER. 1902. Day, Francis and Fayrer, Joseph. Pages 466 and 569–570 (respectively) *in* A Supplement to Allibone's *Critical Dictionary of English Literature and British and American Authors,* Vol. I. J. B. Lippincott, Philadelphia and London.

KIRK, JOHN FOSTER. 1902. Hodgson, Brian; Jerdon, Thomas Caverhill; and Russell, Patrick. Pages 833, 909, and 1900 (respectively) *in* A Supplement to Allibone's *Critical Dictionary of English Literature and British and American Authors*, Vol. 2. J. B. Lippincott, Philadelphia and London.

KUMAR, DEEPAK. 1984. Science in higher education: A study in Victorian India. *Indian Jour. Hist. Sci.* 19(3):253–260.

KUMAR, DEEPAK. 1995. *Science and the Raj.* Oxford Univ. Press, Bombay, Calcutta, Madras, India. 273 pp.

LAMBA, B. S. 1963. Progress of zoological museums in India. *Science & Culture* 29(4):185–188.

LARWOOD, H. J. C. 1961. Science and education in India before the Mutiny. *Ann. Sci.* 17(2):81–96.

LARWOOD, H. J. C. 1962. Western science in India before 1850. *Royal Asiatic Soc.,* 1962:62–76.

LEVITON, ALAN E. and MICHELE L. ALDRICH. 1984. John Anderson (1833–1900): A Zoologist in the Victorian Period. Pages v–xxxv *in* J. Anderson, *Herpetology of Arabia*, 1896. Facsimile Reprints in Herpetology. Society for the Study of Amphibians and Reptiles, Athens, Ohio.

MACLEOD, ROY. 1987. On visiting the "Moving Metropolis": Reflections on the architecture of imperial science. Pages 217–249 *in* Nathan Reingold and Marc Rothenberg, eds., *Scientific Colonialism: A Cross-Cultural Comparison.* Smithsonian Institution Press, Washington, DC.

MARKHAM, SIDNEY FRANK and HAROLD HARGREAVES. 1936. *The Museums of India*. The Museums Association, Chaucer House, London. [6] + 229 pp., 37 pls.
MATHER, PATRICIA. 1986. A Time for a Museum: The History of the Queensland Museum, 1862–1986. *Mem. Queensland Mus.* 24:i–ix + 1–366, illus.
MCCLELLAND, JOHN. 1838. Indian Cyprinidae. *Asiatic Researches* 19:217–471, pls. 37–61.
MCKINNEY, H. LEWIS 1970. Blyth, Edward. Pages 205–207 *in* Hans Berger and Christoph Buys Ballot, eds., *Dictionary of Scientific Biography*, vol. 2. Charles Scribner's Sons, New York.
MOORE, D. T. 1982. Geological collectors and collections of the India Museum, London, 1801–79. *Arch. Nat. Hist.* 10(3):399–427.
MURRAY, JAMES A. 1881. *The Plants and Drugs of Sind: Being a Systematic Account, with Descriptions of the Indigenous Flora and Notices of the Value and Uses of their Products in Commerce, Medicine, and the Arts*. Richardson, London and Bombay. xxxv + 219 pp.
MURRAY, JAMES A. 1884. *The Vertebrate Zoology of Sind: A Systematic Account with Descriptions of All the Known Species of Mammals, Birds, and Reptiles Inhabiting the Province....* Richardson & Co., London and Bombay. xvi + 424 pp., 13 pls.
MURRAY, JAMES A. 1886. *The Reptiles of Sind: A Systematic Account*. Bombay. vi + 92 (3) pp., 7 pls.
MURRAY, JAMES A. 188?. *A Hand-Book to the Geology, Botany, and Zoology of Sind*. (Not seen by authors. Year of publication uncertain.)
OROSZ, JOEL J. 1990. *Curators and Culture: The Museum Movement in America, 1740–1870*. University of Alabama Press, Tuscaloosa, Alabama. xii + 304 pp., 6 figs.
PRAKASH, GYAN. 1992. Science "gone native" in colonial India. *Representations* 40:153–178.
PRAKASH, GYAN. 1999. *Another Reason: Science and the Imagination of Modern India*. Princeton University Press, Princeton, New Jersey. 248 pp., illus. (N.B. This reference is included for completeness; it arrived too late for it to be referenced within our text.)
PRASHAD, B. 1931. The Indian Museum, Calcutta. *Nat. Hist. Mag.* 3(18):33–38.
ROTHSCHILD, MIRIAM. 1983. *Dear Lord Rothschild: Birds, Butterflies & History*. Balaban, Philadelphia. xxiii + 398, 92 photos., 12 col. pls.
ROXBURGH, WILLIAM. 1820–1824. *Flora Indica: or, Descriptions of Indian Plants* [with additions and observations by Nathaniel Wallich; edited by William Carey.] Mission Press, Serampore, India. 2 vols.
ROXBURGH, WILLIAM. 1832. *Flora Indica: or, Descriptions of Indian Plants*. [Printed for] W. Thacker, Serampore, India. 3 vols.
RUMPHIUS, GEORG EBERHARD. 1741–1750. *Herbarium Amboinense... Fransicum Changuion*, J. Catuffe, [etc.], Amstelaedami.
RUSSELL, PATRICK. 1791. *Treatise on the Plague: Containing an Historical Journal, and Medical Account, of the Plague, at Aleppo, in the Years 1760, 1761, and 1762. Also, Remarks on Quarantines, Lazarettos, and the Administration of Police in Times of Pestilence. To which is added, an Appendix, Containing Cases of the Plague; and an Account of the Weather, During the Pestilential Season*. [Printed for] G.G.J. and J. Robinson, London. 12 + 583 + clix pp.
RUSSELL, PATRICK. 1796. *An Account of Indian Serpents, Collected on the Coast of Coromandel; containing Descriptions and Drawings of Each Species; together with Experiments and Remarks on their Several Poisons*. George Nicol, London. vii + 91 pp., 46 pls.
RUSSELL, PATRICK. 1801–1809[1810?]. *A Continualtion of an Account of Indian Serpents; containing Descriptions and Figures, from Specimens and Drawings, transmitted from Various Parts of India, to the Hon. the Court of Directors of the East India Company*. G. and W. Nicol, London. v + ix–xv + 53 + (4) pp., portrait [of Russell], 45 pls. (Note: According to Zhao & Adler [1993:396–397], this volume was published in five parts between 1801 and 1809 [possibly 1810].)
SANTAPAU, H. 1964. The Botanical Survey of India. *Science & Culture* 30(1):2–11.
SCLATER, WILLIAM LUTLEY. 1891. *List of the Snakes in the Indian Museum*. Trustees of the Indian Museum, Calcutta, India. 79 pp.
SCLATER, WILLIAM LUTLEY. 1892. *List of the Batrachia in the Indian Museum*. Trustees of the Indian Museum, London, UK. viii + 43 pp.

SECORD, JAMES A. 1986. The Geological Survey as a research school. *Hist. Sci.* 24(3/65):223–275.
SEN, S. N. 1966. The Character of the Introduction of Western Science in India During the Eighteenth and the Nineteenth Centuries. *Indian Jour. Hist. Sci.* 1(2):112–122.
SHEETS-PYENSON, SUSAN. 1989. *Cathedrals of Science: Development of Colonial Natural History During the Nineteenth Century.* McGill-Queens Univ. Press, Montreal, Canada. 144 pp.
SOMASEKAR, B. 1964. Contribution of the Czech geologist Dr. F. Stoliczka to the Indian geology. *Casopis mineral. geol.* 9(1):115–118, 2 pls.
SPEAR, PERCIVAL. 1961. *India: A Modern History.* Univ. Michigan Press, Ann Arbor. x + 419 + xix pages.
STAFFORD, ROBERT A. 1984. Geological surveys, mineral discoveries, and British expansion, 1835–71. *Jour. Imper. Commonw. Hist.* 12(3):5–32.
STEINDACHNER, FRANZ. 1867. Reptilien. Pages 1–98 and 3 pls. *in Reise der Österreichischen Fregatte Novara um die Erde in den Jahren 1857, 1858, und 1859 unter den Befehlen des Commodore B. von Wüllerstorf-Urbair. Zoology,* vol. 1, pt. 3. Kaiserlich-Königl. Hof-Staatsdruckerei, Vienna, Austria.
STEINDACHNER, FRANZ. 1867. Amphibien. Pages 1–70 and 5 pls. *in Reise der Österreichischen Fregatte Novara um die Erde in den Jahren 1857, 1858, und 1859 unter den Befehlen des Commodore B. von Wüllerstorf-Urbair. Zoology,* vol. 1, pt. 4. Kaiserlich-Königl. Hof-Staatsdruckerei, Vienna, Austria.
STOLICZKA, FERDINAND. 1870. Observations on some Indian and Malayan Amphibia and Reptilia. *Jour. Asiatic Soc. Bengal* 39(2):159–228, pls. 10–12.
STOLICZKA, FERDINAND. 1872. Notes on reptiles, collected by Surgeon F. Day in Sind. *Proc. Asiatic Soc. Bengal* 1872(May):85–92.
STOLICZKA, FERDINAND. 1872. Notes on some new species of Reptilia and Amphibia, collected by Dr. W. Waagen in North-Western Punjab. *Proc. Asiatic Soc. Bengal* 1872(July):124–131.
STROUD, PATRICIA TYSON. 1997. The founding of the Academy of Natural Sciences of Philadelphia in 1812 and its *Journal* in 1817. *Proc. Acad. Nat. Sci. Philadelphia* 147:227–236, figs. 1–8.
SYKES, WILLIAM HENRY. 1838. On the fishes of the Deccan. *Proc. Zool. Soc. London* 4:157–165.
THEOBALD, WILLIAM. 1876. *Descriptive Catalogue of the Reptiles of British India.* Thacker, Spink and Co., Calcutta, India. x + 238 + xxxviii (Synopsis) + xiii (Appendix) pp.
VACCARI, EZIO. 2000. The Museum and the Academy: Geology and Palaeontology in the "Accademia dei Fisicritici" of Siena during the 18th century. Pages 5–25 *in* M. Ghiselin and A. Leviton, eds., *Cultures and Institutions of Natural History.* California Academy of Sciences, Memoir 25.
VISVANATHAN, SHIV. 1985. Organizing for Science: The Making of an Industrial Research Laboratory. Pages 8–38 (Chapt. 2) in *The Rise of Industrial Research I.* Oxford Univ. Press, Delhi, India. Pages 8–38.
WHITE, GILBERT. 1789. *The Natural History and Antiquities of Selborne, in the County of Southampton: with Engravings, and an Appendix ....* [Printed for B. White and Son by] T. Bensley, London. 468 + 12 pp., 6 pls., map. (An 1836 edition containing 19 + 418 pp. was edited by the naturalist Edward Blyth, *q.v.*)
WHITEHEAD, P. J. P., and P. K. TALWAR. 1976. Francis Day (1829–1889) and his Collections of Indian Fishes. *Bull. British Mus. (Nat. Hist.), Hist. Ser.,* 2(1):1–189, 4 pls.
WHITFIELD, PETER. 1998. *New Found Lands: Maps in the History of Exploration.* Routledge, New York. viii + 200, illus.
WIGHT, ROBERT. 1831. *Illustrations of Indian Botany.* J. Murray, London. 10 col. pls.
WIGHT, ROBERT. 1840–1850. *Illustrations of Indian Botany.* [Published for the author by] J. B. Pharaoh, Madras, India. 2 vols. 205 col. pls.
WOOD, CASEY A. 1931. *An Introduction to the Literature of Vertebrate Zoology Based Chiefly on the Titles in the Blacker Library of Zoology ... McGill University, Montreal.* Oxford University Press, London. xix + 643 pp.
ZHAO ER-MI, and KRAIG ADLER. 1993. Herpetology of China. Society for the Study of Amphibians and Reptiles, Ithaca, New York. 522 pp., 38 numbered figs., 25 unnumbers figs., 48 col. pls.

Copyright ©2000 by the California Academy of Sciences
Golden Gate Park, San Francisco, California 94118, USA.
All rights reserved.

The Museums and the Construction of Natural Sciences in Brazil in the 19th Century

MARIA MARGARET LOPES
Instituto de Geociências, UNICAMP.CP.6152
CEP 13083–970 Campinas, São Paulo, Brazil
E-mail: mmlopes@ige.unicamp.br

Since the mid–1860s, the number and the scientific and social importance of museums related to the natural sciences increased significantly in Brazil, an explicit indication of the increasing interest in natural sciences and the consolidation of this field of knowledge. In 1876, the Museu Nacional do Rio de Janeiro (National Museum) — which had existed since 1818 — was renovated while several museums were created in the provinces. In the Amazon, the present-day *Museu Paraense Emilio Goeldi* (Paraense Museum) was organized in Belém in 1866, and the *Museu Botânico do Amazonas* (Botanic Museum) in Manaus in 1883. In the South, the *Museu Paranaense* (Paranaense Museum) was founded in Curitiba by the Society of Acclimatization in 1874, and the *Museu Paulista* was founded in São Paulo in 1894. Moreover, a series of smaller museums was founded in several others capitals of the North-East provinces, such as in Fortaleza, Recife and Salvador, the majority linked to local Institutos Históricos e Geográficos (Historical and Geographical Institutes), which also undertook to collect natural and ethnographical products. This proliferation of local museums and the renewal of the National Museum were the results, in the case of Brazil, of the consolidation of different local elites and regional scientific initiatives that integrated the set of scientific measures implemented by the process of conservative modernization,[1] which characterized Brazil at that time.

To modernize the country and promote agrarian interests, the government would have to ameliorate the training of technical staff by reforming the system of higher education. To address the need for more tillable land, new roads and railways, and new means of transportation, investments had to be directed towards frontier reconnaissance commissions, cartographic teams, geographical surveys and geological services. All this had a strong repercussion, both in the knowledge of the natural framework of the country, and in the extermination of the native populations who occupied the land required for agrarian expansion. Moreover, the government advanced a series of measures relating to public health, urbanization, and immigration. They involved issues "of whitening the race," based on scientific research in anthropology and using the racialist craniometric theories widely accepted at that time. The directors of our museums embraced and disseminated these ideas in order to reach the dream of bringing this country of mulattos to the "heights" of Western civilization.

In fact, this paper touches upon some of issues that are essential to understand the process of institutionalization of the natural sciences in this country. Those issues are related to the profession alization of the naturalists, the dispute for institutional space, and where the local scientific community, having increased in number, sought unification. Discussions focused on which of several institutional models should be adopted that would best foster research on natural history, which by the end of the 19th century had already become highly specialized.

This paper presents, first of all, a short characterization of some aspects of the history of Rio de Janeiro National Museum. It then provides a description of several other museums that were organized in the provinces in order to draw a quick sketch of the contribution of those museums to the development of a natural sciences establishment in Brazil. Lastly, we proceed then to explore the general traits that marked this process.[2]

II. The *Museu Nacional do Rio de Janeiro*: A Metropolitan Museum, with a Universal and Encyclopedic Character

> The reform undertook in 1876 was the beginning of the most fertile, of the greatest activity and most intense splendor in the history of National Museum. It grew a lot in the value of the collection it possessed and in the scientific reputation that it had already acquired until on a par with the best institutions of the same kind in other countries of Europe and America. Its present shine is, if we may say, a reflection of the intense light projected by that renewal, after which came, what we can rightly call, the Golden Age of National Museum. (Lacerda, 1905:37)

The oldest Brazilian Museum, today the *Museu Nacional do Rio de Janeiro* (Rio de Janeiro National Museum), originated from the *"Casa de História Natural"* (House of Natural History) best known as *"Casa dos Pássaros"* (House of Birds). Founded in 1784, this colonial entrepôt, which housed both stuffed collections and live animals, was the first official station for the shipment of natural history products from all Portuguese overseas possessions in the Western Hemisphere to the museums in Lisbon and Coimbra.

The Rio de Janeiro National Museum (Fig. 1), officially created in 1818, inherited the collections and housed civil servants of the former "Casa dos Pássaros," as well as the mineralogical collection, purchased in Freiberg, Saxony and classified by Abraham Gottlob Werner, that had been in the Ajuda Museum in Lisbon. The establishment of the museum may be viewed as a logical outgrowth of the introduction of enlightened policies stemming from the arrival of the Portuguese Royal Family in Brazil and the cultural initiatives it introduced to transform the old colony into the new seat of the Empire.[3]

In contrast to the former colonial entreposto, what was created in Rio de Janeiro, then the center of the Portuguese Empire, was a metropolitan museum of encyclopedic and universal character. The

FIGURE 1. First building of Museu Nacional from 1818 to 1892. Photo: Archives Museu Nacional do Rio de Janeiro.

Rio de Janeiro Museum was created in the model of the greatest European museums, particularly the Muséum d'Histoire Naturelle de Paris, where several of the Rio directors had studied and would continue to study. This concept of globalization, with proper contextual modifications resulting from the development of natural sciences, has continued to the present day. It was reflected throughout the 19th century either in the criteria for the acquisition and exhibition of collections, or in the priority given to international exchanges maintained by the museum.

Because, even in its formative years, the National Museum had metropolitan characteristics, it assembled not only national but also European, Egyptian, and Greek-Roman collections as well as those from former Portuguese colonies in Africa and Asia.

The museum functioned from its founding and throughout most of the 19th century as a kind of government advisory agency for the matters of geology, mining, natural resources and agriculture. These are the roots for the importance of both its chemical analysis laboratory and geological section. The significance of this area of knowledge in the museum was such that throughout the first half-century, museum directors were chosen based on their proficiency in chemistry, geology and mineralogy. And, after an institutional reform in 1842,[4] the museum director was always in charge of the 3rd section, namely Geology, Mineralogy and Physical Sciences. The dedication to analysis of mineral samples — especially coal — which came in from almost all provinces, did not preclude the museum directors from taking an interest in other researches, especially paleontologic investigations. In this regard, the Rio de Janeiro National Museum, under the direction of Frederico Leopoldo Cesar Burlamaque from 1847 to 1866, constituted an institutional landmark in the paleontological research in our country (Lopes, 1999). In 1866, the distinguished Brazilian botanist, Francisco Freire Alemão (Fig. 2), served as director of the museum until he was succeeded by Ladislau Netto in 1874 (Fig. 3).

The institutionalization of anthropological studies began also at the museum and was marked by the particular interest of the French-educated botanist/anthropologist Ladislau Netto (1838–1894), who directed the National Museum between 1870 and 1893. Netto understood the role the museum could play in an international context, thanks to a local particularity, not yet thoroughly studied — a Brazilian "race." Since the end of the 1860s, cranio-metric measures of the Brazilian "race" were undertaken within the museum's 1st Section of

FIGURE 2. Francisco Freire Alemão, (1797-1874) the well-known Brazilian botanist, directed the Museu Nacional do Rio de Janeiro from 1866 to 1874. Photo: Archives Museu Nacional do Rio de Janeiro.

FIGURE 3. Ladislau Netto, director of the Museu Nacional do Rio de Janeiro from 1875 to 1893, was responsible for major scientific changes in the museum. Photo: Archives Museu Nacional do Rio de Janeiro.

Zoology.[5] An institutional reform of the museum in 1876 changed this section into 1st Section of Anthropology, Zoology, Comparative Anatomy and Animal Paleontology. The changes in the names and the order of priority, besides initiating the process of redrawing discipline boundaries, not only reflects the interests of the director himself, but it also illustrates the level of relevance that the collections and research carried on this area had already attained. The field of anthropology was further consolidated in our country by the studies of skull measurements of native races during the 1870s and 1880s by João Batista de Lacerda (1846–1915), a physiologist devoted to Brazilian anthropology, who directed the National Museum between 1895 and 1905.

Scientific education also integrated the contribution of the museum to the process of institutionalization of the natural sciences in Brazil. From its beginning, the National Museum constituted a center of reference and it supported the teaching of the natural sciences. Its founding collections, were, in fact, study collections for the students of the Military School of Engineering of Rio de Janeiro. During the 19th century, members of the museum's staff gave lectures on natural history and mineralogy to the students at the school. The museum also shared classes, teachers, rooms, collections and instruments with the faculties of Engineering and Medicine, as well as with other schools in Rio de Janeiro. The museum was permanently linked to public educational institutions. All the proposals debated in Congress during 1830–1840 aimed at establishing a university in Brazil, and which also gave priority to the teaching of natural and physical sciences, argued that the National Museum was the most logical choice to house such courses. The outstanding fact that highlights the museum's role was its attempt to gain full recognition for the natural sciences. The museum's scientists demanded that the natural sciences be accepted as specific disciplines and not just accessories to the education of physicians and engineers.

But, if the museum and the schools shared a mutual interest in the teaching of the natural sciences, there was also competition between them. Custódio Alves Serrão, the museum director during the 1840s as well as a mineralogist and teacher at Military School, engaged himself in a true scientific and political battle against the elite of physicians of the Court and the military engineers to create a Faculty of Natural History in the Museum.[6] He lost the battle. The Laboratory of Chemistry of the National Museum was transferred for a short period to the Faculty of Medicine. Thus, from 1842 until the end of the century, although the Military School was in charge of the courses of natural sciences, it nonetheless continue to use resources available at the Museum.

What was sought was the equalization of the museum with the other schools of high learning, to improve its scientific, social and political prestige. In fact, the museum's lack of prestige provides evidence that the natural sciences were, in large measure, linked to the possibilities of revealing the ever-dreamt of wealth of natural resources in the country rather than a source of creative ideas through basic research that would put it on a par with its European counterparts. This argument was always remembered by the directors of the museum in their demand for larger budget and more support. Nevertheless, the natural sciences never ceased to be thought of as secondary by the political elite and even by some members of the scientific community because at the time the country was faced with more urgent needs, especially for medical and engineering measures that focused on such concerns as hygiene and public health, urbanization, and the construction of roads to open new agricultural areas for valuable crops, especially coffee, the dominant export of the country.

Ladislau Netto, following Custódio Alves Serrão's ideas, managed, thanks to the big museum renewal of 1876, to establish free courses in the museum. These open courses, conceived as a kind of Faculty of Natural Sciences, were inspired by those courses that Netto had attended at the Muséum d'Histoire Naturelle in Paris. These free lectures drew their audiences from "all the classes of society, ladies, statesmen, physicians, lawyers, journalists, everyone interested in Natural Sciences" (Netto,

1878:185). Even the Emperor D. Pedro II himself often attended the lectures in company of his daughters.

At this time, museums were still one of the very few places engaged in science that were available to the lay public, whom the museums needed for their validation and affirmation. It is clear that in a country still characterized by the mark of slavery, laymen constitued only a small intellectual or economic elite of the main cities. Thus, it was something of a novelty to also include "ladies" in scientific courses given at the museum. Nonetheless, in these courses, the presence of women was, indeed, encouraged, a break with tradition because in Brazil, it was only after the 1880s that women were allowed to attend higher education courses in medicine.

In the decades that followed, these regular museum courses were transformed into public lectures and by 1890, even the courses of the physical and natural sciences given at the School of Engineering were terminated. This fact makes still more relevant, in the process of institutionalization of the natural sciences, the role played by the National Museum as an institutional place for the education and training of naturalists. At the National Museum, laymen, physicians, engineers, and even lawyers became during the 19th century the collectors, taxidermists, botanists, zoologists, paleontologists, geologists, archaeologists and anthropologists of Brazil.

Renewed in 1876, the National Museum blossomed. It lived its "Golden Age" during Ladislau Netto's leadership. Netto in many ways inaugurated a new institutional model. The previous naturalist, engineer, physician directors were lecturers in the Court's schools and therefore worked part time in the museum. However, Ladislau Netto and later João Batista de Lacerda, as well as the directors of sections and the directors of recently created museums, had to work full time, and were required to go through a selective process when initially applying for their positions, which constituted a major step towards professionalization.

Ladislau Netto's projects, which included aquaria and botanical gardens — natural study environments — even if they were not fully implemented, were rather updated in terms of understanding of zoological and botanical studies and aimed at developing areas of expertise still little investigated in the country. Exploration was supported in order to collect products to complete the collections; all collections were greatly incremented, and they reached the figure of 200,000 objects by the turn of the century. The great Brazilian Anthropological Exhibition, organized in 1882, displayed skeletons of large mammals, which are absent, even today in many Brazilian museums. The sections of Botany and Zoology were enlarged and the first laboratory of Experimental Physiology in the country, directed by Louis Couty and Lacerda, was opened in 1880. That laboratory introduced experimental studies in Brazil, notably through studies on curare and snake venom.

The aim was to transform the Museu Nacional into a first order institution that would deserve the title as the most important museum in Brazil, even in Latin America. This transformation implied also the inclusion of the museum into the international scientific movement that was happening within the realm of natural sciences museums. In search of a broader international acknowledgment, Netto hired foreign naturalists to direct various sections of the museum. He participated at international congresses, exchanged collections, and devoted considerable energy to the publication of the *Archivos do Museu Nacional*. Since its beginning in 1876, the "Archivos" together with the collections, played a fundamental role in expanding the international exchanges of the Museum. For instance, every issue of the *Archivos* carried not only the names of corresponding members but also a list of institutions, on all continents, with which the Museum exchanged publications.[7]

Towards the end of the 19th century, the Museu Nacional, already well into another phase of its history, was not the sole museum concerned with the institutionalization of the natural sciences in Brazil. Still struggling with the same difficulties of carrying on research, publications, maintenance and increase of the collection, international exchanges, as well as courses and lectures, the National Museum had to deal with the question of how to adapt its institutional model to the growing demands of specialization and new fields of science.

Lobbying in favor of his own museum model, Ladislau Netto's inspiration and proposals came from the Muséum National d'Histoire Naturelle de Paris. Lacerda, who was in charge of the museum, even though he permitted a certain degree of specialization in the National Museum, he refused to abandon its metropolitan character. Lacerda acknowledged that "even in a general museums like the National Museum of Rio de Janeiro there was a trend towards specialization in certain types of specimens." Specimens *were* either easily obtained in the area where the museum was located, or even from distant regions of another continent, especially when those regions were subject to the political domination of the nation to which the museum belonged. In Lacerda's opinion, this was the case for the British Museum having a specialized section dealing with Egyptian, Assyrian, and Hindu antiquities inasmuch as the imperialist activities of England in those countries helped the exploration of the territories yielding those antiquities. In the case of the Museo de La Plata, it specialized in South American paleontological collections because the vast territory of the Argentinean Republic became a field of excavation for extinct animal bones, unknown in other continents. In South American Ethnography, the National Museum of Rio de Janeiro was the reference (Lacerda, 1912).

In justifying what he considered his ideal for a museum, Lacerda stated that although the British Museum (Natural History), which is located in London's South Kensington district, was one of the most important museums in the world, nonetheless, it was not the model for Brazil's National Museum:

> It [the Museu Nacional] is shaped more by the models of the Muséum d'Histoire Naturelle in Paris than the type of British museums. The division by natural sections, the existence of regular courses and laboratories are features common to both museums. (Lacerda, 1912:42)

But even in comparison to the Muséum de Paris, the Rio de Janeiro museum had its own characteristics. To Lacerda the difference between them was that the laboratories created by the last reform to the Brazilian Museum (1911) had "a more utilitarian goal" than those of the Muséum de Paris. These have become more restricted to "the classical norms being designed only to practical demonstration of a science already built and constituted." The laboratories of the Rio de Janeiro museum applied the practical knowledge to "the elucidation of new questions of the interest of agriculture and industry, which are interconnected to them." But Lacerda met with opposition even among his collaborators. Alipio Miranda Ribeiro, director of the museum's section of Zoology, held the opinion that "at the present time, in which specialties dominate, complex museums are anachronical and without a raison d'être. It is necessary to specialize to excel — we can not delude ourselves much longer — polyvalent researchers are good only for the fossilized period of Athanazius Kirch." (Ribeiro, 1945:61)

Miranda Ribeiro proposed the split of the Rio de Janeiro National Museum into four museums. The Geology, Mineralogy and Paleontology would be united with the Geological Survey and become a Museum of Geology. The section of Botany, grouped with the Botanical Garden, would become the Museum and Botanical Garden. The section of Anthropology would become the Museum of Anthropology and History while the section of Zoology should remain in the National Museum building. The main advantage of these divisions would enable each to hire staff according to the requirements of the specialization. Contrary to these views, the museum remained a complex one, following Lacerda's vision. This institutional trajectory would differ from the other models of Brazilian museums. This fact helps us understand the constant quarrels and opposing positions held by Brazilian museums at the end of the 19th century. Let us digress for a moment and look at the history of some of those other Brazilian museums, after which we can return to some specific aspects of those institutions that might help us understand why museum directors viewed their own institutions as they did.

IH. The Museums in the Amazon
The *Museum Paraense Emílio Goeldi*: From Museum to Research Institution

> The Province of Pará is a paradise to zoologists and specially to ornithologists, and this is enough to understand how glad the naturalists from the British Museum and Mr. Layard (British representative in Pará) [were] when they learned about the *inauguration* of a museum here where in a few years the most complete and diverse specimens of the animal kingdom can be displayed, therefore alleviating the naturalist, the trouble, perils and big expenses in the expeditions trying to find them in the forests and deserts in our hinterland. (Diário do Gram-Pará de 12/7/1872)

The official reports of the government of the Pará Province (Amazon) acknowledge the influence of Louis Agassiz and the Thayer Expedition in the creation of the present-day Museu Paraense Emilio Goeldi by the Sociedade Philomática do Pará in 1866 (Vellozo, 1867). In fact the influence of Agassiz and his expedition on the learned society of Belém was so important that for many decades this fact was considered a landmark in the scientific history of the region. But it is necessary to emphasize that Domingos Soares Ferreira Penna[8] was indeed the organizer of the Museum Paraense, having conceived of and worked for its existence. Given his political position as a liberal and republican in a conservative Monarchy, the merits of Ferreira Penna were obscured by the official historiography of this period.

It is possible to identify the influence of American ideas in the creation of the Museum Paraense if we take into account that in the United States museums were normally founded by private entrepreneurs as opposed to European museums and the existing Brazilian ones that were government sponsored (Lopes, 1994). This was precisely Ferreira Penna's point of view inasmuch as he considered that the Museum should not be government sponsored but rather a private institution supported by private funds. His plans envisioned the Museum as the core of a school of higher education and a center that should foster the studies of natural sciences in the Amazon (Graça, 1871). However, Ferreira Penna was ousted from the museum by political rivals, which hindered the plan for the development of the museum, a plan which had the strong support of the British representative Edgard L. Layard, whom Penna wanted to nominate as the museum's scientific director.[9]

Nonetheless, gathering modest botanical, zoological and archaeological collections from the Amazon, the Paraense Museum, despite all odds, survived and remained open to public visitation. After 1890, the museum entered a new phase of development, enhanced by the arrival in 1894 of a new director, Emil (Emilio) August Goeldi (1859–1917), a Swiss zoologist and former director of the section of Zoology of the National Museum in Rio de Janeiro, who would remain in the position until 1907.

When Goeldi arrived in Pará, he had to start from scratch. However, it was another epoch and museums were changing too. Comfortable appropriations were available, thanks to the rubber being exported from Pará. Thus, Goeldi could count on the necessary resources to build his ideal Museum. At the same time, he also passed a harsh judgment on his predecessors, considering himself as "a kind of landmark separating the past and the future of the Museum." (Goeldi, 1894a:375)

Goeldi managed the transformation of the institution into a scientific museum typical of the end of the 19th century. He proposed that the Paraense Museum should devote itself "to the study, the development and popularization of Natural History and Ethnology of the State of Pará, of the Amazon in particular, and of Brazil, South American and the American continent in general" (Goeldi, 1894b:22). This was accomplished by means of public lectures, of scientific publication — the "Boletim do Museum Paraense" — and through scientific collections classified and subdivided into the sections of Zoology, Botany, Geology and Ethnology, Archaeology and Anthropology, the Botanical Gardens, and the Zoo, as well a wide network of international exchanges. Both the collections and scientific publications show that the museum concentrated on Amazonian zoology and botany while the other disciplines were considered less important. Nonetheless, the Goeldi Museum published more during this period than any other Brazilian museum.

Among the problems common to all Brazilian museums was the fact that buildings were the primary focus, and not just for architectural reasons alone, but more importantly for the scientific concepts underlying them. For instance, Goeldi stated that sometimes he was tempted to construct a huge building for his museum, but resisting the temptation, he chose the "pavilion system," composed of a cluster of smaller, simpler buildings. He considered that small one-story constructions "with free access by all sides to air and sun" were more suitable to "a local hygienic architecture, healthy and rational" than "heavier fortresses." In these statements, Goeldi focuses on issues other than those relating to the conditions of conservation of exhibits. Although in our view his arguments seem far-fetched, they are clearly aimed more at solving problems of conservation and management of research collections and facilities than they are about the public side of a museum. Thus, they also clearly reflect Goeldi's worldview, which favored the future specialization of the Museum. It was not a question of splitting the museum into several specific museums, but rather of creating new "Research Institutes."

FIGURE 4. Staff from the Museu Paraense in 1907. The director, Emílio Goeldi, is sitting at the center, with two administrative women clerks, next to him. Ornithologist Emília Snethlage, the first woman to direct a museum in Brazil, is standing in the first row (second from right). Photo: Archives Museu Paraense Emílio Goeldi.

Managing over time that each section of the museum would have its own pavilion, thus erecting here a Botanical Institute, there an "Mineralogical and Geological Institute", further down an "Ethnographical Institute", I would willingly sacrifice the idea of a new monumental building. (Goeldi, 1902:108)

But Goeldi did not have time to build those institutes. Between 1898 and 1900, Goeldi went to Europe, not only to deal with scientific matters, but mainly to work on the issue of frontier limits between Brazil and the French Guyana. In recognition of his diplomatic skills in behalf of the Brazilian government, the museum changed its name from *Museu Paraense de História Natural e Ethnografia* to *Museu Goeldi* (until 1931).[10] In 1907, Goeldi returned to his native Switzerland, where he taught zoogeography and animal biology at Bern University.

Despite Goeldi's departure and despite serious economic setbacks in Pará due to the decline in revenues coming from rubber exports, which had already begun an irreversible decline, the Museum survived. Goeldi's successors were, in order: Jakob Hüber, a botanist, from 1907 to 1914; and Maria Emilia Snethlage (b.1868–d.1929), an ornithologist of German origin, from 1914 to 1922. Snethlage held a Ph.D. in Natural Philosophy; she had been a zoology assistant at the Berlin Museum, and she became the first woman to direct a scientific museum in Latin America.

FIGURE 5. "Orchard's Building," the first building of the Museu Paraense, after renovation in the 1980s. Photo: Archives Museu Paraense Emilio Goeldi.

Like Emilio Goeldi, who had been held in high esteem by the government, even representing it in diplomatic issues, Jakob Hüber also established close links to the local elite. He was charged, when he was already director of the museum, for instance, with a mission to the Far East to analyze the prospects for Brazilian rubber.

Experiencing the general crisis in the Amazon, after Hüber's death in 1914 and the beginning of the First World War, the museum was practically abandoned, despite the efforts of Emilia Snethlage. Snethlage was eventually dismissed from public office due to her German nationality. Following the war, in 1919, she has reinstated in her position, but she then transferred to the Museu Nacional in Rio de Janeiro, where she continued her studies on the Amazon.

Despite its successive crises, the Museu Paraense Emilio Goeldi survived and today it stands as one of the Amazon's and the nation's leading scientific institutions.

The Search of Specialization in the Amazon:
The *Museu Botânico do Amazonas*

Mr. Derby informs me that a Brazilian who formerly lived in Rio criticized in the Rio press Dr. Netto's administration of the National Museum. After this, this gentleman has been called to head a provincial Museum in Brazil and is now Dr.Netto's rival. He lives in Manaos, Amazonas Province, on the Amazon at the junction with the Rio Negro. He makes frequent journeys into the heart of Brazil on diplomatic and missionary visits as he has great influence with the Indians. (. . .) Any recognition the Smithsonian might make of the existence of the Museum would be highly appreciated by its director Dr. Juan Barbosa Rodrigues (. . .). I think almost anything would be acceptable to a Museum just starting and desirous of enlarging itself and rivaling the Museum at Rio. There is no harm at any rate in pointing out the opportunities for exchange.[11]

This Botanical Museum of the Amazonas was constituted by means of botanical and ethnological collections gathered by Barbosa Rodrigues (1842–1909), an engineer who become one of the most renowned Brazilian botanists and who later directed the Botanical Gardens in Rio de Janeiro after he left the Manaus museum.

The Museu Botânico in Manaus, located deeper inside the forest than the Museu Paraense itself, was a specialized, local museum. It was particularly attuned to the study of the Manaus region and its most striking characteristics — its biological diversity, either natural, as seen in the luxurious vegetation of the forest, or human, as shown in the diversity of ethnicities of the first inhabitants of the region. In the Section of Ethnography, the artifacts representing the 'types' of tribes were kept together with photographs or drawings in an arrangement that might be useful for anthropological studies. Also, no object was allowed to leave the premises except by exchange and then only after a third copy was deposited at the museum. In 1885, despite the lack of funds, the museum was completed. It had a large herbarium consisting of 1,283 Brazilian plant species representing 78 families and 322 genera, with more than 5,000 specimens classified and catalogued, as well as more than 800 vegetable species from the United States, particularly from California, that had been obtained through exchange. The accession list of the Ethnographical Section shows that the Sections' collections had 1,103 classified objects on hand, and that they were representative of the 60 nations of the Amazon valley. According to its by-laws,[12] the Museu Botânico do Amazonas was sanctioned to "mainly study the botany and the chemistry of the flora of the province and divulge its products, cataloguing and keeping under its guard its natural and industrial products." The museum relied on a laboratory for the chemical analysis and a botanical garden for the acclimation of plants. Together with these functions, a science course was to be created with theoretical and practical classes in land survey and agriculture. Despite the constraints in the museum's by-laws, Barbosa Rodrigues did publish several scientific papers on ethnography, archeology and philology of indigenous nations of the Amazon; among them was one that caused trouble for him and his museum until the end of his days in Manaus: "*A Pacificação dos Krichanás*" — The Pacification of the Krichanás (Porto, 1892).

It has been Rodrigues' intention to publish a weekly magazine in French — a language more widely read by the people he wanted to reach than Portuguese; he intended to include reports not only on the discovery of new plants and their descriptions but also historical, geographical and ethnographical information on the region to share these with scientists abroad. It was his intention that this journal would be exchanged with scientific societies and similar institutions in Europe. More down to earth, the Museum by-laws also allowed for a quarterly magazine, which was to publish the results of research carried out in the different sections of the museum (1st Botany, 2nd Chemistry, 3rd Ethnography, 4th History, Geography and Statistics of the Amazon). Here, too, French was to be the preferred language. The journal, *Vellosia*, named in honor of Friar Velloso — a Brazilian botanist of the colonial period — was published only once, its two volumes containing descriptions of new Amazonian plants and paleontological and archeological studies (Rodrigues, 1891). Besides the journal, other articles were published at the time, largely based on Barbosa Rodrigues' own activities at the museum.

The Museu Botânico, set in the heart of the Amazon, brings to mind the structure of museums at the end of the 18th century or the first years of the Museu Nacional in Rio de Janeiro, when a naturalist alone would direct his museum. Barbosa Rodrigues looked after everything, although he was helped in general by his own family, e.g., his wife, with drawings, his sons, as well as private employees, in the cleaning and conservation of the Museum. On the other hand, the museum displayed the characteristics that would distinguish the museums which were to be created in São Paulo in the next decade.

Although the museum functioned rather well, despite the lack of funds, Barbosa Rodrigues, on his arrival in Manaus, encountered strong opposition from political groups who considered themselves harmed by his actions regarding the Krichanás nation.[13] The advent of the Republic did not save the museum, which ceased activities in 1890, but it did save Barbosa Rodrigues who, as a renowned botanist, was promoted that same year to the directorship of the Jardim Botânico do Rio de Janeiro.

IV. Towards a Museum of Mollusks or the History of "a sort of white elephant"

> As you see the place offered was created *ad hoc* for you and if you do not accept it no appointment will be made. I did not enter into all these matters before because I had no desire that you should come here under a sense of personal obligation to me and I should not do so now. However, I see from your letters that you have completely misapprehended the situation... In the first place the government of São Paulo is not specially interested in zoological studies nor in the museum, considering the latter on the contrary as a sort of white elephant, an opinion in which I heartily agree. It consists of a private collection made by an "amateur."...The government did not know what to do with it. I unwillingly accepted the charge in order to preserve what there was of value in the collections and to keep alive the idea of a museum... When I was asked to arrange something for you in São Paulo, I considered the idea of the museum and of zoological work in the Commission as the only practical means of doing what was requested of me and as a way of helping a colleague supposedly in need of such a service.[14]

The origins of the Museu Paulista lie in an old private collection that was rather well known in the city of São Paulo at the end of the 19th century by the nickname "Museu Sertório." The museum was organized in 1894 (Fig. 6), following the initiatives of the North American geologist Orville Adelbert Derby (1851–1915), who had been the director of the Geology, Mineralogy and Physical Sciences Section at the Museu Nacional in Rio de Janeiro from 1879 to 1890. In 1894, Derby was in charge of his own institution, the Commissão Geographica e Geologica de São Paulo (São Paulo Geographical and Geological Commission) (Figueirôa, 1997). Derby planned "to coordinate and modestly develop under the aegis of the Geographical and Geological Commission . . . the several sections of a Natural History Museum"; in fact, he meant to create a position for his former colleague at the Museu Nacional, Hermann von Ihering, so he could continued his zoological and palaeontological studies.[15]

Hermann von Ihering (1850–1930) (Fig. 7) arrived in Brazil in 1880 and occupied the post of traveler-naturalist at the National Museum until 1891. His work covered the most diverse fields in zoology, botany, anthropology and ethnology, but his lifetime work was dedicated to modern mollusks and their palaeozoology. In 1892, Ihering, jobless, accepted in principle, Derby's proposal, which was also accepted by the government of the province of São Paulo. But since his first contact with Derby, von Ihering's aim of occupying the position of zoologist and director of the Geographical and Geological Commission Museum had already changed; his ambition was to hold a position somewhat higher than just the post of Director of a Section.[16] So he accepted the position, but it lasted only one year because, by the following year, he had managed to transform the Museu Paulista into an independent institution, which he then directed for the next 22 years, from 1894 to 1915.

Ihering had read the well-known "Principles of Museum Administration" by George Brown Goode (1895) — the famous assistant secretary of the Smithsonian Institution and director of its

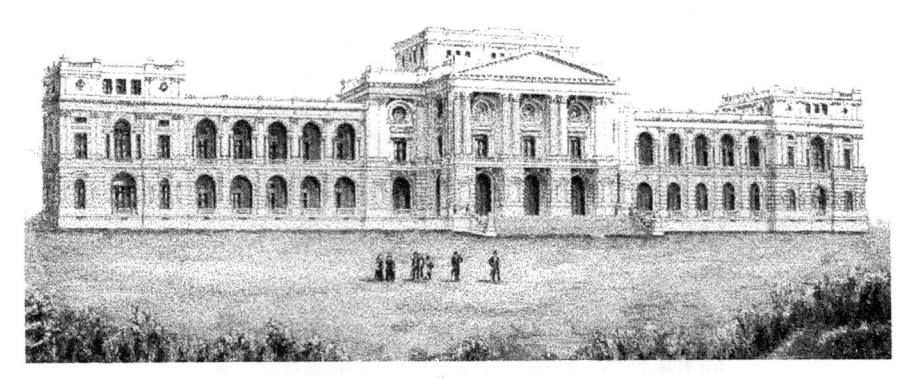

FIGURE 6. Museu Paulista as it appeared in 1895.
From a lithograph published in volume 1 of the *Revista do Museu Paulista*, pl. 1.

National Museum — with whom he entertained a systematic correspondence[17] about his proposals for the organization of the Museum Paulista. Thus, his dream and his plan for the Museu Paulista — in accordance with his own work that had acquired a continental dimension — was the construction of a South American Museum.[18]

Completely at ease with the discussions of his time about different schemes for classifying and arranging natural history collections, Ihering was adept at separating study collections from exhibition collections, an arrangement he instituted at the Museu Paulista from its inception (Ihering, 1895:20). The study collections were, in fact, his main interest, especially those of South American mollusks, and although the Museum was not divided into Sections, the zoological collections were the outstanding collection, followed by ethnographical collections and botanical inventories.

FIGURE 7. Herman Friedrich Albrecht von Ihering, director of the Museu Paulista from 1894 to 1916.
Photo: Archives Museu Paulista.

Besides the study collections, another of Ihering's main concern was to keep the scientific character of the *Revista do Museu Paulista*. Like other museums, the *Revista do Museu Paulista* was clearly an organ for disseminating the wide-ranging scientific writings of the Museum director.

Ihering listed in his reports the names of researchers, both national and foreign, who classified his collections, as well as the names of "illustrious visitors" who came to São Paulo to study the museum's collections and who published their results in the museum's journal. He also stressed the importance of international exchange, which he maintained with museums and scientific societies all over the world; the two he considered most "intimate and extremely advantageous" were the exchanges with the British Museum and National Museum in Washington.[19] He established a wide network with researchers and institutions in South America, especially with the directors of museums in Argentina and Chile, in the Pacific region, which in the long run allowed him to construct his theory on "Continental Bridges."[20]

Just as F. A. Bather (1895) — British Museum curator — who, in his survey of museums linked to the British Empire, divided the museums into metropolitan and colonial ones, or L.V. Coleman (1939) — director of the American Association of Museums — who divided his survey of some 100 Latin-American museums (22 of which were dedicated to natural history) into national, provincial, university, school and private, Ihering also proposed his typology of museums, following a trip to Europe in 1907, with the specific goal of studying the organization of museums. Based on their scientific collections, he distinguished three groups of museums: central, provincial and specialized museums. *Central Museums* included only those located in the great capitals of the main countries of Europe and then only if they had managed to overcome critical problems, sometimes by means of a complete reorganization, to give them proper buildings and a great increase in finance and scientific staff. *Provincial Museums* were characterized, in general, by lack of definitive plans of research, while *Specialized Museums*, for Ihering "constituted, no doubt, what best corresponds to the needs of science, but even then they exist in a very limited number" (Ihering, 1907:441).

Mentioning some small museums of the latter kind in Germany and even some private collectors, Ihering's comments generated a bitter quarrel with the Museu Nacional do Rio de Janeiro. Ihering held that in South America there existed only two "specialized museums," the one he directed in São Paulo, the other under Goeldi's direction in the Amazon. While the Museu Paraense investigated Amazonian themes, the Museu Paulista dedicated itself to the zoological studies of South America, giving special attention to modern and fossil mollusks.

Doubting that the great museums would be able to follow the changes needed by the development of science, Ihering declared that specialized museums are the museums of the future. And, from that base, he argued for what might sound bizarre today — the foundation of a Mollusks' Museum. In fact, he was defending and praising his own speciality, advocating the need for an extreme specialization of museums, to the increasing specialization of science in his day. The Museu Paulista never became exactly the "Mollusk Museum" that Ihering had hoped would solve the crisis of complex museums at the end of the last century. The specialization of science did not engender such museums but, on the contrary, deepened the crisis.

Due to a series of political issues, including the First World War, Ihering stepped down as director of the museum at the end of 1915. In the 1920s, the Museu Paulista was split and the botany section was closed when the Biological Institute was created in 1927. In the 1930s, the zoological collections, largely gathered during Ihering's tenure as director of the museum, were reorganized. Those collections — maybe the largest in South America in regard to neotropic fauna — some 16,000 birds, 4,000 mammals, 3,000 fishes, 2,000 snakes and other reptiles, 120,000 insects and 17,000 mollusks — became the Museum of Zoology, today incorporated into the Universidade de São Paulo. The Museu Paulista has become a museum dedicated to public displays dealing with national history and especially the history of São Paulo and Brazilian ethnography.

Final Considerations

To end these considerations on the contribution of museums to the process of institutionalization of sciences in Brazil, it is important to underline some aspects of the museums movement in the country. Throughout the 19th century it is possible to identify two distinct trajectories in Brazilian museums. The first is represented by the Museu Nacional do Rio de Janeiro, integrating the enlightened Portuguese-Brazilian project; it was the only institution of its kind in Brazil at the time. The second trajectory, dating from the late 1860s, came about when new museums were created in the provinces.

In the first phase, which is not covered in detail in this paper, I could identify another subdivision, the first moment of attempt of rupture with the models of the "cabinet of curiosity-museum," characteristic of the end of the 18th century and based on contemporary scientific ideas that already foresaw the path to specialization to the different field of natural sciences. In this context I refer specifically to the program of research and teaching advanced by Custódio Alves Serrão, — the director of the museum from 1828 to 1846. This was expressed in the new "Regulations" that renewed the National Museum in 1842, through the establishment of four sections: (1) Zoology and Comparative Anatomy; (2) Botany, Agriculture and Mechanical Arts; (3) Mineralogy, Geology and Physical Sciences; and (4) Numismatics, Liberal arts, Archaeology, Usage and Costumes of Modern Nations.

Compared to the earlier period, in the second phase of the history of museums, initiated in the middle of the century during the period of consolidation of Brazilian Empire, natural sciences were not directly involved in the project that consolidated the agrarian, dependent, and slavery driven Brazilian policy. In this context, the emerging community of naturalists was divided by conflicting interests and differing scientific approaches and practices, and thus the conditions were not ripe for it to implement its own agenda. What happened in terms of institutionalization of natural sciences was that timely and important initiatives were undertaken by groups of naturalists who associated themselves with the National Museum. At that institution, activities were organized within the new fields of knowledge that were being introduced in the country, such as paleontology, anthropology and ethnology. The first society of naturalists with a priority dedication to natural sciences — the Sociedade Vellosiana — was organized within the museum, while the first Exploratory Commission — the so-called Comissão Científica de Exploração — best known as "Ceará's Commission," also nicknamed the "Butterflies' Commission," was formed by Brazilian naturalists associated with the National Museum.

Those initiatives, together with the creation of museums in the provinces, the renewal of Museu Nacional in 1876, and the attempts to create the courses of natural sciences in the museum, were part of the efforts that practitioners of science were undertaking to consolidate scientific activities as an autonomous field of knowledge. There was the hope that such activities would confer on them both political prestige and professional recognition in a manner not dissociated from their intention of contributing to universal science, which they thought was not bound by regional or national frontiers.

This was the period (1860–1870) in which scientific naturalism, as an explicitly articulated ideology or a diffuse state of mind, although only surfacing in the beginning of the 19th century, would acquire its fully developed form. Naturalism established the universal goal of scientific method and procedures, and it constituted the ideology that supported the rapid ascent of new professional groups (Barnes and Shapin, 1979). This is also the moment when the position of foreign naturalists in the country began to change. With the expansion of modern sciences, the number of professionals increased, and, consequently, so did the competition for professional positions. Several naturalists came to establish themselves in the "New World" in order to interact from their new home with the international scientific community. Those are the authentic "seekers," so well characterized by Pyenson (1985). In the case of Brazilian museums, we can, perhaps, identify the most important among them, Orville Adelbert Derby, Emil August Goeldi, and Hermann von Ihering, and even Barboza Rodrigues, a "Brazilian Southern foreigner in the Amazon"; all served at one time or another as directors of Sections in the Museu Nacional and latter as directors of their own institutions.

To the above can be added those differing visions about future directions of scientific investigations, that led to disputes and rivalries among national and foreign researchers that took place within the framework of scientific professionalization at the end of the 19th century. For example, these differing visions of the future constitute some of the main reasons for the quarrel between the director of the National Museum in Rio de Janeiro and the director of Museu Paulista in São Paulo that was discussed earlier in this paper. Controversies among national and foreign naturalists that had marked the work of naturalists from the National Museum in previous periods, would surface again during the First World War and profoundly injure directors of German origin, such as Ihering and Emilia Snethlage. Expressing professional interest disguised by nationalist ideas, such controversies were part and parcel of the process that I have pointed to as a search for professional space and consolidation of scientific reputation within the scientific community already established in the country.

In this second phase of the history of Brazilian museums, it is necessary to consider another sub-division that took place in the year 1890. Marked by the development of local museums more than the continuity of the naturalist tradition of National Museum, this phase is clearly delineated by the rupture between the model of a general "Metropolitan," encyclopedic museum, represented by the Rio de Janeiro Museum, and the model of specialized museums created in the more dynamic, economically-developed provinces of the Republic, which assumed a position contrary to the old museum tradition of the Brazilian Empire. Among those distinctive traits of the agencies of these museums in the country, we could consider the scientific investigation and divulgation they undertook based upon the accumulated research in different field of natural sciences. This disclosure was accomplished by means of exhibitions and scientific publications — in fact, these were the only regular Brazilian scientific publications with an international readership and the only ones specialized in natural sciences. In addition, for instance, was the persistence of the directors, albeit not always successful, in creating their own institutional spaces or the inclusion of anthropological, archeological and ethnographic research in their investigation agendas. These studies had not yet freed themselves from the realm of natural sciences, just as some compartmentalized views of modern science do not allow studies to reach their full dimensions. In these human-linked fields, the museum could gather original pieces, sometimes objects that were unique in the world, as the directors liked to point out. They did gather original pieces, especially due to their scientific interest in participating at the hotly debated issue of the times, the "origins of American mankind." The directors were favored by their locations, since the museums were built in regions not yet completely surveyed and investigated, including many Indian nations yet to be exterminated and relegated to a museum.

The creation of the Museu Paulista and Museu Botânico do Amazonas added to the fundamental meaning of the need for more global understanding of the process of institutionalization of sciences in Brazil. In this period they add to the initiatives of the Brazilian State to create institutional spaces. Many of the initiatives were personal and individual ones begun by those seeking a safe harbor that would provide them both salary and support (financial and infrastructure) and allow them to get on with their research and advance their careers.

The Paraense — in the first, pre-Goeldi phase — could, perhaps, be characterized by its role in providing cultural space in a provincial capital, which allowed for local initiatives devoted to natural sciences. Museum directors did not overlook the promotion of courses and lectures, or taking part in national and international exhibitions, and they maintained exchanges with the Museu Nacional in Rio de Janeiro. There were even cases of original investigations, particularly in Brazilian archeology and ethnology, an area where Ferreira Penna excelled.

The Museu do Amazonas characterized itself as an authentic institution of research of the time; it promoted local exhibitions, which were open to the public, and attempts were made to teach courses, but basically it concentrated on botanical research and it exploited the international connections of its director. Its highly specialized character was clearly delimited by Barbosa Rodrigues, even before Ihering advocated the case of specialized museums as a solution to the crisis of these institutions.

Seeking recognition in the civilized world, in the international museum movement, and in the scientific community in both Europe and the United States, each of the directors of Brazilian museums had their own suite of friends and scientific colleagues who were, for the most part, rooted in their individual countries of origin, where they had studied and/or were either related to specific fields of scientific knowledge or shared common museological concepts. Indeed, some of the museum directors could reasonably claim affiliation with one or more of the most famous and well-known museums and research centers. Thus, the Brazilian museum directors drew upon their scientific colleagues elsewhere to help them build their own careers in Brazil, as well as with their projects which had both regional and international dimensions.

In the case of different visions of museums at the dawn of the 20th century in Brazil, Ihering took to the extreme the process of specialization of natural sciences; he had hoped his South American Museum, which specialized in a very precise field of zoology — Mollusks — would become a model. Lacerda, on the other hand, continued to emphasize "national specificity" because he identified the Rio de Janeiro National Museum as a "metropolitan museum," modeling it after the Muséum d'Histoire Naturelle de Paris, this despite the loss of hegemony it had experienced during the century (Limoges, 1980).

Here it is necessary to correct an aspect frequently repeated in the historiography of sciences in Brazil, which deals with how 19th-century foreign naturalist viewed scientific activities in the country and especially at the Rio de Janeiro National Museum. In studies on the institutionalization of natural sciences in Brazil in the 19th century, one constantly comes across foreign reports about the National Museum that portray it as a hoax, a deception in so far as its science was concerned. The National Museum, in those reports, definitely did not measure up to what was expected from it. These reports, which bequeathed us a negative image of ourselves, do not always coincide with records that have been increasingly recovered from the forgotten shelves of our libraries and archives. What strikes me most forceably is that the position taken by foreign naturalists with respect to the Museum, in my opinion, may be best explained by Flora Sussekind (1990) perceptive view of the phrase "Brazil is not far from here," which is taken from a German song about immigration. To her, the phrase can be understood as "an observation made by someone, already living in the country and who does not recognize the expected landscape." Our foreign naturalists had first-hand experience with European museums, and they had developed their own notions about the role of museum in the "new worlds." Naturalist had "ways of seeing, known by heart." They expected to find here a complete museum that would reunite all local products in a way that would help their work. One could, thus, understand the joy of British naturalists when they learned about the creation of a museum at the Amazon forest doorway, which would save them all the "hardness of a tropical forest excursion."

In contrast to what the foreigners expected, what was intended for the capital of the Empire was a Museum that followed European patterns, perhaps incomplete, but with samples representing the whole world, a symbol of urban civilization. Our historiography, even today, has never understood what Egyptian mummies meant in the context of the National Museum.

Agassiz (1975:33) stated that "Rio was during the whole 19th century, the main target of French, English, German, Russian and American scientific expeditions," which could have diminished the scientific interest over this province, but, in his opinion, led to the contrary. "Precisely because all the specimens described or present in the majority of travel reports which originated from Rio and its neighborhood, it was mandatory that all museums wishing to be complete and comprehensive should have original samples of these localities and could check the description of species mentioned." Brazilian naturalists knew the Rio de Janeiro species, they traveled in the outskirts, and even Ladislau Netto began to look for new species in the street market, following Agassiz's advice.[21] However, the scientific interests of Brazilian naturalists, just like those of their foreign counterparts, focused on the search in virgin territory for new species of plants and animals and for archaeological and ethnographical artifacts.

The French naturalist Ferdinand Denis (1980:409), who visited Brazil in the first decade of the 19th century, appears to be an exception, as he put in simple terms the question of how different "invisible things" lay in the eye of the beholder. Dennis states that "a certain traveler observed that among the curiosities of the Rio de Janeiro National Museum there was a swan and a finch. This is very simple and Brazilians would have much to say if they notice the common birds of their fields that we keep in our museums." If we reuse the sense Pomian (1984) attributed to collections of any kind of museum, of "uniting the visible and invisible world," it is possible to understand that the invisible here could be in the street market, as observed by Agassiz. Not everywhere could be called Brazil, the country of exuberant nature and populated by Indian nations with very different life styles than the transplanted Europeans. For the inhabitants of the Court living in Rio de Janeiro, the seat of the Empire, this Brazil *was not far away, but surely it was not there.*

Ihering, Netto, and Lacerda, and even Goeldi's museums do not fit into the category of "colonial museum," with which Bather (1895) characterized the museums of the British Empire and that Sheets-Pyenson (1988) used in her analysis of Canadian, Argentine and Australian museums. From the analysis of the ideals expressed by different directors of Brazilian museums in their practical agencies, it is possible to understand how their ideals were transformed into realities. The directors continuously gathered and classified collections, set up excursions and expeditions, responded to the demands for public institutions, struggled for appropriations, renovated inadequate buildings, gave classes and lectures, started national and international exchanges, published journals, established priority research programs, fought for institutional spaces and got involved with political debates within the realm of consolidation of scientific community in the country. From the point of view of the role played by museological institutions at an international level in the transition to the 20th century, like the major museums of Europe, Asia and elsewhere in the Americas, Brazilian museums, despite their difficulties, served as important research centers for the natural sciences. Our museums assuredly were not mere warehouse of objects, for they tried to assert themselves through the relevance of their scientific production and experimental research, while not neglecting the cataloguing and classifying of their collections. They attempted to respond to current trends in museum development and they did play a pioneer role in the specialization of areas of knowledge in Brazil.

ACKNOWLEDGMENTS

To Susan-Sheets Pyenson, in memoriam, whose work led me to understand the importance of the study of Latin American museums and to Pamela Henson whose support and help were essential to the publication of this article. To FAPESP, for the financial supports on museum researches in 1997 and 1999. I also want to express my appreciation to the three reviewers, all of whom chose not to remain anonymous, Drs. William Brice, Pamela Henson, and Alan Leviton, for their many constructive comments that helped measurably to improve the manuscript.

NOTES

[1] This process — one of its pillars was science —was initiated at the end of the war against Paraguay, in 1870. Only then did the Brazilian elite condemn slavery and dethrone the Monarchy, still reigning in the country, in 1888 and 1889, respectively, to better promote and maintain their own agrarian interests. During this period, although the economic conditions of the country were reasonably stable, thanks to the position of Brazilian coffee in the international market, the social contradictions became more acute and agrarian interests diversified. The coffee planter elite from Rio de Janeiro, who since the mid–19th century had been able to influence the Emperor, began to lose ground to the emerging coffee planters from São Paulo. And, while the sugar cane planters from the northeast harvested their latest important crops, rubber soared in commercial importance, introducing the Amazon to the international scene.

[2] For a more comprehensive overview of Brazilian museums, see Lopes, 1997.

[3] Due to the Napoleonic war, the Portuguese Royal Family came to Rio de Janeiro in 1808. Thanks to this peculiar fact in history, completely different from what happened in other colonial empires, it became necessary to create several institutions, including scientific ones, to provide the infrastructure to the new center of the Portuguese kingdom.

[4] This institutional reform organized the National Museum in four sections: 1st Comparative Anatomy and Zoology; 2nd Botanics, Agriculture and Mechanical Arts; 3rd Mineralogy, Geology and Physical Sciences; 4th Numismatics and Liberal Arts, Archaeology, Uses and Costumes of Modern Nations.

[5] See for instance Doc. Arq. Nac. IE7–64, 20/11/1873. *Relatório do dr. Pizarro sobre a 1ª Seção de Zoolologia e Anatomia Comparada*.

[6] See Arquivos do Museu Nacional Correspondência Oficial — 1833–1842.

[7] For instance, in volume IV issued in 1879, among the publications received from 52 cities around the world, there were some from the United States National Museum — Smithsonian — in Washington; the Muséum National d'Histoire Naturelle de Paris; the Museum of Comparative Zoology in Cambridge [Harvard College], Massachusetts; several botanical, zoological and anthropological associations from several North American and European cities, besides museums from Melbourne, Cairo, Buenos Aires, México and Santiago among others. In 1905, the exchange of "Archivos" encompassed 48 institutions in Brazil and 497 institutions like museums, scientific institutes, geological surveys, government organizations, botanical gardens, and libraries on all continents. (Lopes, 1992)

[8] Domingos Soares Ferreira Penna (1818–1888), a self-taught, itinerant naturalist of the Museu Nacional do Rio de Janeiro, interested in geology and archaeology of the Amazon, held on several occasions political office in the government of the state of Pará and twice directed the Museu Paraense, from 1871 to 1872 and from 1882 to 1884 (Cunha, 1989).

[9] The British representative, Edgard Leopold Layard, a well-known ornithologist who had helped found the South African Museum in Cape Town in 1885, was a close collaborator of the Paraense Museum from the time of his arrival in Brazil in 1872. He promoted an exchange between the two museums, with the donation of an ornithological collection composed of 340 African bird skins.

[10] Decreto n° 933 de 31/12/1900. Actas e Decisões de 1900. Estado do Pará, Belém. Typ. do Diário Official, 1902:366–367.

[11] Private letter A. P. Nilback (Ensign, U.S.N.) to Spencer Baird. Rio de Janeiro, Oct. 13, 1884. Smithsonian Archives, Record Unit 189. Assistant Secretary in charge of the U.S. National Museum, 1860–1908. Incoming Correspondence. Box 90. I am grateful to Pamela Henson and to the staff of the Smithsonian Institution Archives for access to and orientation regarding the vast and important documentation about the interchange between that institution and Brazilian museums of natural history.

[12] By-law number 49 from 22 January 1884, to the Museu Botânico do Amazonas, in:*Vellosia*, 2nd ed., 1891:XIII.

[13] Those Indians who were in constant fights with the settlers in the region, if they cause problems they also

constitute somehow a "source of income." Following each Indian attack, the settlers received a "huge sum to buy gifts and to finance expeditions." If the Indians were, in fact, "pacified," the appropriations would cease and with them "some eight sure votes of unscrupulous State representatives." According to Porto, this was one of the main reasons that kept Barbosa Rodrigues away from the Amazon (Porto, *op. cit.*:71).

[14] Derby correspondence to Herman von Ihering, SP, 23/Jan/1893. I am thankful to Silvia Figueirôa for lending me this valuable correspondence addressed by Derby to Ihering from 29/Jan/1886 until 17/Jan/1915, in total 109 letters, partially unpublished, archived at the Hand-schriftabteilung (Darmm Smlg) da Staatsbibliotek Preussischer Kulturbesitz, Berlin.

[15] Derby correspondence to von Ihering, SP, 12/Oct/1892.

[16] Derby correspondence to von Ihering, SP, 16/Jan/1893.

[17] See Smithsonian Institution Archives (SIA), RU 189, Assistant Secretary in charge of the Museum. Incoming Correspondence. 1860–1908. George Brown Goode Papers, Box 62, Folder 1. Especially the letter dated 25 July 1896, in which Ihering comments about Goode's paper.

[18] "The character of the Museum in general is a South-American museum aimed at the study, of the animal kingdom, its zoological history and the Natural History of human kind". (Museum Paulista By-Laws, article 2°, 1894:4).

[19] Relatórios do Museu Paulista, 1894 a 1911. Ihering kept a systematic correspondence with directors and specialists from the Smithsonian Institution. See especially his letters in SIA, RU 7073 — William Dall Papers (1865–1927) — Box 122, Folder 12; RU 189 — George Brown Goode Papers — Box 62, Folder 1; RU 54 — George Brown Goode, Incoming Correspondence (1883–1896)— Box 4; RU 105 — Division of Birds Records — Box 7, Letters.

[20] His theory on "Continental Bridges," published in the book "Archhelenis and Archinotis" in 1907 in Leipzig had its importance acknowledged by Wegener in his conceptions of "Continental Drift." On Ihering's interchanges network see Lopes and Figueirôa (1994).

[21] Agassiz (op. cit.) stated that in the Rio de Janeiro fish market there were more rare specimens than in the collections of the National Museum, which he considered anachronic during his visit in 1865.

BIBLIOGRAPHY

AGASSIZ, L. e AGASSIZ, E. C. 1975. *Viagem ao Brasil 1865–1866*. Trad. J. E. Filho. Apres. M. G. Ferri. Belo Horizonte, Ed. Itatiaia; São Paulo, Ed. da Universidade de São Paulo, (Reconquista do Brasil; v. 12).

BARNES, B., and SHAPIN, S., eds. 1979. *Natural Order*. (Historical Studies on ScientificCulture.) Sage Focus Ed., London.

BATHER, M. A.1895. Some colonial museums. Pages 193–239 *in Report of Proceedings with the Papers Read at the Fifth Annual General Meeting. Museums Association*. Dublin.

COLEMAN, L. V. 1939. *The Museum in America. A Critical Study*. The American Association of Museums, Washington D.C. (3 vols.)

CUNHA, O. R. da 1989. Domingos Soares Ferreira Penna (1818–1888). Pages 20–47 *in* Oswaldo Cunha, *Talento e Atitude:Estudos Biográficos do Museu Emilio Goeldi, I*. Belém. PR/SCT/CNPq.

DENIS, F. 1980. *Brasil*. EDUSP, São Paulo (Coleção Reconquista do Brasil. vol. 46).

FIGUEIRÔA, S. F. de M. 1997. *As Ciências Geológicas no Brasil:uma História Social e Institucional, 1875–1934*. HUCITEC, São Paulo.

GOELDI, E. A. 1902. Parte Administrativa. *Boletim do Museu Paraense de Historia Natural e Ethnographia (Museu Goeldi)* — Tomo II (Fasciculos 1 — 4) 1900–1902. Typ. de Alfredo Silva & Cia. (Fasc. 1 e 2) Instituto Lauro Sodré (Fasc. 3 e 4). Pará-Brazil.

GOELDI, E. A. 1894a. *Relatório sobre o estado do Museu Paraense, apresentado a S. Exc. o sr. Dr. Governador do Estado do Pará*. Typ. do Diário Official, Belém.

GOELDI, E. A. 1894h. *Regulamento do Museu Paraense*. Typ. do Diário Official, Belém.

GOODE, G. B. 1895. The principles of museum administration. Pages 69–148 *in Reports of Proceedings with the Papers Read at the Sixth Annual General Meeting Held in New Castle-Upon-Tyne, July/1895*. Dulan and Co., London.

GRAÇA, A. 1871. *Relatório apresentado à Assembléia Legislativa Provincial na Segunda Sessão da 17ª Legislatura pelo Presidente da Província, em 15 de agosto de 1871.* Typ. do Diario do Gram-Pará, Belém.

IHERING, H. von. 1895. História do Monumento do Ypiranga e do Museu Paulista. *Rev. Mus. Paulista* 1:9–31, pl. 1.

IHERING, H. von. 1907 (1908). A Organisação actual e futura dos Museus de História Natural. *Rev. Mus. Paulista* 7:431–449. (Volume for 1907 but the "Indice" [Table of Contents] page bears the notation, "Publicado em 12 de Septembro de 1908.")

LACERDA, J. B. de. 1905. *Fastos do Museu Nacional do Rio de Janeiro.* Imprensa Nacional, Rio de Janeiro.

LACERDA, J. B. de. 1912. *Os Museus de História Natural e os Jardins Zoológicos de Paris e de Londres. O Kew Garden.* Papelaria Macedo, Rio de Janeiro.

LIMOGES, C. 1980. The development of the Muséum d'Histoire Naturelle of Paris, c. 1800 — 1914. Pages 211–240 *in* R. Fox and G. Weisz, eds., *The Organization of Science and Technology in France 1808–1914.* Maison des Sciences de l'Homme, Paris and Cambridge University Press, Cambridge.

LOPES, M. M. 1992. Brazilian museums of natural history and international exchanges in the transition to the 20th Century. Pages 193–200 *in* Patrick Petitjean, org., *Science and Empires.* Boston Studies in the Philosophy of Science, 136.

LOPES, M. M. 1994. C. F. Hartt's contribution to Brazilian museums of natural history. *Earth Sci. Hist.* 13 (2):174–179.

LOPES, M. M. 1997. *O Brasil descobre a pesquisa científica:Os Museus e as Ciências Naturais no século XIX.* HUCITEC, São Paulo.

LOPES, M. M. 1999. Sociedades Científicas e Museus na América Latina, no século XIX. Saber y Tiempo. *Revista de História de las Ciencias, Buenos Aires* 7 (2):51–72

LOPES, M. M. and FIGUEIRÔA, S. M. de. 1994. Horizontal interchanges in geological sciences. Pages 1-6 *in Useful and Curious. Geological Enquiries Beyond the World. Pacific-Asia Historical Themes.* 19th International INHIGEO Symposium, Sydney.

NETTO, L. de S. M. 1878. Resumo do Curso de Botânica do Museu Nacional, em 1878 pelo respectivo professor. *Archivos do Museu Nacional* 3:185–199.

POMIAN, K. 1984 Coleção. Pages 51–86 *in* Enciclopédia Einaudi. 1. Memória — História. Porto. Imp. Nac. Casa da Moeda.

PORTO, J. C. 1892. *Histórico do Museu Botânico do Amazonas. Vellosia — Archeologia, Paleontologia. 1885–1888.* 2ªed. Imprensa Nacional, Rio de Janeiro. 2:61–80.

PYENSON, L. 1985. "Functionaries" and "Seekers" in Latin America: missionary diffusion of exact sciences, 1850–1930. *Quipu* 2(3):387–420.

RIBEIRO, A. de M. 1945. *A Comissão Rondon e o Museu Nacional .* (Conferências realizadas pelo Professor, no Museu Nacional do Rio de Janeiro, em 1916). 2ª ed. Min. da Agricultura. Cons. Nac. de Proteção aos Índios. Publicação nº 49. Rio de Janeiro.

RODRIGUES, J. B. 1891. *Vellosia — Contribuições do Museu Botânico do Amazonas.* Botânica, v. I — II 1885–1888. 2ªed. Imprensa Nacional, Rio de Janeiro.

SHEETS-PYENSON, S. 1988. *Cathedrals of Science. The Development of Colonial Natural History Museums during the Late Nineteenth Century.* McGill-Queen's University Press, Montreal.

SÜSSEKIND, F. 1990. *O Brasil não é longe daqui — O narrador, a Viagem.* Cia das Letras. São Paulo.

VELLOZO, P. L. 1867. *Relatório com que o Excellentissimo Senhor Presidente da Província passou a administração da mesma ao Excellentissimo Senhor 1º Vice-Presidente Barão do Arary, no dia 9 de abril de 1867.* Typ. F. Rhossard, Belém.

Spencer Baird's Dream: A U.S. National Museum

PAMELA M. HENSON
Historian, Institutional History Division
Smithsonian Institution Archives, Washington, DC 20560
E-mail: hensonp@osia.si.edu

Many people in the United States and abroad identify the name "Smithsonian Institution" with museums and assume, not unreasonably, that the Smithsonian was founded as a museum. However, museums were not an important part of early planning for the Institution and were even resisted by the first Smithsonian Secretary. A complex mixture of cultural forces and individual initiatives led to the founding of the United States National Museum at the Smithsonian Institution.

To begin at the beginning, in 1826 an English scientist named James Smithson (c.1765–1829) (Fig. 1) wrote his will, leaving his estate to his nephew, Henry James Hungerford. However, he added a peculiar last paragraph in which he stated that should his nephew die without heirs, his estate should go "to the United States of America, to found in Washington under the name of the Smithsonian Institution, an Establishment for the increase & diffusion of knowledge among men."[1] Smithson died three years later in 1829 and his estate went, as stipulated, to his nephew. But in an odd twist of fate, that nephew died without heirs in 1835. In due course, the United States embassy in London was notified of Smithson's unusual gift. President Andrew Jackson sent the matter to the Congress, and a long period of debate began over what to do with these funds.

FIGURE 1. James Smithson (c. 1765–1829), founding donor of the Smithsonian Institution. Portrait by H. Johns, 1816. Smithsonian Institution Archives.

Smithson was the illegitimate son of Hugh Smithson, the Duke of Northumberland, and Elizabeth Macie, a wealthy gentlewoman and the source of his fortune. He had attended Pembroke College, Oxford, where he studied chemistry and mineralogy. He wrote over twenty scientific papers, many on chemical analyses and descriptions of minerals. He was also active in such organizations as the Royal Society of London and the Royal Institution of Great Britain. These organizations were founded with mandates for the increase and useful diffusion of knowledge and so may have served as models. But even among his extensive writings, no real clues can be found as to what Smithson actually intended by an institution "for the increase and diffusion of knowledge."[2]

Early reports in American newspapers assumed that the money would be used to found a national university; they consistently referred to the bequest as being for the "Smithsonian University." Perhaps surprisingly, reactions to news of the bequest were quite mixed. Southern Congressman, such as John C. Calhoun, opposed accepting the bequest, arguing that to create such a national entity would violate the principle of states' rights. Former President John Quincy Adams, now in the House of Representatives, led the supporters of the bequest, and they soon prevailed. On 1 July 1836, Congress authorized President Jackson to pursue the bequest. Richard Rush (Fig. 2), former Ambassador to the Court of St. James's, was dispatched to London to file a suit in the British Chancery Court for the bequest. Smithson's estate was awarded to the United States on 8 May 1838. After Rush disposed of Smithson's holdings and investments, the gift totaled some £104,960.[3]

After the estate was transferred to the United States, it took another eight years of wrangling before the Smithsonian was actually established. Martin Van Buren was now in the White House, and he asked Secretary of State John Forsyth to write to "persons versed in science and familiar with the subject of public education" to solicit "their views as to the mode of disposing of the fund best calculated to meet the intentions of the testator." Former President Adams opposed the creation of a national university, arguing that money from a foreigner should not be used to educate American children. The War of 1812 and the burning of Washington by the English in 1814 still loomed large in people's minds. Accepting a gift from a foreigner, especially an Englishman, for such a purpose was viewed as demeaning to citizens of a democracy. Many educators saw exciting opportunities in Smithson's bequest.[4] They responded to Van Buren's request for ideas with a dizzying range of proposals. An agricultural school, experimental farm, academy for instruction of women, mechanics institute, school of the classics, graduate school, natural history school, and teacher training school were just a few of the ideas put forth. Thomas Cooper, president of South Carolina College, a political radical, wanted a scientific school that would ameliorate social conditions through practical advances. He wrote, "I object to all . . . philosophical literature as calculated only to make men pleasant talkers."

FIGURE 2. Richard Rush (1780–1859), attorney charged with securing Smithson's bequest for the United States. Engraving by J. I. Pease. Smithsonian Institution Archives.

Francis Wayland argued just the opposite! This professor from Brown University wanted a school devoted to the classics. Science, he believed, did not ameliorate social problems but rather provided mankind with more means of destruction, "gratifying to the full the widest love of slaughter." Steven Chapin of Columbian College, which is now The George Washington University, worried that a Smithsonian University would compete with and perhaps destroy his fledgling school in the nation's Capital. Thus he argued for a graduate school that would complement, not compete with, Columbian College.[5]

Former President Adams argued for a national observatory. He considered studying the heavens to be the most exalted of the sciences, thus the most appropriate for this public trust. Senator Rufus Choate and Representative George Perkins Marsh lobbied for a great national library. The Library of Congress was just a small collection in the Capitol and had been destroyed in the 1814 fire. Choate demanded to know, "Why should a German or an Englishman sit down to a repast of five hundred thousand books, and an American scholar, who loves the truth as well as he, be put on something less than half allowance?" In a democracy, he argued, a library would diffuse knowledge much more effectively than a national university. Alexander Dallas Bache, Superintendent of the U.S. Coast Survey, and the great-grandson of Benjamin Franklin, was a supporter of scientific research. He maintained that the bequest should continue Smithson's life work as a scientific research institute.[6]

Others argued for the creation of a great national museum to house the treasures from scientific expeditions and icons of American heroes. A group called the National Institute for the Promotion of the Arts and Sciences had begun a small museum, located in the Patent Office Building. They acquired the scientific specimens from the great United States Exploring Expedition as it traveled around the world during the years 1838 to 1842. Birds, bugs, and baskets from all corners of the globe were displayed for a curious public. The promoters of the National Institute attempted to gain control of the Smithson bequest for their museum.[7]

Legislation was introduced for virtually every one of these ideas and, as the years passed, no agreement was ever reached. The Treasury purchased state bonds with the legacy and the bonds failed to pay as promised. John Quincy Adams and Richard Rush despaired of any solution. Every Tom, Dick, and Harry had a proposal for how he could use the half million dollars. Adams wanted to protect the bequest, "to secure, as from a rattlesnake's fang, the fund and its income, forever from being wasted and dilapidated in bounties to feed the hunger or fatten the leaden idleness of mountebank projectors and shallow worthless pretenders to science."[8]

Part of this problem was American politics, but another part of it was the vagueness of Smithson's will. Many, indeed most, philanthropists are quite specific about how they want their money to be used. Examples include John Harvard's 1638 bequest of money and books to the small Cambridge college that later bore his name and Sir George Cayley's founding of London's Regent Street Polytechnic Institute in 1838 with specific educational goals and administrative structure. These philanthropists design buildings, create organizational charts, specify staff, operating procedures, and programs in excruciating detail. Smithson left no hints, in the will, in his many writings, or in his correspondence with friends and colleagues. He does not seem to have ever even discussed the idea with his circle of friends, such as Dominique François Arago and Davies Gilbert, who were quite surprised by it. The vagueness of Smithson's will made his bequest vulnerable to such debates, to charlatans as well as idealists. It has also contributed to the notion that he tossed the phrase in as an afterthought; that this was not a grand scheme of his.[9]

Despite the difficulties in deciding how to proceed, finally in 1846, a Congressman from New York, William Jervis Hough, managed to craft a compromise bill that included something for virtually everyone. The only provision that had been dropped, oddly enough, was the first, a national university. On 10 August 1846, Congress passed the legislation establishing the Smithsonian, and it was signed into law by President James K. Polk that same day. It contained provisions for basic research, and a building to house a library, a museum, and a lecture hall.[10]

With a mandate as broad as "the increase and diffusion of knowledge," where does one begin? The legislation placed the governance of the Institution in the hands of a Board of Regents, and they prepared a report outlining what they believed were appropriate activities for Smithson's new Institution. Led by Robert Dale Owen, radical reformer from the New Harmony commune in Indiana, they immediately began to plan a building to house the Institution. Owen wanted a building that would exemplify academic ideals and inspire Americans to improve their lot. The Smithsonian "Castle," (Fig. 3) designed by architect James Renwick, evoked the contemplative life of a medieval college.[11]

The Regents' second decision was to select a Secretary to manage the day to day affairs of the Smithsonian. They appointed Joseph Henry (Fig. 4), a professor of physics at the College of New

FIGURE 3. Smithsonian Building or "Castle," c. 1860.
Smithsonian Institution Archives.

Jersey, which is now Princeton. Henry had pioneered research on electromagnetic induction and was the most distinguished scientist in the United States of that day. Henry wanted to focus the Institution on basic scientific research and outlined a "Programme of Organization" to carry out that plan. Henry argued that the Smithsonian was a private research organization, responsible to the international community of science, not a *national* entity. He was reluctant to take on the financial burden of managing large collections and making them available to the public. He believed that museums, libraries, and lecture halls reached only a small local population. Henry had an equally important vision for how the Smithson funds could be used to advance scientific knowledge in the United States and the world, while establishing the nation's reputation as a scientific power. Henry would fund basic research, especially in chemistry and physics, publish the writings of American scholars, coordinate major research projects, and exchange scientific publications between the United States and abroad. He supported acquiring natural history collections for scientific research but did not want a large museum with public exhibits. He strongly opposed the elaborate building being planned by the Regents on the Mall. He would have preferred to rent space in a nearby office building. He did not want to hire a large permanent staff. Instead he wanted to give grants to qualified scientists, much like the National Science Foundation does today.[12]

Since Henry had to have a new building, as ordered by the Regents, he filled it with laboratories for natural history and chemical research, as well as an apparatus room where he could demonstrate state of the art scientific equipment. Despite his opposition, the Regents insisted on a lecture hall, a library and a museum. Henry was quite reluctant to take on the enormous financial and administrative burden of managing a national library and museum. He believed that the costs of managing such collections would force him to turn to the Congress for federal funding and, thereby, subject the young Institution to political influence. Henry wrote, "The answer made to some of these objections has usually been, that the government would grant an annual appropriation for the support of the museum of the exploring expedition. But this would be equally objectionable, since it would annually bring the institution before Congress as a supplicant for government patronage, and ultimately subject it to political influence and control." The best course, Henry believed, was "to ask nothing from Congress . . . to mingle its operations as little as possible with those of the general government. . . ." In time, Henry's words would acquire a ring of truth.[13]

FIGURE 4. Joseph Henry (1799–1878), First Smithsonian Secretary. Photograph by Brady. Smithsonian Institution Archives.

How then did the Smithsonian become the museum complex it is today? To answer that question, let us step back in time to August of 1838, shortly after the United States won its lawsuit for the Smithson estate in the British Court of Chancery. August of 1838 was a busy month for the ports of the young country. On the 19th of August, a fleet of six ships under the command of Lieutenant Charles Wilkes left the port of Hampton Roads, Virginia, on a four year voyage around the globe. This United States Exploring Expedition was designed to establish American presence in international naval power and science. On board was a group of naturalists who would collect a treasure trove of anthropological artifacts, and biological and geological specimens which some twenty years later would form the basis of the United States National Museum.[14]

Later that same month, the 29th of August to be exact, a packet ship, the *Mediator*, arrived in New York from London. On board was Richard Rush, the diplomat and attorney who had successfully sued for the Smithson estate in the British Chancery Court. Rush kept a watchful eye over his cargo — eleven boxes filled with gold sovereigns worth some £104,960, plus 8 shillings and 6 pence, which would be converted into $508,318.46. Rush also transported Smithson's personal effects, his library, and his mineralogical cabinet. Those funds later formed the Institution which would create the United States National Museum. The collections of minerals and books also formed part of its earliest collections. To some this story might seem a classic case of two ships crossing in the night, fates inextricably interwoven, brought together by some strange coincidence of fate.[15]

But in many human affairs, seeming convergences are as much the result of long and careful planning and dreaming, as they are of chance. Such was the case here. The movements of these two ships were carefully watched by one Joel Poinsett (Fig. 5), a planter and amateur naturalist from South Carolina who believed his young country needed a National Museum. As Secretary of War, he insisted that the United States Exploring Expedition include a staff of naturalists to study and collect from the natural resources and peoples of distant lands. And from the time the expedition departed, he worried about where to house the collections when they returned. He saw the answer in the peculiar bequest recently received from Smithson. Poinsett believed such an unusual resource should be used to form a truly great institution which would establish the cultural equality of our new country with Europe and display its wealth of resources.[16]

Although it would take twenty more years and many other individuals for Poinsett's dream to become reality, he did successfully inject the concept of a National Museum into the Congressional debates about how to use Smithson's bequest. And there were strong pressures to create a national museum for the young nation. When the Exploring Expedition collections arrived, they were housed in the Patent Office Building. They were displayed alongside a collection of patent models, James Smithson's mineralogical cabinet, and relics of the pantheon of the new country. These included George Washington's uniform and Benjamin Franklin's printing press. This cabinet of curiosities was managed by the National Institute for the Promotion of the Arts and Sciences which was formed in 1840 by Joel Poinsett and others to secure control of the Smithson bequest and create a National Museum.[17]

FIGURE 5. Joel Roberts Poinsett (1779–1851), founder of the National Institute. Engraved by J. B. Longacre. Smithsonian Institution Archives.

Although ultimately, Poinsett's National Institute failed in its bid to gain control of the Smithson bequest, the exact reverse occurred. Eventually all of the National Institute's collections were transferred to the new Smithsonian. Despite the vision and dedication of Poinsett and his close circle, its staff of amateurs did not understand how to study these artifacts and specimens to increase knowledge or use collections to diffuse knowledge through carefully crafted exhibitions. Exploring Expedition scientists complained about provenance information lost through sloppy handling and specimens destroyed by unprofessional preparation. Titian Ramsey Peale, expedition naturalist and artist, lamented, "my two birds (male and female) made into one, — the legs of one put on another body, hundreds of fine insects put in families without localities, although they came from all parts of the world, — bows in one end of the room — arrows in another with their ends sawed off to make them fit into fancy stands, et cetera, — all for the great end, — the promotion of science." These collections soon overwhelmed the space capacity, staff time and financial resources of the National Institute. Exhibited without context or theme, as a set of curiosities and relics, they were truly the first "Nation's Attic." The public soon lost interest in the Patent Office Building exhibits, and public financial support never materialized for the National Institute. This image of a dilapidated and disorganized collection of curiosities, growing unkempt and unstudied, is probably what worried Secretary Henry, with good cause.[18]

But others saw these collections not as mere relics and natural curiosities. The botanical and zoological collections could serve as the basis for research on the range of distribution of organisms on the North American continent. The relics of George Washington and Thomas Jefferson could be used to tell the story of the founding of the young country. Ethnological artifacts and modern industrial equipment could be used to trace the development of technology from "primitive" civilizations to that pinnacle of technological innovation, the United States. All these could be used in exhibits designed to educate the citizens of a democracy about their history, the fine arts and the natural world. These specimens and artifacts became valuable only when studied and analyzed comparatively, and when the results of that work were shared through research-based publications and exhibits. This vision, soon to be a reality, garnered the public enthusiasm that Poinsett had never been able to secure. Most importantly, this vision of a research museum secured public support in the form of collection donations, additional bequests, and Congressional appropriations which grew annually and ultimately built fine new buildings to create a complex of museums and research institutes unparalleled anywhere in the world.

In the fall of 1850, this new research-based museum approach arrived at the Smithsonian in the form of one Spencer Fullerton Baird (1823–1887) (Fig. 6), naturalist, ornithologist, ichthyologist, and dedicated collector from Carlisle, Pennsylvania. Baird had begun a natural history collection as a young man, aided by his older brother, William M. Baird. He attended Dickinson College in Carlisle, Pennsylvania, receiving the A. B. in 1840, and then studied medicine briefly in New York. On family visits to Philadelphia, Baird visited the Academy of Natural Sciences and became acquainted with many of the prominent naturalists of his day, including John Cassin, Isaac Lea, Samuel G. Morton, and Thomas Nuttall. At the Academy, Baird first saw John James Audubon's folio on American birds. On 4 June 1840, Baird began a correspondence on natural history with the famed bird artist, which lasted for the rest of Audubon's career. By the time Baird graduated from college, he was a well-known member of the small but vibrant natural history community in the United States.[19]

FIGURE 6. Spencer Fullerton Baird (1823–1887), c. 1850, Assistant Secretary of the Smithsonian. Daguerreotype. Smithsonian Institution Archives.

In 1841, Baird heard from his brother, Will, who then worked in Washington for the Treasury Department, about the collection of natural history materials amassed by the United States Exploring Expedition and exhibited by the National Institute. That same year, while studying medicine in New York, he met one of the expedition artists, Titian Ramsey Peale, son of Charles Willson Peale, who ran a museum in New York City. Titian Peale was preparing the ill-fated reports on the birds and mammals collected by the expedition. Baird peppered his brother with questions about the specimens and the naturalists who worked at the National Institute. In 1842, Baird walked from Carlisle, Pennsylvania, to Baltimore, Maryland, and then took a train to Washington to visit Will and see the National Institute collections at the Patent Office Building. Indeed, he hoped he might be appointed curator of the new museum, but as the National Institute foundered, so did Baird's dreams. He settled for a professorship at Dickinson College, teaching chemistry and natural history to its academy and college students. Baird took his students on natural history "rambles" and taught them proper techniques for collecting and preparing specimens. He also devoted considerable energy to improving the college's small museum. On 8 August 1842, he married Mary Churchill, the daughter of family friends, a union that brought as much to Baird's career as his personal life.[20]

Baird devoted his energies to teaching and developing the museum at Dickinson College, but he soon tired of the classroom. When he heard of the founding of the Smithsonian Institution in 1846, with provisions for a museum, his hopes were rekindled. In January of 1847, James Dwight Dana, one of the "scientifics" on the United States Exploring Expedition, wrote to urge Baird to apply for the position of curator of natural history at the new Institution, since Dana did not want the position for himself. In early February 1847, Baird wrote to the new Secretary, Henry, offering his services as the natural history curator and his collections to the new museum. He visited the fledgling Institution several times to plead his case. He solicited recommendations from influential friends, such as John James Audubon, James Buchanan, Asa Gray, and Samuel G. Morton. The natural history community was eager to see a curator appointed to care for the natural history collections. Most influential was George Perkins Marsh, a Congressman and member of the Smithsonian's Board of Regents. Marsh was a family friend of Baird's wife, Mary Churchill Baird, and undertook to advance the young man's career. Secretary Henry was not enthusiastic about establishing a museum and wrote to Baird that he would not hire a curator before construction of the Smithsonian Building was completed, a period of at least five years. He did, however, provide Baird with funds to assist with his natural history collecting and publications since this would fit Henry's plan of supporting scientists' research without hiring a staff. Henry's reluctance to move forward with the museum was a disappointment to many naturalists. Dana wrote to Baird that the new Secretary was "not of the wide comprehensive character I had expected from Henry." On 9 October 1849, the distinguished Harvard naturalist, Louis Agassiz, wrote to Henry to urge him to appoint a natural history curator, recommending Spencer Baird. Marsh solicited support for Baird's candidacy from other Regents and pushed Henry to appoint him Assistant Secretary and natural history curator. Finally, in 1850, Baird was named the first natural history curator, with the title of Assistant Secretary.[21]

Spencer and Will Baird had amassed a large natural history collection which included birds, mammals, reptiles, plants, minerals, and fossils. Baird's two box cars full of personal collections arrived at the young Smithsonian Institution via railroad — the new form of transportation which facilitated the settling of the western half of the continent. As settlements pushed westward, tilling prairie and felling great forests, they forever altered the American environment and landscape. During Baird's first decades at the Smithsonian, the many exploring expeditions sent out west provided a fine opportunity to collect examples of western natural resources. Scientists such as Baird believed it was imperative to study the natural distribution of flora and fauna before it disappeared. The economic development of the country would be spurred by scientific collection and analysis of the natural resources of each region. The distribution of such life forms would be studied to uncover the great laws governing life, especially, in the 1860s, to evaluate Charles Darwin's recently published theory on *The Origin of Species*. For a collector such as Baird, each specimen was a piece of a puzzle, which when compared, contrasted, juxtaposed, and arranged systematically, contributed to a larger picture of the order underlying nature. Natural specimens *were* beautiful, they often *were* curious, but most of all they were precious sources of information. In Baird's view, collections and research were complementary, not competitive. Some research required collections; that gave meaning to the specimens in the collection. A well-documented and researched collection was an asset to American science.[22]

When young Spencer Fullerton Baird joined the staff of the new Smithsonian Institution he had a dream, which he confided in July of 1853 to Regent George Perkins Marsh, his mentor. Baird wrote, "I expect the accumulation of a mass of matter thus collected (which the Institution cannot or will not 'curate' efficiently) to have the effect of forcing our government into establishing a National Museum, of which (let me whisper it) I hope to be director. Still even if this argument don't weigh now; it will one of these days and I am content to wait." At the helm of a National Museum, he could amass a comprehensive collection of the plants, animals, minerals, and ores of North America. The National Museum would house the "type" or definitive example of each species of American flora and fauna, and thus would serve as a national voucher collection for all researchers to consult and compare specimens with. The national collection would serve as the basis for economic exploitation of those natural resources, as well as scientific research to unlock the secrets of nature. When Baird arrived at the Smithsonian, there was a small collection of 6000 natural history specimens. The Exploring Expedition collections and Smithson mineralogical cabinet were still housed at the Patent Office Building, deteriorating through neglect and loss of associated provenance information. He immediately set about working up the Exploring Expedition collections, starting with the reptiles in 1851.[23]

Baird's first years at the Smithsonian were devoted to carrying out Secretary Henry's program of publication of new research and the international exchange of publications. Baird dutifully shepherded other scientists' research through to publication and shipped a huge quantity of exchange publications within and outside the country. At the same time, Baird quietly but relentlessly continued to amass natural history collections. Growing by over ten thousand accessions a year, by 1863, some 86,847 collections had been entered in the catalog, each containing many specimens. Baird at first utilized the network Henry created to collect meteorological information and for the International Exchange Service. From his office, Baird wrote an average of 3500 letters a year, some ten a day. In this way, he established correspondence with interested individuals across the continent and around the world. Baird was a diligent correspondent. An amateur naturalist writing to Baird for the first time would receive a detailed, courteous, and enthusiastic reply. These collectors then sent him Native American artifacts and specimens of plants, rocks, insects, meteorites, birds, and dinosaurs. He rewarded them by listing their names in the annual reports of the Institution, placing them on the mailing list for Smithsonian publications, and, perhaps most enduring, naming a new species after the collector who had sent in the specimen. In his light-hearted manner, Baird wrote in 1853 to his mentor, Marsh, "I fear me I have much to answer for in the way of deluding unsuspecting young (and even old) men to possible destruction from bite of snake, scorpion or centipede, engulfing in caverns while in search of fossil bones, embrace of Krakens when catching starfish on the seas; or some other undescribed species of calamity, the genus, even, of which is not yet known." In these years Baird collected collectors. In this way he was able to bring in vastly more than he could ever collect on his own.[24]

Soldiers on the western frontier, farmers in the newly settled plains, physicians in the growing cities, and trappers and hunters in the Canadian northwest, all sent him plants, animals, rocks, and artifacts. These were carefully collected, documented, and shipped according to instructions printed and distributed by Baird (Fig. 7). If these specimens were to have any scientific value, they had to be properly prepared and documented. As one of the new class of professional researchers, Baird set the standards for American natural history collecting during the second half of the nineteenth century. He prepared circulars and manuals to teach the members of his collecting network what to collect, how to collect, how to prepare, pack and transport specimens, and, very importantly, how to document the specimens they sent. Baird thus ensured that the specimens in his national museum met the emerging scientific standards.[25]

Baird devoted much time to a group of young men whom he taught how to explore, collect, and conduct scientific research. Elliott Coues became an Army surgeon in the West, but devoted his life to ornithology. William Stimpson, Robert Kennicott, Henry Ulke, and Henry Bryant were among Baird's favorite young explorers. A lively group, they dubbed themselves the Megatherium Club

GENERAL DIRECTIONS FOR COLLECTING AND PRESERVING OBJECTS OF NATURAL HISTORY.

The SMITHSONIAN INSTITUTION being desirous of procuring objects of Natural History for its Museum, would respectfully ask assistance of the friends of Science generally, and especially of officers of the Army and Navy. Any specimens of animals, plants, minerals, and fossil remains will be acceptable, particularly such as may be enumerated in the following brief directions for their preservation. All contributions will of course be duly credited to their respective donors, in the Museum and the reports of the Institution. By reference to the annexed letter, it will be seen that the Quartermaster's Department is authorized to receive and forward specimens.

The best way to preserve animals of moderate size is in alcohol. Next to this, rum or whiskey (the stronger the better) may be employed. When spirits cannot be obtained, the following substitutes may be used:

I. GOADBY'S SOLUTION.—A. *The Aluminous fluid*, composed of rock salt, 4 oz.; alum, 2 oz.; corrosive sublimate, 4 grains; boiling water, 2 quarts. B. *The Saline Solution*, composed of rock salt, 8 oz.; corrosive sublimate, 2 grains; boiling water, 1 quart. To be well stirred, strained, and cooled.

II. A strong brine, to be used as hereafter indicated for Goadby's Solution.

III. In extreme cases dry salt may be used, as in salting herring, &c.

The collector should have a small keg, jar, tin box, or other suitable vessel, partially filled with liquor, into which specimens may be thrown as collected. They should be alive, or as near it as possible when this is done, as besides the speedy and little painful death, the animal will be more apt to keep sound. The entrance of the spirit into the cavities of the body should be facilitated by opening the mouth, making a small incision in the abdomen a half or one inch long, and especially by injecting the liquor into the intestines through the anus, by means of a small syringe. After the animal has soaked for some weeks in this liquor, it should be transferred to fresh. Care should be taken not to crowd the specimens too much, and the slightest taint of putridity should be the signal for the employment of fresh spirits. When it is impossible to transfer specimens to fresh spirits from time to time, the strongest alcohol should be originally used.

To use Goadby's Solution, the animal should first be macerated for a few hours in fresh water, to which about half its volume of the concentrated solution may then be added. After soaking thus for some days, the specimens may be transferred to fresh concentrated solution. When the aluminous fluid is used to preserve vertebrate animals, these should not remain in it for more than a few days, after this, they are to be soaked in fresh water, and transferred to the Saline Solution. An immersion of some weeks in the aluminous fluid will cause a destruction of the bones. Specimens must be kept submerged in these fluids.

To pack the specimens for transportation, procure a small keg, which has been properly swelled, by allowing water to stand in it for a day or two, and from this extract the head by knocking off the upper hoops. Great care must be taken to make such marks on the hoops and head, as will assist in their being replaced in precisely the same relative position to each other and the keg, that they originally held. At the bottom of the keg place a layer of tow moistened in liquor, then one of specimens, then another of tow and another of specimens, and so on alternately until the keg is filled. Replace the head, drive down the hoops, and fill completely with spirits by pouring through the bung hole. Allow it to stand at least half an hour, and then supplying the deficiency of the liquor, insert the bung and fasten it securely. An oyster-can or other tin vessel may be used to great advantage, in which case the aperture should be soldered up and the vessel enclosed in a box. A glass jar or bottle may also be employed, but there is always a risk of breaking and leaking. In the absence of tow, chopped straw, fine shavings, or dry grass may be substituted.

Fishes under six inches in length need not have the abdominal incision. Specimens with the scales and fins perfect, should be selected, and if convenient, stitched or pinned in bits of muslin, &c., to preserve the scales. In general, fishes under twelve or fifteen inches in length should be chosen. The skins of larger ones may be put in liquor. It is important to collect even the smallest.

Skulls of quadrupeds may be prepared by boiling in water for a few hours. A little potash or lye added will facilitate the operation. The flesh can then be removed. Skulls of the American Indians and other human races are desirable when they can be obtained, as also the skulls and skeletons of the larger mammalia, as deer, bears, wolves, panthers, foxes, beaver, badger, antelope, rocky mountain sheep, mountain goat, seals, buffalo, wild cat, prairie dogs, marmots, &c., &c.

Birds and mammalia larger than a rat should be skinned. The proper material for the preservation of such skins is arsenic, applied to the inside, either in powder, or mixed with alcohol or water. Such specimens should be perfectly dry before packing away. In the absence of arsenic, skins of large mammalia may be salted down in casks.

Skeletons may be roughly prepared by skinning the animal and removing all the viscera, together with as much of the flesh as possible. The bones should then be exposed to the sun or air until completely dried. Previously, however, the brain of large animals should be removed, by separating the skull from the spine, and extracting the contents through the large hole in the back of the head. In case it becomes necessary to disjoint a skeleton, care should be taken to attach a common mark to all the pieces, especially when more than one individual is packed in the same box.

Specimens of the following kinds, preserved in spirits, are particularly desired:—SMALL QUADRUPEDS, as field mice, shrews, moles, bats, squirrels, weasels.—REPTILES, as snakes, lizards, scorpions, (so-called) frogs, toads, tree frogs, and, above all, the salamanders, or lizards without scales, found in water or under logs and stones, known by the various names of hellbender, young alligator, ground puppy, water puppy, &c. FISH of all kinds, especially the gars, perch, pike, sunfish, chubs, suckers, minnows, and other fresh water species. Also the skulls, teeth and bones of animals in general, and especially the fossil remains of teeth and bones, found in marl-pits, rocks, caves, and the superficial soil.

INSECTS, BUGS, &c.—The harder kinds may be put in liquor as above, but the vessel or bottles should not be very large. Butterflies, wasps, flies, &c., may be pinned in boxes, or packed in layers with soft paper or cotton. Minute kinds should be carefully sought under stones, bark, dung, or flowers, or swept with a small net from grass or leaves. They may be put in quills, or small cones of paper, one in each.—They may be killed by immersing the bottles, &c., in which they are collected, in hot water, or exposing them to the vapor of ether.

Marine shells, crabs, worms, sea cucumbers, star fishes, sea urchins, and polypes should be put in spirit and in small vessels, so as to prevent too great pressure. Sea urchins and star fishes may also be dried after having been previously immersed for a minute or two in boiling water, and packed up in cotton, or any soft material which may be at hand.

Shells without the animals, skulls, bones, fossils, minerals, &c., should be packed so as to prevent attrition, in separate pieces of paper, or in cotton, grass, sawdust, &c., leaving no vacancy in the box. All specimens should be accompanied by marks indicating the locality whence obtained.

SPENCER F. BAIRD,
Assist. Secretary of the Smithsonian Institution, in charge of the Nat. Hist. Dept.

[COPY.]

QUARTERMASTER GENERAL'S OFFICE,
Washington City, March 31st, 1848.

COL.:—I am in receipt of Professor Baird's letter with your endorsement, dated the 25th instant. In reply, I have to inform you, that where public wagons are returning empty, from the interior to the depots on the coast, and public vessels returning from Mexico or Texas, to New Orleans, or other ports in the United States, specimens can be transported and kept in public stores, as requested by Professor Baird, free of expense, but that no money can be paid for expenses, it being contrary to law.

I remain, Colonel,
Very respectfully,
Your obedient servant,
THOS. S. JESUP, *Q. M. Gen.*

COL. S. CHURCHILL,
Ins. Gen. U. S. A.

FIGURE 7a. General Directions for Collecting and Preserving Objects of Natural History, and Special Desiderata, c. 1850. Smithsonian Institution Archives.

SPECIAL DESIDERATA.

As comparatively little is known of the animals and plants of the country west of the Mississippi and Gulf of Mexico, the attention of officers of the army, and others, is especially invited to this region. Of the fresh water fishes, trout, grayling, minnows, &c., little or nothing is on record, and the same may be said of the marine species. The reptiles, birds, smaller mammalia, (squirrels, marmots, gophers, pouched rats, hares, &c.,) and other animals should also be carefully collected.

This region likewise abounds in fossil bones, teeth, &c., of the greatest interest, especially in those portions known as "Mauvaises Terres," or "Bad Lands," and occuring along the Missouri and its tributaries, White River, Milk River, Platte, Eau qui Court, &c. The banks and beds of these and other streams, likewise contain rich treasures of fossil bones. Similar remains are to be looked for in all caves, peat bogs, alluvial soil, marl pits, fissures in rocks, and other localities throughout North America.

A list of the principal species of large North American animals is subjoined, with reference to the collection of skulls and skeletons. For the purpose of having complete series in the different stages of age and sex, and for supplying other Museums, it is desirable to have a considerable number of the skulls of each species. When possible, at least one skeleton should be procured. It must, however, be remembered, that a single tooth or bone, of an animal, in the absence of anything more, will be of importance. *Each specimen should, as far as practicable, have the age, sex, and locality distinctly marked on the bone in pen or pencil.*

HUMAN RACES, civilized and uncivilized.	HARES.	OCELOT.
BUFFALO.	LARGE WOLF, black, white, or grey.	OUNCE.
MUSK OX.	LOBOS WOLF.	TIGER CAT.
MOUNTAIN SHEEP, or BIGHORN.	PRAIRIE WOLF.	WILD CAT.
CALIFORNIA WILD SHEEP.	COYOTE.	LYNX.
MOUNTAIN GOAT.	INDIAN DOG.	CIVET CAT, or BASSARIS.
ANTELOPE.	FOXES, all species.	ARMADILLO.
ELK.	SEA OTTER.	PECCARY, or MEXICAN HOG.
LITTLE ELK.	COMMON OTTER.	WALRUS, or MORSE.
MOOSE.	GRIZZLY BEAR.	SEALS.
REINDEER, or CARABOU.	WHITE BEAR.	PORPOISES.
BLACK TAIL DEER, of Rocky Mountains	BEARS, other species.	DOLPHINS.
" " " of the Pacific.	RACCOON, especially from California.	WHALES.
MULE DEER.	BADGER.	MANATEE, or SEA COW.
WHITE TAIL DEER.	WOLVERENE, or CARCAJOU.	
DEER—other species.	FISHER.	
BEAVER.	MARTEN.	ALLIGATOR.
PRAIRIE DOG.	PANTHER.	SHARKS, STINGREES, RAYS, DEVIL
MARMOTS.	JAGUAR.	FISH; teeth, jaws, and vertebræ.

FIGURE 7b. General Directions for Collecting and Preserving Objects of Natural History, and Special Desiderata, c. 1850. Smithsonian Institution Archives.

(Fig. 8) after a spectacular fossil sloth recently uncovered. Baird juggled funds to support them financially, allowed them to live in the towers and basement of the Castle, and used them to both acquire collections and disseminate more research than he could produce on his own. Baird knew, as we do today, that he could increase his research productivity geometrically if he also brought in and trained young and eager students. The Smithsonian may not have become the National University, but it soon became a center for honing the research skills of young scholars interested in natural history and collections based research. Baird's considerable skills as a mentor ensured that these young naturalists remained in the Smithsonian fold, unlike his colleague at the Museum of Comparative Zoology, Louis Agassiz. These young natural history enthusiasts did, however, experience the dangers Baird had so lightly alluded to; the young Kennicott, for instance, lost his life on an expedition to Russian-America in 1865. But others, such as William Healey Dall, went on to spend long careers as curators at the new National Museum.[26]

Baird ensured that well-trained naturalists accompanied the government exploring expeditions to the western part of the continent and that their collections came to the Smithsonian. In 1857 alone he took in specimens from ten government expeditions and six private exploring parties. He sent instructions on how to collect, preserve, document, and ship the specimens and arranged free shipment on railways, boats, and through the mails. Additional collections were sent from Russian-America, Mexico and South America. The fact that Baird's father-in-law, Brigadier General Sylvester Churchill, was Inspector General for the United States Army greatly facilitated his requests for collecting assistance from soldiers. Indeed, Baird's list of collectors included such military luminaries as General George B. McClellan, Captain David Farragut, and Commodore Matthew C. Perry.[27]

FIGURE 8. Members of the "Megatherium Club," clockwise from upper right: Henry Ulke, Henry Bryant, William Stimpson, and Robert Kennicott, c. 1860s. Smithsonian Institution Archives.

Within the first two decades of his arrival at the Smithsonian, Baird equipped the six surveys for railroad routes across the continent, including the Frémont, Gunnison, Stevens, Whipple, and Williamson surveys. He also equipped the naturalists on the United States and Mexican Boundary Survey, the Navy Survey of the La Plata River and its tributaries, the United States Naval Astronomical Expedition to Chile, the Ringgold and Rodgers exploration of the China Seas and Behring's Straits, and Elisha Kent Kane's exploration of the west coast of Greenland and Smith's Sound. The 1870s saw the surveys of the Territories, under Hayden, Powell, and Wheeler. From 1850 to 1877, the Smithsonian received specimens from more than 245 expeditions to all reaches of the globe.[28]

Congressional support was forthcoming for these western exploring expeditions in part because of their practical focus. Expeditions leaders such as Ferdinand Vandiveer Hayden and John Wesley Powell were interested in both advancing science and economic development of the West. Hayden viewed locating coal deposits, mineral veins, timber stands, agricultural resources, grazing lands, water, irrigation sites, and tourist spas as the duty of the territorial geologist. Powell's interest in the West was as an environment for settlement, as much as it was in its geology and archeology. By working closely with figures such as Hayden and Powell who emphasized the economic value of their work, Baird ensured that his naturalists accompanied military and commercial exploring expeditions, and the surveys received strong Congressional and popular support.[29]

Baird also developed the nucleus of a national paleontological collection during his four decades at the Smithsonian. In 1858, Fielding B. Meek was appointed Resident Collaborator in Paleontology at the National Museum and resided in the Smithsonian Castle from 1861 until his death in 1876. A veteran of state geological surveys in Iowa, Minnesota, New York, and Wisconsin, as well as the Hayden surveys, Meek brought expertise in systematics and stratigraphy. He worked diligently on publications from the collections amassed by the surveys. By the time the United States Geological Survey was established in 1879, the U.S. National Museum had sufficiently established itself as the national repository that the legislation directed that all specimens and artifacts collected by the U.S.G.S., when no longer needed for research, were to be deposited in the National Museum.[30]

Baird also encouraged the transfer of parts of the National Institute collections to the Smithsonian in 1857 and again in 1862. As room after room filled with specimens, Baird continued to play a major role in publishing the results of research on the collections made by the United States Exploring Expedition and other surveys. In this way, he ensured that they were worked on and described by competent, experienced scientists. The last of the National Institute collections, however, were not transferred to the Smithsonian's National Museum until 1883 when was Baird was Secretary. These transfers included historical artifacts, such as George Washington's military tent and field kit, as well as scientific specimens. A collection of art on display in the Castle attracted visitors as well. Portraits and busts of classical subjects, as well as important Americans and scientists, were displayed for public viewing. A collection of American Indian paintings by John Mix Stanley also received a great deal of interest. Thus, within a few years of its opening, the Castle had become a popular place to visit in the nation's Capital, with collections in art, history, and science.[31]

During his first two decades as Assistant Secretary at the Smithsonian, Baird dutifully continued to harry printers and ship an endless stream of publications for Secretary Henry. He had watched closely in 1855 as Henry fired the other Assistant Secretary, Charles Coffin Jewett, in a dispute over creation of a National Library. The Institution had been receiving a copy of all works submitted for copyright and had amassed a fine collection of other books, especially in art history. These included portfolios with copies of such masters as Rembrandt and da Vinci. But Secretary Henry did not believe the Smithson bequest was sufficient to pay for scientific research, a museum, *and* a national library. When Jewett pushed too hard for the National Library, Henry dismissed him and suggested that the Smithsonian should dispose of some of the collections which were filling up every available inch of the Castle. In his 1856 report, Henry proposed that the government take back all the collections the Smithsonian had accumulated thus far and even purchase the Smithsonian Building to house the collections. Henry could then operate his program from much reduced space. The Congress did not take Henry up on his offer, but rather sent more and more treasures to the Castle.[32]

The Institution had received art works, historical "relics," and scientific specimens from its earliest days. The Smithsonian was pushed into becoming the National Museum because the young nation was just beginning to establish a national collection and had no way to care for it. As the generation of founding fathers died off and entered a national pantheon, their personal possessions were collected as relics. These artifacts of everyday life soon gained iconic status as they came to stand for the ideals, values, and accomplishments of the men who had once used them. Painters offered images of great American figures as inspiration for the citizens of a democracy. Scholars brought copies of the great art works of Greece, Rome, and the Renaissance to educate the masses. As these new collections filled the nooks and crannies of the Castle, Henry had finally agreed in 1858 to accept a Congressional appropriation to care for them, with the fiction that the appropriation for the United States National Museum was to the Department of the Interior, not the Smithsonian. Henry accepted the government funding reluctantly, concerned that such funding would make the Institution an annual supplicant to the Congress and expose the Smithsonian to political influence.[33]

Baird simply did not share Henry's concern about loss of freedom when accepting public funding; thus, as Assistant Secretary and later Secretary, he sought Congressional appropriations for museums, expeditions, buildings, fisheries research, and international expositions. Baird knew his vision for a great national museum was too big for the Smithson bequest alone and would require federal appropriations for its care. Baird watched over the collections carefully as the Civil War raged around the Smithsonian Building, and the National Museum passed safely through that national crisis. But shortly before the war ended, the Institution faced its second major crisis, one that gave Secretary Henry additional justification for disposing of the collections.[34]

Disaster struck these early national collections as they went up in flames when fire erupted in the Castle in 1865. Among the objects destroyed in the fire were the John Mix Stanley Indian portraits, James Smithson's papers and mineralogical cabinet, and a collection of scientific instruments. The fireproofed flooring of the second story spared the natural history collections and the library. However, Secretary Henry used the fire to argue that the Smithsonian could not serve as a responsible custodian for the national collections. The library was deposited at the Library of Congress and the art collection was split between the Library of Congress and the private Corcoran Gallery of Art. Baird worked quietly to ensure that his scientific collections would not suffer a similar fate. Despite his efforts, the botanical collections had been sent to the new United States Department of Agriculture in 1862, and the insect collections followed in 1866; that same year the human anatomical collections were sent to the Army Medical Museum. But the remainder of the natural history collections stayed in the Smithsonian Castle. Henry and Baird danced a complex *pas de deux* during these years, Henry grudgingly allowing Baird to bring in ever more materials. I cannot but think that the younger Baird sustained himself through these hard times with the thought, "I am content to wait — I'll be here long after you're gone, Professor Henry."[35]

Baird sought to prove the research value of the zoological collections by preparing — and commissioning others to prepare — monographs on them. A stream of publications emanated from the Institution during these years. But Baird's focus on a national voucher collection can be seen clearly in his publication record. Unlike his colleague, and at times competitor, Louis Agassiz of Harvard, Baird did not pursue theoretical analysis of his biological specimens, develop grand classification schemes, or propose ideal mechanisms to explain life forms. His only analytical work was "The Distribution and Migration of North American Birds." Baird had quickly accepted Darwin's new theory, but did not seek to expand on it in his work. Baird published reports describing the specimens from each expedition and massive catalogs of the national collections, such as his catalogs of the mammal and bird collections of the National Museum. These publications made the National Museum's collections a resource for other scientists and for analyses of economic potential. Baird did not amass collections to further his personal research program, as many of his colleagues did; he collected to establish a grand natural resource in the form of a museum.[36]

The great collections amassed in nineteenth century Europe and North America created an empirical base for new studies of phylogeny, morphology, and geographical distribution. The sheer number of specimens in each taxonomic group demanded specialization, as well. No longer could one naturalist hope to be an expert on all of zoology, or even all insects or birds. This enormous empirical base demanded years of study by specialists and encouraged the professionalization of science. These new curatorial demands also allowed Baird to increase the staff of the National Museum.[37]

Baird was also able to garner Congressional and popular support by demonstrating the practical value of his collections to a larger audience. In 1866 he had testified before Congress about the value of natural resources in Russian-America. Although Alaska was called "Seward's folly," Baird has been credited with arguing that Alaska possessed a wide range of natural resources, far beyond the value of the asking price. He could point to the collections from Russian-America sent in by such expeditions as the 1865 Western Union Telegraph Expedition. The intrepid young explorers he mentored, such as Robert Kennicott, William Stimpson, and William Healey Dall, went out on these expeditions and amassed vast collections which served both scientific and economic purposes.[38]

In 1872 Baird made a major step forward towards his goal when Secretary Henry gave him full responsibility for management of the United States National Museum. Baird now devoted much of his time to supervising staff, preparing budgets and acquiring new collections. Perhaps Henry had now become resigned to the existence of the National Museum and saw his best course as placing it in Baird's hands, freeing him to focus on promoting research and publications. After 1870, the National Museum was on firmer ground and grew rapidly as the nation expanded west. Baird encouraged other natural history museums throughout the country, distributing duplicate specimens to the steadily increasing number of museums on college campuses and in the rapidly growing cities.[39]

Baird's biggest acquisition arrived in the 1870s after Secretary Henry recommended that he be appointed to an interagency committee to prepare the government exhibits for the Centennial Exposition in Philadelphia in 1876. The Congressional legislation introduced for the government exhibit in Philadelphia had an interesting proviso. It stated that the appropriation was to be considered a *loan* and if income from the exhibition was sufficient for the exposition directors to repay the loan, Congress would then allow part of those funds to be used to construct a new building for the National Museum. Although that language was left out of the final version of the appropriation, it opened the door to a National Museum building. Perhaps motivated in part by this possibility, and with help from a talented young assistant, George Brown Goode, Baird produced award winning exhibits that received great public acclaim and gave the Smithsonian national visibility. The exhibit consisted of two sections, one on the Smithsonian Institution itself, emphasizing its research programs, and a second section which focused on the natural history of North America, including botany, zoology, ethnology, and mineralogy. This section emphasized the economic importance of these natural resources. The government exhibition was considered by many to be the most successful section of this immensely popular exposition. Baird now had a national, even international, audience and acclaim for his museum program.[40]

Baird's most important triumph, however, came as he was able to convince most of the Centennial exhibitors to avoid the hassle and expense of shipping their displays home by donating them to the Smithsonian. When the train pulled in to Union Station this time, it had sixty box cars filled with materials for the National Museum. Finally Baird had exceeded the capacity of the Castle, and so he stored his collections in the Armory Building until he secured Congressional appropriations for a National Museum building.[41]

After Secretary Henry's death in 1878, Baird was immediately named the second Smithsonian Secretary. His first priority was securing a new museum building, so he turned his attention to Capitol Hill. In 1879, Congress did, indeed, allocate funds for the new National Museum Building. Like Henry, Baird did not wish to waste money on a monumental building. He proposed instead a simple structure similar to the government exhibition building at the Centennial Exposition that had been designed by General Montgomery C. Meigs. No wood was to be used in the construction, ensuring that the building would be fireproof, and avoiding another disaster like the 1865 Castle fire. Baird fought successfully to have the building placed next to the Castle, despite concerns that it would obstruct the view of that building. He argued that operating a distant facility was far too costly in terms of staff and operating costs–it would even require new sewer lines. Ground was broken on 17 April 1879 on the Smithsonian Building "Annex." Baird carefully watched over the construction of his new museum, brick by brick. A high-powered building committee, including General Meigs, General William Tecumseh Sherman, a Smithsonian Regent and chair of the Building Committee, and Peter Parker, also a Regent, assisted Baird with construction of the building designed by architect Adolf Cluss. The building was completed on time and within budget (Fig. 9). Per square foot, it was the cheapest permanent government building ever built. It had 80,000 square feet of exhibit space. When the National Museum opened in 1881, it was the fulfillment of the dream Baird had penned to George Perkins Marsh so many years before.[42]

In Baird's first annual report as Secretary, he paid lip service to Henry's vision, but Henry's "Programme of Organization" for the Smithsonian and the fiction that the museum was really part of the Interior Department soon disappeared from the annual reports. Baird devoted his tenure as Secretary to placing the museum on a firm foundation. He did not share his predecessor's concerns about accepting government funds and quickly sought increased funding for all aspects of the National Museum's activities.[43]

The first event in the new building, before its exhibits were installed, was the Inaugural Ball for

FIGURE 9. United States National Museum, c. 1881. Smithsonian Institution Archives.

President James Garfield and Vice-President Chester A. Arthur, attended by 7,000 people on March 4, 1881. A wooden floor was laid, 10,000 bins for hats and coats were erected, 3000 gas lights were installed, banners and buntings were hung from the balconies, and two electric lights were installed in the rotunda. While Henry might have deplored such a political activity at the Institution, Baird accepted the price of government funding.[44]

As soon as the permanent floor was laid, the work of installing exhibits began. Massive specimens of marine mammals were hoisted into place. A team of watchmen and laborers was hired for the building. The National Museum Building opened to the public in October of 1881, and in its first full year, 1882, the guards counted some 167,455 visitors. Initially the ground floor was completely open and devoted to exhibits. The halls were furnished with mahogany exhibit cases that were eight feet, eight inches long, to fit the architectural design of the building (Fig. 10). The cases were easy to move, so exhibits could be reconfigured without great difficulty. The cases themselves served as the partitions between exhibits. The cases were dust-proof and insect-proof, with special Yale locks, and each case was wired with an electric alarm that ran to the superintendent's office.[45]

The National Museum was new in philosophy, as well as building and cases. Credit for this belongs to Baird's assistant, George Brown Goode (Fig. 11), who became the leading figure in American museum theory and display. He had visited all the major museums in Europe, and then

FIGURE 10. Hall of Comparative Anatomy in the new United States National Museum, c. 1881. Smithsonian Institution Archives.

developed his own "democratic" approach. In Goode's view, the early Smithsonian collections had been a museum of research. When the Smithsonian accepted the government collections, it became a museum of record, the official repository for objects of art, culture, and science. Goode's new museum was also a museum of education. Goode believed that the role of the National Museum was to teach and uplift the citizens of a democracy, not merely amuse or entertain.[46]

Goode established a comprehensive classification system of the world, from the inorganic, to plants, to animals, to man. Each of these groups showed a progression from the simple to the complex. The exhibits were designed to convey the place of each object in a great world order. Although an ichthyologist by training, Goode was also interested in history and the meaning of human artifacts. To Goode and his colleagues, objects were a window to the past. His colleague, Otis T. Mason wrote, "...the people of the world have left their history most fully recorded in the works of their hands." The late nineteenth century was the Progressive Era, and the Smithsonian's museum philosophy reflected the prevailing point of view. Mason's ethnological exhibits traced an evolutionary progression of human civilizations, from the "primitive" to contemporary America, based on technological advancement. Goode's museum of research, record, and education sought a comprehensive display of the inorganic, organic, and human worlds, to engage visitors with the specimens and artifacts on display.[47]

FIGURE 11. George Brown Goode (1851–1896), Assistant Secretary in charge of the United States National Museum, c. 1887. Smithsonian Institution Archives.

With a new building, Baird was able to expand the staff of the National Museum as well. By 1886, his staff included Goode and Romyn Hitchcock, Arts and Industries; Dr. H. G. Beyer, Materia Medica; Otis T. Mason and William Henry Holmes, Ethnology; Charles Rau, Antiquities; Frederick William True, Mammals; Robert Ridgway and Leonhard Stejneger, Birds; Captain Charles E. Bendire, Oology; Henry C. Yarrow, Reptiles; Tarleton H. Bean, Fishes; William Healey Dall and Robert E. C. Stearns, Mollusks; Charles V. Riley, Entomology; Richard Rathbun, Marine Invertebrates; Charles D. Walcott, Invertebrate Fossils; Charles A. White, Mesozoic Paleontology; Lester F. Ward and Frank H. Knowlton, Fossils and Recent Plants; F. W. Clarke and W. S. Yeates, Minerals; and George P. Merrill, Lithology and Physical Geology. Many of Baird's curators held honorary appointments; they either received no salary for their work or were paid by another government agency. Nevertheless the pace and range of work at the National Museum had increased rapidly under Baird's guidance.[48]

Baird (Fig. 12) accepted new responsibilities for the Smithsonian, such as the Bureau of Ethnology, led by John Wesley Powell. With strong support from Congress, Baird encouraged the B. of E. ethnologists to collect artifacts and pursue archaeological investigations, as well as study Native American life and languages. All collections acquired by these ethnologists would, of course, come to the National Museum. In this case, again, there were strong pressures from the general public and the Congress to document vanishing Native American culture, especially through artifacts. Baird worried that the most valuable ethnological and geological materials were being purchased for

European collections. As a matter of national pride, Baird joined many citizens and Congressmen in believing that the United States needed to have the premier collection of these materials.[49]

Smithsonian exhibits appeared at almost every late nineteenth century exposition, often winning awards as they showcased the National Museum and taught visitors about their history and natural world. The Smithsonian presented displays at the International Fisheries Exhibition in London in 1880, the International Fisheries Exhibition in Berlin in 1883, Boston's Foreign Exhibition in 1883, Chicago Railway Exhibition in 1883, International Electrical Exhibition in Philadelphia in 1884, Southern Exposition in Louisville in 1884, the Industrial Exposition in Cincinnati in 1884, the World's Industrial and Cotton Exposition in New Orleans in 1885, Minneapolis Industrial Exposition in 1887, Centennial Exposition of the Ohio Valley in 1888, the Marietta, Ohio, Exposition in 1889, the Paris International Exposition in 1889, the Patent Centennial in 1891, the Columbian Historical Exposition in Madrid in 1893, the World's Columbian Exposition in Chicago in 1893, and the Cotton States and International Exposition of 1895 in Atlanta. A steady stream of exhibits made the National Museum a household world within the United States and abroad.[50]

FIGURE 12. Spencer Fullerton Baird, c. 1878, second Smithsonian Secretary. Smithsonian Institution Archives.

Baird also served, without salary, at his own insistence, as U. S. Commissioner of Fish and Fisheries, a joint appointment with his Smithsonian duties. As Fish Commissioner, he conducted research on the decline of the fishing industry in the North Atlantic. He established the marine biology station at Woods Hole, Massachusetts, and oversaw a network of smaller stations. Fish Commission boats, such as the steamer *Albatross*, made extensive collections of marine fauna, which were studied and then accessioned into the national collections. Baird also produced award winning exhibits on the fisheries industry at the London and Berlin Fisheries Expositions. At the Centennial Exposition in Philadelphia and other international expositions, Baird's natural history displays emphasized both scientific value and economic importance. National collections were, then, a resource for both scientific research and economic development. In this and many other smaller ways, Baird cultivated the growth of both research and the national collections. And when all else failed, Baird purchased the collections with his personal funds or wrote a personal check to an explorer to be sure he could collect specimens properly and ship them back to the Institution.[51]

To Baird then, stewardship of the National Museum did not require a choice between research and collections. As pointed out earlier, he held that some research required collections, other research did not. Thus, research was the activity that gave meaning to the individual objects that formed a collection. An artifact or specimen provided information to the scholar, stored information for future studies, and served as a teaching tool in public exhibits. Without research, the National Museum would remain the cabinet of curiosities displayed by the earlier National Institute. With research, the National Collections became a new type of vehicle for economic development, public education, and the advancement of American science and culture, transporting casual visitors and serious scholars alike to exotic lands, vanishing landscapes, and the backrooms where democracy was plotted and secured. Not ephemeral in nature, the National Collections would also travel through time as a vehicle for the increase and diffusion of knowledge not only for the present but for generations to come.

In 1884–1885 Joseph Henry's fears about accepting federal funds for the National Museum proved well-grounded, as Spencer Baird faced the most difficult days of his career. The Congress held hearings about the fate of both the United States National Museum and the United States Fish Commission, as part of a general attack on government science programs. Some critics questioned Baird's management of the two organizations and his handling of federal funds. Discontented staff members and disappointed office seekers added fuel to the fires. Ironically, the Congress then proposed the solution that Henry had so ardently desired twenty years before — that the National Museum and Fish Commission be separated from the Smithsonian Institution. Baird worried that the positions of director of the National Museum and director of the Fish Commission would become political plums and lose their scholarly status. Eventually the U.S. Fish Commission was separated from the Smithsonian, but the United States National Museum remained within the Institution's aegis. The vitriolic personal attacks that were part of this episode took their toll on the aging and infirmed Baird.[52]

By the time he died in 1887, Baird had achieved his dream of a comprehensive National Museum. When he arrived in 1850, the Smithsonian housed some 6000 specimens, but at his death, the National Museum had grown to over 2.5 million lots of artifacts and specimens in art, history, anthropology, and science. The National Museum consisted of thirty-one departments under the care of twenty-six curators, although only seven were on the museum's payroll. Honorary curators from the U.S. Fish Commission, United States Geological Survey, Bureau of Ethnology, United States Army, and United States Navy carried out the work of the National Museum alongside its small but growing paid staff. The museum's annual visitorship was counted as 315,114 for that year. Baird left his dream in the hands of a committed younger colleague who would ensure that his vision for the Smithsonian would prevail. As Assistant Secretary in charge of the United States National Museum, Goode lived less than a decade longer than his much older mentor, but in his short life he established museum arrangement and display as a professional field and secured for the United States National Museum a reputation as the premier museum in the country.[53]

As is the usual case, by the time Baird died in 1887, the National Collections had already outgrown the new National Museum Building. Indeed, by 1882, Baird was requesting a new building from the Congress. The third Secretary, Samuel Pierpont Langley (Fig. 13), continued to make this request annually for more than a decade after Baird' death. Balconies were constructed to create more exhibit space; exhibit halls were closed to provide additional storage space; and cases of specimens crowded higher and higher along hallways (Fig. 14). Some two decades passed until the

FIGURE 13. Samuel Pierpont Langley (1834–1906), third Smithsonian Secretary, c. 1887. Smithsonian Institution Archives.

"new" National Museum was built across the Mall. Designed by architect J. D. Hornblower, this monumental building reflected the iconic status the Smithsonian's collections had achieved. It opened in 1910 to house the anthropology, natural history, and art collections (Fig. 15). Today it is known as the Natural History Building.[54]

In the decades since, the Smithsonian has evolved into a complex of sixteen museums in Washington, D.C., and New York City, devoted to the arts, history, and the sciences. These are the Anacostia Museum, Arts and Industries Building, Cooper-Hewitt Museum, the Freer and Sackler Galleries, Hirshhorn Museum and Sculpture Garden, National Air and Space Museum, National Museum of African Art, National Museum of American Art, National Museum of American History, National Museum of the American Indian, National Museum of Natural History, National Portrait Gallery, National Postal Museum, National Zoological Park, and Renwick Gallery. By the 150th anniversary of its founding in 1996, the Institution housed over 140 million objects in its national collections.[55]

With vision and plenty of hard work, Baird was able to achieve his dream of building a great national museum and, in doing so, substantially alter the direction of the Smithsonian Institution. Poinsett's efforts set the stage by having a provision for a museum in the Smithsonian's enabling

FIGURE 14. Ethnology workroom in the United States National Museum, 1890s (since renamed the Arts & Industries Building following completion of the "new" National Museum, now the Natural History Building, in 1910). Smithsonian Institution Archives.

FIGURE 15. The "new" United States National Museum, 1911, now known as the Natural History Building. Smithsonian Institution Archives.

legislation. Many prominent citizens and politicians called for amassing national collections and creating a national museum. Exploring expeditions sent to the nation's capital the nucleus of a national voucher collection. Baird's personal goals met the needs of the country to establish a great museum where a national identity could be forged. He was able to direct those impulses to the Smithsonian and translate them into actual support for his vision. In the many decades since his death, his one United States National Museum has grown and diversified into the largest complex of art, history and science museums in the world, perhaps surpassing even his dreams for how to use Smithson's bequest.

NOTES

[1] Paul H. Oehser, *The Smithsonian Institution* (New York: Praeger Publishers, 1970), pp. 13–15; draft of James Smithson's will, October 1826. James Smithson Collection, box 1, Smithsonian Institution Archives [SIA], Record Unit [RU] 7000.

[2] Oehser, *Smithsonian*, pp. 4–8, 12–15.

[3] *The National Intelligencer*, 16 October 1835, 17 February 1836, and 2 May 1836; William Jones Rhees, ed., *The Smithsonian Institution: Documents Relative to Its Origin and History* (Washington: Smithsonian Institution, 1879), pp. 141–154.

[4] Rhees, *Smithsonian Documents*, pp. 148–154.

[5] Rhees, *Smithsonian Documents*, pp. 158–169, 172–198, 837–842, 856–859.

[6] Rhees, *Smithsonian Documents*, pp. 126, 208–229, 247, 262, 306–331, 337, 349–350, 354, 409–410, 467, 499, 763–802, 930–943; Wilcomb E. Washburn, ed., *The Great Design: two lectures on the Smithson bequest by John Quincy Adams* (Washington, D.C.: Smithsonian Institution, 1965).

[7] Rhees, *Smithsonian Documents*, pp. 200–201, 239–241, 899–909; Sally G. Kohlstedt, "A Step Toward Scientific Self-Identity in the United States: The Failure of the National Institute, 1844," in *Science in America since 1820*, Nathan Reingold, ed. (New York: Science History Publications, 1976), pp. 79–89, 101–103.

[8] Rhees, *Smithsonian Documents*, pp. 167–171, 226–228, 236–242, 246, 249–260, 262–265, 295–305, 356–364, 803–836; Washburn, *Great Design*.

[9] Oehser, *Smithsonian*, pp. 11, 18; Charles H. Gibbs-Smith, *Sir George Cayley (1773–1857)* (London: Her Majesty's Stationery Office, 1968), pp. 12, 15; "Harvard, John," *Dictionary of American Biography* (New York: Charles Scribner's Sons, 1959), pp. 371–372. For history of research on Smithson's colleagues, see folders 10–14 in box 4, and folder 3 in box 5, James Smithson Collection, RU 7000, SIA; William Jones Rhees, *James Smithson and His Bequest*, Smithsonian Miscellaneous Collections, volume 21, number 330 (Washington, D.C.: Smithsonian Institution, 1880), pp. 11–13.

[10] Rhees, *Smithsonian Documents*, pp. 430–431, 469–473; Oehser, *Smithsonian*, pp. 20–25.

[11] Rhees, *Smithsonian Documents*, pp. 930–960; Oehser, *Smithsonian*, pp. 26–27; Cynthia R. Field, Richard E. Stamm, and Heather P. Ewing, *The Castle: An Illustrated History of the Smithsonian Building* (Washington, D.C.: Smithsonian Institution Press, 1993), pp. 4–21; and Kenneth Hafertepe, *America's Castle: The Evolution of the Smithsonian Building and Its Institution, 1840–1878* (Washington, D.C.: Smithsonian Institution Press, 1984), pp. 12–21, 37–39, 47, 50–55, 59–61.

[12] Rhees, *Smithsonian Documents*, pp. 930–960; Oehser, *Smithsonian*, pp. 27–32; Marc Rothenberg, et al., eds, *The Papers of Joseph Henry*, Vol. 7, *The Smithsonian Years, January 1847–December 1849* (Washington, D.C.: Smithsonian Institution Press, 1996), pp. xiii–xxii; Wilcomb E. Washburn, "Joseph Henry's Conception of the Purpose of the Smithsonian Institution," in *A Cabinet of Curiosities: Five Episodes in the Evolution of American Museums*, Whitfield J. Bell, Jr., ed. (Charlottesville: University Press of Virginia, 1967), pp. 108–143.

[13] Washburn, "Henry's Conception," 129–143; Marc Rothenberg, et al., eds., *The Papers of Joseph Henry*, Vol. 8, *The Smithsonian Years, January 1850–December 1853* (Washington, D.C.: Smithsonian Institution Press, 1998), pp. xviii–xxvii; *Fourth Annual Report of the Board of Regents of the Smithsonian Institution for 1849* (Washington: by the Printers to the Senate, 1850), pp. 20–21.

[14] Herman J. Viola and Carolyn Margolis, eds., *Magnificent Voyagers, The United States Exploring Expedition, 1838–1842*. (Washington,D.C.: Smithsonian Institution Press, 1985), pp. 9–23, 227–253.

[15] Rhees, *Smithsonian Documents*, pp. 107–122; Oehser, *Smithsonian*, pp. 17–18.

[16] Kohlstedt, "National Institute," pp. 83–87; Viola, *Magnificent Voyagers*, pp. 227–233.

[17] Kohlstedt, "National Institute," pp. 87–89; Viola, *Magnificent Voyagers*, pp. 227–241; George Brown Goode, "The Genesis of the United States National Museum," in *Annual Report of the Board of Regents of the Smithsonian Institution for 1897*, Part 2: *A Memorial of George Brown Goode* (Washington: Government Printing Office, 1898), pp. 83–145.

[18] Kohlstedt, "National Institute," pp. 89, 95–99, 103; Viola, *Magnificent Voyagers*, pp. 47, 243–253; Goode, "Genesis of National Museum," pp. 113–142.

[19] William Healey Dall, *Spencer Fullerton Baird; A Biography* (Philadelphia: J. B. Lippincott Company, 1915), pp. 34–56, 61, 67, 73–75; J. Ruthven Deane, "Unpublished Letters of John James Audubon and Spencer F. Baird," *Auk* 21(1904):255–259, 23(1906):194–201, 318–334, 24(1907):53–70.

[20] Dall, *Baird*, pp. 52–53, 56–57, 59, 62, 70–73, 132, 140–144, 164, 203; Spencer F. Baird, *Hints for preserving objects of natural history prepared by Professor S. F. Baird for Dickinson College, Carlisle, Pennsylvania* (Carlisle: Gitt & Hinckley, 1846); Sally Gregory Kohlstedt, "Curiosities and Cabinets: Natural History Museums and Education on the Antebellum Campus," *Isis* 79(1988):405–406, 411.

[21] Dall, *Baird*, pp. 155–167, 180–182, 185–201; Kohlstedt, "Natural History Museums," p. 425.

[22] Dall, *Baird*, pp. 158–159, 179; Edward F. Rivinus and Elizabeth Youssef, *Spencer Baird of the Smithsonian* (Washington, D.C.: Smithsonian Institution Press, 1992), p. 44; Charles Darwin, *The Origin of Species* (London: John Murray, 1859).

[23] Dall, *Baird*, pp. 304–305; Rivinus, *Baird of Smithsonian*, pp. 153–155; Charles F. Girard, *Herpetology*,

prepared under the superintendence of S. F. Baird (Philadelphia: C. Sherman & Son, 1858); Pamela M. Henson, "Spencer Baird Had a Different Vision for Research at the Smithsonian," *Smithsonian Research Reports* 83(Winter 1996):5–6.

[24] Dall, *Baird*, pp. 287–301, 308–310, 336, 339; Rivinus, *Baird of Smithsonian*, pp. 57–60; *Annual Report of the Board of Regents of the Smithsonian Institution, 1863* (Washington: Government Printing Office, 1864), pp. 58; William A. Deiss, "Spencer F. Baird and his Collectors," *Journal of the Society for the Bibliography of Natural History* 9(4[1980]):635–645; Frederick William True, "Exploration Work of the Smithsonian Institution," in *The Smithsonian Institution, 1846–1896. The History of Its First Half Century*, George Brown Goode, ed. (Washington: Smithsonian Institution, 1897), pp. 477–478.

[25] Spencer F. Baird, "General Directions for Collecting and Preserving Objects of Natural History," SIA, RU 65, Chief Clerk, 1846–1933, Forms, Circulars, and Announcements, volume 1, "Directions for collecting, preserving, and transporting specimens of natural history, prepared for the use of the Smithsonian Institution," *Smithsonian Miscellaneous Collections*, vol. 2, article 7 (Washington: Smithsonian Institution, 1859), and *Circular in reference to shipping fresh fish and other animals* (Washington: Smithsonian Institution, 1881); Nathan Reingold, "Definitions and Speculations: The Professionalization of Science in America in the Nineteenth Century," in *Science, American Style* (New Brunswick: Rutgers University Press, 1991), pp. 24–53.

[26] Dall, *Baird*, pp. 307–308, 333–335, 342–352, 357–366, 381; Deiss, "Baird and Collectors," pp. 641–642; Rivinus, *Baird of Smithsonian*, pp. 85–89, 94–105, 117, 163–169; True, "Exploration Work," 475–477. For a discussion of Agassiz's difficult relationships with his students, see Ralph Dexter, "The 'Salem Secession' of Agassiz Zoologists," *Essex Institute Historical Collections*, 101(1[1965]):27–39.

[27] Dall, *Baird*, pp. 305, 313–314, 318, 321–322, 330–334; Rivinus, *Baird of Smithsonian*, pp. 61–62; *Annual Report of the Board of Regents of the Smithsonian Institution for 1857* (Washington: William A. Harris, Printer, 1858), pp. 34, 46–49.

[28] True, "Exploration Work," 459–467; "List of the More Important Explorations and Expeditions, the collections of which have constituted the principal sources of supply to the National Museum, with indication of the department of the government under which prosecuted," *Annual Report of the Board of Regents of the Smithsonian Institution for 1877* (Washington: Government Printing Office, 1878), pp. 105–117.

[29] William H. Goetzmann, *Exploration and Empire: The Explorer and Scientist in the Winning of the American West* (New York: Alfred A. Knopf, 1966), pp. 496–498, 501–502, 515–516, 527–529, 562–563, 572–576; Philip J. Pauly, *Biologists and the Promise of American Life: From Meriweather Lewis to Alfred Kinsey* (Princeton: Princeton University Press, 2000).

[30] Clifford M. Nelson and Ellis L. Yochelson, "Organizing Federal Paleontology in the United States, 1858–1907," *Journal of the Society for the Bibliography of Natural History* 9(4[1980]):607–609.

[31] Hartley H. Bartlett, "The Reports of the Wilkes Expedition, and the Work of the Specialists in Science," *Proceedings of the American Philosophical Society* 82(1940):601–705; Girard, *Herpetology*; *Annual Report of the Board of Regents of the Smithsonian Institution for 1858* (Washington: William A. Harris, Printer, 1859), pp. 52–56; *Annual Report of the Board of Regents of the Smithsonian Institution for 1862* (Washington: Government Printing Office, 1863), p. 56; *Annual Report of the Board of Regents of the Smithsonian Institution for 1883* (Washington: Government Printing Office, 1885), p. 177; William Jones Rhees, *An Account of the Smithsonian Institution, Its Founder, Building, Operations, etc.* (Washington: Thomas McGill, Printer, 1857), and *Visitor's Guide to the Smithsonian Institution and United States National Museum in Washington* (Washington: Judd & Detweiler, Printers, 1886).

[32] Dall, *Baird*, pp. 313–317; Oehser, *Smithsonian*, pp. 38–39; Rhees, *Smithsonian Documents*, p. 589; Joseph Henry, "Report of the Secretary for 1856," *Annual Report of the Board of Regents of the Smithsonian Institution for 1856* (Washington: Cornelius Wendell, Printer, 1857), pp. 17–22; U.S. House, 33rd Congress, 2nd Session, Journal of the House Select Committee, House Documents, No. 141 (1855); Jean V. Matthews, *Rufus Choate: The Law and Civic Virtue* (Philadelphia: Temple University Press, 1980), pp. 129–130, 138–146.

[33] Oehser, *Smithsonian*, pp. 88–89; Pamela M. Henson, "'Objects of Curious Research': The History of Science and Technology at the Smithsonian," *Isis* 90(1999):S249–S242.

[34] Rivinus, *Baird of Smithsonian*, pp. 64–65.

[35] Dall, *Baird*, pp. 378, 385–386; Field, *Castle*, pp. 78–80, 123–124; *Annual Report of the Board of Regents*

of the Smithsonian Institution, 1866 (Washington: Government Printing Office, 1867), pp. 13–17; Oehser, *Smithsonian*, p. 187. The art, botanical, entomological, and physical anthropology collections were later returned to the U.S. National Museum.

[36] Rivinus, *Baird of Smithsonian*, pp. 63–66; George Brown Goode, "The Published Writings of Spencer Fullerton Baird, 1843–1882," *Bulletin of the United States National Museum*, vol. 20 (Washington: Government Printing Office, 1883); Spencer F. Baird and C. Girard, *Catalogue of North American reptiles in the Museum of the Smithsonian Institution* (Washington: Smithsonian Institution, 1853); Spencer F. Baird, *Catalogue of North American mammals: chiefly in the museum of the Smithsonian Institution* (Washington: Smithsonian Institution, 1857), "The Distribution and Migration of North American Birds," *American Journal of Arts and Sciences*, 2nd series, 41(January–May 1866):78–90, 184–192, 337–347, *Review of American birds, in the Museum of the Smithsonian Institution* (Washington: Smithsonian Institution, 1864–1866), and *Mammals of the Boundary: with notes by the naturalists of the survey* (Washington: C. Wendell, Printer, 1859?); Louis Agassiz, *Essay on Classification* (London: n.p., 1859), and *Contributions to the Natural History of the United States of America* (Boston: Little, Brown and Co., 1857–1862).

[37] Paul L. Farber, "The Transformation of Natural History in the Nineteenth Century," *Journal of the History of Biology* 15(1[Spring 1982]):145–152; Reingold, "Professionalization of Science," pp. 44–48.

[38] Dall, *Baird*, pp. 367–378; Debra Lindsay, *Science in the Subarctic: Trappers, Traders, and the Smithsonian Institution* (Washington, D.C.: Smithsonian Institution Press, 1993), passim. Lindsay and others question the role of the National Museum's collections in influencing the purchase of Alaska.

[39] Dall, *Baird*, p. 389; Rivinus, *Baird of Smithsonian*, p. 122; Kohlstedt, "Natural History Museums," 425–426.

[40] Dall, *Baird*, pp. 391–392; Rivinus, *Baird of Smithsonian*, pp. 123–125; Robert Post, *1876: A Centennial Exposition* (Washington, D.C.: Smithsonian Institution Press, 1976), pp. 77–79; Robert W. Rydell, *All the World's A Fair: Visions of Empire at American International Expositions, 1876–1916* (Chicago: University of Chicago Press, 1984),pp. 19–27, 44.

[41] Rivinus, *Baird of Smithsonian*, pp. 124–125, 190.

[42] Dall, *Baird*, pp. 393–395; Oehser, *Smithsonian*, pp. 189–190; *A Handbook to the National Museum at the Smithsonian Institution, Washington* (New York: Brentano, 1886).

[43] Dall, *Baird*, pp. 393–395; Henson, "Baird's Vision," pp. 5–6; Oehser, *Smithsonian*, pp. 40–44; Rivinus, *Baird of Smithsonian*, pp. 127–130; Theodore D. A. Cockerell, *Spencer Fullerton Baird and the U.S. National Museum* (Mount Vernon, Iowa: n.p., 1942), pp. 1–7, reprinted from *Bios* 8, 1.

[44] Oehser, *Smithsonian*, pp. 189–190.

[45] *Annual Report of the Board of Regents of the Smithsonian Institution for 1882* (Washington: Government Printing Office, 1884), pp. 119–120, 124–126.

[46] Edward P. Alexander, "George Brown Goode and the Smithsonian Museums: A National Museum of Cultural History," in *Museum Masters: Their Museums and Their Influence* (Nashville, Tenn.: American Association for State and Local History, 1983), pp. 277–310; Sally G. Kohlstedt, "History in a Natural History Museum: George Brown Goode and the Smithsonian Institution," *The Public Historian* 10(2[Spring 1988]): 7–26, and "Preface," in *The Origins of Natural Science in America: The Essays of George Brown Goode*, Kohlstedt, ed., (Washington, D.C.: Smithsonian Institution Press, 1991), pp. 11–15; George Brown Goode, "Museum-History and Museums of History," (1888), and "The Museums of the Future," (1889), reprinted in Kohlstedt, *Origins*, pp. 297–319, 321–348.

[47] Curtis M. Hinsley, *The Smithsonian and American Indian: Making a Moral Anthropology in Victorian America* (Washington, D.C.: Smithsonian Institution Press, 1994), pp. 84–94, 97–99; Kohlstedt, "Goode and Smithsonian," 13–14, 25–26; Rydell, *World's A Fair*, pp. 57–60, 98–99; *Annual Report for 1882*, pp. 128–130.

[48] *Annual Report of the Board of Regents of the Smithsonian Institution for 1886* (Washington: Government Printing Office, 1889), pp. 36–51.

[49] Dall, *Baird*, pp. 387–388; Hinsley, *Smithsonian and American Indian*, pp. 139–140, 147–164; True, "Exploration Work," pp. 467, 470–474; Neil Merton Judd, *The Bureau of American Ethnology: A Partial History* (Norman: University of Oklahoma Press, 1967), pp. 3–4, 6–18.

[50] Rydell, *World's A Fair*, p. 43.

[51] Dall, *Baird*, pp. 388, 416–432; True, "Exploration Work," pp. 467, 469–470; Dean C. Allard, *Spencer Fullerton Baird and the U.S. Fish Commission* (New York: Arno Press, 1978), passim.

[52] Dall, *Baird*, pp. 402–405.

[53] Dall, *Baird*, pp. 408; Kohlstedt, *Origins of Natural Science*, pp. 4–6, 11–15; Oehser, *Smithsonian*, pp. 44–47; *Annual Report of the Board of Regents of the Smithsonian Institution for 1887* (Washington: Government Printing Office, 1889), pp. 17–18.

[54] *Annual Report for 1882*, pp. 5–10; *Annual Report for 1887*, p. 17; Richard Rathbun, "The United States National Museum: An Account of the Buildings Occupied by the National Collections," in *The Report of the United States National Museum for 1903* (Washington, D.C.: Government Printing Office, 1905), pp. 263–296; Ellis L. Yochelson, *The National Museum of Natural History, 75 Years in the Natural History Building* (Washington, D.C.: Smithsonian Institution Press, 1985), pp. 19, 23–27.

[55] *E Pluribus Unum: This Divine Paradox, Report of the Commission on the Future of the Smithsonian Institution* (Washington, D.C.: Smithsonian Institution, 1983), pp. 34–35; *Smithsonian Year, 1996* (Washington, D.C.: Smithsonian Institution Press, 1996), passim.

Paleontology in Washington DC
A Brief History of Institutional Change
Or the Waxing and Waning
of Two Disparate Organizations

ELLIS L. YOCHELSON
Research Associate, National Museum of Natural History
Washington, DC 20560-0121 and U. S. Geological Survey (retired)
E-mail: yochelson.ellis@nmnh.si.edu

Study of fossils in Washington began about 150 years ago when F. B. Meek came to the Smithsonian Institution; he identified fossils for the purpose of dating the age of rocks collected by government expeditions and territorial surveys. In 1879, the U.S. Geological Survey (USGS) was founded; paleontologists who were housed in the United States National Museum (USNM) building were an integral part of this organization. Collections were transferred to the Museum for curation, which generally was also done by the personnel of the Geological Survey.

In 1894, the Museum finally employed a paleontologist, Charles Schuchert, and in 1897, when the Museum was reorganized, he became a member of the new Department of Geology. Until after the second World War, the Museum had less than half a dozen professionals, in total, despite the move to a new larger building in 1910. Most Geological Survey paleontologists moved to the new site and they significantly increased in number during that interval.

After the second World War, both organizations grew; again the USGS was far larger. The Geological Survey professionals were still mainly concerned with age determination by fossils, but a larger variety of kinds were studied in increasing detail. With the addition of wings to the Museum, there came dramatic increase in staff, especially for the Survey. Formation of the Department of Paleobiology in 1963, by splitting the Department of Geology, resulted in a gradual shift of the Museum staff to problem-oriented issues. USGS efforts on age determination of rocks by their enclosed fossils were officially ended in 1995.

Paleontology first appeared in Washington nearly two centuries ago. During Thomas Jefferson's first term as President, one room in the President's House[1] was used to display fossil bones from Big Bone Lick, Kentucky, and from a cave in what is now West Virginia. Jefferson's interests in matters scientific were used against him by political opponents, and, legend has it, some of the bones were later ground up for fertilizer. That may be an appropriate metaphor, for further developments depended on permanent organizational structures.

Not too many decades later, two disparate organizations came into being in Washington, DC, the Smithsonian Institution's National Museum of Natural History and the U. S. Geological Survey. Although each had a distinct mission, they both were interested in paleontology, and, for an impressive length of time, the staffs of the two worked together more or less in harmony. Since their foundings, each organization has had about three scientific generations of paleontologists; even so, remarkably few persons were involved. Also, over time, a significant number of aides and some clerical staff and even scientists who began with, for instance, the USGS switched allegiances and moved to the Museum, and more rarely *vice versa*.

---
[1] "White House" did not come into use until after the painting to conceal the fires set in 1814 by the British.

In what follows, it may seem dull to use names and mention specialties, rather than convey the grand sweep of events. Nevertheless, I believe this approach provides a better notion of just how small was the Federal involvement in the science of paleontology, yet how successful it was. It also provides anyone interested in the history of study of a particular group of organisms or segment of geologic time, a name or two to investigate further. Besides, it is people who make most events, and history of events without mentioning individuals can be remarkably colorless. The names of generals are often recorded, but the forgotten "spear bearers" at least deserve a mention. The technicians who carried the water bottles for the spear bearers, that is, broke rocks, inked numbers on fossils, made thin-sections, typed manuscripts, and produced photographs have not been recorded, but their immense contribution in keeping scientists productive should not be ignored.

The Smithsonian Institution

In 1829, the Englishman James Smithson died, and in 1836, his estate became a gift to the people of America. In 1840, the National Institute, a private organization, was set up in Washington with the hope of obtaining the Smithson bequest; Institute members collected all manner of items and may have had a few fossils. The National Institute had a display in the new Patent Office Building (Evelyn 1985). Two years later, Congress established the official National Cabinet of Curiosities mainly to house the collections of the United States Exploring Expedition (1838–1842), made under the command of Charles Wilkes (Stanton 1975). Because there was no other place in Washington, DC, to store them, the Federal expedition collections were nominally given to the care of the Institute. By 1846, when it became apparent that the National Institute was not to receive the Smithson bequest, that organization rapidly declined and, before long, the fledgling Smithsonian Institution fell heir to its collections.

On August 10, 1846, the Smithsonian Institution (SI) was founded as a public trust for the American public. In present-day terminology, it might be classified as quasi-governmental. Though it was not clear what the Institution was to accomplish, one of the functions laid out in the founding legislation was that of a museum. On December 3, the American physicist Joseph Henry was elected as the first Smithsonian Secretary (Oehser 1949). Long before Henry had gained fame as a physicist, he had helped survey a near-wilderness road across New York and thus had acquired a feeling for topography and geology. Even before the Institution had its own building, Henry scheduled public lectures, including one in 1849 on geology. He also instituted a publication program, and by the early 1850s, the Institution had published three papers on paleontology, at a time when there were few outlets in America for scientific papers. Although the exterior of the Smithsonian "Castle," the first of the many buildings that make up the present-day Smithsonian complex on Washington, DC's "Mall," was completed by 1851 (Fig. 1), interior construction went slowly, and Henry did not move into the building, literally (it became his home!), until 1856 (Hafetepe 1984).

In 1850, Henry hired Spencer Fullerton Baird as an Assistant Secretary (Rivinus and Youseff 1992). Though he was no paleontologist, Baird established publication standards for many of the Federal western exploring expeditions, in which reports on the fossils that were collected played a prominent role. Baird's advice resulted in better illustrations and descriptions of the specimens. The Smithsonian gave advice, helped in the selection of scientific personnel, provided some scientific equipment, and — rarely — funds, to various exploring parties. Despite initial resistance and occasional objections from Henry, Baird energetically pursued the acquisition of both biological and fossil specimens for the Institution's collections.

Early on, in part because of the language in the founding legislation, it was determined that natural

FIGURE 1. The Smithsonian Institution Castle, possibly taken between 1856 and 1860, looking southwest. Courtesy Smithsonian Institution Archives (SIA #45934-A).

history collections from the General Land Office and various government expeditions were to come to the Institution for safe keeping. For example, specimens described by David Dale Owen in his survey of the Iowa, Wisconsin and Minnesota territories are still to be found in the type collections.

By the time Henry moved into the Castle in 1856, mismanagement of the Wilkes collections had become a "Washington" scandal. In response, in 1857, Congress appropriated $17,000 for cases, transfer, and maintenance of these collections. During 1857 and 1858, the Wilkes materials came to the Castle. Thus, without any Federal organization being formally established by Congressional mandate, the United States National Museum (USNM) came into existence as a government bureau administered by a non-governmental organization. The General Land Office material came earlier than transfer of the Wilkes material, but whether it in any way laid the groundwork for the National Museum is uncertain.

Despite what has been written, Henry was not opposed to collections as such. He was concerned, understandably, about the continual cost of maintaining a museum collection. He agreed to take the Wilkes material only after an annual sum for curation was promised. Until his death in 1878, Henry tried unsuccessfully to have the National Museum transferred away from Smithsonian administration. He was even eager to sell the Castle as an inducement to the government to take the USNM off his hands. Yet, by 1880, under the stewardship of Spencer Fullerton Baird, Henry's successor as Smithsonian Secretary, construction was begun on a new museum building (Fig. 2) to house the growing collections that had been accumulating in the Castle and the exhibits from the Centennial Exposition in Philadelphia.

FIGURE 2. The United States National Museum building under construction, probably in 1880. The photograph is taken from the Castle looking east. Courtesy Smithsonian Institution Archives (SIA #742).

The Meek Era and Ephemeral Government Surveys

More or less coordinate with the transfer of national collections, Henry rescued — the word is deliberately chosen — Fielding Bradford Meek (1817–1876) (Fig. 3) from the clutches of James Hall in Albany and brought him to the Institution in 1858 (Nelson 1987). Hall was the State Paleontologist of New York, and, at that time in the United States, Albany was the center for study of fossils. At the Smithsonian, Meek was literally a scholar in residence, as he received no salary from the Institution but had the privilege of living in his office in the south tower of the Castle, his abode from 1861 until his death in 1876; earlier, he lived under a staircase. During his lifetime, Meek published descriptions of fossils from every group of invertebrate fossils and discussed specimens gathered from rocks of every age from Cambrian to Recent.

In determining the age of rocks by fossils, one compares the fossils from an unknown area with those whose relative age within an established general sedimentary sequence is known. One cannot understand structural complications nor interpret the geologic history of an area unless the sequence and relative ages of the sedimentary rocks are known. Meek was the premier biostratigraphic paleontologist in 19th Century America, not just because he was one of the first, but because he was so remarkably accurate in age determinations, especially in the western regions where virtually nothing was known of the details of geology.

Meek worked on contract for several state geological surveys, most notably Illinois. After the Civil War, major Federally-financed territorial surveys replaced more transitory expeditions (Rabbitt

1979). The four principal surveys were those headed by Hayden, King, Powell, and Wheeler (Bartlett 1962); only King completed his assigned survey area. Among Meek's many other accomplishments, he described fossils for all four of the Federal territorial surveys (Nelson and Yochelson 1980).

One function of a museum is to maintain collections. The National Museum ably performed its responsibility as a museum of record and these early Federally-collected fossils are, as of this writing, still safe in Washington. Meek made the critical curatorial decision that collections were to be arranged in stratigraphic order, that is by age of the rocks, rather than in biologic order. Since the primary objective of paleontology at that time was to provide the relative age of strata from unknown areas, this arrangement best supported that effort. Meek also determined that where relatively large number of specimens were available, "duplicates" were to be distributed to colleagues and schools, so that the collections did not grow too large. Years later this policy was changed, but for most of the last half of the 19th Century, collections were donated by the Institution.

During Meek's last years, his career overlapped with that of Charles Abiathar White (1826–1910) (Fig. 4), who left the Iowa Geological Survey to become paleontologist/geologist for the Hayden Territorial Survey. White is best known for his studies of Mesozoic fossils. William Healey Dall (1845–1927) (Fig. 5) also appeared on the Washington scene as an explorer-naturalist in Alaska and was in residence in the Castle for a time in 1868. He was concerned with study of Recent mollusks and, to a lesser extent at that time, their Cenozoic ancestors. Dall had no permanent position until 1881 when he obtained employment with the United States Coast Survey.

There was no organized study of vertebrate paleontology or paleobotany in Washington during the 1860s and 1870s.

Transition to Permanent Structure and Staff

On March 3, 1879, the U. S. Geological Survey (USGS) was founded, as a bureau of the Department of Interior. Its establishment provided a permanent Federal organization for geology; Clarence King was appointed director. Charles Doolittle Walcott (1850–1927) (Fig. 6) became USGS employee number 20 (Yochelson 1967). He was hired as a temporary geological assistant at $50 per month, not as a paleontologist. After a year, he became a permanent assistant geologist at $1,200 per year. White had gone to Europe, and did not return to Washington until after the USGS was formed; on his return, apparently he was on the staff of the USNM briefly, though in all likelihood, this was an honorary appointment. Almost immediately, Walcott and White had a disagreement concerning who would study some of Walcott's 1879 collections from the Colorado Plateau. White did not win the argument.

When the new USNM building was completed, space was made available for USGS paleontologists. After less than two years, King had left the Geological survey, and John Wesley Powell was appointed director; Powell also continued to run the Bureau of Ethnology, which was founded in 1879 and was more or less under the Smithsonian. Whereas King was concerned with support for the mining industry, Powell was more concerned with basic investigations. He was far more liberal in allowing paleontologists to pursue publication and not simply confine their activities to rote identification for age determination.

At the start of the fiscal year on July 1, 1881, employee number 64, White, was hired as a geologist at $2,000 per year and moved into the new building. He remained with the USGS until the 1892 appropriations catastrophe. Another important figure in the building was Lester Frank Ward (1841–1913) (Fig. 7) who joined the USGS at the same time as White at an annual salary of $1,800. Ward was a sociologist but, as this field was outside the purview of the USGS, Powell hired Ward to work

FIGURES 3–6. (3) Fielding B. Meek, an illustrious paleontologist (SIA #77-9498); (4) Charles A. White, in charge of Mesozoic paleontology (SIA #78–15937); (5) William Healey Dall, in charge of Cenozoic paleontology (SIA #A–1145); (6) Charles Doolittle Walcott, about 1887. Figures 3–5 courtesy Smithsonian Institution Archives.

FIGURE 7. Lester F. Ward, in charge of paleobotany, and Miss Morehead (later Mrs. F. Knowlton) in his office, the inner room at the east end of the south balcony in the USNM, probably taken in 1886. Courtesy Smithsonian Institution Archives (SIA #85-10257).

on "vegetable paleontology." Ward learned on the job and became an excellent paleontologist. Meanwhile, he laid the foundation for sociology in America in his spare time; Ward remained in Washington until 1907 when he left to become a professor at Brown University.

During May 1882, Walcott was given an honorary appointment as assistant curator of fossil invertebrates in the National Museum, and he also settled into the new red brick building completed earlier the previous year. Vertebrate paleontology gained a position on the USGS in 1882 when Othniel Charles Marsh (1831–1899) of Yale University was appointed employee number 87 by Powell, at $4,000 per year. In 1883, two of the 25 statutory positions in the Geological Survey were for paleontologists. Marsh had one, and Walcott the other, at $2,000 per year.

In 1884, Dall transferred to the Geological Survey as employee number 253, though he remained in the Smithsonian Castle and was not in the Museum building. Dall had an office in one of the towers, but spilled over onto a balcony in the Great Hall. By July 1, 1884, the Geologic Branch of the USGS had five formal divisions, one of which was paleontology (Rabbitt, 1980). This in turn had five parts, each with its own leader: Walcott for Paleozoic; White for Mesozoic; and Dall for Cenozoic. The fourth was vertebrate paleontology under Marsh, who never had an office in Washington, and, the fifth, paleobotany under Ward. The Museum had comparable divisions, staffed by the same people. The multiplicity of titles may have been to avoid any personality clashes.

All of the paleontologic divisions had assistants, some of whom went on to greater things. Two of Walcott's assistants for a short time were Robert Thomas Hill (1858–1941) who left the survey after a few years for a varied career, associated mainly with geology in Texas, and Timothy William Stanton (1860–1953) (Fig. 8) who joined in 1889 and remained with the USGS throughout his professional career, as a Mesozoic specialist and, later, Chief Paleontologist.

After a few years, a tradition developed of having an understudy for each mature specialist. Often these persons began as aides or technicians. Thus, Charles David White (1862–1935) (Fig. 9) was hired in 1886 as a draftsman for Lester Ward, but he soon developed his own speciality in Paleozoic paleobotany.

The United States National Museum

From several aspects, 1879 was a key year because, along with the founding of the USGS, a separate building for the United States National Museum was finally authorized. Construction was completed in 1881 on the red brick rectangle east of the Castle (and west of the much later circular Hirshhorn Gallery). Originally designed to be a temporary building to house exhibits which had been at the 1876 Philadelphia Centennial Exposition, it stands to this day, still occupying space on the Mall just east of the Castle; a century of repair costs — even corrected for inflation — have many times exceeded its construction cost. Within the barn-like building, the Museum geologist George Perkins Merrill had an office, but the USNM staff did not include any paid paleontologist.

In truth, the USNM had practically no staff. To find specialists, the Smithsonian gave "honorary" appointments, a practice started long before the separate Museum building became a reality. Those who received this honor were expected to do the work of the Museum, while being paid by another agency or serving as volunteers. For example, the Museum division of mollusks and Dall were synonymous throughout his long career, and during his "retirement" years, until his death in 1928.

When George Brown Goode was director of the USNM, the "honorary" concept was pushed to an extreme. In effect, anyone who could be convinced to do work for the Museum, would be given a title and often would be made head of his own department. By the 1890s, the Museum had more than twenty departments: the activities of each were noted in the USNM Annual Report. The annual reports of the USGS also list the activities of its paleontologists, thereby allowing one to note the difference between the research-oriented and the curatorial-oriented efforts of the same individual.

Honorary appointments, under different names, are still given with the same understanding of contributions to the Museum. With only one or two exceptions, the USGS paleontologists who had offices at the USNM have also been honorary research associates. For generations, many scientists outside the city assumed that every paleontologist in Washington was on the Smithsonian staff, whereas actually they were paid by two different Federal agencies with two quite different missions.

The 1879 Organic Act founding the USGS specified that collections were to be transferred to the USNM, when no longer needed for research. The act clearly established that the Museum was to be the national repository for Federal natural history material. So far as paleontology was concerned, at this time it was the role of the USGS paleontologists to study the fossils obtained during field work for the purpose of dating the rocks, and the role of the USNM was to serve as a museum of record, safeguarding those collections. The term "museum of record" is that of Goode, who emphasized a tripartite function of museums, the other two being education and research.

Along with the legalities was an informal arrangement, like that with the Bureau of Ethnology and, later, the Biological Survey, wherein one organization did field work and the other curated the material which was obtained. To provide a brief summary of the next century, the rate of transfer of collections from the Geological Survey has waxed and waned, being governed by time, space, and individual temperament. Likewise, there has been exchange of individuals from Survey to Museum and, more rarely, in the opposite direction.

Problems for the U. S. Geological Survey

Through a complex political situation involving irrigation in the West and personal dislike of Powell, in 1892 the USGS came under attack by Congress. Slashing the budget affected the entire

FIGURES 8–9. (8) A mature T. W. Stanton, first chief of P&S section, helping to collect a *Triceratops*. Courtesy U. S. Geological Survey Photographic Library (A. L. Beekley Collection #278); (9) David White, paleobotanist, probably taken after 1913 during his tenure as Chief Geologist. Courtesy Smithsonian Institution Archives (SIA #99–10019; a second copy in "Portraits" files, Photographic Library, U. S. Geological Survey, Denver).

organization but was particularly hard on paleontology. Funds for its study were cut by 70% and the paid staff went from twenty-eight to seven. This science has the dubious distinction of being one of the few disciplines to be singled out for ridicule by Congress. For example, "What use has the Government for paleontology? What functions of the Government are carried on by means of paleontology? Not only has the Government no use for it as government, but paleontological work is not even necessary to the proper construction of a geologic map." The monograph by Marsh on Cretaceous toothed-birds, published years earlier by the King territorial survey of the 40th Parallel, became for Congress the symbol of government waste, as powerful as any discussed in the latter part of the 20th Century.

One positive result in this dismal situation was that Walcott was promoted to the new position of Chief Paleontologist, bringing all the diminished five parts of paleontology under one head. He saved some people by having them transferred to the USNM staff. There the young paleobotanist Frank Hall Knowlton (1860–1926) remained on a payroll and, in better times a few years later, he returned to the Geological Survey. David White was among the few USGS paleontologists who survived the slaughter.

In the midst of all this upheaval, Walcott was responsible for preparing a large display of rocks and minerals for the Chicago Columbian Exposition of 1893. Several persons received temporary jobs from Exposition funds.

Although Walcott was appointed Geologist-in-Charge of Geology and Paleontology in 1893, even with his immediate efforts, life as a government employee got worse before it became better.

Matters began to improve the next year after he became Director. Walcott was able to increase the number of paleontologists by assigning them as members of field parties, effectively shielding them and the study of fossils from Congressional wrath. He recovered several of those lost and added George Herbert Girty (1869–1939) (Fig. 10) to study Late Paleozoic faunas. Headquarters for the USGS were in the Hoee Iron Building on F Street NW, now the site of the National Press Club Building. Paleontologists at the Museum had to walk over to Hoee Building each payday. The USNM building was crowded and a few paleontologists were housed in the Hoee Building, which provided even less satisfactory space than the cluttered Museum. Just before the turn of the century Edward Oscar Ulrich (1857–1944) (Fig. 11) was added to the staff to work on Lower Paleozoic faunas and was housed in the crowded Hoee Building.

In 1900, the paleontologists in the Geologic Branch of the USGS were finally gathered into a division with T. W. Stanton in charge. Although the USGS budget had increased dramatically since 1894, it was only about this time that Walcott was finally able to restore some of the funds for paleontology which had been cut in 1892. Four years later, this division became the Paleontology and Stratigraphy Section, and remained the longest-lived administrative subdivision within the Geological Survey. Even under one head, the five-part internal subdivision by ages and specialties remained in place, though this had little impact, except for convenience in maintaining a separate locality catalogue for each group.

Another important function, tangentially associated with the section, was the Committee on Geologic Names. The Chief of the Section for years was also head of the Committee, which

FIGURES 10–11. (10) George Herbert Girty, specialist on upper Paleozoic fossils; (11) Edward O. Ulrich, specialist on lower Paleozoic fossils, at his desk in Hoee Iron Building (date unknown, but probably between 1900 and 1910). Courtesy Smithsonian Institution Archives (SIA # 85-4022).

determined the name and age of formations and standardized usage in USGS publications. Years later, Stanton followed in Walcott's footsteps when he too became Chief Geologist of the Geological Survey; and, as the number of paleontologists grew, the Names Committee was made a separate position with its own head and staff.

As it had been when the paleontologists were directly attached to mapping parties, the prime emphasis was providing dates for rocks. The geologists sent in fossils for "Examination and Report" (E&R), and the E&R became the principal internal product. Eventual publication of studies by the paleontologists on submitted fossils and those that they collected when visiting field parties documented for the world the richness of the fossil record in the United States.

Once USGS funding began to increase in the latter part of the 1890s, Walcott followed the lead of Powell by using academic paleontologists, such as Samuel Hubbard Scudder (1837–1911) of Harvard University, as part-time contract employees. Though these men were not on the Washington scene, their collections eventually came to the USNM; Scudder's fossil insects remain a prime possession. Perhaps the most noteworthy name in this category is Henry Shaler Williams (1847–1918) of Cornell University who worked extensively on the Devonian fossils of New York and contributed many fossils to the collections.

USNM Expansion

After Walcott became Chief Geologist, he no longer had time to curate fossils. Charles Schuchert (1858–1942) (Fig. 12) had been hired by Walcott to help prepare an exhibit of crinoid slabs for the 1893 Columbian Exposition in Chicago and, after that job, he came to Washington with the USGS. When Walcott became director, he could no longer spend much time at the Museum building, so in 1894, Schuchert was transferred to the USNM staff and became the first paid staff member responsible for paleontology in that organization. Indeed, a Department of Paleontology was established in the USNM with Walcott as Honorary Curator and Schuchert as Assistant Curator (Gilmore, 1941). In addition to his curatorial duties, Schuchert began detailed studies of fossil brachiopods.

During parts of 1897 and 1898, in addition to his position as director of the Geological Survey, Walcott was also served as Acting Assistant Secretary [of the Smithsonian Institution] in Charge of the National Museum (Yochelson, 1998). During this interval, he reorganized the Museum into three departments; Schuchert became a staff member in the Department of Geology. For those interested in chains of command, presumably honorary curator Walcott was subservient to paid employee Schuchert, who reported to Head Curator G. P. Merrill, who reported to Acting Assistant Secretary Walcott. According to a manuscript by Merrill, the division was originally

FIGURE 12. Charles Schuchert in 1910 when the Yale University Professor was elected to the National Academy of Sciences. Published by permission of the Peabody Museum of Natural History.

named "Stratigraphic Paleontology" quite in keeping with the USGS direction of effort. One key decision made at that time was that Cenozoic fossils would be assigned to the Department of Geology, rather than to the Division of Mollusks, which was within the Department of Biology. Merrill wrote a history of geology at the Museum, in part to publicize the efforts of his new department. He was quite clear as to what his staff was supposed to do. "The National Museum is not organized primarily as a bureau of research, but rather as a museum of record, a place for the preservation of the types of past investigations. The first duty of its officials relates, then, to the care of the collections" (Merrill 1901:122).

When Marsh died in 1899, the Federal vertebrate collections that he had assembled at Yale University came to Washington (Gilmore 1941). Frederic Augustus Lucas (1852–1929) of the USNM was sent to pack the specimens and he became an acting curator of fossil vertebrates until he left the Museum in 1904. Because in gathering vertebrates Marsh had intertwined Federal funds, university grants, and private money, Walcott (1900) thought it appropriate to explain what fossils had come to Washington and the history of the material. With this large collection, overnight the USNM became a center for the study of fossil vertebrates.

Charles Whitney Gilmore (1874–1945) (Fig. 13) was hired by the Museum as a vertebrate preparator in 1903 and James William Gidley (1866–1931) joined him two years later; probably they were housed in the old Armory building, where the Hirshhorn Museum is now located, as the brick museum was filled to overflowing. Both men gradually worked their way up to professional status as the fossil vertebrates and fossil invertebrates were variously shuffled around through several internal reorganizations within the Department of Geology. Gilmore made his name with study of fossil reptiles and Gidley with that of fossil mammals (Gilmore 1941).

After Marsh's death in 1899, the Geological Survey did not employ another vertebrate paleontologist for more than half-a-century, presumably because the field was so well covered by the USNM. As more or less a mirror image, paleobotany remained a prime USGS specialty. In 1889, Albert Charles Peale (1849–1914) of the USGS came to the museum building, and after being fired in 1892, had a temporary position before joining the Museum staff in 1898, but his work on the paleobotanical collections was entirely curatorial. There was a tacit agreement that, on the rare occasions where a staff member could be hired, neither organization would duplicate the specialty of the other; and this arrangement persisted for more than half a century.

FIGURE 13. Charles Whitney Gilmore, first vertebrate paleontologist at the U. S. National Museum. Courtesy Department of Paleobiology, National Museum of Natural History.

After a decade at the National Museum, Schuchert moved to Yale University, and, though he had not even completed grade school, Schuchert's brachiopod studies impressed his academic colleagues. After all, his origins were in Cincinnati, Ohio, a key paleontological training ground of the 19th Century. In 1902, before Schuchert moved from Washington, Ray Smith Bassler (1871–

1961) (Fig. 14), another Cincinnati product, joined the Department of Geology as a preparator. After two years he transferred to the USGS, only to return to the Museum staff when Schuchert left government employment.

From the time of the reorganization of 1897, a few private individuals were also associated with the Department in an honorary capacity. Noteworthy among these was Frank Springer (1848–1927), who had made money in New Mexico, but had a passion for crinoids. He left his collections and a small endowment to the Museum with a stipulation that the collection be housed in a separate room in which his portrait hung.

Personality Problems in the USGS

According to legend, Girty shared an office in the Museum with Schuchert and the latter's off-key whistling drove Girty, a concert pianist, wild. For reasons unknown, Girty also later developed a low opinion of Walcott. Ulrich was originally housed in the Hoee Building, but, in 1910, he transferred to the new museum building. At some date, now unknown, but before 1910, Girty and his collections were transferred to the Hoce Building.

FIGURE 14. Ray Smith Bassler, technician to second Head of Department of Geology, standing in southwest corner of USNM by wooden cases containing drawers of fossils. Courtesy Department of Paleobiology, National Museum of Natural History.

Whether Ulrich and Girty were physically adjacent for a short time is irrelevant to their profound differences. Ulrich's goal was to revise the Paleozoic stratigraphic column, but when he reached into the Upper Paleozoic, Girty objected and beat him off. Their styles were fundamentally different, Girty produced tome after tome for the Geological Survey, whereas Ulrich published increasing less on fossils. Notwithstanding that, Ulrich was closely connected to the Museum; for much of Bassler's earlier career, he was second author with Ulrich on a variety of fossil groups.

When most of the Geological Survey moved in 1917 to a new building that also housed the administration of the Interior Department, Girty moved with them, while the other paleontologists remained on the Mall. The isolation of Girty and his staff from other paleontologists probably played a part in the long delay of the USGS in recognizing the Mississippian and Pennsylvanian periods. This was somewhat balanced by the refusal of the Geological Survey to recognize the new segments of geologic time propounded by Ulrich (Weiss and Yochelson, 1995).

Another notable disagreement of this generation was between Stanton and Knowlton on the placement of the Mesozoic-Cenozoic boundary in the western United States; whether the interpretations provided by one group of organisms should be given more weight than those of another group of organism remains an unresolved scientific problem.

One should not presume that because there is no further mention of problems that either the USGS or the USNM were one big happy family. There were divisions within both organizations and among the members of each staff. These differences were internal and personal; except indirectly, such disagreements and personality clashes had no effect on the course of the science. Seemingly,

140   CULTURES AND INSTITUTIONS OF NATURAL HISTORY

until the late 1940s, most Geological Survey collections were transferred to the Museum more or less automatically, apart from those of Girty, which remained physically separate.

New Quarters

One of Walcott's last acts in 1898, in his capacity as Acting Assistant Secretary, was to obtain planning money for a new museum building. Smithsonian Institution Secretary Samuel Pierpoint Langley died in February, 1906, and in January, 1907 Walcott became the fourth Secretary, with an office and laboratory in the Castle. He continued to run the Geological Survey as well as the Smithsonian until April of that year, yet he still had time to plan his first field season in western Canada. Throughout his tenure as Secretary, Walcott was in the field for 18 seasons (Fig. 15); he actively collected in western Canada and described many Cambrian fossils. His most famous accomplishment was the discovery, collection, and description of the Middle Cambrian Burgess Shale biota (Yochelson, 1996).

FIGURE 15. Charles Doolittle Walcott, in charge of Paleozoic paleontology, and Helena B. Walcott on their honeymoon in Newfoundland collecting trilobites. Taken in 1888.
Courtesy U. S. Geological Survey Photographic Library (C. D. Walcott Collection, #62).

FIGURE 16. The "new" National Museum under construction, taken looking north from the Castle. The vertebrate paleontologists were on the ground floor of the east wing, partially obscured by trees in the foreground. Courtesy Smithsonian Institution Archives (SIA #18546).

FIGURE 17. Main office of the Department of Geology in the new National Museum. Probably taken in 1911 or 1912 There is a blemish in the negative, not a leaking roof. Courtesy Smithsonian Institution Archives (SIA #1273).

Lancaster Demorest Burling (1882–1975), who had been Walcott's personal assistant on the USGS, transferred to the USNM in 1907 where he remained for five years, until leaving for a position with the Geological Survey of Canada. His place was partially filled in 1914 when Charles Elmer Resser (1889–1943) was employed by the Museum to study Cambrian fossils in the Division of Invertebrate Paleontology and Paleobotany of the Department of Geology. Resser assisted Walcott at times in the laboratory and went to field areas in the west as directed by him, but he was never a true assistant as was Burling. Resser published almost nothing until after Walcott's death in 1927.

The next significant historical event after Walcott became Secretary, was completion of the "new" National Museum, the natural history building on the north side of the Mall (Fig. 16). In 1910, the paleontologists and their collections moved from the red brick building into far more luxurious quarters (Yochelson, 1985) (Fig. 17). The old place was renamed the Arts & Industries Building and housed cultural and technological exhibits, with a minimal staff of curators. By comparison, the new quarters for paleontology were luxurious. The third floor corridor on the east side housed Geological Survey Mesozoic and Paleozoic paleontologists and paleobotanists, including those formerly in the Hoee Building — except for Girty. Old customs die hard and Dall, the USGS Cenozoic paleontologist, was on the west side of the building, his collections intermixed with the modern shells of the Division of Mollusks.

Invertebrate paleontologists of the USNM Department of Geology were on the south side of the building; but Bassler and, later, Resser constituted the staff for invertebrates for nearly two decades. It is superfluous to note that the Geological Survey staff was far larger. Gilmore and his vertebrate colleagues held forth on the east side of the ground floor. Because of the need to fill exhibit halls, a relatively large number of vertebrate preparators was employed for years reconstructing skeletons.

There is no indication of the size of the USGS/USNM fossil collections when they were transferred to the new building. It is known that much material had been in storage for years and, finally, could be put in cases making examination of the material far easier. There was a gradual shift from wooden cases to those of steel, lessening the danger of fire. The space for more cases also must have been an incentive for increased effort in collecting, mainly by the USGS paleontologists and by Walcott. By the 1940s, little unused space remained and most fossil collections were in cases which were stacked 9 feet high. Meanwhile, the limited staff of the Museum began to develop "biologic" collections of selected organisms, in contrast to stratigraphic collections of the entire fauna of a locality.

One important consequence of the move was new public display space. Four halls were devoted to paleontology and preparing exhibits was officially a job for the Museum staff. Peale made major contributions to the hall of paleobotany, and the vertebrate paleontologists eventually filled two halls with skeletons. How much assistance Bassler received in organizing the invertebrate hall is no longer known. For the next forty years, the exhibits remained essentially unchanged.

USGS 1910–1941

With new office space, the USGS hired Edwin Kirk (1884–1955), an echinoderm specialist, and a mid-Paleozoic biostratigrapher. He was considered by the geologists to be a phenomenal man in determining the age of rocks in the field and did yeoman work in the Great Basin and Alaska before losing a leg in a quarry accident; he continued to come to the museum after retirement and died at his desk. Paleobotanist White became U. S. Geological Survey Chief Geologist in 1913. He returned full-time to paleontology at the new museum building in 1922, but was in frail health after a stroke.

Within the Geologic Division of the USGS, a separate section on coastal plain investigations was organized in 1913 and headed by Thomas Wayland Vaughan (1870–1952) (Rabbitt 1986). Vaughan later left Washington to become head of Scripps Oceanographic Institute, but, late in life, a retired Vaughan returned to the USNM and to his study of scleractinian corals. Others in the Coastal Plain Section who were housed in the new building included Lloyd William Stephenson (1876–1962), a specialist on Cretaceous mollusks, Charles Wythe Cooke (1887–1971), who studied echinoids, and Julia Anna Gardner (1882–1960) (Fig. 18), specialist on Cenozoic mollusks and a pioneer in paleoecological interpretation of fossils. These names are familiar worldwide to all students of younger fossils.

In 1913 Wendell Phillips Woodring (1891–1983) was hired, though he may not have been in the Coastal Plain Section; he left in 1927 for a three year teaching stint, but returned to the Washington fold. In 1922, Stephenson became head of the Coastal Plain Section, which he led for the next 15 years, until the paleontologists of that group were transferred to the Paleontology and Stratigraphy Section. That name was commonly shortened to P&S and occasionally referred to by some field geologists as "Pull and Strut." Near the end of World War I, John Bernard Reeside Jr. (1889–1958) (Fig. 19) was hired to work on the Cretaceous. There then came a pause in growth.

Surprisingly, despite the great depression, 1930 saw new faces in the P&S Section. Josiah Bridge (1896–1953) came, presumably as an understudy of Ulrich on lower Paleozoic fossils and stratigraphy. He soon joined the group of geologists who could not agree with Ulrich's notions of unique faunas in rocks he had named the Ozarkian and Canadian. James Steele Williams (1896–1957) also came to Washington in 1930 to understudy the aging Girty and was housed in the main Interior Building, though later he moved to another Interior department building. A few years later, Lloyd

FIGURES 18–19. (18) Julia Anna Gardner, first woman paleontologist in the U.S. Geological Survey; (19) A young John B. Reeside, Jr., second chief of P&S Section, U.S. Geological Survey. Courtesy U. S. Geological Survey, Photographic Library (Portraits #341 and 1034 respectively).

George Henbest (1900–1987) was hired to work on Paleozoic fusulinids and, in a sense, he became the first Geological Survey micropaleontologist in Washington.

As still another 1930 hire, the Paleozoic paleobotanist Charles Brian Read (1907–1979) arrived in Washington, more or less to understudy White but, after a decade, he transferred to other Geological Survey activities. When he was appointed in 1931, Kenneth Elmo Lohman (1897–1996) also was housed in the USGS headquarters, for there was no more space in the new museum building; Lohman continued his study of fossil diatoms begun at the California Institute of Technology.

The outstanding "character" among the new group of post-1919 paleontologists was the Cenozoic paleobotanist Roland Wilbur Brown (1893–1961), hired in 1929. Along with plants, he became involved in problematica and acquired all sorts of esoteric paleontologic information. Brown was also a scholar of Latin and Greek and, though "Brownie" was renowned for his penny-pinching, it was the pennies he saved that allowed him in 1954 to publish privately his famous book *Composition of Scientific Words*, which has become the bible for anyone coining a new specific or generic name in systematic biology or paleontology. Brown also left a large endowment to the National Museum for the study of paleobotany.

In 1940, Ralph Willard Imlay (1908–1989), a Jurassic ammonite specialist, joined the P&S Section. He, Stephenson, and Reeside occupied adjacent offices. All worked and wrote extensively and had no time for chit-chat; their offices were referred to as the "hall of silent men." As an indication of productivity, during one month in the 1970s, Imlay was the author of five percent of all the Professional Papers published by the USGS.

Woodring, Gardner and other USGS paleontologists studying Cenozoic fossils had their offices near Dall on the west side of the building. So little is known of Ralph Bentley Stewart (1901–1957) and his Geological Survey career that it is uncertain when he arrived to consider the California fossil mollusks; it may not have been until the 1940s.

During 1931, Stanton was appointed USGS Acting Chief Geologist and was given the job on a permanent basis the following year; despite his advanced age, Stanton served until 1935. With Stanton's move upward, Reeside, another Cretaceous specialist, headed the Section in 1932 and held that position for the next nineteen years.

USNM 1910–1941

Following the death of Merrill, in 1929, Bassler became Head of the Department of Geology in the Museum and occupied the position until retirement in 1948 (Yochelson 1985a); he remained around his office until a few years before his death in 1961. In 1930, the Department employed Gustav Arthur Cooper (1902–   ) (Fig. 20); this was the best decision of Bassler's career. Cooper left the museum building in 1987, fifty-seven years later, 15 years after his official retirement in 1972. As Cooper occasionally recounted, "Mr. Resser studied the Cambrian trilobites and Cooper had to care for all other fossils." He specialized on the study of fossil and Recent brachiopods, dramatically improved curatorial practices, and accumulated extensive collections. Cooper produced many monographs which contributed significantly to Paleozoic stratigraphy and in some ways his work was comparable to that of the USGS paleontologists. Nevertheless, he was equally interested in the life habits, phylogeny, and classification of the brachiopods. He was, without a doubt, the outstanding Museum paleontologist of the 20th Century.

A year after Gidley died in 1931, the Museum hired Charles Lewis Gazin (1904–1996) to continue research on Cenozoic mammals; he retired in 1970, but maintained his research effort for a

FIGURE 20. G. Arthur Cooper, last Head of Geology and first Chairman of Paleobiology, and Mrs. Cooper in his office on the south side of the "new" National Museum Building. Taken June 1954. Courtesy Smithsonian Institution Archives (SIA #85-4051).

few more years. Gazin had previously worked a year or so for the USGS, but for some reason did not like the organization.

From the early 1920s onward, funds were short for both the Geological Survey and Museum, but especially the latter. The great depression made a bad situation worse. The Museum had no money for cases, drawers or trays, but the Geological Survey would scrape together funds and lend these items. On several occasions, Cooper joined USGS paleontologists on field trips as, apart from salaries, there was essentially no funding for the Museum.

World War II

The Second World War affected everyone. The P&S Section was essentially reduced to Reeside and Brown; both had served as Lieutenants in the First World War. Williams and Helen Margaret Duncan (1910–1971), interested in Paleozoic bryozoans, went off to look for fluorite. Jean Milton Berdan (1916–   ), another woman interested in Lower Paleozoic ostracodes, was involved in water resources work.

Mackenzie Gordon, Jr. (1913–1992), later to make his name studying goniatites, looked for bauxite in Arkansas, and Preston Ercelle Cloud (1912–1991) (Fig. 21) was sent to find bauxite in

Alabama. Cloud left the USGS after the War but then returned in 1949. Josiah Bridge headed the entire bauxite program and did not return to P&S until a few years before his death in 1954. Israel Gregory Sohn (1911–2000), who had started as a technician in 1941, went to Military Geology and then searched for bentonite clays in Montana. In Military Geology, Julia Gardner studied tiny mollusks and foraminifers in sand ballast from a captured Japanese fire balloons and, combined with Lohman's analysis of the diatoms, located the launching site in Japan.

As far as the Museum staff was involved, vertebrate paleontology contributed members to the armed forces, and Gazin was an officer. Cooper accompanied Imlay in studies of stratigraphy in Mexico in the hopes of increasing oil production. After Resser died in 1943, Cooper constituted the entire staff of the Division of Invertebrate Paleontology and Paleobotany.

Also, as a consequence of the war, there was serious concern that Washington would be bombed. Shortly before 1941, illustrated material had been separated from the general collections as had the type specimens much earlier. So, with the onset of war, the illustrated material and the types were moved from the museum to off-site storage in limestone caves in Virginia. As a result of this, the Department came to maintain three kinds of collections: "type material," which included illustrated specimens; biological sets; and stratigraphic collections. Although many museums maintain their illustrated material in order by the publication in which they are described, the fossil holdings at the USNM are so huge that the "type" collections, including illustrated material, are maintained in cases in alphabetical order adjacent to, but separate from, the "biological" collections.

FIGURE 21. Preston E. Cloud, first chief of the USGS P&S Branch, taken about 1970, in his later years after leaving the USGS. Published by permission of the National Academy of Sciences.

Post-War Boom in USGS

In 1946, William Aubry Cobban moved into the Mesozoic Hall of Silent Men, and continued the tradition of silently writing extensive monographs. Beginning in 1948, the USGS expanded dramatically and the sections became branches. Williams and other Upper Paleozoic paleontologists were transferred to the not quite so new museum building to provide more space in another USGS building. They brought with them about 200 6-foot cases of fossils which had to be stored in the east attic. Jack Elwood Smedley began work on the Permian in 1947 and remained for about a decade before transferring to another part of the USGS.

Along with the old hands who came back from war-time assignments, a few former assistants had worked their way up. I. G. Sohn, for instance, went from the search for clay deposits during the war to the post-war study of ostracodes, and Wilbert Henry Hass (?–1959), who had joined P&S during the 1930s as a technician, now worked on conodonts.

When Joseph Augustine Cushman (1881–1949), a USGS contract employee for many years, died, his foraminifer collection, along with Ruth Todd (1913–1984), who had started work for the Geological Survey in Cushman's laboratory in 1941, and Todd's assistant, Doris Low, came to the P&S Branch (1949). As a result, the branch expanded its space on the third floor of the museum into the southeast corridor.

Following the administrative change wherein USGS sections became branches, in the fall of 1949 Reeside stepped down and Cloud became Chief of the Paleontology and Stratigraphy Branch (Fig. 21). A dramatic new era of expansion began. About this time, Harry Stephen Ladd (1899–1982), experienced in the National Park Service before his stint in war-time USGS administration, transferred to the branch and started his post-war investigations of Cenozoic rocks on the Pacific Islands. He also completed the massive treatise on paleoecology begun by Vaughan and was, at least, the grandfather of the deep-sea drilling program.

Cloud hired a whole series of people, comparable to the increase of two decades earlier. In 1949, Arthur James Boucot was brought in, a graduate student working on Paleozoic brachiopods under Cloud; and the following year, Cloud hired Allison Ralph Palmer, who had just completed his degree and was deep into investigations of Cambrian trilobites. In 1951, he hired the Paleozoic paleobotanist Sergius Harry Mamay, who had completed a post-doctorate year in England studying Carboniferous plants. In the space of one year, 1952, Cloud employed Richard Stanton Boardman, who was completing a thesis on Devonian bryozoans; Raymond Charles Douglass, who was to do research on larger foraminifers and fusulinids; and Ellis Leon Yochelson, beginning a thesis on Permian gastropods.

Not only did Cloud want more people to serve the needs of the large increase of USGS geologists who were mapping, but he also wanted groups of fossils which had been little exploited to be made more useful for stratigraphic purposes. These people, and those who followed, tended to concentrate on a particular group of fossils and were more specialized than those who had preceded them. Though the conventional groups of fossils for age determination were studied in ever more detail, new groups were being investigated and utilized in increasing numbers. A second minor theme of these new hires was more emphasis on consideration of environments of deposition and on paleoecological interpretation of fossils.

Notwithstanding more time for longer-term research, the main emphasis was still on support for the field geologists, and all material sent in was to be reported on within a few months. A delay in an answer to an inquiry based on fossils led to a chastising by the Chief. Commonly, the younger paleontologists were out each summer visiting field parties to provide on-the-spot assistance.

After a second floor geological exhibit hall was closed, P&S expanded into "Stone Hall" for a decade, an office area nearly as uncomfortable as the attic storage area. Paleobotanist James Morton Schopf (1911–1978) was in the Branch for a year, but he saw better opportunities with the Fuels Branch and set up his own laboratory in Columbus, Ohio.

William Jasper Sando (1927–1996) joined the branch in 1954, was detailed to another position for two years and in 1956 began study of Mississippian corals of the West, dying shortly after his retirement in 1993. Norman Fredrick Sohl (1924–1991) arrived in 1954 to work on the Cretaceous of the Gulf Coast and later the Caribbean, and brought a little noise into the "Hall of Silent Men." In 1954, Robert Ballin Neuman moved from elsewhere in the USGS to the museum building, but he did not officially join the Branch to study of Lower Paleozoic brachiopods until a decade later; he retired in 1980, but is still busy as a volunteer and museum research associate.

The great expansion of the USGS led to creation of P&S branch offices in Denver, Colorado, and Menlo Park, California. Cobban moved to Denver and others were hired directly for that facility.

Richard Rezak came to Washington to study algae, both Precambrian and Recent; he then moved to Denver, to the oil industry, and to academia. Later, Ellen James Moore, who had been Julia Gardner's assistant, moved to the Menlo Park facility to study Cenozoic mollusks of the West Coast. In 1955, Dwight Willard Taylor, a specialist on nonmarine gastropods, came to P&S in Washington for several years before moving West; he left the USGS in 1967. Jack Albert Wolfe, a Mesozoic paleobotanist, began in Washington and then transferred to Denver for a long and noteworthy career. However, a number of Geological Survey paleontologists who had distinguished careers in the Denver and Menlo Park offices were never in Washington, except as occasional visitors and are not included in this account.

William Albert Oliver, Jr. came from Brown University in 1957 to work on Devonian corals. At the time, there was so little obvious distinction between paleontologists of the USGS and USNM that he was offered a position with both the Department staff and P&S Branch, and given his choice. Ultimately, he accepted the position with the Geological Survey. The Survey had more money for field work and assistants, as well as a ready outlet for publication, but his decision may have been influenced by the fact that, under Cloud, detailed concentration on a particular group of fossils was strongly encouraged. The day of faunal studies of a formation had passed.

Although Cloud took a year in Europe during his tenure, he was the branch chief until 1961. Charles Warren Merriam (1905–1974) had come East from Menlo Park, California, to be Acting Chief during that year, and took over again with the understanding that his earlier year as Acting Chief would be included in his term of office. It had become the custom throughout the USGS that a branch chief served five years. In 1961, a few months after stepping down as branch chief, Cloud left the Geological Survey. Merriam hired John Warfield Huddle (1907–1975) from the University of Kentucky to revive the studied of conodonts, but sadly, like Hass, he also died of cancer. Whether the heavy liquids used in concentration of conodonts were responsible is uncertain, but greater safety precautions with these liquids were installed.

Being a young paleontologist for the USGS did not suit everyone; Boucot left for a teaching career in 1956, but continued his study of brachiopods. Margaret Jean Hough, the first USGS vertebrate paleontologist since Marsh, came to the museum in the 1950s and left in 1960 for an academic position. A few years later, Palmer also left for the joys of academia.

USGS studies in vertebrate paleontology finally found a focus when Frank Clifford Whitmore, Jr. transferred to P&S Branch in 1959, after more than a decade as Chief of Military Geology Branch. Since the early 1950s, John Thomas Dutro, Jr. maintained an office at the Museum as a paleontologist with the Alaska Branch; he strengthened the Paleozoic contingent when, in 1956, he transferred to P&S Branch.

Post-War Change for USNM

After the war, the USNM began rebuilding its staff, though on a modest scale. Alfred Richard Loeblich, Jr. (1914–1994) joined the staff in 1946, originally to study bryozoans, but because of conflict with Bassler's interest in that group, he soon began to study foraminifers, starting his new investigations by helping to move Cushman's collection to Washington. The transfer of the Cushman collection of foraminfers to the USNM, made it the premier organization for study of this group of microfossils. Loeblich remained in the Department for just over a decade, leaving in 1957 for an oil research laboratory, and, ultimately, a university.

David Hosbrook Dunkle (1911–1984) came in 1947 to start a program in the study of fossil fish; as one of the rare examples of Museum to Geological Survey transfer, he spent 1961–1963 overseas with a USGS mission. It was a surprise when he resigned in 1968 to move to the Cleveland Museum. Arthur Leroy Bowsher joined the Department in 1948 for a year, transferred to the USGS for a year to work in Alaska, returned to the Department staff for a year to study crinoids, and then left again in 1951 for a career with the USGS before moving to the oil business in the late–1950s. David Nicol arrived in 1949, the first Museum Cenozoic specialist; after eight years, he also left to teach at Southern Illinois University.

Turnover of staff within the Department was significant during the 1940s and 1950s and, relative to the size of the two groups, it was far higher than among Geological Survey paleontologists. No single cause is obvious but, as slow as the rate of promotion was in the Survey, it was even slower within the Museum.

To move to a more positive point, just before the start of World War II, Cooper had brought back a few small pieces of Permian limestone from west Texas and extracted fossil brachiopods using hydrochloric acid. In the post-war years, an annual trip to gather more and more blocks became a ritual. The blocks were acidified in a temporary building in the east courtyard, leaving a residue of magnificent fossils. "By spending the same time on the outcrop, collecting limestone blocks rather than loose specimens, the number of specimens increases by many orders of magnitude.... Silicified fossils are not sturdy. We have leaped from storing rocks to storing objects as delicate as butterflies" (Yochelson, 1969, 599). Millions of brachiopods accumulated along with a variety of other invertebrates. Research Associate James Brookes Knight (1880–1960) retired from Princeton and spent a few months each year in Washington examining the Permian snails.

Following Bassler's retirement, mineralogist William Foshag was appointed Head Curator of the Department of Geology (Yochelson, 1985a). In 1956, Cooper became Head Curator, and he had plans for division and reorganization into a Department of Mineral Sciences and a Department of Paleobiology.

Cooper hired Porter Martin Kier in 1957 to examine echinoids. After completing his thesis under Geological Survey auspices, in 1957, Boardman transferred to the Museum's Department of Geology; his view was that paleontologists should be concerned with biology of the organism and less interested in its age. To strengthen study of fossil vertebrates, Peter Paul Vaughn came in 1958, but left in 1960 for academia. Nicholas Hotton III (1921–1999) arrived in 1959 to wrestle with the fossil reptiles and had a distinguished career before retirement. Erle Galen Kauffmann was hired in 1960 and established himself as one who brought in enormous collections of Cretaceous invertebrates. Sohl of the USGS and he collaborated closely but, in 1980, Kauffmann left for the University of Colorado. Richard Cifelli (1923–1984) joined the staff in 1960 to look after the foraminifers; his career was cut short by cancer.

The USNM staff continued to be "poor relations" relative to its counterpart in the P&S Branch. Funds for field work were in short supply and, more commonly than not, it was the USGS that bought new cases, drawers, and specimen trays. Neither organization had sufficient technical support, but P&S had relatively more than those in USNM. Perhaps the single greatest daily annoyance to the Museum's "have nots" was that USGS offices had window air conditioners. These actually had little effect, for the building was brick faced with thick granite and soaked up heat from March onward to the late fall, but they were symbolic.

Girty had set a tone in not transferring the Late Paleozoic collections to the USNM. Eventually his type specimens were added to the collections, but the bulk of the material remained the property of the Department of Interior. Likewise, most of the Paleozoic collections made during the time that Cloud was branch chief and for years thereafter were not transferred. The Museum continued to receive material but, increasingly, its staff was more concerned with research of their own choosing than with curation of the growing collections. The Geological Survey collections were well curated, but neither they nor the National Museum were particularly zealous in the joint duties of transfer of material.

During the 1950s and 1960s, the younger members of P&S and the Department of Geology/Paleobiology socialized. As families grew and commuting became more difficult, there was less interaction between the groups. The intimate association between Museum and Geological Survey eroded slightly as organizational memory was lost. For both groups of paleontologists who were beginning their careers, promotion depended on productivity. Among a few of the people, an unspoken feeling was that the bright lights in the Geological Survey were wasting their careers in aiding field men and, conversely, obtuse problems of no practical importance were being pursued by some members of the Department.

One of the problems faced by the Department staff was that of the outdated public displays. Eventually, four new halls were completed (Yochelson, 1985). It was a painful process and required a great deal of time and effort. Except for occasional and minor contributions, the staff of P&S was not involved. Still later, several of these exhibit halls were completely redone.

More New Quarters and Staff

New space was one major event of the next decade for the two groups. An air conditioned east wing with six research floors was added to the building in 1962. Formerly, the USGS placed between two and four people in each room in the main building, but now finally P&S had the entire third floor of the wing and part of the fifth and first floors in this new facility. Those in the Department of Paleobiology occupied most of the first floor, all of second and some of the fifth. Along with the new space for people came new space for empty cases and new space for collections.

Shortly after the move to new space in the east wing, the organization of the Department of Paleobiology ensued. In 1963, Cooper became the first in charge of the new Department of Paleobiology; he also held the title of Chairman rather than Head Curator (Yochelson, 1985a), another change from the past. Although it may have seemed trivial at the time, "paleontology" was not in the title and use of "paleobiology" in retrospect signified a break with past tradition. A certain amount of research had always been done by members of both the Department and P&S Branch staffs, depending in part on individual temperament and time available; but this title was a clear signal that the Museum was shifting more toward research.

Dutro became chief of P&S Branch in 1962 in the new quarters and he was followed by Sohl in 1968. Under both, the staff continued to expand slightly and identifying fossils and writing descriptions continued on more or less an even keel. Almost immediately after the move in 1963, John Pojeta, Jr. was hired to help support USGS mapping in the state of Kentucky. The Geological Survey started its own program of dissolving limestone blocks to obtain silicified fossils from the older rocks of that state. P&S used the Museum acid room in the east wing basement. The same year Olgarts Karklins came to study Kentucky bryozoans.

Blake Winfield Blackwelder arrived in 1972 to study Tertiary fossils for the USGS and stayed until 1981 before switching to the oil business. Harlan Richard Bergquist (1908–1982), who began by studied microfossils for the Alaskan Branch, transferred to P&S at the Museum about 1967. Anita Gertrude Harris, who began as a preparator and went on to become USGS map editor, came back to P&S Branch and, among other accomplishments, developed the conodont alteration index (CAI), a major tool for investigations of oil prospects of a region; she retired in 1997. As a result of a project to study Miocene at the Calvert Cliffs nuclear power plant, Lauke Ward came as a technician; he was the last in the Branch to work his way up to professional status before he resigned to help organize a new natural history museum in Virginia.

In 1962, Thomas George Gibson began working on Cenozoic foraminifers. Joseph Ernest Hazel came in 1964 to work on younger ostracodes. Richard Monroe Forester was hired in 1975 to add to the ostracode effort; he was at the museum and then Reston before moving to Denver. Elisabeth M. Brower started as a technician in Washington, but came into her own with ostracodes, after transferring to Denver. Laurel Mary Bybell was another person added in 1975; she has the distinction of being the first of the group to be moved to Reston, Virginia, in 1978, occupying a huge empty space to reserve it for future use. Norman John Silberling was hired in 1975 for the Menlo Park office; some time later he came to P&S in Washington for a year and, when he returned to California, some cases of Triassic fossils left the Museum with him. Now retired, Silberling continues Triassic work in Denver. John Edward Repetski came in 1975 to work on Lower Paleozoic conodonts for the P&S Branch. In 1969, Michael E. Taylor filled the long vacant spot in the study of Cambrian trilobites, before he transferred to Denver; when he moved a significant part of the Cambrian collection moved with him, and it remained in Denver when he retired in 1995.

Again developments of the Museum paralleled the USGS on a more modest scale. The first paleobotanist came to the department when Francis Maurice Hueber joined in 1962 to study Devonian plants. Martin Alexander Buzas came in 1963 to strengthen research in foraminifers. The year 1964 was a banner year for the Department; it added four new members. Richard Hall Benson came from teaching at Kansas to a career with ostracodes and study of the Cenozoic of the Mediterranean region. Clayton Edward Ray began studying fossil mammals with emphasis on marine forms and has continued on since retirement in 1996. Walter Adey began studying fossil algae, switched to Recent forms and marine ecosystems, and formed a unit separate from the department in 1984. Kenneth M. Towe began to worry about oxygen in the Precambrian atmosphere and other more esoteric matters until his retirement, also in 1996. It is symbolic of a future division of approach that, whereas the Smithsonian telephone directory listed a biological specialty for both the Geological Survey paleontologists and those in the Department, Towe's specialty was listed as "electron microscope."

The Department staff expanded a little more. Thomas Richard Waller started looking at scallops as a staff member in 1966 and has continued apace. Alan Herbert Cheetham left the academic life at Louisiana State University in 1967 to concentrate on Cenozoic bryozoans in Washington. However, like some members of the P&S Branch, the Department was not for everyone; Richard Ashby Robison came in 1966 to study trilobites, intensely disliked commuting, and left in 1967.

By mid–1964, a west wing of the building was completed and was available for occupancy. The paleobotanical contingent of P&S and the Department moved again to new quarters. Now that there was space, Lohman moved to the west wing from another USGS building. Paleobotanist Leo Joseph Hickey was added to the departmental staff in 1969, but in 1980 the Yale Peabody Museum called, and he answered the call.

The 1960s were the golden time for paleontology in Washington. It was the heyday of the P&S Branch with 31 professionals and 35 support staff on its rolls at the USNM. The Museum's departmental staff was approximately half that size, but together, and in one capacity or another, some 90 persons were examining fossils. Apart from institutes in Nanjing and Moscow, the USNM housed the largest concentration of paleontologists in one establishment in the world. Indeed, it has been stated informally, that the large contingent of USGS personnel was a strong reason for building the east wing.

After the USNM departmental reorganization was in place and functioning well, Cooper stepped down in 1967 and Kier became Chairman of Paleobiology. By then, the USNM had also established five years as a term for a chairman. In 1969, the United States National Museum metamorphosed into the National Museum of Natural History (NMNH); at the insistence of the curators, the abbreviation used to designate specimens remains USNM.

Robert John Emry was hired in 1971 and took up the task of investigating early Cenozoic mammals, replacing Gazin, who retired in 1970. In 1973, immediately after his term as Department Chairman, Kier became director of the National Museum of Natural History, serving until 1980. He returned briefly to the Department to look at a few more fossil echinoids, then having seen them all, or at least most of them, he retired. James Francis Mello, who had been hired by the Geological Survey's P&S Branch to study Cretaceous foraminifers in 1962, developed a taste for administration by 1970 and transferred to the office of the Chief Geologist. Three years later, Kier appointed Mello as Assistant Director and Mello remained in administration for about a decade, before returning to foraminifers for a year or so and then taking an early retirement.

Cooper had received a grant from the National Science Foundation to continue his work on silicified Permian brachiopods and, in 1957, Richard Evans Grant (1927–1994) came to Washington. When this grant money was expended, he joined the P&S Branch and continued to assist Cooper in preparing and describing Permian brachiopods.

Whereas the Chief of P&S Branch was appointed by the Chief Geologist, the Chairman of the Department was elected by the staff, subject to final approval by the Museum director. At least twice in the history of Paleobiology, a staff member who wanted the position worried other staff members to the extent that he was not elected. In 1973, Grant transferred to the Department staff, moving from the third floor to the second, and followed Porter Kier as the next departmental chairman; because of a major departmental split, bringing in an "outside" person resolved the dilemma. Grant's fatal heart attack in December, 1994, shocked everyone. Earlier, however, Martin Buzas had followed Grant as Chairman and had served for nearly six years, from 1977–1982.

Tarnish on the Golden Age

The new wings provided air conditioning, far better lighting and much needed space for offices and collections. Still, there was a disadvantage in being spread among four floors. One practical point is that in the main part of the building there was only one toilet on the third floor. Sooner or later, P&S Branch and Department members met and exchanged a few words. The new wings provided many rest rooms, but increased the isolation of the two groups and to some extent within each group. Slight though this contact may have been and humorous though it may seem, this was another factor in divergence of the two groups. One must keep in mind that museums tend to attract people who are to some extent the antithesis of gregarious sales people. Further, the longer one pursues a speciality, the less time one has to socialize, even among peers. This is one of differences between academic institutions and museums.

When Norman Sohl stepped down as USGS Branch Chief, Joseph Hazel took over the position from 1973–1978. Thomas Woodrow Henry was hired to study marine invertebrates from the Pennsylvanian stratotype section, and remained at the museum building for nearly a decade, before moving to Denver. When he moved, the bulk of the Late Paleozoic Geological Survey fossil collection went to Denver with him.

More significantly in the history of that organization, the completion in the 1970s of a new building for the U. S. Geological Survey at Reston, Virginia, provided for more expansion. Almost all of the new staff were in the field of micropaleontology and primarily oriented toward younger

Cenozoic rocks, rather than older Paleozoic strata, and again toward groups of fossils which had not been studied by USGS specialists.

Of profound significance, for the first time since Geological Survey paleontologists were in Washington, their headquarters left the Museum. Hazel transferred the office of the Branch Chief of P&S Branch to Reston, and left the Geological Survey for the oil business in 1983. Hazel was followed as Branch Chief by William V. Sliter (1935–1997), a foraminifer specialist who, like Merriam, came east from Menlo Park, and had scant knowledge of the Museum contingent or the history of USGS-USNM relations. Thomas Mark Cronin was hired in 1978, had at office at NMNH, and continued the tradition in ostracode studies.

Next, several paleontologists who had been at the museum transferred to Reston. These included Cronin, Gibson, Harris, Karklins and Repetski in the early 1980s. From the standpoint of collections, moving the microfossils was relatively easy. When Sohl transferred to Reston, a number of large, heavy cases went with him. On the other hand, Pojeta went to Reston but kept most of his collections at the Museum. Whitmore was not transferred to Reston; he retired in 1984, but like most retirees he kept right on pursuing his research.

Bruce Wardlaw holds the all-time record for moving. He had a post-doctorate with the Museum Department, followed by a post-doctorate with the USGS P&S Branch, followed by USGS employment in Washington and then Reston, followed by a move to Denver and a return to Reston. Along the way he switched from brachiopods to conodonts, because they are a more useful biostratigraphic group. Large scale programs of dissolving limestone to extract fossils ceased, in part because of environmental regulations and, in part, because of poor original design and construction of the facilities in the aging east wing.

Decline and Fall at USGS

During 1979, the USGS began a major change in organization. One step was to shift to programmatic research. Whereas the tradition had been that P&S was a "service" organization, with every Chief from Cloud onward urging more time for independent research, now identification of fossils for field parties was downgraded. More or less simultaneously, budget problems developed. Several middle management administrators seized this as a reason to detail for several months some paleontologists at the Museum to proof-read regulations for the Office of Surface Mining. Protests to the branch chief were to no avail.

Funds for field work began to decline, but especially so for the paleontologists. As paleontologists no longer visited field parties, the number of collections sent in for examination and report began to decline, for it was assumed that there was no reason to collect fossils which would not be studied. It was a self-fulfilling prophesy.

In 1984, Sliter was followed as Branch Chief, for a very few months, by Taylor, the only time Branch headquarters was in Denver. Later in 1984, Richard Z. Poore, yet another foraminifer person moving east from California, was appointed branch chief and returned P&S Branch headquarters to Reston. Poore chose to emphasize investigations of paleoclimatology of the late Cenozoic.

Poore had no prior experience or understanding of the relationship that had existed among Museum and Geological Survey staff and administrations, and the acting director of the museum, at that time, likewise, had no knowledge of this past history. As a consequence, P&S paleontologists were strongly encouraged to move to Reston, even though this meant smaller quarters for them. In 1988, Repetski, Harris, and Pojeta were moved out of the building. Eventually only a few persons interested in Paleozoic megafossils remained in Washington.

FIGURE 22. John Pojeta, Jr. (1999).
Photo courtesy Alan Leviton.

FIGURE 23. John Thomas Dutro, Jr. (1999).
Photo courtesy Alan Leviton.

Retirements of the USGS post-war generation of paleontologists had started with Neuman in 1980, Mamay in 1982, Whitmore in 1984 and Yochelson in 1985; Oliver and Sando both retired in 1993. The Museum generously provided offices for those who remained in Washington, and they continued as Research Associates in the Department. Pojeta took over as Branch Chief from Poore in 1989; after Pojeta's retirement in 1994 (Fig. 22), he too returned to the Museum as another full-time working retiree. Wardlaw became Chief of P&S Branch in 1994, following Pojeta. Gibson came back to the Museum as a retiree in 1995.

Dutro (Fig. 23), the last P&S Branch paleontologist at the Museum, officially retired in 1994 — though, like others, he is still active — and the last technician, Keith Moore, retired in July, 1995. The long tenure of Geological Survey paleontologists in the Museum, which had begun in 1881, ended. Later that year, other USGS paleontologists were lost by a government reduction in force, not only at Reston, but also at Denver and Menlo Park.

During the mid-1990s, an administrative decision was made that there were no longer to be any branches with national responsibilities. On October 1, 1995, the Paleontology and Stratigraphy Branch was dissolved and the few remaining Geological Survey paleontologists were scattered to other projects. A new director in 1999 commented "We have been accused of never wanting to stop anything, but we have ended programs. A lot of stratigraphy and paleontology programs, for example, aren't around anymore . . ." (Molina, 1999:11). Apparently whatever paleontologists might have contributed in the past, they will not, in the foreseeable future, have the opportunity again to aid the Geological Survey.

The Last Quarter Century in the Museum's Department of Paleobiology

Cooper's reorganization included adding a division for sedimentologists. The hope in part was that this might lead to an active role for the Museum in the Deep Sea Drilling Program and, in part, might lead to paleoecological investigations. Jack W. Pierce was the first sedimentologist, arriving in 1965. M. Grant Gross came in 1966 but left in less than two years; it was such a short stay that it is not listed in *American Men and Women of Science*. Daniel Jean Stanley arrived later in 1966.

Although interesting research resulted from the group, neither hope was realized. In one sense the sedimentologists are not germane to the story, but in another sense they were part of the group making decisions on policy and on hiring; two sedimentologists served as departmental chairman.

Ian George MacIntyre, who came to Museum in 1970 and joined the Department in 1972 to work on coral reefs, primarily recent ones, took over the duties as departmental chairman from Buzas. The first woman on the Paleobiology staff was Anna Kay Behrensmeyer, hired in 1981 and specializing in vertebrate taphonomy, that is what processes affect the bones after an animal dies; she moved up to Acting Associate Director for Research in 1993, and returned full-time to the Department in 1996.

When MacIntyre stepped down, Pierce, a sedimentologist not closely allied to any group of fossils, became chairman. Money problems that beset the USGS affected the Museum at about the same time. It is generally agreed that Pierce's administration was not a happy time, but it is equally agreed that this was because of external developments over which he had no control. He retired in 1995.

Notwithstanding these problems, Pierce was still able to increase the staff. Scott Lewis Wing was added to the staff in 1984 to work on Cretaceous-Tertiary floras; after a museum post-doctorate, he was employed by the P&S Branch for a short time before joining the Department staff. In 1985, William Anthony DiMichele came from the University of Washington to study Late Paleozoic plants; he was briefly in the west wing of the building. In only a few years, he became Department Chairman, following Pierce.

Perhaps the most symbolic event of this period was in 1987 when Cooper left the Museum after 57 years of faithful service to paleontology. A Museum Support Center, a few miles from Washington, was opened in 1983 and, in another symbolic event, the first collections of fossils were moved there a week following Cooper's departure. Other internal space moves resulted in the paleobotanists joining their fellow paleontologists in the east wing.

A 1990 addition to the departmental staff was Douglas Hamilton Erwin, concerned with Permian history and its snails, among many other interests, Also in 1990, Brian Thomas Huber, joined the staff and added more strength to the world's largest collection of foraminifers, along with his interest in correlation by foraminfers of some of the deep seas cores. Conrad Columbus Labandiera, came in 1992 and opened a new field for the department in his investigations of fossil insects. A reasonable generalization is that, during the time P&S was in dramatic decline, the Department more or less remained steady and has since been slightly strengthened. Ray retired in 1996 but still comes to the museum occasionally.

Although a specialty is given above for the paleontologists on the Museum staff, this is not a truly accurate description. The philosophy of hiring had shifted, and an extreme expression of this is that, to fill a vacancy, the best paleontologist should be hired, the fossil group of which the person had most knowledge being secondary. One consequence of this is that few on the current staff are investigating Paleozoic rocks or fossils. Overall, the rate of collecting fossils has also declined dramatically relative to the 1960s.

Another new development is more emphasis on international studies. Paleontology has always been broad in intellectual outlook, but employment for the Department of Interior required a great deal of ingenuity for a paleontologist to spend much time overseas. In contrast, the stricture on the Museum's Department in this regard was concerned with funding rather than philosophy. During the 1980s the Department became strongly international in the research efforts of its staff.

In 1996, Richard H. Benson became Department Chairman. The Walcott Fund, which had been taken away by the Director's office during Pierce's tenure, was returned to the Department. The Department staff is still strong, but the number of professional positions has declined slightly from its high point in the 1960s. John Michael Pandolfi was added to the staff in 1996, his prime interest being in coral reefs. There is hope for a dinosaur specialist, but the Museum has never had one and in light of the public interest in these fossils, this lack of a staff person is bizarre. Still, with its smaller staff, the Department of Paleobiology cannot provide the coverage of fossil groups that was available in the 1960s and 1970s when Geological Survey and Museum paleontology were both strong.

Transfer of collections to the Museum Support Center has continued. There are probably more fossils out of the Museum building than in it, and examining these collections is more complex and time consuming than when the cases were at hand. The material which Sohl moved to Reston has been returned to Washington. Collections located at the former P&S offices in Denver and Menlo Park[2] remain at those locations, and they cannot be completely transferred to the Museum because of space limitations. These include collections which had been in Washington at one time and were removed when USGS paleontologists left for these centers. Apart from the preservation of type specimens, the concept of a museum of record is no longer a significant concern. Major reconstruction within the east wing presents new and varied problems for the working scientists, though there is assurance from the administration that all will be well by 2002, 2003, or a year or so after, at the latest.

Unfortunately, this history must end on that down note. Yet, the story of paleontology in Washington has been one of ups and downs, so that one can only hope that, in a few years, the pendulum will swing again and that more paleontologists will join those still at the National Museum of Natural History.

Research Trends

One extreme approach to fossils is to be concerned only with the age of the rocks that yield them. Another extreme is to be concerned only with the biology of the organism, and ignore its age. It has been argued that paleontologists combine these approaches but they are neither geologists or biologists (Knight, 1947). Ancillary to this division, somewhere between "pure" biostratigraphy and "pure" paleobiology lies the discipline of paleoecology. The environments of the past are significant, but relatively few persons classify themselves as paleoecologists; in a sense that discipline has been subsumed within paleobiology.

Another aspect of research should be considered. Most paleontologists of the first and second generation were concerned with megafossils, easily studied, at least at a first stage. Following the First World War, emphasis began to shift to microfossils, requiring a microscope at all stages. During the last half of the 20th Century, ultramicrofossils, requiring the scanning electron microscope, have become increasingly significant. The Washington paleontologists covered all parts of the stratigraphic column, but their greatest area of specialist knowledge was in the Paleozoic. This is now a portion of time essentially neglected, and indeed few of those remaining in Washington are interested in fossils much older than the Cretaceous.

Summing this up and allowing for many exceptions, 1850–1925 may be characterized as an era overwhelmingly concerned with biostratigraphy, at least as far as invertebrate fossils were concerned. After the time of Meek, research was conducted by the paleontologists of the Geological Survey. Those few on the staff of the Museum worked hard, but because they were so few their efforts do not

---

[2] In 1999, the Menlo Park Mesozoic and Cenozoic collections, primarily Alaskan in origin, were transferred to the Museum of Paleontology at the University of California, Berkeley.

loom large. Like their counterparts, at least some of the studies were directed toward biostratigraphy. One need only look at the correlations charts published by the Geological Society of America to see the importance of the P&S staff and of Cooper from the Museum.

In marked contract, the last quarter of the 20th Century has seen an overwhelming emphasis on paleobiology. From 1925 through 1975, both approaches were employed. As the practical problems of age determination and correlation were resolved and as geophysical investigations of the subsurface became more important, the need to have paleontologists study both large and small fossils in relation to geologic problems declined in both the Federal and private sectors.

The end of paleontology in the Geological Survey is a classic example of success being the cause of failure. In the final analysis, it was forces within the Geological Survey that first minimized and then destroyed the field of paleontology. Ostensibly, these were all budget driven during the 1980s, yet the Museum had equally severe funding difficulties but was able to support its scientists. From the 1960s onward, the Geological Survey and the Museum had different objectives. The wonder is not that they had diverged, but that they existed in harmony under one roof for a century. Despite this difference in approach, retirees from the Geological Survey continue to conduct research at the Museum. This is an independent proof that changing views between administrators of the two organizations as to the kind of research which should be conducted had no direct effect on the course of events among individuals.

If one defines a "golden age" by number of persons employed, paleontology in Washington has passed its time in the sun and, indeed, the study of fossils is in decline worldwide. This should not be taken to mean that investigations of evolution, speciation or extinction are any less important. If Meek returned to the Museum a century after his death, though he would have been impressed with far better microscopes and lighting, and astounded by some of the groups of microfossils, nevertheless he would have understood what was being studied and why. Today, on the other hand, he would be bewildered by the kinds of problems addressed. It is an inaccurate metaphor that the modem-connected computer has replaced the geologic hammer, yet there is a kernel of truth in the observation. To a large extent, interest has shifted away from detailed study of particular groups of fossils.

Possibly, paleobiology will bring new intellectual advances. However, determining the significance of ideas on, say, life habit of a extinct organism, against the significance of determining the age of a rock from an unknown area, makes the classic problem of comparing apples and oranges appear to be child's play. Equally important, the great days of collecting fossils are over, for they are a non-renewable resource. Increasingly older collections will have to be mined for data and will of necessity produce somewhat skewed results. Nevertheless, that is better than considering fossils as icons, to be observed only from afar and not studied at all.

Private Biases Based on Examination of the Two Organizations

1. Working scientists in an organization are best supervised by a working scientist. The supervisor, in turn, must have the confidence and support of the higher levels of administration. The fewer the levels-the better!

2. For any museum or museum-like organization, collections and their proper care are fundamental. Collections are not the "end all," but they are the "be all" and "do all" of such places. Preserving the past and documenting past accomplishments are functions of a civilization.

3. Collection-based scientists should be near the collections they might want to study. Dead storage is an accurate descriptive term, as items relocated from areas of human activity lead to "out-of-sight, out-of-mind," and loss of their utility as intellectual stimulants. So far as the confusion

engendered by transfer of offices of scientists purely for the benefit of administrators, three moves is approximately equivalent to one fire.

4. The best and most enduring work is not necessarily done in the best physical environment. Lots of nice new space is fine, but it does not guarantee a good product. Required reading for everyone, but particularly for administrators, should be C. Northcote Parkinson's book *Parkinson's Law*.

5. Many scientists are *prima donnas* and do not necessarily interact well with colleagues. However, more often than not, isolation from other colleagues results in much routine publication, but a limited number of good ideas. The dual concepts of a "critical mass" of scientists and "optimum size" need to be more carefully explored in organizational structure.

6. Routine tasks done by highly trained people is a waste of money and time. Proper assistance is a key feature of a well-run organization. The best labor saving device is not a machine, but someone else doing the routine work.

7. Expansion in good times is fine. Hiring too many people of the same age, no matter how much promise they have, is not good. Organizations may age, but generally it is the aging staff without the infusion of new ideas from young people that causes problems, not the organizational framework.

8. Scientists should expect to be supported for long periods and encouraged to produce definitive works, rather than short term products. Anathema is too mild a word for the concept of annual programmatic research. Cutting paper work in an organization by trusting the staff would have the great benefit of forcing most "bean counters" to move elsewhere.

ACKNOWLEDGMENTS

This work is modified from an unpublished document prepared in 1996 by Yochelson and J. Thomas Dutro, Jr.; it also draws on Nelson and Yochelson (1980). Clifford Nelson also provided hard-to-find information on the careers of several early government paleontologists. Alan E. Leviton and Michael Ghiselin generously invited me to participate in a 1998 symposium at the California Academy of Sciences; subsequently, J. Thomas Dutro, Jr., William A. Oliver, Jr., Michele L. Aldrich, and Alan Leviton labored to make substantial improvements in its organization, not always at first to my liking! The staffs of the Smithsonian Institution Archives and USGS Photographic Library contributed significantly to the visual aspects of this summary.

REFERENCES

BARTLETT, R. A. 1962. *Great Surveys of the American West*. University of Oklahoma Press, Norman, Oklahoma. 408 pp.
EVELYN, D. E. 1985. The National Gallery at the Patent Office: 226–241. In H. J. Voila and C. Margolis, eds., *Magnificent Voyagers*. Smithsonian Institution Press, Washington, DC. 302 pp.
GILMORE, C. W. 1941. *A history of the Division of Vertebrate Paleontology in the United States National Museum*. Proceedings of the United States National Museum 90:305–377.
HAFERTEPE, K. 1984. *America's Castle*. Smithsonian Institution Press, Washington, DC. 180 pp.
KNIGHT, J. B. 1947. Paleontologist or Geologist. *Geological Society of America, Bulletin* 58:281–286.
MERRILL, G. P. 1901. The Department of Geology in the National Museum. *American Geologist* 28:107–123.
MOLNIA, B. F. 1999. Meet Charles Groat, Director of the U. S. Geological Survey (Part 2). *GSA Today* (September 1999):10–13.
NELSON, C. M. 1987. Meek in Albany 1852–1858. *Earth Sciences History* 6:40–46.
NELSON, C. M., and E. L. YOCHELSON. 1980. Organizing Federal paleontology in the United States, 1858–1907. *Journal of the Society for the Bibliography of Natural History* 9 (4):607–618.

OEHSER, P. H. 1949. *Sons of Science: The Story of the Smithsonian Institution and Its Leaders.* Henry Schuman, New York. 220 pp.

RABBITT, M. C. 1979. *Minerals, Lands, and Geology, for the Common Defense and the General Welfare: Volume 1, Before 1879.* United States Government Printing Office, Washington, DC. 331 pp.

RABBITT, M. C. 1980. *Minerals, Lands, and Geology, for the Common Defense and the General Welfare: Volume 2, 1879–1904.* United States Government Printing Office, Washington, DC. 407 pp.

RABBITT, M. C. 1986. *Minerals, Lands, and Geology, for the Common Defense and the General Welfare: Volume 3, 1904–1939.* United States Government Printing Office, Washington, DC. 479 pp.

RIVINUS, E. F. and E. M. YOUSSEF. 1992. *Spencer Baird of the Smithsonian.* Smithsonian Institution Press, Washington, DC. 228 pp.

STANTON, W. 1975. *The Great United States Exploring Expedition of 1838–1842.* University of California Press, Berkeley, California. 433 pp.

WALCOTT, C. D. 1900. Correspondence relating to collections of vertebrate fossils made by the late Professor O. C. Marsh. *Science* 11:21–24.

WEISS, M. and E. L. YOCHELSON. 1995. Ozarkian and Canadian systems: Gone and nearly forgotten: Pages 41-44 *in* J. D. Cooper, M. L. Droser, and S. C. Finney, eds., *Ordovician Odyssey: Short Papers for the Seventh International Symposium on the Ordovician System.* Pacific Section, Society for Sedimentary Geology, Fullerton, California. 498 pp.

YOCHELSON, E. L. 1967. Charles Doolittle Walcott 1859–1927. *National Academy of Sciences, Biographical Memoirs* 39:471–540.

YOCHELSON, E. L. 1969. Fossils — the how and why of collecting and storing. *Proceedings of the Biological Society of Washington* 82:585–601.

YOCHELSON, E. L. 1985. *The National Museum of Natural History: 75 years in the Natural History Building.* Smithsonian Institution Press, Washington, DC. 210 pp.

YOCHELSON, E. L. 1985a. The role and development of the Smithsonian Institution in the American geological community. Pages 337–354 *in* E. T. Drake and W. M. Jordan, eds., *Geologists and Ideas: A history of North American Geology.* Geological Society of America, Centennial Special Volume 1. Geological Society of America, Boulder, Colorado.

YOCHELSON, E. L. 1996. Discovery, collection, and description of the Middle Cambrian Burgess Shale Biota by Charles Doolittle Walcott. *Proceedings of the American Philosophical Society* 146 (4): 469–545.

YOCHELSON, E. L. 1998. *Charles Doolittle Walcott, Paleontologist.* Kent State University Press, Kent, Ohio. 510 pp.

Samurai at the Smithsonian
First Japanese Visitors to Western Museum in the U.S.

KAE TAKARABE
1-29-105 Kamimura-cho
Showa-ku, Nagoya, Japan 466-0802
E-mail: takarabe@info.human.nagoya-u.ac.jp

In 1860, at the very end of the Edo era, the Tokugawa Shogunate sent a mission, so-called Man'en Gannen Mission, to the United States of America in order to ratify the Japan-U.S. Treaty of Amity and Commerce. The mission members were the first official Japanese visitors to the U.S. with the exception of a few castaways.

In Edo [Tokyo] in 1603, a leading samurai was appointed by the emperor as his Shogun and with this designation he set up a feudal government, the Tokugawa Shogunate. In the three hundred year-long and peaceful Edo era, the status system of samurai-farmer-artisan-merchant became established and at the top of this were the samurai (samurai was a male-only status). The samurai were at first professional soldiers who fought with swords; however, under the peaceful circumstances that prevailed, gradually they became the learned officials of bureaucracy.

At the time Commodore Matthew C. Perry's squadron of ships arrived in 1853, Japan had been more or less shut off from the rest of the world for more than two hundred years in a self-imposed isolation. Nevertheless, there was a steady shift toward the opinion that Japan should open its doors and actively encourage the introduction of advanced foreign ideas. Being eager to obtain first-hand knowledge of the advanced country, some progressive officials conceived of the signing of the treaty as presenting an opportunity to tour in the United States. Strong opposition to the establishment of international relations, however, still existed within the country, and a political shakeup in the Shogunate brought about the downfall of these progressive officials, so that they were not able to travel as ambassadors.

Finally, in October, 1859, the post of the Ambassador was assigned to Masaoki Shimmi, a new Foreign Affairs Commissioner. Having served as Shogun's chamberlain for years, Shimmi was a refined gentleman, which was his major credential for appointment to an ambassadorship. The post of the Vice-Ambassador went to Norimasa Muragaki, another Foreign Affairs Commissioner. His experience in various posts in the Shogunate bureaucracy was recognized. Apparently, however, both Shimmi and Muragaki were less imaginative than the original innovative officials with respect to both experience in foreign affairs and eagerness to obtain foreign knowledge. The third ambassador was Censor [Counselor] Tadamasa Oguri, of the Censor's Office, who had a reputation for intelligence (Fig. 1). The three ambassadors were accompanied by seventeen officials, fifty-one servants, and six cooks. Most of the servants and cooks were samurai; so interested were they to participate in the mission, they were willing to take less prestigious positions in order to travel. Thus, the mission was composed largely of intellectuals.[1]

Leaving Edo on February 9, 1860, the seventy-seven mission members arrived in Washington, D.C., on May 14, having traveled by way of Honolulu, San Francisco, and Panama. During their 25-day stay in Washington, they exchanged the treaty ratification documents, attended official functions, and visited places of interest, among them being the Smithsonian Institution.[2] It was the first Japanese visit on record to a Western museum. At that time, the Smithsonian building contained a natural history "museum" along with other facilities, which would be identified as the precedents of both a science and technology museum and an art museum.

The purpose of this paper is to examine one of the least understood aspects of scientific contacts between Japan and the West at the end of the Edo era — in short, the *Japanese reception* of a Western-style natural history museum. I will first describe Japanese traditional exhibitions in the Edo era, and then trace how the Japanese mission came to visit the Smithsonian Institution. Finally I will interpret mission members' understandings and perceptions of the Institution and its museum.

1. Two Kinds of Exhibitions in the Edo Era

Toward the end of the Edo era, several official missions and many students who were sent to the West had the opportunity to see Western-style museums and exhibitions. Such experiences led to the opening of the first national exhibitions of products in Tokyo in 1871 because the new Meiji government was eager to encourage industries to catch up with the advanced countries of Europe and America. Furthermore, this form of exhibition was familiar to the people because two kinds

FIGURE. 1 Ambassadors of Man'en Gannen Mission. Left to right standing: Morita and Naruse; seated: Shimmi, Oguri, and Muragaki. (*The New York Illustrated News*, May 19, 1860)

of private exhibitions — Yakuhin'e and De-kaicho — had already been held during the Edo era. It should be noted that Japanese-style museums and exhibitions, in their earliest stages, developed together in Japan.[3] Because I believe that the objects displayed at the national exhibitions as well as the experiences with them in time must have had some impact on the creation of a national museum, let us first examine the configurations of the two Japanese traditional exhibitions that existed before the reception of Western-style museums.

(1) Yakuhin'e

Yakuhin'e was a kind of temporary exhibition of natural objects from various regions. Its purpose was to promote Honzogaku. Honzogaku, that is research on medicinal plants, animals, and minerals, had been introduced into Japan from China around the fifth or sixth century. In the earliest days of the Edo era — at the beginning of the seventeenth century — a systematic book, *Honzo Komoku* (1596), was introduced from China and stimulated Honzogaku. As *Honzo Komoku* gradually came to be understood and digested, Japanese "products," that is native Japanese plants, animals, and minerals, became objects to be dealt with. This trend culminated in *Yamato Honzo* (1708), in which 1362 species, including 358 Japanese indigenous products, were classified.[4]

Meanwhile, in its self-imposed isolation, Japan traded only with the Netherlands and China. In the mid-seventeenth century, two books, Rembert Dodoens's *Cruydt boeck* (Dutch version, 1644) on plants and John Johnstone's *Naeukeurige beschryving van de natuur der vier-voetige dieren, vissen en bloedloze waterdieren, vogelen, kronkeldieren, slangen en draken* (Dutch version, 1660) on animals, were introduced to Japan. These books were used by physicians and naturalists throughout the Edo era. Thus, in spite of its isolation, European natural history was introduced to Japan by way of Dutch books.[5]

With the development of Honzogaku, the first Yakuhin'e was held in Edo in 1757. This exhibition was arranged so that naturalists might exchange their knowledge about natural objects. One hundred and eighty objects were exhibited. Six years later, the advocate of Yakuhin'e, Gennai Hiraga, published *Butsurui Hinshitsu* (1763), an illustrated book in which he described 360 specimens chosen from about 2000 objects that had been exhibited at five previous Yakuhin'es. He had bought several Dutch natural history books, such as the ones mentioned above, and introduced knowledge on Dutch natural history in his *Butsurui Hinshitsu*. Because Gennai wanted to keep his exhibition academic, he forbade people from exhibiting freakish objects, such as entertaining deformities.[6]

As Yakuhin'e gradually spread among the large cities, such as Kyoto, Osaka, and Nagoya, and smaller towns, they became more popularized. A medical school in Nagoya, for example, has held a Yakuhin'e in Igakukan [medical building] on June 10 every year since 1831. From the beginning, this exhibition was open to the public. It included such unusual and rare objects as a mounted tiger, a mounted striped-mouse, a dried thorned-crab, various minerals, the skin of a large sea otter, a living snake with two heads, a living white bird [an albino raven], fossils, dried fish, sea shells, a living wild boar in a cage, a black raccoon dog, a crane, a stork, a living salamander in a tub, a mounted paradisean-bird, a mounted Senzanko, the dried skin of a large snake, as well as wooden and coppered human skeletons, which also served as teaching aids in the medical school. "Deposited carrot [maybe] from the lord" and dried bear's gall bladder were exhibited on the stand because they were very precious medicine (Fig. 2).[7] Thus, as time passed, entertainment became one of the aims of these exhibitions. However, considering that specimens such as animals, plants, and minerals were exhibited at these events, Yakuhin'e can be taken as a foundation of a natural history museum.

(2) De-kaicho

Shrines and temples sometimes open their secret statues of Buddha and God to the people in order to spread their dogmas. Such temporary exhibitions of treasures were known as Kaicho. The Edo era had two kinds of Kaicho; one was I-kaicho, the other De-kaicho. I-kaicho means that the secret statues, along with other treasures, were open to the public in the shrines and temples where their statues usually were set. De-kaicho means that local shrines and temples transported their treasures, including statues of Buddha and God, to big cities and opened them there to the public. Such exhibitions enabled the shrines and temples to collect donations as well as spread their dogmas. De-kaicho exhibitions were quite popular.

The first De-kaicho is said to have been held in the 1670s. Ekoin, a temple in Edo, often offered use of its land and buildings so that local shrines and temples could exhibit their treasures there. A catalog of collections exhibited at a De-kaicho was sometimes published.[8] When the De-kaicho of Horyuji in Nara was held in Edo in 1842, the objects used daily by the first Empress Suiko, such as shoes, appeared in the catalog. At the same time, shows, such as menageries and magic, were often held on the grounds outside. Many people came to Kaicho festivals (Fig. 3). Indeed, such festivals became entertainment for the people. On the other hand, considering the genuine antiquities that were exhibited inside the building, De-kaicho can be taken as another form of foundation of a natural history museum.

One would think that the tradition of exhibitions, such as Yakuhin'e and De-kaicho, would have

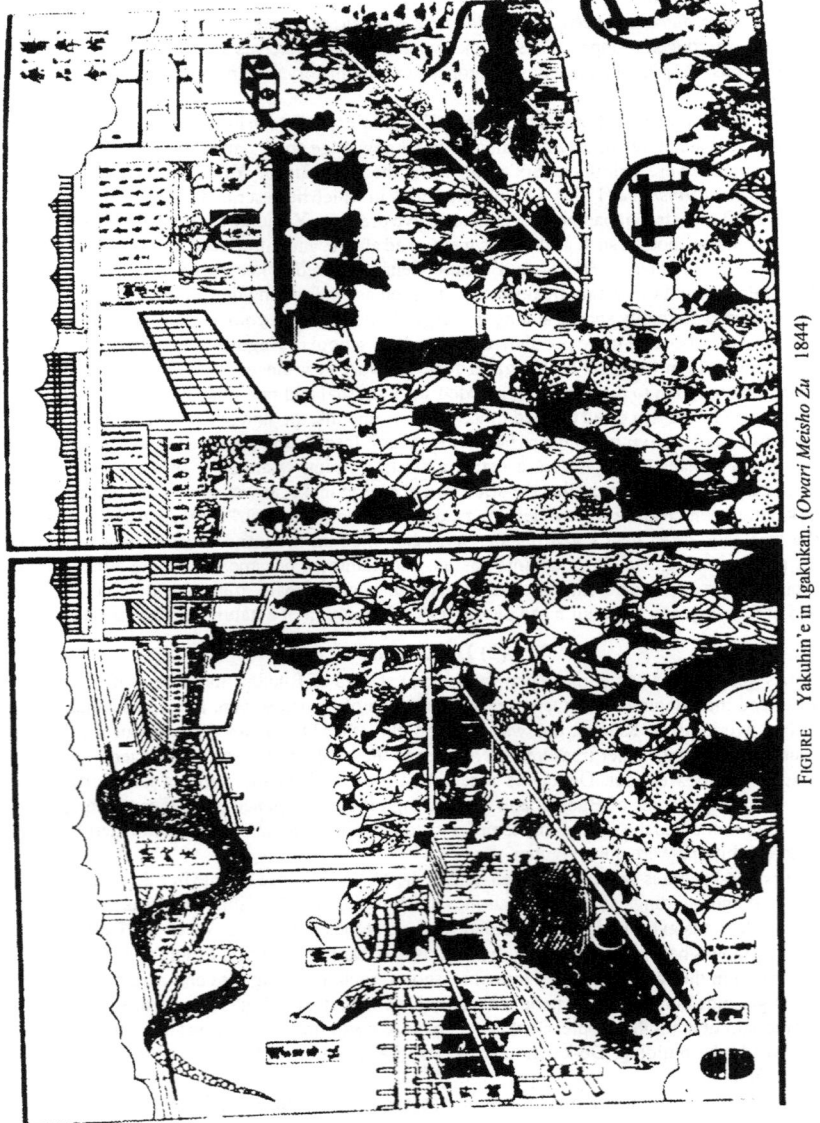

FIGURE Yakuhin'e in Igakukan. (*Owari Meisho Zu* 1844)

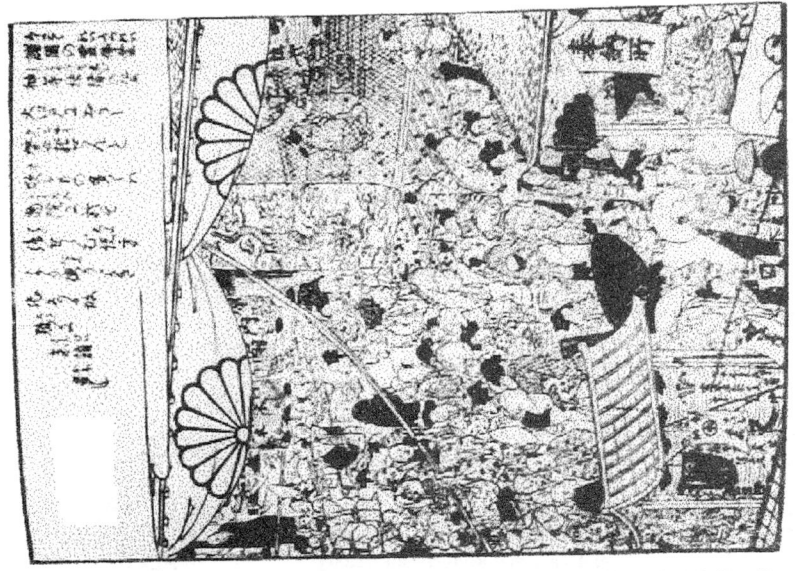

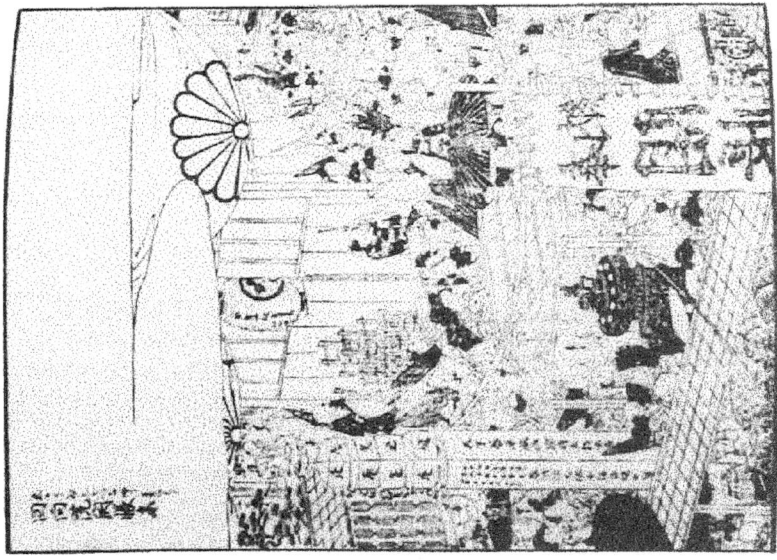

FIGURE De-kaichō in Ekoin. (*Edo Meisho Zue*, 1834–1836)

enabled Japan easily to accept Western-style exhibitions and museums. However, it should not be overlooked that the knowledge about Western museums was introduced to Japan mainly through translating foreign books. The Tokugawa Shogunate managed Bansho-shirabesho, a Research Center to investigate foreign books. Introductory articles on European museums, including such things as the description of the Egypt rooms in the British Museum, the Berlin Museum, and the Natural History Museum in Paris, appeared in the Dutch magazine, *Nederlandsch Magazijn* (1839, 1849), copies of which were imported by Bansho-shirabesho. Considering that the Japanese translation of selected passages of those magazines was published as *Gyokuseki Shirin*, at least some researchers must have read the articles on European museums, though it is not clear whether or not such knowledge had any impact on the later creation of a national museum.[9]

2. Henry's Invitation to the Smithsonian

Secretary of the Smithsonian Institution, Joseph Henry (Fig 4), was eager to invite the Japanese mission to the Institution. He wrote a letter directly to President James Buchanan, in which he referred to Captain John Rodgers who had participated in the North Pacific Exploring and Surveying Expedition. At the Liu-Kiu Islands [Okinawa], Rogers landed a detachment of marines and forced the Okinawans to guarantee the performance of their obligations under their treaty with the United States. He was also responsible for surveying the coast of Japan and the sea of Okhotsk.[10] Thus, he became well acquainted with Japanese history and manners and customs. When Henry met Rodgers later, Rodgers made a series of suggestions in regard to the treatment of the mission from Japan. At Henry's urging, he put them in writing. Among Rodgers' suggestions are the following:

FIGURE 4. Joseph Henry, Secretary of the Smithsonian Institution. Courtesy Smithsonian Institution Archives (10668).

> The only means by which this embassy can be favorably impressed with the superiority of our civilization and institutions is to give them a clear idea of our science, our arts, our arms, and our government. For this purpose the Embassy should be introduced to different institutions of learning ... For example, a series of experimental illustrations in science might be given to them at the Smithsonian Institution, in which some of the most interesting results of modern discoveries should be exhibited.[11]

Henry tried to impress President Buchanan with the importance of the Smithsonian Institution, and referring to Rodgers' suggestions said,

> One of the suggestions [by Captain Rodgers] alludes to the cooperation of the Smithsonian Institution, and I need scarcely say in behalf of this establishment that any services which may be required in the line indicated, will be cheerfully rendered.[12]

Meanwhile, a Naval Commission was organized in Washington, D. C., to take charge of the Japanese mission to the United States. It consisted of Captain Samuel F. Du Pont, Commander Sidney Lee, Lieutenant David Porter, C. J. MacDonald (secretary), and A. C. Portman (interpreter). Because Du Pont, Lee, and Porter participated in Commodore Perry's Japan expedition, it was no surprise that they were selected to take charge of the Japanese mission. The commission was supposed to arrange the places for the mission to visit.[13] After this commission had been organized, Henry wrote several letters to Captain Du Pont in order to invite the Japanese to the Smithsonian Institution. The final letter from Henry to Du Pont, dated May 30, shows that Henry had a chance, in private, to extend the Japanese an invitation to visit the Institution. In this letter, Henry also wrote that they had made extensive preparations for doing honor to the Japanese and that he intended to demonstrate the galvanic battery.[14] Three days later, on June 2, the Japanese ambassadors did visit the Smithsonian Institution.

From this series of letters, both Rodgers and Henry's strong sense of superiority about American civilization, including its institutions, is very clear. Henry was eager to demonstrate his latest experiments at the Smithsonian Institution in order to impress the Japanese visitors. Because of his academic interest in electricity, in these letters Henry emphasized his desire to demonstrate the galvanic battery experiment. However, the experiment was not the only thing shown to the Japanese mission; the Smithsonian collection was also shown to them.

TABLE 1. Schedule of mission members' visit to the Smithsonian Institution. Henry's experiments were carried out on June 2.

Date	Member	Age	Executive Position
5.21	Kanae Sano	30	Servant of Masuzu
5.26	Masakiyo Yanagawa	25	Servant of Shimmi
	Sadayu Tamamushi	37	Servant of Shimmi
	Tadazane Nonomura	43	Servant of Muragaki
	Yoshikoto Fukushima	19	Servant of Oguri
	Tetsuta Kimura	31	Servant of Oguri
	Hidenaga Sato	37	Cook
5.31	Shunjiro Masuzu	32	Under Officer of the Treasurer
	Tameyoshi Hitaka	24	Official of the Censor
	Ryugen Miyazaki	34	Physician
	Hakugen Murayama	32	Surgeon
6.2	Masaoki Shimmi	40	Ambassador
	Norimasa Muragaki	48	Vice-Ambassador
	Motonori Namura	34	Chief Interpreter
6.5	Okataro Morita	49	Treasurer
	Jugoro Tsukahara	36	Official of the Ambassadors
	Onojiro Tateishi	17	Junior Interpreter

3. Mission Members' Perceptions of the Smithsonian

The above-mentioned Henry letters could lead to a misunderstanding that none of the mission members visited the Institution until June 2. Indeed, it seems to be true that Henry was interested in showing his experiments only to the Japanese official ambassadors and not other members of the mission, such as their servants. However, not only did other mission members visit the Institution when they had time (Table 1),[15] but all of the mission members who did visit the Institution were samurai.

In order to assess mission members' understandings and perceptions of the Smithsonian Institution, especially its natural history museum, and to the actual conditions and organizations as they were in 1860, reference can be made to impressions as recorded in a number of personal diaries.[16]

(1) Smithsonian Institution

The Smithsonian Institution is an extensive museum and research complex, today including 16 museums, the National Zoological Park, and research centers.[17] The Institution was established in

Washington, D. C., in 1846, based on the property which James Smithson bequeathed "to the United States of America, to found at Washington, under the name of the Smithsonian Institution, an Establishment for the increase and diffusion of knowledge among men."[18] When Japanese mission members visited the Institution, it had pursued various fields of research such as astronomy, geography, meteorology, geology, botany, physiology, comparative anatomy, zoology, natural history, terrestrial magnetism, antiquities, and (comparative) philology.[19]

As to the Institution as a whole, the mission members who had just toured the building (and had not observed Henry's experiments) understood the Institution as "the place to collect rare objects from various regions" or "the place for deposit of treasury." On the other hand, the members who had both observed Henry's experiments and toured the building got different impressions. The Vice-Ambassador Muragaki, for example, wrote in his diary that it was "a mansion which contained rare objects or in which the truth of things got revealed."[16(e)] Furthermore, Interpreter Motonori Namura wrote of it as "an office where machines such as electricity are deposited."[16(g)] Such machines seem to have greatly impressed Namura.

The Smithsonian building, which we have come to know as "the Castle," was completed on the Mall in 1855. Most early government buildings being light in tone, the Castle was the Romanesque style of dark red sandstone with towers and battlements. It had a stunning impact.[20] The Japanese mission visited the Institution a scant five years after the building had been completed. As to the external appearance of the building, most mission members described it as "huge" and "temple-like." Some of members referred to a fence around the building site; others noticed two cross-shaped gateposts. Tetsuta Kimura, for example, in his diary illustrated the gateposts as well as the building (Figs. 5a–b). According to him, the gateposts were made so that only one visitor could enter through them. On the other hand, Sadayu Tamamushi understood that they were used to avoid being crowded or a carriage's entrance. The interior of the building contained a museum, an apparatus room, a picture gallery, a lecture room, a library, a publication room, and other rooms such as laboratories.

How did mission members perceive such facilities?

(2) Museum Hall

Henry thought the increase of knowledge more important than its diffusion. "The increase of knowledge is much more difficult," Henry insisted, "and in reference to the bearing of this institution on the character of our country and the welfare of mankind much more important than the diffusion of knowledge. There are at this time thousands of institutions actively engaged in the diffusion of knowledge in our country, but not a single one which gives direct support to its increase."[21] In his opinion, original researches requiring difficult experiments should be carried out in the Institution.

He had little sympathy for the congressional mandate to create a library and a museum because he viewed institutions of that kind as repositories of knowledge already acquired, not as contributors to its increase. Therefore, Henry did not want to use his limited resources to improve and maintain a museum. Reflecting Henry's policy, the collections already stored in the Smithsonian Institution were not fully displayed to the public owing to the lack of suitable cases, although they were accessible to naturalists and in constant use by them.

However, the time came when Henry was forced to change his own stance. Congress in March, 1857, made an appropriation for the construction of suitable cases to be installed in the Smithsonian hall to contain the natural history collection of the Wilkes Exploring Expedition and others belonging to the government.[22] Congress also agreed to pay for moving expenses and four thousand dollars yearly for maintenance. Since 1840 these collections, up to then, had been stored in the Patent Office

FIGURE. 5a. Kimura's illustration of the Smithsonian Institution.
(Tetsuta Kimura, *Kobeiki*, Seichosha: 1974)

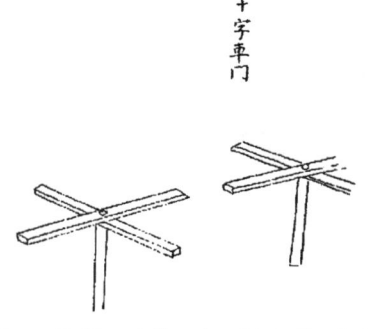

スミツワシヨチヱン

十字平門

FIGURE. 5b. Kimura's illustration of the Smithsonian's two cross-shaped gateposts.
(Tetsuta Kimura, *Kobeiki*, Seichosha: 1974)

Building (Fig. 6) under Joel Pointsett's National Institute for the Advancement of Science.[23] In 1858, they were finally moved to the Castle and appropriately arranged.

Eventually, Henry himself came to terms with the museum mandate, noting in the Institution's *Annual Report for 1858*, that "The principal event of importance in the history of the Institution during the past year is the transfer of the government collections from the Patent Office to the large room of the Smithsonian Building."[24] This action by Congress was significant because it vastly increased the museum role of the Smithsonian. Assistant Secretary Spencer Baird promptly became curator of the museum collections and operations.[25] Baird, whose interests lay in the natural rather than physical sciences, believed that the way to find basic truths in scientific research was to assemble large collections of physical specimens and to develop conclusions from careful comparisons of tangible objects.[26] Under his guidance, the museum developed rapidly. Thus, it should be noted that Japanese mission visited the Institution only two years after the various collections had been transferred from the Patent Office, in short, after the museum role increased. According to the *Annual Report of the Smithsonian Institution for 1860*, the museum devoted itself to the completion of its series of specimens illustrating the natural history of North America. Nearly all the mammals, the North American birds, and the exotic water birds exhibited in the museum, were labeled with both scientific and vernacular names. A large number of skins of North American mammals and birds not previously exhibited were mounted and placed in cases. All the old stands of mounted specimens were replaced by new ones. Duplicate specimens were prepared for distribution to the principal museums in the world. Some scientific catalogs had already been published by the Institution.[27] Thus,

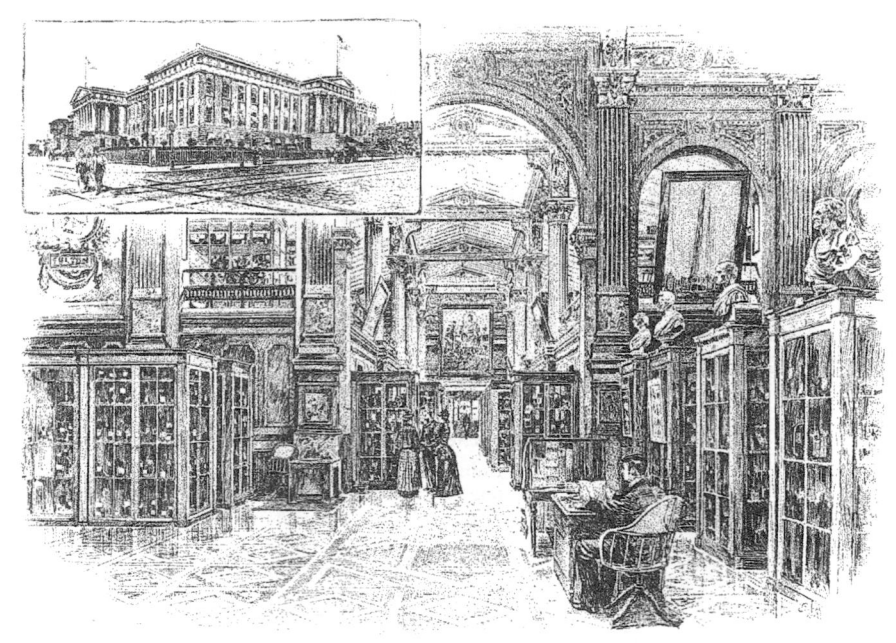

FIGURE 6. Patent Office Building interior.
Courtesy Smithsonian Institution Archives.

TABLE 2. Entries in the Record Books of the Smithsonian Collection. (*Annual Report of the Smithsonian Institution*, 1860)

Objects	1851	1852	1853	1854	1855	1856	1857	1858	1859	1860
Skeletons and skulls	911	1074	1190	1275	2050	3060	3340	3413	3650	4350
Mammals		114	198	351	1200	2046	3200	3226	3750	4575
Birds				4353	4425	5855	8766	11390	15913	20875
Reptiles						106	239	4370	4616	4683
Fishes						155	613	1136	1740	2975
Eggs of birds								1032	2525	4425
Crustacea								939	939	979
Mollusks									2000	8832
Radiates									1100	1308
Fossils									171	705
Minerals									793	1132
Ethnological specimens										550
TOTALS	911	1188	1388	5979	7675	11222	16158	25506	37197	55389

by the time the mission visited the Smithsonian, its museum had already undergone a transformation with respect to both volume of collections and their arrangement or classification (Table 2).

The collections of the museum were exhibited both on the first floor and on the mezzanine of the main building (Fig. 7). A ground plan of the museum and collections of the museum hall at that time suggests that the Smithsonian building housed a natural history museum that included botany, zoology, mineralogy, and anthropology and archeology (Fig. 8, Table 3).[28] The museum of the Smithsonian Institution had responded to the idea of Charles Willson Peale, who had founded the first popular museum in America, that all people should come face-to-face with nature in a museum.[29]

The museum hall was so huge that it greatly impressed many of the mission members, who made reference to its size in their diaries. Masakiyo Yanagawa, who had visited the Patent Office Building five days earlier, tried to compare these two halls of collections. First, he thought that both halls were identical and described them as "a kind of Igakukan." His reference to Igakukan [medical building] suggests that he had been to a Yakuhin'e at which the natural history exhibition was held in the Igakukan, or that at least he had heard about it. But, he then concluded that the hall of the Smithsonian was "bigger and had more various objects."[16(l)]

The museum hall contained various collections, such as rare mammals, birds, insects, fish, and objects from all over the world. Such collections may have overwhelmed the visiting mission members. Tamamushi, for example, expressed that "every collection" was "amazing."[16(k)] Tadazane Nonomura correctly pointed out that collections were classified, noting in his diary that "birds,

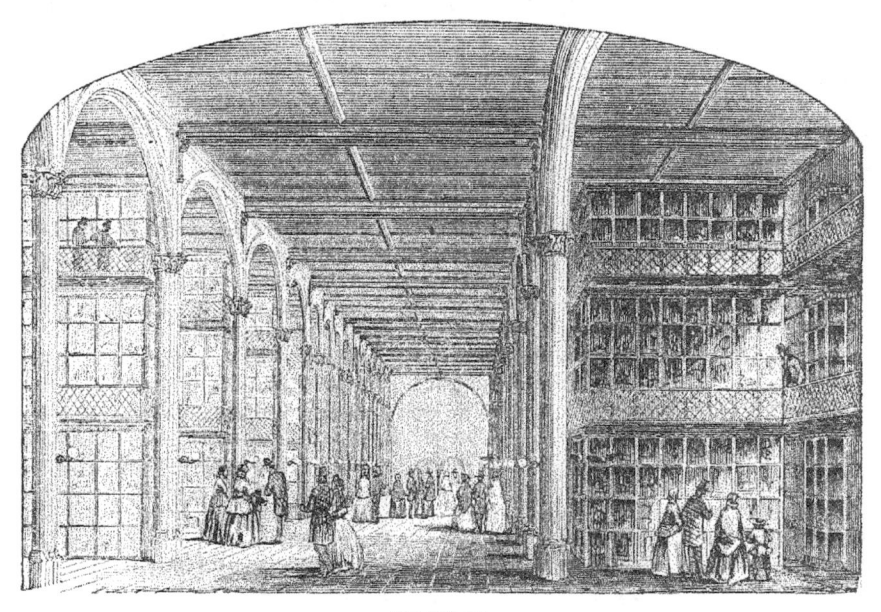

FIGURE 7. Museum Hall of the Smithsonian Institution. Courtesy Smithsonian Institution Archives (91–17967).

First Floor

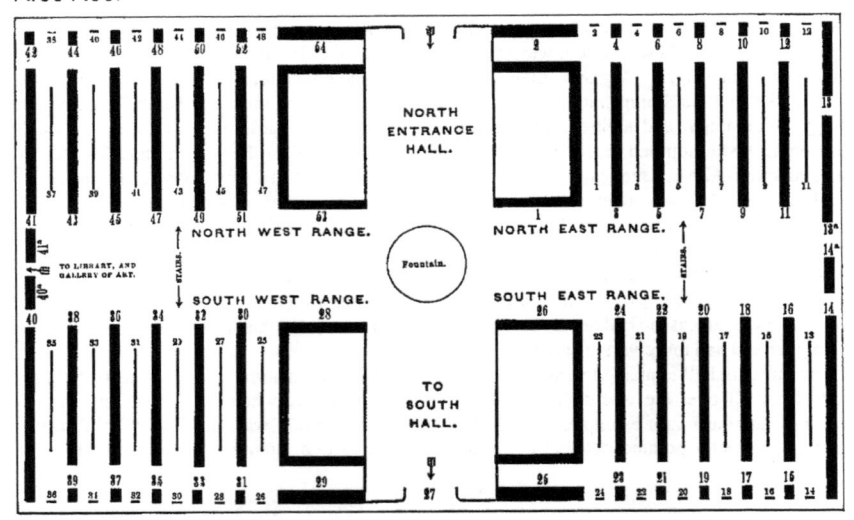

Mezzanine

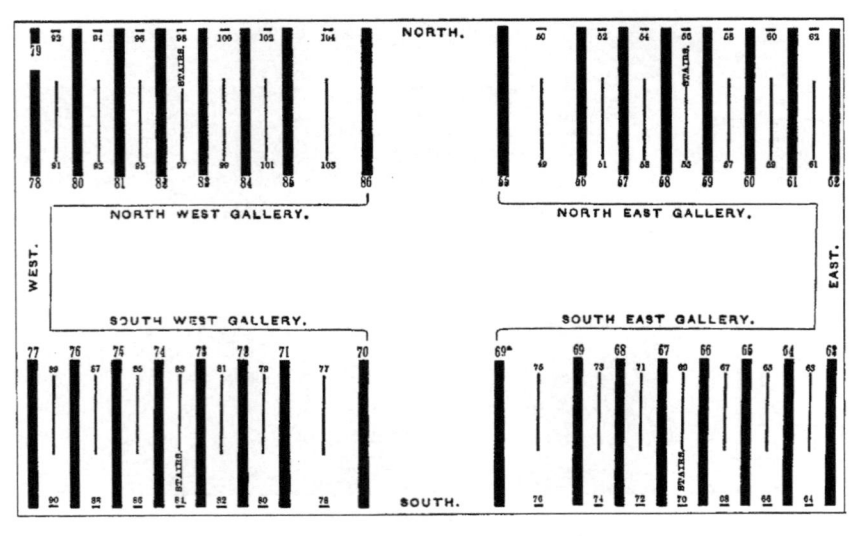

FIGURE 8. Museum of the Smithsonian Institution. Black lines: upright cases; light lines: table and window cases. After William J. Rhees, *An Account of the Smithsonian Institution, its Founder, Building, Operations, etc.*, Collins Printer, 1863.

TABLE 3. Collections of Museum Hall. (From William J. Rhees, *An Account of the Smithsonian Institution, its Founder, Building, Operations, etc.*, Collins Printer, 1863)

First Floor	Northeast Range	Mammals, foreign birds, North American fishes
	Southeast Range	North American birds, reptiles, some marine animals
	Northwest Range	Genera of fishes, foreign birds, reptiles
	Southwest Range	Mammals, radiates, crustaceans, reptiles, fishes of North Pacific Exploring Expedition
	South Hall	Sarcophagus from Beirut, plank from redwood tree (California), copper from Lake Superior mines, living alligator from Georgia, idols from Nicaragua
Mezzanine	Northeast Gallery	Collections of mineralogy, geology, paleontology
	Southeast Gallery	Human skulls, skulls and skeletons, skins of reptiles and fishes, botany
	Northwest Gallery	Ethnological collections from East Indies, China, Japan, South America, Africa, mummies from Egypt and Peru
	Southwest Gallery	Ethnological collections from the Feejee, Sandwich, Marquesas, New Zealand, and other islands
Table Cases		Center of hall→East end: Nests, eggs, meteorite, ores
		Center of hall→West end: Shells, turtles

mammals, fish, turtles, snakes, and shells are grouped into such parts."[16(h)] Kimura described not only the groupings of the objects but also the labels that related to them.[16(e)] Both scientific and vernacular names appeared on the labels. Hidenaga Sato referred to the process of collecting specimens, writing that "Whenever American people go to other states and obtain rare objects, the objects are supposed to be kept here [the Smithsonian Institution]."[16(j)] In addition, many members were interested in the upright glass cases in which specimens were displayed. In Japan, glass sheets were not produced at that time. Kanae Sano, for example, noted them as "cabinets with sliding-glasses like Shoji [Japanese sliding paper screen]."[16(i)]

The arrangement of displays in the museum interested the visitors. Mammals, birds, fish, amphibians, and reptiles were on the first floor. Mission members were particularly engaged by the mounted mammals and birds and admired the elaborateness of them. Nonomura, for example, described that "skins of mammals and birds were removed from the bodies and something were stuffed into the skin. The colors of their skins and eyes are quite the same as living ones."[16(h)] Among the mounted animals, the great apes such as orangutans and gorillas especially fascinated members — which brings to mind the fact that Europeans were themselves puzzled when they first came face to face with great apes in the seventeenth and eighteenth centuries. During the Edo era, Japanese had almost no chance directly to observe living great apes. Living orangutans had been brought to Nagasaki in 1792 and again in 1800, but owing to the cold climate, they did not survive long. Thus, few people had a chance to see them. A Japanese doctor who had observed two different orangutans described them in his book on Western natural history. The doctor illustrated two orangutans; one copied from Dutch books, the other a copy of a sketch of the above-mentioned orangutan in Nagasaki. He concluded that the sketch of the Nagasaki orangutan was right. The skins of the orangutans, which had died in Nagasaki, were stored in a certain house; one of them is said to have been exhibited in Yakuhin'e in Edo in 1838.[30]

The only person to refer to the sea mammals on display was Muragaki. He described them as "sea cows and seals which I saw in Ezo."[16(e)] Muragaki was once an official in Ezo [Hokkaido, a northern island], where he explored to cultivate the land. Considering his background, it is not surprising that they interested him. In a like manner, only Sato described lions, noting that "There are quite differences between a lion exhibited here and a lion appeared on Japanese paintings; the face of the former is longer than the latter and the former has long hair from its neck to shoulder."[16(j)] Living lions were not brought to Japan until 1865. Accordingly, Sato was forced to rely on lions that appeared in Japanese paintings as his reference point. In the eighteenth century, some people who had seen a lion in Western natural history books, also said that it was quite different from the Japanese painting of a lion.[31] Indeed, a Japanese traditional lion on paintings had a round face with curly hair! Sato also described "a deer whose antlers look like open-hands." It could be a moose or an elk; however, it is not clear which one he had in mind. He continued to write that "The deer is as big as a horse and was once used, instead of a horse, to draw a cart."[16(j)] It may have been an Arctic reindeer.

These descriptions remind us again of the fact that the mission members were samurai, who had little knowledge about Western natural history. Owing to the lack of such knowledge, mission members tried to understand such unfamiliar objects, relying on individual limited experience. At that time, Japanese physicians and naturalists had already learned something of Western natural history, especially through Dutch publications, and so they were familiar with such illustrations. Therefore, the physician Ryugen Miyazaki and surgeon Hakugen Murayama, both of whom had visited the Institution, would have been much more familiar with the collections than other mission members. It is, therefore, regrettable that they did not write a little about the Institution in their respective diaries.[16(f)]

As mentioned above, mammals and birds were exhibited as mounted forms. On the other hand, amphibians and reptiles were soaked in alcohol and placed in glass bottles. Some members were surprised to see so many specimens of snakes. Muragaki directly expressed his "unpleasant" feelings when he saw too many snakes and serpents.

In addition to these collections, a dress, worn by a famous American Arctic explorer, Dr. Elisha Kent Kane, was brought to the museum by him and also exhibited on the first floor. The dress was made of animal skins, including fox, bear, and bird.[32] Only Tamamushi noted that "there is a doll made out of hide. It is about 180 to 210 centimeters high. They say that an American doctor wore the dress when he went to a cold country."[16(k)] Tamamushi had once been an official assigned to explore in Ezo. All explorers in Ezo wore such fur dresses at that time. Accordingly, Dr. Kane's fur dress may have been familiar to Tamamushi.

Other anthropological collections were exhibited on the mezzanine. Most of them had been transferred from the Patent Office in 1858. Thus, the objects brought by Perry's Japan Expedition were exhibited there.[33] The Japanese objects attracted mission members' attention and in their diaries they referred to many objects such as lacquer ware, silk such as Noshime[plain] and Chirimen[lit], cotton fabric, Mino-gami[mulberry fiber], pottery vase, fans, umbrellas, smoking pipes, Kamidana [family Shinto altar], wooden clogs, straw raincoat, samurai sword, polearm, lance, tools such as chisels, nail, plane, hoe sickle, ploughshare, and dolls. They described these items in detail. In addition, Okataro Morita paid attention to the sender of an exhibited letter. The sender, Mantaro Matsuzaki, who had studied Confucianism, was one of Morita's acquaintances. Because Morita had worked at Gakumonjo [Shogunate Learning Center], he had become acquainted with Matsuzaki. Tamamushi, who had earlier visited the Patent Office, wrote that "there are more Japanese objects [here] than the Patent Office."[16(k)]

On the other hand, the various objects brought from Japan, which was in its self-imposed isolation, so overwhelmed Sano that he could not help thinking about the purpose of the collection.

Some years before, Commodore Perry collected Japanese clothes such as female jackets and white underwears. In the other cabinets, there are Japanese swords and farm implements. Even Japanese objects have been collected in this way, and so we cannot tell how many objects there are from other countries with which this country has been in friendly relations for a long time. In this place, there are various rare objects from all over the world. I cannot have any ability to think of the purpose of the place. I guess that it is the place to collect various objects, to show them to the public, and to broaden people's knowledge. I have no time to take my eyes off such objects.[16(i)]

When he was in Japan, Sano had learned Dutch and how to use guns, and he took part in this mission in order to learn Western tactics and the art of navigation. Although he may have been unfamiliar with exhibitions such as Yakuhin'e, he correctly understood the nature of the museum as the place to "collect various objects, to show them to the public, and to broaden people's knowledge."

Other anthropological objects which drew the special attention of mission members were mummies from Egypt and Peru. Although mummies had been brought to Japan since the end of the sixteenth century, mummy imports were rare. After reaching Japan, whole bodies were ordinarily powdered into medicine. Accordingly, few people ever had a chance to see a mummy as a whole. The medicine itself was so expensive that people could not obtain it easily.[34]

About the mummies on display, Tamamushi wrote that they made him "feel dread." Vice-Ambassador Muragaki recorded this impression in his diary:

. dried human bodies[mummies] . . . are standing. I cannot tell their sexual differences. It is said that such objects should be exhibited here in order to find the truth of everything from all over the world. However, to display human bodies as well as other birds, mammals, insects, and fish astonishes me so much. They [American people] are worth being called barbarians.[16(e)]

Interestingly, he thought that displaying human mummies along with other animals was an indication of American barbarity, contrary to Secretary Henry's intention to show off the latest science at the Smithsonian Institution. Muragaki was not an ultranationalist; however, he was not able to free himself from his Japanese sense of values.

Apart from the anthropological collections, Yanagawa noted that there were "a lot of stones such as gold, silver, copper, and iron produced from various countries" on the mezzanine.

In the South Hall, there were so-called eye-catchers such as a sarcophagus from Beirut (Syria), a plank from a California redwood tree, copper from Lake Superior mines, a living alligator from Georgia, and idols from Nicaragua.[35] An alligator kept alive in a water tank especially interested many mission members. Someone let the alligator out of the tank and then struck it with a stick so that in anger it opened its large mouth. Muragaki was surprised to see so large a mouth opening. Though he correctly identified the species as a Wani [alligator or crocodile], he wrote that it had "scales on the back" and its appearance looked like "a gecko." During the Edo era, Japanese had little chance to observe directly living alligators, although a specimen of alligator was exhibited in Yakuhin'e in Edo in 1838.[36]

Despite some misunderstandings about each collection, mission members generally seem to have correctly perceived that the museum hall kept animals, plants, minerals, and anthropological objects so that visitors could see them.

(3) Apparatus Room and Henry's Experiments

There was an apparatus room on the second floor in the main building (Fig. 9). The room was not only equipped with collections of scientific instruments but also arranged to allow for some scientific experiments. Most of those machines had been donated by Dr. Robert Hare of Philadelphia,

FIGURE 9. Apparatus Room of the Smithsonian Institution.
Courtesy Smithsonian Institution Archives (43804–G).

who had accumulated much of the apparatus during his twenty-nine years as professor of chemistry at the University of Pennsylvania Medical School. His large electrical machine was on an elevated platform of the room. The hair of a person sitting in the throne-like chair on the platform under the machine was supposed to be made to stand on end as a result of an electric charge.[37]

In addition to the Hare collections, the room contained a full set of pneumatic instruments constructed for the Smithsonian Institution, a set of ingenious instruments for illustrating wave motion, Page's electro-magnetic instrument, and a large Fresnel lens used in light-houses. Furthermore, the room had a hydroelectric machine imported from Germany by the Institution itself. The machine gave a constant succession of sparks, and charged a battery of sixteen large jars in thirty seconds.[38]

On June 2, as mentioned above, Henry demonstrated various experiments in this room. Only ambassadors with two interpreters and some officials had a chance to see the experiments:

> Mission members were trying to separate Magdeburg hemispheres in vain; they were not able to easily separate his hand from the mouth of a vacuum glass bottle, either. They observed charcoal burned by discharged electricity and iron acted by electromagnet. They also tried to grip the handle of storage battery.[39]

Otto von Guericke's 17th century "Magdeburg hemispheres" experiment, in which air is evacuated from within a hollow sphere, making it almost impossible to separate the two halves of the sphere without letting air back in, shows that air can exert enormous pressure. Japanese mission members tried to separate the hemispheres in vain. An American company later advertised its glue by making use of the event (Fig. 10). Concerning his experience there, Muragaki noted that "There are various electric machines. Lightning in the dark. I saw various magic."[16(e)] Secretary Henry intended to show off the latest science. Indeed, it is not surprising that Muragaki would be amazed at Henry's experiments; he was not a scientist and he had no scientific knowledge to evaluate it correctly.

Other members of the mission, who visited the apparatus room at times other than when Henry gave his demonstrations on June 2, were able only to observe the machines that were in the room. What interested those mission members most was the Fresnel lens, though they referred to it as a big mirror. Yoshikoto Fukushima, for example, recorded the following details:

FIGURE 10. Advertisement of glue by Spalding. *Man'en Gannen Kenbei Shisetsu Zuroku.*

> There is a big mirror. It is about 150 centimeters wide. It is round with a big stand. It is nine-centimeter thick glass and both faces can reflect something. When we look at our own images in it, the images become more than twice. How unique it is![16(a)]

Fukushima's description highlights both what interested him and his understanding of the device. Morita, on the other hand, described the functioning of the lens more correctly in observing that "When we go behind a square mirror, our own images on the front become ten times as large as ourselves."[16(d)] In that room, according to Kimura's report, there were also other apparatus such as a telescope, a terrestrial globe, and a celestial globe. Because these members were not able to observe Henry's experiments, they seem to have perceived the apparatus room as the place where various machines were exhibited rather than a place in which experiments were performed. Indeed, the room could be identified as setting a precedent of a science and technological museum.

(4) Gallery of Art

One important feature of the art gallery (Fig. 11) was the interesting series of portraits, mostly full size, of over one hundred and fifty North American Indians, with sketches of scenery. These portraits were all taken from life and were accurate representations of the peculiar features of prominent individuals of forty-three different tribes. The room also contained a marble statue, a copy of the celebrated work of art in Rome, the "Dying Gladiator."[40] Many of the mission members referred to the gallery in their diaries. Kimura, for example, described what he saw as follows:

> White stone was carved into the shape of a person. The person was naked and the privates parts were covered with an oak leaf. There was a bleeding wound under the arm; the wound was pressed by the left hand. Lots of pains .... On every side of the room there were portraits. The people looked different from those of today because they had lived in the old times.[16(c)]

At that time, Japanese were not familiar with such a marble statue, and so many members became interested in it. They also paid attention to the portraits of Native Americans. However they did not have the capability to see through the suggestion of the gallery — the sculpture indicated a conscious

FIGURE 11. Gallery of Art of the Smithsonian Institution. Courtesy Smithsonian Institution Archives (43804-D).

visual comparison between the plight of the Native American peoples and the dying heroes of a classical world.[41]

Muragaki was distracted by entirely unrelated objects in the room. For instance, he wrote "On the wall were also hung specimens of the hair of the successive Presidents. This reveals that they [American people] are not courteous at all."[16(e)] The hair to which Muragaki referred was on display in an exhibit called "Hair of the Presidents of the United States with other Persons of Distinction, Prepared and Arranged by John Varden, February, 1853." Included in this exhibit was a collection of tiny locks of hair, identified by name-tags as coming from the first fourteen Presidents, from George Washington through Franklin Pierce. The hair of the Presidents was supposed to call to mind the memory of national leaders and the continuity of power. However, Muragaki misread it as a sign of disrespect for leaders.[42] Henry's intention to show off American superiority did not work well again.

Other facilities in the building also attracted the attention of mission members. Yanagawa, for example, described a lecture room on the second floor in detail:

> In the building was a lecture platform built up high above the floor. In front of it were many seats. On the walls of the hall there were pictures portraying the sorrows and joys of life from birth to death. By the side of the platform there was a recumbent statue carved in marble of a nude woman larger than life size.[6(l)]

As we have seen above, there was a natural history museum in the Smithsonian Building. There were also precedents both of a science and technology museum and of an art museum. At the Smithsonian, Henry intended to show off American superiority in science. Generally speaking, the American side, including Henry himself, seemed to have been content with the results of Japanese visit to the Institution. The Journal of the Commission, in Charge of the Japanese Embassy to the U.S., for example, observed that the Smithsonian Institution offered the delegation an opportunity to see "a number of interesting experiments in physics and chemistry, which had prepared with great care," and also "the library and the valuable collection of specimens of natural history, as well as the innumerable objects of interest and curiosity from all parts of the world."[43]

Although mission members did not have enough scientific knowledge to appreciate fully all they had seen, they tried to understand the Smithsonian Institution, its several facilities, and its collections. Each member picked up on those objects that teased his curiosity and described them in his diary.

Conclusions

The experiences of the Japanese mission members at the Smithsonian Institution did not have any immediate effect on the founding of the first natural history museum in Japan.[44] The mission's influence, or lack of it, was inextricably linked to other historical events, and to understand the situation, we must take into consideration Japanese political conditions as they existed at the time. Under the slogan "Respect the Emperor and Expel the Aliens," the anti-Shogunate movement had become more serious during the mission members' absence. The Shogunate government had been forced to change its foreign policies; it was trying to keep foreign influence to minimum. Accordingly, the Shogunate gave the returning mission a cool reception, not even firing a salute when their ship entered the harbor. Meanwhile, America's East Asian policy had become inactive because of the Civil War (1861–1865).

Following the Meiji Restoration in 1868, three of the previous ambassadors in the mission were not asked to serve the new government. Therefore, the mission is often said to have had little impact on the new government. Their experiences at the Smithsonian, however, should not be underestimated, considering the indirect influence they had that led to the creation of the first Japanese museum.

First, it is obvious that advanced technology reported by the ambassadors was not overlooked by the Meiji government, because the government's first overseas mission visited the United States, in 1872, before going to Europe.[44] Along with advanced technology, their knowledge about the Smithsonian would also have been handed down to the Meiji government through mission members' diaries and reports. When the Japanese mission was about to give Lewis Cass, U.S. Secretary of State, splendid specimens of Japanese skill, he declined the offer. That is because American officials could not accept presents from any foreign authority without the assent of Congress. Such presents were supposed to become the property of the nation and had to be deposited in a place where they would be open for public inspection.[45] Muragaki had correctly noted the event and its reason in his diary. The event was significant in that Muragaki had learned that objects could be deposited in a place that was open to the public. Thus, the nature of a museum as well as the description of the Smithsonian museum would certainly have been handed down to the Meiji government through his diary. Furthermore, copies of their diaries and reports continued to be read quietly but earnestly among the public, in spite of the serious anti-Shogunate movement, and they survived until the Meiji era.

Second, five members — Tameyoshi Hitaka, Shunjiro Masuzu, Kawasaki, Sano, and Sato — participated in the Mission to Europe in 1862. Namura also took part in the Mission to Russia in 1866. On both occasions, they had opportunity to observe other Western museums. Masuzu, for example, wrote about a museum in London, presumably the British Museum. The knowledge they had obtained at the Smithsonian probably served as a reference point for their later visits to other Western museums.

Third, because several mission members became teachers, they had opportunity to inform their students about the United States. The mission members' knowledge would, thus, have been passed on to the next generation. For example, two of Tamamushi's students accompanied a certain person to study at the U. S. Naval Academy in Annapolis. Assuredly, Tamamushi's knowledge about America must have been passed on to these students.

Fourth, according to Muragaki's diary, Henry gave him a book on the Smithsonian Institution. It cannot now be located. However, it may have been the *Guide to the Smithsonian Institution* or the *Annual Report*. Generally, books acquired as gifts by mission members while visiting the U.S. were deposited in the Shogunate Foreign Research Center and were available to the staff of the Center and other researchers.

It is true that the mission members' experiences at the Smithsonian did not have any immediate or direct effect upon the creation of Japan's first natural history museum, but the importance of these experiences should not be underestimated as a scientific contact in the process of Japanese reception of Western natural history museums.

NOTES

[1] Jiro Numata, "Bakumatsu no Kengai Shisetsu ni tsuite," *Seiyokenbunshu*, Iwanami Shoten, 1974:600–607.
[2] The mission members also visited the exhibited hall of the Patent Office Building in Washington, D. C. and P. T. Barnum's museum in New York.
[3] Tokyo Kokuritsu Hakubutsukan ed., *Tokyo Kokuritsu Hakubutsukan Hyakunenshi*, 1973:60.
[4] Ichiro Yabe, *Edo no Honzo*, Saiensu sha, 1984: 62–66.
[5] Ibid.:125–135.
[6] Ibid.:135–142.
[7] Saburo Nishimura, *Bunmei no Naka no Hakubutsugaku*, Kinokuniya Shoten, 1999:472–474.
[8] Tokyo Kokuritsu Hakubutsukan ed., *op. cit.*:7.
[9] Ibid.:8–9.
[10] Dumas Malone ed., *Dictionary of American Biography* 16, Charles Scribner's Sons, 1935:77–78.
[11] Rodgers' suggestions, W9–9757, Hagley Library Archives.
[12] Henry to the President, 26 April 1860, W9- 9756, Hagley Library Archives.
[13] Journal of the Commission, in Charge of the Japanese Embassy to the United States 1860, W9–18480, Hagley Library Archives.
[14] Henry to Du Pont, 30 May 1860, W9–9992, Hagley Library Archives.
[15] According to the *New York Herald* on June 4, five senior members of the mission with two interpreters visited the Institution on June 2. Registration Books of the Smithsonian Institution in 1860 are missing; therefore the schedule is based on mission members' diaries. However, the members who described the visit on June 2 were only two: the vice ambassador Muragaki and an interpreter Namura.
[16] Mission members' perceptions were based on their diaries as follows:
(a) Yoshikoto Fukushima, "Kokai Nisshi," *Man'en Gannen kenbeishisetsu Shiryoshusei 3*, Kazama Shobo, 1960:279–400.
(b) Tameyoshi Hitaka, "Beiko Nisshi," *Man'en Gannen kenbeishisetsu Shiryoshusei 2*, Kazama Shoho, 1961:1–43.
(c) Tetsuta Kimura, *Kobeiki*, Seichosha:1974.
(d) Okataro Morita, "Ako Nikki," *Man'en Gannen kenbeishisetsu Shiryoshusei 1*, Kazama Shobo, 1961:1–270.
(e) Norimasa Muragaki, "Kenbeishi Nikki," *Kengaishisetsu Nikkisanshu 1*, Nihon Shiseki Kyokai, 1928:1–207.
(f) Hakugen Murayama, "Hoshi Nichiroku," *Man'en Gannen kenbeishisetsu Shiryoshusei 2*, *op. cit.*:279–343.
(g) Motonori Namura, "Ako Nikki," *Man'en Gannen kenbeishisetsu Shiryoshusei 2*, *op. cit.*:191–277.

(h) Tadazane Nonomura, "Kokai Nichiroku," *Man'en Gannen kenbeishisetsu Shiryoshusei 3*, op. cit.:131–277.
(i) Kanae Sano, *Man'en Gannen Hobei Nikki*, Kanazawa Bunka Kyokai, 1946.
(j) Hidenaga Sato, "Beiko Nikki", *Kengaishisetsu Nikkisanshu 1*, op. cit.:405–510.
(k) Sadayu Tamamushi, "Kobei Nichiroku," *Seiyokenbunshu*, op. cit.:7–259
(l) Masakiyo Yanagawa, "Kokai Nikki," *Kengaishisetsu Nikkisanshu 1*, op. cit.:209–404.
The diaries of Muragaki and Yanagawa are translated in English.

[17] Ellen Cochran Hirzy ed., *Official Guide to the Smithsonian*, 1996:4.

[18] Cynthia R. Field, et al., *The Castle: An Illustrated History of the Smithsonian Building*, Smithsonian Institution Press, 1993:1.

[19] William J. Rhees, *An Account of the Smithsonian Institution, its Founder, Building, Operations, etc.*, T. McGill Printer, Washington, D.C., 1857:8–9.

[20] Cynthia R. Field, et al., op. cit.:1.

[21] Albert E. Moyer, *Joseph Henry: The Rise of an American Scientist*, Smithsonian Institution Press, 1997:249–250.

[22] William J. Rhees, op. cit.:23.

[23] Edward P. Alexander, *Museum Masters*, American Association for State and Local History, 1983:285.

[24] Joseph Henry, "Report of the Secretary for 1858," *Annual Report of Smithsonian Institution, 1858*, Smithsonian Institution, 1859:13.

[25] E. F. Rivinus and E. M. Youssef, *Spencer Baird of the Smithsonian*, Smithsonian Institution Press, 1992:64.

[26] Ibid.:133.

[27] Spencer Baird, "Appendix to the Report of the Secretary," *Annual Report of Smithsonian Institution, 1860*, Smithsonian Institution, 1861:72–77.

[28] Edward P. Alexander, *Museums in Motion: An Introduction to the History and Functions of Museums*, American Association for State and Local History, 1976:51–53.

[29] Charles Coleman Sellers, *Mr. Peale's Museum*, W. W. Norton & Co. Inc., 1980:332.

[30] Takao Kajishima, *Shiryo Nihon Dobutsushi*, Yasaka Shobo, 1997:529–531. Ichiro Yabe, op. cit.:152–155. Gentaku Otsuki, *Ran'entekiho*, 1817. Saburo Nishimura, op. cit.:474–475.

[31] Takao Kajishima, op. cit.:559–561.

[32] William J. Rhees, *An Account of the Smithsonian Institution, its Founder, Building, Operations, etc.*, Collins Printer, Philadelphia, 1863:68.

[33] Ibid.:72–73. Chang-su Houchins, "Artifacts of Diplomacy: Smithsonian Collections from Commodore Matthew Perry's Japan Expedition (1853–1854)," *Smithsonian Contributions to Anthropology* no. 37, Smithsonian Institution Press,1995.

[34] Ichiro Yabe, op. cit.:159–161.

[35] William J. Rhees, *An Account of the Smithsonian Institution, its Founder, Building, Operations, etc.*, T. McGill Printer, Washington, D.C., 1857:18–19.

[36] Takao Kajishima, op. cit.:364–365. Saburo Nishimura, op. cit.:142–143.

[37] Cynthia R. Field, et al., op. cit.:75.

[38] William J. Rhees, *An Account of the Smithsonian Institution, its Founder, Building, Operations, etc.*, T. McGill Printer, Washington, D.C., 1857:24–26.

[39] Takeki Osatake, *Bakumatsu Kengai Shisetsu Monogatari*, Jitsugyono Nihonsha, 1948:65–66.

[40] William J. Rhees, *An Account of the Smithsonian Institution, its Founder, Building, Operations, etc.*, T. McGill Printer, Washington, D.C., 1857:27.

[41] Cynthia R. Field, et al., op. cit.:77.

[42] Etsuko Taketani, "Brief Communication: Samurai Ambassadors and the Smithsonian Institute in 1860," *Journal of the American Oriental Society* 115:479–481(1995).

[43] Journal of the Commission, in Charge of the Japanese Embassy to the United States 1860, W9–18480, Hagley Library Archives.

[44] Tadashi Aruga, "The First Japanese Mission to the United States 1860," *Abroad in America: Visitors to the New Nation 1776–1914*, Addison-Wesley Publishing Company: 143 (1976).

[45] Journal of the Commission, in Charge of the Japanese Embassy to the United States 1860, W9–18480 Hagley Library Archives.

Copyright ©2000 by the California Academy of Sciences
Golden Gate Park, San Francisco, California 94118, USA.
All rights reserved.

Sciences and The Smithsonian Institution 1852-1906

MICHELE L. ALDRICH[a] and ALAN E. LEVITON[b]
[a] Science and Technology Studies Program, Cornell University, Ithaca, New York
(address for correspondence: 24 Elm Street, Hatfield, Massachusetts 01038)
E-mail: 73061.2420@compuserve.com
[b] California Academy of Sciences, Golden Gate Park, San Francisco, California 94118
E-mail: aleviton@calacademy.org

On July 9, 1846, Rear Admiral John D. Sloat's American squadron entered San Francisco Bay and raised the U.S. flag over Yerba Buena; two days earlier, it had been raised over the custom house in Monterey, about 100 miles south of San Francisco. Before the 1849 Gold Rush, Yerba Buena had been a sleepy little village; with the Gold Rush and California's admission to the Union in 1850, the population of the town, renamed San Francisco, grew enormously (Figs. 1, 2).

On April 4, 1853, seven men met in the law offices of Lewis W. Sloat to discuss the formation of a scientific society, which they proposed to be known as The California Academy of Natural Sciences. Lewis Sloat was, at the time, the City Commissioner of Deeds. He was also a nephew of Admiral Sloat whose squadron, in 1846, raised the American flag at Yerba Buena. Another was Charles Farris, a physician who lived in San Jose.

FIGURE 1. San Francisco, winter 1849–1850. From Soulé, 1855.

FIGURE 2. San Francisco in 1854. From Soulé, 1855.[1]

Nothing is known of Farris except that he attended a few early meetings but then left the state sometime in the summer or fall of 1853. The third was Henry Gibbons, who had come from Philadelphia a few years earlier, and who had a successful medical practice in San Francisco. Gibbons had wide-ranging interests, which included meteorology, botany, and fishes. Albert Kellogg was among the seven; also a physician, he had a pharmacy in San Francisco, but his interests in botany were too distracting, and he often neglected his responsibilities to the pharmacy. Thomas Nevins was San Francisco's first superintendent of public schools as well as an attorney. John Boardman Trask (Fig. 3) practiced medicine and, though Yale-educated, he did not at the time have an M.D. (the M.D. was not yet a requirement to establish a practice as a physician). His interests were in geology and, in 1853, he published two maps and the first of several reports on the geology of California, all based on surveys he had begun three years earlier. Finally, the seventh founder was Andrew Randall (Fig. 4), about whom there is some confusion. Contrary to much of what has been said in print, Randall came to California overland with the Col. James Collier party that had departed from Fort Leavenworth, Kansas, on 17 May 1849 (Foreman, 1937:12). He was not with the Sloat party when it entered Monterey Bay, as oral tradition has it (see, for example, Miller, 1944). At the time of the flag-raising in 1846, Randall was an assistant to David Dale Owen on Owen's Federal Survey of the Northwest Territory, which included Minnesota and Wisconsin. Randall arrived in California in 1850 and took up residence for a short time in Monterey before moving to San Francisco where he entered in business dealings as a financier. By 1856, Randall was in debt in excess of $67,000 to one Joseph Hetherington, a gambler in the city. On July 24, 1856, in public, Hetherington shot Randall dead. Five days later, on July 29, while the Academy heard about the trees of California, the city's notorious vigilante committee took Hetherington from the jail and hanged him. The militia was called out but the commander said that without an issue of small arms from the army's armory, the militia could not intervene. The militia's commander was William Tecumseh Sherman, at the time a San Francisco banker.[2]

FIGURE 3. John Boardman Trask (1863). California Academy of Sciences Archives.

FIGURE 4. Andrew Randall. California Academy of Sciences Archives.

Henry's Meteorological Network

One of the first scientific efforts of the Academy was to get involved in the meteorological network established by Joseph Henry (Fig. 5), Secretary of the Smithsonian Institution in Washington, D.C. In September 1853, Henry was elected an honorary member of the Academy. Less than three months later,

FIGURE 5. Joseph Henry. Smithsonian Institution Archives (RU 95, Neg. #26452).

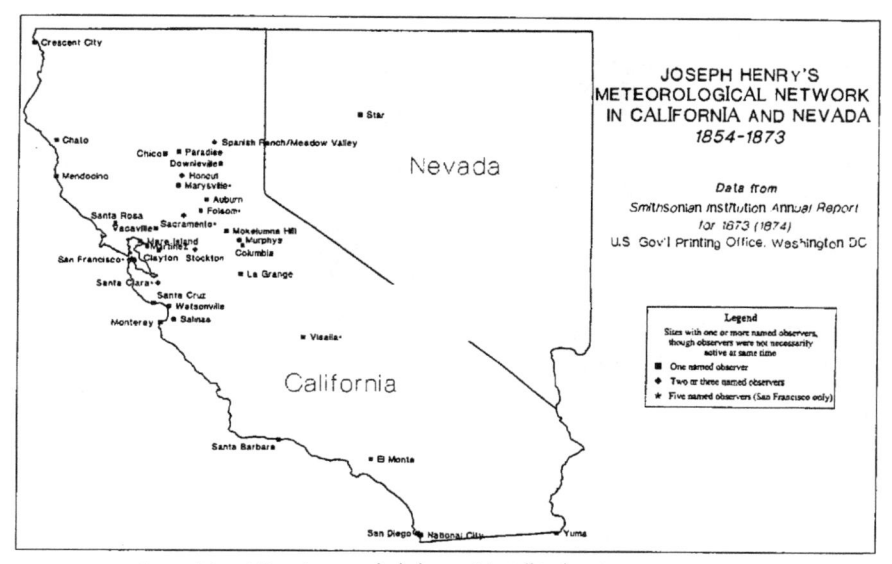

FIGURE 6. Joseph Henry's meteorological network in California and Nevada, 1854–1873.

on December 19, he offered to assist the Academy in getting meteorological and magnetic instruments and, by January 16, 1854, he had ordered the instruments. Henry offered that the Smithsonian would pay the freight charges to ship the instruments to San Francisco, but the Academy had to pay the cost of the instruments themselves.[3] The significance of the meteorological network, insofar as California is concerned, is noteworthy. The network was especially strong along the Sierra foothills (Fig. 6), where most of the population was concentrated because of the gold mining. When weather comes in from the Pacific, especially during the winter months, air moving up the Sierra slope, cools and storms develop. This meteorological phenomenon was an important test case for some of the theories of storms that were being discussed in the United States, including ones that especially interested Joseph Henry.[4] It was vital to have a sizable California network to gather data. The only problem was that there was only one observer in Nevada, on the rain shadow side, and because that observer was only active for a couple of years, it was hard to draw any firm conclusions.

Another peculiarity of Henry's California network was that there were lots of observers in the Bay area (Fig. 7). The earliest person of whom we have record was a post-surgeon stationed at the Presidio, on the north side of the San Francisco peninsula; his records dated back to 1852. Heavy coverage in the Bay area was required because it has a complicated micro-climate.[5] As anybody who has been there

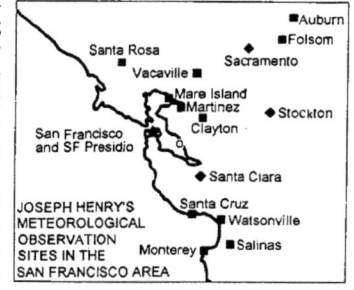

FIGURE 7. Joseph Henry's meteorological network in the San Francisco Bay Area in the 1850s.

FIGURE 8. Henry Gibbons. California Academy of Sciences Archives.

FIGURE 9. William Gibbons. Bancroft Library, University of California, Berkeley.

knows, you can have sun on one side of the peninsula and fog and cold on the other. To quote Mark Twain, "the coldest winter I ever spent was a summer in San Francisco."

Interest in the meteorological network at the Academy continued for a number of years even though the Academy observations were sometimes erratic. In the fall of 1868, Henry Gibbons (Fig. 8) visited Joseph Henry in Washington, where Henry briefed him on the importance of the telegraph for rapid reporting of weather.[6] Speed was crucial in later years in order to make meteorological observations more useful for forecasting. In 1871, Joseph Henry visited San Francisco and the Academy where he presented a preview of his forthcoming rainfall article[7] and also spoke about the importance of science in general.

Publications

The next Smithsonian involvement with the Academy centered on its publications program. William Gibbons (Fig. 9), who we believe was Henry Gibbons' brother, had read papers on viviparous fishes in June, 1853. His remarks were published in *The Pacific* (Fig. 10), a Congregationalist newspaper in San Francisco self-described as "of high literary character."[8] Spencer Fullerton Baird (Fig. 11), Joseph Henry's second in command at the Smithsonian Institution, wrote a starchy letter in early 1854 saying that science would not recognize the priority of papers published in newspapers. Gibbons disagreed and the Academy passed a resolution on March 27, 1854 stating: "In view of the isolated condition of this Academy from other societies, we will regard every publication of new species which has been or may be made through the daily papers of this city as substantial evidence of priority of discovery."[9] Also, and unbeknownst to Baird, Gibbons' viviparous fishes papers had anticipated the work that was published about the same time by Louis Agassiz. Agassiz, on learning of Gibbons' remarks as published in the newspapers a few days before his own publication appeared, sent a letter to the Academy, which was received April 3, accepting the priority of Gibbons's paper.[10] At the same meeting the Academy also set up a committee to look into ways of establishing a more formal scientific program of publications. In September, 1854, the Academy arranged for the more elegant presentation of its transactions with *The Pacific*. What they did was, essentially, reset the type from the newspaper into a journal format.

In October 1854, Baird received a copy of the new publication and said that he now saw no problems with scientists acknowledging priority from that. He also advised them on how to properly date the sheets.[11] On January 22, 1855, Baird was elected an honorary member. He continued to advise the Academy on matters relating to its publications program, on one occasion remarking that

FIGURE 10. *The Pacific*, San Francisco's Congregationalist's newspaper that sent reporters to Academy meetings and then published the proceedings. Papers given by Academy members in which new species were described were published verbatim. This continued until September, 1854, at which time the Academy began issuing its own publication, the *Proceedings of the California Academy of Natural Sciences*.

FIGURE 11. Spencer Fullerton Baird. Smithsonian Institution Archives (RU 95, Neg. #64750).

FIGURE 12. William Healey Dall. Smithsonian Institution Archives (RU 95, Neg. #SA–1156).

FIGURE 13. James Graham Cooper. California Academy of Sciences Archives.

250 copies was too few and advising at least 500 of each part be printed. As it turned out, Baird was correct. The 1854 *Proceedings* had to be reprinted in 1873 because of demand.

Newspaper publication of scientific work reported at Academy meetings served another function — in its early days, it was the Academy's principal form of popular outreach inasmuch as it did not yet have a museum that it could open to the public. The daily and weekly papers in San Francisco, among them, the *San Francisco Daily Bulletin*, the *Alta California*, and the *Scientific and Mining Press*, sent representatives to the Academy's weekly meetings. Even one of the city's German language newspapers covered the Academy. Despite his initial criticism of newspaper publication, Baird himself eventually came to terms with the idea of popularizing science in this way, especially in the 1870s when he began his own dissemination of science through *Harper's* and the *New York Tribune*.[12] Popularization through the public media, however, proved to be a mixed blessing to scientists. William Dall (Fig. 12) and James Cooper (Fig. 13), for example, both complained about the inaccuracy of the reports and their inability to check proof before something came out in the newspaper.[13]

Building the Collections and Library at the Academy

A major problem that quickly emerged during the early years of the Academy was that of finding a home for the rapidly growing collections of artifacts and biological specimens. In the 1850s, Academy members met in a series of rented rooms. The Academy was perpetually short of funds so that the landlords, Lewis Sloat and Col. Nevins (Fig. 14), both Academy members, often "forgave" the rent.[14] But, the needs of the fledgling organization could not be easily dismissed. The 1860s began with serious agitation for a new building. The Geological Survey of California was started under Josiah Dwight Whitney (Fig. 15) who, on his arrival in San Francisco, became a member of the Academy, as did other Survey staff. Whitney's was a large field-party effort, much different from Trask's reconnaissance efforts during the early 1850s. Initially, Whitney sent his type specimens of rocks, plants and animals to the Smithsonian Institution. But in 1861, he drew up a plan under which the collections from the Survey would be split, with the agricultural ones — mostly botany — going to the Agricultural Society in Sacramento for a museum there. The general natural history specimens — geological and zoological specimens that were unrelated to agriculture — would be given to the California Academy of Natural Sciences to form the nucleus of a state museum, which itself would be managed by the Academy on behalf of the Survey. The collections deposited with the Academy would remain under state geological survey control until the Survey was finished, and then they would pass on to the Academy. Whitney even went so far as to submit a floor plan for Spencer Baird to look over.[15] However, the scheme was derailed by a combination of politics and lack of money. Even if Whitney had gone through with his plans, the arrangement would have had trouble because the managing board included two politicians and only one scientist.

In the 1870s, Dall desperately wrote to Baird that he could not work in the cold, damp rooms of the Academy. In 1872, Harvard zoologist Louis Agassiz visited San Francisco on his return from his South American expedition and, in place of a scientific report, gave a rabble-rousing lecture on the past successes of the Academy, on the need to support science, and the need for a new home for the Academy. Academy member Robert Stearns (Fig. 16) told Baird about Agassiz's paper and speculated that it should finally result in material aid to the Academy once monetary conditions improved.[16]

In 1873, George Davidson, then president of the Academy, wrote to Joseph Henry about a lot that had been deeded to the Academy by San Francisco entrepreneur James Lick (Fig. 17) and asked Henry whether he could write a letter of thanks to the benefactor that the Academy could also use to

FIGURE 14. Col. Thomas Nevins. California Academy of Sciences Archives.

FIGURE 15. Josiah Dwight Whitney. Smithsonian Institution Archives (RU 7177, Neg. #78–106).

FIGURE 16. Robert Edwards Carter Stearns. Bancroft Library, University of California, Berkeley.

FIGURE 17. James Lick. California Academy of Sciences Archives.

approach other philanthropists to raise money for the building itself. Lick's original offer had a number of drawbacks and the Smithsonian was kept well-apprised of them. Dall wrote to warn Baird about Lick's earlier offers to other San Francisco groups who were then unable to raise the money to erect suitable structures. For instance, initially, Lick did not permit the Academy to take out a mortgage, and he placed other restrictions on the gift, notably that the Academy had only two years to raise the funds and erect a building.

On March 10, 1873, Henry's letter to Lick in response to Davidson's request began by drawing an analogy between Lick and James Smithson and waxed eloquent for five pages in Victorian prose about what a fine benefactor Lick was for science, how he would have immortality, and so forth. On page six, Henry got down to brass tacks; he warned Lick that to be successful, the building would require curators, maintenance, and a research program.[17] This letter was taken seriously because, by October 1873, Lick had modified the plan and included a bequest to pay for a building and to endow its maintenance. Although James Lick died on October 1, 1876, it was some years before the interminable wrangling over Lick's estate ended and monies were released to the Academy for the purposes intended.

Meanwhile, in 1874 the Academy and its collections moved into the old First Congregationalist Church on the southwest corner of California and Dupont Streets.[18] They were to stay there until the new building was completed in 1891. This church building was described by Robert Stearns as "smelling of hell and brimstone," and it was not adequate for the display of the Academy's rapidly growing accessions. In 1882, for instance, through the largess of railroad magnates Charles Crocker and Leland Stanford, for the sum of $8,000 each, the Academy acquired a large natural history collection from Ward's Natural History establishment that, at the time, was being displayed in San Francisco at the Mercantile Library. This collection, thereafter known as the Crocker-Stanford Collection in Geology, Mineralogy, and Natural History,[19] remained on display in the Mercantile Library. This proved unacceptable and, in 1884, the collection had to be moved and stored in the old church where dampness and mold took their toll.[20] In 1888, the Academy finally started to build its own home, a project that took three years to complete. It consisted of two buildings, one fronting on Market Street (Fig. 18), the second immediately behind and connected to the Market Street building by a bridge at the level of the second floor. You can see the sign "California Academy of Sciences." One entered through the front hall, went up the Grand Staircase and walked through the bridge corridor to the rear building, which was the actual museum area. The front building was dedicated to offices, which the Academy rented out for income.[21] The museum building featured exhibits that had been previously displayed in

FIGURE 18. Facade of the Academy's Market Street building. This building was used for commercial purposes. A second building behind this one supported the Museum. California Academy of Sciences Archives.

FIGURE 19. Main exhibit floor of the Academy's museum building, circa 1902. The mammoth restoration was among the items purchased from Wards Scientific Establishment in 1882 and first on display at the Mercantile Library. California Academy of Sciences Archives.

the Mercantile Library, then, in part, in the Congregationalist Church, and finally in all their glory in the new building (Fig. 19).[22]

The founders of the Academy overwhelmingly were collectors of natural history specimens, but the Academy's resources in the 1850s were miniscule and all too often one reads in the minute books, "no cash" (Hittell in Leviton & Aldrich, 1997:22).[23] In 1857, William Orville Ayres (Fig. 20) wrote to Spencer Baird at the Smithsonian saying that the entire small-bird collection fit in a large cigar box.[24] Initially, there were manifold advantages to sending collections to the Smithsonian rather than keeping them in the Academy. In exchange for the specimens, the scientists received publications or Eastern material for comparison, and sometimes they were paid for their collections. Nevertheless, there was a problem of competition between the Smithsonian and the Academy, and also there were plenty of other individuals who competed with Baird to get collections from California. Louis Agassiz, in particular, paid well and often walked off with the choicest material.[25] However, George Davidson favored the of the Academy of Natural Sciences of Philadelphia, and sent them his "personal" collections, as he called them. This practice irritated Baird, because to ship them Davidson had used the Smithsonian exchange system. Davidson would box the material, take it to the wharf,

FIGURE 20. William Orville Ayres. California Academy of Sciences Archives.

and ask that it be loaded onto the steamer ahead of other packages going to the Smithsonian. Davidson used the system to get the collections to the Smithsonian, and then Baird had to trans-ship it to Philadelphia.[26] There were also a number of Europeans who came to San Francisco and collected in cooperation with the Academy. Among them were Franz Steindachner and Baron Ferdinand Richthofen. Richthofen, especially, made the California scientists nervous because he shipped all of his fossils back to Prussia and the Californians rushed to get their descriptions out in their own journal before Richthofen's friends scooped them.[27]

There were several conflicts with Smithsonian personnel about priority in describing new species. Early on, Charles Girard and William Ayers clashed over birds, but the most long-standing dispute was between Theodore Gill (Fig. 21), who had arguments with both Ayers and William Lockington regarding fish taxonomy. Gill had the U.S. Exploring Expedition material, giving him what he considered proprietary rights on all North Pacific fishes. Gill was severe in his criticism of Ayers and, in fact, of anyone who tread upon what he considered his turf. At one point Ayers described the shark genus *Notorhynchus*, which Gill first rejected, but later redescribed using the Ayres' genus and species names but attributing them to himself (the dispute was finally resolved in Ayres' favor by strict application of the International Code of Zoological Nomenclature). The westerners regarded Gill as an arm-chair naturalist who had the print resources of the Library of Congress available to him, which stirred up a great deal of resentment. In 1881, Gill was still fighting with William Lockington over fishes.[28] Baird sometimes mediated these conflicts but sometimes he was a source of irritation himself. At one point he received a box of specimens from James Cooper that had material for the Smithsonian and for two other collections. Baird went through the box, took what he wanted, adjusted the invoices for the others, and sent them on. The result was that Cooper ended up about $80 short, because he was selling his other specimens.[29]

FIGURE 21. Theodore Nicolas Gill. Smithson-ian Institution Archives (RU 95, Neg. #SA–602).

A major problem for the Smithsonian in terms of collecting in the West was making its exchange system work. Several Academy members, such as Benjamin Redding, were professionals in the transportation companies in the West and were vital to the economical running and the success of the Smithsonian exchange system. The earliest notable example is Samuel Hubbard of the Pacific Mail Steamship Company. The Pacific Mail designated a certain number of cubic feet on every steamer that left San Francisco for shipping material under the Smithsonian exchange system and did not charge for it. Before the advent of the railroad, that was the only way to ship bulky packages.[30]

California's attitude toward the railroad changed over time and affected the shipping of scientific specimens. There was initial euphoria over the idea of the railroad; it was begun in 1863 from Oakland and the feeling was that it would bind the nation and end the economic isolation of California. Californians took great pride in its construction up to 1869, but the railroad did not bring the prosperity and the population that the state expected, and it was the first experience many of them had with a large eastern-style corporation. Furthermore, the four men who headed the Central Railroad, Leland Stanford, Collis Huntington, Charles Crocker, and Mark Hopkins, were not especially gentle, lovable people.[31] There were endless rate disputes, especially over the issue of short- and long-haul, and science was caught in the middle. When Baird asked for free, or at least favorable, rates on the railroad, he was lumped in with the big farmers and friends of the "big four" who were getting favors. The legislature passed laws against this practice and for a while the Smithsonian exchange system got bogged down by the resulting requirements.[32] At least two of the rail magnates were active in the Academy, Crocker and Stanford, and they regarded scientific work in the West as part of the civilizing of the area that would contribute directly to the success of the rails.

In terms of the mid-level personnel on the Central Pacific Railroad, the most useful to Baird was Benjamin Redding, the land agent who previously had served as California's Secretary of State as well as the state's fish commissioner. The Central Pacific had been financed by bonds, loans, construction grants, and by large grants of land, which were then sold off. It was Redding's responsibility to sell the land and, during his tenure, this was handled reasonably fairly.[33] The situation described in Frank Norris's novel, *The Octopus*, in which the land agent lures people to develop the land and then jacks up the prices, portrayed a later agent.

In contrast to the Pacific Mail Steamship and Central Pacific Railroad, Baird had a notable lack of success in getting any rate reduction from Wells Fargo, which operated as a Federal Express of the West. Wells Fargo served the same function as Adams Express in the East in terms of getting small packages transported rapidly. Wells Fargo contracted with the railroads to do that but also tracked the freight as it crossed the country. Scientists involved in Wells Fargo during this early period never could help Baird get free shipments or even preferential rates.[34]

Ostensibly, the Smithsonian exchange was for European materials, primarily publications. But the Academy scientists and Baird used the exchange system for moving domestic packages and scientific specimens as well. The Academy would package its books, and while still in San Francisco add whatever postage was necessary to cover mail from Washington, D.C. to the final destinations along the East Coast or Europe. It then would ship a box of packaged books to the Smithsonian. On arrival in Washington, Baird had only to drop the separately packaged books in the mail in Washington. This kept the material intact instead of spread out all over the place and was much more successful and significantly less costly than mailing multiple packages directly from San Francisco. The Academy also became an important trans-shipping agent for the Smithsonian on the West Coast.[35]

Another feature of the exchange system was that the California Academy and the Smithsonian Institution used it to introduce species from the West to the East, and vice versa. In 1874, Stearns sent Baird eleven species of conifer seeds and fourteen species of flowers to try to establish in the East. Similarly, in his capacity as fish commissioner, Redding introduced shad to the West and attempted to introduce the Pacific salmon to the East.[36] The scientists were aware of the downside risks of this kind of transaction; the English sparrow was universally condemned, and they had seen introduced plant species crowd out desirable natives.

An aside, an incident related to the exchange system for shipment of specimens by the Academy to the Smithsonian, occurred in 1887. The Academy accidentally used a large container of alcohol that the Smithsonian had set aside for David Starr Jordan, who was still in Indiana at the time. This was seen as a serious violation of IRS interstate regulations, because if the alcohol were not used by the person who initially paid the bond — in this case, the Smithsonian — then large taxes were due; furthermore, both parties' bonds could be suspended. Baird and Reese took up the matter and wrote the Commissioner of Internal Revenue a letter explaining what had happened. In a letter that amazes one when read today, the Commissioner replied, in essence, "it was used for the purpose for which it was designed, so I don't see that this is an issue; and neither of the bonds are threatened."[37]

Another cooperative arrangement between the Smithsonian and the California Academy involved what was called "the great want of books here, which has been the bane of workers." In the

1860s, foreign scientific publications flowed in 50 to 100 at a time under the exchange system. In 1873, Baird told Robert Stearns that [Secretary Joseph] Henry had finally decided what to do with the duplicate books left over from transfer of the Smithsonian library to the Library of Congress. The Secretary had decreed that the world of science needed a first-class reference library at the greatest possible distance from the Smithsonian. Several institutions qualified, and Baird urged Dall to have the Academy write first to preempt them.[38] George Davidson took the hint and in November asked Henry for the books and, on the 12th of December, Henry wrote to Davidson informing him that fifteen cartons were shipped, "consisting of all the duplicates of publications... in the possession of the Smithsonian Institution...," over 2,000 volumes, weighing 3,000 to 4,000 pounds. Some of them were broken sets but those were easy to fill and accessions to the library from the Smithsonian continued. Other institutions also sent books, including major donations from the Academy of Sciences of Philadelphia; these were especially welcome following the devastating 1906 San Francisco earthquake and fire that left the Academy's physical plant in ruins.[39]

Staffing the Academy

With the Lick bequest, the Academy was no longer preoccupied with money or survival, although the handling of the new wealth certainly raised a whole set of new problems, but it was not the end to change and innovation, especially in staffing. The personnel within the Academy differed somewhat from that in eastern scientific establishments. Eusebius Molera (Fig. 22) was one of the prominent Hispanic professionals in San Francisco at the time. Born in 1846, he was a civil engineer and architect. In May of 1873, he became a member of the Academy, frequently presented papers on a variety of subjects and, in 1886, was elected to the Academy's Board of Trustees, on which he served for some years. Because of his architectural and engineering background, he was very active while the building was going up. His main scientific interest, apart from mathematics and engineering, was Aztec calendars, on which he published a major paper.[40]

FIGURE 22. Eusebius Molera. California Academy of Sciences Archives.

Theoretically, women could join the Academy since its founding in 1853, but they did not actually start attending meetings until the early 1870s, and several joined *en bloc* in 1878. Women began giving papers at the Academy in 1881 and continued to do so with increasing frequency thereafter. They also donated large collections, Mrs. E. D. Crocker being especially noteworthy in that regard.[41] In June 1883, Mary Katharine Layne [Curran] (Fig. 23), who had received an M.D. degree from the University of California several years earlier, became the first woman curator hired by the Academy. She was a botanist, and within six months had moved from an unpaid to a paid position. Rosa Smith (later Rosa Smith Eigenmann) (Fig. 24) was appointed Curator of Fishes in February 1884. In 1892, on the recommendation of [Mary] Katharine Layne [Curran] Brandegee (Katharine had by this time had married Townshend Brandegee), Alice Eastwood (Fig. 25) was appointed to the botany department.[42]

After Baird died in 1887, the Academy's relations with the Smithsonian Institution changed, but it was also a sign of the times. Now, instead of Secretary of the Smithsonian to President of the California Academy, relations became scientist to scientist. For instance, John Van Denburgh (Fig.

FIGURE 23. Mary Katharine Layne (Curran) (Brandegee). Hunt Institute for Botanical Documentation, Carnegie-Mellon University.

FIGURE 24. Carl and Rosa Smith Eigenmann, November 1889. Courtesy Scripps Institution of Oceanography Archives

FIGURE 25. Alice Eastwood. California Academy of Sciences Archives.

FIGURE 26. John Van Denburgh. California Academy of Sciences Archives.

26), the Academy's Curator of Herpetology, carried on correspondence and exchanged specimens with Leonhard Stejneger, his counterpart at the Smithsonian's National Museum.[43] The botanists, notably Alice Eastwood and Katharine Brandegee and her husband Townshend, are also good examples of this shift in activity. Katharine Brandegee and Alice Eastwood corresponded with and exchanged specimens with Joseph Nelson Rose and C. L. Pollard in the Smithsonian's National Museum's Division of Plants, and with George Vasey and Frederick Vernon Coville in the Department of Agriculture's Botany Division, whose connection with the Smithsonian was indirect, through the Department of Agriculture and the National Herbarium. Plant culture was among the things that interested the botanists most, especially Alice Eastwood. As earlier with the publication exchange system, Eastwood asked for Eastern aquatic plants to be shipped to her because the sportsmen's club wanted to plant them to attract ducks; she in turn sent seeds back to the Eastern scientists to watch their development.[44] This was a different use, not connected with introduction of the materials there; propagation was being studied as a scientific issue. Eastern scientists advised Alice Eastwood and her colleagues on preservation techniques, and there was, of course, the ongoing loan and exchange of plants that persists to this day among curators of nearly all major natural history museums. During these years, Eastwood was adding 5,000 to 10,000 plants a year to the Academy's herbarium, so she was extremely active in the field. In 1902, on one trip, carrying her luggage on her back, she walked 22 miles into the Coast Ranges when the temperature was 104 in the shade, stayed overnight, and walked back the next day.[45] And because samples of western plants were eagerly sought by eastern curators for their herbaria, which is one reason why the exchange system among herbaria and other museum collections works, Eastwood was able to build a major herbarium in near-record time. The process and etiquette of exchanging and priority had been understood and regularized for some time. Scientists collected to fill in gaps in their collections and to write papers, some jointly, and they helped one another with identifications. If a new species was found in material shipped East, the eastern scientist was welcome to identify it, but the western scientist expected that the description would be published in the California Academy's *Proceedings* series and that the types would be sent back. The eastern scientist could retain a sample from the duplicates.

This peaceful and productive chapter in the Academy's history ended abruptly on April 18, 1906 when a heavy earthquake hit the area. The earthquake's epicenter was in Marin County, 20 miles north of San Francisco. It cracked the city's water mains and that made it nearly impossible to put out the fires, which actually did most of the damage (Fig. 27–28). The morning of the earthquake several of the curators went to the Museum to examine the damage. The stairs and the bridge between the two buildings had collapsed. The galleries' floors — cement-reinforced, among the first in San Francisco — remained intact. The curators started to rescue the types and records. The people mainly involved in this were Alice Eastwood, John Van Denburgh, Curator of Herpetology, Leverett Loomis, Director of the Museum, and Mary Hyde, the Librarian. Before the fire reached the Academy's building, they managed to get out a few type specimens, mostly from the herbarium, and the entomology and herpetology collections, the Museum catalogues, a few books from the Library, most of the minute books of Academy meetings dating back to 1853, and a 324-page manuscript of a history of the Academy that had just been completed by Theodore Hittell (see Leviton and Aldrich, 1997).[46]

Within six months of this devastating event, the schooner *Academy* returned from its voyage. It had left in 1905 to collect in the Galapagos Archipelago, where it spent over a year. When the schooner returned in November 1906, the collections were stored in a walled-off portion of the building (Fig. 29).[47] The damage to the Academy was widely publicized in letters to Washington scientists, especially Edward Nelson, who saw to it that those letters were published in *Science* magazine.[48] Many offers came to help rebuild the Academy's scientific collections. The Smithsonian, for instance,

FIGURES 27–28. (27) The remains of the California Academy of Sciences following the devastating earthquake and fire of 18–19 April, 1906. The elevator shaft alone remains standing of the Market Street building; the building immediately behind and to the left was the Academy's museum building. (28) The interior of the Academy's museum building following the devastating earthquake and fire of 18–19 April, 1906, California Academy of Sciences Archives.

198 CULTURES AND INSTITUTIONS OF NATURAL HISTORY

FIGURE 29. Walled-off space made available in the earthquake-damaged museum building for storage of the Galapagos collections on return of the Schooner *Academy* in November, 1906, seven months after the earthquake and fire had substantially destroyed the Academy's buildings on Market Street. California Academy of Sciences Archives.

FIGURE 30. Book plate acknowledging the donation of books to the Academy's Library replacing those lost in the April 18, 1906 earthquake and fire that destroyed the Academy's buildings. California Academy of Sciences Library.

offered to send plants to Alice Eastwood to refurbish the herbarium but she asked them to delay until a new building was put up. Julius Hurter sent Van Denburgh collections of eastern amphibians.[49] And, almost immediately, to replenish the Library, the Smithsonian responded by donating thousands of books to the Academy, as did other organizations, like the Academy of Natural Sciences of Philadelphia (Fig. 30), and 170 other organizations, including several European book dealers.

The Smithsonian Institution began in 1846, less than ten years before the Academy was founded a continent apart. The Institution had an endowment left by James Smithson that supported the research program envisioned by Joseph Henry, while its museum was funded largely from Congressional appropriations. The Academy struggled financially for years, until the Lick funds enabled it to operate on a steady basis; by then, Henry was able to guide the Academy's donor to make his gift more helpful to western science. Meanwhile, Henry himself benefited from the Academy's commitment to research in the form of participation in his meteorological data gathering. His assistant and successor, Spencer Baird, also had a symbiotic relation with the Academy, in part through an ongoing correspondence with Academy-based scientists, such as William Healey Dall and Robert Stears, but also, for instance, in receiving collections from the West Coast for the Smithsonian's museum in exchange for advising the Academy on and assisting in the distribution of the latter's scientific publications. The Academy became the western outlet for the Smithsonian's extra library accessions, a crucial resource before the growth of major university libraries in the West. As both institutions matured, an equilibrium came about, with curators exchanging specimens and information, and publishing in each other's reports and journals. By the end of the century, their mutual relationship became a major factor in defining science in the United States.

ACKNOWLEDGMENTS

A large amount of the material for what has been presented here came from the Smithsonian Archives and could not have been collected without the diligence of Bill Cox, Bruce Kirby, Tammy Peters, Terrica Gibson, Susan 'Woody' Glenn, Pamela Henson and all the other people who assisted. Josephine Jamison, the Archives' patient and understanding receptionist, allowed herself to be drafted by the two impetuous researchers on more than one occasion. Everybody was very cooperative. We also acknowledge the assistance of the Henry Papers in dealing with the issue of meteorology; both Kathleen Dorman and Marc Rothenberg were of great assistance. An early version of this paper was presented in 1996 in Washington, D.C. on the occasion of the 150th anniversary of the Smithsonian Institution. A taped version of that talk was transcribed by Ms Caroline Farquhar to whom we are indebted for her faithful rendering of the presentation in hard copy. Anita Karg, archivist at the Hunt Institute for Botanical Documentation, Carnegie-Mellon University, Pittsburgh, as always, was extremely helpful in locating portraits of hard-to-find individuals. The Bancroft Library, University of California, Berkeley, kindly permitted us to use several portraits from their collection, as did the Scripps Institution of Oceanography Archives. We are indebted to two reviewers, J. Thomas Dutro, Jr. and Pamela Henson, for their helpful comments and criticisms. And last, but assuredly not least, at the California Academy of Sciences, archivist Michele Wellck and Special Collections librarian Karren Elsbrend gave unstintingly of their time in response to our many needs to access their unique collections.

NOTES

Note bene: The "Hittell" references cited below refer to a now published 324-page handwritten manuscript that had been saved from the earthquake and fire that devastated the California Academy of Sciences on 18 April 1906. The manuscript was among the few items saved by

Academy staff on the scene. It was resurrected and edited by Leviton and Aldrich (see Leviton, Alan E., and Michele L. Aldrich, 1997, *Theodore Henry Hittell's The California Academy of Sciences, 1853–1906*. San Francisco: California Academy of Sciences, xv + 623 pp., 144 illus.), with significant additions to the original Hittell text by the editors; the editors were also responsible for all footnotes and for the appendices with the exceptions of Appendix A and Appendix H (Appendix A was written by Hittell and presented orally in 1903, Appendix H was prepared by G. W. Dickie, L. M. Loomis, and R. Pratt as a memorial for Hittell; it was published in 1918). The editors also are responsible for choosing the illustrations that accompany the text. As noted earlier in this volume (see Ertter, pp. 203), for convenience and consistency, quotes and references from this source are cited simply as Hittell, unless derived from the footnotes or appendices that were added by the editors.

[1] Soulé, Frank, John H. Gihon, and Joseph Nisbet. 1855. *The Annals of San Francisco; Containing a Summary of the History of the First Discovery, Settlement, Progress, and Present Condition of California, and a Complete History of All the Important Events Connected with Its Great City: to which are added, Biographical Memoirs of Some Prominent Citizens*. D. Appleton & Co., New York, San Francisco, London. 824 pp., illus.

[2] Hittell, pp. 11–19 and 46–48. On Henry Gibbons, see *National Cyclopedia of American Biography* (1889), vol. 7, p. 287. On Kellogg, see Anonymous (but probably penned by Katharine Brandegee), "Dr. Albert Kellogg," *Zoe*, vol. IV (April 1893), p. 1–2. On Randall, see Clay Preston Butler, *Andrew Randall: Editor and Geologist; Founder of the California Academy of Natural Sciences*, in two manuscript volumes (undated but assembled sometime before 1982) in the Archives of the California Academy of Sciences; see also Grant Foreman, *The Adventures of James Collier: First Collector of the Port of San Francisco* (Chicago: Black Cat Press, 1937, 61 pp.). On Trask, see Alan Leviton and Michele Aldrich, *John Boardman Trask: Physician-Geologist in California, 1850–1879* in Leviton et al., *Frontiers of Geological Exploration of Western North America*, Pacific Division Amer. Assoc. Advance. Science, San Francisco (1982), pp. 37–69. On Sloat, see Robert C. Miller, *Calif. Hist. Soc. Quart.* (1942, vol. 21, no. 4, p. 363–364), also *Pacific Discovery* (1953, vol. 6, no. 2, pp. 18–25); Ewan, *San Francisco as a Mecca for Nineteenth Century Naturalists*, in E. Babcock et al., eds., *A Century of Progress in the Natural Sciences*, California Academy of Sciences, San Francisco (1953), p. 9. On Nevins, see references for Sloat (*op. cit.*), p. 9.

[3] Hittell, pp. 21–24.

[4] James Rodger Fleming, *Meteorology in America, 1800–1870* (Baltimore: Johns Hopkins University Press, 1990, xii + 264 pp.), pp. xx–xxii, 81–82, 101, 127–128, 132, 135, and 170–172.

[5] Smithsonian Institution, Annual Reports for 1852–1860 (Washington DC: Smithsonian Institution, 1853–1861) inclusive provide the names of observers in Henry's weather network. Marc Rothenberg and Kathleen Dorman graciously shared their insights into the relevance of observations on California for Henry's ideas. Their work on the weather network is embodied in vols. 7 et seq. of *The Papers of Joseph Henry* (Washington DC: Smithsonian Institution Press, 1996).

[6] Hittell, p. 107.

[7] Hittell, p. 135.

[8] William Gibbons, fish articles, *The Pacific*.

[9] Hittell, p. 29. Gibbons to Baird, 14 September 1854, vol 7, p. 272, Assistant Secretary Incoming Correspondence, RU 52, Smithsonian Institution Archives (hereafter SIA). Baird to CAS early 1854.

[10] Loc. cit.

[11] Baird to W. Gibbons, 10 October 1854, vol. 9, p. 353, Outgoing Assistant Secretary Correspondence, RU 53, SIA, transcribed in Hittell, pp. 33–34.

[12] Baird to Dall, 1 December 1873, Box 7, William Dall Personal Papers, RU 7073, SIA. E. F. Rivinus and E. M. Youssef, *Spencer Baird of the Smithsonian* (Washington DC: Smithsonian Institution Press, 1992), pp. 118-119.

[13] Cooper to Baird, 18 February and 18 April 1871, vol. II, pp. 294-296 and 299, RU 52, SIA. Dall to Meek, 30 May 1869, Box 2, folder 1, Fielding B. Meek Papers, RU 7062, SIA. (Note: The Dall to Meek letter does not bear a year. However, based on other evidence, namely a letter from Meek to Dall dated 24 May 1869 to which

this letter appears to be a response (N.B. the Dall to Meek letter begins, "Yours was duly recd and I hasten to reply ...," the year seems probable [according to W. Cox, SIA Archives [pers. commun., Cox to Leviton, 14 July 2000], "The Dall to Meek letter ... is simply dated May 30, ... no year. But, I'm almost positive it was written in 1869. The Dall collection contains a letter from Meek dated May 24, 1869, which discusses the same tertiary rocks of Alaska.")

[14] Hittell, pp. 22–23.
[15] Vol. 24, pp. 292 et seq., Record Unit 52, SIA, transcribed and sketch reproduced in Hittell, pp. 512–513.
[16] Dall to Baird, 29 December 1872, Box 18, RU 7002, SIA. Hittell, pp. 146–147. Stearns to Baird, 23 October 1872 and 27 January 1874, Box 36, folder 13, RU 52.
[17] Hittell, pp. 151–153. The letters are cited and transcribed or summarized there: Davidson to Henry, 19 February 1873, vol. 162, p. 147 and 3 April 1873, vol. 132, p. 486–487 in Secretary Incoming Correspondence, vol. 162, p. 147, RU 26, SIA, and Henry to James Lick, 10 March 1873, Secretary Outgoing Correspondence, vol. 33, p. 40, Record Unit 33, SIA. See also Dall to Baird, 23 February 1873, Box 18, RU 7002 and Stearns to Baird, 17 October 1873, Box 36, folder 13, RU 52.
[18] Hittell, pp. 164-165.
[19] Hittell, pp. 243–244, 248, 269–271.
[20] Hittell, pp. 280.
[21] Hittell, pp. 318–326.
[22] Hittell, pp. 243–245 and 323–325.
[23] Hittell, p. 22.
[24] Ayres to Baird, 18 May 1859, vol. 16, p. 30, RU 52.
[25] Baird to Dall, 8 November 1872 and 18 March 1873, Box 7 RU 7073. Stearns to Baird, 17 November 1873, Box 36, folder 13, RU 52.
[26] Baird to Dall, 17 November 1873, Box 7, RU 7073.
[27] Stearns to Baird 23 October 1872, Box 36, folder 13, RU 32.
[28] Hittell, pp. 35, 43, 64, 69, 196, and 239. Based in part on letters as follows: Ayres to Baird, 19 July 1859, Box 14, item 110 in Baird Personal Papers, Record Unit 7002, SIA and Lockington to Dall, 21 December 1878, Box 13, folder 25, Dall Personal Papers, Record Unit 7073, SIA.
[29] Cooper to Baird 20 January 1874, vol. II, p. 326, RU 52.
[30] Hittell, p. 85 and Stearns to Baird, 9 December 1873 and 27 January 1874, Box 36, folder 13, RU 52. Letters from Academy members in RU 26 (Secretary Incoming Correspondence) routinely mention shipping via the Pacific Mail boats.
[31] William Francis Deverell, *Railroad Crossing: Californians and the Railroad, 1850–1910* (1994, University of California Press, Berkeley, xiii + 278 pp.), pp. 3–18. Stearns to Baird, 19 May 1873, Box 36, folder 13, RU 52, where Stearns says "Everything is badly mixed and jumbled since the railroad was completed — and the outlook is not promising."
[32] Hittell, p. 170, based largely on letters of Redding to Baird in Assistant Secretary Incoming Correspondence, Record Unit 52, SIA.
[33] Hittell, pp. 169–170.
[34] Baird to Dall, 13 October 1872, Box 7, RU 7073.
[35] Baird's official correspondence at the SIA is replete with letters documenting this. See for example letters from Trask, Ayres, Stearns, Dall, and Cooper.
[36] The salmon story has been told by other authorities. Among the older literature, the most useful to us is Dean Allard, *Spencer Fullerton Baird and the U.S. Fish Commission* (New York: Arno Press, 1978), pp. 137–157 and 266–268. For a comprehensive recent survey of writings on the topic, see Joseph E. Taylor, *Making Salmon: An Environmental History of the Northwest Fisheries Crisis* (Seattle: University of Washington Press, 1999), p. 380–385. Allard also deals with the shad question, pp. 136–137 and 143. On seeds, see Stearns to Baird, 31 January 1874, Box 36, folder 13, RU 32.
[37] Joseph Miller to William Rhees, 4 June 1887, RU 33.
[38] Dall to Baird, 28 December 1873, Box 18, RU 52. Baird to Dall, 17 December 1873, Box 7, R 7073. Hittell, pp. 42, 80, 164–165, and 196. George Davidson to Joseph Henry, 29 November 1873 and 24 December

1873, vol. 136, p. 232 and vol. 142, p. 1, Secretary Incoming Correspondence, Record Unit 26, SIA. Stearns to Baird, 27 January 1874, Box 36, RU 52, confirms arrival of 15 cases of books, as yet unopened, because of move of the Academy into the old First Congregationalist Chuch building as its temporary quarters.

[39] Hittell, pp. 478–479 and 561–567.

[40] Molera's biography appeared in the *Transactions* of the Technical Society of the Pacific Coast, an engineering society in which he was active.

[41] Hittell, pp. 21, 206, 211, 232–233, and 246–247.

[42] Biographical sketches for Katharine and Townshend Brandegee see William A. Setchell, "Townshend Stith Brandegee and Mary Katharine (Layne) (Curran) Brandegee," *Univ. California Publ. Botany* (1926, vol. 13, no. 9, pp. 155–178, pls. 13–14); also Frank S. and Carol D. Crosswhite, "*The Plant Collecting Brandegees, with emphasis on Katharine Brandegee as a liberated woman scientist of early California,*" *Desert Plants* (1985, vol. 7, no. 3, pp. 128–162), Elizabeth Rush, "On her terms: Katharine Brandegee: First woman of Western botany," *Pacific Discovery* (1997, vol. 50, no. 1, pp. 22–27, 6 illus.), and Nancy G. Slack, "Mary Katharine Brandegee," *American National Biography* (1999), vol. 7, pp. 414–417 and "Townshend Stith Brandegee" (*op. cit.*), pp. 417–418. Several biographical sketches of Alice Eastwood exist but see in particular Frank Mace MacFarland in the *Proceedings of the California Academy of Sciences* (1949, ser. 4, vol. 25, pp. ix–xxiv), Carol Green Wilson's *Alice Eastwood's Wonderland*, (San Francisco: California Academy of Sciences, 1955, 222 pp.), "Eastwood, Alice," in *Notable American Women: The Modern Period. A Biographical Dictionary* (edited by B. Sicherman, et al., 1980, Cambridge: Belknap Press, Harvard University), pp. 79–80, and more recently, Elizabeth Keeney, "Alice Eastwood," *American National Biography* (1999), vol. 7, pp. 255–256. A brief biographical sketch and portrait of Rosa Smith Eigenmann appear on p. 15 of *Women in Science: A Selection of 16 Significant Contributors*, published by the San Diego Supercomputer Center (1997) (a copy of this publication can be found in the GS Myers/AE Leviton Biographical and Portrait Files of Natural History, Department of Herpetology, California Academy of Sciences).

[43] John Van Denburgh correspondence with Leonhard Stejneger, January 15, 1906 to June 17, 1927, Department of Herpetology Archives, California Academy of Sciences.

[44] Eastwood to Joseph Rose, 15 November 1894, Box 9, US National Museum, Division of Plants, Record Unit 221, SIA.

[45] Hittell, p. 364, quoting Alice Eastwood to Joseph Rose, 27 August 1896, and Eastwood to Rose, 11 August 1902, Box 9, RU 221.

[46] Hittell, pp. 467–474 and 499–506.

[47] Hittell, pp. 446–449, 461–466, 477 and 481.

[48] Hittell, pp. 475–476, 499, and 505–506. The *Science* magazine versions appeared in New Series, vol. 23 (25 May 1906), pp. 824–826. Four of the original letters are in Box 4, folder 2 (Eastwood) and Box 7, folder 1 (Loomis) of E. N. Nelson and E. A. Goldman Collection, Record Unit 7364, SIA, and the fifth is in Box 9, Eastwood folder, of US National Museum, Division of Plants, record Unit 221, SIA. They are transcribed in Hittell, pp. 500–506. We thank William Cox of the Smithsonian Institution Archives for drawing our attention to them.

[49] Julius Hurter to John Van Denburgh correspondence, December 17, 1906 to August 11, 1916, Department of Herpetology Archives, California Academy of Sciences.

Copyright ©2000 by the California Academy of Sciences
Golden Gate Park, San Francisco, California 94118, USA.
All rights reserved.

People, Plants, and Politics: The Development of Institution-Based Botany in California 1853–1906

BARBARA ERTTER
University and Jepson Herbaria
University of California, Berkeley, CA 94720 2465
E-mail: ertter@uclink4.berkeley.edu

The second half of the nineteenth century witnessed the almost overnight transformation of a remote outpost into the bustling metropolis of San Francisco, situated in the midst of an undescribed wealth of biological diversity. This period accordingly also saw the founding and development of most of the major scientific institutions of California: the California Academy of Sciences, the California Geological Survey, the University of California, and Stanford University. As demonstrated by a focus on the botanical component, the early histories of these institutions are tightly intertwined, with overlapping casts of colorful personalities. Those who exerted the greatest influence on botany during this period were Albert Kellogg, Hans Hermann Behr, Josiah Dwight Whitney, William Henry Brewer, Henry Nicholas Bolander, Mary Katharine Layne Curran Brandegee, Edward Lee Greene, Harvey Willson Harkness, William Russel Dudley, and Townshend Stith Brandegee.

Botanists in California have long been a popular topic for biographical sketches, due in large part to the dramatic exploits and colorful personalities of such well-known figures as David Douglas (e.g., Marwood, 1973), William Henry Brewer (Farquhar, 1930), Edward Lee Greene (McIntosh, 1983; McVaugh, 1983), and Alice Eastwood (Wilson, 1955). More recently significant attention has been given to Katharine Brandegee (Crosswhite & Crosswhite, 1985; Bonta, 1991; Rush, 1997), making up for nearly a century of undeserved obscurity. These biographical sketches, however, generally focus on a single person, and as a result have failed to capture the rich interplay of personalities, the feuds and alliances, that left their indelible marks on the fledgling scientific institutions of California. The origins of these institutions are themselves intertwined, due to the overlapping and shifting involvement of many of these same individuals. Critical "missing pieces" have been provided by the recent publication of Theodore Henry Hittell's manuscript history of the California Academy of Sciences, which had languished in the Academy archives since 1906.[1]

Only Gleanings Left to Us of the Present Day

From a beginning-of-the-21st century perspective, it is difficult to appreciate that California was, at the beginning of the 19th century, one of the farthest corners of the earth, accessible from the Atlantic only by a long and arduous voyage around Cape Horn, or by an even more hazardous overland voyage through uncharted wilderness. Long after thriving colonial cities had been established in

---

[1] Resurrected and edited by Leviton and Aldrich (1997), with significant additions to the original Hittell text by the editors; the editors are also responsible for all footnotes and for the appendices with the exceptions of Appendix A and Appendix H (Appendix A was written by Hittell and presented orally in 1903; Appendix H was prepared by G. W. Dickie, L. M. Loomis, and R. Pratt as a memorial for Hittell). For convenience, quotes and references from this invaluable source are cited herein simply as Hittell, unless derived from the footnotes or appendices that were added by the editors.

Mexico and along the South American coastline, only tenuous footholds existed in western North America. Even as Spanish, English, and Russian settlements became established along the Pacific coast of the continent, visiting ships routinely depended on the Hawaiian Islands as the closest outpost of Western civilization where provisions could be reliably obtained.

The gradual colonization changed abruptly and dramatically with the discovery of gold in California in 1849, leading to the nearly overnight appearance of a full-fledged city in the heart of prime botanical hunting ground. The gold rush soon peaked, with the bulk of miners moving on to newly discovered fields outside of California, but the rise of new industries (e.g., whaling) ensured that the young city of San Francisco could support the rise of culture and learning. It was still very much an outpost of civilization, however, and would remain isolated from the centers of culture in the eastern United States for nearly two decades, until the completion of the first transcontinental railroad in 1869.

It was in this setting, in 1853, that seven gentlemen scholars met to establish the California Academy of Natural Sciences. The situation is perhaps unparalleled, wherein the intellectual resources of an isolated 19th century city were situated intimately with so much uncatalogued biological diversity. The very first issue of the Academy's *Proceedings,* for example, included the description of a new fish that was being sold in local markets, *Labrus pulcher* Ayres. Plants provided an equally rich source of novelties, with well more than half of the currently known flora of California remaining to be discovered and catalogued (Ertter, 2000). This fact, however, was not fully appreciated at the time. In 1858, for example, Thomas Bridges wrote to his mentor in England, Sir William J. Hooker:

> I can scarcely describe to you how pleasing and gratifying it has been to me to learn that in my collections you have found some new and rare plants — I was partially under the impression that from the labours of Douglas, Hartweg, Jeffrey, Lobb and other travelers from Europe with the many United States Exploring Expeditions that little or nothing remained to be discovered and only gleanings were left to those of us of the present day. (quoted in Jepson, 1933, pp. 85–86)

That Good-hearted and Impractible Fellow

At the time the Academy was founded, "science" was mostly not a profession but rather a joint pursuit of amateurs, often as members of "philosophical" or "natural science" organizations. Very few of the botanists during the 19th century, men or women, held professional positions. Two of the primary exceptions were John Torrey, professor at Columbia College, and his protégé Asa Gray, who founded the herbarium at Harvard University. Working together, Torrey and Gray represented botanical authority in North America and were attempting a massive synthesis, *A Flora of North America.*

The seven founders of the Academy exemplified the gentleman scholar approach to natural science, with the members meeting weekly in a rented room to present their scholarly findings. The proceedings of these meetings were initially published in local newspapers *(Daily Alta California* and *The Pacific),* only retroactively collated into volumes that could be used for exchange (Hittell, p. 33; Curran, 1887). Prospective new members had to be nominated and elected, with not all applicants successful. Curatorships were also elected offices, rotating and unsalaried at least during the early years. The only financial resources were membership dues ($1 per month), with the growth of both library and collections accordingly dependent on contributions and exchange programs. By the end of the third year, in 1855, the library consisted of 65 books, and a single cabinet was shared by all curators (Hittell, p. 38). This represented the height of scientific resources on the West Coast at that time.

Several of the founders and other early members had at least some interest in botany, if only as a then-essential part of medical practice. Dr. William P. Gibbons, for example, although primarily interested in ichthyology, also became an expert on the logged-over redwood forest in the Oakland Hills (Hittell, p. 91; Gibbons, 1893). The founder whose name became synonymous with this phase of California botany, however, was Dr. Albert Kellogg (Fig. 1), whose passion for plants was at the expense of his profession as a physician: "Dr. Kellogg, who kept a drug-store, was almost too much engrossed with hunting and working over new plants to patiently wait upon customers" (Hittell, p. 35). One of his subsequent supporters noted that:

> [Kellogg] practiced his profession... with success in all but what pertained to his own needs. He was careful to enter in his books, the account of every fee due him, and as careful (or careless) never to present a bill. It was the opinion of one who knew him in those days, that he did not once, in all his career as a physician, request a payment. Naturally, he failed to obtain in medicine the means of subsistence, and abandoned his profession. (Greene, 1887:146)

FIGURE 1. Albert Kellogg. Courtesy Jepson Herbarium Archives University of California, Berkeley.

Instead, Kellogg devoted his time to the botanical riches surrounding him, with enthusiasm taking the place of formal training:

> Dr. Kellogg would not have claimed for himself the place of a scientific botanist, nor have wished others to claim it for him. He had a great love for all forms of plant life, more particularly of trees; and he had a keen eye for detecting varietal and specific differences. He was fond of sketching them and writing about them; and when writing upon a species which he thought was new to science (and, in his earlier years of California life he met with many which scientific botanists knew nothing of), he liked to give it a Latin name and a formal description; but his terminology was somewhat original and his way of making Latin adjectives even more so. (Greene, 1887, pp. 148–149)

Among Kellogg's originalities was his fondness for Biblical references, such as his choice of *Marah* for a genus of wild cucumbers. Although a Latin derivation for the generic name is commonly stated (e.g., Schlising, 1993), Kellogg's protologue indicates instead a Hebrew origin, with the tantalizing note that "The significance of the name we have chosen would be better understood by perusing Exodus xv:22–26" (Kellogg, 1855:38). This leads one to the following passage, as Moses led the Hebrews through the wilderness: "When they came to Marah, they could not drink the water because it was bitter. That is why it was called Marah [Bitterness]." The use of *Marah* as a genus name was challenged by Torrey and Gray on the grounds that "it was neither a native nor a personal name, nor one derived from either Greek or Latin," a charge countered by Kellogg's defenders; e.g., "It is a name taken from a literature with which we are all familiar, and its application appears a sufficiently happy one to any person who has accidentally tasted the copious watery juice of the fruit" (Curran, 1885:129–130).

Independent of any eccentricities, Kellogg's devotion to the Academy endeared him to his fellow members. As a result, and in recognition of his financial straits, Kellogg's unpaid dues were canceled in 1864 (Hittell, p. 68), he was declared the first life member two years later (Hittell, p. 80), and in 1868 he became the first member to receive a salary "raised by subscription," as special assistant to the Secretary (Hittell, p. 103). Asa Gray, on the other hand, while referring to Kellogg as "that good-hearted and impractible fellow" (quoted in Dupree, 1959:396), provided the following advice to another California botanist, John Gill Lemmon: "If you knew what a nuisance in the science Dr. Kellogg's name is — good meaning soul that he be, you would not envy his botanical reputation" (quoted in Dupree, 1959:398).

He Gave It the Name of His Backbiter

Although the original members were all self-taught naturalists, this changed after the first year, with the arrival of Dr. Hans Hermann Behr (Fig. 2). A scion of German aristocracy, Behr had studied medicine and natural science at the universities of Halle, Wurzburg, and Berlin. He then traveled in Australia, the East Indies, South America, and the Philippines, becoming acquainted with the botany, entomology, and native languages of the various countries (Gutzkow et al., 1905). His professional contacts, especially in Australia, played a subsequent role in the development of California science, including horticulture.

Behr joined the Academy in 1854:

> Into this group of worthy but little-schooled gentlemen came Behr with his thorough scientific training, his solid learning, his rich experience gathered during long and successful travels, and his ability to distinguish the truly new and interesting from observations and discoveries that had been made before. (Gutzkow et al., 1905:3)

FIGURE 2. Hans Hermann Behr. Courtesy California Academy of Sciences Archives.

In addition to his training and experience, Behr's copy of Endlicher's *Genera Plantarum* also proved an invaluable addition to the Academy's scientific resources.

Parallel to Kellogg, Behr had trouble making a living as physician, but for different reasons:

> He was outspoken in his opinions and a sworn enemy to scientific humbugs and professional quacks. This characteristic ... made him many enemies and [was] not favorable to his financial success as a practitioner. One of the most obnoxious of his adversaries was a doctor, or so-called doctor, who had charge of a local German newspaper and for a time filled its columns with abuse of Dr. Behr, particularly on account of his being a member of the Catholic Church and asserting that he was a 'Jesuit' of the most sinister designs — a calumny which had more or less effect upon its object's professional clientage. (Hittell, pp. 427–428)

Behr had his revenge, however: "on discovering a particularly despicable and obnoxious new species of louse, he gave it scientifically the name of his backbiter" (Hittell, p. 428).

Behr is primarily remembered as an entomologist, but his botanical contributions were also significant. In addition to describing several new species (e.g., *Cordylanthus palustre, Oxybaphus froebelii*), he also left us with the most complete description of the original vegetation of San Francisco

(Behr, 1884, 1888, 1891, 1896). However, what might be Behr's most significant impact is a matter of speculation; specifically, the decision of members of Academy, with a library of less than 100 books and no access to authenticated comparative material, to publish new species independent of established authority. Given Behr's aristocratic background and solid scientific credentials, it is reasonable to speculate that his self-assuredness inspired, or at least bolstered, inclinations towards autonomous publication of new species. One area where Behr and his frontier colleagues parted ways, however, was in the use of Latin: "It met with no encouragement from the Academy, partly because the members generally were not as good Latinists as Dr. Behr and partly because is was felt that plain English was better, or certainly good enough" (Hittell, p. 37).

In whatever language, the right to autonomous publication was resisted by Eastern and European scientists, who considered Academy members to be "amateurs and upstarts" (Hittell, p. 29). After the priority of publication of several new species in the *Proceedings* was ignored, the Academy accordingly passed the following resolutions in 1854:

> Resolved, That in view of the isolated condition of this Academy from other societies, we will regard every publication of new species, which has been or which may be made through the daily papers of this city, as substantial evidence of priority of discovery.
>
> Resolved, That the corresponding secretary be directed to furnish to other scientific bodies a copy of the above resolution, accompanying it with explanations which have led to this conclusion. (Hittell, p. 29)

The battle for scientific recognition continued for years, with the Academy never backing down, and full acceptance was eventually attained. This is indicated in an 1881 presentation of a new *Ranunculus* by John Gill Lemmon, one of the many self-taught botanists in California who became Academy members, which also reiterates the rationale for autonomous publication of new species even in the face of limited library resources:

> [Lemmon] proceeded to say that he had been encouraged by Dr. Asa Gray to make descriptions of new species, even if all the literature upon the subject were not on hand or available. There were only ten libraries in the world where all the botanical works were to be found, and only one of these on this continent. We had only a nucleus of one here in California. He said he was therefore, on account of want of all the most recent publications, apt to make a mistake and name as new something that had already been described. It had been the custom of some Eastern men to describe all sorts of California plants from any kind of specimens, without ever having seen them grow, and take the chances as to their being new and the descriptions accurate; and they had not infrequently received credit which should have remained in California.... Dr. Behr said that California botanists had been roughly handled by Eastern scientists for describing old things; that is, plants already described; but they did not take into consideration the fact of the want of scientific literature on the Pacific Coast. (Hittell, p. 239)

A Hallmark of Enlightened State Administration

By 1860, the flush of Gold Rush wealth was well past and new directions of economic development were sorely needed. The young state of California was accordingly receptive to the concept of a state geological survey, already established in many eastern and midwestern states as "a hallmark of enlightened state administration, a source of local cultural pride, and the means whereby exploitable resources might be cheaply located and advertised to would-be investors" (Goetzmann, 1966:355). Farquhar (1930:xv) credits Stephen J. Field, a Supreme Court justice, with convincing "the more sober minds of the state that definite scientific knowledge was needed to give better direction to the development of resources." According to Brewster (1909:183), however, "The credit . . . belongs in some small measure to her who was born Elizabeth Whitney. It had been her dream, from the time she married and went to California to live, to have her beloved brother at once her neighbor and the head of a state survey."

Elizabeth's "beloved brother," Josiah Dwight Whitney (Fig. 3), a veteran of several state surveys in the Midwest, was among those lobbying vigorously for a California geological survey. As a result of these collective activities, on 21 April 1860, Governor John G. Downey signed into law the following legislation that would have a lasting impact on the natural history of California:

> J. D. Whitney is hereby appointed State Geologist, whose duty it shall be, with the aid of such assistants as he may appoint, to make an accurate and complete Geological Survey of the State, and to furnish, in his Report of the same, proper maps and diagrams thereof, with a full and scientific description of its rocks, fossils, soils, and minerals, and of its botanical and zoological productions, together with specimens of the same, which specimens shall be properly labeled and arranged, and deposited in such place as shall be hereafter provided for that purpose by the legislature. (quoted in Brewster, 1909, pp. 184–185)

FIGURE 3. Josiah Dwight Whitney. Courtesy Courtesy Smithsonian Institution Archive (Neg. # 78-106).

Although Whitney was married and had recently become a father, the men he hired as assistants would all have to be single, in that the funds available for salaries were insufficient to support dependents (Brewster, 1909). One of these men was William Henry Brewer (Fig. 4), a graduate of Sheffield Scientific School and chemistry professor in Pennsylvania whose expertise centered around agriculture. Tragically, Brewer's wife had recently died following childbirth, and the son shortly afterwards, so Whitney's offer represented a way to escape unhappy associations (Farquhar, 1930). Brewer proved to be ideal, not only filling the role of botanist but becoming Whitney's right-hand man.

Whitney and family, Brewer, and other members of the initial core arrived in San Francisco on 14 November 1860, to a gratifying reception: "the survey was popular; the Governor friendly. The newspapers were complimentary, and chronicled every movement of the surveyors. Prominent citizens called, to make the acquaintance of the staff" (Brewster, 1909:191). The Survey team outfitted itself and immediately began field work, starting in southern California.

FIGURE 4. William Henry Brewer. Courtesy University Herbarium Archives, University of California, Berkeley.

While Brewer stayed with the field crew, Whitney periodically spent his time lobbying in Sacramento to obtain continued funding. His efforts paid off the first year, with sufficient appropriations to hire three more men: Dr. James Graham Cooper as surgeon-naturalist, Charles F. Hoffmann as topographer, and William More Gabb as paleontologist. Troubles in the state Treasury began at the same time, however, with the result that salaries were not available for months, not only for the Survey, but for all State officers, up to and including the governor. Funds were borrowed to allow the Survey to proceed, with much of the money obtained from Whitney's well-to-do father (Brewster, 1909).

Alas, disastrous winter floods of 1861–1862 devastated the California economy and further depleted the Treasury. Throughout the state most bridges were gone, roads were washed out, and communication was accordingly cut off. Kept indoors by the incessant rains, the Survey members became active in the California Academy of Natural Sciences. Although a setback to the Survey, this might very well have ensured the survival of the struggling young Academy, which only two years previously had been described by John Xantus as "in a deplorable condition," with only eleven members and a collection "entirely eaten by the miriads of mice and rates [sic]" (quoted in Leviton & Aldrich, 1997:51). According to Hittell (p. 54), participation by Survey members "put a sort of new life into the institution, and gave it an impetus which materially assisted in enabling it to continue its struggle for existence and in the end to triumph over all obstacles." At the annual election of 6 January 1862, Brewer was elected corresponding secretary; Whitney, librarian; Cooper, curator of zoology; and Gabb, curator of paleontology. Another addition to the Academy the same year was Henry Nicholas Bolander (Fig. 5), who had moved to California for reasons of health (Jepson, 1898). A school teacher by profession, with botanical training from Leo Lesquereux, Bolander immediately become interested in the local flora, with special attention paid to grasses and cryptograms.

FIGURE 5. Henry Nicholas Bolander. Courtesy California Academy of Sciences Archives.

Petroleum Is What Has Killed Us

Once the rains let up, and by dint of additional borrowing and frugal use of funds, the Survey resumed, though downscaled. In spite of continued accomplishments in the field, however, long-term prospects for the Survey dwindled. By mid-year, the State owed Whitney $15,000, and the initial enthusiasm for a state survey had decidedly cooled. In an 1862 letter, Whitney noted that "State officers would be my best friends if I would be their confidential adviser in their interest in claims and stocks, but as it is, I do not know one of them who cares a rye-straw for the work [of the Survey]" (Letter from Whitney to S. F. Baird, 15 December 1862, quoted in Leviton & Aldrich, 1997:66). This included Downey, who, as Governor in 1860, had signed the act bringing the Survey into existence, but who was now "down on [the Survey] because Professor Whitney would not use his official influence as State Geologist to aid him in mining speculations" (Brewer in Farquhar, 1930, letter of 20 September 1863, p. 452). Whitney's discouragement is evident in another letter:

> I do not think there is any fear that the survey will be formally killed, but am rather disposed to think that the appropriation may be so small that I shall not feel disposed to carry on the work any longer. . . . I cannot afford the wear and tear of mind and body merely to make a piddling

survey with one or two assistants, and the necessity of making economy the predominating thought. (Letter from Whitney to G. J. Brush, 5 June 1862, quoted in Brewster, 1909:219–220)

The Survey nevertheless continued into 1863, with the Civil War at its height. Brewer noted that "the Union element is vastly in the majority [in California], unconditionally loyal. This state has had so many southern scoundrels in office that the people are afraid of them" (Brewer in Farquhar, 1930, letter of 26 July 1863, p. 427). When surveying around Lake Tahoe, Brewer later commented:

> Its Indian name, Tahoe, was dropped and it was called after Governor Bigler, a Democratic politician. He was once of some notoriety here, since he has turned "Secesh" [secessionist] all the Union papers have raised the cry to have his name dropped, and the old Indian name has been revived and will probably prevail. (Brewer in Farquhar, 1930, letter of 23 August 1863, p. 442)

In the midst of the 1863 field season, in the face of uncertain funding, Brewer was offered a part-time professorship in chemistry at the private College of California in Oakland, and subsequently taught at least one course (Constance, 1978). Whitney continued to alternate his time among the field crew, Sacramento, and San Francisco, presenting a paper to the Academy in May in which he summarized the accomplishments of the Survey to date (Hittell, p. 65). Among the most significant events of 1863, however, was a chance encounter by Brewer, on a steamer from Sacramento, with two recent graduates of his alma mater: James Terry Gardner and Clarence King. Both young men joined the Survey, initially as volunteers, with King eventually going on to become, in 1879, the first director of the United States Geological Survey.

In 1864, Whitney returned to the East to initiate the printing of the Survey reports, "for printing in California cost three times its proper price, and engraving was not to be had on any terms" (Brewster, 1909:235–236). Even thus separated from California, he was not out of reach of a new challenge that threatened the very credibility of the Survey. Although the petroleum reserves of the Santa Barbara area had been noted by the Survey, they had not been deemed to be of immediate economic value, in that existing technologies and uses (primarily as a substitute for dwindling whale-oil) had been developed only for kerosene-grade petroleum, such as that coming out of the Pennsylvania oil fields, not for the thick crude that characterized the Santa Barbara deposits. Nevertheless, in 1864 speculation fever for Santa Barbara petroleum was triggered, and the effectiveness and credibility of the Survey was called into serious question for overlooking such a seemingly valuable resource. Whitney, as State Geologist, took it upon himself to challenge claims of the petroleum's value, sending one assistant back to Santa Barbara to verify the Survey's initial evaluation of the asphaltum's negligible economic potential under existing technology. "Petroleum fever" nevertheless continued to build, and the credibility of the Survey to fall, until an independent study in 1865 exhaustively tested samples from all the major sites in southern California, found none matching the sample used for promotional purposes, and accordingly suggested that refined Pennsylvania oil had been substituted in a deliberate swindle (Goetzmann, 1966:381). Unfortunately, vindication came too late for the California Geological Survey ever fully to regain its initial prestige and state support, especially against a background of continued financial difficulties and a prolonged Civil War.

The botanical component of the Survey had been eliminated from the 1864 budget, though Brewer nevertheless collected a hundred or so specimens while pursuing the mandated portions of the Survey. This phase of botanical activity ended abruptly, however, when Brewer, at the end of the 1864 field season, received an offer of a professorship in Yale. In spite of "the cheering news that we would probably be paid up in January next" (Brewer in Farquhar, 1930, letter of 22 December 1864,

p. 564), the lukewarm prospects for the Survey could not compete against such a prestigious post. Even when support for the Survey temporarily improved the following year, the botanical component was never fully reinstated. Instead, Bolander was periodically hired, apparently on a contract basis, to collect in those areas where Brewer had not been (e.g., the North Coast Ranges, which had been the stronghold of hostile Indians). Cooper also made some significant botanical collections, primarily in conjunction with a winter spent at Fort Mohave (Brewer et al., 1876:vii).

Bolander was even more active in the Academy than Brewer had been, becoming curator of botany in 1865 and publishing the first catalogue of plants of San Francisco (Bolander, 1870). He was also a member of the committee that amended the constitution and dropped "Natural" from the name of the Academy in 1868 (Hittell, pp. 93, 95). Whitney, returning from the East, also became actively involved in the California scene, being elected to the Academy presidency in 1867, planning for the proposed state University, and heading a board of three commissioners to manage the newly established Yosemite Park (Brewster, 1909). The importance of Survey participation in the life of the Academy is evidenced in a letter from Whitney at this time:

> [O]f late I have been much engaged with the affairs of the California Academy, as we have had to move into and fit up new rooms, and have tried to resuscitate it in general. We seem now to be in a fair way to live; but when I came back last year, it seemed as if it was as dead as a doornail. (quoted in Ewan, 1955:19)

The Survey itself, however, continued its downhill slide, as summarized by Whitney:

> The prospects of the survey remain as uncertain as ever. Two committees have been at the office and exhibited even more than their usual amount of stupidity and ignorance. Since the Yosemite Valley bill [to give settlers 160 acres apiece] passed over the Governor's veto, I feel so disgusted with California that I can hardly stand it much longer. Still I am running the survey along in a small way at my own expense, waiting to see what the jackasses at Sacramento will do.... I am told, on good authority, that this legislature is by far more corrupt and reckless than any of its predecessors. It is a fact — at least everybody believes it to be — that votes can only be had this year by purchase. (J. D. Whitney to W. D. Whitney, 26 February 1868, quoted in Brewster, 1909:264)

> 'Petroleum' is what has killed us. By the word 'petroleum,' understand the desire to sell worthless property for large sums and the impolicy of having anybody around to interfere with the little game. (J. D. Whitney to W. D. Whitney, 13 April 1868, quoted in Brewster, 1909:266–267)

Thus, in spite of a supportive governor and a testimonial from the Academy to the Legislature in favor of the Survey (Hittell, p. 100), funding temporarily ceased. Even before the axe fell, Bolander, Kellogg, and Behr had withdrawn from any further Survey-related activities in a show of solidarity for Whitney (Leviton & Aldrich, 1997:101), a move that would prove more permanent for them than for Whitney. At the 20 April 1868 meeting of the Academy, a report strongly condemning the "abrupt and shabby" discontinuance of the State Geological Survey was accepted, approved, and adopted (Hittell, p. 100). At a subsequent meeting, Bolander, as corresponding secretary, "stated that he had received two letters from scientific men in the East, commenting in such violent terms of condemnation on the recent action of the Legislature in superseding the State Geological Survey that he declined to read them publicly" (Hittell, p. 102). Nevertheless, "As the discontinuance of the Survey deprived Professor Whitney of his occupation in California and necessitated his return to the East, he resigned his office as president of the Academy and accompanied his withdrawal with a few farewell remarks" (Hittell, p. 100).

An Asylum for Rebel Professors

The same year (1868) that a hostile Legislature pulled the plug on the State Geological Survey saw the establishment of the University of California, by the merger of the private College of California in Oakland with a proposed State Agricultural, Mining, and Mechanical Arts College (Constance, 1978; Stadtman, 1970). It is reasonable to assume that this was not strictly a coincidence; at the very least, the University represented an equally prestigious alternative to the Survey for the State to parade before the general public and the nation at large, and one more palatable to those legislators who had a personal vendetta against Whitney. If so, there is some irony in the fact that Whitney had played a significant role in the founding of the University, and even served as chairman for the commission that drafted the plans for the State University (Brewster, 1909; Stadtman, 1970).

In 1861, Whitney had prepared "Outline of a plan for the disposal and care of the specimens collected by the State Geological Survey of California," in which he proposed that the specimens be divided among the State Agricultural Society at Sacramento and the California Academy of Natural Sciences (Appendix E in Leviton & Aldrich, 1997:512–513):

> The State Agricultural Society shall receive a full set of the plants, soils, and other specimens illustrating the agricultural resources of the State; also a set of the rocks, minerals and ores, exhibiting its geological structure and mineral wealth. These shall be arranged in the hall of the Society, in a room or rooms provided for that purpose and fitted with cases by the Society. The arranging and labeling of the specimens shall be done by the geological corps.
>
> The remainder of the specimens collected on the Survey shall be deposited in a building to be erected at San Francisco and called the 'State Museum.' This building shall be erected by private funds subscribed by the citizens of San Francisco and the State in general, aided by an equal amount furnished by the Legislature. The Governor, the President of the Academy, and the State Geologist shall constitute the committee to take charge of the erection of the building, purchase a suitable lot of land, and make the other necessary arrangements.

Whitney proceeded to draft a proposed floorplan for a State Museum, to serve as the headquarters for the Survey during its existence and subsequently to revert fully to the Academy, "to be used by them as a place of meeting, and for all the purposes required by the Academy, and it shall be the duty of the Academy to keep the collections in order, to make such additions to them as they may be able to do, and to make the whole museum available as far as possible, and is consistent with its safety, for the purposes of scientific and popular education."

However, the passage of the Morrill Act in 1862, providing grants of land for state agricultural colleges,[2] led the California state legislature to turn its sights instead on "establishing a State University, embracing an Agricultural College, a School of Mining and a Museum, including the geological collections of the State" (Hittell, p. 65). Whitney accordingly chose to put his influence where it would do the most good, serving as chairman for the commission that drafted the plans for the future State University (Brewster, 1909:241). His proposal, known as the "Museum Plan," was based on the rationale that:

---

[2] The Morrill Act, or Agricultural College Land Grant Act, was signed into law on 2 July 1862 by Abraham Lincoln. It gave each state 30,000 acres of public land per senator and congressman, for the purpose of "the endowment, support, and maintenance of at least one college where the leading object shall be, without excluding other scientific and classical studies, and including military tactics, to teach such branches of learning as are related to agriculture and the mechanical arts, in such a manner as the legislatures of the States may respectively prescribe, in order to promote the liberal and practical education of the industrial classes in the several pursuits and professions in life" (quoted in Stadtman, 1970:25). The Morrill Act also provided the funds for the new professorship at Yale that was used to entice Brewer away from the California Geological Survey (Slack, 1993).

[T]he establishment of the Geological Survey was in fact the first step towards the production of a State University. Without the information to be obtained by that Survey, no thorough instruction was possible on this coast, either in geography, geology, or natural history; for the student of these branches requires to be taught in that which is about him, and with which he is brought into daily contact, as well as that which is distant and only theoretically important. (quoted in Stadtman, 1970:27)

Although Whitney's full proposal proved overly ambitious, Section 24 of the Organic Act bringing the University of California into existence (Assembly Bill 583) specified that:

The collections made by the State Geological Survey shall belong to the University, and the Regents shall, in their plans, have in view the early and secure arrangement of the same for the use of the students of the University, so soon as the geological survey shall be completed, and of giving access to the same to the public at large and to visitors from abroad; and shall in every respect, by acts of courtesy and accommodation, encourage the visits of persons of scientific tastes and acquirements from other portions of the United States and of Europe, to California. The said collections shall be arranged by the resident Professors of the University in a building by themselves, which shall be denominated the 'Museum of the University.' . . . the Board of Regents may allow duplicates to be taken from said collections of the State Geological Survey and made a part of some other museum under the care of an incorporated Academy of science, which shall become responsible for the custody and return of same.

There is at least some evidence of mutual support and sharing of resources, at least in the scientific realm, between the fledgling University (Fig. 6), the Survey, and the Academy. Following the precedent of Brewer, who had a brief association with the College of California before returning East,

FIGURE 6. University of California, Berkeley, from the east looking toward San Francisco Bay (Harmon Gymnasium, South Hall, North Hall, and Mechanical Arts, 1879). Courtesy Bancroft Library, University of California, Berkeley (Image 3:228).

members of the Survey and the Academy taught several courses at the University during its early years: Forestry by Bolander, Field Botany by Kellogg and Gibbons, and Lower Forms of Vegetable Life (e.g., fungi) by Harvey W. Harkness (Constance, 1978). A special meeting of the Academy in 1875 was held at Berkeley, at the invitation of University President Gilman, at which it was remarked that "the Academy would have to depend mainly upon the University to fill its ranks as time thinned it of pioneers" (Hittell, p. 181). Bolander even served as an *ex officio* Regent in 1871–1875, by virtue of his position as State Superintendent of Public Instruction at that time (Stadtman et al., 1967).

Bolander's brief presence notwithstanding, relations between the Regents of the University and the Survey were another matter. At the final demise of the Survey, Whitney noted that "I have not the support but the opposition of the Regents of the University" (Letter from Whitney to F. von Richthofen, 1 June 1877, quoted in Brewster, 1909:333). Antagonism between the Regents and the Academy is also evident, such that a verbal proposition by the Regents in 1870 to incorporate the Academy as part of the University was "very decidedly objected to" (Hittell, p. 123). James Cooper zoologist for the Survey and director of the Academy museum at the time, was particularly vehement in his rebuttal:

> ... the Academy is flourishing considering the hard times and laughs at the wise professors and regents of the University who kindly informed us that we must be swallowed up in that Asylum for rebel Professors or be extinguished. On the contrary they have managed so recklessly that their President admits they are on the verge of bankruptcy, and nothing but a liberal appropriation by the Legislature will save them! This will be had ... as the University is a popular hobby & will probably swallow up all that the state has to give. (Letter from Cooper to S.F. Baird, 24 March 1871, quoted in Leviton & Aldrich, 1993:123)

Succumbed to Stupidity and Malignity

Following the legislative setbacks of 1868, Whitney returned to his professorship at Harvard, rented Asa Gray's garden home, and prepared two more volumes of Survey reports and a popular scientific guide to the Yosemite Valley region, all at his own expense (Brewster, 1909). In the winter of 1869–1870, he returned to California to take up the battle anew:

> As soon ... as the new legislature convened, Whitney repaired to California and laid siege to the new body. Of his scientific friends in the East, Dana, Henry, Guyot, and Agassiz gave special aid; while of the Californians, Leland Stanford lent the weight of his very considerable influence and Edward Tompkins, who was state senator, took charge of the details of the campaign. Governor Haight was, as always, favorable. Among them the bill went through. (Brewster, 1909;269–270)

The 1870 appropriation allowed the field crew to be reassembled, though without a botanical component. Furthermore, the Survey no longer held its original appeal even to Whitney: "I can do other scientific work which will bring me in just as much scientific reputation as this, without half the wear and tear which this survey demands, and for which I am getting less fitted as I get older." (Letter from Whitney to wife, 13 August 1870, quoted in Brewster, 1909:275). Whitney's malaise apparently extended to his involvement in Academy affairs, where his report on the Survey at the 4 December 1871 meeting (Hittell, p. 138) may have also marked his final appearance. The following year, he disparagingly indicated that the Academy was now in the hands of "business men" (quoted in Leviton and Aldrich, 1997:138), presumably referring to the newly established Board of Trustees (Hittell, p. 130).

Support for the Survey made it through the 1872 legislature, but there subsequently turned out to be no funds available for it in the Treasury (Brewster, 1909). At a special meeting of the Trustees of the Academy, a petition was drawn up to be sent to the State Legislature:

> The Trustees of the California Academy of Sciences, as requested by an unanimous vote of that body, respectfully pray that a liberal appropriation may be made at this session of the Legislature for the continuance of the State Geological Survey and the publications thereof as at present organized and conducted under the direction of Professor J. D. Whitney. (Hittell, p. 142)

At a subsequent meeting, the esteemed visiting scientist Louis Agassiz, after praising the Academy, "also spoke of the excellent and valuable work of the State Geological Survey, and of the bright promise of the University of California for the cultivation, promotion, and diffusion of knowledge" (Hittell, p. 146). At the same meeting were John Torrey, botanist extraordinaire from New York, and, as an introductory appearance, Daniel Coit Gilman (Fig. 7), president-elect of the University.

Contrary to Cooper's previously quoted glib statement that "the University is a popular hobby & will probably swallow up all that the state has to give," Whitney and Gilman soon found themselves united in battle against a common foe in the form of the 1874 legislature. Gilman's efforts at academic innovation ran afoul of "the social unrest of the 1870s, when California's farmers and workingmen were challenging established wealth, established authority, and established intellectual values, [and] found the University, even as it then existed, too rich for the needs of the common man" (Stadtman, 1970:69). As a result, just one year after the Berkeley campus opened, Whitney wrote:

FIGURE 7. Daniel Coit Gilman (1872). Courtesy Bancroft Library, University of California, Berkeley.

> Gilman is engaged in a hard fight to save the University from the claws of the grangers who want to make a manual-labor school of it. Gilman feels very much discouraged, especially as he now realizes fully that a state institution must always be in hot water. For each legislature can undo the work of its predecessors, and they have full power to pull down and alter as they please. Already, by the New Code, all the Regents are appointed by the Governor, and by the constitution of the state, can hold office only for four years, so that politics and change must ever be the predominating elements in the concern. (Letter from J.D. Whitney to W.D. Whitney, 3 March 1874, quoted in Brewster, 1909:288)

Gilman resigned the following year, accepting a post at Johns Hopkins University in Maryland. As for the Survey, Whitney at last threw in the towel for good:

> The survey has succumbed to the stupidity and malignity of the legislature, backed by the same characteristics on the part of the Governor. The Committee reported in favor of continuing the work, putting it under the supervision of a 'Board of Survey' . . . I would not have acted under this had it passed, and had the place been offered to me; but the discussion turned entirely on me and my work, without any hint of the possibility of the employment of any one else. I was accused of having given all the collections to Harvard; and it was stated over and over again,

that the survey had been run by me for the benefit of Harvard University! (Letter from J.D. Whitney to W.D. Whitney, 19 March 1874, quoted in Brewster, 1909:289-290)

The Generosity of a Few Citizens

The insinuation that Whitney was acting on behalf of Harvard at the expense of California was grounded in the reality that Harvard University was in fact where at least the botanical specimens were sent for processing. This violation of the Academy's efforts at autonomous publication of the California flora triggered this summary by Gibbons:

> three sets [of California plants] have been made up; one for the California Academy of Sciences; one for the University of California; while one has been sent out of the State, and eastern botanists have the credit of devoting their time to working it up, in occasional paroxysms, without remuneration. It would have been far better for the interests of the State and of science had this [California Geological] commission never existed
>
> California scientists would have accomplished more work, without aid from the State, than has thus far, to all practical purposes, been achieved by the commission. (quoted in Ewan, 1955:20)

Nevertheless, in spite of Gibbons' confidence in his colleagues' abilities, an undertaking of the magnitude of a brand new state flora, especially up to Brewer's and Whitney's standards, required the resources and expertise that could only be found at an established major herbarium. Most vascular plant specimens from the Survey were accordingly shipped to Harvard University, where Asa Gray was feverishly working on his and John Torrey's magnum opus, *A Flora of North America*. Part and parcel with his work on the *Flora*, Gray was not only willing but needed to have the flood of new collections from the western regions pass through his hands (Dupree, 1959).

After leaving the Survey and taking up a professorship at Yale, Brewer joined in the time-consuming task of analyzing collections, writing treatments, and assembling the whole into what would become the first complete flora of California. However, although the original legislation mandated that the reports of the Survey be copyrighted and sold for the benefit of the common school fund, no funds were allocated, so that Brewer's efforts took the form of a labor of love:

> I received no pay whatever after the closing of my connection with the Survey of California — neither for the time nor the expense in working up results. I spent an aggregate of two years time — a little more rather than less — and over two thousand dollars in cash, besides deducting another one thousand dollars from my salary from college because of time taken out from my work — that is, absence during term time at work on my plants at the Cambridge Herbarium. (quoted in Farquhar, 1930:xxiii)

Whitney was eventually able to secure additional State funding for the publication of several Survey reports, but not for botany. Instead, a select group of California's wealthier citizens, at the urging of University President Gilman, came forth and provided the necessary funds from their own pockets: Leland Stanford, D. O. Mills, Lloyd Tevis, James C. Flood, Charles McLaughlin, Robert B. Woodward, William Norris, John O. Earl, Henry Pierce, Oliver Eldridge, and S. Clinton Hastings. As a result, Sereno Watson, who had become familiar with the western flora while serving as botanist for Clarence King's spin-off survey of the Fortieth Parallel (Watson, 1871; Davis, 1994), was employed to finish what Gray and Brewer had started. Whitney summarized the situation in the introduction to the first of the resultant two volumes (Brewer et al., 1876; Watson, 1880):

> The Survey not being able to pay any one for devoting his whole time to this investigation, the

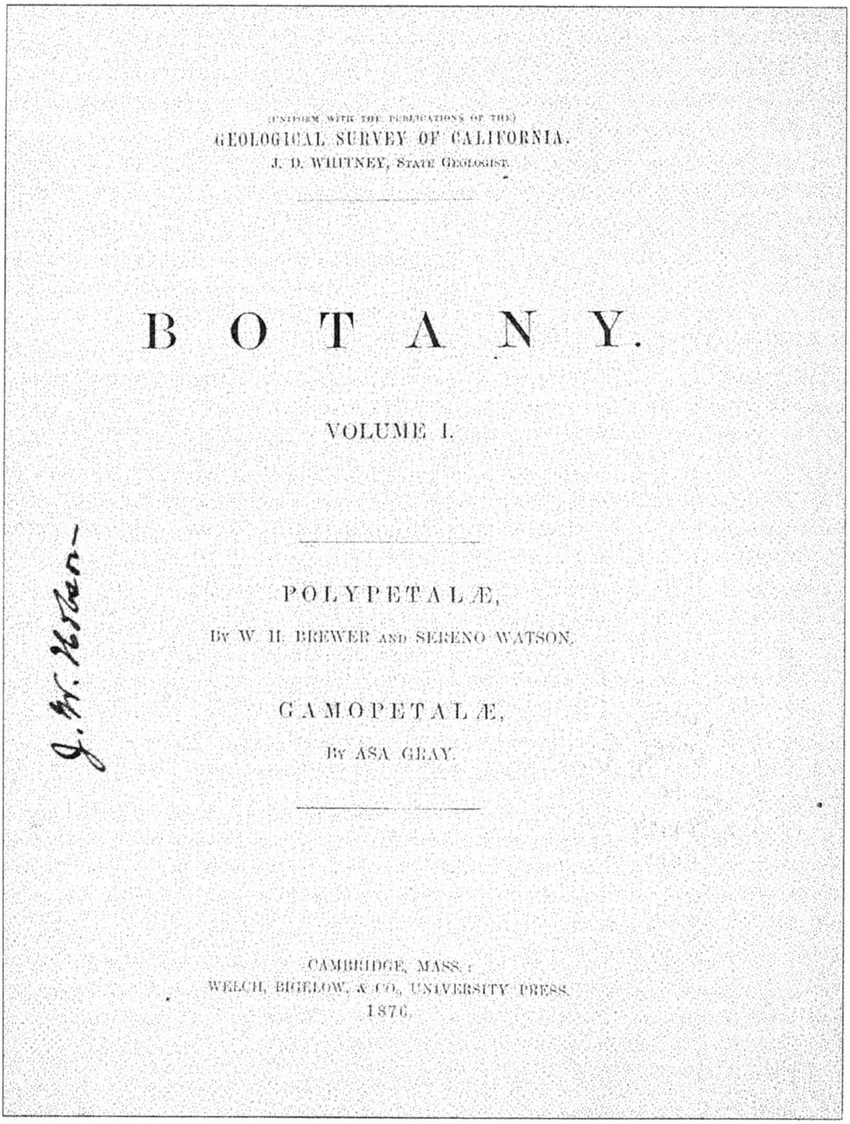

(UNIFORM WITH THE PUBLICATIONS OF THE)
GEOLOGICAL SURVEY OF CALIFORNIA.
J. D. WHITNEY, State Geologist.

BOTANY.

VOLUME I.

POLYPETALÆ,
BY W. H. BREWER AND SERENO WATSON.

GAMOPETALÆ,
BY ASA GRAY.

CAMBRIDGE, MASS.:
WELCH, BIGELOW, & CO., UNIVERSITY PRESS.
1876.

FIGURE 8. Title page of the botany volume for the California Geological Survey.

year 1874 had been reached and the printing had not yet begun. The Legislature of 1873–74 put an end to the work by refusing any further appropriations for the Survey, and the present volume would have remained unpublished, had it not been for the generosity of a few citizens of San Francisco, who came forward and placed in the hands of the [former] State Geologist a sum sufficient to insure the publication of one volume of the Flora of California. (Brewer et al., 1876:viii–ix)

In recognition of the collective contributions and efforts of all involved, the Academy passed a motion "that the names of the contributors should be enrolled upon the records of the Academy as Benefactors of Science. And it was further ordered that honorable mention should be made and recorded of Professor Asa Gray, Professor J. D. Whitney, Professor Watson and Professor William H. Brewer for their personal devotion, without pecuniary considerations, to the work" (Hittell, p. 182).

The Extent of Botanical Activity at that Time

Although the first set of the botanical collections amassed by the California Geological Survey still resides in the Gray Herbarium at Harvard University, a duplicate set was eventually deposited at the University of California, forming the core of the current University Herbarium. Although tradition has it that this herbarium was established in 1872 with the receipt of the Survey specimens, the earliest extant records in the herbarium archives concerning Survey material date only from 1901, by which time the herbarium already contained nearly 27,000 specimens. The earliest "Herbarium Records" book in the University Herbarium archives begins in 1898, at which time 24,179 specimens were censused. On pp. 152–153 is the following entry:

Prof. Brewer's donation of State Survey Specimens, 1901. Under date of Oct. 24, 1901 Mr. Coville [botanist for the U.S. Department of Agriculture, where the U.S. National Herbarium was then housed] wrote to Prof. Setchell as follows: 'At the request of Professor W.H. Brewer, I send to you by mail today a set [of] 1,714 specimens of his collections of 1860 to 1867 on which the Botany of California was largely based. The specimens are to be the property of the University of California. Professor Brewer will probably write you farther regarding them'.

Although the exact number is not tabulated, there are probably significantly more than 1,714 California Geological Survey specimens among the current holdings of the University Herbarium, including numerous duplicates.

It is evident nevertheless that there was strong support for botany nearly from the University's inception, as befit the provisions of a land grant university. The establishment of a College of Agriculture was given first priority by the Organic Act, with the Secretary of the Board of Regents instructed to "receive and distribute such rare and valuable seeds, plants, shrubbery and trees . . . as may be adapted to our climates and soils, or to purposes of experiment therein" (Sec. 16). In his 1872–1873 report, President Gilman called for "a professor whose province it is to teach the Laws of Vegetation — all that pertains to the growth and structure of plants, of Botany; in its scientific and economic aspects; and there should also be a competent gardener, and perhaps a forester employed at once to take charge of the grounds" (quoted in Constance, 1978:2).

The first full-time faculty member to teach botany courses was Joseph LeConte (Fig. 9), Professor of Geology, Natural History, and Botany, whose appointment in 1869 placed him among the original faculty of the newly established university. LeConte and his brother John, heirs of a cotton plantation in Georgia, had actively pursued positions at the new university, seeking a refuge from the social upheaval and privations of the Reconstructionist South (Stephens, 1982). The botanical component expanded significantly in 1875, when Bavarian-born Eugene W. Hilgard (Fig. 10) was recruited. Hilgard promptly took on the challenge of developing the full-fledged College of Agriculture required by the Organic Act and campaigned for by Bolander in his capacity as an *ex officio* Regent (Stadtman, 1979; Stadtman et al., 1967; Weislander, 1965), and also established the Agricultural Experiment Station (taking advantage of the 1887 Hatch Act [Stadtman, 1970]). The LeConte brothers and Hilgard (who had spent a significant portion of his professional life in Mississippi) are presumably high on the list of "rebel Professors" scorned by Cooper (quoted earlier). All three were nevertheless elected resident members of the Academy, the LeConte brothers in 1870 (Hittell, p. 120) and Hilgard in 1896 (Hittell, p. 367), though none played a particularly active role in Academy affairs.

As previously noted, some botany courses were also offered by Bolander, Kellogg, and Gibbons, all of whom had strong Academy involvement. In addition, visiting lecturers were occasionally employed, providing us with the following account by Charles E. Bessey:

> Arriving in Oakland we were advised that it would be best for us to find quarters in town rather than to attempt to do so in Berkeley, then only a much scattered village of but a few people. A horse car ran towards Berkeley at long intervals, and a couple of miles out in the country it stopped in a discouraged sort of way, and the passengers were obligated to wait on an open platform for a smaller car drawn by a single mule at a very slow place. In time, however, the car brought one to the edge of the University grounds, at that time marked by a brook and a fine California Laurel tree. We crossed the brook on a plank, and walked a little distance to the two buildings which housed the University of that day. I think it took a full hour to make the trip from Oakland to Berkeley. (quoted in Constance, 1978:3)

FIGURE 9. Joseph LeConte. Courtesy Bancroft Library, University of California, Berkeley (Image 13:4419).

FIGURE 10. Eugene W. Hilgard. Courtesy Bancroft Library, University of California, Berkeley (Image 13:281).

In spite of the steady growth of the University, the Academy remained the botanical center for the San Francisco Bay Area. This is evidenced by the following 1914 account by Samuel Bonsall Parish, the first resident botanist in southern California, reminiscing on a visit to the Bay Area some "thirty odd years" earlier:

> Berkeley at that time was not a botanical center by any means. I remember coming over from San Francisco . . . to call upon the only working botanist in Berkeley. I suppose there was somebody up at the University, tho I do not know. But the only working botanist was the Rev. E. L. Greene, afterwards Professor of Botany in the University, but who was at that time [1881–1884] rector of a little wooden church [St. Mark's Episcopal Church]. . . . I came over

and attended the morning service and afterwards went with the rector to his home and we talked about plants the rest of the evening. That seemed to be the extent of botanical activity in Berkeley at that time. What activity there was on the coast of California at that time centered in San Francisco at the old Academy of Sciences, which then occupied a church at the top of the hill, and the botanical department was located in the gallery of the old church. There were perhaps three or four persons in the Academy who were more or less interested in botany. *(Madroño* 1:71, 1922)

Parish goes on to describe Behr as "the best educated botanist," whose interest had turned to spiders; Kellogg, "in his shirt sleeves and his old red flannel waistcoat, making drawings of twigs"; Kellogg's co-worker, William Harford; and Harvey Harkness, who was working on fungi. More will be said on Greene, Harford, and Harkness later, but noteworthy at this point, in the absence of any mention by Parish, is the person who was possibly already curator of botany at this time: Mary Katharine Curran.

I Began to Make Myself Useful

The connection of Mary Katharine (Kate) Layne Curran Brandegee (Fig. 11) to California botany originates with the founding of the Toland Medical College in 1864, which was accepted as the University's medical school in 1873 (Stadtman, 1970). When the recently widowed Curran decided to pursue a medical career in 1875, at the age of 31 (Dupree & Gade, 1971), she was only two years behind Lucy Wanzer, the first woman to force her way into the University's medical school; Curran presumably faced many of the same obstacles. Wanzer's admission had required a reluctant ruling by the Regents that the Organic Act of the University gave an equal opportunity to both sexes, but significant resistance remained. The dean of the medical school encouraged Wanzer's fellow students to make her so uncomfortable that she would choose to leave (Doyle, 1934). One anecdote is particularly priceless both for showing the degree of hazing, and the spirit that allowed Wanzer to persist:

FIGURE 11. Mary Katharine (Kate) Layne Curran Brandegee. Courtesy Hunt Institute for Botanical Documentation, Carnegie-Mellon University.

When [Wanzer] was present at an eye clinic, the professor in charge stated: 'A woman has no business to study medicine. If she does, she ought to have her ovaries removed.' She quietly replied: 'If that is true, the men students ought also to have their testicles removed!' (Doyle, 1934:239)

As a separate but closely affiliated college, the California College of Pharmacy was established in 1872, becoming part of the University only two months later. Beginning in 1874, College of Pharmacy courses were taught in the Toland Medical College building, on Stockton Street between Chestnut and Francisco streets. This location was only about a mile away from the Academy, which was at that time at the corner of California and Dupont (now Grant) streets. This made it convenient for Behr to be a professor at the College of Pharmacy, teaching botany as the basis for a large percentage of the available pharmacopoeia. While pursuing her medical degree, Curran accordingly came under the tutelage of Behr. As described by Wanzer:

> We were all much interested in Materia Medica. Our professor was a very busy man and could not always give the time he wished to give to the subject: Therefore Mrs. Curran with a number of us who were members of the Academy of Sciences decided to go out with the Pharmaceutical Class — Dr. Herman Behr our instructor — and study the flora and plant life of the bay region usually Marin, Contra Costa and San Mateo Counties. Whatever was collected of value or of special interest was taken or given to the Academy of Sciences. Mrs. Curran was a very close student and observer — so also was Dr. Behr and his deep interest in the Academy — and the flora and plant life of California had a charm for the entire class. (Letter from Lucy Wanzer to Eleanor Stockton [Curran's niece], 25 July 1925, in UC Herbarium archives)

Curran received her M.D. in 1878 (with honors, according to Wanzer [see above, Wanzer to Stockton]), but was subsequently unsuccessful in establishing a medical practice (Setchell, 1926). As noted by Rush (1997), this cannot be ascribed simply to her gender, in that several other women were practicing medicine in San Francisco, including Wanzer. Although retaining a lifelong interest in medicine (Herre, ca. 1960), Curran accordingly began spending more and more time at the Academy, where, with Behr's backing, she was elected a member in 1879, only one year after the first women were accepted as members.[3] Curran did not begin as a botanist (her first presentation to the Academy was "On Caenums of the Hare" [Hittell, p. 242]), and she confessed decades later that "With me botany was accidental. I would have preferred the study of birds or more strongly still, the study of insects" (quoted in Setchell, 1926:168). Independent of her initial orientation, Curran eventually found her niche in the herbarium: "As a member of the California Academy of Sciences in San Francisco, with considerable spare time on my hands, I began to make myself useful especially about the herbarium, which was in a shocking condition" (quoted in Setchell, 1926:167).

As a result, in 1883 Curran was appointed joint curator of botany with mycologist Justin P. Moore, who was also serving as first vice-president (Hittell, p. 252).[4] The following four years the curatorship was held jointly with Edward Lee Greene (Greene listed first in 1884 and 1886 [Hittell, pp. 266, 278], Curran first in 1887 [Hittell, p. 283]), after which she was sole curator until 1892. As an exception rather than the rule for curators at that time, Curran was awarded a salary of $40 per month (Hittell, p. 260), and in 1885, was furthermore elected an honorary life member (Hittell, p. 272). In choosing to provide her with a salary, it was noted that Curran had "for many months given her whole time to the proper arrangement and classification of the botanical collections of [the] Academy, and travels at her own expense to different parts of the country to fill wants in the collection, etc. From knowledge of her successful labors on this special unit, the Council unanimously recommends this action" (Hittell, pp. 260–261). As examples of her contributions to Academy curation, Curran standardized herbarium sheet size, instituted a new method of gluing specimens, provided packets "containing fragments for lending," and advocated the mounting of multiple collections on a single sheet[5] (Brandegee, 1901b). She also donated three volumes of Bentham and Hooker's *Genera Plantarum* to the Academy (Hittell, p. 264).

In addition, Curran revived an outlet for Academy publications, which had languished for some

---

[3] The election of women as members finally implemented a policy adopted by the Academy the year of its founding: "on motion by Dr. A. Kellogg, Resolved, as the sense of this society that we highly approve of the aid of females in every department of natural science, and that we earnestly invite their cooperation" (Hittell, p. 21).

[4] Justin P. Moore was sole curator of botany in 1882. Previous curators had been Albert Kellogg, Dr. T. L. Andrews (1855), Hiram G. Bloomer, and Henry N. Bolander.

[5] This last policy has been the bane of subsequent curators, who are routinely faced with the need to divide sheets on which more than one species (as currently circumscribed) were mounted.

years (as discussed later). In 1884, she instituted the *Bulletin of the California Academy of Sciences*, serving as "acting editor" (Hittell, p. 267; Crosswhite & Crosswhite, 1985). The first volume of the *Bulletin* contains one of her most significant scientific contributions (Curran, 1885), a careful and critical evaluation of all the plant species described over the preceding three decades by Kellogg, Behr, and Bolander, taking advantage of the newly available *Botany of California* (Brewer et al., 1876; Watson, 1880). As noted in her introduction:

> When the arrangement of the Herbarium of the Academy was undertaken two years ago, the necessity of bringing these scattered descriptions of species together in some form, soon became apparent . . . The preparation of this list has been a matter of more difficulty than would be supposed, on account of the scattered and fragmentary condition of the material. The types of many of the species have disappeared from the herbarium, and many have been identified from drawings by Dr. Kellogg, which have only recently become accessible to us. In the labor of identification, the writer has received the constant advice and assistance of the Rev. E. L. Greene. (Curran, 1885:128)

A Gentleman, Well and Carefully Dressed

Curran's generous words refer to Edward Lee Greene (Fig. 12), who had informally received his botanical training from the expatriate Swedish naturalist, Thure Kumlein (Greene, 1888), and had been ordained an Episcopal priest in 1873. Greene was subsequently assigned to a series of parishes in Colorado, New Mexico, and California (McIntosh, 1983). When assigned to Vallejo in 1874, he became a member of the Academy (Hittell, p. 170), but then was relocated out of the state after one year. He returned to the Bay Area seven years later, to become rector of St. Mark's in Berkeley in 1881. Greene quickly resumed his association with the Academy, was elected a resident member in April 1883 (Hittell, p. 260), and, as previously noted, served as joint curator of botany with Curran in 1884–1887.

Although Jones (1932, 1933) credits Greene with giving Curran her botanical training, it is evident that she was already active in the Academy before Greene's arrival, under the tutelage of Behr. It is nevertheless quite possible that Greene's long-standing passion for botany encouraged her own newfound interest in the subject, as suggested by Ewan (1942). In any event, at the beginning of their association there are only indications of mutual support and respect, including joint field work (e.g., to Donner Lake [Greene, 1885:78]). Greene named a *Mimulus, Astragalus,* and *Senecio* after Curran, using her maiden name of "layneae," and referred to her as "my zealous, clear-seeing and most efficient co-laborer in the field of California botany" (Greene, 1885:84).

FIGURE 12. Edward Lee Greene. Courtesy Setchell Collection, University Herbarium Archives, University of California, Berkeley.

Alas, the relationship soon deteriorated, eventually leading to full-fledged warfare. By the 1890s, the following kinds of comments characterized Curran's [by then Brandegee] increasingly sharp criticisms in her published reviews of Greene's work: "The specific descriptions of Mr. Greene are a disgrace to botany" (Brandegee, 1893b:65), and: "A year or two before his death Dr. Gray dubbed

[Greene] 'The New Rafinesque.' In this he was unjust to Rafinesque who was at once a great egotist, a little mad, and somewhat of a genius. Prof. Greene lacks the genius" (Brandegee, 1894:420). Greene in his turn referred to Curran/Brandegee as a "she devil" (Jones, 1932, 1933), an opinion shared by at least some other male contemporaries (e.g., Britton, 1891).

Greene's animosity was passed on to his protégé, Willis Linn Jepson (Fig. 13), as discussed in greater detail later in this paper. The passage presented as evidence here, recalling Jepson's romanticized first meeting with Greene, serves also to provide a rich description of Academy facilities at the time. Jepson casts Curran as an "unkempt woman" with "an unpleasant voice," only grudgingly helpful and clearly (and properly) subordinate to the eulogized Greene:

> In a June of the early eighties of the last century a lad came out of the edge of the bordering foothills of the Sacramento Valley and set his face towards San Francisco on a great quest. Beneath the facetiousness of a smart reporter's newspaper article he had derived the existence of the California Academy of Sciences which harbored a staff of 'worthy fossils' laboring in behalf of the advancement of science and which contained, above all things else, to the boy's mind, an herbarium — an ordered collection of plants. The lad climbed the broad stone steps rising to Dr. Stone's old church on the corner of California and Dupont streets and knocked on the great door, timidly at first and, growing bolder, yet again and again and again.
>
> After a while there came down the narrow choir stairs one who inquired in an unpleasant voice what he was doing there. And without waiting for a reply the woman — for it was a woman — demanded to know why he should be knocking and calling all away from their work. The lad looked at the unkempt woman, found tongue and in a few words told his story. The woman regarded him for a space as if in astonishment, and then said shortly, 'Come up.' The lad followed her up the stairs.
>
> At the top of the stairs the gallery of the old brick church opened out before his shining eyes, filled with rows and rows of the most wonderful herbarium cases, such an array, the boy was sure, as the world had never seen before. The woman showed him the plants he wished to see, explained the herbarium, and answered his questions. Meantime he noticed a gentleman, well and carefully dressed, sitting at a table, intently studying the plants before him and occasionally writing. His face was youngish and clean-shaven, his skin clear and slightly ruddy, his features regular and full, but most remarkable was his thick head of hair which was not gray, but white as cotton. 'That,' said the woman, 'is Mr. Greene. He is studying in the Herbarium and is now engaged on a revision of Mimulus. Very able revisions of Eschscholtzia, Brodiaea, and other California genera, he has already completed. He is a very wonderful man.' Upon that she took the boy along the gallery to the table where the botanist sat, who then looked up from his work, greeted the lad and laid down his pen. The lad saw that his eye was bright and kindly, and his voice carried a certain richness akin to mellowness. (Jepson, 1918:24)

FIGURE 13. Willis Linn Jepson (1899). Courtesy Setchell Collection, University Herbarium Archives, University of California, Berkeley.

An entry in one of Jepson's voluminous notebooks is also revealing, not only of Jepson's opinion of Curran/Brandegee but perhaps of his own vulnerabilities:

> [Mrs. Brandegee's] life has been a peppery one. Undoubtedly with a genuine interest in botany and with real ability, she has yet used her botany to gratify personal hatreds. It has been used as a means of attacking someone whom she chose to dislike. And it was necessary for her to have some one to attack. It was her life to 'follow up' the work some one was publishing and find in it as many mistakes as possible. It is needless to say that any one can find plenty of occupation at such a task. (Jepson fieldbook 25:23, 31 May 1912, Jepson Herbarium archives)

In contrast, Setchell claimed that "her outbreaks of sarcasm were professional rather than personal and she was amazed at those who could not distinguish between the two, to her, very different attitudes" (Setchell, 1926:168). Support for this statement is provided by Curran/Brandegee's comment on Per Axel Rydberg, a splitter on par with Greene: "We disagree constantly but get along very well, and I tell him I like him much better than his botany" (Letter from K. Brandegee to T.S. Brandegee, from New York, 28 September 1913, in UC Herbarium archives). She was furthermore capable of poking fun at herself in this regard, e.g.: "Fernald just read me a criticism of the new edition of Britton & Brown, that is nearly as sarcastic as some of mine" (letter from K. Brandegee to T.S. Brandegee, from Harvard, 11 October 1913, in UC Herbarium archives). This latter quote also makes the point that Curran/Brandegee's acid pen, rather than setting her apart from her male colleagues, was instead a common characteristic of the era.

This point was among those noted by Albert W.C.T. Herre (ca. 1960) in his diatribe in defense of Curran/Brandegee, which was more personal than factual in nature (e.g., taking aim at Greene's alleged homosexuality). She had other defenders as well, most notably Marcus E. Jones (1932, 1933), who, like Herre, knew her only during the later periods of her life. Jones' highly opinionated biographies are riddled with factual flaws; e.g., stating Carson City, Nevada, as Curran/Brandegee's birthplace (Jones, 1933), rather than Tennessee, as she herself reports (Setchell, 1926). Nevertheless, in addition to being exceptionally entertaining, Jones's biographies are a rich source of character sketches such as the following:

> It is said of [Katharine Brandegee] that she was a very beautiful young woman. As I knew her she was a person rather angular and unconventional, with a very strong face, compelling consideration and respect without an effort on her part ... Her mind was masculine in its grasp, philosophical, discriminative to the last degree, and her keenness of observation and memory of things, and capacity to correlate was marvelous. I was always impressed by the mental grasp she had on any subject she tackled. (Jones, 1932, p. 267 of reprint)

Jones' comments on Greene, on the other hand, were significantly less complimentary: e.g., "Greene's hatred of people was limited only by his capacity to define them" (Jones, 1932, p. 267 of reprint).

There are nevertheless hints of an eventual reconciliation with Greene, in which a homesick Katharine socialized with an increasingly isolated Greene (who was by this time residing in Washington, D.C.) during her 1913 tour of eastern herbaria:

> Mr. Greene is full of gossip and is rather frank in his opinion of the pinhead selfishness of most of the botanists about the department [= the U.S. National Herbarium].... He took me out to lunch and we luxuriated riotously at ten cents per. He is as scary of the street cars and autos as a country girl and grabbed me hysterically at every crossing. If it had not rained I would have gone out botanizing with him yesterday — violets. (Letter from K. Brandegee to T.S. Brandegee, from Washington, D.C., 17 November 1913, in UC Herbarium archives)

To Sneer at Misguided Mortals Who Differ

Given the prominent roles that Curran/Brandegee and Greene subsequently played in California botany, the question of what triggered their mutual animosity has relevance beyond the purely biographical. Several possibilities can be inferred, all of which might have been involved to a greater or lesser extent. For example, Ewan's suggestion that "her particular vitriolic criticisms of Greene were surely in part the aftermath of unrequited love" (Ewan, 1942:773), although vociferously challenged by Herre (ca. 1960) and dismissed by Crosswhite and Crosswhite (1985), cannot be completely ruled out. After all, Curran was a recent widow, Greene was described as markedly handsome, and the fact that the falling-out coincided with her marriage to Townshend Brandegee certainly indicates that at least an element of spurned interest could have been involved.

Even if true, however, the emotional undercurrent probably only added intensity to a diversity of equally compelling reasons for mutual animosity. High on the list is the dramatic divergence between their taxonomic philosophies, which recapitulated as personal drama the battles that permeated the biological community following the publication of Charles Darwin's theories of natural selection and the origin of species. Following her mentor Behr (e.g., Behr, 1884), Curran became an early convert of the Darwinian interpretation of natural history. In contrast, as befit his religious orientation, Greene remained steadfast to creationist doctrine, to the disdain of Curran/Brandegee:

> He openly contemns [sic], as inconsistent with the Mosaic record, the theory of evolution held in greater or lesser degree by almost all biologists, and proclaims his belief in the special creation and the fixity of species, taking occasional opportunity to sneer at the misguided mortals who differ from him. (Brandegee, 1893b, p. 64)

Greene's philosophy predisposed him to treat all recognizable variants as distinct species, even at the expense of consigning inconvenient intermediates to the waste bin as "the works of the devil" (*fide* Herre, ca. 1960:3). In Curran/Brandegee's disparaging view:

> Mr. Greene . . . makes it perfectly evident that a species is not with him as with most of us a form of life with characters sufficiently and constantly different from others to admit of a clear description and with a name conveniently expressing relationship, but a distinct entity not necessarily in any close relation to other forms now or previously on the earth and to be hunted to its remotest lair properly labeled and put away on shelf for all time. This kind of botany was taught, probably, in the middle ages to which Mr. Greene properly belongs. (Brandegee, 1893b, p. 65)

Putting her disdain for Greene's approach into action, with perhaps a personal vendetta adding incentive, Curran/Brandegee dedicated much of her subsequent career to critically evaluating Greene's species, even to the extent of revisiting type localities to study what variation existed in the living population (Ewan, 1942). Many of her herbarium specimens clearly demonstrate this focus, such that the entire sheet is filled with a stunning diversity of flowers representing infraspecific variation within a population (e.g., *Calochortus luteus, Clarkia biloba*). In addition, she was an early proponent of experimental systematics:

> The life history of a single species, its limit of variation, and its hybrids, if any, would be far more useful than a dozen 'decades' of new violets or Senecios. A few years ago I happened upon a very instructive object lesson of this kind. . . . [Luther] Burbank informed me that he had transferred a single plant [of *Zauschneria*] from a locality not far away, and saving all the seeds produced by this self-fertilized individual, had planted them to see what variations he could get. In this row were all the forms, both of flower and foliage, which have been observed in the genus,

except the extreme narrow or revolute leaf which is climatal variation of drier regions. A few experiments of this kind would rid us of a host of species. (Brandegee, 1901a:96)

In this also she was following Behr, who in the preface to his flora of San Francisco noted that:

Many of our Californian species split into numerous variations, which mingle frequently with variations of related, equally variable species. Some of these variations owe their existence to hybridization; and this circumstance is probably the reason why several species described and characterized by different authors have not been found again. In annuals such spurious species will only reappear occasionally. Questionable types can be investigated only by cultivation. Up to this time California does not possess a botanical garden or experimental grounds where such questions could be definitely settled. (Behr, 1888:3–4)

Ironically, while Behr and Curran/Brandegee shared philosophies that represented the cutting edge of botanical inquiry at that time, and which draw our sense of kinship in the current day, it was Greene who had the better appreciation of how much undescribed diversity still existed in California, even by late 20th century standards (Ertter, 2000). Contrary to Curran/Brandegee's assessment that "It is safe to say that not more than one in ten of [Greene's] species is tenable, and probably one in fifteen or twenty would be nearer the mark" (Brandegee, 1893b:64), a respectable 70% of those species described by Greene while he was residing in California have stood the test of time (McVaugh, 1983). On the other hand, Curran/Brandegee's propensity towards explaining variation as representing intraspecific diversity or resulting from hybridization meant that, in spite of a career spent in the midst of unrecognized novelties, she described only a handful of California's wealth of species (tellingly, mostly *before* her rift with Greene; e.g., Curran, 1884). So extreme was this propensity that her husband in later years "sometimes humorously remarked that he thought her flora [of California, never completed] would finally contain only a single species" (Setchell, 1926:166).

For the Want of Confidence in Its Management

Another prominent explanation for the rift between Curran and Greene, which is most relevant to the institutional focus of the current narrative, is their respective alignment in opposing camps in the Academy politics that peaked in the late 1880s. Although the acrimonious elections of 1887, which resulted in the election of an opposition slate of officers, are clearly recorded, the issues at stake are to some extent a matter of conjecture. The most illuminating document in this regard is the 1887 Reform Ticket (copy in UC Herbarium archives), which presents as stated goals:

- To reform the Administration of the affairs of this Society.
- To save and protect its property from rot and waste.
- To advance the cause of Science instead of the aggrandizement or profit of individuals.
- To furnish suitable buildings or rooms, indispensable for its Museum, Laboratory, and Officers.
- To provide for the publication of the *Proceedings* — neglected for years.
- To put the Society in a position of respectability before the world, such as to deserve the large Bequests and Donations which are being withheld for the want of confidence in its management.
- And generally; to make the California Academy of Sciences a success in furtherance of the hopes and desires of its friends.

These are serious charges, ranging from inadequately housed collections to alienated donors, and are presumably aimed at George Davidson (Fig. 14), a well-respected member of the United States

Coast Survey who had been president of the Academy for the previous 16 years. According to Ewan (1987:6), "For sixty years he was the best known scientist on the Pacific Coast." In the bitterly contested election of 1887, which resulted in a complete turnover of the slate of officers, Davidson was ousted by Harvey Willson Harkness (Fig. 15). Harkness, a retired physician with a strong mycological interest, had significant political connections; for example, at the ceremony of completing the Transcontinental Railway in 1869, he was "chosen to present, on behalf of the State of California, the golden spike used upon that occasion" (Hittell, p. 441). According to Hittell, "an antagonism had been growing between Professor Davidson and Dr. Harkness, which to a considerable extent involved their friends" (Hittell, p. 277), with Greene apparently in the Davidson camp and Curran in Harkness's.

FIGURE 14. George Davidson. Courtesy California Academy of Sciences Archives.

FIGURE 15. Harvey Willson Harkness. Courtesy California Academy of Sciences Archives.

Tantalizing evidence of how visible this episode in Academy politics was beyond the walls of the institution can be seen in a subsequent address by David Starr Jordan, who replaced Harkness as President of the Academy in 1896:

> For some time previous to my election the Academy membership had been divided into two warring factions — one led by Dr. Davidson, the other by Dr. Harkness ... Both men were vigorous and rather intolerant, a combination of qualities which was not rare in pioneer days, and disrupted more than one California organization even as it affected the famous 'society on the Stanislow.' Indeed, it is reputed that the discords in the institution furnished the motive for Bret Harte's satirical verse. (quoted in Ewan, 1955:37)

Before the reasons for Greene's and Curran's alignments in the opposing camps can be understood, the issues underlying the antagonism against Davidson must first be discerned. The most obvious explanation, ironically enough, involves the bequest that singlehandedly changed the Academy from a scholarly club into a full-fledged scientific institution: that of prominent philanthropist James Lick, "the eccentric cabinetmaker whose investments had made him a millionaire" (Stadtman, 1970:108). Lick's attentions had been turned to the Academy by Hiram G. Bloomer, one of the early members with an interest in botany, best known for his membership in San Francisco's notorious Vigilance Committee. According to Jepson (1899:165–166), "Bloomer was the first to interest Mr. Lick in the nature and extent of scientific work, to explain the needs of its devotees, and to introduce him to the Academy."

This Fine Building, in Which We Meet

High on the list of Academy's needs was a suitable permanent home for the increasingly valuable library and natural history collections, which had long outgrown the solitary shared cabinet of the 1850s. For the first two decades of its existence, the Academy occupied quarters at 622 Clay Street, "at the generous sufferance of Pioche, Bayerque & Co." However, the building was damaged in an 1865 earthquake, "to such an extent as to induce those in charge of the library and collections to pack them up and store them where they would not be exposed to the weather" (Hittell, p. 79). Rooms were subsequently rented at the corner of Montgomery and Sacramento streets, but these also proved inadequate, so two years later the Academy returned to its previous site once repairs had been effected (Hittell, p. 84).

In 1869, the San Francisco authorities reserved an "Outside-Land lot," near the corner of Point Lobos and First Avenues, "for the purposes of an 'Academy of Sciences'" (Hittell, pp. 108–109). No building funds were allocated, however, and Academy income ($1,760 in 1868) was woefully inadequate for undertaking a construction project. Instead, in 1874 the Academy relocated to the former First Congregational Church on California and Dupont (now Grant) streets (Hittell, p. 164). The short-comings of this facility for natural history collections quickly became evident:

> [T]he old First Congregational Church . . . had been built in 1853 of brick made with salt water, which had been so poorly burned and were so soft that they absorbed moisture like a sponge and did not dry out from one rainy season to another. . . . A deep foundation had been necessary for the foundation of this structure, and into this excavation the water from the hill continually seeped, keeping the foundation walls constantly soaked. (Hittell, p. 280)

Lick's initial gift therefore appeared as a godsend: the deed to a piece of land on Market Street, near the southwestern corner with Fourth Street, worth $150,000 (Hittell, pp. 151–152). When first offered in 1873 (the same year that Lick was elected a life member of the Academy), the deed carried several stipulations: "that the premises should be used and devoted solely and exclusively for scientific purposes, and none other," and that:

> The Academy was required to erect and maintain on the premises, and covering the whole lot except a small space in the rear for light and ventilation, a substantial and elegant brick edifice, three stories in height, with a substantial granite front faced with appropriate scientific emblems; and its structure and design should be classic and such as would readily distinguish it from buildings used for business or commercial purposes. (Hittell, p. 151)

Two years were designated in which the Academy was supposed to come up with the funds necessary to build such a magnificent structure, with $200,000 estimated to be the amount necessary for construction and maintenance (Hittell, p. 153), or else the deed would be forfeit. Although the Academy had previously been the recipient of other relatively large bequests,[6] this was a seriously daunting prospect. Over the next several years the deed was accordingly modified, and in 1875 (the same year Curran entered medical school) the property was donated to the Academy outright, with no stipulations attached (Hittell, p. 186).

This still left the Academy unsure what to do with the prime downtown real estate, since even a more modest facility was well beyond the members' means. Lick's death in 1876, while suitably mourned, looked to provide an answer, in that his Trust Deed specified that, after certain bequests

---

[6] Foremost among these was $20,000 from Charles Crocker in 1881, "in aid of scientific research under the auspices of the Academy" (Hittell, p. 237). This established the Crocker Scientific Investigation Fund, which played a significant role in subsequent years, including as the source of curatorial salaries. Crocker himself was elected an honorary life member in 1882 (Hittell, p. 241).

were filled (including $700,000 to establish the Lick Observatory [Hittell, p. 186]), the remainder of his estate was to be divided between the Academy and the Society of California Pioneers (Hittell, p. 187). The will, however, was contested by a son who had been left out of the inheritance (Hittell, p. 199), and the Academy was accordingly unable to draw from the Trust Deed until 1879. Funds were then available as a mortgage with the Lick Trustees, but exactly how much the Academy's share of the estate would turn out to be was not immediately apparent. In fact, it was not until 1895 that it could be determined that the Academy's portion of the Trust Deed was the princely sum of $604,654.08 (Hittell, p. 357), more than the most optimistic expectations.

The ironic result was that, rather than catapulting the Academy into more wealth than it had ever dreamed of, the immediate impact of Lick's munificence was a period of extreme indebtedness, due to the need to pay property taxes on the Market Street property (e.g., $1,444.50 in 1876 [Hittell, p. 192]). The Board of Supervisors of the City and County of San Francisco even attempted a suit against the Academy for taxes on the "Outside-Land lot" in 1885 (Hittell, p. 183), and then proceeded to "confiscate" the land for "school purposes" in 1887 (Hittell, p. 289).[7] The financial situation was so dire that in 1879 there was concern that there would be "no other course open to them except that of closing the Academy" (Hittell, p. 221).

Even after mortgages could be obtained against the Lick Trust, there was evidently disagreement within the Academy as to when and how the new wealth was best allocated, especially given that its exact magnitude was not yet known. This dissension is accordingly what lies behind the 1887 Reform Ticket. For example, as one controversial belt-tightening move, publication of the *Proceedings* had been suspended in 1877 (Hittell, p. 205), depriving the members both of an outlet for publication and of their main exchange item for library materials from other institutions. The *Proceedings* did not reappear until 1889 (Hittell, p. 302), several years after Curran had instituted the *Bulletin* as an interim publication outlet.

Even more pressing, however, was the continued deterioration of the First Congregational Church as suitable facilities for housing the collections. By 1886, "the metal roof had rusted and rotted away; and a new roof was necessary, or other quarters, before it rained again" (Hittell, p 280). Although some repairs were subsequently effected, Behr chose to remove his personal collection to preserve it from damage, and even "asked to be excused from serving as curator of entomology as long as the Academy occupied the building it was then in" (Hittell, p. 278).

Although new quarters were obviously a high priority, and the Academy had now both the land and means to construct its long-desired permanent home, the decision to proceed was delayed by critical disagreement on the best use of the Market Street property. When Lick's original stipulations were withdrawn in 1875, as previously discussed, the prospect of using such a prime piece of downtown real estate as income-generating property became an attractive option (e.g., Hittell, p. 263). Such a use would not only provide a permanent source of funds for Academy activities, but would also support the maintenance of a facility that could either be purchased or constructed at a less expensive site.

Although Harkness is recorded as being "favorable to selling the Market Street lot" (Hittell, p. 263), planning and construction on the property began almost immediately following the election of the Harkness slate, implying that some crucial deadlock had been broken. The solution to the income vs. museum question was elegant: a commercial building was built facing Market Street (Fig. 16), with a central portal leading to a back building, which housed the Academy's offices, collections, and display areas (Hittell, pp. 319–324). The new building was completed in time for the 5 January

---

[7] This move was challenged by the Academy, eventually resulting in a suit brought against the City and County of San Francisco, and the Board of Education (which had begun building on the lot), in 1890 (Hittell, pp. 290, 299, 307).

1891 annual meeting of the Academy. Confirmation of Harkness's hand in its construction is provided by the following tribute, given at a 1905 meeting:

> It was during [Harkness's] incumbency as president that this fine building, in which we meet, was designed, erected and dedicated as the home of science in this great metropolis of the Pacific Coast. He placed its corner-stone, and gratuitously labored with a sort of fatherly superintendent interest over every part of its construction, watching with jealous inspection every brick that was laid and every trowel that was handled in its building. And when it was completed, it was he, more perhaps that any other, that directed and guarded the careful removal and transportation of its treasures from the dark, dingy, dusty and dilapidated old quarters on Dupont Street to the bright, airy and well-kept galleries above us. (Hittell, 1905:6)

As counterpoint views, David Starr Jordan, in the 1896 presidential address quoted previously, described the result as "a large office building . . . [with] the museum occupying cramped quarters at the rear" (quoted in Ewan, 1955, p. 37). In later years Curran's successor, Alice Eastwood, likewise expressed her dissatisfaction with the Market Street facility, accusing Harkness of a lack of concern for the well-being of the collections after shading caused by a newly built adjacent structure created a humidity problem in the herbarium (Wilson, 1955).

FIGURE 16. California Academy of Sciences, Market Street Building. Courtesy California Academy of Sciences Archives.

Friend and Protector of the Gentle Kellogg

This account does not yet answer the question of why the 1887 election would have contributed to the rift between Curran and Greene, given that they both presumably appreciated the pressing need for suitable collections space and a publication outlet. Curran is well-established as a backer of the opposition slate; given that she was editing the *Bulletin,* it is reasonable to speculate that she may have even printed the Reform Ticket. Behr was her mentor, and Harkness had also given her early encouragement and support.[8] A contemporary newspaper account implies that the female voting bloc determined the election (Leviton & Aldrich, 1997:288), and Jepson (1933:84) outright states that "the first political upheaval of the Academy [was] largely engineered by Mrs. Mary K. Curran." At least one other contemporary shared a similar view, as shown in a letter from Charles Christopher Parry, a venerable western botanist, to S. B. Parish:

---

[8] However, a mushroom that Harkness initially indicated would be named after Curran (Hittell, p. 243) was instead described as *Polyploclum californicum* Harkness, now treated as *Gyrophragmium californicum* (Harkness) Morse (Zeller, 1943).

Acad[em]y affairs as you will infer are run *a la Curran* and nobody else has anything to say in the matter — Greene draws off to Berkeley — how long this state of things may last *quien sabe*. I enclose Harkness's inaugural written as I understand by Curran. (quoted in Ewan, 1955:32)

Parry's comments refer to the termination of joint curatorship by Greene and Curran, with indications of implications beyond botany. The reasons for Greene's opposition to the new administration are not clearly stated, but are probably based at least in part on loyalty to Kellogg. Kellogg's antipathy to the new regime was so severe that, upon his death several months after the elections, he chose not to leave his botanical drawings to the Academy. So acrimonious was this issue that when Gibbons read a paper "regarding the drawings of the late Dr. Albert Kellogg and his reasons for not leaving them to the Academy while the present administration was in power," it was resolved "After a great many desultory remarks . . . that the paper was not in proper tone and should not be received by the Academy" (Hittell, p. 299). Greene's loyalties to Kellogg and defiance of the new administration can be inferred from Greene's involvement in publishing Kellogg's drawings, as noted in an 1889 meeting:

There was some discussion as to the publication of a new volume, entitled 'West American Oaks' by Dr. Albert Kellogg. It was edited by Edward L. Greene and contained matter and particularly drawings, which seemed to have been prepared by Dr. Kellogg while in the employ of the Academy and was claimed to belong to the Academy. After Dr. Kellogg's death, Dr. William P. Gibbons, E. L. Greene and a few others seem to have published the book as a work independent of the Academy. (Hittell, p. 303)

The reasons for Kellogg's antagonism to the Harkness administration are not explicitly stated, and would seem to be at odds with his best interests. Not only were his precious specimens, like Behr's, threatened by deteriorating facilities, but the cessation of the *Proceedings* undermined his hard-won battle for autonomous publication. This is clearly noted in his biographical sketch attributed to Curran/Brandegee:

During the years 1877–1883 publication by the California Academy of Sciences ceased, and with the exception of a few which appeared in a San Francisco newspaper, the Rural Press, the species described by [Kellogg] thereafter remained in the herbarium of the California Academy of Sciences with the MS. diagnoses. Several of these, as *Eunanus angustus* [Gray], *Sphaeralcea fulva* [Greene], *Calyptridium nudum* [Greene], etc., have been described, either wholly or in part, from the types of Dr. Kellogg's unpublished species, and no mention made of his work. (Brandegee, 1893a:1)

What apparently mattered most to Kellogg was his personal ties to Davidson, perhaps developed when Kellogg and Davidson participated in an 1867 expedition to the newly acquired territory of Alaska. The strength of this friendship is seen in Davidson's reminiscence: "We lived in the same contracted temporary deck cabin for four or five months under many trials and inconveniences, and the sweetness of [Kellogg's] character was as pervading and refreshing as the beauty and fragrance of the flowers he gathered" (quoted in Ewan, 1955:11). Kellogg would have also felt personally affected by the ouster of William G. W. Harford (Fig. 17), who was also on the Alaska expedition and who, as Director of Museum, was among those who lost his position in the insurrection. Primarily a concholo-

FIGURE 17. William Harford. Courtesy California Academy of Sciences Archives.

gist, Harford had particular significance to the botanical community as "the friend and protector of the gentle Kellogg, especially in Kellogg's later years" (Jepson, 1933:84). The two men made extensive plant collections together in California and Oregon in 1868 and 1869, and at least during Kellogg's last years shared a house in Alameda (Jepson, 1933).

With the loss of his paid position at the Academy in 1887, Harford spent the next four years at the University, as an assistant to James John Rivers, "Curator of the Museum at the University of California" (Jepson, 1933:84).[9] The University may have acted as a stronghold for resistance to the new Academy administration in general, as evidenced by the appearance of Joseph LeConte as candidate for Academy president on an unsuccessful opposition ticket in the 1890 election (Hittell, p. 306). LeConte's disdain for Academy politics is clearly stated: "Under the presidency of J. D. Whitney the Academy was prosperous and held a high position among the scientific institutions of our country; but from that time, because of internal dissensions, it dropped lower and lower" (quoted in Ewan, 1955:32).

The Faithful of His Flock Behind Him

As mentioned by Parry in his letter to Parish (previously quoted), Greene had also taken refuge at Berkeley, in a successful bid for the first strictly botanical appointment at the University of California, in 1885. Eugene Hilgard had vigorously lobbied for such a position, which was included in the President's report for 1884–86:

> It is important that a separate department of general and economic Botany should be formed, and that a Professor of Botany should be appointed at a salary of $3,000 a year. He will require an assistant for the purpose of taking charge of the herbarium and aiding in instruction of the classes at $600 a year. The formation of a large herbarium should be seriously begun. (quoted in Constance, 1978:4)

Greene's career move was dictated not only by Academy affairs, but also by the fact that Greene had converted to Catholicism in 1884 and accordingly lost his post as rector of St. Mark's Episcopal Church in Berkeley. He did not go quietly, however, and his subsequent attempts to teach Catholic doctrine to a congregation that was ultra-Protestant aroused strenuous objections (McIntosh, 1983). As a result:

> It was a case, not without precedent, in which the vestry locked the doors of the church against the priest; and we have preserved for us the picture of the Reverend Mr. Greene, in surplice, passing down Bancroft Way, an axe over his shoulder and the faithful of his flock behind him, beating down the doors of St. Mark's and leading his people in to service, sermon and benediction. That service, the legend runs, was his last office in the Episcopal Church. (Jepson, 1918:26–27)

Although Greene had previously taught an occasional course for the University, for a stipend of $900 per year (Constance, 1978), he was now a full-time professional botanist for the first time in his career. In 1890 he became chair of the new Department of Botany (Fig. 18), established within the College of Natural Sciences "to meet the wants of students not caring for the courses in the colleges of applied science" (quoted in Constance, 1978:4). Greene was assisted by Marshall Avery Howe,

---

[9] The only reference to James J. Rivers in the Centennial Record of the University of California (Stadtman et al., 1967) is the enigmatic note by Smith (1967:85) that Rivers was "curator of the University Museum from 1881 to 1895, [and] was also active in entomology," along with Hilgard. This appears to be the only mention of a "University Museum" in the Centennial Record. Ewan (1995:30), who provides slightly more information, refers to Rivers as Curator of Organic Natural History. The fate of either the "University Museum" or "Organic Natural History" has not been determined.

FIGURE 18. UC botany lab and herbarium in South Hall, 1893 (with Willis Linn Jepson, Marshall Howe, Ivar Tidestrom, and Joseph Burtt-Davy). Courtesy University Herbarium Archives, University of California, Berkeley.

as instructor of vegetal structure, morphology, and cryptogamic botany. Joseph Burtt-Davy (Fig. 19) joined the faculty in 1892, teaching economic and commercial botany, with special attention paid to grasses and early range studies. Willis Linn Jepson became Greene's assistant even before receiving his Ph.D. in botany in 1899 (the first at the University), after which he was promoted to assistant professor. Another noteworthy student was Ivar Tidestrom, who made an early start on establishing a botanical garden.

With the burst of activity in Berkeley, the Academy was no longer the only center for botanical activity in the San Francisco Bay Area. *Erythea*, founded in 1893 and primarily edited by Jepson, served as an alternate (and strictly botanical) professional outlet to Academy publications and *Zoe* (discussed later).[10] It became the outlet of choice for members of the Chamisso Botanical Club, which was organized at the University in 1891, "by officers and students interested in botanical work. The promoters of the club had especially in view the collection of material upon which to found local plant-lists" (Jepson,

FIGURE 19. Joseph Burtt-Davy (1899). Courtesy University Herbarium Archives, University of California, Berkeley.

---

[10] Greene had previously founded his own journal, *Pittonia*, in 1887. This was, however, used almost exclusively as his personal publication outlet, saving him from having to submit his work to be reviewed and approved by his critics.

1894:171). Members staked out individual territories, in which trespassing by rivals was discouraged, with one exception: "Professor Greene as the Great Chief was of course free from all restrictions. We had too much to gain from his friendship to object to his hunting on our grounds" (Frederick Theodore Bioletti, quoted in Ewan, 1955:35). One of Greene's disciples, Elmer Reginald Drew, went on to become a professor of physics at Stanford, and most of the other Chamisso club members also found prestigious posts (Ewan, 1955).

The hive of activity continued after Greene resigned in 1895, to accept a post at Catholic University in Washington, D.C. He was accompanied by Tidestrom, and also took his herbarium with him (which was eventually deposited at the University of Notre Dame). After some concern that Hilgard would succeed in claiming botany for the College of Agriculture, departmental autonomy in the College of Natural Sciences was assured with the recruitment of William Albert Setchell (Fig. 20) as professor and chair (Constance, 1978). Setchell brought formal training from Yale and Harvard, along with broad interests in phycology, plant evolution, and phytogeography. He was elected a member of the Academy in 1895 (Hittell, p. 359), but does not appear to have been overly active beyond presenting a few papers and serving on the publication committee (Hittell, p. 404). Howe also departed, to be replaced by W. J.

FIGURE 20. William Setchell (circa 1892–1894). Courtesy Setchell Collection, University Herbarium Archives, University of California, Berkeley.

FIGURE 21. Botany Building, University of California, Berkeley (circa 1898). Courtesy University Herbarium Archives, University of California, Berkeley.

V. Osterhout as co-instructor with Jepson while both worked to complete doctoral degrees (Constance, 1978). It was during this period, in 1897, that the Department of Botany and herbarium moved from their original quarters in South Hall, which had been taken over by the College of Agriculture (Stadtman, 1970:146), to a new two-story Botany Building (Fig. 21) on the north bank of Strawberry Creek (Constance, 1978).

It Surely Was a Droll Affair

Coinciding with Greene's crisis of faith, Curran's life was also undergoing a major change, due to the arrival of Townshend Stith Brandegee (Fig. 22) in San Francisco. Brandegee, a graduate of the Sheffield Scientific School and veteran of several territorial surveys (e.g., the Hayden survey in 1875), arrived in California in 1885, to collect trunk samples of various trees for the American Museum of Natural History in New York (Setchell, 1926; Ewan, 1942). As recorded by Marcus E. Jones, one of Greene's most opinionated detractors, with a liberal amount of hyperbole and post-facto speculation:

FIGURE 22. Townshend Stith Brandegee. Courtesy University Herbarium Archives University of California, Berkeley.

> It was opportune that Brandegee came to California at this time with a lot of Columbia Basin and north Pacific plants to name, for he was the oldest and most accomplished botanist in the country, and his presence would command respect and dispel the aura that Greene had cast about himself like a human god. Brandegee never squabbled. He was a very insignificant looking and little man who did not have to blow about himself (like Greene) to be heard. The atmosphere cleared at once, and everyone saw the beginning of a new era. Mrs. Curran fell 'insanely in love' with Brandegee, as she put it in a letter to her sister. It surely was a droll affair, a most intensely masculine woman desperately in love with the most retiring and effeminate man, and both of them dead in earnest about it, the man too with other women buzzing around like flies in fly-time. (Jones, 1933:15)

Curran and Brandegee married in 1889; their honeymoon was a collecting trip on foot from San Diego to San Francisco. It was at this time that Mary K. Curran became Katharine (Kate) Brandegee: "My first name being the same as my mother's, I was never called by it, and on marriage to Mr. Brandegee it was dropped as making an unwieldy combination" (quoted in Setchell, 1926:168). Townshend had a sufficient inheritance ($49,000 in Jones, 1932; only $40,000 in Jones, 1933) for financial independence, and to initiate a new journal, *Zoe*, in 1890, initially with assistance from Harkness (later repaid). Overtly founded "as a medium for recording in accessible form the numerous, often unconnected observations, pertaining more particularly to the western part of North America, made by amateurs as well as working naturalists" (anonymous introduction to Vol. 1, 1890), *Zoe* also specifically served to provide Katharine a freer rein for her published critiques of others' works (Setchell, 1926; Crosswhite & Crosswhite, 1985).

In 1891, Katharine started the California Botanical Club, a counterpart of the California Zoological Club, to serve the growing community of regional botanists. At its inception, the club encompassed professionals and amateurs alike, including among its early members such well-known western botanists as W. C. Cusick, L. F. Henderson, Thomas Howell, M. E. Jones, S. B. Parish, and W. N. Suksdorf (Brandegee, 1892). As perhaps the first botanical club on the West Coast, it was highly popular for group excursions (Setchell, 1926), and resulted in the publication of initial floristic surveys of Yosemite Park (Brandegee, 1891) and San Francisco (Brandegee, 1892). In spite of the early professional involvement, however, the club's focus apparently soon shifted to local enthusiasts, especially women, with the club serving as both a social outlet and a source of volunteer assistance and funding for the Academy's herbarium.[11]

The same year that the California Botanical Club was founded saw the first appearance at the Academy of Alice Eastwood, a young schoolteacher and self-taught botanist from Colorado (Wilson, 1955; Moore, 1996). The Brandegees were impressed enough with Eastwood during her 1891 visit that they encouraged her to move to San Francisco the following year, at which time Katharine gave up her salary so that Eastwood could be hired as joint curator of botany, at $80 per month (Hittell, p. 337). Additional funding was approved for an assistant in the botany department at $40 per month, a position filled in 1893 by Effie A. McIllriach (Hittell, p. 339).[12] Katharine herself received a formal accolade from the Academy, in the form of a resolution "that the zeal and efficiency evinced by Mrs. Brandegee during the years of her labors in the herbarium had been such as to merit our highest commendation" (Hittell, p. 338).

Shortly thereafter, in 1894, the Brandegees left San Francisco and moved to San Diego, leaving Eastwood in charge of the herbarium and the California Botanical Club. The announced reasons for the Brandegees' move were "partly for the more agreeable climate and partly to be nearer the chosen field of Mr. Brandegee's botanical labors [Mexico]" *(Zoe* 4:421, 1894), but the proximity to Katharine's sister in Ramona, as well as the distance from Academy politics, might have likewise factored in. The ample space for a year-round botanical garden (Fig. 23), on the mesa above San Diego, could have also tempted Katharine with the opportunity to begin putting into practice her incipient leanings towards experimental systematics.

FIGURE 23. The Brandegee garden and brick herbarium in San Diego. Courtesy University Herbarium Archives, University of California, Berkeley

---

[11] The professional function was subsequently claimed by the California Botanical Society, founded by Jepson in 1913 (Ewan, 1987).

[12] McIllriach's duties were later changed to assistant secretary and librarian for the Academy, a position she "was relieved of" after becoming Mrs. Cloudsley Rutter in 1902. However, she continued to receive a monthly salary for supervising and proof-reading Academy publications (Hittell, p. 406).

Botany Taught According to Modern Methods

The flowering of botanical activity at the University of California, and the beginning of what would become the decades-long Eastwood era in botany at the Academy (Wilson, 1955; Moore, 1996; Chickering, 1989), coincided with the inception of the third major institutional center for botany in the San Francisco Bay Area, when Stanford University opened its doors in 1892. Leland Stanford, founder of the university, had been a staunch supporter of the California Geological Survey and was one of the benefactors whose private funds allowed the completion and publication of *Botany of California* (Brewer et al., 1876; Watson, 1880). In 1881, Stanford had also been a nominee for the University of California Regency, at which time there was the possibility of Stanford bestowing his philanthropic intent to "do something for education" on the existing University, but politics intervened, such that "Stanford was lost to the University's cause forever after" (Stadtman, 1970:95).

A published announcement of the opening of Stanford University, technically anonymous, was undoubtedly written by Curran/Brandegee, hurling as it does yet one more stone at Greene (also technically anonymous), at the time when Greene was on the faculty at Berkeley:

> Prof. W[illiam] R[ussel] Dudley [Fig. 24], late of Cornell, has taken the chair of systematic botany at Stanford University. With such men as he and Prof. Douglas H. Campbell [Fig. 25] in charge of the botanical work at Stanford University, where botany is taught according to modern methods, we may expect to have in time, a body of resident botanists whose entire stock of botanical knowledge is not confined to the possession of a limited terminology and a large capacity for discovering new species that do not exist. (*Zoe* 3:378, 1893)

Dudley's focus was the systematics of vascular plants, especially conifers, combining traditional with experimental methodologies acquired during studies in Europe in 1887. The other two faculty in the botany department, Douglas Houghton Campbell and George James Pierce, were even more representative of the increasingly laboratory-oriented "new botany," with expertise in cryptogamic botany and plant physiology respectively. The resultant emphasis on "modern methods," as lauded in the preceding quote, presages the eventual decision by Stanford University to divest itself from traditional systematics entirely in the 1970s, when the herbarium and other natural history collections were transferred to and merged with those of the California Academy of Sciences (Timby, 1998; Chickering, 1989).

Traditional systematics nevertheless had a strong presence

FIGURE 24. William Russel Dudley. Courtesy Department of Botany, California Academy of Sciences

FIGURE 25. Douglas Houghton Campbell. Courtesy Department of Botany, California Academy of Sciences.

at Stanford University during its early years, with perhaps the first significant gift to the University consisting of the William H. Harvey collection of 70,000 herbarium specimens. This largesse, several times larger than the contemporaneous herbarium at the University of California, was used by Stanford University's first president, David Starr Jordan, to recruit Dudley from Cornell University, where Dudley had become Jordan's successor as instructor of botany (Timby, 1998). Unfortunately, conditions at the fledgling university were far from ideal following Dudley's arrival in 1892, in that Leland Stanford died the next year. As a result, "the university entered upon a period of anxiety and privation, which was only tided over by the noble and self-sacrificing devotion of Mrs. Stanford" (Campbell, 1913:12–13). Dudley's office, laboratory, and herbarium during this period were accordingly all housed in the attic of a shop building. In spite of these poor facilities and various health problems, Dudley built up the herbarium (which was subsequently named in his honor) to some 120,000 specimens by the time of his retirement in 1910 (Timby, 1998).

Conservation provided a further arena where Dudley played a significant pioneering role in California, especially concerning the preservation of coast redwoods and Sierran big trees. In this capacity Dudley served as an early officer for another venerable institution established in California during this period: the Sierra Club. Now ranked among the world's foremost conservation organizations, the Sierra Club was founded in 1892 by John Muir and three professors from the University of California (including Willis L. Jepson), with Jordan, Kellogg, and LeConte among its early officers (Slack, 1993). As a different expression of the same goal, Dudley also attempted to establish a forestry program at Stanford University, but lost out to the University of California (Wieslander, 1965).

In the end, Dudley's contributions to the botanical legacy consisted largely of his collections, his conservation efforts, and his students (listed on pp. 29–32 of his memorial volume, and including his eventual successor, LeRoy Abrams), rather than substantial publications or institutional involvement. This is presumably due in large part to his sensitive personality, in kinship with Kellogg's poetic soul of a generation earlier, which left him ill-equipped to elbow his way onto the battleground that characterized the field of his day. As summed up in his eulogy by the Vice President of Stanford, John Branner, who had been a student, classmate, and fraternity brother of Dudley at Cornell University, in words that are just as relevant today:

> To be rather than to appear was the steadfast principle of [Dudley's] life. Modesty, gentleness, unobtrusiveness, decorum, and purity of life were his most prominent characteristics. He never did anything for the sake of display; he never courted popularity. His whole life, within and without, was one long, living protest against vulgarity in all its forms.... I am sure my friend would not thank me to apologize for the modest part he played in this or any other community, but in closing I am constrained to say a word on behalf of him and all such men: It behooves us not to lose sight of this blessed truth, that there are fine men and women in this world of ours — and plenty of them, too — who keep out of the limelights, whose names we never see in the headlines of the newspapers, but who lead quiet, sane, and wholesome lives. Such people always suggest to me the foundations of a great structure. These foundations lie deep within the surface of the ground; we never see them; we seldom think of them; they are not decorated with flying flags or written across with gaudy colors or blazing electric lights. But they stand fast and firm, and the stability and the real worth of the entire superstructure depends upon them. (Branner, 1913:8, 10)

Both Dudley and Campbell (though not Pierce) quickly became active members of the Academy, with Dudley serving with Setchell on the editorial committee for botany, but it was Jordan who played the most prominent role in Academy affairs. In 1896, Jordan was elected president of the Academy on the slate that finally ousted the Harkness administration, which had been in power for nearly a decade, ushering in a new era of close ties between the Academy and the universities:

> [I]t was deemed proper to give the presidency to Professor David Starr Jordan, president of Leland Stanford, Jr. University; and apparently as a counterpoise, the first vice-presidency to Professor William E. Ritter of the University of California. It was the start of what was commonly known as the 'University Regime of the Academy,' which lasted seven years. (Hittell, p. 360)

Harkness apparently retired voluntarily in favor of Jordan, who claims to have "then endeavored, with fair success, to put an end to the old feud" (quoted in Ewan, 1955:37).

They Gave Unstintedly of Their Resources

During this period the Brandegees pursued a diversity of activities from their idyllic retreat on the outskirts of San Diego: collecting extensively in California and Mexico, publishing in *Zoe*, and perhaps putting some of Katharine's ideas on experimental taxonomy to the test in their magnificent garden. Unfortunately, the "agreeable climate" of San Diego ultimately proved to be incompatible with Katharine Brandegee's health, and the isolation from research centers also took its toll. As a result, twelve years after leaving the Academy, Katharine wrote to Setchell, then chair of the Department of Botany at the University of California:

> You remember that I have found the summer climate not to agree with me in San Diego In consideration of this fact I will try to induce Mr. Brandegee to part with his herbarium. It has absorbed too much of our means to be given away, and as I would much prefer it went to the University, I desire your opinion as to the feasibility of disposing of it to the Regents.
> There are about 50,000 sheets averaging I suppose nearly two specimens to the sheet (two collections) in small plants sometimes as many as ten or a dozen from different localities are mounted on the same sheet, as they do at Harvard, and there are about 200 types. We would transfer the whole herbarium, library, cases, etc. to the University — for $100 a month for the remainder of our lives. — We would prefer selling outright, but this plan would probably be much to the advantage of the University.
> This would at once give the University the best herbarium and the best working library on the coast, and we would deposit therein all our future types. (undated letter from K. Brandegee to Setchell, UC Herbarium archives)

Arrangements were subsequently made whereby, in exchange for the donation of their extensive library and herbarium, the Brandegees would have full use of the University's facilities (but apparently not the requested remuneration). Townshend was appointed Honorary Curator and thereafter devoted most of his time to describing the flood of new species sent to the Brandegees by Carl Albert Purpus from Mexico.[13] As for Katharine: "Without compensation and refusing all personal or official recognition or commendation, she labored in the Herbarium of the University of California for fourteen years, as regularly and as faithfully as if she had held a salaried position. She gave to it of her best and was content to feel that she had contributed her quota toward a better knowledge of the flora of California" (Setchell, 1926:168).

The Brandegee Herbarium and Brandegee Library were collectively the single most significant contribution ever received by the University Herbarium. A total of 76,166 specimens was presented in August 1906, effectively doubling the size of the existing herbarium (censused at 74,800 on 1 July

---
[13] Carl Albert Purpus, a freelance botanical collector from Germany, was appointed botanical collector without pay for the herbarium in 1907 (Herbarium Records, p. 109, University Herbarium archives). His initial contact with the Brandegees, at first Katharine, occurred in 1894, about the time that they moved to San Diego (Sousa, 1969; Ertter, 1988).

1906) and allowing the University of California herbarium to draw ahead of Stanford University's. The library was equally valuable, making readily available an outstanding selection of rare botanical literature. Back issues of *Zoe* were also turned over to the University, with the provision that funds from the sale of same were to be used for subscriptions to botanical journals. The Brandegee donation coincided with the availability of new fire-proof quarters for the University Herbarium on the third floor of the new Hearst Mining Building, where one room was designated the Brandegee Room (p. 106–108 of Herbarium Records, University Herbarium archives).

The Brandegees' generosity was posthumously acknowledged by Setchell:

> In 1906, shortly after central California had received its baptism by earthquake and fire, there came to the University of California two botanists, husband and wife, who devoted all their accumulations of knowledge to the service of the University and entrusted all their books and specimens to its guardianship. They gave untiringly and unstintedly of their services and of their resources to the herbarium from the time of their coming to the time of their passing away. Their generosity and their devotion have placed in their debt all those botanists who in future years will come to the University to study the systematic botany of the western United States and of Mexico — a study made possible because of the rich and abundant material given to the University by these unselfish workers. (Setchell, 1926:155)

At the time the Brandegees chose to move to Berkeley, Greene had been gone for nearly a decade, but at least some of the enmity had been passed on to his protégé Jepson; it was, after all, while the Brandegees were at Berkeley that Jepson wrote his tribute to Greene, in which Katharine was cast as

FIGURE 26. Katharine and Townshend Brandegee (date unknown).
Courtesy University Herbarium Archives, University of California, Berkeley.

an "unkempt woman" with "an unpleasant voice" (Jepson, 1918). In contrast, Jepson is one of the few authors whose floristic work Katharine had previously approved, as indicated by her review of the results of his doctoral work, *Flora of Western Middle California:* "Throughout the book there is evident the most careful and painstaking proof reading and considering the difficulties encountered in a Flora of even a restricted region of California, the author is to be congratulated on having done so well" (Brandegee, 1901c:146). In addition to loyalty to Greene, Jepson's antagonism to Katharine might have resulted from his personal animosity toward Setchell, who he had initially admired but with whom he then become disenchanted (mss. in Jepson archives). The Brandegees were obviously at the University under Setchell's aegis, and as such may have represented a perceived assault on Jepson's aspirations to being the ultimate authority on the California vascular flora.

As a result of interactions with another member of the Setchell camp, Harvey Monroe Hall (Fig. 27), Katharine might have even exerted a subtle influence on the future direction of botany at Stanford, which she had already (albeit anonymously) commended as the place

FIGURE 27. Harvey Monroe Hall. Courtesy University Herbarium Archives, University of California, Berkeley.

"where botany is taught according to modern methods" (*Zoe* 3:378, 1893). Hall received his Ph.D. at Berkeley the same year the Brandegees arrived, after already having earned undergraduate and Master's degrees there and becoming Burtt-Davy's replacement on the botany department faculty (Babcock, 1934; Constance, 1978). He also became the first paid assistant in the herbarium in 1902 (at $400 per annum) and was placed in charge of the herbarium a few months later when Jepson stepped down (p. 104 of Herbarium Records, University Herbarium archives).[14]

Setchell credits Harvey and his wife Carlotta Case Hall (a fellow student at Berkeley, with an interest in ferns) with providing much of the biographical information on the Brandegees, implying well-developed social ties (Setchell, 1926:178). One can easily imagine the conversations that must have occurred between Katharine and Harvey on their shared philosophies of systematics, which Hall would eventually have a chance to develop when he subsequently accepted a position with the newly established Carnegie Institute of Washington at Stanford University. Echoing Katharine, and even Behr, with such statements as "experimental and quantitative methods promise to turn taxonomy from a field overgrown with personal opinions to one in which scientific proof is supreme" (quoted in Babcock, 1934:359), Hall is recognized as one of the founders of experimental taxonomy, or biosystematics, pioneered at the Carnegie Institute in the first half of the 20th century.

My Own Destroyed Work I Do Not Lament

As noted in Setchell's tribute, the year of the Brandegees' return to the Bay Area was the same

---

[14] The position of herbarium assistant was then filled by Harriet A. Walker, a graduate of Mt. Holyoke College with twelve years experience in the botany department of Wellesley College and three months in the Gray Herbarium. Walker spent the remaining 22 years of her career at the University Herbarium, making extensive collections and eventually leaving a substantial endowment for the ongoing support of the herbarium (Jepson, 1929).

year of the great San Francisco Earthquake and Fire. Regular earthquakes had been well known in the San Francisco area, to the extent that at one point it had jokingly been suggested that the Academy appoint a curator of earthquakes "whose duty it should be to collect specimens of earthquakes and place them in the museum, taking care, however, to purge such specimens of their gases to avoid dangerous consequences" (Hittell, pp. 117–118), but the magnitude of the one that occurred in the morning of April 18, 1906, was far beyond any that had previously been experienced. The Academy building, Harkness's proud legacy, had been designed to be fireproof (Hittell, p. 321), but a full-fledged firestorm proved more than it could withstand (Fig. 28). The building had in fact survived the earthquake with only moderate damage, but after the fire what remained was a gutted shell (Hittell, pp. 471–474). Essentially the entire library of some 15,000 volumes was destroyed (Hittell, p. 473), as well as the vast bulk of the collections. Due to the heroic efforts of Eastwood and others, who braved a broken stairwell to the upper floors in order to rescue what was deemed most valuable, the type specimens and other particularly significant subsets of the natural history collections were saved from the approaching flames, as were various records and documents, including Hittell's unfinished manuscript (Hittell, p. 472; Wilson, 1955; Moore, 1996). In a single catastrophic event, what was undoubtedly the largest and most significant botanical collection on the West Coast at that time was reduced to a mere 1,497 specimens (Chickering, 1989), whose intrinsic value admittedly far exceeded the numbers alone.

FIGURE 28. Remains of the California Academy of Sciences following the earthquake and fire, April 18, 1906. The building seen in the left rear is the remains of the Museum; the rubble of the front Market Street building has been largely cleared. Courtesy California Academy of Sciences Archives.

One room of the gutted building actually survived well enough to be repaired for temporary storage (Hittell, p. 477), but new quarters were essential for general Academy functions. A temporary office was first rented at 1806 Post Street (Hittell, p. 474), followed by "more ample and convenient quarters" at 1812 Gough Street (Hittell, p. 477). Here began the rebuilding of the Academy's natural history collections and library, helped greatly by the flood of generous donations sent by other institutions around the world (listed in Appendix M of Leviton & Aldrich, 1997:561–563). Rather than rebuilding a new museum on the Market Street property, the Academy chose to lease that property for commercial purposes, eventually selling it in the mid-1980s. For its own purposes, the

Academy negotiated to have new facilities housed in Golden Gate Park, opening the doors of the first of a seven-building complex to the public in 1915 (Leviton & Aldrich, 1997:505).

Within this setting, it would obviously have been both fitting and a magnificent boon if the Brandegees had donated their library and herbarium to the Academy that had once served as their professional home, and why they chose not to is a question that begs to be addressed. One possible explanation is that the Brandegees were in need of immediate, not future, working facilities, and convenient housing would also have been hard to come by in post-Fire San Francisco. However, a letter from Leverett Mills Loomis, director of the Academy's museum, claims that adequate facilities were available by June 1906: "The Academy has secured fine temporary quarters [at Gough Street], and we have ample room for books and specimens. In short, we are ready to receive everything now — while the tear is still in the eye" (letter from Loomis to E.W. Nelson, 4 June 1906, quoted in Leviton & Aldrich, 1997:505). It is also unclear if the Brandegees had approached Setchell before or after the earthquake destroyed the Academy.

One might further speculate that, with Harkness no longer president, Katharine might have felt less than welcome at the scene of her earlier political battles. Perhaps she also felt it would be awkward finding a niche in the herbarium where her successor now reigned supreme. As analyzed by Moore (1996), the on-going relationship between Brandegee and Eastwood combined elements of both fond support and professional rivalry, setting the stage for a complex tension that would have made coexistence under the same roof decidedly uncomfortable. Consider, for example, the following evaluation of Eastwood's taxonomic abilities by Brandegee:

> I was informed that Miss Eastwood had arranged [Harvard's] Lupines, whereupon I presented them with my opinion of Miss E. from a botanical standpoint. I show on the enclosed card her arrangement. Of course about half the species won't go into any of these groups, and they are stuck in higgledepiggledy. As an exhibition of pure idiocy, it must be hard to match. (Letter from K. Brandegee to T. S. Brandegee, from Harvard, 11 October 1913, in UC Herbarium archives)

However, Alice Eastwood (Fig. 29), who had gained fame because of her efforts to save the botanical type specimens, had also taken shelter at Berkeley, at least temporarily:

> Things can be sent to me at 2705 Hearst Avenue, Berkeley. I am in Geo. Hansen's house.... I do not want botanical stuff sent [to the Academy address at Post Street] as I cannot attend to it while I can at my own place and with the use of the library and herbarium at the Univ. of Calif. I think that I wrote you that Prof. Setchell had most hospitably put everything at my service and had given me the use of a room. (Letter from Eastwood to E.W. Nelson, 22 May 1906, quoted in Leviton & Aldrich, 1997:504)

As previously noted, Berkeley already housed another rival claimant to the throne of expertise in the California flora, in the form of Greene's successor Jepson. However, it is evident that Setchell and Hall, who befriended the Brandegees, were fully in charge

FIGURE 29. Alice Eastwood, possibly taken about 1910, wearing a floral hat with which she became identified. Courtesy California Academy of Sciences Archives.

by this time, with Jepson already becoming marginalized within the departmental power structure. We are nevertheless left with the bizarre image of the Brandegees, Eastwood, and Jepson all working under the same roof, apparently doing their best to ignore each other's presence, with the exception of occasional sniping. A marvelous example of the last-named activity is provided by Jepson's notes, under an entry for Eastwood:

> Has been working in our herbarium more or less since August, 1906. More cocksure and unscientific than ever. She brought in the Manzanitas. Before Mrs. Brandegee she said: 'Any one who says these two species of mine are not distinct is a fool.' Said Mrs. B. quietly: 'No one would say that they are not distinct but they have both been described before'! (Jepson field book 16: 198, 1906, in Jepson Herbarium archives)

Other letters by Eastwood during this time carry clues that political factors may have been a determining factor for the Brandegees' decision, specifically involving the director of the Academy's museum at that time, Leverett Mills Loomis. It is evident that Eastwood at least had a serious distrust of Loomis, with an initial "stiff upper lip" giving way to an increasingly pessimistic attitude concerning the fate of botany at the Academy:

> I do not feel the loss to be mine but it is a great loss to the scientific world and an irreparable loss to California. My own destroyed work I do not lament, for it was a joy to me while I did it and I can still have the same joy in starting it again. . . . I am beginning already to recollect and intend to go to type localities as much as possible and shall not hesitate to beg hospitality of my friends. I expect to have very little aid from the Acad. but have a tiny income of my own and can get along I feel sure. The Bot. Dept. has a fund of $5000. of its very own besides. I feel sure that the Board of Trustees will not permit Loomis to divert all the funds to his own particular ends. (Letter from Eastwood to E.W. Nelson, 7 May 1906, quoted in Leviton & Aldrich, 1997:500–503)

> I am not at all sanguine about the future of the botanical department of the Academy; for those who are in charge act as if they were hostile to it and me and give me no help whatever. I even had a bill sent me for dues not long ago, for the first time since I have been connected. It is all so uncertain that for the present, it is best for you as for me to do nothing and plan nothing. (Letter from Eastwood to J.N. Rose, 2 May 1907, quoted in Leviton & Aldrich, 1997:505–506)

If Loomis's policies and personality were in fact instrumental in diverting the Brandegees' herbarium and library from the Academy to Berkeley, it was not the only time that blame can be laid on his doorstep for the University profiting at the Academy's expense. According to Barbara Stein (pers. comm., 1998), Annie Alexander's displeasure with Loomis's curatorial policies probably influenced her decision to establish and generously endow both the Museum of Vertebrate Zoology and the Museum of Paleontology at Berkeley, rather than at the Academy.

EPILOGUE

Independent of Loomis's impact, and in spite of Eastwood's reservations, botany at the Academy did recover, and went on to thrive and interact with the other scientific institutions in the San Francisco Bay Area to the present day. Eastwood, Jepson, Setchell, and Hall all continued to make significant contributions to California botany, as did Dudley's student and successor, LeRoy Abrams. Other major centers sprang up elsewhere; at the San Diego Natural History Museum, Rancho Santa Ana Botanic Garden, and the new campuses of the University of California in Los Angeles and Davis. However, the period from the founding of the Academy to its destruction in 1906 represents a well-circumscribed era, with a suitable stopping place. It has also been one of the least known eras in California's botanical history, undoubtedly in large part because of the massive disruption caused by the 1906 Earthquake. It has been the goal of the current paper to rectify this situation, by bringing back to light the extensive foundation that was laid by Kellogg, Behr, Brewer, Bolander, Curran/Brandegee, Greene, Dudley, and their contemporaries.

ACKNOWLEDGMENTS

The thoughtful and helpful criticisms of Nancy Slack and Thomas Daniel, who served as reviewers, are gratefully acknowledged, as are the many stimulating discussions with Slack, Robert Ornduff, Patricia Moore, Richard Beidleman, Lincoln Constance, Peter Raven, James L. Reveal, Betty Smocovitis, Elizabeth Rush, Anne Zwinger, Marcia Bonta, Arnold Tiehm, Annetta Carter, David Charlet, Patricia L. Packard, Elihu Gerson, Michael Ghiselin, Alan Leviton, Michele Aldrich, Sara Timby, Elizabeth McClintock, Barbara Stein, and numerous others (whose names regrettably escape me at present). The generosity of Sharon Kingsland in making available her insightful manuscript (provisionally entitled "An American Science: A Study in Ecology, Evolution, and Society") is deeply appreciated. Special mention goes to Richard Beidleman for unearthing the treasures in Jepson's fieldbooks, and to Isabelle Tavares for successfully tracking down the fate of "*Polyplocium Curranii.*"

LITERATURE CITED

BABCOCK, ERNEST BROWN. 1934. Harvey Monroe Hall. *University of California Publications in Botany* 17:355–368.
BEHR, HANS HERMANN. 1884. *Synopsis of the Genera of Vascular Plants in the Vicinity of San Francisco, with an Attempt to Arrange Them According to Evolutionary Principles.* Payot, Upham & Co., San Francisco, California. 165 pp.
BEHR, HANS HERMANN. 1888. *Flora of the Vicinity of San Francisco.* [privately published, San Francisco]. 364 pp. + xiv [appendix].
BEHR, HANS HERMANN. 1891. Botanical reminiscences. *Zoe* 2:2–6.
BEHR, HANS HERMANN. 1896. Botanical reminiscences of San Francisco. *Erythea* 4:168–178.
BOLANDER, HENRY N. 1870. *A Catalogue of the Plants Growing in the Vicinity of San Francisco.* A. Roman & Co., San Francisco, California. 43 pp.
BONTA, MARCIA MYERS. 1991. *Women in the Field: America's Pioneering Woman Naturalists.* Texas A&M University Press, College Station. 299 pp.
BRANDEGEE, KATHARINE. 1891. The flora of Yo Semite. *Zoe* 2:155–167.
BRANDEGEE, KATHARINE. 1892. Catalogue of the flowering plants and ferns growing spontaneously in the city of San Francisco. *Zoe* 2:334–390.
BRANDEGEE, KATHARINE. 1893a. Dr. Albert Kellogg. *Zoe* 4:1–2.
BRANDEGEE, KATHARINE. 1893b. The botanical writings of Edward L. Greene. *Zoe* 4:63–103.
BRANDEGEE, KATHARINE. 1894. [Review of] "Manual of the Bay Region Botany." *Zoe* 4:417–420.
BRANDEGEE, KATHARINE. 1901a. Some sources of error in genera and species. *Zoe* 5:91–98.
BRANDEGEE, KATHARINE. 1901b. The size of herbarium sheets. *Zoe* 5:138–139.
BRANDEGEE, KATHARINE. 1901c. [Review of] *Flora of Western Middle California,* by Willis Linn Jepson. *Zoe* 5:142–146.
BRANNER, JOHN CASPER. 1913. William Russel Dudley. Pages 7–10 in *Dudley Memorial Volume.* Leland Stanford Junior University Publications, University Series.
BREWER, WILLIAM HENRY, SERENO WATSON, and ASA GRAY. 1876. *Botany [of California],* vol. 1. Welch, Bigelow, & Co., University Press, Cambridge, Massachusetts. 628 pp.
BREWSTER, E. T. 1909. *Life and Letters of Josiah Dwight Whitney.* Houghton Mifflin Company, Boston and New York. 411 pp.

BRITTON, NATHANIEL L. 1891. On Mrs. Brandegee's review of my list of state and local floras. *Zoe* 1:344–346.
CAMPBELL, DOUGLAS HOUGHTON. 1913. William Russel Dudley. Pages 11–15 in *Dudley Memorial Volume*. Leland Stanford Junior University Publications, University Series.
CHICKERING, SHERMAN. 1989. Growing herbaria at the California Academy of Sciences. *Fremontia* 17(1):3–10.
CONSTANCE, LINCOLN. 1978. *Botany at Berkeley: The First Hundred Years*. Department of Botany, University of California, Berkeley. 21 pp., 100 photos on 37 unnumbered pages.
CROSSWHITE, FRANK S., and CAROL D. CROSSWHITE. 1985. The plant collecting Brandegees, with emphasis on Katharine Brandegee as a liberated woman scientist of early California. *Desert Plants* 7(3):128–139, 158–163.
CURRAN, MARY KATHARINE. 1884. New species of Californian plants. *Bulletin of the California Academy of Sciences* 1:12–13.
CURRAN, MARY KATHARINE. 1885. List of plants described in California, principally in the Proc. of the Cal. Acad. of Sciences, by Dr. Albert Kellogg, Dr. H. H. Behr, and Mr. H. N. Bolander; with an attempt at their identification. *Bulletin of the California Academy of Sciences* 1:128–151.
CURRAN, MARY KATHARINE. 1887. Priority of Dr. Kellogg's genus *Marah* over *Megarrhiza* Torr. *Bulletin of the California Academy of Sciences* 2:521–524.
DAVIS, LIAM H. 1994. Sereno Watson: Early California botanist. *Fremontia* 22(3):20–23.
DOYLE, HELEN MCKNIGHT. 1934. *A Child Went Forth. The Autobiography of Dr. Helen McKnight Doyle*. Gotham House, New York. 364 pp.
DUPREE, A. HUNTER. 1959. *Asa Gray*. Harvard University Press, Massachusetts. 505 pp.
DUPREE, A. HUNTER, and MARJAN L. GADE. 1971. Brandegee, Mary Katharine Layne Curran. Pages 228–229 in E.T. James, ed., *Notable American Women, 1607–1950*, vol. 1. Harvard University Press, Cambridge, Massachusetts.
ERTTER, BARBARA. 1988. C. A. Purpus: His collecting trips in the Sierra Nevada and Owens Valley, California, 1895–1898. Pages 303–309 in Clarence A. Hall, Jr., and Victoria Doyle-Jones, eds., *Plant Biology of Eastern California*. White Mountain Research Station, University of California, Los Angeles.
ERTTER, BARBARA. 2000. Floristic surprises in North America north of Mexico. *Annals of the Missouri Botanical Garden* 87(1): 81–109.
EWAN, JOSEPH. 1942. Bibliographical miscellany — IV. A bibliogeographical guide to the Brandegee botanical collections. *American Midland Naturalist* 27:772–789.
EWAN, JOSEPH. 1955. San Francisco as a mecca for nineteenth century naturalists. Pages 1–63 in Ernest B. Babcock, J. Wyatt Durham, and George S. Myers, eds., *A Century of Progress in the Natural Sciences 1853–1953*. California Academy of Sciences, San Francisco.
EWAN, JOSEPH. 1987. Roots of the California Botanical Society. *Madroño* 24:1–17.
FARQUHAR, FRANCIS P. 1930. *Up and Down California in 1860–1864: The Journal of William H. Brewer*. Yale University Press, New Haven, Connecticut. 601 pp.
GIBBONS, William P. 1893. The redwood in the Oakland hills. *Erythea* 1:161–166.
GOETZMANN, WILLIAM H. 1966. *Exploration & Empire: The Explorer and the Scientist in the Winning of the American West*. Random House, Inc., New York (Vintage Books edition). 656 pp + xviii pp. [index].
GREENE, EDWARD LEE. 1885. Studies in the botany of California and parts adjacent. *Bulletin of the California Academy of Sciences* 1:66–127.
GREENE, EDWARD LEE. 1887. Biographical notice of Dr. Albert Kellogg. *Pittonia* 1:145–151.
GREENE, EDWARD LEE. 1888. Sketch of the life of Thure Kumlien, A. M. *Pittonia* 1:250–260.
GUTZKOW, FREDERICK, GEORGE CHISMORE, and ALICE EASTWOOD. 1905. *Doctor Hans Herman Behr*. [Memorial printed by] California Academy of Sciences, San Francisco. 7 pp., photo.
HERRE, ALBERT W. C. T. [ca. 1960.] *Katherine [sic] Brandegee: A reply to a fantasy by J. Ewan*. Printed by the author, University of Washington, Seattle. 6 pp.
HITTELL, THEODORE HENRY. 1905. *In memory of President Harkness*. [Memorial printed by] California Academy of Sciences, San Francisco. 6 pp.
HITTELL, THEODORE HENRY. [sans date: see Leviton & Aldrich, 1997].
JEPSON, WILLIS L. 1894. Chamisso Botanical Club. *Erythea* 2:171–172.

JEPSON, WILLIS L. 1898. Dr. Henry N. Bolander, botanical explorer. *Erythea* 6:100–107.
JEPSON, WILLIS L. 1899. Biographical sketch of H. G. Bloomer. *Erythea* 7:163–166.
JEPSON, WILLIS L. 1918. Edward Lee Greene, the man and botanist. *Newman Hall Review* [Berkeley] 1:24–29.
JEPSON, WILLIS L. 1929. Harriet A. Walker. *Madroño* 1:261.
JEPSON, WILLIS L. 1933. The Botanical Explorers of California — VIII. William G. W. Harford; Thomas Bridges. *Madroño* 2:83–88.
JONES, MARCUS E. 1932. Katherine Brandegee, a Biography. Mary Katherine (Layne) (Curran) Brandegee. *Desert Plant Life* 4:41, 51, 65, 70. [reprinted in *Cactus and Succulent Journal* of the Cactus and Succulent Society of America 41:266–269, 1969.]
JONES, MARCUS E. 1933. Mrs. T. S. Brandegee. *Contributions to Western Botany* 18:12–18.
KELLOGG, ALBERT. 1855. [Marah.] *Proceedings of California Academy of Natural Sciences* 1 [2nd edition, 1873]:37–38.
LEVITON, ALAN E., and MICHELE L. ALDRICH, eds. 1997. *Theodore Henry Hittell's The California Academy of Sciences: A Narrative History, 1853–1906*. California Academy of Sciences, San Francisco. xv + 623 pp., 145 illus.
MARWOOD, WILLIAM. 1973. *Traveller in a Vanished Landscape: The Life and Times of David Douglas*. Clarkson N. Potter, New York. 244 pp.
MCINTOSH, ROBERT P. 1983. Edward Lee Greene: the man. Pages 18–53 *in* F. N. Egerton, ed., *Landmarks of Botanical History: Edward Lee Greene*. Part 1. Hunt Institute for Botanical Documentation, Carnegie-Mellon University. Stanford University Press.
MCVAUGH, R. 1983. Edward Lee Greene: an appraisal of his contribution to botany. Pages 54–84 *in* F. N. Egerton, ed., *Landmarks of Botanical History: Edward Lee Greene*. Part 1. Hunt Institute for Botanical Documentation, Carnegie-Mellon University. Stanford University Press, California.
MOORE, PATRICIA. 1996. *Cultivating Science in the Field: Alice Eastwood, Ynes Mexia and California Botany, 1980–1940*. Ph.D. dissertation. Department of History, University of California, Los Angeles.
RUSH, ELIZABETH. 1997. On her terms: Katharine Brandegee: first woman of western botany. *Pacific Discovery* 50(1):22–27.
SCHLISING, ROBERT L. 1993. Cucurbitaceae. Pages 535–538 *in* James C. Hickman, ed., *The Jepson Manual: Higher Plants of California*. University of California Press, Berkeley.
SETCHELL, WILLIAM ALBERT. 1926. Townshend Stith Brandegee and Mary Katharine (Layne) (Curran) Brandegee. *University of California Publications in Botany* 13:155–178.
SLACK, NANCY G. 1993. Botanical exploration of California from Menzies to Muir (1786) with special emphasis on the Sierra Nevada. Pages 195–242 *in* Sally M. Miller, ed., *John Muir, Life and Works*. University of New Mexico Press.
SMITH, RAY F. 1967. Entomology and Parasitology [Department]. Pages 85–86 *in* V. A. Stadtman and Centennial Publications Staff. *The Centennial Record of the University of California*. University of California, Berkeley.
SOUSA SANCHEZ, MARIO. 1969. Las colecciones botanicas de C. A. Purpus en Mexico: periodo 1898–1925. *University of California Publications in Botany* 51:i–ix, 1–36.
STADTMAN, V. A. 1970. *The University of California, 1868–1968*. McGraw Hill Book Company, New York. 594 pp.
STADTMAN, V. A., and CENTENNIAL PUBLICATIONS STAFF. 1967. *The Centennial Record of the University of California*. University of California, Berkeley. 586 pp.
STEPHENS, LESTER D. 1982. *Joseph LeConte: Gentle Prophet of Evolution*. Louisiana State University Press, Baton Rouge. 340 pp.
TIMBY, SARA. 1998. The Dudley Herbarium. *Sandstone & Tile* 22(4):3–15.
WATSON, SERENO. 1871. *Botany*. *In* Clarence King, Report U. S. Geological Exploration of the Fortieth Parallel, vol. 5. Government Printing Office, Washington, D.C. 525 pp.
WATSON, SERENO. 1880. *Botany [of California]*, vol. 2. Little, Brown, and Company, Boston. 559 pp.
WIESLANDER, A. EVERETT. 1865. The beginnings: 1873–1912. Pages 1–22 *in* Casamajor, Paul, ed., *Forestry Education at the University of California: The First Fifty Years*. California Alumni Foresters, Berkeley.

WILSON, CAROL GREEN. 1955. *Alice Eastwood's Wonderland: The Adventures of a Botanist.* California Academy of Sciences, San Francisco. 222 pp.

ZELLER, S. M. 1943. North American species of *Galeropsis, Gyrophragmium, Longia,* and *Montagnea. Mycologia* 35:409–421.

Agassiz's Notions of a Museum
The Vision and the Myth

MARY PICKARD WINSOR
Institute for the History and Philosophy of Science and Technology
University of Toronto and Victoria College
73 Queen's Park Crescent, Toronto, Ontario M5S 1K7 Canada
E-mail: mwinsor@chass.utoronto.ca

> When I had Dr. Hagen here to show him how I wanted the Crustacea put up, he was appalled, so different are my notions of a Museum from those prevailing even among the most advanced students. — Louis Agassiz, July 21, 1868[1]

Visitors to the Museum of Comparative Zoology at Harvard may feel that its arrays of stuffed animals are rather old-fashioned, but I can testify that in the late 1950s the exhibits looked even more antique than they do today. As a high school student working there summers, peering into cases crowded with crabshells or pickled fishes, I could slip back in my imagination to the nineteenth century, for in fact many of the specimens and their arrangement, and even some of the labels, dated from the 1880s. I was aware that the museum had been founded by Louis Agassiz a hundred years earlier, in 1859. I also knew that the building had grown in stages, for I was told that the room in which I worked, in Bill Clench's Mollusk Department, was older than the rooms where the public stared at stuffed sharks.[2] I am sure I assumed the museum had simply grown in size over the years, without changing its nature. Many years later, while writing a book on the MCZ, I arrived at a very different picture of its development (Winsor, 1991). Close reading of the yearly *Annual Reports* (which include statements from the curatorial staff as well as the director) led me to conclude that the museum's early decades were fundamentally different from the mature

FIGURE 1. 1892 photograph of the MCZ's first floor "Synoptic Room — Zoological" viewed from the gallery level. Beneath the life-size model of an octopus are cases containing examples of mammals, birds, reptiles, fish, and the major invertebrate groups. By permission of the Ernst Mayr Library of the Museum of Comparatve Zoology, Harvard University. Copyright President and Fellows of Harvard College.

249

museum. The metaphor of growth so commonly applied to institutions, as if they were living things, will not do for Agassiz's museum, unless perhaps we recall the life story of a butterfly. The schemes that Louis Agassiz nursed in the 1860s for arranging his museum had scant resemblance to the chaotic reality that sorely tried the patience of his supporters, and scant resemblance too to the arrangement ordering the museum in the 1880s and later.

In his heyday, Agassiz was distinctly proud of his novel ideas about museum arrangement; my epigraph refers to his new employee, the distinguished German entomologist Hermann Hagen. What probably appalled Hagen was not so much the novelty of Agassiz's "notions of a Museum," but that his scheme would greatly multiply curatorial labor. Hagen and the other assistants were to make considerable progress by 1870 in dissuading the MCZ's founder from his pet plans. After Louis Agassiz's death in 1873, the impractical notions of museum arrangement he had cherished were consigned to oblivion, and this happened not just through the ordinary forgetfulness of later generations, but because of the steadfast loyalty of his only son. In the late 1870s and 1880s, Alexander Agassiz transformed the MCZ into an impressively modern museum, and he made sure the museum's successes reflected back upon his father's reputation. Inspecting the hapless schemes of Louis Agassiz, who, in spite of all his faults, was a man of passionate vision, we find at their core a robust faith that collections of specimens are a powerful tool for uncovering new biological knowledge.

Alexander Agassiz's Thoroughly Modern Museum

Come back with me, please, and let us visit together the MCZ when its exhibit halls were new. A number of large photographs taken in 1892 display the museum's interior (Figs. 1–5).[3] The rooms in Figures 1, 2, and 3 were two stories high, though of modest width; the upper row of windows, avoided by the photographer, supplied sunlight to the gallery level, where a walkway was supported by slender iron columns. The stairway leading to the galleries is visible in Figure 2 on the right. Although these photographs contain considerable information, what they cannot convey is the impression that those rooms could make on 19th century visitors. In the 1880s, techniques of taxidermy were improving rapidly, so that a mounted deer, bison, or even hummingbird looked much more life-

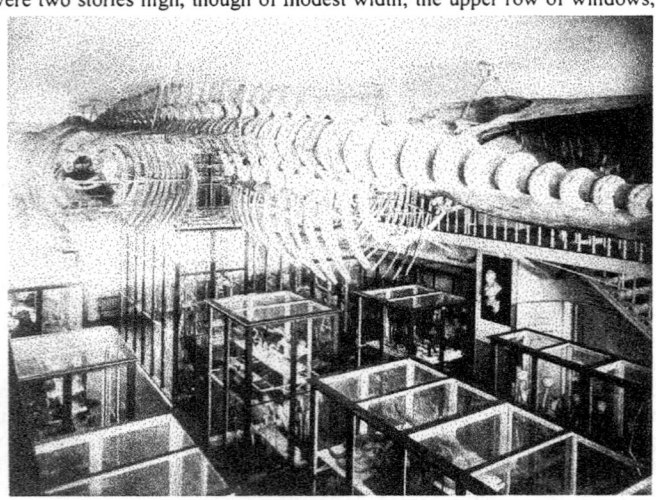

FIGURE 2. 1892 photograph of the MCZ's third floor "Systematic Collection — Mammals" viewed from the gallery level.
By permission of the Ernst Mayr Library of the Museum of Comparatve Zoology, Harvard University. Copyright President and Fellows of Harvard College.

like than had been possible even ten years before. The lack of background or vegetation around the specimens would disappoint no one, for museum dioramas were a thing of the future (Wonders, 1993).

One visitor has left us a record of his impressions, although he was by no means a disinterested reporter. The great English naturalist Alfred Russel Wallace, while on a lecture tour of the United States, went twice to the MCZ, during November and December of 1886 (Wallace, 1905). He was welcomed by Alexander Agassiz, who had every reason to be proud as he conducted Wallace through the exhibit halls and behind the scenes. A self-made millionaire, the younger Agassiz had supervised and paid for the MCZ's recent expansion. Wallace inspected the research collections, where row after row of specimens were stored in cabinets of drawers, he saw the library, and he walked through the public exhibition rooms with their glass cases and neat labels. He described his visit in the popular English magazine *The Fortnightly Review*. In its day, his article added a bit to Wallace's small income as well as giving encouragement those who were striving to upgrade old museums; now it serves as a precious source of evidence about the historic MCZ.

FIGURE 3. 1892 photograph of the MCZ's third floor "Systematic Collection of Radiates." By permission of the Ernst Mayr Library of the Museum of Comparatve Zoology, Harvard University. Copyright President and Fellows of Harvard College.

Although never himself employed in a museum, Wallace was an exceptionally well-informed observer; before his American trip he had written endorsements of the importance of public museums of natural history (Wallace, 1869; 1870; 1873; 1882). He seized this opportunity to preach to his countrymen about museum policy. In spite of the vast quantity of material that has accumulated in the British Museum, Wallace declared,

> the Harvard Museum is far in advance of ours as an educational institution, whether as regards the general public, the private student, or the specialist; and as it is probably equally in advance of every European museum, some general account of it may be both interesting and instructive, especially to those who have felt themselves bewildered by the countless masses of unorganized specimens exhibited in the gloomy halls and galleries of our national institution. (Wallace, 1887:347)

The natural history department of the British Museum in London had only recently moved from Bloomsbury to South Kensington, where a building had been specially designed for it. The elaborate new museum had been designed under the direction of Richard Owen after more than twenty years of debate (Stearn, 1981; Girouard, 1981; Rupke, 1988; Forgan, 1994). It was opened to the public between 1881 and 1883, so how could its halls, only six years old or less, be "unorganized" and "gloomy"? Wallace's criticisms were presumably not aimed at Owen, now retired, but at those curators who were resisting the reforms of his successor, William H. Flower. There was one display in South Kensington reportedly quite pleasing to visitors: a series of British birds, each pair mounted on appropriate vegetation in natural poses with their nest and eggs (Gunther, 1975; Wonders, 1993). Wallace acknowledges the effort as "interesting," but otherwise, he complains,

> the great bulk of the collection still consists of the old specimens exhibited in the old way, in an interminable series of over-crowded wall-cases, while all attempt at any effective presentation of the various aspects and problems of natural history, as now understood, is as far off as ever. What may be done in this direction, and how a museum should be constructed and arranged, so as to combine the maximum of utility with economy of space and of money, will be best shown by an account of the Museum of Comparative Zoology at Harvard. (Wallace, 1887:348–349)

By "natural history, as now understood," Wallace meant evolution.

His phrase "how a museum should be constructed and arranged" encompasses two related but distinct issues: how specimens are arranged within each room, and how much access to those rooms is allowed to the general public as opposed to serious students and expert researchers. Wallace begins with the question of public access. "The first thing to be noticed is the small proportion of the whole building open to the general public, as compared with that devoted to the preservation and study of the bulk of the collections" (Wallace, 1887:350). In the rooms housing most of the museum's specimens, there is space well designed for study, the tables situated at the windows so that chosen specimens can be examined in sunlight, Wallace notes approvingly. We can see one such workroom in Figure 4. Alexander Agassiz explains in his *Annual Reports* how he transformed the original building to achieve the large number of non-public rooms.[4] Originally the building, constructed to Louis Agassiz's specifications, consisted of a basement plus only two complete floors; each room was tall, with two rows of windows and a gallery, and the layout of all the rooms was the same. The structure (but not the contents) of those original rooms is clear in Figure 3. Additions to the building during the founder's lifetime, which doubled its length, followed the same design (except that the roof of

FIGURE 4. 1892 photograph of the MCZ's first floor paleontological workroom. By permission of the Ernst Mayr Library of the Museum of Comparatve Zoology, Harvard University. Copyright President and Fellows of Harvard College.

the whole was raised to add a top floor). Alexander Agassiz increased the floorspace by adding sections to the building and by flooring across the galleries in many of the rooms. Figure 4 shows a side effect of that process; in one of the paleontological storage and work rooms on the main floor, the floor of the old gallery is visible as the plastered portion of the ceiling, contrasting with the underside of the new second floor level.[5] Alexander Agassiz announced in 1876 his intention of flooring over most of the galleries (*Annual Report*, 1875).

Gray's 1864 Proposal to Separate the Exhibits

The policy Wallace was praising in 1887, that most of a museum's collection should be stored away from public view, had originated in the mind of John Edward Gray of the British Museum about 30 years before. Gray spelled it out in a public address of September 1864; printed in October, Gray's speech was widely distributed and discussed by museum workers everywhere (Köstering, 1999, and Nyhart, personal communication).[6] His exposition was forceful and unambiguous. Public museums have two distinct objects, Gray said:

> 1st, the diffusion of instruction and rational amusement among the mass of the people; and 2nd, to afford the scientific student every possible means of examining and studying the specimens of which the museum consists
>
> What the largest class of visitors, the general public, want, is a collection of the more interesting objects so arranged as to afford the greatest possible amount of information in a moderate space, and to be obtained, as it were, at a glance. On the the other hand, the scientific student requires to have under his eyes and in his hands the most complete collection of specimens that can be brought together, and in such a condition as to admit of the most minute examination . .
>
> In the futile attempt to combine these two purposes in one consecutive arrangement, the modern museum entirely fails in both particulars . . . .
>
> . . . for the purposes of scientific study, the most complete collection . . . would be best kept in cabinets or boxes from which light and dust would be excluded, in rooms especially devoted to the purpose, and not in galleries open to the general public . . . . (Gray, 1864:284–286)

Since today this is how most major museums are designed, it may be hard for us to understand what a disturbing departure from existing policy Gray's plan was. Yet, during the preceding centuries of museum evolution, from the Renaissance through the Enlightenment, there was no reason to differentiate between specimens according to audience, and whenever the public helped pay the bills, it seemed important to make as large a show as possible. Gray's boss, Richard Owen, rejected the idea that much of the natural history collection at the British Museum should be hidden away, although Owen did propose that visitors would be helped to understand the whole collection if selected specimens were used as a kind of introduction to the rest. What Owen called an "index museum" would be examples illustrating the main taxonomic groups (Rupke, 1994).

When Alexander Agassiz took charge of the MCZ, after his father's death, he explicitly set out his commitment to Gray's plan (without mentioning Gray).

> The number of [planned] exhibition-rooms will undoubtedly seem small, compared with the total amount of space, to those who are accustomed to wander through room after room of such museums as the British Museum, the Jardin des Plantes; and still smaller, when compared with the new museums contemplated in London, Vienna, and Berlin. This brings us to the fundamental difference existing between the two systems possible in museums: one of which is to place before the public everything in a single series; the other to make such a selection from the general collection, and also such other combinations and special expositions, that, while the Museum retains in its stores the archives of the science, the exhibition may place before the public an

exposition of the problems of natural science in a condensed and easily intelligible form. (*Annual Report*, 1875:12)

Alexander Agassiz had announced this policy as early as 1876, not, as I have wrongly stated, 1878 (Winsor, 1991). The United States National Museum of the Smithsonian in Washington adopted this plan in 1881, as Berlin did around 1888, while Paris and London dragged their heels (Winsor, in press).

Wallace, in his 1887 article, moved on from the collections behind the scenes to the rooms open to the public, and detailed the themes which governed their content. Some of his remarks echo Gray's views, that with only a limited number of specimens on show, visitors have a chance of making sense of what they see; other remarks of Wallace's have to do with the particular choices of what specimens are grouped together.

> On entering the building the visitor finds opposite to him an open room, over which is painted in large letters, "Synoptic Room — Zoology,"

(His description fits exactly the room in Figure 1, where the words "Synoptic Room" can be seen on the door at lower right. He calls the room "open" because it is two stories high. Wallace mentions a "suspended . . . model of a gigantic cuttle-fish twenty feet in diameter." The octopus was generally termed a "cuttlefish" and was labelled, the photograph shows, with both names.)

> . . . this room contains a Synopsis, by means of typical examples, of the whole animal kingdom . . . . its contents and purpose are clearly indicated to every visitor, each group and each specimen being also well and descriptively labelled . . . the specimens are comparatively few in number, not crowded together, and so arranged and grouped as to show at the same time the wonderfully varied forms of animal life, as well as the unity of type that prevails in each of the great primary groups . . . . (Wallace, 1887:352)

Gray's policy called for the labelling of every specimen and each glass case. Alexander Agassiz went a step further and made a point of labelling each room (Annual Report, 1875:13). The idea of the MCZ's Synoptic Room was the same as Owen's Index Museum, planned but never installed in London.

Next Wallace describes five rooms, all with gallery levels, in which specimens are arranged taxonomically: a large room for the mammals, with whale skeletons (Fig. 2), and four others containing representative birds, fishes, crustacea, insects, mollusks, echinoderms, coelenterates, worms, and sponges.[7] In Figure 3, the labelling of some corals is visible, including fossils in the table cases, but we cannot see the "beautiful glass models" of sea anemones that caught Wallace's attention. Each of these "systematic collections" is a synopsis of one taxonomic group, just as the first room gave a synopsis of the whole animal kingdom, but in his report Wallace adopts the museum's term rather than repeating the word "synopsis." Wallace stresses that while individual specimens may later be replaced by better ones, the number of specimens will not increase, "because they are already quite as numerous as the average intelligence even of well-educated persons can properly understand" (Wallace, 1887:353).

Wallace then moves on to a set of rooms arranged according to a different principle, and one especially close to his own heart. Wallace had written three books arguing that biogeography provided powerful evidence for evolution, so no wonder he admired

> the special feature of the museum, and that which is most to be commended, the presentation to the public of the main facts of the geographical distribution of animals. This is done by means

of seven rooms, each one devoted to the characteristic animals of one great division of the earth or ocean

He explains that one room of the museum is devoted to the fauna of North America, another to animals of South America. Comparing this to the room containing African fauna, Wallace declares,

> The most cursory inspection of these two rooms will teach the visitors a lesson in natural history that he will not learn by a dozen visits to our great national storehouse at South Kensington -- the lesson that each continent has its peculiar forms of life, and that the greatest similarity in geographical position and climate may be accompanied by a complete diversity in the animal inhabitants.

Wallace reports the contents of the Indo-Malayan room, the one for the fauna of Europe including Siberia, and finally Australia. He concludes his tour of the faunal rooms by declaring,

> It is a remarkable thing that so interesting and instructive a mode of arranging a museum, and one so eminently calculated to impress and educate the general public, has never been adopted in any of the great collections of Europe . . . . It is a striking proof of the want of any clear perception of the true uses and functions of museums that pervade the governing bodies of such institutions, and also perhaps, of the deadening influence of routine and red-tapeism in rendering any such radical change as this almost impossible. (Wallace, 1887:357)[8]

Wallace also saw two more faunal rooms in preparation, for the Atlantic Ocean (Fig. 5) and the Pacific, plus four rooms on the first floor not yet open to the public, intended to display fossils of the Cambrian, Devonian, Jurassic, and Tertiary periods. Envisioning the future, the Englishman was beside himself.

FIGURE 5. 1892 photograph of the MCZ's third floor "Faunal Collection." By permission of the Ernst Mayr Library of the Museum of Comparatve Zoology, Harvard University. Copyright President and Fellows of Harvard College.

The last room of the series will be devoted to the Tertiary deposits, and will show the many curious lines of modification by which our most highly-specialised animals have been developed. If some of the preceding rooms contain the most marvellous products of remote ages, here assuredly will be the culminating point of interest in seeing the curious changes by which our existing cattle and horses, sheep, deer, and pigs, our wolves, bears, and lions, have been gradually modified from fewer and more generalised ancestral types. Of all the great im-

> provements in public museum arrangement which we owe to the late Professor Agassiz and his
> son, there is none so valuable as this. Let any one walk along the vast palaeontological gallery
> at South Kensington, and note the crowded heaps of detached bones and jaws and teeth of fossil
> elephants and other animals, all set up in costly, mahogany and glass cases for the public to stare
> at . . . all crowded together in one vast confusing series from which no clear ideas can possibly
> be obtained, except that numbers of strange animals, which are now extinct, did once live upon
> the globe, and he will certainly admit the imperfections of this mode of exhibition, as profitless
> and puzzling to the general public as it is wasteful of valuable space and inconvenient to the
> student or the specialist. (Wallace, 1887:358)

But plans and their realization are two different things. Nine years would pass before two of the paleontological exhibit rooms were opened, the third after another nine years (*Annual Report*, 1895–1896, 1904–1905). It is not clear if "the culminating point of interest," the Tertiary room, was ever finished.

Based on Wallace's understanding of the planned fossil exhibits as well as the geographic and taxonomic rooms already open, and because Alexander Agassiz assured him that the "general plan of the building and the arrangement of the contents were carried out in accordance with Professor [Louis] Agassiz's views" (Wallace, 1887, p. 349), Wallace saw an irony that he could use to further shame his countrymen into remedial action. Towards the close of his article he wrote,

> It is surely an anomaly that the naturalist who was most opposed to the theory of evolution should
> be the first to arrange his museum in such a way as best to illustrate that theory, while in the land
> of Darwin no step has been taken to escape from the monotonous routine of one great systematic
> series of crowded specimens arranged in lofty halls and palatial galleries, which may excite
> wonder but which are calculated to teach no definite lesson. (Wallace, 1887:358–359)

Everyone knew that Louis Agassiz was a leading opponent of evolution (a theory his son quietly accepted), and that Wallace was Darwin's co-discoverer and a staunch ally, so this was powerful rhetoric. Was it really true, however, that Louis Agassiz had designed the museum arrangement Wallace saw in 1886?

The Myth of Louis Agassiz's Founding Plan

If Wallace's information about the MCZ's history came from the mouth of Alexander Agassiz and from copies of the *Annual Reports*, as is most likely, he could certainly have concluded that all its virtues should be credited to the father. Alexander Agassiz asserted that when Louis Agassiz died, "and indeed far earlier, from the very beginning of the institution, the general plan was sketched out in the mind of the founder" (*Annual Report*, 1882–1883:3). Indeed, he had even pointed out how ironic it was that his father's plans now seemed so evolutionary. A year before Wallace's visit Alexander Agassiz had reported:

> By a strange coincidence the foundation of the Museum dates from the publication of the "Origin
> of Species." Of course so powerful a movement in the scientific thought of the time could not
> fail to modify the problems which the institution was intended to illustrate and to solve. Yet the
> usefulness of the plans laid down for the Museum remains unimpaired by the new methods of
> treating questions of affinity, of origin, of geographical and geological distribution. Should the
> synoptic, the systematic, the faunal, and the paleontological collections cease to bear the
> interpretation given to them by the founder, their interest and importance, even for the advocates
> of the new biology, would not be one whit lessened . . . .
> The plans of the founder have been realized, perhaps, far beyond his most sanguine expecta-
> tions . . . . (*Annual Report*, 1884–1885:4–5)

Wallace most likely had a copy of this report before him when he composed his article.

Wallace would have had no reason to cross-examine Alexander Agassiz about possible differences between the museum of the 1880s, Louis Agassiz's ideas in the last years of his life, and Louis Agassiz's ideas in 1859. The evidence that tells us that a policy like Gray's was not part of Agassiz's thinking in 1859 forces us to interpret Alexander Agassiz's statements about the "founder's plans" as referring only to the principle of synoptic, systematic, and faunal arrangements, not to the separation of exhibit halls from scientific storage. On close examination, one finds Alexander Agassiz making no explicit claim that his father originated the concept of separating research from exhibit rooms.

That claim was first made a few years later, by a museum director from Dresden, Adolf Bernhard Meyer (1840–1911).

> As far back as 1860, L. Agassiz, perhaps the first to carefully consider such a plan, had developed the principles on which he meant to separate an exhibition collection for visitors from a scientific collection for investigators . . . . He actually carried out these plans a few years later. (Meyer, 1905: 93–94)[9]

Meyer had paid an official visit to the MCZ between October 5 and 19, 1899. At that time, both Alexander Agassiz and the museum's Keeper, William McMichael Woodworth, were away, leaving Samuel Henshaw in charge (*Annual Report*, 1899–1900:7–8). Alexander Agassiz supplied Meyer with material, however, sending several *Annual Reports*, the printed version of his 1902 remarks on MCZ history, and the reference to a lecture Louis Agassiz delivered on July 11, 1860.[10] It was that reference, which Meyer gives as a footnote, that lends authority to his statement. Speaking to the Mercantile Library Association in Boston, Louis Agassiz had proclaimed his intention to arrange his museum by subdividing the specimens into synoptic, faunal, paleontological and other collections (L. Agassiz, 1862).[11] Yet nowhere in that speech had Louis Agassiz suggested the kind of differences in public access to any of these collections which lay at the heart of Gray's policy.

Meyer's easy assertion that Louis Agassiz "actually carried out these plans a few years later" warns us not to trust him as an historical source. Louis Agassiz's own *Annual Reports* boast no such success; instead they explain why his mushrooming collection cannot yet be arranged as it ought to be. The state of the museum at the time of Louis Agassiz's death in 1873 was described, ten years later, by Alexander Agassiz, as one of "confusion."

> . . the difficulties involved in the initiation of so large an undertaking prevented Professor Agassiz from developing his schemes. From want of rooms and of means for proper distribution, the immense accessions constantly accumulating upon his hands invaded, little by little, the space devoted to special objects. It became evident, at the time of his death, that nothing short of a radical rearrangement of the collections could bring out his plans and give them distinct expression. This rearrangement has been completed only within the past year, and no sign of the former confusion, due to a too rapid accumulation of material, is left. (*Annual Report*, 1882–1883:3).

Clearly Meyer had been encouraged to imagine that the "general plan" in Louis Agassiz's mind from the very beginning had included the separation of exhibits from research material as well as the concept of faunal versus synoptic collections, but his own reading of the documents was uncritical.

Samuel Henshaw repeated the gist of Meyer's claim in 1907 (*Annual Report*, 1906–1907:3), but this does not constitute fresh evidence. Henshaw's association with the Agassiz Museum dated from 1891 when Hagen fell ill. Curator from 1904, Henshaw did his best to please the retired Agassiz. Henshaw's 1907 story of the museum's history carried the authority of his office, but he was surely reading the same documents Meyer was, as well as talking to Alexander Agassiz. Meyer's statement is evidently the source for subsequent claims to the same effect, such as L. V. Coleman's (1939, 2:249).

If the plans Alexander Agassiz put into effect in the 1870s and 1880s had really been present in Louis Agassiz's mind in 1859, he would deserve credit for the innovations advocated by Gray in 1864. What record is there enabling us to reconstruct Louis Agassiz's early ideas of museum arrangement? In 1854 he had declared that he wanted to create a museum "which . . . would be as important for science as those founded by John Hunter in London or by Cuvier in the Jardin des Plantes" (Lurie, 1960:215). Both of these, the Museum of the Royal College of Surgeons and the Muséum d'Histoire naturelle, were research institutions whose collections were used by professors to teach medical and other advanced students. The public was admitted at certain times to make whatever sense they could of those same specimens. This did not mean, however, that every specimen in such museums was equally open to view. Special furniture, like cabinets for household china, held some specimens on open shelves, others behind glass, and others in drawers or behind doors, so the contents of each room would be experienced differently by the casual visitor glancing at what was open to view and by the expert who would be pulling out the drawers.

The first time Agassiz announced that his museum would be unusual in its arrangement was on December 21, 1859, speaking at the Boston Society of Natural History.

> In the great collections, he said, even that at the British Museum, the sole object seems hitherto to have been to exhibit animals according to the supposed natural affinities...he intended to arrange the Cambridge Zoölogical Museum in a totally different manner, viz: according to natural zoölogical provinces; in this way, he hoped to be able to define such provinces, which as yet were but imperfectly known, and to arrive at important conclusions on the correlations of animals of the different classes. (L. Agassiz, 1861)

The belief that geographic distribution of species is as much a part of God's order as are the patterns studied by morphologists, embryologists, and paleontologists was an idea Agassiz promoted in the "Essay on Classification" he had published in 1857 (L. Agassiz, 1962).

This report of remarks made shortly after his collections were transferred to the new MCZ provides a striking clue to Agassiz's thinking. Here we find a novel and intriguing idea: the notion that attempting to arrange animals by "natural zoölogical provinces" will help him discover those provinces. Thus the process of arrangement becomes a form of research, which is a very different thing than constructing didactic exhibits, whose function is to display relationships already known.

The report of his 1859 Boston Society comments continues,

> He intended to do the same with fossils, showing independent creations and distinct zoölogical provinces in geological as well as modern times. For purposes of study and comparison, to this he purposed to add a very small collection of typical genera and species, exhibiting the natural affinities of animals, — also a third collection, exhibiting the embryonic series of every animal type, — a fourth, embracing the domesticated animals, to show what are species, varieties, breeds, &c., with such products from them as have a commercial value, — and finally, a museum of men, skulls, skeletons, &c., for the study of the human races. (L. Agassiz, 1861)

To maintain that a policy like Gray's was in Agassiz's mind at the founding of his museum, one must deal with the fact that on these public occasions he omitted to mention it. Neither the layout of the rooms, which were all the same, nor the language of his letters and speeches, makes any mention of spaces dedicated to different purposes. Rather, he seemed to assume that, like Hunter and Cuvier, he could invite outsiders to see what his students saw; in a speech of January 1859, he explicitly promised that were he given enough space he could "allow free access to the rooms for the public as well as the students . . ." (L. Agassiz, 1859).

One could conjecture, in support of Meyer's claim, that Agassiz intended to exclude the public from the working core of his collection but did not say so for fear of weakening the public's willingness to support his museum financially. Such a conjecture would violate the historians' sacred principle that people are presumed to mean what they say unless there is compelling evidence to the contrary. In this case, such evidence may seem to exist, consisting of Louis Agassiz's jealous reaction when Gray's paper appeared. He confessed himself afraid of losing credit to Gray. In the MCZ's *Annual Report*, after complaining that lack of space prevents him from arranging his specimens as he intends, Agassiz says,

> I regret the more any delay in that respect, since I see that the directors of other Museums begin to feel the imperfections of the present arrangement of their collections, and are proposing as new, schemes identical with those which for many years have been in active operation with us. I would particularly refer to the recent suggestions of Dr. J. E. Gray . . . the burden of which coincides, though on a limited scale, with what we have been doing upon a much more extended plan for several years past. (Annual Report, 1864:13)

But what was it that Agassiz had been doing which Gray now proposed? The separation between research rooms and public rooms in Gray's proposal was fundamental and absolute, not "on a limited scale." Gray also mentioned another innovation that did closely coincide with what Agassiz had advocated publically. Agassiz wanted to allocate his specimens into several distinct series or collections, and one of these, the synoptic, was suitable for novices. His 1860 lecture had eloquently set out the problem the synoptic collection was designed to solve, the massing of hundreds of thousands of specimens in one great taxonomic series.

> No human intelligence can take in such an assemblage. Not long ago I visited, until I was tired of it, the magnificent and immense collection of birds of the British Museum. Rather than teaching me, it made me dizzy. There one finds, one may say, all the known birds, one beside the next, so similar in species and family and so uniform in appearance, that the most active and searching eye can neither detect nor remember the differences. The spirit is confused . . . . (L. Agassiz, 1862:537)

(His London visit, in 1859, had included meetings with Gray, so there may be some doubt as to the complete independence of their ideas.)

> It was there that I was struck with this idea, that a museum arranged only in order to exhibit all zoological facts fails in its purpose; because the naturalist cannot, without constantly retracing his steps, see how the various ducks, for example, differ from one another. A collection which will put everything that is different under the observer's eyes in a small space, leaving to the side what is similar, will answer much better the needs of those seeking to educate themselves. (L. Agassiz, 1862:537)

Gray's paper addressed the same problem, stating that the

> general visitor perceives little else than a chaos of specimens, of which the bulk of those placed in close proximity are so nearly alike that he can scarcely perceive any difference between them . . . the eye both of the general visitor and of the student becomes confused by the number of the specimens . . . . (Gray, 1865:76)

Gray suggested that a few selected specimens could be arranged in special cases, one to show the classes of the animal kingdom, another the orders of each class, and so on. This synoptic or index idea could have been the point that generated Agassiz's fear of being upstaged, and Agassiz's idea of faunal collections certainly constituted "a much more extended plan" than Gray's. We are not forced to conclude that Gray's policy of splitting a museum into public and restricted collections was a secret scheme of Agassiz's.

Louis Agassiz's 1867 Instructions to Hagen

Although Agassiz was proud of the ideas he had explained to audiences in Boston in 1859 and 1860, Alexander Agassiz would later remember them as "ideas which had floated vaguely through Professor Agassiz's mind" (A. Agassiz, 1902). Alexander Agassiz was twenty-four years of age when the museum was founded and deeply involved in assisting in its management. His term "floated vaguely" points to the distance between his father's inspirational Boston lectures and the challenges faced within the museum's walls, where "everything had to be sacrificed to the exigencies of the collections, which accumulated at first far too rapidly for their proper arrangement" (*Annual Report*, 1877–1878:4). (So loyally did he guard his father's reputation, however, that the term "floated vaguely" present in the typescript of his 1902 talk was deleted from the printed version that was sent to Meyer.)[12] By the mid-1860s, however, vague ideas would no longer do. The student assistants of the museum's first years were replaced by full-time employees. Hiring the entomologist Philip R. Uhler in 1864, Agassiz wrote a letter setting out the conditions of work, including the requirement that insect specimens should form four distinct series, namely: Special Systematic Collections for each order, Faunal Collections for each zoological province, Embryological Collections, and Anatomical Collections.[13] The Faunal and Embryonic had been mentioned in his 1859 Boston lecture, the Anatomical was the arrangement of Hunter and Cuvier, and the Special Systematic was described as "*single* representatives of each species with the view of illustrating their affinities." It would, thus, be much richer than a synopsis or index, where a whole family or order is represented by an individual, but leaner than the full collection, where for some species scores or hundreds of specimens were preserved.

In 1867, Louis Agassiz, safely home after an expedition to Brazil, refreshed and excited, resumed control of the MCZ (thus releasing his son to run the copper mine which later made him rich). The MCZ's *Annual Reports* for that year and the next contain numerous mentions by the museum assistants of various instructions Agassiz had issued, tailored for each department. Uhler left for a better paying post, and in the middle of October, 1867, Hermann Hagen arrived to replace him (Winsor, 1991). A 13-page manuscript labelled, in Hagen's distinctive script, "(Instructions given by Prof. L. Agassiz October 1867)" survives. The document itself is not in Hagen's handwriting, nor in Agassiz's; presumably it was dictated by Agassiz to an amanuensis. My transcription of it is published, by permission of the Museum of Comparative Zoology Archives, Harvard University, as an appendix to this paper. It deserves a closer study than I gave it in 1991.

Agassiz's 1867 instructions spell out the "notions of a Museum" that appalled Hagen, and we have to agree that they were utterly "different... from those prevailing even among the most advanced students." Gray's lucid exposition of the advantages of dedicating some rooms to research and other rooms to exhibits had been circulating for three years, yet Agassiz says nothing about specimens or collections being open or closed to the public, except for a comment that the synoptical collection will be useful to beginning students and to visitors. The prevailing notion was that a museum had a single collection, subdivided taxonomically, yet Agassiz demanded the four separate collections he had specified to Uhler.

Within the 1867 document, three of the four headings — "General Systematic Collection,"

"Faunal Collections," and "Synoptical Collection" — resemble the titles Wallace later saw painted on the walls of the exhibition rooms. On closer examination, however, interesting differences emerge. The 1867 Synoptical Collection illustrated the taxonomic groups of insects, while Alexander Agassiz used the term only for his synopsis of the whole animal kingdom. Thus, the Synoptical concept of 1867 was realized in Alexander Agassiz' public Systematic Collection of insects. Nothing in the later exhibits seen by Wallace corresponded to what was meant by the term "Systematic" in 1867. Louis Agassiz explained to Hagen that a General Systematic Collection should contain only specimens identified to species by a trustworthy authority, making it, "as it were, a register, systematically arranged, of authentic specimens, the identification of which may be trusted" (L. Agassiz, 1867:1).[14] We can only conjecture what the rationale was for separating such specimens from others. Many of the specimens arriving in the MCZ were newly collected by all manner of people, and so the scientific name appropriate to each specimen would either not exist or be open to doubt; at other times recognized naturalists or their heirs sold or donated a collection to the museum, and in those cases the identification already attached to each specimen was part of the value of the collection. (Agassiz told Hagen that labels in an expert's handwriting should be carefully retained.) Probably by establishing this series Agassiz hoped to protect material of archival value from careless treatment. We may think these correspond to the "type" specimens which, in modern museums, are usually distinctly marked and segregated, but types must have been named by the one person who first christened that particular species, whereas in 1867 Agassiz was proposing that the identification can have been made by any skilled taxonomist. Hagen must have seen in this instruction a source of unending labor, for because he was an expert himself, every time he made a firm identification of a specimen he would have to transfer it into this series. A specimen of which the collecting locality was not known would be welcome in this series, for an expert determination of its name would make the specimen a useful reference object.

Agassiz's 1867 instructions to Hagen included what he called a "structural" collection, by which he meant a series of specimens dissected to reveal internal anatomy. He emphasized that its purpose was not to study the physiology of organs (which was the purpose of the comparative anatomy of Hunter and Cuvier) but to display the characteristic features of taxa; this was a continuation of the theory he had announced in his "Essay on Classification" that each taxonomic category, from genus and species up to order and class, had distinct kinds of characters.[15]

The "Faunal Collections" of the 1867 instructions must have been what Alexander Agassiz was remembering when he created a set of rooms ordered geographically, but Louis Agassiz's concept was utterly at odds with the small displays of typical examples of a few major regions his son mounted. Louis Agassiz told Hagen that all specimens of which the place of origin is precisely known must be arranged geographically rather than taxonomically. If he continued to go on collecting trips, and invite contributions from naturalists and admirers whom he educated about the importance of precise collecting data, most of the specimens entering the building would go to the faunal collections. Any specimen with only a general provenance, such as "Switzerland," is not allowed in this series. Such a specimen could not even be retained in the MCZ, unless its specific name has been authoritively determined; it will be cast into the pile of "duplicates" waiting to be sent to a less fussy museum in trade for something more scientifically useful, or else it would be dissected and join the "Structural" series. The faunal collections will be works in progress, Agassiz explains, demanding "great discretion, & an unknown amount of patience to start rightly . . ." (p. 4), because the appropriate geographic boundaries are not yet known. Here we recognize an elaboration of Agassiz's sketch of 1859, when he told the Boston Society of Natural History that the boundaries of unknown zoological provinces would be discovered in the process of arranging his specimens. Certainly Agassiz in 1867 did not have in mind areas as large as the ones his son would later use to define exhibits — North America, Africa, Indo-Asia — for he tells Hagen that there may be "three faunæ within ten miles of Cambridge . . ." (1867:5). Great discretion would surely be needed, to arrange things by province when the provincial boundaries are unknown.

In practical terms, the scheme may have been less fantastic than it sounds, and perhaps even reflected a common occurence in his growing museum. When he or one of his collectors packed material in the field, the contents of boxes or kegs would be taxonomically heterogeneous (various families of animals, unsorted), but geographically homogeneous (all collected in one locality). Such a container could be immediately placed in the faunal collection without even being unpacked. To satisfy Agassiz's conviction that natural faunal provinces exist, however, all the museum staff would have to have been contributing to the same enterprise. The birds, mammals, fish, mollusks, and insects of eastern Massachusetts should be arranged together, all helping to reveal the boundaries of the several faunal provinces that might exist there. Yet, there is no hint in Agassiz's several instructions that the assistants in charge of those different taxa were to meld their faunal collections.

Agassiz tells Hagen that faunal collections "may be of great importance for the progress of Science," (p. 4), which reminds us of the high hopes he cherished for biogeography. After the correlation of fossil forms to embryos had convinced him, early in his career, that zoology was the study of God's unfolding plan, he then decided that animal distribution was another grand topic for a similar breakthrough. Lamarck's theory, in Agassiz's view, gave physical agents the responsibility for life, which was absurd. In 1848 he explained what he expected from biogeography:

> The geographic distribution of organized beings displays more fully the direct intervention of a Supreme Intelligence in the plan of the Creation, than any other adaptation in the physical world . . . . evidence must rest upon direct observation and induction, just as fully as mathematics claims the right to settle all questions about measurable things. There will be no *scientific* evidence of God's working in nature until naturalists have shown that the whole Creation is the *expression of a thought*, and not the *product of physical agents*. Now what stronger evidence of thoughtful adaptation can there be, than the various combinations of similar, though specifically different[,] assemblages of animals and plants repeated all over the world, under the most uniform and the most diversified circumstances? (L. Agassiz, 1850:144–145)

Later, when confronted by Darwinism, Agassiz again hoped that this latest version of the old error could be disproved by showing that distributional patterns made no sense physically but displayed the workings of divine intelligence. He made this point explicit in his Boston address of 1860, and explained it to his companions on their way to Brazil in 1865 (L. Agassiz and E. C. Agassiz, 1868:8–9; Winsor, 1991:144–145).

In content and in method, Agassiz's biogeography is a confusing mix of the familiar and the strange. His repeated insistence that collectors must record localities with precision, that specimens were scientifically useless if identified only by the port where they were purchased, seems modern. Scientists today, however, explain fauna and flora as complex products of historical events, many of them essentially accidental, but Agassiz's views excluded accident, evolution, and even historical contingency; he believed that species were divinely created extending over their full natural range (L. Agassiz, 1962:44-45).

How far his world view differed from ours is vividly shown by one example from his 1857 "Essay on Classification." In one family of lizards, the skinks, he knew more than thirty genera, ranging from ones with four legs having five toes on each foot, to others with four, three, two or only one toe, down to two-legged species, ending with the snake-like legless skinks. Agassiz made a list arranged by the number of legs and toes and concluded triumphantly (L. Agassiz, 1962:51), "Who can look at this diagram, and not recognize in its arrangement the combinations of thought?" Noting where each genus lives, he was satisfied to find that

> the home of these animals stands in no relation whatsoever to their zoological arrangement. On the contrary, the most remote genera may occur in the same country, while the most closely related may live far apart . . . . they are scattered all over the globe, but not so that there could be any connection between the combinations of their structural characters and their homes. (L. Agassiz, 1962:50, 52)

The pattern of limb number showed thought, and the lack of pattern of distribution showed freedom; "such freedom indicates selection, and not the working of the law of necessity" (p. 51). (His meaning is that the Creator exercised freedom in selecting where to place His creatures. Agassiz did not know that "selection" would be a key word in Darwin's theory, which was still secret when Agassiz wrote this.) Agassiz passed over in silence the lack of freedom in the distribution of species within each genus, whose contiguous homes accord well with the hypothesis of common ancestry.

In one of Agassiz's remarks about the numerical arrangement of skink legs and toes there lies an intriguing clue to his thinking about museum arrangement. Although the taxonomic hierarchy he presents is based on one "drawn up [by Leopoldo Fitzinger {Vienna}, copied by August-Marie-Constant Duméril and Gabriel Bibron {Paris}] to classify animals preserved in the Museum of the Jardin des Plantes in Paris," its orderly pattern or "arrangement . . . is in reality inscribed in Nature by these animals themselves and is only read off when they are bought together and compared side by side" (p. 51). Thus, for Agassiz, arranging specimens in a museum is not a matter of imposing our order on nature's chaos, but an opportunity to "read off" an order really present in nature but only discerned through the medium of the museum.

As I was struggling to picture how this idea of a geographically-arranged collection would work, my memory lit upon those long-ago summers, when one of my jobs was to make entries in a geographical card file, a tool the Mollusk Department was experimenting with to aid biogeographic research. Politically-bounded areas, such as nations or the states of the U.S.A., each had a card, onto which I entered the department's holdings. This meant methodically combing the taxonomically-arranged collection, drawer after drawer, and copying onto the cards the accession number, scientific name and particular locality from each specimen's label. The hope was that queries could be answered, about the fauna of Florida for example. Perhaps because of this experience, my first reaction to Agassiz's instructions to Hagen was, why didn't he just make a card file? It is simpler to arrange and rearrange bits of stiff paper than to move specimens, or to copy data from the Massachusetts card onto new Eastern Massachusetts and Western Massachusetts cards. (Later, in California, Joseph Grinnell, clear-eyed in his commitment to using museums as tools for the study of ecological regions, would nevertheless arrange the specimens themselves in taxonomic order [Griesemer, 1990].) Yet, when Agassiz first formulated his novel concept of faunal collections, card files were not the standard tool of data management they later became. Libraries, including the one in the MCZ, kept catalogues in the form of bound books. I imagine that even if some state-of-the-art champion of card files had explained their virtues to Louis Agassiz in 1867, he would have stuck to his own scheme; he would have explained that effective comparison requires objects, not just the names of objects, to be brought together.

In the museums Agassiz admired — the great Muséum d'Histoire naturelle in Paris, where Louis Agassiz spent several crucial months in 1832, and the Museum of the Royal College of Surgeons based on John Hunter's collections — specimens were arranged in two different ways. Comparative anatomists ordered material by physiological system, while zoologists followed taxonomic groups.

Thus both Hunter and Cuvier, as anatomists, organized material by function, such as the skeletal system, digestive system, reproductive system and so on; they would place a horse's skeleton beside the skeleton of a pig, while the horse's stomach was located elsewhere, laid out for comparison next to the stomach of a pig. Except for Cuvier, the zoologists in the Paris museum were assigned responsibility along taxonomic lines: Latreille the insects, Lamarck the other invertebrates, Lacépède the fish and reptiles, Geoffroy St.-Hilaire the mammals and birds. Agassiz invented a new term, "comparative zoology," to signal that his museum would build upon both traditions, zoology and comparative anatomy.

Always a loyal soldier, Hagen responded to the 1867 instructions by proposing a modified version of Agassiz's plan, suggesting practical reasons for excluding the public from the workspace.

> Since most of these collections require to be kept as much excluded from light and air as possible, there will be a collection for public exhibition, containing species remarkable for their beauty, or as being either useful or obnoxious; besides, a collection representing types of families, and genera for entomological students. The other collections will always be accessible on special application, or for purposes of study. (*Annual Report*, 1868:30)

The very formulation — the insects are especially delicate, they will still be accessible — implies that Hagen knew he was proposing an exception to the policy Agassiz intended for the rest of his collections.

Louis Agassiz clearly intended, in his 1867 instructions as in 1859, that the faunal collections would allow scientists to uncover new truths about nature. And his hopes soon bore fruit, for the assistant in charge of birds reported, "In connection with the faunal arrangment of the collection, a special investigation of the Geographical Distribution of the Birds of North America has been commenced" (*Annual Report*, 1868:24). Thus did Joel Asaph Allen begin the biogeographic studies for which he is still remembered. For the most part, though, the complexity of Agassiz's plans weighed against their ever being accomplished, and his friends worried that he would die without having left a clear impression of his ideas in the arrangement of his museum.

The plan that Alexander Agassiz executed did honor to his father's memory by including both the idea of synopsis and of geographic arrangement in the public rooms, but in each research department, where the vast majority of specimens were stored in a single taxonomic arrangement, Louis Agassiz's novel notions were forgotten. There are hints in the *Annual Reports* that this shift in plan was underway even before Louis Agassiz's death, having begun soon after Hagen and other curatorial staff were faced with the practical difficulties of following Agassiz's instructions. During the planning of the building expansion that took place in 1871–1872, father and son very likely discussed museum arrangement. If so, Alexander Agassiz's attribution of the "general plan" to his father may not have been disingenuous.

From this distance, Alexander Agassiz's reasons for celebrating his father are as transparent as Wallace's frustrations at the slow reform of British and Continental museums. What of our own motives and interests? Is the job of historians only to set the record straight? Here the evidence, while not strong enough to assign credits, is enough to justify withholding priority for Gray's policy from Louis Agassiz. Yet, our interest in the past surely includes the appreciation of unfamiliar ways of thought, and we can be inspired by schemes that failed as well as by those that succeeded. The strengths of Gray's proposals were proven when, after considerable delay, museum directors began to adopt them (Nyhart, 1998). In contrast, Louis Agassiz's "notions of a Museum. . ., so different. from those prevailing even among the most advanced students," were stillborn. It may be that they were so fraught with false assumptions and impracticalities that any attempt to implement them was doomed. Yet, his utopian vision of a museum where researchers' tentative arrangements would be exposed to public gaze, that is, where there is no separation between exploration and teaching, has a certain charm missing from Gray's sensible plan.

ACKNOWLEDGMENTS

I am grateful to Michael Ghiselin, who invited me to the California Academy of Sciences in May, 1994, and to him and Giovanni Pinna, who together invited me to the Museo Civico di Storia Naturale di Milano in November, 1996, for two congenial workshops which caused me to explore this story more thoroughly than I had done in 1991. On those occasions, I profitted from stimulating discussions with Paula Findlen, James Griesemer, Kevin Padian, David Lindberg, Nick Arnold, Claudine Cohen, and especially with the remarkable Elihu Gerson. I also received helpful advice from Peter Stevens, Sharon Kingsland, and Lynn Nyhart. Staff of the Museum of Comparative Zoology's Ernst Mayr Library, notably Robert Young and Dana Fisher, provided generous assistance at critical moments. The suggestions offered by two anonymous referees improved my presentation, but I thank Alan Leviton for allowing some of my fancies to stand. My research was supported by the Social Sciences and Humanities Research Council of Canada, through the University of Toronto and Victoria University.

NOTES

[1] Louis Agassiz to Theodore Lyman, July 21, 1868. Lyman Family Papers, Massachusetts Historical Society, Boston.

[2] The space I occupied on the fourth floor was similar to that on the second floor pictured in Winsor (1991, p. 220).

[3] In the *Annual Report* for 1892-93, Alexander Agassiz wrote, ". . . considerable time was spent by the Professors and Instructors in preparing an exhibit for the [World's] Columbian Exposition [in Chicago], specially intended to illustrate the methods of instruction, and forming a part of the Harvard University exhibit. The Museum sent plans of the Building, prepared under the supervision of Dr. Wolff, who also charged himself with advising the Harvard Camera Club in regard to the views of the most characteristic Exhibition Rooms of the Museum which accompanied them. The plans, and the photographs taken by the Camera Club and by Mr. J. L. Gardner, will be hereafter most useful . . ." (p. 4). In my 1991 book, others from this set are reproduced (figs. 34, 35, and 39).

[4] He includes complete floorplans, first in 1878 and again in 1889; the later ones are reproduced in Winsor (1991:184–189).

[5] The location of this room can be seen in Winsor (1991:185, fig. 29); the *Annual Report* for 1875 gives plans that show its gallery. Another of the oldest rooms, at gallery level, can be seen in fig. 43 (p. 220).

[6] Lynn K. Nyhart mentions evidence for the early impact of Gray's ideas in a book on German museums now in progress.

[7] Of the five systematic rooms, the only one open to the public today is that for mammals, the others having been made into workrooms by being floored across at the gallery level. Wallace saw two whale skeletons in the mammal room, for the sperm whale in Figure 2 was added a few years later (*Annual Report*, 1890–1891:4). Thankfully the museum authorities have been sensitive enough to this room's history that the words "Systematic Collection of Mammals" remain painted on the wall.

[8] Wallace relates his frustration with petty museum red tape in his 1905 autobiography, vol. 2, pp. 376–377.

[9] Meyer (1905) is a translation of Meyer (1904), where the original reads "Schon 1860 hatte L. Agassiz, vielleicht als erster, die Grundsätze entwickelt,*) nach denen er in dem vergleichend zoologischen Museum, das er in Cambridge in den Vereinigten Staaten einzurichten hatte, eine Schausammlung für den Besucher von einer wissenschaftlichen Sammlung für den Forscher zu trennen beabsichtigte, was er denn auch weniges Jahre später ausführte" (pp. 93–94).

[10] I am indebted to Dana Fisher, Special Collections Assistant at the Ernst Mayr Library, for locating the Meyer correspondence and summarizing its contents for me.

[11] The lecture was delivered in English but published in French, because his Boston audience included George-Auguste Matile (1807–1881), who sent a report of what Agassiz had said back to Switzerland, where it was published.

[12] I am indebted to Dana Fisher, Special Collections Assistant at the Ernst Mayr Library, for comparing the two versions of Alexander Agassiz's 1902 speech.

[13] L. Agassiz to P. R. Uhler, 6 April 1864, Special Collections, Ernst Mayr Library, Museum of Comparative Zoology, Cambridge, Massachusetts.

[14] References to the 1867 "Instructions" are to the page numbers of the manuscript, indicated in brackets in my transcript.

[15] I discuss this taxonomic idea in Winsor (1991:19–27), but my claim there that he fell silent about this idea soon after publishing his 1857 "Essay on Classification" is mistaken, for clearly he still hoped to find support for it within his museum in the late 1860s.

LITERATURE CITED

AGASSIZ, A. 1902. Remarks [on completion of Geological Museum, 1902]. Typescript in possession of Anna Prince Jones.

AGASSIZ, L. 1850. *Lake Superior: Its Physical Character, Vegetation, and Animals, Compared with Those of Other and Similar Regions*. Gould, Kendall and Lincoln, Boston.

AGASSIZ, L. 1859. [speech to Visiting Committee of Lawrence Scientific School, January 1859] *American Journal of Science* 27: 295–299.

AGASSIZ, L. 1861. [the best arrangement of a Zoölogical Museum] *Proceedings of the Boston Society of Natural History* 7:191–192.

AGASSIZ, L. 1862. Des Musées d'Histoire naturelle. *Bibliothéque Universelle* 14:527–551.

AGASSIZ, L. 1867. Instructions given by Prof. L. Agassiz, October 1867. Manuscript UAV.298.367 *in* Special Collections, Ernst Mayr Library, Museum of Comparative Zoology, Cambridge, Massachusetts.

AGASSIZ, L. 1962. *Essay on Classification* [1857], edited by E. Lurie. Belknap Press, Cambridge.

AGASSIZ, L. and AGASSIZ, E. C. 1868. *A Journey in Brazil*. Ticknor & Fields, Boston.

ANNUAL REPORT OF THE MUSEUM OF COMPARATIVE ZOOLOGY. Published by the MCZ starting in 1860, it is cited according to the period covered, not the year of publication.

COLEMAN, L. V. 1939. *The Museum in America: A Critical Study*. American Association of Museums, Washington. 3 vols.

CUVIER, G. 1803. Notice sur l'établissement de la collection d'anatomie comparée du Muséum. *Annales du Muséum d'Histoire Naturelle* 2:409–414.

FLOWER, W. H. 1898. "Modern museums" (Presidential address to the Museums Association, 1893) in his *Essays on Museums and Other Subjects Connected with Natural History*, pp. 30–53. MacMillan, London.

FORGAN, S. 1994. The architecture of display: museums, universities and objects in nineteenth-century Britain. *History of Science* 32:139–162.

GIROUARD, M. 1981. *Alfred Waterhouse and the Natural History Museum*. British Museum (Natural History) London.

GRAY, J. E. 1864. On museums, their use and improvement, and on the acclimatization of animals. *Annals and Magazine of Natural History* 14:283–297 (reprinted in *Report of the British Association for the Advancement of Science* 1865:75–86).

GRIESEMER, J. R. 1990. Modeling in the museum: on the role of remnant models in the work of Joseph Grinnell. *Biology and Philosophy* 5:3–36.

GUNTHER, A. E. 1975. *A Century of Zoology at the British Museum through the Lives of Two Keepers: 1815–1914*. Dawsons, London.

KÖSTERING, S. 1999. Museumsbau und Museumsreform: Plazierung, Gebäude- und Raumkonzeptionen von Naturkundemuseen in Deutschland, 1871–1914. Pages 159–176 *in* A. Geus, T. Junker, H.-J. Rheinberger, eds., *Repräsentationsformen in den biologischen Wissenschaften.* (Beiträge zur 5. Jahrestagung der DGGTB [Deutsche gesellschaft für Geschichte und Theorie der Biologie] in Tübingen 1996 und zur 7. Jahrestagung in Neuburg a.d. Donau 1998.) *Verhandlungen zur Geschichte und Theorie der Biologie,* Bd. 3. Berlin.

LURIE, E. 1963. *Louis Agassiz: A Life in Science.* University of Chicago Press, Chicago.

LYMAN FAMILY PAPERS, Massachusetts Historical Society, Boston.

MEYER, A. B. 1904. Das Bestreben der americanischen naturwissenschaftlichen Museen, breitern Schichten des Volkes zu dienen. Pages 93–96 in *Die Museen als Volksbildungsstätten, Schriften der Centralstelle für Arbeiter-Wohlfahrtseinrichtungen* no. 25. Carl Heymann, Berlin.

MEYER, A. B. 1905. Efforts of the American natural history museums to increase their usefulness. Pages 93–94 in *Annual Report of the Smithsonian Institution, U.S. National Museum for 1903.* Government Printing Office, Washington, D.C.

NYHART, L. K. 1998. Civic and economic zoology in nineteenth-century Germany: the "Living Communities" of Karl Möbius. *Isis* 89:605–630.

RUPKE, N. A. 1988. The road to Albertopolis: Richard Owen (1894–1892) and the founding of the British Museum of Natural History. Pages 63–89 in N. A. Rupke, ed., *Science, Politics and the Public Good: Essays in honour of Margaret Gowing.* Macmillan Press, London.

RUPKE, N. A. 1994. *Richard Owen: Victorian Naturalist.* Yale University Press, New Haven.

STEARN, W. T. 1981. *The Natural History Museum at South Kensington: A History of the British Museum (Natural History) 1753–1980.* Heinemann, London.

WALLACE, A. R. 1869. Museums for the people. *MacMillan's Magazine* 19:244–250.

WALLACE, A. R. 1870. [Comments on Sclater's paper]. *Nature* 2:465.

WALLACE, A. R. 1873. East India Museum. *Nature* 8:5.

WALLACE, A. R. 1882. [Review of H. Housman, *The Story of Our Museum.*] *Nature* 25:407–408.

WALLACE, A. R. 1887. American museums: the Museum of Comparative Zoology, Harvard University. *Fortnightly Review* 42:347-359.

WALLACE, A. R. 1905. *My Life: A Record of Events and Opinions.* Chapman and Hall, London. 2 vols.

WINSOR, M. P. 1991. *Reading the Shape of Nature.* University of Chicago Press, Chicago.

WINSOR, M. P. In press. "Museums." *Cambridge History of Science,* vol. 6.

WONDERS, K. 1993. *Habitat Dioramas.* Uppsala University Press, Uppsala.

APPENDIX

Transcription of handwritten document UAV.298.367 in the Special Collections of the
Ernst Mayr Library, Museum of Comparative Zoology, Harvard University

(Instructions given by Prof. L. Agassiz October 1867)
[This written by Hermann Hagen. Text dictated by Louis Agassiz to an unknown amanuensis.]

General systematic Collection

This Collection is to record all the work done in the Museum, to identify the specimens: — it is not intended to exhibit the characteristic features of the species — This will be done in the faunal collections. The systematic collection is to be, as it were, a register, systematically arranged, of authentic specimens, the identification of which may be trusted: select specimens of all the species, which have been named by recognized authorities ought therefore to be put up in this Collection, & as far as possible provided with labels in the hand writing of those who named them. It is equally desirable that the origin of these species should be well authenticated, & the precise origin of the specimen ought to be recorded, on the label, with the name; but specimens, the origin of which is unknown are not to be excluded from the systematic collection whenever their name has been identified by trust worthy authorities.

With reference to the arrangment of the Collections still in bulk in the Museum, only such specimens should at first be transferred to the systematic Collection which are already

[*p. 2*] labelled by some acknowledged authority. & if the specimens are numerous, only one or two should be transferred to the systematic collections, and the rest reserved for the faunal Collections. In disposing of the specimens, the following considerations should serve as a guide. Whenever the specimens are exactly alike & no essential differences exist between the males & females, one specimen alone should be transferred to the systematic collection; — but whenever there exist marked sexual differences, a pair should be selected, & the original label should be transferred to the systematic collection with the specimens: — a new label is to be written out to remain with the specimens that are not transferred to the Systematic Collection, — this new label is to contain every information which the original label furnished. The specimens so provided with new labels may now be transferred to the faunal Collections to which they belong, if they are provided with an authentic indication of their origin; but if the origin is doubtful or only general, the specimen had better be transferred to the duplicates, rather than to the faunal collections.

[*p. 3*] Faunal Collections

All the specimens gathered in the Museum, the origin of which is perfectly authentic ought to serve as basis for the arrangment of faunal collections. It is of no consequence whether the specimens are named or not; all that is required to give them a place in the faunal collections is that there should be no doubt as to their origin; & by this I mean not in a general way the country in which they were collected, or even the state; but the special locality must be known:— specimens labelled as collected in Brazil, or Australia, or in the United States, or in Europe have no claim to a place in a faunal Collection: if from Switzerland it must be known whether they were collected in the Jura, or in the plain, or in the Alps, in Subalpine, or higher Alpine regions etc. If in France, whether in the Pyrrenees, or Mountains of Auvergne, or the Cevennes, or in the lowlands of the West, or in the departments along the Mediterranean, or in those bordering the British Channel etc. Specimens from Europe without such precise locality must be transferred to the systematic Collection, when carefully named, or treated as duplicates. The same applies to specimens from all other parts of the world; and North American

[*p. 4*] insects, in the Museum, not carefully labelled in this way may be put up in the systematic collection, if they are provided with authentic labels, or with the duplicates for our foreign exchange.

In collecting specimens for the faunal Collections it ought to be remembered that these collections are to afford information, which is not recorded with sufficient accuracy or to a sufficient extent elsewhere, and that when fairly arranged they may be of great importance for the progress of Science. As it is impossible beforehand to determine within what geographical areas these faunæ are circumscribed, nor indeed where their centre & their periphery may be, the first attempts at an arrangement must at all events be considered as provisional. It is indeed possible that the most valuable collections we possess have been gathered in localities where two faunæ meet, & in a manner overlap one another. It is therefore possible that even those collections we possess from the best authenticated localities are a mixture of two distinct faunæ, & may therefore furnish no accurate indication of the zoological character of either the one, or the other of these faunæ. It will require great discretion, & an unknown amount of patience to start rightly in laying a foundation for these faunal collections — I conceive for instance that the neighborhood of Boston & Cambridge [p. 5] afford special difficulties in studying the faunal arrangement of the insects. Guided by the little experience I have thus far had, I believe that to the east of the hills of Somerville, excluding the immediate sea-shore, the fauna will partake of the character of Maine, south of the White Mountains, — while the flats of Charles river & East and South Boston, Dorchester etc — will share the character of the maritime shore throughout New England. If this be true, it is evident that a collection made promiscuously within ten miles of Cambridge, with this place as a centre, would contain representatives of two distinct faunæ, and I have satisfied myself that the summit of the prominent hills about Waltham nourish species which belong to the White Mountain fauna. There are therefore three faunæ within ten miles of Cambridge, & it is evident therefore that the collection, embracing all the insects that may be found within ten miles of Cambridge would be a mixture of three different faunæ. As the faunal Collections are intended to exhibit the species in their natural relation to their homes, the specimens for these collections should be so selected as to represent each species in all its stages of growth with everything that may illustrate its history —

In the first place it should contain

[p. 6] a good many adult specimens with all their varieties, and in the case of insects, undergoing metamorphosis, it should contain several chrysalids, in all their stages, & also a number of eggs. In the case of insects with imperfect metamorphosis, such as the grasshoppers, it should contain a series of immature specimens of all sizes, from their first escape from the egg to maturity, & eggs also — In the second place and with reference to insects remarkable for their skill in building shelter or otherwise providing for their progeny, all these structures should be carefully collected. {{The question as to the best arrangement of all these materials will require farther thought & consideration.

As long as the natural boundaries of the different faunæ are not confidently ascertained, it would seem preferable to include the perfect insects only in the systematic arrangement of the faunal collections; and to arrange the larvæ, with the various structures of these insects separately, & it is my opinion that in the end it will be desirable to devise an arrangement that will admit of a combination of all these things in one series, & thus disclose which are the industrious insects, & which are not, which are useful & which injurious to man, animals & vegetation, & which undergo a more perfect metamorphosis, or none at all. It will be particularly desirable to keep up a regular intercourse with farmers & agriculturalists in order to give them desirable information, & to obtain from them large supplies of insects invading cultivated lands and the regular crops of our gardens & fields.

[p. 7] Synoptical Collection

The Class of insects is so numerous that a systematic collection embracing all the species we now possess in the Museum would be of little use to students, who have not yet made much progress in the knowledge of these animals. To satisfy the wants of this class of visitors & students, it is desirable to put up a synoptical collection, containing only a limited number of representatives of the different orders, families & genera of insects. It will at first be difficult to find the true limits of a synoptical collection, & in the beginning we must in a great measure be guided by our supplies, admitting perhaps such species to represent their genus, which are not the most characteristic, but may be the only one we possess.

In course of time we may replace those species by others that will answer the purpose better. Groups that are largely represented in nature should also have several representatives in this synoptical collection, while groups which are not numerous should be indicated by few species, so that the student, at the very outset, learns, even from so small a collection as this must of necessity remain, what are in reality the numeric proportions of different types of insects.

I hold for instance that among the carnivorous beetles, Manticora should be represented by a single specimen, Cicindela by half a dozen of the different types of one genus, such as

[*p. 8*] Germanica, Hybrida, Maritima, Chinensis &c — Cychrus by one single specimen — Calisona by one single specimen. Carabus by ten or twelve of the different types, Procrustes by a single specimen — and so on; so that the whole collection of Cleoptera [*sic*] may be included in two or three cases, — the different families being separated by an interval & labelled in larger letters, — and the genera separated by a smaller interval & labelled in smaller letters.

I think the whole collection of Orthoptera might be at first contained in a single case, that of Lepidoptera may occupy three cases, — that of Hymenoptera two cases etc — But the proper measure of all this must be ascertained by experiment. As this synoptic collection is to give to the students the first idea of the systematic relation of the class or insects & their general character, — it ought to contain all the indications that may be furnished concerning the metamorphoses of the insects selected to represent their natural groups, & in putting up the larvæ by the side of the perfect insect, the student may be taught in the very beginning that the scientific study of Entomology does not consist mainly in an investigation of the characteristics of the perfect insects but should embrace all their stages of growth. Preparations, exhibiting the most obvious characters of the principal groups,

[*p. 9*] such as the structure of the wings and the parts of the mouth, should be placed at the head of each larger group. Students, who enter the laboratory with the view of studying insects may be directed to make such preparations, and when successful their work may be put up in this synoptic collection. In former years I caused Mr. Scudder, Packard & Shurtleff, while they were students in the laboratory, to make a good many such preparations; but they were never properly put up, & have been allowed to decay.

[*p. 10*] Structural Collection

There is one side of the study of insects which is rarely represented by special collections even in the largest & best organized Zoölogical Museums, and only finds its place in Museums of Comparative Anatomy. I think that the isolation of anatomical investigation of insects from their zoölogical study is greatly detrimental to the scientific progress of entomology. At all events in a Museum, which has the name of a Museum of Comparative Zoölogy, and which is therefore not intended to contain merely zoölogical specimens, but to illustrate at the same time the anatomical structure of all the objects it embraces, such a separation of the collections into an anatomical & a zoölogical collection is not admissable. I hold therefore that our entomological collection must embrace anatomical preparations, illustrating in the fullest manner the anatomical stucture of all the articulates. But here the preparations necessary for this purpose ought to be arranged in a different manner from that usually adopted in anatomical Museums. The aim of the Museum of Comparative Zoölogy is not to illustrate the functions of the organs of insects, as contrasted with those of the other great types of the Animal Kingdom; it cannot be our object

[*p. 11*] to illustrate the various modifications of the nervous system through the whole series of articulates, or the various forms of the digestive, respitory [*sic*] or reproductive organs. Our object must be to show what are the combinations of these different systems of organs in each of the more comprehensive, & in all the subordinate groups of the type of articulates.

Thus I would have preparations made to show what are the characteristic, structural features of the type of articulates as a whole, & these preparations should not enter into any exhibition of any anatomical detail by which insects for instance may be distinguished from Crustacea, or Crustacea from worms; but only such anatomical preparations which show the characters common to them all, whether in their perfect condition, or in their larval state. The second series of preparations should exhibit all the anatomical characters, which distinguish the classes of articulates one from the other — that is to say, the anatomical peculiarities, which distinguish the insects as a class from the Crustacea as a class, and the worms from both.

The result of this study must decide the limitations of the classes, & teach us for instance whether the insects proper constitute a different class from the Arachnids & the Myriapods, or whether all three belong to one class. The same investigation must settle the question

[*p. 12*] whether Annelids & Helminths belong to one & the same class, or form two distinct classes, and whether the Rotifera are to be associated with the worms, or with the Crustacea. {{The third series of preparations ought to illustrate the anatomical characters of the orders in each class, & these preparations will decide for instance such questions as whether Myriapods, Arachnids and true insects are orders of one and the same class, or not, or whether Coleoptera, Orthoptera, Neuroptera, Hymenoptera, Lepidoptera, Hemiptera, Diptera &c are natural divisions of the character of orders, or not; for I hold that such questions can no longer be left to the arbitrary decision of entomologists; but are subjects to be decided by special scientific investigations. {{The fourth series of preparations ought to illustrate the anatomical characters of all the natural families in each of the larger groups of the Articulates, & these preparations are to decide whether the many groups, which have been called families by entomologists are really natural families, deserving to be considered as such, or may be groups of a higher, or lower standing: {{Finally the fifth series of preparations ought to illustrate the anatomical characters of each genus deserving a place in the natural system as a genus.

[*p. 13*] The various structures built by insects, such as the nests of bees, and all the various means which insects employ to provide for their existence, or that of their progeny, are natural manifestations of their faculties, which we commonly call instinct. But inasmuch as insects of allied groups, and which have therefore a similar anatomical structure build in a similar way, it seems natural to assume that all these industries of the different insects are as many manifestations of their diversified structures.

I hold therefore that all the various productions of the different groups of insects are to be considered as much as characteristics of their respective groups, as the various implements of different races among men are characteristic of their intellectual capacity, and therefore I hold that representations of the various characteristic industries of the different types of insects ought to be included in this structural collection. I do not mean to say that we should put by complete collections of these industrial products in the structural collection; for the endless diversity of these products belongs to the faunal collections, but I would include in the stuctural collections specimens of each kind of insect industry, which characterises a special mode of life, & is therefore indicative of a special faculty in the insects from which they originate.

A Bioeconomic Perspective on the Organization of the Naples Zoological Station

MICHAEL T. GHISELIN[a] and CHRISTIANE GROEBEN[b]

[a] Center for the History and Philosophy of Science, California Academy of Sciences, Golden Gate Park, San Francisco, California 94118 USA (E-mail: 110640.3011@compuserve.com);
[b] Stazione Zoologica «Anton Dohrn», Villa Comunale, 80121 Napoli, Italy (E-mail: groeben@alpha.szn.it)

Marine stations are widely recognized as an important kind of scientific institution, and historians have devoted a considerable amount of attention to them (Benson, 1995). One reason is that they can be pleasant places to work, not just for scientists, but for historians too. Another is that some very important research has been done at them. Such research forms major chapters in the biographies and autobiographies of many biologists. The institutional setting is crucial to the understanding of what went on.

A particularly important example of such an institution is the Zoological Station at Naples, Italy. It was a remarkably successful institution, and its success can be largely attributed to the organizational and administrative genius of its founder, Anton Dohrn (1840–1909) (Fig. 1). Indeed, Dohrn's performance in creating the institution has led to a de-emphasis by historians of his accomplishments as a scientist. Here we shall argue to the contrary. Dohrn was in fact a good scientist, and the kind of science that he did helps to explain his success as an administrator. He was a comparative anatomist with a functional outlook, and that may help to explain his capacity to understand how things are, and should be, organized.

It is important to emphasize the difference between such a functional anatomical approach, and the kind of morphology that traditionally has treated function as of no particular interest (see Reif, 1983; Ghiselin, 1994, 1996). Dohrn treated the organism as a coadapted system of interdependent parts, and the station as he created it had just such organismal qualities. One point that

FIGURE 1. Anton Dohrn.

emerges from the present study is the manner in which labor was both divided and combined within the organization. The traditional theory of the division of labor that goes back to Adam Smith tended to presuppose that the further tasks are subdivided, the better. Bioeconomists have emphasized the advantages of combining labor as well as dividing it (Ghiselin, 1974, 1978). Combining functions within an organization is particularly important where there is a need for communication among its subdivisions.

In the present essay we look at Dohrn's accomplishment from a broadly economic point of view. For those unfamiliar with recent developments in the science of economics, it should be stressed at the outset that we are only incidentally concerned with the financial aspect of the enterprise. Economics is the science of resources; it is not by definition a social science and has no necessary connection with business (Ghiselin, 1986). We are rather concerned with how organisms obtain and allocate resources, including their time and their skills. It does not matter whether we apply optimal foraging theory to a shore-bird or a marine biologist: the laws and principles are one and the same. For those interested in the more traditional aspects of economics, there is already an outstanding book by Partsch (1980) that provides detailed information about the funding of the Station and its political circumstances. The literature on Dohrn and the Station contains a lot of material that can be pressed into service in such an analysis as this (Kühn, 1950; Fischer, 1980; Groeben, 1985; Heuss, 1991; Ghiselin and Groeben, 1997). We should also give credit to an excellent, but brief, article written from the managerial point of view (De Masi, 1987).

Scope

Investigative behavior often includes moving from one place to another. That takes time and energy that might be expended in some other way. If equipment is involved, or if there are specimens to be brought back, there is a cost of carriage additional to that of transporting the scientist. It therefore stands to reason that a scientist undertaking an excursion into the field will engage in the sort of economic behavior that characterizes animal life in general. Various steps will be taken to maximize the amount of return on time and other resources that are invested. If the field work involves hiking and camping out, the economic rationale may be much the same as that of a recreational hiker and camper. One uses light-weight equipment and keeps it to a minimum. Gear may be shared with traveling companions.

Scientists, however, have somewhat different goals and interests from those of tourists. A look at how scientific excursions to the shore gave rise to permanent bases of operation there should help to explain why such laboratories came to exist. We can then press the analysis a bit further, and see how the manner in which the Naples laboratory was organized also illustrates some important principles of institutional economic organization.

This study focuses on marine biology, a science for which permanent laboratories at the shore have had a particularly important role. Similar considerations might be made for other disciplines, such as limnology. Marine biology, of course, has also been done on board ships, which solve some of the traveling scientist's problems but create others. Let us say just a few words about this mode of operation as part of the introductory background material. Transport by water is cheap, and a passenger on board a ship can have a fairly large amount of equipment with him: perhaps a substantial library. Space, however, is at a premium on ships, and for this and other reasons it is harder to work on board than on shore. A lot of scientists who worked on board ships did so attached to teams that were sent out for exploration or other purposes. Darwin is a familiar example. A common practice was to combine the labor of medical and scientific personnel on board: good examples are Darwin's friends and supporters Thomas Henry Huxley (1825–1895) and Joseph Dalton Hooker (1817–1911). A ship's doctor's essential duties could be discharged on a part-time basis under routine conditions. However, the arrangement could be rather unsatisfactory from the scientist's point of view. Dohrn actually took advantage of such situations; he set up a training program in marine biology so that Italian naval officers could do something useful in their spare time (Groeben 1988). Where the ship's captain wanted to go was not necessarily where the scientist did. Dedicated research vessels designed and operated to serve the scientists' needs were a later development. They were also expensive. Even the Challenger expedition of the late nineteenth century, however well equipped and staffed it was scientifically, had its tasks largely determined by the government's priorities and of course things have never changed altogether (Ghiselin, 1989).

Traditional Excursions

Scientists might travel by themselves or with one or a few companions. There were distinct limitations in the amount of equipment that they could take with them as baggage. From the accounts of travelers who were on their own much of the time, there were some basic pieces of equipment that may be treated as fixed costs: a microscope, rudimentary collecting gear, materials for dissecting, drawing, and preserving. Traveling in pairs or small groups has the advantage that certain items might be shared. There could be more division of labor within the kit of equipment that was carried. They could also provide one another with other things that they valued, such as intellectual companionship (and perhaps drinking companionship).

It makes sense, therefore, that groups of scientists, including teachers with their students, would make a joint venture of a visit to the shore. Professor Johannes Müller (1801–1858) of Berlin was largely responsible for the tradition of annual trips to Helgoland (Fig. 2) (Florey, 1995; Zissler, 1995). Both his student Ernst Haeckel (1834–1919) (in 1854) and Haeckel's student Dohrn (in 1865) participated in such trips. So did a lot of other important nineteenth century biologists.

Among German scientists there was also a most venerable tradition of traveling to Italy. There was a superb role model in Goethe's travels as described in his *Italienische Reise*. There was not just a mystique, but outright mysticism, in Goethe's quest for the *Urpflanze*. It is hard to say how much mystical baggage Haeckel took with him, but he made a literary-artistic bash of his trip to Italy in 1859 and 1860, just as the Darwinian Revolution was beginning (Haeckel, 1921). Haeckel's (1862) monograph on Radiolaria, which initiated his campaign for Darwinism, was based on work done in Italy.

FIGURE 2. Haeckel (standing right), Dohrn (standing left) and students at Helgoland, August 1865.

The scientific travelers found quite a number of good places to visit, most notably Messina with its rich semi-tropical biota (Groeben, 1996). Somewhat to the north lay Naples, and there were also various sites, such as Villefranche-sur-Mer, along the Riviera, Trieste and finally Naples. But they did not have fixed bases of operation. When in Naples, Haeckel set himself up in rented rooms on the water front. Others, such as the Russians Kowalevsky and Metschnikoff, obviously did much the same. From favorite sites to more permanent establishments at such sites is not a big step, but there were both incentives and disincentives. Among the incentives were, of course, the solution of such problems as the cost of carriage already mentioned. Another important incentive was the reduction of various transaction costs. The travelers had to negotiate for such amenities as housing. They might also need to arrange for the rental of boats or the assistance of local fishermen. This might take a considerable amount of time. The disincentives may be a bit less obvious. Mobility allowed the scientists to get away from circumstances that prove unsatisfactory. It also meant that they could visit a larger range and variety of sites. This was particularly important for those whose work depended upon such variety, especially systematists. We should also note that in the beginning the relative advantages of the various sites was still being explored, and that the needs of the scientists were changing. It was hard to predict what site would be optimal for a permanent base. And unless a substantial number of scientists could agree that a site would be optimal, they could not enjoy the economies of scale that result from all of them working together in the same place. Therefore, any number of reasons would inhibit them from sinking capital into such an establishment, over and above whether such capital was available.

Karl Ernst von Baer (1792–1876) was generally recognized as the greatest of living embryologists when Dohrn sought his assistance in founding the Station (see Groeben, 1993). Von Baer was strongly supportive, and also helpful because of his ability to influence the Russian government and scientific establishment. His enthusiasm no doubt had something to do with his frustrations in attempting to work in temporary quarters. In 1845 he had great difficulty obtaining sea-urchin embryos at Trieste. Towards the end of his stay he succeeded, but the chambermaid, not knowing what they were, threw them out.

Early Efforts to Establish a Permanent Laboratory

Carl Vogt (1817–1895) was a zoologist and geologist who was notorious for his materialistic philosophy. He also was an enthusiast for evolutionary thinking at a time when it was considered reprehensible but still had some following, especially among political dissidents. Vogt translated the *Vestiges of the Natural History of Creation*, a popular work on evolution published anonymously by Robert Chambers (1844, 1847), from English into German (Vogt, 1858). Vogt's efforts to establish a permanent marine laboratory, and also the advice and assistance that he gave to Dohrn, have been described in considerable detail by Groeben (1998). He worked at Nice during the winters of 1846–1847 and 1850–1852. In the early 1860s he attempted to establish a permanent laboratory, first at Nice, then Villefranche, and finally at Naples, but without success. His radical politics and lack of the proper connections may have had something to do with it, but probably the need was not yet strongly felt by enough of the scientific community. The more conservative Frenchman Henri de Lacaze-Duthiers (1821–1901) was more successful. He established a laboratory at Roscoff in the north of France at around the same time that Dohrn established the Naples laboratory (Pruvot, 1902).

Anton Dohrn (1840–1909) had certain advantages over Vogt. Not the least was the circumstances of his family. Because his father was a rich industrialist and a serious amateur entomologist, he was well connected both politically and scientifically. Anton Dohrn worked on insects early in his career, but switched to crustaceans when he came under the influence of Darwinian thinking. He studied at Königsberg, Bonn, Jena and Berlin. Dohrn was associated with Haeckel at Jena early in his career, but broke with him partly on philosophical grounds. They were together at Helgoland in the summer of 1865, which was the year before Haeckel's *Generelle Morphologie* was published. Dohrn's shift away from insects, the topic of his doctoral dissertation (Dohrn, 1865), to other arthropods and especially crustaceans, occurred that year as well. The rationale for this shift is clear enough. The science of phylogenetics had become recognized, and ambitious scientists were now looking for more remote connections among organisms. The principle of embryonic recapitulation was propounded by Fritz Müller (1864) and then given a central place in Haeckel's approach (Haeckel, 1866). The early branching events in the metazoan tree had taken place in the sea, and that is were Dohrn and others began to look in order to fill in the big picture. They were not disappointed. A. O. Kowalevsky (1866) was able to relate the vertebrates to a particular group of invertebrates on the basis of the larvae of tunicates. Dohrn's choice of crustaceans as material was perhaps serendipitous, but it put him in a particularly good position to understand Darwin's barnacle phylogenetics. Correspondence between

Darwin and Dohrn began on 26 November 1867 and Dohrn visited Darwin on 26 September 1870. Darwin was a strong supporter of Dohrn's efforts to found the Station (Groeben, 1982).

Dohrn habilitated at Jena on 11 November 1867, thus becoming a junior faculty member in Haeckel's department. In 1868 Dohrn spent several months with David Robertson (1806–1896) near Glasgow, Scotland. He had a home near the water and the advantages must have been quite evident. While there he invented a portable aquarium (Fig. 3) for the use of scientists. This he took with him to Messina in October where he worked together with the young Russian zoologist Nikolai Miklucho Maclay (1846–1888). At that time Dohrn began to take steps to found a permanent station at Messina. It would be one of many small stations in various localities. He discussed his plans with Vogt and others.

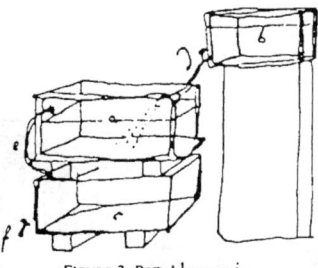

FIGURE 3. Portable aquaria.

The Naples Station

In 1870 Dohrn decided to build the station at Naples (Fig. 4) rather than Messina. There were several reasons for choosing Naples. It had a good biota, and it was reasonably accessible. But the reason most often given was Dohrn's idea of associating it with a public aquarium. Naples was a major tourist center, and the price of admission would provide an economic base for the scientific enterprise. Once the station was built it did indeed contain a superb public aquarium, and it did bring in a substantial amount of income. However, the net receipts were somewhat disappointing, and the aquarium never sufficed to cover the expenses of the Station. There are both advantages and disadvantages to such an integration of a profit-making enterprise into what is basically a non-profit institution. The sometimes unreliable nature of the income is one example of a disadvantage. The tastes of tourists are apt to change. And there were cholera outbreaks in Naples that kept both tourists and scientists away. On the positive side, the combination lowered fixed costs. A seawater system, with all its pumps and pipes, is costly both to build and to maintain, but serving both the aquarium and the laboratories lowered the fixed costs. Likewise there were advantages with respect to obtaining animals for both research and display. The supply department branched out and sold collections of preserved specimens. The techniques for anesthetizing and preserving the specimens were worked out in house, largely through the efforts of Salvatore Lo Bianco (1860–1910) (Fig. 5), who joined the staff at the age of fourteen and became a scientist in his own right. The practical need for scientists to know when the animals were available and reproducing led to publications that were of no small interest from the point of view of pure science (Lo Bianco, 1888, 1899, 1909). For some time the preservation techniques were kept a trade secret, which is, of course, a standard means of creating and maintaining a monopoly. It turned out, however, that publishing the techniques used in preservation had no significant effect on sales because Dohrn had a sufficiently effective organization that others could not compete with his. One problem with the arrangement was that fishermen who brought in specimens wanted to maintain their own monopoly and not reveal where the specimens came from. This tended to militate against the scientists collecting and observing the organisms that they studied in the field (Fig. 6). Dohrn considered the possibility of supplying living organisms, but decided that doing so would over-extend the station's resources. Transport of living animals over long distances was still quite difficult in those days and a laboratory at Rovigo had already specialized in this service.

FIGURE 4. Stazione Zoologica «Anton Dohrn», 1875, engraving.

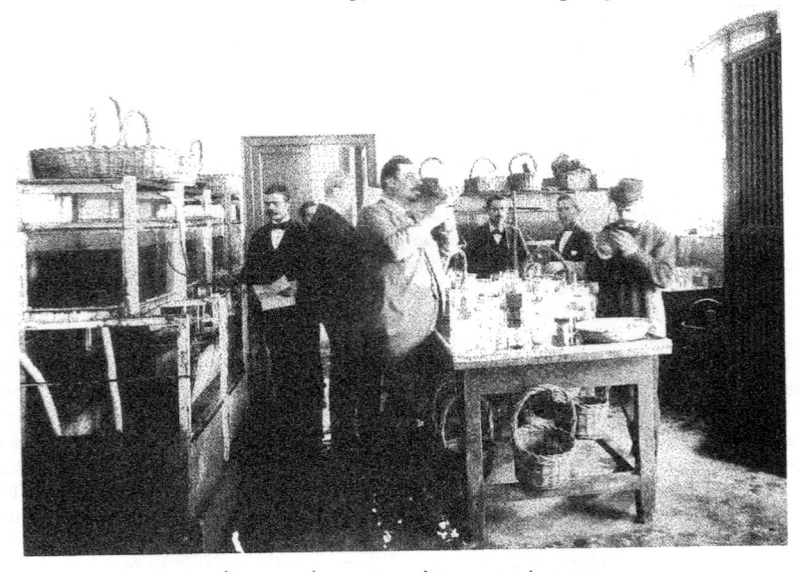

FIGURE 5. Salvatore Lo Bianco (3rd from left) in the Sorting Room, ca. 1890.

FIGURE 6. Diver (Harry Luman Russell) stepping down into the water, 1891.

The real monetary base lay elsewhere. Dohrn used a lot of his personal fortune plus contributions from his father to build and equip the Station; it remained his property and was passed on to his heirs. There were also substantial contributions from other wealthy persons and a subvention from the German government. He might have charged the visiting scientists "bench fees" for using the facilities. However, he did something much more creative and subtle, which was to create the "table" system. He had governments, universities, and other institutions, such as the British Association for the Advancement of Science, pay a sort of retainer. Dohrn would then make the facilities available to the scientists, who applied to the sponsoring institution for permission to use the table. This gave Dohrn a means of pressuring governments to fund the Station and its activities, and to do so on a regular basis. There was a drawback, however, insofar as not all governments were equally inclined to fund tables. This was most conspicuously the case with France, which had recently suffered a humiliating defeat at the hands of Prussia. The American Women's Table (Fig. 7) is a particularly good example of Dohrn's attempt to create a truly cosmopolitan institution (Sloan, 1978).

How the Station was Run and Organized

The advantages of working at the Station are abundantly clear from the lavish praise bestowed by those who took advantage of them (Boveri, 1910; Driesch, 1951; Metschnikoff quoted in Ghiselin and Groeben, 1997). All the *Gastforscher* had to do was let the administration know what would be needed and Dohrn's staff would do their best to see that it was available. The rest was a matter of packing one's baggage and taking the train or a ship. Although unusual equipment might have to be included in the baggage or sent ahead, the usual reagents and the like were already in place. Housing was pre-arranged, and the animals that had been requested would be there and ready for use when the scientists arrived for work the first day. There was a very competent staff, including Dohrn's Assistants, who were themselves working scientists and who were able to provide all sorts of advice.

FIGURE 7. Nettie Stevens at a microscope.

The Assistants were responsible for much of the high-level infrastructure. Because they were expected to be productive scientists, they had a vested interest in the quality of that infrastructure. A good example is the library. It had all the latest journals and much else besides. Dohrn's personal library served as the nucleus, and he requested and obtained all sorts of donations, especially in kind.

There were also the publications of the Station, mainly sent out to publicize work done there, but reciprocated to some extent by other institutions. The *Mittheilungen aus der Zoologischen Station zu Neapel, zugleich ein Repertorium für Mittelmeerkunde*, which appeared at more or less regular intervals beginning in 1879, provided a convenient outlet for work that was done at the Station, including that of Dohrn and his staff. There was also a series of taxonomic monographs, *Fauna und Flora des Golfes von Neapel und der angrenzenden Meeres-Abschnitte*, the first of which was published in 1880. It was sold by subscription thereby increasing sales and lowering costs. Well-to-do book collectors who were not professional scientists often subscribed, partly because the plates turned out to be so attractive, further increasing the press runs. Such monographs are useful scientific infrastructure. However, publishing the series also helped to support the Assistants, and constituted a major part of their scientific output. Dohrn wrote the one on pycnogonids himself (see below). And finally there was an abstracting journal, *Zoologischer Jahresbericht*. It was supposed to compete with the *Zoological Record* and similar journals, and the first report, for 1879, was published in 1880. Again, it helped to support the Assistants, but there were other benefits. Authors sent reprints of their publications, and these made their way into the Station's library. Also, producing the reports helped to keep the staff and the other scientists working there up to date on the latest developments in research.

Another enterprise was research and development in microtechnique (Ankel, 1963). Dohrn established close linkages with the German dye industry and manufacturers of equipment such as microtomes and microscopes (Zeiss in particular sent sets of instruments). His staff tested the equipment and developed the procedures for its use, making them available for the visiting scientists. The scientists on the one hand had access to the latest technology, and on the other hand tested it out in practice. The program was very successful. Scientists went to the Station for the purpose of learning the techniques as well as availing themselves of the services. One result was a manual of microtechnique, upon which later ones were modelled (Lee and Mayer, 1898 and later editions).

The Intellectual Economy

One of the major advantages enjoyed by scientists while working at the Station was the opportunity it afforded for communication with colleagues (Fig. 8). Dohrn referred to it as a permanent zoological congress. The scientists who worked there often praised this aspect of life at the Station. Unfortunately for historians, we have virtually no record of the scientists' conversations. We do know that they got together for parties, that they often met at a wine shop, and that they took excursions together (Eisig, 1916; Driesch, 1951). A little material on what they said to one another has turned up in the correspondence, but how much can be recovered is an open question.

Continued Growth and Expansion

The Station was a non-profit organization, even though it raised money by selling goods and services. There is at least one good reason why non-profit organizations exist: they supply high-quality information (Weisbrod, 1988). What has been said here about the Station, including the personal contacts between scientists from all over the civilized world, supports this interpretation. It provided a kind of infrastructure that was highly valued by the scientific community for that very reason. However, it did not meet all of everybody's needs, and it met the needs of some scientists more than others. For that reason Dohrn's goal of establishing an institution devoted to the study of evolution was not fully realized.

FIGURE 8. Tea at the Stazione.

Centralization allowed for a larger institution, with concomitant economies of scale. The library, for example, could have a larger number of books and journals per user. However, there are disadvantages to having just one such institution, some of them more obvious than others. The farther the scientists had to travel to reach the Station the less the incentive to go there, especially for shorter periods of time. Distance seems to have been one factor in getting governmental support for tables. And finally, rich though the Naples fauna was, it did not include all the animals of interest to zoologists. There was still an incentive for traveling from place to place, and this helped to encourage the founding of laboratories that to some extent competed with the one at Naples. Dohrn had, in fact, originally intended to establish a series of stations in various places, but it was not to his advantage to dilute the effort.

There are some remarkable similarities between the Naples laboratory and others such as those at Plymouth and Woods Hole (Groeben, 1985; Maienschein, 1985; Monroy and Groeben, 1985). This is hardly surprising because the Naples laboratory was the inspiration for the rest, and there was plenty of opportunity for imitation. However, there were important differences. Teaching was an important activity at Woods Hole, and it helped to strengthen the activities of the laboratory (Russell-Hunter, 1985). A teaching program often gives faculty an opportunity that would otherwise not be possible to work at the shore. Dohrn, however, felt that courses were quite unnecessary and that they would interfere with his ideals with respect to freedom of research.

One way that Dohrn managed to increase the demand for the facilities of the station was to enlarge the scope of its activities. Although called a zoological station, its activities included botany and other sciences. The original building, opened in September 1873, was supplemented by a physiological laboratory, with a new building for it opened in October 1888. To accommodate an even more expanded program in physiology, microbiology and other disciplines, a third building was erected; it opened in 1906. Dohrn's original intent had been to create a center for evolutionary research, but he insisted on giving the scientists working at the Station complete intellectual freedom. He believed that physiology and other branches of biology would help realize his own Darwinian goals. Things did not turn out quite as he had hoped.

The kind of evolutionary biology that the Station was originally intended to support was mainly systematics based on comparative anatomy and embryology. The systematic monographs that were produced at the station generally included revisions of entire groups and were not limited to the Naples fauna and flora, although that was their focus. For higher-level classification and phylogeny, the opportunities lay in studying the anatomy, and more especially the embryology, of a representative sample of animals, especially ones with primitive traits. Organisms of great interest were, in fact, available at Naples. However, good material, and different material, was also available elsewhere. This encouraged the practice of working at other locations. For systematic work it was advantageous to have living organisms available to study. However, much research was carried out on preserved materials, and ones that had been made up into slides for microscopy. In many ways it was more convenient and efficient to study such preserved material in museums, including those run by universities, even if they were prepared at Naples.

Towards the end of the nineteenth century comparative anatomy and embryology became somewhat less fashionable, and there was increasing hostility toward Darwinism and evolution. There was an increasing emphasis on experimental, in contradistinction to comparative, embryology. Such experimental embryology required a reliable supply of the appropriate (living) organisms and a reliable supply of sea-water. These conditions were admirably met at the Station. Likewise, the experimental work could be carried out on a more narrow range of organisms. Therefore, the Station was even more attractive to the experimental biologists than it was to the comparative ones. There was considerable rivalry between the two factions, partly because of anti-evolutionism, partly because of a scarcity of academic chairs in Germany.

The standard account of what happened has been somewhat distorted by efforts of the experimentalists and their apologists to discredit the comparative, or as they usually put it, "descriptive" approach (I. Müller, 1975). The traditional historiography suggests that the experimental approach replaced the comparative. It seems more accurate to say that something was added. The Station expanded, and the systematists kept their research programs going. It is true, however, that a succession of disciplines has flourished, with the result that the kind of biology that Anton Dohrn practiced and fostered ceased to attract the proportion of young scientists that it did in the early years of the Station. In a letter to Reinhard Dohrn dated December 1, 1913, Edwin S. Goodrich of Oxford wrote: "So many young zoologists have been diverted to Mendelism & other special studies that it is quite difficult to find a sufficient number to fill the various tables at seaside laboratories."

Success and Failure

Dohrn's success as an administrator has been so impressive that the traditional historiography has used it as an excuse for denigrating him as a scientist. Irmgard Müller (in Groeben 1975:17) says that Dohrn had little urge for discovery and that "It did not appear to him as so important to make discoveries for himself, it was only important to him that they were so made." Yes, he facilitated the work of others, but not without furthering his own research career. We should remember that university professors then as now were expected to allocate a substantial amount of their time to teaching, administration, and research. Dohrn stopped teaching, and that allowed him to allocate a larger proportion of his effort to administration, but he never gave up research. The station was, in fact, designed and organized so as to facilitate his own research program. He was interested in the phylogeny of marine arthropods. His monograph on pycnogonids (Dohrn, 1881) addressed the sort of phylogenetic questions that he was asking when he first conceived of the Station. While he was creating it, he had some ideas about the origin of vertebrates, which he published in an influential little book (Dohrn, 1875; Ghiselin, 1994). As time permitted, he carried out extensive researches on the anatomy and embryology of lower vertebrates, to which are devoted 1,577 pages of the *Mittheilungen*. Much of the research carried out by his staff addressed questions that were germane to his own research. And he took full advantage of the Station's ability to provide him with specimens, microscope slides, and other resources. One reason why the Station was so well designed and administered was that Dohrn, like all good scientists, acted out of self-interest, not altruism.

Dohrn died in 1909, but leadership was taken over by his son Reinhard who was also an able administrator, and had a degree in science as well (R. Dohrn, 1908; Groeben 1983). The institution had been so successful that it was kept going much as it had until World War I. That event was catastrophic for the scientific community, and the weakening of international cooperation both during and after the war is a good example. Although the Station was put back in operation after both world wars, and still exists, it is no longer considered the Mecca of marine biology. For a while it was basically an Italian laboratory, albeit an outstanding one, rather than an international one. After a period of uncertainty, strong leadership was provided by Gaetano Salvatore, who served as President from 1987 until his death in 1997. It took about ten years to restore the international character of the Station, because it was necessary to change from the table system to one based on staff research. There has also been a concerted effort to have the Station function as a venue for scientific meetings, often of an international character.

What has been said here of course applies, so far as general principles go, to a wide variety of scientific organizations. Museums, for example. A comparative approach might lead to a better understanding of those principles themselves. Their application to particulars does not fundamentally alter the kind of narrative that emerges in more traditional approaches to intellectual and institutional history. Rather it places such narrative on a more solid foundation in causality.

REFERENCES

ANKEL, WULF EMMO. 1963. Paul Mayer 1848–1923, Anton Dohrn 1840–1909. Pages 251–261 *in* H. Freund and A. Berg, eds., *Geschichte der Mikroskopie: Leben und Werk grosser Forscher*, vol. 1. Umschau Verlag, Frankfurt am Main.

BENSON, KEITH R. 1995. The development of the research mission in marine biology stations. *Helgoländer Meeresuntersuchungen* 49:409–416.

BOVERI, THEODOR. 1910. *Anton Dohrn: Gedächtnisrede gehalten auf dem Internationalen Zoologenkongress in Graz am 18. August 1910*. Verlag von S. Hirzel, Leipzig. 41 pp.

CHAMBERS, ROBERT. 1844. *Vestiges of the Natural History of Creation*, 1st edition. John Churchill, London. vi + 390 pp., Published anonymously.

CHAMBERS, ROBERT. 1847. *Vestiges of the Natural History of Creation*, 6th edition. John Churchill, London. iv + 512 pp., Published anonymously.

DE MASI, DOMENICO. 1987. La fabbrica della scienza. *Rivista IBM* 24:2–17.

DOHRN, ANTON. 1865. *Quaedam de anatomia herpeterorum*. Privately Published Dissertation, Vratislava. 39 pp., 1 plate.
DOHRN, ANTON. 1875. *Der Ursprung der Wirbelthiere und das Princip des Functionswechsels — Genealogische Skizzen von Anton Dohrn*. Wilhelm Engelmann, Leipzig. xv + 87 pp.
DOHRN, ANTON. 1881. *Die Pantopoden des Golfes von Neapel und der angrenzenden Meeres-Abschnitte*. Fauna und Flora des Golfes von Neapel, III. Wilhelm Engelmann, Leipzig. viii + 252 pp., XVII Taf.
DOHRN, REINHARD. 1908. Ueber die Augen einiger Tiefseemacruren. Aus dem Material der Deutschen Tiefsee-Expedition 1898–99. Ph.D. Dissertation. Marburg.
DRIESCH, HANS. 1951. *Lebenserinnerungen. Aufzeichnungen eines Forschers und Denkers in entscheidender Zeit*. Ernst Reinhardt, Basel. 311 pp.
EISIG, HUGO. 1916. Arnold Lang und die Zoologische Station in Neapel. Pages 56–126 *in* E. Haeckel, K. Hescheler, and H. Eisig, eds., *Aus dem Leben und Wirken von Arnold Lang. Dem Andenken des Freundes und Lehrers gewidmet*. Verlag von Gustav Fischer, Jena.
FISCHER, JEAN-LOUIS. 1980. L'aspect social et politique des relations épistolaires entre quelques savants français et la Station zoologique de Naples de 1878 à 1912. *Revue d'Histoire des Sciences* 33:225–251.
FLOREY, ERNST. 1995. Highlights and sidelights of early biology in Helgoland. *Helgoländer Meeresuntersuchungen* 49:77–101.
GHISELIN, MICHAEL T. 1974. *The Economy of Nature and the Evolution of Sex*. University of California Press, Berkeley. xii + 364 pp.
GHISELIN, MICHAEL T. 1978. The economy of the body. *American Economic Review* 68:233–237.
GHISELIN, MICHAEL T. 1986. Principles and prospects for general economy. Pages 21–31 *in* Gerard Radnitzky and Peter Bernholz, eds., *Economic Imperialism: the Economic Approach Applied outside the Field of Economics*. PWPA Press, New York.
GHISELIN, MICHAEL T. 1989. Science, government and the exploration of coral reefs. Pages 207–220 *in* R. C. Amacher and R. E. Meiners, eds., *Federal support of higher education*. Paragon House, New York.
GHISELIN, MICHAEL T. 1994. The Origin of Vertebrates and the Principle of Succession of Functions. Genealogical Sketches by Anton Dohrn. 1875. An English translation from the German, introduction and bibliography. *History and Philosophy of the Life Sciences* 16(1):5–98.
GHISELIN, MICHAEL T. 1996. Charles Darwin, Fritz Müller, Anton Dohrn, and the origin of evolutionary physiological anatomy. Pages 49–58 *in* G. Pinna and M. Ghiselin, eds., Systematic Biology as an Historical Science. *Memorie della Società Italiana di Scienze Naturali e del Museo Civico di Storia Naturale di Milano* 22(1).
GHISELIN, MICHAEL T., and CHRISTIANE GROEBEN. 1997. Elias Metschnikoff, Anton Dohrn, and the metazoan common ancestor. *Journal of the History of Biology* 30:211–228.
GROEBEN, CHRISTIANE, ed. 1982. *Charles Darwin 1809–1882, Anton Dohrn 1840–1909: Correspondence*. Macchiaroli, Napoli. 118 pp.
GROEBEN, CHRISTIANE, ed. 1983. Reinhard Dohrn 1880–1962. Reden, Briefe und Veröffentlichungen zum 100. Geburtstag. Springer-Verlag, Berlin. viii + 91 pp.
GROEBEN, CHRISTIANE. 1985. Anton Dohrn — the statesman of Darwinism. *Biological Bulletin* 168(Supplement):4–25.
GROEBEN, CHRISTIANE. 1993. Karl Ernst von Baer – Anton Dohrn. Correspondence. *Transactions of the American Philosophical Society* 83(3):1–156.
GROEBEN, CHRISTIANE. 1996. Naturalisti a Napoli nella prima metà dell'800. Pages 76–84 *in* F. Cacciapuoti, C. Groeben, and J. Massarese, eds., *Il Sogno Mediterraneo: Tedeschi a Napoli al Tempo di Goethe e di Leopardi*. Gaetano Macchiaroli Editore, Napoli.
GROEBEN, CHRISTIANE. 1998. «Le précurseur du plan», la contribution de Carl Vogt à la fondation des stations marines. Pages 287–312 *in* J.-C. Pont, D. Bui, F. Dubosson, and J. Lacki, eds., *Carl Vogt: Science, Philosophie et Politique (1817–1895)*. Georg, Chêne-Bourg.
GROEBEN, CHRISTIANE, and IRMGARD MÜLLER. 1975. *The Naples Zoological Station at the Time of Anton Dohrn*. Stazione Zoologica, Naples. 110 pp.

HAECKEL, ERNST. 1862. *Die Radiolarien. (Rhizopoda Radiaria.)*. Georg Reimer, Berlin. xiv + 572 pp., Taf. I–XXXV.
HAECKEL, ERNST. 1866. *Generelle Morphologie der Organismen. Allgemeine Grundzüge der organischen Formen-Wissenschaft, mechanisch begründet durch die von Charles Darwin reformirte Descendenz-Theorie*. Verlag von Georg Reimer, Berlin. xxxii + 574 + clx + 462 pp., Taf. I–II, I–VIII.
HAECKEL, ERNST. 1921. *Italienfahrt: Briefe an die Braut 1859/1860*. Verlag von K. F. Koehler, Leipzig. viii + 184 pp.
HEUSS, THEODOR. 1991. *Anton Dohrn: a Life for Science*. Edited by Christiane Groeben; contribution by Margret Boveri; introduction by Karl Josef Partsch; translated by Liselotte Dieckmann. Springer-Verlag, Berlin. xxxvi + 401 pp.
KOWALEVSKY, A. O. 1866. Entwickelungsgeschichte der einfachen Ascidien. *Mémoires de l'Académie Impériale des Sciences de Saint-Pétersbourg*, ser. 7, 10(15):1–19, Taf. I–III.
KÜHN, ALFRED. 1950. Anton Dohrn und die Zoologie seiner Zeit. *Pubblicazioni della Stazione Zoologica di Napoli* (Supplemento):1–205.
LEE, A. B., and PAUL MAYER. 1898. *Grundzüge der mikroskopischen Technik für Zoologen und Anatomen*, 1st edition. R. Friedländer & Sohn, Berlin. ix + 470 pp.
LO BIANCO, SALVATORE. 1888. Notize biologiche riguardanti specialmente il periodo di maturità sessuale degli animali del Golfo di Napoli. *Mittheilungen aus der Zoologischen Station zu Neapel* 8:383–400.
LO BIANCO, SALVATORE. 1899. Notize biologiche riguardanti specialmente il periodo di maturità sessuale degli animali del Golfo di Napoli. *Mittheilungen aus der Zoologischen Station zu Neapel* 13:448–573.
LO BIANCO, SALVATORE. 1909. Notize biologiche riguardanti specialmente il periodo di maturità sessuale degli animali del Golfo di Napoli. *Mittheilungen aus der Zoologischen Station zu Neapel* 19:513–763.
MAIENSCHEIN, JANE. 1985. Agassiz, Hyatt, Whitman, and the birth of the Marine Biological Laboratory. *Biological Bulletin* 168(Supplement):26–34.
MONROY, ALBERTO, and CHRISTIANE GROEBEN. 1985. The "new" embryology at the Zoological Station and at the Marine Biological Laboratory. *Biological Bulletin* 168(Supplement):35–43.
MÜLLER, FRITZ. 1864. *Für Darwin*. Verlag von Wilhelm Engelmann, Leipzig. iii + 91 pp.
MÜLLER, IRMGARD. 1975. Die Wandlung embryologischer Forschung von der deskriptiven zur experimentellen Phase unter dem Einfluss der Zoologischen Station in Neapel. *Medizinhistorisches Journal* 10:191–218.
PARTSCH, KARL JOSEF. 1980. *Die Zoologische Station in Neapel. Modell internationaler Wissenschaftszusammenarbeit*. In W. Treue, ed., *Studien zu Naturwissenschaft, Technik und Wirtschaft im Neunzehnten Jahrhundert*, Band 11. Vandenhoeck & Ruprecht, Göttingen. 369 pp.
PRUVOT, G. 1902. Henri de Lacaze-Duthiers. *Archives de Zoologie Expérimentale et Générale*, ser. 3, 10:1–78.
REIF, WOLF-ERNST. 1983. Functional morphology and evolutionary ecology. *Paläontologische Zeitschrift* 57:255–266.
RUSSELL-HUNTER, W. D. 1985. An evolutionary century at Woods Hole: instruction in invertebrate zoology. *Biological Bulletin* 168(Supplement):88–98.
SLOAN, JAN BUTIN. 1978. The founding of the Naples Table Association for Promoting Scientific Research by Women. *Signs* 4:208–216.
VOGT, CARL, ed. 1858. *Natürliche Geschichte der Schöpfung des Weltalls, der Erde und der auf ihr befindlichen Organismen, begründet auf die durch die Wissenschaft errungenen Thatsachen*, 2nd edition. Translation of *The Natural History of Creation*, by Robert Chambers, from the Sixth English Edition. Verlag von Friedrich Vieweg und Sohn, Braunschweig. vii + 330 pp.
WEISBROD, BURTON A. 1988. *The Nonprofit Economy*. Harvard University Press, Cambridge. xi + 251 pp.
ZISSLER, DIETER. 1995. Five scientists on excursion — a picture of marine biology on Helgoland before 1892. *Helgoländer Meeresuntersuchungen* 49:103–112.

Copyright ©2000 by the California Academy of Sciences
Golden Gate Park, San Francisco, California 94118, USA.
All rights reserved.

The Institutions of Natural History versus Herbert Spencer 1890–1895

DANIEL BECQUEMONT
Université de Lille III
Lille, France

Herbert Spencer's biological philosophy, in its entirety, implied the harmony between progress in complexity and functional diversification, supported by the inherited effects of use and disuse, an idea which was tolerated by professional scientists in the 1860s, when Spencer began to write the thousands of pages of his synthetic philosophy.

In the 1880s and 1890s, when Natural Sciences and their institutions (the Plymouth Laboratory of the Marine Biological Association for instance) had acquired a new power and a new prestige, and had formed a new generation of evolutionary biologists, trained in cytology, embryology, and other fields of research, such as August Weismann, Edwin Ray Lankester and George Romanes, his theories could be more openly criticized, and his theory of functional modifications was rejected, bringing about the collapse of his whole philosophical system.

La philosophie biologique d'Herbert Spencer, dans sa totalité, impliquait une harmonie entre progrès en complexité et diversification fonctionnelle, appuyés sur les effets héritables de l'usage et du non-usage, idée tolérée par les scientifiques professionnels des années 60, où Spencer commençait à rédiger les milliers de pages qui composent sa philosophie synthétique.

Dans les années 1880 et 1890, alors que les sciences naturelles et leurs institutions, par exemple le Laboratoire de Plymouth de l'Association de Biologie Marine, avaient acquis pouvoir et prestige, et avaient formé une nouvelle génération de biologistes évolutionnistes, experts en cytologie, embryologie et autres domaines de recherche, tels qu'August Weismann, Edwin Ray Lankester, et George Romanes, ses théories furent ouvertement critiquées, et son concept de modification fonctionnelle fut rejeté, ce qui entraîna l'effondrement de l'ensemble de son système philosophique.

Herbert Spencer's synthetic philosophy, in the late 1870s, was immensely popular all over the world, and he was probably the most widely read philosopher in those years. In his synthetic philosophy, from the *First Principles* to his *Principles of Sociology*, he had founded his cosmic and social system on laws of evolution, which implied integration of matter and dissipation of movement, matter evolving from indefinite incoherent homogeneity to definite and coherent heterogeneity. This law in its smallest details rested on a belief in the harmony between progress in complexity and functional diversification.

Direct Equilibration

Spencer's main argument was that evolution at large (in the physical world, in nature and in society) accounted for the greatest happiness of the greatest number. It implied the existence of a cosmic benevolence favouring the increase of happiness as species evolved towards more progress and more perfection.

FIGURE 1. Herbert Spencer.
Courtesy G.S.Myers/A.E.Leviton Portrait File in
Natural History, California Academy of Sciences.

By its essential nature, the process must everywhere produce greater fitness to the conditions of existence, be they what may . . . there is in all cases a progressive adaptation . . . thus the evils accompanying adaptation are ever being self-eliminated.[1]

Biological evolution could be explained at a last resort by the universal laws stated in the *First Principles*, laws of redistribution of matter and movement:

From an external point of view, astronomic rhythms wrought upon the organisms continuous changes, stimulated by the law of the multiplication of the effects and thus brought to an extreme degree of complexity.

From an internal point of view, "functional modifications" caused by changes in circumstances affected the "organic aggregates," hence a structure growing in complexity, defined by Spencer as a "gravitation of the structure from a state of homogeneity to a state of heterogeneity . . . we see that a liability to be unfolded arises from the actions and reactions between organisms and their fluctuating environments."[2] Spencer thus reduced — or enlarged according to the stand one takes — the laws of biological evolution to the physical laws of the *First Principles*.

One could consider all the functionally-wrought modifications as a search for a direct equilibration, described in purely physical terms. The smallest change in the environment disturbed the fragile

---
[1] H. Spencer, 1864, *Principles of Biology*, vol. I. Chapman, London, p. 355.
[2] Spencer, *Principles*, p. 421.

and temporary balance between live beings and their environment, giving birth to an excess or force exerted by the environment upon the organism, or, on the contrary, by the organism on the environment. Then a new process of equilibration took place, bringing about a new change in the structure of the organism, readjusting the balance between live beings and their environment. Such was the real definition of adaptation, and — he stated very briefly — there were many arguments in favour of the idea that the changes in structure occasioned by functional changes were transmitted by heredity

This general theory of inherited direct modification was for Spencer the core of the theory of evolution.

Indirect Equilibration or the Survival of the Fittest

Spencer's theory of direct equilibration had satisfied him till the *Origin of Species*; but now he was compelled, either to criticize Darwin's theory as incompatible with his own or to enlarge and adapt it in order to take natural selection into account. He chose the second solution, with his secondary law of indirect equilibration.

Direct equilibration could take place, he went on to explain, only if all the individuals of a same species could adapt themselves to a change in the environment. But some changes in the environment did not affect directly the function, and could affect individuals in different ways. He went on to explain, always in purely physical terms, that the individuals of a same species were also submitted to secondary deviations in the response of organisms to their environments. They gave birth to a number of secondary modifications (similar, one may suppose, to Darwin's small variations), so that the individuals of a same species were slightly different from each other. Some were better adapted than others.

> The individuals whose functions are most out of equilibrium with the modified aggregate of external forces, will be those to die . . . And by the continual destruction of the individuals that are the least capable of maintaining their equilibria in presence of this new incident force, there must eventually be arrived at an altered type completely in equilibrium with the altered conditions.[3]

This was the survival of the fittest, "which I have sought to express in mechanical terms."[4] Such was, Spencer went on to say, Darwin's great discovery: "This more special mode of action, Mr. Darwin has been the first to perceive. To him we owe the discovery that natural selection is capable of producing fitness between organisms and their circumstances."[5] Thus Spencer reduced Darwin's theory to a mere device of elimination. Spencer considered this as an "obvious truth," if not a truism.

> We see that plants may become better adapted, or re-adapted, to the aggregate of surrounding agencies, not through any direct action of such agencies upon them, but through their indirect action . . . through the destruction by them of the individuals which are less congruous with them, and the survival of those which are most congruous with them.[6]

The theory of natural selection, thus reinterpreted by Spencer, could be integrated, as a secondary process, or perhaps even as a mere accelerator of Spencer's primary laws of direct equilibration, in Spencer's biological principles, expressed in "purely mechanical terms."

Spencer's homage to Darwin is thus part of his strategy to absorb Darwin's theses into his general

---

[3] Spencer, *Principles*, p. 444.
[4] Spencer, *Principles*, p. 445.
[5] Spencer, *Principles*, p. 445.
[6] Spencer, *Principles*, p. 447.

principles of the synthetic philosophy. Every part of Darwin's argumentation in the first theoretical part of the *Origin of Species* is reduced to a mechanical type of argument. To summarize:

(1) Darwin tried to advance various hypotheses on heredity which supported his theory of natural selection. Spencer considered that his theory of functional modifications transmitted to the offspring was enough to account for every fact concerning heredity.

(2) The Darwinian metaphor of the struggle for existence connected together relationships between individuals of a same species, relationships between species, and relationships between live beings occupying a given station and their environment. All these were brought together into a complex unity. Spencer cut the Darwinian concept into two halves. On the first level, he considered the relationship between species and their changing environment and their progressive modifications through the inheritance of characters acquired by use (or declining by non-use). As a general rule, individuals were directly adapted to their conditions of life by direct equilibration. On a second and secondary level, the differences of ability between individuals induced a survival of the fittest individuals and an extinction of the less fit, giving birth to an indirect form of equilibration. The extinction of the less fit seemed to be considered by Spencer as concerning only some individuals.

(3) In mechanical terms, the idea of natural selection could be more advantageously expressed by the "survival of the fittest." It was a secondary process, accounting with great subtlety for some facts which could not be expressed by direct equilibration, but it was hierarchically submitted to the idea of direct adaptation by functionally-acquired modifications. It was brought into activity only when one or some factors in the environment did not act continuously or frequently upon individuals. It could be considered in many cases as an accelerator of the changes of habit required by the changing environment.

Spencer concluded that the Darwinian theory took its real meaning in terms of modifications of equilibrium, submitted to the synthetic philosophy. Natural selection conformed to the same mechanical principles as every other form of equilibration.

Spencer's biological hypothesis, though, rested on the hypothesis of the inheritance of modifications functionally acquired by use (or non-use). Darwin, he said, had failed to see that many morphological facts could easily be explained as results of functionally-wrought modifications transmitted to the offspring and increasing from generation to generation.

This integration of the theory of natural selection into Spencer's principles went together with a systematic effort to reduce biological phenomena to mechanical explanations. For Spencer "survival of the fittest" was a better expression than "natural selection" because it was a more mechanical explanation.

As an example, there runs throughout the *Principles of Biology* a constant theme, that of "functionally-wrought modifications" transmitted to the offspring (in modern terms inheritance of acquired characters or "Lamarckism"). These functional modifications always imply progress in complexity and diversification, a more complex structure, a better form of adaptation. This theme is overtly considered by Spencer as a mechanistic version, applied to live beings, of his theory of the improvement of the human mind by a continuous increase of energy, ingeniosity, complexity, inducing a constant moral advance towards perfection. Human labour (considered under his two aspects of human force and ethical value) and functionally-wrought modifications formed the two aspects of a "labour-value," representing human energy and the source of economic value. Spencer's deep and obstinate commitment to the concept of functional modifications, as a last resort, refers to his cult of human effort — display of mechanical force and ethical value — as the supreme value, extended from society to all organic beings. If the thesis was questioned or criticized, Spencer's whole system was in danger.

Spencer was not a biologist. He did not make a clear distinction between the examples he mentioned and scientific proofs. He was certainly well read in biology; he had written his *Principles of Biology*, submitting them before publication to his friends T. H. Huxley and J. Hooker (botanist and director of Kew Gardens) to avoid any gross biological mistake. But the *Principles of Biology* were to a certain extent old fashioned, a book belonging to an XVIIIth century tradition which did not draw a distinction between biological studies and philosophical principles. Nevertheless, there was no immediate contradiction to his theories — notwithstanding the strictures that may have come from Huxley and Hooker — from professional scientists or their institutions.

Huxley had been the founder of the Imperial School of Science and Technology; he had founded the famous X-club (1864), whose aim was to influence scientific institutions from the inside, and develop evolutionary studies. From 1859, and in response to the debates which had followed, the importance of a body of professional scientists was recognized. The members of the X-club advocated the defense of "pure science," implying a method, and an ethical position, a model of rationality which could have its say even in politics. The X-club, though it was an unofficial society (with a very limited number of members), had a strong influence on such institutions as the Royal Society (of which Huxley was to become president in 1887), the British Association for the Advancement of Science, and the Linnean Society. Huxley was the promoter in his country of the development of laboratory biology. But Huxley — who was a personal friend of Spencer's — never criticized him on points of detail. Spencer, actually, was a member of the X-club himself, the only member of it who was not linked to any institution.

Another institution — and one that was to become one of the most famous editorial institutions in natural history, was the review *Nature*. It was the successor of another journal, *The Reader*, founded in 1865. This review was directed by Huxley, Tyndall, and Galton (Darwin and Spencer were shareholders), and Spencer wrote four articles in it. The "review" failed, but, after an editorial reorganization, was issued again under the name of *Nature*.

In the 1860s, in spite of the growing importance of scientific institutions and the development of laboratory biology, there existed some kind of complicity between scientific institutions and Spencer, an amateur biologist and a philosopher whose popularity was on its way to conquer the whole world. The reasons for this were probably that laboratory biology had not yet taken a full consciousness of its importance, and, more generally, that the distinction between "pure science" and biological philosophy was not yet clearly drawn.

More particularly, Spencer enjoyed immense prestige as having been one of the first thinkers to state evolutionary principles in the 1850s. This allowed him to influence the first generation of professional biologists in the 1860s who were at the head of the most important institutions and who were impressed by his philosophical biology (even Darwin was impressed). Some of them, such as Huxley or Hooker, were his friends and had played a part in the working out of the *Principles of Biology*.

The most important theoretical argument remains nevertheless the fact that the status of Darwin's theory of natural selection was at that time uncertain. Huxley himself considered it as an interesting hypothesis, which had yet to be demonstrated, while Hooker interpreted it in a very narrow sense. Many biologists agreed with the idea that natural selection did not explain everything, nor even a very large number of facts, and admitted that evolutionary biology had to be supported by the direct action of use and disuse and the inheritance of acquired characters. Young biologists who were starting their careers in the early seventies, such as Weismann in Germany, Edwin Ray Lankester, or George Romanes, did not yet question Spencer's theory, which rested entirely on this assumption.

A New Generation of Evolutionary Biologists, New and More Prestigious Institutions

In the 1880s and the 1890s the situation had changed, and a new generation of scientists came to the fore, supported by new institutions which enabled them to develop their studies in cytology, morphology, embryological studies. One of the most important of these institutions was certainly the Zoological Station in Naples, directed by Anton Dohrn, which played a major part in the formation of Weismann, Lankester and to a lesser extent Romanes. The three men acquired there a deep knowledge of marine animals. If Weismann remained most of his life a professor at the university of Freiburg, Lankester and Romanes played a very important part in the development of new institutions, the opening up of new laboratories. August Weismann, in Germany, was a physician who had specialized in insects and crustaceans, taught at the University of Freiburg, and studied hydrozoa in Naples, though weak eyesight partly removed him from laboratory studies. Ray Lankester had been a pupil of Ludwig, Haeckel and Huxley, then taught at the universities of London and later Oxford, and became the editor of the *Quarterly Journal of Microscopical Science*. He had specialized in embryology and was influenced by the morphophysiological approach of Anton Dohrn.

As an example of such new institutions we may take the Marine Biological Association, founded in 1884, inspired by Dohrn's Zoological Station, under the leadership of Huxley, whose aim was "the establishment and maintenance of a marine laboratory . . . similar to, if not quite so extensive as, Dr Dohrn's Zoological Station at Naples." At the opening meeting, Ray Lankester, who was to be the first secretary of the Society, pleaded in favour of the collaboration of "pure science" and practical ends:

> Even if no end was to be served by such a station except those of pure science, these in our estimation are so important as to justify the movement which has secured such influential support. The utility in its highest sense and even in its lowest sense of encouraging scientific research may now be recognized in all civilized countries. All the most practical discoveries have been made by men who were not seeking for them, but whose sole aim was to satisfy a noble inquisitiveness. Our government encourages science in the magnificent establishments at Bloomsbury and South Kensington, and subsidizes . . . 1000 £ for the proposed station.[7]

Huxley, at the same meeting, mentioned Dohrn's support for the project, and summarized in a few words the impact and necessity of new institutions for the development of evolutionary biology:

> The establishment of laboratories for the observation of the fauna and flora of the seas has now taken place in most civilized countries, and is, in fact, a necessary consequence of the great changes which have taken place in the whole of the aims of biological science . . . In order to understand the living beings now, it is no longer sufficient to be acquainted with its outside, as in the days of our forefathers, or even with its inside, so far as obvious anatomy is concerned...We now, in order to understand the being, relations and affinities of an animal, have to go through the whole course of existence beyond, in order to trace out the successive stages of development from the egg; and this can be done with a precision and accuracy which in my young days we had no conception of . . . A more directly practical reason exists. We possess good fisheries, which are more or less regulated by legislation . . . Hitherto, such regulations have been made in an almost entirely haphazard manner, because of the want of knowledge of the habits, the mode of life of the food fish.[8]

The Duke of Argyll, apparently more concerned by "pure science," mentioned as an example

---

[7] *Journal of the Marine Biological Association*, vol. I, March 1884.
[8] *op. cit.*

the new theory which considered flat fish as a form of degeneration from the round fish, stressing what was becoming at the time an important issue of evolutionary biology, the idea of degeneration, and concluding "the sea is the area in which and out of which we can best get at some of the secrets of organic life." The prestige of a scientific institution, the part played by "pure science" in economic issues, the importance of sea life for evolutionary biology, allusions to the theory of degeneration, expressed in these speeches, testify to the new power and the scientific interests of the institutions of natural history in the 1880s.

Ray Lankester, later, was to found a Laboratory of Comparative Anatomy at Oxford, and later in 1898 became director of the Natural History Department of the British Museum. There was hardly any naturalist in those days who occupied more prestigious institutional positions.

Spencer's conception of what was a scientific experiment was very remote from that of the second generation of Darwinian scientists who were professionals, inserted in a scientific community, working in laboratories, members of scientific institutions, who did not consider Spencer's theories with such awe, or at least respect, as did the Darwinians of the first generation.

There was now a new generation of laboratory men who did not know Spencer personally and were not impressed by his synthetic philosophy, and who had a high view of their scientific achievements and did not think very highly of "principles" or "philosophy of biology." The important thing to note is that most of this new generation tried to enlarge the scope of natural selection.

Extension of the Theory of Natural Selection to Degeneration

Weismann and Lankester questioned and rejected the idea of an inheritance of acquired characters. They had met at a meeting in Manchester in 1887 on "Are acquired characters hereditary?" with Geddes, Poulton, Hartog. Both of them had studied at the Zoological Station at Naples, directed by Dohrn (Lankester in 1874, Weismann in 1881, at the time when Weismann questioned for the first time the idea of acquired inherited characters). Both of them were interested, not only in evolutionary progress (what Lankester called increase in the complexity of structure), but in extending the concept of natural selection to alleged facts of degeneration (what Lankester called diminution of the complexity in structure). Dohrn, as early as 1875, had maintained that some of the structural changes of animals in the course of evolution were not progressive, but that in many cases a process of simplification, or degeneration, had taken place. The idea of an inheritance of acquired characters, though it had been expressed by Lamarck under the form of laws, was rather a millenary conception of common sense, which began to be seriously questioned in connection with problems of degeneration, and the observation of marine animals. The relationship between this rejection of the inheritance of acquired characters and the extension of the theory of natural selection to many cases of degeneration may not seem obvious today, but the two fields of research fused together under the form of a rejection of the concept of inheritable action of use and disuse transmitted to the offspring.

August Weismann's theory — which dissociated the germinative cells from the somatic ones, thus denying any possibility of functionally-wrought modifications being transmitted to the offspring — rejected the action of use and disuse as a factor of heredity.

A new form of Darwinism developed, supported by Wallace, Ray Lankester, and to a certain extent by George Romanes. Spencer, committed to the inheritance of acquired characters, could but reject it. He was then compelled to criticize more openly Darwin's theory, and took a different stand. He gave up his strategy of absorbing Darwin's theory, and lay more stress on the insufficiency of natural selection.

In 1886, in two articles in *The Nineteenth Century*, Spencer took a rather defensive position, and admitted that he had neglected the theory of natural selection in his first articles and even in the *Principles of Biology*. But the efficiency of natural selection, he went on to say, did not imply that the inheritance of functionally-wrought modifications (now called inheritance of acquired characters) did not play any part in the evolutionary process. Darwin himself, he argued, maintained that functional modifications due to use and non use played an important part, a statement which Darwin's disciples were prone to forget.

Panmixia

But this defensive stand could not be maintained against the impact of the neo-Darwinism developed by Weismann, Wallace, and Lankester in the early eighties.

Weismann had developed his theory of the continuity of the germ-plasm, and the immortality of the reproductive cells. Death, he maintained, was a trait which had been selected among somatic cells as as advantage which favoured a "division of labour" among cells. He was then led to criticize the Lamarckian — and Spencerian — ideas of inheritable variations as the effect of use and disuse. As natural selection was to explain not only the numerous cases of advance in complexity of structure, but also cases of simplification (degeneration), he mostly criticized the idea of degeneration caused by the disuse of an organ transmitted to the offspring, and he put forward his theory of Panmixia.

When there was no longer, owing to changes in the conditions of life, any use for an organ, this organ ceased to be the object of natural selection. Consequently, all possible variations of this organ had an equal chance of surviving. The equal survival value of all these possible variations led to a gradual dwindling of the organ by intermixing. Besides, variation in the direction of greatly diminished size or structure in the organ became then advantageous as causing a diminished tax on the organism: the variations in the direction of diminution of a useless organ became useful and were selected, whereas the variations in the direction of excessive size tended to die without reproducing. Thus disuse was not the cause of the dwindling of useless organs, which took place by the selection of diminutive variations.

Ray Lankester, in his essay on "Degeneration. A chapter in Darwinism,"[9] had more generally maintained that natural selection opened three possibilities: balance of an organ (status quo), elaboration (increase), or degeneration (diminution). He mentioned many instances of the latter case among parasites, but also lizards (dwindling of limbs), cirripedia and ascidians. At that time, Lankester did not openly criticize the Spencerian theory of a direct action of the environment through the action of disuse, but his claim that natural selection could account for many facts of degeneration implicitly undermined Spencer's theory. His theory of heredity was not Weismann's; he believed rather in "physiological units" (Spencer's own words) and in pangenesis.

The issue was not only for Spencer a matter of biology. In his synthetic philosophy, from the *First Principles* to his *Principles of Sociology*, he had founded his cosmic and social system on laws of evolution (integration of matter and dissipation of movement, matter evolving from indefinite incoherent homogeneity to definite and coherent heterogeneity), which were laws of progress. This progress rested on a resolute faith in the cooperation between structure (increase in complexity) and function (action of circumstances on live beings, society), in the same way that physical and intellectual exertion (i.e., labour) led man forward through the division of labour (diversification and integration) towards higher degrees of civilization, and this was transmitted to subsequent generations. In other, more modern words, Spencer did not draw any distinction between inheritance and heredity. His whole synthetic theory, physical, social, and biological, rested on the inheritance of

---

[9] Published in *The Advancement of Science*, 1890.

acquired characters. Biological facts which tended to question the issue, and stressed the importance of degeneration, endangered his whole philosophy, at a time when Spencer was the most popular — and most read — philosopher in the world. Francis Balfour had asserted that the whole Spencerian system would collapse if Spencer's theory of heredity turned out to be wrong.

This can account for the fact that the polemics which took place in the 1890s about the inheritance of acquired characters were published first in *Nature*, a scientific periodical, but found their full scope in *The Contemporary Review*, a political, social and cultural review.

Polemics in *Nature* (1890)

Hostilities started when in February 1890 Weismann published an article in *Nature* in which he repeated his views on the non-inheritance of acquired characters, panmixia, and the continuity of the germ-plasm. He gave as an example Brown Boveri's experiment proving that among live beings the body of the ovum contributes nothing to its inheritance. "I believe I have proved that organs no longer in use become rudimentary, and must disappear solely by panmixia; not through the direct action of disuse, but because natural selection no longer maintains their standard structure."[10] He linked closely his theory of panmixia with his theories on the lapse into mortality of somatic cells as a trait acquired by natural selection. A differentiation in the somatic cells occurring, "the death of these cells would not be detrimental to the species, since its continuance is ensured by the immortal germ cells."

In the same issue of *Nature*, Ray Lankester also questioned the inheritance of acquired characters, taking as an example the migration of the eyes of the flat fish. He explaining it by the selection of a possible "sport," rejecting the idea of an action of muscles pulling out the eye, followed by the inheritance of this acquired character to the next generation. Lankester's argument about Darwin was rather a devious one: he tried to maintain that "Darwin was not really interested with the question as to whether acquired characters were transmitted or not," and always preferred, when it occurred to him, another explanation. He had often attributed to natural selection modifications which common sense ascribed too easily to use and disuse, such as wingless island birds, or the defective eye of the mole. Actually, when there was no longer any use for an organ, the equal survival of all possible variations led to the dwindling and possible loss of the organ. Besides, variations in the direction of greatly diminished size were advantageous in causing a diminished tax on the organism. If there were variations in the direction of an excessive diminution of a useless organ (as, for instance, tailless cats or hornless sheep), they would tend to survive as being less taxed, whilst the complementary variations in the direction of excessive size tend in the struggle to die without reproducing, owing to their awkwardness and their relatively greater burden in life. It was clear that panmixia could lead rapidly to the dwindling and eventual extinction of a disused organ without any transmission of acquired parental characters. He went so far as to say that Darwin himself had formulated the idea of panmixia in the sixth edition of the *Origin of Species*.[11] When he used such phrases as "due to disuse," he did not mean necessarily such effects as Lamarck assumed, but may have meant the effects of disuse due to panmixia which, Lankester added, had not yet been proved.

---

[10] "A theory of heredity," *Nature*, February 1890, p. 318.

[11] "Thus, as I believe, natural selection will tend in the long run to reduce any part in the organization as soon as it becomes, through changes of habits, superfluous" (*Origin of Species*, John Murray, London, 1872, 6th ed., p. 118) or "If it could be proved that every part of the organization tends to vary in a greater degree towards diminution than augmentation of size, then we should be able to understand how an organ which had become useless would be rendered, independently of the effects of disuse, rudimentary, and would be at last suppressed" (p. 401).

Spencer's Reply

Spencer replied in *Nature*[12] stating that Darwin himself had frequently referred to the action of use and disuse, for instance in the example of the shortening of the wings of oceanic birds, and in Darwin's observations on tame ducks. Spencer concluded that Weismann did not bring any new proof of his theory. In a new letter to the editor on panmixia, he gave the example of the drooping ears of some domestic animals, which could be explained by non use and not by panmixia.

Spencer, in a way, agreed with Balfour and understood that this idea of functionally-wrought modifications was the basis of his whole system: he wrote as a conclusion:

> I have, indeed, been led to suspend for a short time my proper work, only by consciousness of transcendent importance of the question. As I have before contended, a right answer to the question whether acquired characters are on the whole inherited, underlies right beliefs, not only in biology and psychology, but also in education, ethics and politics.

The board of directors of *Nature* — among whom Hooker, who had carefully re-read *Principles of Biology* before it was published twenty years earlier — was more and more reluctant to publish Spencer's articles, and welcomed on the contrary articles from Weismann and his supporters. Spencer, scientifically more and more isolated, had to publish his views in the *Contemporary Review* (three articles in 1893, one in 1895). This shift from a scientific review to a social and political paper is in itself a symbol of Spencer's rejection by the institutions of natural science.

1893 *The Contemporary Review*

In "The Inadequacy of Natural Selection,"[14] Spencer argued in favour of the inheritance of acquired characters, criticized panmixia, advocated use and non-use as factors of evolution. He stood more and more openly in favour of a kind of group selection, where almost all the individuals of a same species were approximately affected in the same way by modifications in the conditions of life entailing functional modifications. He lay more stress on the coadaptation of cooperative parts, gave instances of evolution by use and non-use, and even mentioned telegony (a word used by Weismann) as an important proof of his own theory of heredity.

Spencer's view of evolution now centered on the concept of numerous variations, almost uniform, oriented in the same direction by incident forces. The tenet of the survival of the fittest had been reduced to a sort of elimination of a few unadapted forms or an accelerator of functional modifications. Such was Spencer's view of evolution in the 1890s, and it was very remote from Darwin's theory. Spencer added that to pretend, as Weismann did, that natural selection was the sole mechanism of evolution, and to deny the inheritance of acquired characters, was "absurd and disproved," and constituted a perversion of Darwinism, a form of biological fetishism.

Spencer's Experiment

In the same article, Spencer based his "experiment" on the different gradations of the sense of touch in the tips of the fingers. He explained that if "natural selection or the survival of the fittest is the cause, then it is required to show that each degree of endowment has advantaged the possessor to such an extent that life has been — even infrequently — preserved by it." He noted that all the

---

[12] "The inheritance of acquired characters," *Nature*, March 6, 1890, was not an article but a letter to the editor.
[13] H. Spencer, *Principles of Biology*, vol. II. Chapman, London, p. 650.
[14] H. Spencer, "The inadequacy of natural selection," *The Contemporary Review*, February 1893.

different parts of the surface of the fingertips had become widely unlike in perceptiveness owing to some cause.

> And, if the cause alleged is natural selection, then it is necessary to show that the greater degree of power possessed by this part than by that, has not only conduced to the maintenance of life, but has conduced so much that an individual in whom a variation had produced better adjustment to needs, thereby maintained life when some others lost it; and that among the descendants inheriting this variation, there was a derived advantage, such as enabled them to multiply more than the descendants of individuals not possessing it.[15]

But if this distribution of tactual perceptiveness could not be explained by the survival of the fittest, how could it be explained? "This cause is the inheritance of acquired characters" he affirmed. To check this, he said, "I have made some experiments."

Taking a pair of compasses, if the points were closed nearly, less on an average than one twelfth of an inch apart, the end of the forefingers could not perceive that there were two points; they could if the distance between the two points was more than one twelfth.

So Spencer tested two (1) youths from a nearby School for the Blind (their sensitiveness must have been exercised by reading from raised letters), and found out that they could distinguish two points when only 1/14th of an inch apart, though they had very thick and coarse skins on their fingertips.

Then he tested two skilled music composers, who had a degree of discrimination reaching 1/17.

The result of this experiment was "that we have clear proof that constant exercise of the tactual nervous structures leads to further development."[17]

The same reasoning could be applied to taste and tongue sensitiveness. In the latter case, the sensitivity was seen to be connected with eating and speech, but it had no selection value. However, it could easily be explained by the inheritance of acquired characters. The decrease in size of the human jaw could not either be due to any advantage in the struggle for life, "so natural selection cannot be to cause of the diminution of the jaw and its appendage."[18]

"The Inadequacy of Natural Selection," II, March 1883

The idea of cooperative parts was for Spencer a strong obstacle to the sufficiency of natural selection. They could not have been solely adjusted by the survival of the fittest, as proved by the example of the extinct Irish elk whose immense antlers implied great modifications of adjacent bones and muscles, and strengthening of the fore legs. Many facts (he did not clarify which ones) proved that they could not vary together. Spencer developed the same form of reasoning for the neck of the giraffe.

If there occurred some changes in an organ which adapted it better to the creature's needs, the use of the organ demanded the cooperation of other organs, so that the changes in one organ were of no service unless the cooperative organs were also changed. When cooperative parts changed simultaneously, they either increased or decreased *together* simultaneously, or they all simultaneously increased or decreased *independently*, or they varied in such degrees as to be serviceable for the new end.

But "if such modifications of structure produced by modifications of function as we see take

---

[15] Spencer, Inadequacy, p. 154.
[16] Spencer, Inadequacy, p. 155.
[17] Spencer, Inadequacy, p. 156.
[18] Spencer, Inadequacy, p. 162.

place in each individual, are in any measure transmissible to descendants, then all these coadaptations are easily accounted for ... In some cases this inheritance of acquired characters suffices by itself to exploit the facts; and in other cases it explains it suffices when taken in combination with the selection of favourable variations."[19]

Spencer then took a critical look at Weismann's theories: he mentioned a few (dubious) examples, such as hereditary diseases (relying on Pasteur) and telegony, referring to Lord Moreton's famous quagga mentioned in the archive of the Royal College of Surgeons, relying on the theory of impregnation. "These facts are fatal to Weismann's theory," he claimed. There was no independence of the reproductive cells, but there existed protoplasmic connections between the reproductive cells and the somatic ones. Darwin himself had fully recognized the inheritance of acquired characters.

> What are the facts proving the inheritance of acquired characters ? ask those who deny it ?
> They might be asked a counter-question: "What are the facts that disprove it? ... Not a single case can be named in which panmixia is a proved cause of diminution.[20]

Romanes' Reply[21]

In this article, Romanes flattered himself on having been "the first evolutionist to have questioned the belief in use inheritance." When Darwin had experimented on the inherited effects of use and disuse, Romanes went on, he had worked on the bones of domesticated ducks, comparing tame and wild animals of different ages, but had not attempted to measure use. Romanes referred to a previous article in which he had advanced his own theory of a withdrawal of natural selection: "minus variations have as good a chance as plus variations: the average size of the part concerned will therefore decrease. I called this cessation of selection."[22]

Galton, Dohrn and Lankester, he went on to say, had expressed similar views, but they had not mentioned "cessation of selection." Weismann utilized the principle but, Romanes added, "he had not read my articles and called it panmixia."[23] He went so far as to assert that in a private conversation Darwin had admitted the idea of a "cessation of selection." According to Romanes, panmixia was a passive cessation of selection, to be distinguished from "economy of nutrition," which implied "an active hostility of selection to the part undergoing degeneration,"[24] a reversal of selection. The cessation of selection had no relationship to natural selection, it was a negative condition, a stoppage. Economy of nutrition was a positive cause of degeneration, a turning round of the selective process from activity maintaining to actively destroying an organ. Spencer, Romanes went on, did not seem to understand the difference between cessation of selection and economy of nutrition. He thought only in terms of degeneration by economy of nutrition (a very old theory, dating back at least to Aristotle) and not cessation of selection (developed by Romanes, Dohrn, Lankester, and Weismann).

Weismann in the *Contemporary Review*

Weismann decided in 1893 to summarize his views as a reply to Spencer, not in *Nature*, but also in *The Contemporary Review*.[25] He demonstrated not only the progressive development of variations through natural selection, but also degenerative changes and disappearance of whole organs. He was

---

[19] H. Spencer, "The inadequacy of natural selection," II, *The Contemporary Review*, March 1893, pp. 445–446.
[20] Spencer, Inadequacy II, p. 448.
[21] G. Romanes, "Mr. Herbert Spencer on natural selection," *The Contemporary Review*, April 1893, p. 499.
[22] Romanes, *Spencer*, p. 501.
[23] Romanes, *Spencer*, p. 502.
[24] Romanes, *Spencer*, p. 504.
[25] A. Weismann, "The all-sufficiency of natural selection," *The Contemporary Review*, 64, Oct. 1893.

led, once more, to support his idea of the all-sufficiency of natural selection with his theory of panmixia. External influences could act only in a selective way on changes that had already occurred in the germ-plasm, and regressive changes were caused by variations that occurred in the primary constituents. Natural selection not only brought about the development of a part but must actively caused it to be retained. Unless selection continued, the organ that lost its specialized importance tended to diminish. Panmixia was perhaps not totally satisfactory, but was a step on the way to germinal selection acting on hereditary units. When Spencer said that among blind animals in caves the suppression of the eye caused no economy, he neglected the non-expenditure of special materials and special activities for the production of an eye. "It can be, I say, achieved by natural selection of the most deficient in eyesight in caves."

> I hold it demonstrated that all hereditary adaptation rests on natural selection...it is not merely an accessory principle, which only comes into operation when the assumed transmission of functional variations fails, but it is the chief principle in the variations of the organisms; and compared to it, the primary variation which is due to the direct action of external influences on the germ plasm, is of very secondary importance . . . When my opponents set me down as an ultra Darwinist, who takes a one-sided and exaggerated view of the principle discovered by the great naturalist, perhaps they may make an impression on some of the timid souls who always act on the supposition that the juste milieu is proper . . . Only very gradually have I learned the full scope of the principle of selection, and certainly I have been led beyond Darwin's conclusion. Progress in sciences usually involves a struggle against deep-rooted prejudices; such was the belief in the transmission of acquired characters . . . my work has not been to exaggerate, but to complete.[26]

This did not imply that Weismann's theory of the continuity of the germ-plasm received full acceptance from biologists in the last years of the 19th century. On the contrary, many neo-Lamark-ian theories developed in those years. But the slightest criticism of Spencer's views on progress towards more complexity due to functional modifications could be fatal to his synthetic philosophy.

Actually Spencer was not the only thinker of the time to consider with such disgust the non-inheritance of acquired characters. Moralists, attached to the idea of work as improving man's character, his intellectual and ethical powers, supporters of classical economics or more generally of the labour theory of value also rejected this assumption. How could man be improved if the characters he had acquired or bettered in the course of his life could not be transmitted to his offspring ? Bernard Shaw, and Sidney and Beatrice Webb, rejected it with a similar indignation. But Spencer did feel that a new period was opening, and that his system of synthetic philosophy was falling to pieces.

His system had been already impaired by the discoveries of thermodynamics (which went against his notion of force and equilibrium) and the political evolution of his own country (a reinforcement of the role played by the State), but this did not endanger the validity of the whole system. Neo-Darwinism, on the contrary, meant the collapse of the whole fabric. In order to defend his system, Spencer had to give up his strategy of absorbing the theory of natural selection, and, in the 1890s came very near to rejecting it in its entirety.

In *The Contemporary Review*, Spencer replied and added "Considerations on Professor's Weismann's theories" (May 1893), "A rejoinder to Professor Weismann" (December 93), "Weismannism once more" (October 94), "Heredity once more" (October 95). But, on the whole, he felt he had lost. Rejected by *Nature*, Spencer was also rejected by the survivors of the first generations of Darwinians, Hooker and Wallace, who sided against his views. He found himself supported only by social thinkers who were not biologists (Allen, Shaw, Sidney Webb). He could see that his whole

---
[26] *The Contemporary Review*, 64, Oct. 1893, p. 443.

system of synthetic philosophy was falling to pieces. A new generation of biologists, supported by the power and prestige of scientific institutions, such as Weismann, Lankester, Romanes, had shattered his belief in a universal law of progress, resting on the inherited effects of use and disuse.

At the same time he was deeply shocked by the new functions assumed by the State. The second law of thermodynamics also ran counter to his system. He began to think in terms of social and political regression, if not degeneration. He even thought of a possible period of dissolution of the universe in a remote period "leading us towards death." He died in 1902.

The Awkward Embrace[1]

LÉO F. LAPORTE*
Department of Earth Sciences
University of California, Santa Cruz
Santa Cruz, California 95064
E-mail: laporte@cats.ucsc.edu

I have a debt, a loyalty to the [American] museum; the best place for me to do what I wanted to do. — G. G. Simpson

George Gaylord Simpson spent virtually his whole professional life as an employee of natural history museums. In 1927, at age 25, Simpson joined the American Museum of Natural History as assistant curator of vertebrate paleontology. He resigned that position in 1959 to accept appointment as Alexander Agassiz Professor at the Museum of Comparative Zoology (MCZ) at Harvard University where he remained until 1970. Professionally very accomplished from the outset, Simpson expected — and usually received — from both institutions all the prerogatives and privileges he thought due him as the leading American, if not world, student of fossil mammals in particular and more generally of ancient-life history and evolution. But his appointments were clouded by Simpson's resentments to presumed personal affronts from colleagues, first when being considered for an appointment at Yale, and then during his tenure at the American Museum. His reasons for not accepting an appointment at Yale and his departure from both the American Museum and Harvard were marked by misunderstanding and professional grievance.

Yet despite these mostly self-inflicted difficulties and an ongoing inflated sense of what was due him, Simpson thrived scientifically to a degree not otherwise possible anywhere else. This was certainly true, at least, at the American Museum, as Simpson was quick to acknowledge in old age: "I have a debt, a loyalty to the [American] museum; the best place for me to do what I wanted to do."[2] This was somewhat less true at the MCZ where his second five-year, extended appointment as Agassiz Professor was complicated by his declining health and that of his wife, Anne Roe, as well as by the absence of the magnificent fossil mammal collection of the American Museum.

Prelude to the American Museum Appointment

After receiving his doctorate from Yale University, Simpson continued his study of Mesozoic mammals at the British Museum (Natural History). There was an informal understanding that upon his return to the U.S. he would take up an appointment in vertebrate paleontology at Yale's Peabody Museum. However, Simpson's ongoing marital problems came to the attention of his Yale colleagues and formal application for the appointment was suddenly in doubt, because his estranged wife had complained to the spouse of a senior administrator about Simpson's shortcomings as husband and father. During a visit to London, Richard Swann Lull (1867–1957), professor and curator of vertebrate paleontology at the Peabody Museum and Simpson's dissertation adviser, raised the issue with Simpson. Simpson satisfied Lull with his version of his marital problems and, soon after, Yale made a formal offer to Simpson to join the Peabody Museum. But Simpson remained resentful because he felt that any personal domestic troubles he was having were none of Yale's business.[3]

* Current mailing address: 430 Nimitz Avenue, Redwood City, CA 94061–4226.

William Diller Matthew (1871–1930), vertebrate paleontologist at the American Museum, also visited Simpson in London and discussed the possibility of Simpson's coming to the American Museum. Matthew was well acquainted with Simpson, who had been his field assistant in Texas several years before and, as a paleomammalogist himself, was familiar with Simpson's important Mesozoic mammal work. Soon after, Simpson had a second job offer, this time from the American Museum. He weighed both equally attractive offers and decided on the American Museum, because he "declined to go [to Yale] where my prospective associates had been so willing to believe me a scoundrel."[4] As he wrote years later, his going to the American Museum "was a crucial point, indeed the most crucial point in my professional development."[5]

Simpson Joins the American Museum

During the early part of 1927, Matthew was discussing with the University of California the offer of an appointment as head of the newly re-created department of paleontology.[6] His discussions with Simpson, therefore, about the latter's joining the American Museum were undoubtedly intended to prepare the way for Simpson to succeed him, although this was not made known to Simpson at the time. Years later, Simpson claimed that it was Matthew's recommendation that brought him "in at the bottom of the department" when Matthew "went out at the top."[7] Matthew departed for Berkeley in the summer of 1927, and Simpson began his appointment as assistant curator of vertebrate paleontology on November 1st, shortly after his return from his post-doctoral year in London, at a salary of $2500 (or about $27,500 in current dollars) with "further increase in salary & position to be the reward of effort."[8]

Simpson's initial museum colleagues included Henry Fairfield Osborn (1857–1935), president of the museum and department chairman; Barnum Brown (1873–1963), curator of reptiles and acting department chairman; Walter Granger (1872–1941), curator of fossil mammals; and William King Gregory (1876–1970), research associate in paleontology. Edwin ("Ned") Harris Colbert (b. 1905), a graduate student at Columbia University, joined the department as Osborn's research assistant several years later in 1930, became assistant curator in 1933, and was awarded his Ph.D. under Gregory's tutelage in 1935. Later, following the Second World War, other close associates of Simpson's included Bobb Schaeffer (b. 1913), curator of fossil fishes, and Norman Dennis Newell (b. 1909), curator of fossil invertebrates. Barnum Brown immediately put Simpson to work: "He thought all young squirts should start at the bottom, so he started me at preparation in the laboratory. I was twenty-five, father of a family [of three daughters], and had been working at a professional level for several years, but he was fifty-four and incomparably more experienced. I quite enjoyed my initiation in the laboratory. I liked and admired the men there, and it was interesting to prepare some relatively primitive mammals, which I was later allowed to study and publish."[9]

Young squirt or not and despite the affable tone of the above recollection, Simpson must have felt a little put down by this initial assignment. For at the time of his appointment, Simpson had published four abstracts, 11 articles (one of which was with his soon-to-be museum colleague W. K. Gregory as co-author), five reviews, and two popular pieces; he had in press at least seven more articles and two major monographs, and a number of other works in progress. Despite his relative youth, Simpson had already established himself as the world's authority on Mesozoic mammals and through his writings and travel was known to virtually all the leading vertebrate paleontologists of the day. Within a year, however, his past achievements and obvious potential were recognized by his promotion to associate curator of vertebrate paleontology.

American Museum Research and Expeditions

Employment by one of the world's leading museums of natural history that imposed no formal teaching or administrative responsibilities provided Simpson with unusual opportunities for research, some to his liking, some not. Among the specimens that Barnum Brown had Simpson prepare were some Paleocene mammals that he, Brown, had collected in Montana, and which Simpson then studied and published on. Having finished his study of Mesozoic mammals, this new work propelled Simpson into a major research effort on the Paleocene and Eocene mammals of North America that was to last, on and off, throughout his tenure at the museum. His attention was also turning to the rich early Tertiary geology and paleontology of Patagonia whose mammal faunas bore uncertain relationships to those of the rest of the world. Of less importance to these long-term research interests were other museum collections of various Tertiary ages and locales within the United States that he worked up as part of his curatorial responsibilities.[10]

The stock market crash of 1929 had major financial impact on the museum. The private financial contributions of New York wealthy patrons that H. F. Osborn had so assiduously cultivated for more than two decades now declined sharply.[11] Ned Colbert, Simpson's colleague, has referred to the Depression Era as "the restricted years" at the museum, because until then "any activities beyond the usual ones depended upon help from interested citizens who had money to contribute."[12] Because Simpson's research program required collecting expeditions of some sustained duration, he took personal initiative to seek out support from one of the museum's wealthy benefactors, Horace Scarritt, a New York City investment banker and broker.[13] As Simpson later recalled, "This took some persuasion and more than a few drinking bouts."[14] Scarritt's money flowed as freely as his liquor for he ended up supporting three of Simpson's major fossil-collecting expeditions: two to Patagonia in 1930–31 and 1933–34 and one to Montana in 1935. Simpson recognized Scarritt's crucial support by naming an extinct South American hoofed-herbivore of early Tertiary age *Scarrittia canquelensis*.[15]

The Patagonian expedition had the full encouragement if not financial support of Osborn, and grew out of an earlier cooperative plan between the museum and the University of Tübingen, which subsequently had to back out owing to a lack of funds. Much of the American Museum's reputation and renown had been built upon such foreign scientific research expeditions, and Simpson's plans were thus in keeping with a museum tradition so carefully nurtured by Osborn.

Simpson left for Patagonia in the summer of 1930, returning the following fall to New York. Seven months were spent in the field working out the stratigraphy and age of the mammal-bearing deposits as well as collecting specimens, some 300 in all. After his assistant returned to the museum with the fossils where they began to be prepared for detailed study, Simpson passed the next five months visiting the fossil collections in the museums of Buenos Aires and La Plata.[16]

This sojourn to South America resulted in Simpson's first book, *Attending Marvels*, which not only continued the long tradition of the American Museum, strongly encouraged by Osborn, to bring attention of its research to the public, but it also made Simpson himself known to the non-paleontological world.[17] A radio interview in New York City and front-page coverage in the *New York Times Book Review* immediately followed publication of the book. Simpson clearly had the intention of bringing his research to a broader, educated public. As he remarked in the foreword of the book, "This is an account of a scientific expedition, but it is more concerned with people and events than with science . . . voyages to the far corners of the earth [have] interest and excitement not dependent on technical accomplishments."[18] Simpson was undoubtedly motivated by a genuine interest in popular scientific education, but possibly he also wanted to keep the museum's benefactors in the fold, given the toll that the Depression was having on continued museum support. Increasingly hereafter, Simpson and the American Museum were to become closely associated, if not synonymous, in the educated public's mind as was already the case with his colleague, the anthropologist Margaret Mead.

After the first year-long Patagonian trip, Simpson returned to Patagonia for another eight months in 1933–1934, returning to New York via Paris and Moscow where he tried, unsuccessfully, to arrange a trip to Mongolia. In between his South American expeditions, Simpson spent two long summers in 1932 and 1935 collecting Paleocene mammals in Montana. And, of course, when not in the field, Simpson continued to publish the results of this and other research. During this hectic professional pace Simpson's personal life began to improve. He finally obtained a divorce from his wife in 1938 and immediately married Anne Roe, whom he knew from his childhood in Denver and with whom he had been living surreptitiously for the previous several years. From September 1938 to May 1939, they went off together to collect fossils in Venezuela where Simpson had been invited by the government to expand the search for Pleistocene mammals. Despite unusual heavy rains, Simpson made a large but not particularly well-preserved collection that was arduously prepared by American Museum technicians and partially described by Simpson and one of his graduate students. Before the study of the fossils had been completed, a subsequent change of government in Venezuela claimed that the fossils had been stolen by Simpson and it demanded that all the fossils be returned, which they were.[19]

By his travels, fossil-collecting expeditions, and resultant prolific publication during the 1930s Simpson increasingly strengthened his reputation as a vertebrate paleontologist and the leading student of fossil mammals. His place within the American Museum certainly seemed secure as one of its best known scientists. However, the appointment of a new museum director a few years later was to change all this.

New Directions with a New Director

In the late 1930s, decreasing private and public support of the museum with resultant increasing deficits, turnover of directors, and lack of agreement between the administration and the scientific staff about policies and programs, led to a crisis of leadership at the top. Eventually, in early 1941, the president of the University of Michigan, Dr. Alexander Ruthven, was asked to make a study of the museum. His single most important recommendation to the trustees the following fall was that the director, Roy Chapman Andrews, be replaced. Within several months Dr. Albert Parr, director of Yale's Peabody Museum, was named the new director, taking office in June, 1942.[20]

Parr then began a series of important changes including setting up a formal schedule for salaries and promotions, making the museum more effective in public education, and developing exhibits that instructed more actively than merely displaying objects, however exotic and unfamiliar. Simpson personally soon benefited, receiving a significant raise in salary that was later followed by promotion to curator after having been stalled as associate curator for 18 years despite his obvious achievements and increasing reputation. However, Parr's most provocative initiative was to "de-emphasize evolutionary studies and taxonomic zoology as much as possible." Parr thought that evolution had become an established scientific fact and that further study would add little new knowledge so that the museum's limited resources should be placed elsewhere. Not only was this viewpoint anathema to Simpson, but Parr added insult to injury by further recommending that the department of paleontology be abolished, which was done in summer 1942. The three paleontologists — Simpson, Colbert, and Otto Haas — were assigned to other departments (mammals, reptiles, and invertebrates, respectively).[21]

Perhaps because of the turmoil going on at the American Museum, Simpson received an offer about this time of a Stirling Professorship at Yale University that he provisionally accepted.[22] Provisionally, because he was also considering enlistment in the U.S. Army now that the United States was seriously engaged in the Second World War. At age 40 and a married man with five dependents (his wife and four daughters), Simpson could have avoided military service, but nevertheless he enlisted, obtaining a Captaincy in December, 1942, thereby distancing himself from the problems he was facing at the museum. In June, 1943, while serving in North Africa in military intelligence under General Eisenhower's command, Simpson reiterated his opposition to Parr's reorganization plan to a museum official: "A whole new chapter in the history of evolutionary theory is just beginning. It is almost incredible that the Museum, with its great tradition of interest in evolutionary studies, is not taking a more leading part in this work."[23] Part of that tradition, of course, was Simpson's own work about to be crowned by publication of his book *Tempo and Mode in Evolution*.[24]

By the time Simpson was released from active military service in December 1944, Parr had relented on his scheme of reorganization, so Simpson declined the Yale offer and took up the chairmanship of the new department of geology and paleontology.[25] The rift between Parr and Simpson was apparently healed, and the next decade and a half would become what Simpson years later called his "halcyon period."[26] He gathered up honors, degrees, medals, and prizes from universities and scientific societies from around the world. His list of publications grew and included a number of texts (one of which was translated into more than a dozen languages) and popular books, many scientific monographs, and innumerable articles, reviews, and letters to the editor. He became formally associated with the departments of geology and of zoology at Columbia University, offering graduate seminars on fossil mammals and on evolution. He served on several governing councils of professional societies, and was elected president of the Society of Vertebrate Paleontology and of the Society for the Study of Evolution, both of which he helped found. Besides bringing glory and distinction upon himself, these honors of course also brought honor to the American Museum.

Simpson as Administrator

Simpson's administrative style during his tenure as chairman of the department of geology and paleontology, from 1944 to 1958 at the American Museum, was well described by his long-time museum colleague Norman D. Newell.[27] Newell has said that Simpson was very cordial when he showed up at the American Museum after the war to take up his appointment as curator of fossil invertebrates, but Simpson had failed to anticipated what Newell would need in the way of facilities. They walked all over the museum and could not find any available space, so Newell was temporarily housed for six months with a comparative anatomist. Newell was "irate — I was a member of Simpson's team and he ignored me." Newell kept prodding and finally went to see Parr, the museum director, and space was found immediately on the fifth floor in a dead-storage area. The fifth floor was then completely renovated for the whole department, but first starting with Simpson's area, then that of Colbert, curator of fossil reptiles, and finally down the line to Newell's. All this work took another six months.

With Simpson, there was no socializing among the departmental scientists and staff, so "things got tense and unhappy. Technicians in vertebrate paleontology were often at odds with the technicians in invertebrate paleontology, so that problems got exaggerated and distorted." Newell found it difficult to become acquainted with Simpson who was "just a name, a ghost . . . . I found him extraordinarily shy."

According to Newell, Simpson never saw himself as a solver of administrative or staff problems nor even as an arbitrator. Only under duress did Simpson take responsibility for the departments of fossil invertebrates and of mineralogy, which were both formally under him. For example Newell, who also had an appointment at Columbia University as a professor of geology, was once accused by another colleague in his department of spending too much museum time with students. They were at an impasse over this, so Newell insisted they go discuss it with Simpson to settle the issue. After ten minutes of total silence following initial explanation of what the problem was, Newell had to pry out of Simpson just what his responsibilities were, and in the end Simpson backed Newell.

Newell observed that with all Simpson's travels, Colbert who was next in seniority got stuck with the departmental administrative chores but his decisions had to be approved by Simpson — several were reversed months later when Simpson returned to the museum — despite Simpson's prior assurance to Colbert that he would backup whatever Colbert decided. But one important decision by Colbert did not get overturned by Simpson. Renovation of the exhibition halls was discussed at one rare departmental meeting

FIGURE 1. George Gaylord Simpson at his desk at the American Museum of Natural History in the 1950s.

and Simpson wanted straight-forward Halls of the Paleozoic, Mesozoic, and Cenozoic eras. Colbert, on the other hand, as curator of fossil reptiles, of course wanted the dinosaurs segregated and treated separately. Newell agreed with Colbert because, obviously, his invertebrate ammonites would be overshadowed if the dinosaurs were displayed with them in the proposed Mesozoic hall. Bobb Schaeffer, curator of fossil fishes, remembered this incident too. He and Colbert privately discussed from all sides Simpson's plan to design the displays chronologically, or so they thought. But when they went to talk to Simpson, he immediately turned their logic upside down, and before they knew it they were back outside in the corridor. They had gotten nowhere. Nevertheless, this was one time that Colbert's opinion carried the day, because while Simpson was away in South America, Colbert went ahead and had the dinosaur halls done as he wished.[28]

Newell became restive over the lack of endowment for his department of fossil invertebrates, and like Simpson he did not hesitate to try to raise private funds. However, Simpson was not keen on Newell getting oil company support for his research, and when Newell did receive oil money for work in South America, Simpson told him to be very careful that he was not consulting for the oil industry by using the museum's prestige. Because Simpson was not at all enthusiastic about this arrangement, Newell had a contract written up between the oil company and the museum that would permit the company to see any written manuscript being sent out for publication, which would, *de facto*, give the company about one year's lead time before the information became fully public. Simpson also did not look with favor on Newell's oil company support for his Permian Reef study in West Texas. Newell had to go to Parr for his approval, which he quickly gave because of the financial pinch the museum was in, despite the fact that the trustees wanted all new, private money to go into a general fund to maintain the museum and not to individual research projects.

Colbert was more succinct in his judgment of Simpson's administrative skills. "He was just so-so, average, as an administrator. I've got a theory that every administrator thinks he's a better administrator than he really is. Simpson often didn't tell us what he was going to do. He was a lone wolf in everything."[29]

Accident in Brazil

In the summer of 1956, Simpson participated in a joint Brazilian-American Museum expedition to a remote region in the headwaters of the Amazon River to collect mammalian fossils. Two months into the trip, while a camp site was being cleared, a felled tree struck Simpson, and as he later wrote "it hit my head, giving me a concussion; my left shoulder, dislocating it; my back, bruising it; and my legs, dislocating my left ankle and shattering my right leg with a compound fracture of tibia and fibula.... That event changed my life quite radically."[30] The remoteness of the accident resulted in a week's delay before Simpson received adequate medical treatment. Its seriousness meant that for two years he was unable to pay full attention to his responsibilities as chairman of the department. Or at least that is how it was perceived by the museum director, his former nemesis Parr, and by several colleagues in his own department.

According to Newell, he had urged Simpson not to go to Brazil, arguing that from his experience one could not do much real paleontology in heavy jungle: few outcrops, thick vegetative cover, deep soils. Instead, Newell suggested that Simpson work the flanks of the Andes where there were many oil concessions whose companies would be willing to assist his research. Besides, the outcrops were much better and the geology better known. Newell urged Simpson to contact the appropriate oil companies, but Simpson paid no attention to his advice.

Simpson's morale after the Brazil accident was very low; eventually he was up and about, but quite lame. He was mostly part-time for two years, and when he did return to work full-time in 1958, he received an invitation from the Brazilian Academy of Sciences to visit. Simpson told Colbert that he would have to again cover administratively for him. As Mayr recalled, "Colbert rebelled, was beside himself with rage. He refused to run the vertebrate paleontology department without real authority, despite Simpson's assurance that he'd back him up on all decisions." When Parr heard about this, "he said no more overseas trips! Simpson resigned on the spot."[31]

Already in the year before, Newell and some of his colleagues had asked Parr to relieve Simpson of his administrative responsibilities, but Parr said no. Newell had a serious and cordial discussion about this with Simpson, asking why he did not simply resign the chairmanship thereby resolving all these difficulties. Simpson said that since Colbert was the next senior man it was up to him to take on the departmental responsibilities while he was away. Simpson added that his not resigning the chairmanship was not a question of prestige, but rather "that it wouldn't be fair to Colbert to burden him with that assignment."[32]

Colbert himself recollected that after the Brazil accident Simpson was effectively away from the museum for about two years. Colbert would go to the hospital or Simpson's nearby apartment to talk about departmental business. "We had to get decisions made, but he didn't want to talk about them. It was a chore, no great honor, to be chairman. For two to three years I was virtually doing all of it, but I lacked a certain amount of authority. Finally, Parr discussed it with the trustees and they suggested that I take over as chairman. I was very dubious. I didn't think Simpson would go along with that. Parr went to tell him and apparently they had one helluva row."[33]

Schaeffer corroborates the circumstances surrounding this event, although more tartly than Colbert. He suspects "Colbert groused to Parr that he was doing all the work, and Parr said he'd talk to Simpson about it. Parr went up to Simpson's apartment and Simpson got all hot under the collar."

He believes that Simpson was convinced that Colbert and Parr "connived and contrived" to get him out of the chairmanship.[34]

Although Mayr had by then already left the American Museum for Harvard and the Museum of Comparative Zoology, his explanation of the blowup at the museum was that it had been long festering. "Colbert worked for Simpson for years, doing all the routine departmental work while Simpson insisted on reserving all the policy decisions for himself. Colbert finally went to Parr to complain that his research was suffering by being acting chairman. Colbert either wanted to be chairman or relieved of the hack work. Parr called Simpson in and said 'Look here...'. Simpson felt that Colbert stabbed him in the back and never forgave him."[35]

"Plus Ça Change..."

When Parr asked Simpson to resign the chairmanship, Simpson was infuriated — as he later said, "I resigned rather than accept such a humiliating situation."[36] Not long afterward, it must have stuck in Simpson's craw that he had to request permission from Colbert — now chairman — to accept an invitation to attend the 300th anniversary of the Royal Society of London: "I presume that there will be no serious objection from you or from the director [Parr]... but in view of the recent discussion of the inadvisability of absenting myself from the museum, I would like reassurance on that point."[37]

Simpson's dissatisfaction with his situation soon led to an offer of appointment as an Alexander Agassiz professorship at Harvard's Museum of Comparative Zoology, offered through the good graces of the Director and his colleague, A. S. Romer. Accompanying his formal letter of resignation, Simpson attached a memo to Parr with a copy to Colbert where he announced his MCZ appointment, effective 1 September 1959. In that memo, Simpson expresses "loyalty and affection" for the museum, but he cannot resist a parting shot. "My essential reason for leaving now is that I am offered a position elsewhere that will make my final professional years more useful and productive than they would be likely to be at the Museum. A scientific staff member in a department here active in exhibition and other direct public services, even if not nominally involved in administration, finds that a large proportion of his time is taken up by routine, sometimes necessary and sometimes, frankly, unnecessary or futile and in either case not satisfyingly productive. Thirty-odd years of that is enough, and the Museum, even with recent improvement, in this respect does not really and adequately provide for relief of its senior staff members from sheer routine. It, therefore, becomes only sensible to move on to an institution that can and does provide fuller freedom for scientific activity at this advanced stage in a career.

"There are, of course, other and more personal considerations involved, but these are of secondary importance and I will not dwell on them. I will mention only one: the fact that I have become partially but permanently crippled. It has not been suggested that this injury, which occurred in the service of the Museum, makes me incapable of holding a curatorial position, but it has resulted in certain restrictions and suggestions as to future activities that are uncongenial to me."[38]

In a letter to his sister Martha, Simpson described in glowing terms what he thought the new appointment would require — and not require — of him. "I do have an offer of a better job: Agassiz Professor at Harvard. More money & literally no duties — just to sit & think if so disposed, & occasionally to say a kind word to students (but no teaching!) & other faculty. Free, too, to come & go as I please. The professorship explicitly does not require even residence in Cambridge... There are drawbacks of course: leaving the [fossil] collections I'm working on — but Ned [Colbert] & Bert Parr would probably be so glad to see me go that they'd lend collections to Harvard for my work."[39]

In a letter to his mother a few weeks later, Simpson repeated this rosy picture: "I have been offered a good job at Harvard University . . . [that] pays well & has no duties except to write & do such research as I please. (No teaching, which I do not like — I mean, I do not like to teach & do not have to though I will be a professor.)"[40]

Simpson's colleagues at the museum and Columbia University were quite surprised at his resignation. Schaeffer and John Moore, professor of zoology at Columbia, went to see Simpson to try to talk him out of going to Harvard. Simpson listened without comment to their urgings. His only reply was to say that he really did want to watch the ball game that was soon coming up on television.[41] Newell thought that "The MCZ appointment was a pretty sore arrangement. Simpson was the only person in an enormous dead storage area."[42]

Although strictly speaking, Agassiz Professors did not need to be in residence or to teach, in fact there was some *de facto* pressure to expand their responsibilities. The reason for this was that Agassiz professorships were renewable five-year appointments that did not carry tenure. Agassiz professors were, therefore, given tenured joint appointments in Harvard departments to ensure continued association with the university if and when the term Agassiz appointments lapsed, and thus Simpson also held appointments in both biology and geology. While departmental appointments were *pro forma*, some additional duties were implied, such as teaching an occasional course, working with graduate students, sitting on campus committees — the very activities that Simpson had found "not satisfyingly productive" at the American Museum.

Ernest Williams, who held just such a joint appointment as an Agassiz professor and biology professor, thinks "these distinctions were probably not made clear to Simpson at his time of appointment by the director, Alfred Romer, who liked to get along with people."[43] Mayr, who succeeded Romer as MCZ director, recalled that the MCZ had "fantastic possibilities for Simpson, with all of the benefits and none of the usual obligations; not a single Ph.D. student and away much of the time. He could have taught more than he did, but instead he just gave a few lectures in my course on evolution, and the rest of the time just sat there."[44] Nevertheless, Simpson did continue to thrive at the MCZ, much as he did at the American Museum, at least for the first four years, traveling even more extensively, giving invited lectures, and garnering still more awards and honors, including the National Medal of Science from President Lyndon Johnson in 1966. The MCZ, too, must have been pleased to have Simpson, because a year after his initial appointment Simpson turned down the offer of directorship of the MCZ and instead recommended his colleague Ernst Mayr.[45]

His relations with the American Museum, however, remained strained. In his autobiography, Simpson mentions, among other grudges, that "I had planned a monograph on the fossil marsupials of North America and many specimens were made available to me, but I was refused access to the crucial collection [of didelphids] at my old institution, the American Museum of Natural History, and I therefore had to abandon that plan."[46] The particular specimens he wanted were already being studied by a Columbia University graduate student working under the direction of Simpson's successor at the museum, Malcolm C. McKenna. As with some other disagreements, this was another one where Simpson overreacted. McKenna recalls that "He wanted the material 'right now' [but] it was in use by someone with a legitimate claim to keep [it] on loan . . . for a while. There was a hot exchange of correspondence. Simpson thereafter declared he'd never set foot in the museum again."[47]

In 1964, the beginning of his next five-year appointment as Agassiz professor, both Simpson and his wife suffered "his and her heart attacks." The health of each declined, compounding Simpson's own medical problems resulting from the Brazilian accident. Later, in 1967, Simpson and his wife decided to move to Tucson, Arizona, because the Cambridge winters were getting ever more difficult for them, especially for Anne Roe who was prone to recurrent pneumonia attacks. Simpson wrote MCZ director Ernst Mayr, saying he was ready to resign his Agassiz professorship. Mayr went to the dean and they instead agreed that Simpson was a special case so he was given the remaining years of his second five-year appointment without residence requirements, at half-pay, and with his fringe benefits continued. When time came for re-appointment in 1969, Simpson wrote Mayr and said how he greatly appreciated the arrangement and that he would like the next five-year appointment the same way. This time, however, Mayr and the dean "both had a good laugh and said no — which Simpson resented bitterly."[48] It would seem that Simpson was being unrealistic with this request, given that he was in his late sixties, in poor health, and some twenty-three hundred miles from his home institution. Moreover, the Museum of Comparative Zoology with its limited Agassiz Professorship funds was in no position to offer Simpson such a sinecure, which is what he apparently expected as his due.

Simpson thus ended his ten-year association with the MCZ and accepted a half-time appointment in the department of geosciences at the University of Arizona, which lasted until he finally retired in June 1982 at the age of 80. Because he was overage when first appointed, Simpson had to be reappointed, each year, by "special action of the [Arizona] State Board of Regents."[49]

Conclusion

Given the magnitude of Simpson's achievements based upon his voluminous publications and their quality as judged from the many honors and awards he received, it is clear that Simpson was one of the leading scientists of the middle-half of the 20th century. Simpson therefore was not exercising illusions of personal grandeur in expecting more than usual consideration and freedom of operation from his museum employers. However, it is also clear that these expectations were at times inflated, going beyond the bounds of what was reasonable in terms of other people's needs and interests and responsibilities. He may have thought himself a completely free agent and able to do as he pleased, but in the real world of institutional employment, he was not and could not.

FIGURE 2. Simpson at his desk in his office annex, Tucson, Arizona, in early 1980s.

No doubt many of Simpson's problems with his museum employers were the result of his personal traits of being shy, socially awkward, and disinclined to engage in one-on-one debate, however mild. In short, he not only was a difficult person to deal with but he had no interest in dealing with people. His genuine scientific achievements and the very visible rewards that came with them also encouraged an attitude of feeling that he was in the right, justifiably so or not.

Museum research had great appeal for Simpson whose only interest was in his lifeless fossils and their evolutionary history. He was clearly unsuited for academic employment, his only other professional option. However, even in a museum, Simpson could not avoid people: his institutional superiors, professional associates, and graduate students — all of whom he kept arm's length. Simpson thus often made life for himself and others difficult and unpleasant.

Finally, is there a broader lesson to be learned here about ornery individuals and institutional personality? I think not, because Simpson was *sui generis* in so many ways, scientifically and temperamentally, that his resultant behavior must also be recognized as simply one-of-a-kind.

NOTES

[1] The expression "awkward embrace" was coined by Joan Simpson Burns, Simpson's third daughter, and used by her for the title of her book that examines what former editor-in-chief of *Time* magazine, Hedley Donovan, called "the balance between the rights — or possibilities — of the individual, and the necessities — or claims — of organized society." It seems thoroughly appropriate to extend the metaphor to the particular case of the tension between her father's needs as a highly creative scientist and those of his museum employers as institutions of academic and popular education. (Burns, 1975, *Awkward Embrace — The Creative Artist and the Institution in America*, Alfred Knopf, New York, p. xv.)

[2] Simpson interview with the author, 18 August 1981, Tucson, Arizona.

[3] The description of Simpson's negotiations with Yale and the American Museum is based upon several sources, including Simpson's autobiography, *Concession to the Improbable* (Yale University Press, 1978, p. 38 ff.); letters to his parents and sister at the time that provide more specific details about the Yale and AMNH offers, informal and formal, and Simpson's protracted consideration thereof (*Simple Curiosity: Letters from George Gaylord Simpson to His Family, 1921–1970*, University of California Press, 1987, p. 60, 67, 70, 73, 80, 87, 89, 91); and unpaginated autobiographical notes (*MS* Collection 31, Simpson Papers, American Philosophical Society Archives, Philadelphia).

[4] Simpson, 1978, *Concession*, p. 38.

[5] Work cited, p. 38.

[6] Edwin H. Colbert, 1992, *William Diller Matthew: Paleontologist* (Columbia University Press, p. 215 ff.).

[7] Simpson, 1978, *Concession*, p. 38.

[8] Simpson, 1985, *Simple Curiosity*, p. 87.

[9] Simpson, 1978, *Concession*, p. 39.

[10] Work cited, p. 41.

[11] See John M. Kennedy, 1968, "Philanthropy and Science in New York City: The American Museum of Natural History, 1868–1968," esp. 219 ff. (Yale University dissertation, University Microfilms, Inc., Ann Arbor, Michigan, 277 p.); and Ronald Rainger, 1991, *Agenda for Antiquity: Henry Fairfield Osborn & Vertebrate Paleontology at the American Museum of Natural History, 1890–1935*, University of Alabama Press, Tuscaloosa, 360 p.).

[12] Colbert, 1980, *Fossil Hunter's Notebook*, p. 85 (E. P. Dutton, New York).

[13] Obituary, *New York Times*, 17 May 1949, p. 26.

[14] Simpson, 1934, *Attending Marvels*, p. 302 (The Macmillan Co., New York).

[15] "These were the very animals of which we had seen one small fragment almost three years earlier. Dozens of them! Hundreds perhaps! Complete skeletons weathering out of the ancient rocks where they had lain for millions of years undisturbed! One of these, crushed flat but perfect down to the last joint, is now on display as a treasure of the American Museum in New York and another is in the National Museum in Washington. As the

animals did prove to have been totally unknown to science, I named them *Scarrittia* after the patron of our expeditions." (Simpson, 1941, "How We Knew Where to Dig," p. 209 in *Through Hell and High Water*, S. S. Cramer, editor, R. McBridge and Co., New York.) At the end of Simpson's article, the editor adds: "*Scarrittia canquelensis* ... was about the size of a horse, but stockier and heavier built. It was cumbersome ... herbivorous, browsing on leaves and twigs rather than grazing on grasses. It probably had no tail. It is unrelated to anything ... today."

[16] Although the Patagonian expedition had a sound scientific basis, the year-long overseas trip had the added benefit for Simpson of relief from his marital woes. His marriage was in trouble practically from the first and went downhill quickly thereafter. By summer 1930, when he departed for South America, Simpson had been estranged from his wife, more or less continuously from the time he left Yale to go to the British Museum; he was finally legally separated from her the year after he returned.

[17] Simpson, 1934, *Attending Marvels*. As Kennedy points out "This kind of outdoor science pleased Professor Osborn's wealthy Wall Street trustees and their friends. They particularly liked the museum's combination of exploration and science with the 'traditional American' entrepreneurial virtues of 'boldness' and 'hard work'" (Kennedy, 1968, "Philanthropy and Science," p. 157). Rainger, too, notes that "Osborn operated as a salesman who promoted new projects to museum administrators, authored popular articles in leading newspapers and magazines, and employed rhetoric, exaggeration, and supreme confidence to acquire economic and political support for major projects in what was otherwise an expensive, non-practical, and peripheral field of inquiry [vertebrate paleontology]." (Rainger, 1991, *Agenda for Antiquity*, p. 3.)

[18] Simpson, 1934, *Attending Marvels*, p. xxiv-xxv.

[19] Simpson, 1978, *Concession*, p. 95.

[20] Kennedy, 1968, "Philanthropy and Science," p. 224 ff.

[21] Work cited, p. 241.

[22] Simpson, 1978, *Concession*, p. 38.

[23] Quoted in Kennedy, 1968, "Philanthropy and Science," p. 246.

[24] Simpson, 1944, *Tempo and Mode* (Columbia University Press, New York, 237 p.). Ironically, three other works that are considered important in the "consolidation of the evolutionary synthesis" in the late 1930s/early 1940s were based on the Jesup Lectures at Columbia University, a program of public instruction funded by the late Morris K. Jesup, a wealthy Museum founder and former president who hired the young Henry Fairfield Osborn to start the Department of Paleontology (Douglas J. Preston, 1986, *Dinosaurs in the Attic*, St. Martin's Press, New York, p. 64).

[25] Simpson, 1978, *Concession*, p. 38-39.

[26] Work cited, p. 129.

[27] Norman D. Newell interview with the author, 29-30 May 1979, Las Vegas, Nev.

[28] Bobb Schaeffer interview with the author, 6 Nov. 1980, New York City.

[29] Colbert interview with the author, 7 July 1982, Flagstaff, Ariz.

[30] Simpson, 1978, *Concession*, p. 170.

[31] Ernst Mayr interview with the author, 22 October 1980, Cambridge, Mass. (See also note 48.)

[32] Newell interview.

[33] Colbert interview. Anne Roe, Simpson's wife, had another perspective. She noted that the relationship between her husband and Parr prior to Simpson's resignation "had suddenly turned antagonistic." Simpson did not know why Parr would no longer talk to him or why he would leave the staff room when Simpson entered. For a long time, Anne thought her husband imagined these slights, until she saw Parr turn away from her husband at a museum Christmas party. Sometime later, Simpson discovered that Parr had found out that Parr's grant proposal to the National Science Foundation had been turned down upon Simpson's recommendation. As for Simpson's wanting to remain chairman of the department, Anne had asked her husband why he did not resign, letting Colbert takeover. "After all it was just extra worry and work for him anyway." Simpson replied that he would except he was afraid he would not continue to get the support he needed to carry on his research. (Anne Roe Simpson interview with the author, 17-18 December 1985, Tucson, Ariz.)

[34] Schaeffer interview.

[35] Mayr interview. (See also note 48.)

[36] Simpson, 1978, *Concession*, p. 170.
[37] Simpson to Colbert letter, 23 September 1958 (*MS* Collection 31, Simpson Papers, American Philosophical Society Archives, Philadelphia).
[38] Simpson to Parr letter, 17 April 1959.
[39] Simpson, 1987, *Simple Curiosity*, p. 294, emphasis in the original.
[40] Work cited, p. 295.
[41] J. Moore interview with the author, 14 June 1979, Riverside, Calif.
[42] Newell interview.
[43] Ernest E. Williams interview with the author, 3 October 1980, Cambridge, Mass.
[44] Mayr interview.
[45] Simpson, 1978, *Concession*, p. 195. (See also note 48.)
[46] Work cited, p. 219.
[47] Malcolm McKenna E-mail to the author, 9 September 1998.
[48] Mayr interview. In his review of this chapter, Mayr wanted to correct the record because, since my interview with him, he had learned about Simpson's resignation directly from Parr. According to Parr, when Simpson was fully recovered from his accident, Parr offered him two options. Either Simpson could return full-time to the departmental chairmanship or resign and take upon an appointment as senior scientist. Simpson angrily refused both offers and immediately contacted Romer at the MCZ, asking him for an appointment there as Alexander Agassiz professor, to which Romer agreed. Furthermore, Parr vigorously denied that Colbert had any direct role in Simpson's resignation. Mayr also did not believe that Romer offered Simpson the directorship of the MCZ, given Simpson's personality and previous administrative record at the AMNH. On the contrary, Mayr himself was being groomed by Romer for the directorship. (Mayr review, 27 April 1999).
[49] Simpson, 1978, *Concession*, p. 218.

An Essay on the History of the Biosystematists of the San Francisco Bay Area

WILLIAM Z. LIDICKER, JR.
Museum of Vertebrate Zoology
University of California, Berkeley, CA 94720
E-mail: lidicker@socrates.berkeley.edu

For more than 60 years the Biosystematists of the Bay Area has served as an intellectual focus and integrating influence among the evolutionary biologists of the region. Its membership included many influential contributors to the evolutionary synthesis, as well as a host of leading figures in evolutionary biology over the decades of its existence. The group's history is significant also in that it represents an experiment in the effectiveness of promoting scientific progress through interdisciplinary discourse among peers spiced with a dose of collegiality. This essay summarizes the organization's format, membership, and structure, reports on its founding and early history, documents its transition away from an all-male society, and records the officers that provided its leadership. Future research will assemble what can be learned about its programs, and hence reveal the extent and depth of its intellectual concerns.

Sometimes, quite unpredictably, seemingly minor events result in unanticipated historical paths. This is an account of how a privately published book with a heretical message, *The Atlantic Rift and its Meaning* (Baker, 1932), helped trigger a 63-year experiment in interdisciplinary discourse among evolutionary biologists. For over 60 years the Biosystematists has been a San Francisco Bay Area institution unique in its format and an intellectual *tour de force* in its influence both locally and nationally. It was founded in 1936 with the unusual attitude that interdisciplinary discourse combined with a dose of social collegiality could spawn scientific breakthroughs as well as personal intellectual growth. Although such an idea was not novel, it was definitely not the standard behavior of scientists at the time, at least in North America, and even now, while increasingly often expressed, it is more an idealized goal in science than a reality. This forward-looking cohort of scientists was comprised of systematists and geneticists associated with various academic institutions in the San Francisco Bay Area.

The format for this new organization was to meet generally once a month with a dinner followed by discussion. Meeting venues alternated among the institutions involved, but the University of California at Berkeley soon became the most utilized site because of its central location. Attendance at meetings varied, but the modal number was about 30. Early membership in the Biosystematists included important contributors to the evolutionary "new synthesis" (Smocovitis, 1997). Among them were Jens Clausen, William Hiesey, David Keck, Alden Miller, and Ledyard Stebbins. Richard Goldschmidt was also an early member although his contribution to the evolutionary synthesis is still debated (Dietrich, 1995; Mayr, 1997). Much later (early 1970s) Theodosius Dobzhansky participated while he was retired and living in Davis, California. According to V. B. Smocovitis (pers. commun.), when Dobzhansky was at the California Institute of Technology in Pasadena, he often visited Berkeley to confer with geneticist I. Michael Lerner, and at such times attended meetings of the Biosystematists. In 1970, the group flexed its political muscle by writing an open letter (27 January) to Max Rafferty, then California State Superintendent of Public Education, opposing the inclusion of creationist ideas in the teaching of evolution.

The group prided itself on its informal and minimal administrative structure (no dues were collected for at least the first 40 years), one consequence of which was that records of its activities were not systematically preserved. Over the decades, the Biosystematists naturally changed in many ways, adjusting its format, enlarging its membership base (Table 1), experimenting with different administrative structures, and broadening its concept of what constituted evolutionary biology. Such changes were not always accomplished without controversy, but change after all was a comfortable intellectual concept for evolutionary biologists. Nevertheless, throughout this long period, the group remained faithful to its basic tenets of interdisciplinary discussion among peers, informality, and collegiality. Consistent with this philosophy, Biosystematists was a "membership by invitation" only organization. While the criteria for membership evolved, there was a semi-formal procedure for joining during most of these 60 years. At first, members were required to have a PhD degree or equivalent experience and to have an established program of independent research in some aspect of evolutionary biology. Effectively, this restricted membership to those at Bay Area institutions of higher learning, including the California Academy of Sciences. Gradually, the second requirement became relaxed, but not the first. Another early requirement was that prospective members be resident in the Bay Area for one year before becoming eligible. This seems to have been largely ignored after

TABLE 1. Membership numbers for the Biosystematists based on counts from surviving membership lists. The sometimes violent fluctuations in numbers can be attributed to the occasional purging of inactive or non-paying (after 1977) members. After 1993, the numbers refer to a mailing list as formal membership was abolished.

Year	Number of members
1936/37	15 (est.)
1938	~20
1939/40	27
1940	30
1948	38
1949/50	43
1950/51	47
1953/54	58
1954/55	60
1955/56	63
1968	84
1971	131
1972/73	139
1974/75	59
1977/78	164
1984/85	151
1986	58
1987/88	153
1994/95	175
1995/96	110
1996/97	122
1997/98	130
1998/99	142

just a few years, but the notion that members should be long-term residents of the area persisted through the 1980s. The rule was that nominees for membership should be able to attend meetings for at least one year after election. Shorter term residents, such as post-doctoral fellows, would be welcome as guests. The last formal statement of membership requirements was in a letter from D. R. Kaplan, Chair of the Council, dated 9 October 1991. Criteria included: a professional position in the area, record of research accomplishment, regular attendance on a long-term basis, and ability to present a seminar to the group.

At each meeting, there was a formality of welcoming any new members and introducing guests. Nominations for membership were made in writing and submitted to a membership committee that would review whether or not the nominee fit the above criteria. During some intervals, the Executive Committee, if there were one, or the Secretary acted as the membership committee (see below). In 1993/1994, the membership committee concept was abolished. In about 1977, institutional budgets having become extremely constrained, a $1 annual dues was initiated in order to pay for postage. Dues remained at this rate up to the present time, except that in about 1994 they were raised to $2 for a couple of years to alleviate a deficit. In recent years, electronic mail has reduced mailing costs, and dues collection has become sporadic.

Although there was not an identifiable single defining moment, by 1998 the organization had changed in ways that were more fundamental than it had previously experienced. For some, this signaled the end of an era identified by the above philosophy, and for others it meant re-positioning the organization more appropriately for the next 60 years. Perhaps both are true. For many members, these recent modernizations of the organization triggered an interest in the history of the group and a concomitant reassessment of its accomplishments. For instance, Michael T. Ghiselin of the California Academy of Sciences arranged for an archive to be established at that institution. And, in September 1998, I undertook the task of assembling as much historical data as I could on the organization, a task made complicated and frustrating by the informal and minimal administrative structure that had characterized it. The late John H. Thomas of Stanford University had served for a few years as an informal archivist but for health reasons gradually withdrew from playing an active role. The material that he was able to accumulate was, however, extremely helpful to me in my efforts. I have been a member of the Biosystematists since the autumn of 1957, and maintained an active involvement to the present time, except for a few sabbatical leave absences. I began my present investigation by sending a memorandum to all long-term members of the group soliciting their help. Useful input was received over the subsequent months from the following individuals. I am most grateful to them for their assistance.

John A. Chemsak	Lincoln Constance
Howell V. Daly	Barbara Ertter
Michael T. Ghiselin	Joseph T. Gregory
Nancy Vivrette Haller	Tomio Iwamoto
Ned K. Johnson	Harold W. Kerster
Elizabeth B. McClintock	Brent D. Mishler
Robert Ornduff	Jerry A. Powell
Charles M. Rick	G. Ledyard Stebbins
Barbara R. Stein	Marvalee H. Wake

What follows are (1) an account of the first decade of the organization's existence (2) a discussion of the controversy surrounding women members, and (3) a compilation of the group's officers. Information on programs is currently being assembled and will be presented later.

The most common type of programs were status reports by members on their on-going research, followed by extensive discussion. Sometimes the speaker was a visitor or post-doctoral fellow, and sometimes there were panel discussions. Generally the group scheduled a weekend field trip meeting once a year, and these excursions usually involved multiple speakers. Figure 1 shows a group of four members looking for salamanders following a successful weekend symposium at Bodega Marine Laboratory (13–14 February 1970). In this case the topic was the raging controversy over molecular clocks, and we called the symposium "Phyletics without fossils." There is also in existence an excellent photograph of the group attending a weekend field trip in May 1946 (see Figure 2; also Smocovitis, 1997, fig. 5).

The First Decade

Because of the informal nature of the Biosystematists, few documents concerning the early years of the organization seem to have survived. Even the date of the first meeting has been controversial. In 1978, the regular May meeting of the group (9 May) was devoted to a symposium on its history, a belated 40th anniversary celebration. There were seven speakers at this well attended event, all of whom were founding, or nearly founding, members. David Keck and Ira Wiggins expressed the opinion that the first meeting was in 1935, and there was no dissenting view expressed at that time. Earlier, William Hiesey, another founding member, wrote to Lincoln Constance (19 January 1974) that he thought the group began in "about 1935." A second meeting on the history of the organization, this time led by Betty Smocovitis, an historian, was held on 8 September 1998. At that time Ledyard

FIGURE 1. A group of happy Biosystematists looking for salamanders on their way home from a successful symposium at the Bodega Marine Laboratory, 14 February 1970.
Left to right: Vincent M. Sarich, Allan C. Wilson, William Z. Lidicker, Jr., and David B. Wake.
Photo by Oliver P. Pearson.

Stebbins said that he was sure the first meeting was in 1937 or possibly 1936 (see also Smocovitis, 1994, 1997). And so the matter stood, except to note that it seemed to me that a 1935 starting date was a little early in view of the other events (see below) known to have preceded the group's establishment.

Recently, I discovered a letter that seems to solve the mystery. On 28 September 1938, Herbert L. Mason wrote to Robert C. Miller, then Director of the California Academy of Sciences, inviting him to attend the October meeting of the group. He commented further that this meeting would mark the beginning of the organization's third year. This means that the first meeting was in fact held in October 1936, a date quite compatible with other information. There was no disagreement among early members that this first meeting occurred in October in the library of the Carnegie Institution of Washington at Stanford University. David Keck was the first speaker and his topic was a privately published book by Howard Bigelow Baker (1932) on continental drift. The second meeting was held in Berkeley (2093 Life Sciences Bldg.), and the third was at Stanford's Dudley Herbarium in the former Natural History Museum.

No one person clearly emerges as deserving credit for starting the group. Jens Clausen is frequently mentioned as the initial coordinator, but David Keck and William Hiesey each felt that they were initially and critically involved in the first steps toward its organization. These three formed such an integrated intellectual team that it is probably impossible to know which individual was responsible for which ideas, and over time each could legitimately claim ownership of any group thoughts. Clausen was the senior member of the team, and so it is understandable that he was viewed by others as the initial leader. David Keck, however, gave the most plausible story when he addressed the group at its 9 May 1978 panel discussion. He recalled that in December 1934 the AAAS meetings were in Pittsburgh. Keck arrived just after the meetings ended, his arrival delayed because of the birth of his daughter on 26 December. He had discussions with a group from the Carnegie Museum and others, and conceived the idea for a biosystematics group. Contributing to this germ was his fortuitous discovery of the book by H. B. Baker (1932) on continental drift and his consequent realization of the potential for inter-disciplinary exchange. On his return to Stanford, he claims to have discussed the idea with colleagues and subsequently took the lead in organizing the group. This claim is supported by Herbert Mason who remembered meeting with Keck "and others" in Berkeley to discuss possible interest by Berkeley faculty in participating. Hiesey also gives Keck credit for being the originator of the idea for monthly meetings in the Bay Area (letter to Lincoln Constance dated 19 January 1974). Moreover, Robert Usinger who was a member from about 1938, states that "the Biosystematists' organization was started by David Keck of the Carnegie Institution at Stanford" (Usinger, 1972:68).

Another development that may have helped Keck and others formulate their idea for the new organization was that a group with similar objectives had formed in the East. It was centered in New York with Columbia University and the American Museum of Natural History being the primary institutions involved (Smocovitis, 1994:249–250). The leader of this group was L. C. Dunn with other notables such G. G. Simpson, E. Mayr, and Theodosius Dobzhansky being involved. Ira Wiggins mentioned a group in the East similar to the Biosystematists in a letter to Lincoln Constance on 13 June 1971, which probably referred to this one in New York. Wiggins claimed, however, that the eastern group folded within five years. While this may be true, it is this eastern assemblage of prominent evolutionists that led eventually (1946) to the formation of the Society for the Study of Evolution (Smocovitis, 1994). Members of the Biosystematists clearly were also involved in this event as its agenda for the 5 February 1946 meeting included a discussion of the new organization, to be established at the AAAS meetings in March of that year, with a consideration of possible nominations for officers.

In passing it may be noted that the Biosystematists model was followed by others. In the 1950s and early 1960s there was a Southern California Biosystematists (D. R. Savage, pers. commun.), and the long-lasting (but now defunct) Kennicott Club of Chicago may have had similar objectives. This latter club actually preceded the Biosystematists by a few years, and was an association of working naturalists, rather than evolutionary biologists (O. Pergams and F. A. Pitelka, pers. commun.).

The origin of the name "Biosystematists" is also of considerable interest. A name for the fledgling organization was apparently discussed " around the table" at the group's third meeting. Both Ledyard Stebbins and George S. Myers recall (1978) that Gordon Ferris might have suggested the name, but Hiesey gives this credit to Ernest B. Babcock (1974 letter). Botanists generally credit the term "biosystematics" to Camp and Gilly (1943), but clearly this is wrong (also Smocovitis, pers. commun.). In a letter to Robert C. Miller dated 15 July 1940, the organization was referred to as "The Biosystematists." It was consistently called " Biosystematists" until 1998 when "Bay Area Biosystematists (BABS)" unceremoniously appeared.

There is no record of charter members of the group. Aside from the three leaders based at Stanford, E. B. Babcock took the lead in recruiting faculty from Berkeley. According to Keck, Joseph Grinnell, Director of the Museum of Vertebrate Zoology, was invited to join but declined, recommending his young colleague Seth B. Benson. The California Academy of Sciences was also soon involved through R. C. Miller, and some early meetings were held there as well. One initial member, H. E. McMinn, was from Mills College. Thus the evidence suggests that the following 14 were among the initial participants:

LeRoy Abrams (Stanford Univ.)	Ernest B. Babcock (Univ. Calif., Berkeley)
Seth B. Benson (Univ. Calif., Berkeley)	Ralph Chaney (Univ. Calif., Berkeley)
Jens Clausen (Carnegie Institution)	Gordon F. Ferris (Stanford Univ.)
William M. Hiesey (Carnegie Inst.)	David D. Keck (Carnegie Institution)
Herbert L. Mason (Univ. Calif., Berkeley)	Howard E. McMinn (Mills College)
Alden H. Miller (Univ. Calif., Berkeley)	George S. Myers (Stanford Univ.)
G. Ledyard Stebbins (Univ. Calif., Berkeley)	Ira L. Wiggins (Stanford Univ.)

By 1939/40 there were 27 members (Table 1), including such notables as Lincoln Constance, Richard B. Goldschmidt, Robert C. Miller, and Robert L. Usinger.

Not much is known about the officers and programs during this first decade of the group's existence. Jens Clausen was likely the coordinator for the first two years, and Herbert Mason may have done this job for 1938/39 (cf., his invitation letter to R. C. Miller of 28 September 1938). Aside from the initial program in October 1936, the next record of a program was for November 1938 when D. I. Axelrod spoke on the origin of the Californian element in the flora of California. For 1939/40, we have a list of seven speakers and dates, but no topics. To this list is appended the interesting comment that "speakers will arrange for a place to eat and will send out notices of meetings." In February and March 1941 the program was, respectively: E. G. Linsley on the evolution of floral relationships in bees, and R. C. Miller on geography and evolution — a motion picture on the Galapagos Islands by David Lack. Stebbins and Goldschmidt were probably program officers for this academic year. We do have a partial program for 1941/42 which was assembled by these two leaders in May of 1941. For the four meetings of October 1941 through January 1942, 16 of the 22 chapters in Julian Huxley's "The New Synthesis" were reviewed. Reviewers and alternates were assigned and four chapters were covered each meeting. In 1942/43 the program chairman was Goldschmidt, and

Stebbins wrote a letter to members implying that he was in charge (25 September 1942). The letter expressed concerns about the group being able to continue to meet with gasoline rationing and dim-out restrictions imposed by World War II. Stebbins suggested Saturday afternoon meetings ("as last year") in San Francisco (either at the California Academy of Sciences or at the University of California's Extension Division on Powell Street) both of which could be reached easily with public transportation. Apparently, the organization was relatively inactive from this time until the end of the war, but did meet at least occasionally. Stebbins seems to have been coordinator (Secretary?) in 1945/46, and we know there were meetings in at least February (R. A. Stirton on evolutionary progress in the horses) and May. The May meeting was at the Placerville Forest Genetics Station, and a remarkable photograph exists from this event (Figure 2). There are 21 people in the photo, four of whom were hosts from the Station and two may have been guests, leaving 15 Biosystematists members (including seven of the "charter" members).

Although major gaps remain in the historical record for this decade, it seems appropriate to pull together what we do have at this time. Hopefully, additional information will be found, perhaps with this essay serving as an encouragement for others to search through old files.

FIGURE 2. Biosystematists at Placerville Forest Genetics Station, 11–12 May 1946.
Standing (Left to right): H. E. McMinn*, G. F. Ferris*, E. G. Linsley, H. Graham, L. Adams, C. Y. Chang (guest), E. B. Babcock*, W. E. Castle (guest), R. H. Weidman (Sta. pers.), R. B. Goldschmidt, G. S. Myers*
Front row (Left to right): R. C. Miller, G. L. Stebbins*, C. O. Sauer, H. L. Mason*, I. L. Wiggins*, L. Constance, N. Mirov (Sta. pers.), P. Stockwell (Sta. pers.), W. Cummings (Sta. pers.), and H. Kirby.
Photo courtesy A. Leviton (G.S.Myers/A.E.Leviton Biographical Photo File, California Academy of Sciences).

* = charter members.

Breaking the Gender Barrier in the Biosystematists

In the last few years, the view has been expressed in meetings of the Biosystematists and elsewhere that the organization was blatantly sexist until quite recently. Smocovitis (1994:249) makes the unreferenced assertion that "women and graduate students were strictly excluded from the society until the early 1970s, when they were admitted after much discussion." Since this interpretation of history does not match the recollections of at least some long-term members, it seemed useful to assemble whatever data that I could relevant to the subject. Graduate students, incidentally, were not admitted as members until the last few years because they did not fit the membership requirement of having a PhD or equivalent level of experience. They were, however, always welcomed at meetings as invited guests (while still graduate students, R. L. Usinger attended meetings as early as 1938 as did F. A. Pitelka starting in 1941).

There were in fact no women on the membership rolls of the Biosystematists until 1971, a period of almost 35 years. At least for the earlier part of this interval, most of the long- term members believed that this fact merely reflected the scarcity of women in evolutionary biology in the Bay Area during that period. As recently as September 1998, Ledyard Stebbins, one of the founding members, claimed simply that in the early years no woman met the criteria for membership, which as explained earlier were fairly restrictive. When the subject came up at the 1978 "40th anniversary" meeting of the society, Seth Benson jokingly noted the argument that he had heard to the effect that " women would not understand an organization that did not have any women in it." Another speaker at that symposium, Herbert Mason, commented that "the group had no objection to women; we just did not invite them." In spite of this superficially benign situation, at least a few female biologists felt that they should have been invited to join and were not (including Annetta Carter and Elizabeth B. McClintock).

Certainly toward the end of this 35 year period there were women scientists in the area who likely would have qualified for membership, even by the fairly severe early standards. Some women did attend as guests, just as graduate students did. Although there were no records kept of such instances, some members recall two women guests: Aloha (Hanna) Alava, research associate of Curt Stern, and Olga Pavlovsky, research associate of Theodosius Dobzhansky. Of course it might be argued that although these two held PhD degrees they did not have independent research programs, and hence did not qualify as members. There is evidence, however, that a few members did object on principle to opening membership to females. Based on correspondence or in some cases on recollections of others, the following were known or alleged to have objected at one time or another to including women as members of the society: Jens Clausen, Paul Hurd, Herbert Mason, and Ira Wiggins. In a letter to Lincoln Constance, then chairman of the Executive Committee, Wiggins wrote on 13 June 1971, as a member of this committee, that he was withdrawing his objections to admitting women to the group. He added the interesting explanation that he had heretofore been opposed to opening the group to women because "founders of Biosystematists in the east, before we set our group up in business included females and within five years infighting had wrecked the group and it ceased to function."

From the perspective of most members of the Biosystematists who were participating before 1971, the gender issue rarely surfaced, and no one can recall it reaching the level of a "discussion" or debate. I think I remember a single instance in which a woman was suggested for membership before 1971. A senior member of the group simply explained that she did not qualify according to the group's criteria, and the matter was dropped. Jerry Powell, who became a member in 1961, says (in litt., February 1999) "I do not remember there being any controversy about Biosystematists being a "men only club"; although some older members may have objected when the first women were suggested . . ."

The revolution occurred in 1971 (this incidentally was also a high year for membership numbers; see Table 1). In letters, John H. Thomas nominated Elizabeth B. McClintock on 15 April, George W. Barlow nominated Margaret Bradbury on 29 April, Marvalee Wake was nominated by Ned K. Johnson on 4 June, and about that time Ledyard Stebbins nominated Earleen Atchison Rupert and Dorothy Lowery. The discussions within the Executive Committee (Lincoln Constance, chairman, Ira Wiggins, George Lindsay, and Harman T. Spieth) on these historically important nominations were recorded in (1) a letter of 8 June from Constance to the rest of the committee supporting four of these women nominees (not including Lowery), (2) a note from Lindsay to Constance dated 10 June saying "I think it is time to admit female members . . .", and pointing to the excellent qualifications of M. Wake, and (3) the aforementioned letter by Wiggins dated 13 June endorsing three women candidates and accepting the evaluations of Stebbins for the other two. After discussion by the Executive Committee, these five women were approved for membership along with three men. On 17 July, Constance wrote to outgoing Secretary Ned Johnson instructing him to add these eight names to the membership list.

Following this 1971 breakthrough, women were regularly admitted to membership, and no further opposition to this development has been found in the written records or recalled by members. In 1975, Nancy Vivrette (now Haller) was appointed the first woman Secretary, and she served two terms (1975/76 and 1976/77). Not surprisingly, the organization has survived.

Officers of the Biosystematists

This compilation is based on my own records, the results of a solicitation for information extended to 30 long-term members of the organization (including one charter member), and from a search through five boxes of documents on the Biosystematists in the archives at Stanford University courtesy of John H. Thomas. Information is scarce, especially for the years before 1950 largely because the group was informal, had a minimal administrative structure with few records being preserved, and had until 1986 no written charter of any kind.

The ensuing list of officers not only documents who have been the leaders of the organization but also tracks the group's efforts to experiment with different administrative arrangements. Responsibility for leadership varied from a single officer, the Secretary (e.g., 1949/50 to 1962/63), up to 12 or 13 officers (e.g., 1986/87 to 1992/93). The most common arrangement was for a single Program Officer or Secretary backed up by an Executive Committee whose main responsibility was to appoint the Secretary each year. Very little information has been located for the first decade (1936–1946), and that which was found is mentioned in the section above on that decade. Likewise, no information on officers was discovered for fall 1946 through the summer of 1949, except that in February 1948 Ledyard Stebbins sent out a meeting announcement and membership list suggesting that he served in this capacity in 1947/48. Perhaps he was Secretary for the period 1946/47 through 1948/49 (as well as earlier). The following compilation starts with the academic year 1949/50. Figure 3 was taken on the occasion of a belated 40th anniversary meeting in May, 1978. Of the ten Secretaries serving between then and 1957/58, nine are shown plus Stebbins.

In preparing this account of officers, I have become impressed with how poor unaided personal memories can be. Moreover, suppositions with sufficient repetition can become viewed as "facts." For the benefit of future researchers, note that one source of confusion comes from the organization adhering roughly to an academic calendar. Decisions were usually made in May regarding the

FIGURE 3. Ten Secretaries of the Biosystematists assembled for a belated 40th anniversary celebration, Botanical Gardens University of California, Berkeley, 9 May 1978. Left to right: Robert Ornduff, G. Ledyard Stebbins, Ned K. Johnson, William Z. Lidicker, Jr., George F. Papenfuss, Howell V. Daly, Jr., Seth B. Benson, Nancy Vivrette, Jerry A. Powell, William A. Clemens. Photo by Perry Mulleany; courtesy of N. Vivrette (Haller).

leadership for the next academic year, and sometimes documents listing officers do not make it explicit that they are for the *next* year. Also summer intervals are sometimes covered by the out-going officers and sometimes by the new ones. In at least one year, the new officers did not take over until early December.

In the following tabulation, names are given in full only the first time the person is mentioned; thereafter only family names are used. Note how the titles of the various positions change over time. Since there were no written rules, changes came easily. Even after a formal set of organizational rules was adopted in 1986, it was followed only until the autumn of 1993; a new format was adopted in 1995. As noted, major changes in the organization's structure and philosophy occurred in 1998.

Officers: 1949 to 2000 (by academic years)

1949/50 to 1956/57 (8 years) — Secretary: Robert L. Usinger
1957/58 to 1959/60 (3 years) — Secretary: Seth B. Benson
1960/61 — Secretary: Paul D. Hurd, Jr.
1961/62 to 1962/63 (2 years) — No information, but, by interpolation, Hurd was likely Secretary.
1963/64 — Secretary: Hurd
    Membership Committee (this committee was also charged with appointing the Secretary so served as an executive committee): Alden H. Miller (Chairman), William. M. Hiesey, George E. Lindsay, Charles M. Rick, Usinger
    Committee on Organization (this *ad hoc* committee gave its report in April; it consisted of an eight-point resolution): Ruben A. Stirton (Chairman), Benson, Hurd, John M. Tucker, Ira L. Wiggins

1964/65 to 1965/66 (2 years) — Secretary: Hurd. I assume that the Membership Committee continued. There is some evidence that in the second of these years, the Secretarial duties were shared among Hurd, Usinger, and John A. Chemsak.
1966/67 — Secretary: Ned K. Johnson
    Executive Committee — Usinger (Chairman), Lindsay, Rick, Wiggins
1967/68 — Secretary: Robert Ornduff
    Executive Committee — Lindsay (Chairman), probably Rick and Wiggins cont. (Usinger died in 1968)
1968/69 — Secretary: Howell V. Daly
    Executive Committee: Lindsay resigned 30 Oct. 1968 and was replaced as Chairman by Hurd; Wiggins, Rick (Ornduff and Johnson may have been added later in the year).
1969/70 — Secretary: William Z. Lidicker, Jr.
    Executive Committee: Hurd (Chairman), Lindsay, Herman T. Spieth, Wiggins (Rick seems to have been acting as Chairman on 19 May 1970, possibly as Hurd resigned to go to the Smithsonian Institution about this time.)
1970/71 — Secretary: Johnson
    Executive Committee: Lincoln Constance (Chairman), Lindsay, Spieth, Wiggins (A note was found that this committee also served as the membership committee which it probably did since its inception in 1966.)
1971/72 — Secretary: Johnson continued until early December when William A. Clemens took over.
    Executive Committee: Constance (Chairman), Lindsay, Spieth, Wiggins
    Membership Committee: Lindsay, Spieth, Wiggins (Note: This is the only year until 1985 when separate Membership and Executive committees were formed.)
1972/73 — Secretary: Clemens
    Executive Committee: Constance (Chair), Lindsay, Spieth, Wiggins
    Membership Committee: no information; probably combined with Executive Committee
1973/74 — Secretary: Clemens continued into the Fall (with assistance from Constance), but was then replaced by Jerry A. Powell (assisted in the Spring by Chemsak)
    Executive Committee: Evert I. Schlinger (Chair), Lidicker, Tucker, William N. Eschmeyer, and a fifth position for someone from Stanford was unfilled
    Membership Committee: no further mention of this committee was found until 1985, so presumably its duties were reassumed by the Executive Committee
1974/75 — Secretary: Powell
    Executive Committee: Schlinger (Chair), Lidicker, Tucker, Eschmeyer, John H. Thomas
1975/76 — Secretary: Nancy Vivrette
    Executive Committee: Schlinger (Chair), Lidicker, no record of others (probably also Thomas)
1976/77 — Secretary: Vivrette
    Executive Committee: Schlinger (Chair), Lidicker, Thomas
1977/78 — Secretary: George F. Papenfuss
    Executive Committee: cont.
1978/79 to 1979/80 (2 years) — Secretary: Joseph T. Gregory
    Executive Committee: cont.
1980/81 to 1984/85 (5 years) — Secretary: G. Ledyard Stebbins (except that during Dec. through March of 81/82 Schlinger and Lidicker substituted for Stebbins)
    Executive Committee: cont.
1985/86 — Secretary: Stebbins
    Executive Committee: cont.
    Council: A "Plan for the Future" of the organization was drafted by the Executive Committee and adopted in the Spring. It called for an 8-person Council and a Membership Committee which were established as follows: Council — Schlinger (prob. Chair), Lidicker, Thomas, Stebbins,

O. Ray Collins, David H. Kavanaugh, Kevin Padian, John Hafernik; Membership Committee: Thomas (Chair), Lidicker (Chair as of May 1986), Padian

By 10 April 1986, Barbara Ertter was functioning as the Treasurer/Recording Secretary.

1986/87 — Program Chair: Collins
Council: Thomas (Chair), Ertter (Recording Secretary), Lidicker, Collins, Padian, Kavanaugh, Hafernik, Rick
Membership Committee: Lidicker (Chair), Padian, Thomas

1987/88 — All officers continuing except that Padian became Chair of the Membership Committee

1988/89 — Program Chair: Thomas
Council: Thomas (Chair), Ertter (Recording Secretary), Daphne Fautin, Hafernik, Lidicker, Padian, Collins, Rick
Membership Committee: Padian (Chair), Hafernik, Rick

1989/90 — Program Chair: Thomas cont.
Council: Padian (Chair), Thomas, Ertter (Membership Secretary), Fautin, Hafernik, Rick, Powell, Donald R. Kaplan
Membership Committee: Hafernik (Chair), Padian, Rick, Powell

1990/91 — Program Chair: Thomas cont.
Council: Padian (Chair), Ertter (Membership Secretary), Thomas, Hafernik, Tomio Iwamoto, Kaplan, Powell, Rick
Membership Committee: Hafernik (Chair), Powell, Rick

1991/92 — Program Chairperson: Padian
Council: Kaplan (Chair), Ertter (Membership Secretary), Hafernik, Iwamoto, Powell Thomas, Padian, Grady L. Webster
Membership Committee: Powell (Chair), Hafernik, Iwamoto, Thomas, Webster

1992/93 — Program Chair: Charles Quibell
Council: Kaplan (Chair), Ertter (Membership Secretary), Hafernik, Iwamoto, Powell, Quibell, Thomas, Webster
Membership Committee: cont.

1993/94 — Program Chair: Quibell cont.
Council: cont.
Membership Committee: Powell (Chair), no other members recorded; abolished mid-year

1994/95 — Program Committee: Michael T. Ghiselin, Lidicker, Brent D. Mishler
Social Chairman: Quibell, assisted by Lidicker
Executive Committee: Kaplan (Chair), Harold W. Kerster (Recording Secretary), Quibell, Lidicker, Ghiselin, Mishler. In February 1995, Mishler's suggestion for changing to only three officers was adopted.

1995/96 to 1996/97 (two years) — Program Chair: Ghiselin (with assistance from Mishler and Lidicker)
Social Chair: Lidicker
Corresponding Secretary/Treasurer: Kerster

1997/98 — Program Chair: Mishler
Social Chair: Ghiselin
Secretary/Treasurer: Kerster

1998/99 — Program Committee: Marty Wojciechowski (Chair), Peter Fritsch, Kelly Steele, Dennis Wall
Social Chair: Ghiselin
Secretary/ Treasurer: Kerster

1999/2000 — Program Chair: Mishler
Social Chair: Wojciechowski
Secretary/Treasurer: Kerster

EPILOGUE

I hope this document will inspire an appreciation for what the Biosystematists has contributed to progress in evolutionary biology as well as to the personal enhancement of the lives and careers of its members. It has also been an interesting experiment in the sociology of science. That the Biosystematists has operated at the forefront of evolutionary biology in the broadest sense is perhaps obvious from its membership. Its key role in the development and elaboration of the evolutionary synthesis has been emphasized (see also Smocovitis, 1997). However, an examination of the table of contents in any modern textbook of evolution (see Futuyma, 1998 as a good example) reveals the complete correspondence between these subjects and the interests and contributions of Biosystematist members. A perusal of the literature cited in the Futuyma text finds the publications of at least 39 members, not counting those of their former students.

Perhaps this essay will also trigger the discovery of new information that can help to fill the many gaps remaining in this history. The material on which it is based will be deposited in the archives at the California Academy of Sciences and also posted on the Biosystematists' web page (http://ucjeps.herb.berkeley.edu/bryolab/babs).

ACKNOWLEDGMENTS

In addition to the 17 long-term members who provided valuable information and insights listed above, I am grateful to the following persons who contributed data, important leads to information, and/or encouragement: Richard Beidleman, Oliver Pergams, Frank Pitelka, Betty Smocovitis, David Wake, and Marty Wojciechowski.

Librarians at the archives of Stanford University and the California Academy of Sciences, and at the BioSciences Library in Berkeley were most cordial and helpful.

Alan Leviton, O. P. Pearson, and Nancy Vivrette each kindly contributed a photograph.

Helpful reviews of earlier versions of this manuscript were provided by A. Leviton, L. N. Lidicker, F. A. Pitelka, V. B. Smocovitis, and B. R. Stein, and I am grateful to them for their important contributions.

LITERATURE CITED

BAKER, H. B. 1932. *The Atlantic Rift and its Meaning*. Privately published (106 copies), 305 pp.
CAMP, W. H. and C. L. Gilly. 1943. The structure and origin of species. *Brittonia* 4: 323–385.
DIETRICH, M. R. 1995. Richard Goldschmidt's heresies and the evolutionary synthesis. *Journal of the History of Biology* 28:431–461.
FUTUYMA, D. J. 1998. *Evolutionary Biology*, 3rd ed. Sinauer Assoc., Sutherland, Mass. 810 pp.
MAYR, E. 1997. Goldschmidt and the evolutionary synthesis: a response. *Journal of the History of Biology* 30:31–33.
SMOCOVITIS, V. B. 1994. Organizing evolution: founding the society for the study of evolution (1939–1950). *Journal of the History of Biology* 27:241–309.
SMOCOVITIS, V. B. 1997. G. Ledyard Stebbins, Jr. and the evolutionary synthesis (1924–1950). *American Journal of Botany* 84:1625–1637.
USINGER, R. L. 1972. *Robert Leslie Usinger: An Autobiography of an Entomologist*. Pacific Coast Entomological Society, California Academy of Sciences, San Francisco. 330 pp.

Copyright ©2000 by the California Academy of Sciences
Golden Gate Park, San Francisco, California 94118, USA.
All rights reserved.

Scientific Research versus Public Exhibits
A Schizophrenic Aspect of Natural History Museums

GIOVANNI PINNA
Museo Civico di Storia Naturale
Corso Venezia 55, 20121 Milan, Italy
E-mail:jjpin@iol.it

That which I am going to discuss is based above all on my knowledge of European museums, knowledge acquired in the years I served as Director of the Museum of Natural History in Milan, and following that, as President of the Italian Committee of the International Council of Museums.

At least in Europe, the natural history museums have for some time been concerned with an economic and productive crisis that has its roots in a crisis of identity and that as far as concerns the major institutions increasingly gives rise to a type of "schizophrenia." The first signs of this crisis appeared in the 1970s, when the policies of the Conservative English government compelled the Natural History Museum of London to review their economic strategies, and beyond that, their relationship with the public. This was done with the aim of augmenting their drastically reduced income. The strategy pursued by the London museum became one of transforming exhibits so as to attract the greatest possible number of paying visitors. A further strategy was to expand the space devoted to commercial activity, such as the bookshop, gift shop, cafeteria, and so on. This inevitably led to a reduction in the incisiveness of the museum's activities in education and cultural outreach and at the same time to an increase in the entertainment aspect of natural sciences. The more spectacular results of this strategy have been (1) the destruction of certain exhibits of great scientific and educational interest, such as exhibits dedicated to mammalian fossils, and replacing them with a "bazaar" for children's toys, and (2) the creation of exhibits such as one based on a "robot dinosaur," in which the aspect of an entertaining spectacle prevails over cultural and scientific content.

All this did not take place without polemics. In 1989 and 1990, the English press attacked the management of the museum, which, on the one hand, had decided to diminish funding for research, while on the other had decided to send a delegation of exhibit staff to Disneyland to study the means of communication in use in that amusement park.

What happened to the London museum shows that when faced with economic difficulties, natural history museums immediately debate their scientific role, and do not succeed in facing such difficulties without renouncing their identity as cultural institutions. This is due both (1) to the fact that, in the majority of the more advanced nations, the cultural content of the natural sciences has been minimized, and (2) to the schizophrenia from which most natural museums suffer, a schizophrenia evident in the separation of (a) their role as a scientific research center, and (b) their role in cultural transmission.

During the last twenty years, the major natural history museums all over the world have pursued a policy of separation between scientific activity and activity in cultural transmission. These museums, then, have entrusted each of these aspects to different staff within the bounds of the museums, staff who, in many cases, rarely speak amongst themselves. In extreme cases, it has come to a point where the creation of the museum's permanent exhibits — which are the most powerful instrument of cultural transmission for the museum — has been entrusted to organizations outside the museum itself. By creation I mean not only the architectonic or graphic design, but also the selection and the disposition of its contents. This happened, for example, at the American Museum of Natural History, which chose to entrust the creation of part of its own paleontology exhibits to the organization of Ralph Appelbaum (1997), which specializes in creations for every type of museum, and operates in many museums outside of Europe. The consequence of such a choice is that the real scientific culture of each museum rarely enters into the exhibitions and so rarely gets transmitted to the public. The exhibits lose, then, their originality, and every museum becomes just like every other museum. I believe that the most striking example of this separation between the scientific product of the museum, and that which the museum dispenses to the public, is the Grande Galérie de l'Evolution of the Muséum National d'Histoire Naturelle in Paris. There, the scientific culture accumulated by the museum in the field of evolution during the past hundred years that separate Buffon from Gaudry is relegated to small glass cases on the top floor of the gallery (Laissus, 1995).

If the exhibits of a museum do not convey the culture of that museum, it is quite probable that they do not convey any culture at all. The Grande Galérie just cited provides some general information that concerns the theme of biodiversity. This is a theme that the museums of natural history adopted following the Rio de Janeiro conference in 1992; they believed that this might be able to provide a strategy fit to escape from the "cul de sac" into which the separation between scientific production and cultural diffusion had inevitably taken them. They did so, however, in the belief that they could do so without being compelled to correct the underlying problem. The reuniting of the functions of scientific research and cultural diffusion (and, that is to say, of the intellectual organization and construction of the exhibits and the production in general of the explanatory material that accompanies these exhibits) is, in fact, strongly opposed. It is opposed both by the curators of the museum, who retain the function of cultural transmission belittling of their role as researchers, and by museum personnel involved in the exhibits, who fear losing their jobs and their power. Finally, firms specializing in the creation of exhibits also oppose it, since they fear losing interesting contracts.

The theme of biodiversity had the function of reintroducing both the role of the collections and the scientific aspects of the museums of natural history, areas that were both benefiting from the always-minimal consideration of the public and the donors and funding agencies. There was always more consideration given the didactic aspect of the museums of natural history, and there was a question, therefore, as to what the reasons were for maintaining their costly organizations of conservation and scientific research. As the museum came to be identified with its exhibits and solely with its didactic functions, it was able to construct an excellent institution without a scientific research structure and collections; this was realized, for example, some years back in Munich.

For various reasons, the theme of biodiversity has not provided appreciable results (Pinna, 1997), in the return of the scientific role of natural history museums. Above all, that is because this theme was treated as no more than a new name for an old function of the natural history museums, museums that were created and grew for almost three centuries on the basis of the necessity for documentating the biodiversity that was increasing side by side with a growth in geographic and scientific research. This failure has made it clear that the dichotomy between scientific research and cultural diffusion has become today more acute. It has also made it clear that there is an increasingly marked separation between what the museum produces culturally and scientifically, and what it displays to the public in its exhibits. Ahead of high-level scientific research, that which comes provided to the public in the exhibits is an image of nature and natural sciences that is quite general, and, if one makes an exception for material concerning the protection of the environment, an image that is not at all problematic. The scientific culture presented in the halls of the natural history museums is not an adult culture, and does not correspond to scientific thought. Therefore, it should not surprise us if such institutions are considered more and more to be museums for children, the mission of which ends up being no more than to supplement the school.

The most recent example comes from the new Technology Museum in San Jose, opened to the public on 31 October 1998, the puerile content of which has been criticized in the *San Francisco Chronicle* of October 30, 1998.

Today the museums of natural history rarely ask themselves if their role ought to exceed the confines of pedagogical didacticism. They also rarely ask themselves if they should assume a higher role, that of disseminating scientific thought at the level of the "big questions" and not at the level of "notions," thus becoming a tool for the meeting of the two aforementioned cultures. Not pondering these questions, the natural history museums do not even pay attention to the problem of how to disseminate the culture of science itself.

As regards the diffusion of scientific culture, one cannot deny that the majority of museums of natural history are the last refuge of "Positivism." Many museums are positivist in the very placement of the natural objects in the exhibits, effected through successive systematic steps. The majority of the museums are positivist because they deny the importance of historical process in the learning of science, and have thus suppressed the history of the exhibits themselves. Once more, there is the example of the Grande Galérie de l'Evolution in the Paris museum, about which Michael Ruse in his volume *Monad to Man* (1996 Harvard University Press) says "you are guided on a trail from life's earliest forms to our own species." But there are also examples in all those museums which have adopted the cladistic as method for exhibiting of the phylogenesis of diverse organic groups.

I still agree to this day with the anonymous editorial in the journal *Nature* ("Cladistics and evolution on display," *Nature*, 1981, 292:395–396), published in response to the polemics stirred up by the cladistic exhibits created by the British Museum (Natural History) on the dinosaurs (1979) and on evolution of man (1980). This editorial put in doubt the validity of the cladistic as a method for presenting evolution to the public. I maintain that in fact cladistics in its extreme form is able to reconstruct the phylogenesis of a group, but is not able to explain it. In other words, I maintain that it can not be used in museum exhibits to recount the history of life, insofar as it constitutes only the first step of an historical reconstruction; it does not respond to the question of where, how, and why, a given fact has appended.

For the museums to become instruments for the diffusion of scientific thought, it is not enough to find the modalities of expression; it is indispensable that they also acquire the capacity to elaborate in a critical manner all that concerns science, and to display its results to the public. They should also abandon, for example, all the sensationalism typical of other types of media. To give one example, museums should no longer present any more the "cosmic catastrophe that destroyed the dinosaurs" to the public, nourishing the recourse to the catastrophic, the supernatural, and the miraculous in the explanation of natural phenomena. The museums should not present such concepts unless they themselves are scientifically convinced that such hypotheses might be worthy of being proposed.

A critical analysis that precedes the exhibits is possible only if the museums possess a scientific research structure, and if such a structure organizes directly, or collaborates fully, in the construction of the exhibits. If this is done, the schizophrenia of the natural history museums will be overcome, through the melding of their scientific role with their educational role. In addition, two important results will be achieved concerning the goals of the future development of these institutions: the justification of the existence of costly research organizations within the museums, and a higher role in the diffusion of scientific thought.

If, on the contrary, the museums try to overcome their economic difficulties by reducing the scientific content in what they present to the public, and by making the attractions more spectacular, they will act exactly like commercial television, giving the public what the public wants, and not contributing to the cultural growth of society.

BIBLIOGRAPHY

ANONYMOUS. 1981. Cladistics and evolution on display. *Nature* 292:395–396.
APPLEBAUM, R. 1997. Progettare il museo del XXI secolo. American Museum of Natural History. Pages 236–242 *in* Basso Peressut L., ed., *Stanze della Meraviglia*. Clueb, Bologna (Italy).
HALSTEAD, L. B. 1980. Museums of errors. *Nature* 288:208.
LAISSUS, Y. 1955. *Le Muséum national d'Histoire naturelle*. Gallimard, Paris (France).
PINNA, G. 1997. *Fondamenti Teorici per un Museo di Storia Naturale*. Jaca Book, Milan (Italy).
RUSE, M. 1996. *Monad to Man*. Harvard University Press, Camrbidge, Massachusetts.

Copyright ©2000 by the California Academy of Sciences
Golden Gate Park, San Francisco, California 94118, USA.
All rights reserved.

A Philosophy for Natural History Museums

GIOVANNI PINNA
Museo Civico di Storia Naturale
Corso Venezia 55, 20121 Milan, Italy
E-mail:jjpin@iol.it

During history there was a precise sequence of events that brought about the progressive evolution of the institution that today, thanks to the spirit of the French Revolution, is called the "natural history museum."

Born in the Renaissance as an eclectic place for the preservation of natural curiosities, it was open to a few particularly curious friends of the prince or of wise collectors. It developed in the XVIIth century as a place aimed at accumulating indispensable material for the study of natural history, open only to science lovers. In the XVIIIth century, through the deep European Revolution, the museum of natural history became a place for research, study and public education at the same time. It could be visited not only by scholars, but also by the general populous. Once the fires of the French revolution had been appeased, it took on the shape and functions that it would keep for more than one and a half centuries.

These are the shape and the functions of the modern museum which, by means of the accumulation of collections, are dedicated on the one hand to research on nature and its laws, and on the other hand to the spreading of scientific culture and of science's achievements. For one and a half centuries, the natural history museum developed a scientific and a social vocation in parallel and fostered the spreading of an awareness of science's achievements in the societies where these museums operated. These were the museums until the development of contemporary society, that is until the development of a *modus vivendi* shared by the whole industrialized western world, dominated by an economy based on rapid changes that actually denies immediate productivity and that tends to consider long-term productive structures, such as public institutions dedicated to society's cultural growth, as economically unsustainable.

The undoubted success the museum had until the second half of this century is due to the sublime mix that this kind of institution created between sacred and profane, between scientific vocation and social vocation, a mix that took the shape of a very simple formula: to join the social and scientific roles within the same people.

The joining of the two roles within the same people allowed the museum to promulgate the same scientific ideas it produced, without limiting itself, as school education does, to the illustration of scientific achievements carried out by others, in other places. Those who were in charge of scientific research in the museum had, at the same time, the task to promulgate the results of such research. The actions of scientific research and of scientific communication, therefore, became two subsequent stages of the same process, not separated by any discontinuity. This made every museum an individual cultural subject: each museum was different from every other, and each museum was the interpreter of the society that set it up and that allowed its survival and activity.

Until a few years ago, the public exhibits of museums of natural history, expressing their different scientific cultures, were inspired by the awareness of their own cultural specificity and by the need of museum scientists themselves to maintain relationships with the public and, in particular, to operate in the exhibition halls. Hence, for example, the comparative anatomy and paleontology exhibit of the Muséum National d'Histoire Naturelle of Paris, produced in the second half of last century, mirrored

Albert Gaudry's idea of concatenation of the animal world; the equine evolution exhibit carried out at the beginning of this century by the American Museum of New York mirrored Henry Fairfield Osborn's orthogenetic ideas; and, more recently, the dinosaurs exhibit carried out between the 70s and the 80s at the Natural History Museum of London mirrored the cladistic vision that at that time was a dominant idea among many paleontologists of the London museum.

Today things are changing. In the last few years, we have witnessed the separation of the scientific role from the educational and social roles of many museums. In the exhibition halls of these institutes, it is not the museum's specialists who speak with the public but anonymous teams specialized in the setting up exhibits and in so-called museum didactics. Museums delegated the relationship with the public, that is their social role, to people who were alien to the museum's culture, while the culturally productive portion of the museum enclosed itself within an "ivory tower" that was dedicated to pure research and not aimed at the social spreading of ideas and discoveries. Since those teams that are specialized in exhibition didactics have to adjust to a general pattern that, as such, does not have its own cultural identity, the museum loses its culture for the benefit of this general pattern. As a final result, concerning the relationships of a museum with its public, museums have lost their individuality.

The outcome is disappointing. The exhibits and cultural spreading modalities of the natural history museums are becoming stereotypes, nearly always identical, often repetitive, and lacking individuality and representivity. Therefore, what now distinguishes the exhibits of a Japanese museum from an American, German or French museum is not content, which should mirror different cultural backgrounds, but only the language of the texts that accompany the exhibited materials.

I believe that the reason for the present political and social weaknesses of science museums lies in this separation of roles that has led to the loss of each museum's individual culture. This is dangerous because it leads to financial and, therefore, cultural weakness as well.

By delegating cultural communication actions to teams alien to a museum's culture, museums inevitably took on a trivial educational function, the one that could be carried out by external teams, which lack a defining original culture of their own. Natural history museums, having abdicated their primary role of disseminating scientific ideas, culturally isolated themselves; they did not participate, as did other museum typologies, in the cultural growth of the societies in which they operated, thus deepening the gap between scientific and humanistic cultures.

All this is proven by the transformation of most of the museums of natural history. Over time they neglected an adult public and became almost exclusively places for schoolchildren. For this reason, their cultural incidence within society grew weaker. Thus, many came to face economic difficulties that led to a further weakened their scientific research potential and forced them to turn into small Disneylands to make up for lost revenue. And this, in turn, led to a further weakening of their cultural potential.

Today natural history museums are realizing that the weakening of their cultural presence within society inevitably leads to economic impoverishment and, as a result, to a decrease in their scientific production. But instead of carrying out a policy based on the reinsertion of their scientific culture into society, they devise policies that, in my opinion, will most probably not be successful. In other words, they play all their cards on the renewal of what has always been the fundamental role of scientific museums, that is to gather and preserve nature record for descendants and for science. This ancient role has been called "global inventory of biodiversity," and it has been stated that it represents an entirely new function for scientific museums, worthy as such to be financed by governments.

Beyond the undoubted value of a global inventory of biodiversity, the idea of basing the importance and, therefore, the future existence of scientific museums on a topical function, born together with the museums themselves at least three hundred years ago, is, in my opinion, not only trivial, but also dangerous. The idea that museums seem only recently to have discovered, by emphasizing biodiversity, their role as nature's archives is equivalent to denying the scientific and cultural bases of the museum itself and to denying that in the past the scientific museum played any role in the investigation of the world and nature. It is, in fact, equivalent to denying the history of the museum itself.

It is not by emphasizing the study of biodiversity, that is by emphasizing a purely scientific aspect, that natural history museums can reassume their cultural role; this will take place only by reinserting the museum into society, by elevating the museum's social role. But what is the museum's social role about? As Kristozof Pomian (1987) states, it is certain that the collections or single objects preserved by museums are symbols, or metaphors, able to link the real world with its own space and time to the world they come from or that they represent that which has different space and time, and is therefore invisible in the real world. Therefore, the museum, containing and showing these objects and collections, becomes the place where communication between real and invisible takes place, a link between those who observe the objects and what the objects represent. Now, since society gives objects a collective symbolic meaning, museums become places where society can establish a relationship with the objects and their collective meanings. They are, thus, places where society can connect with its own history, its own artistic or scientific production capability, its own economic or political power, that is with all that represents the nature, the roots and the culture of that society.

The idea that the museum's role is, above all, that of being an identification object, therefore providing society with cohesion (role), is neither new nor original. In France, where the cultural bases of this idea lie on the Revolution, this idea has since long been widely dealt with (the chapter "The state as a mediator of national memory" in Jean-Michel Leniaud's book [1992] is revealing). Therefore, the museum's social role is represented by its capacity to represent society by means of the meaning of its own collections; the more important the meaning given to the objects preserved in the museum, the greater the museum's ability to be the mediator of social and cultural cohesion, this independently of the typology, the size, and the importance of the museum, and of the size, the wealth and the degree of social development of the community. Whether societies are aware of it or not, this social role is the museum's main function. It justifies its existence, its status as a public institution; it justified its birth in the past; it prevents its destruction; and, today, it justifies the creation of new museums in all communities of the world.

The role of identification object played both by the cultural heritage and by the institutions preserving and exploiting such heritage is fundamental to every society. No society survives the loss of its own heritage of history, art or science, since such loss corresponds to collective memory's oblivion, which in its turn changes society from a set of individuals sharing the same heritage into a set of isolated individuals. This is a breaking-down or fragmentation process that is well known to conquerors, for whom a conquest was total and final only through sack aimed at destruction, removal or at least scattering of the cultural heritage of the people to be subjugated.

By gathering and preserving objects proving the history, tradition, art, scientific knowledge, glory, and power of the peoples in other words all that defines a society's or a nation's essence museums are, therefore, institutions where the society or the nation finds an aggregation and identification point. But the identification relationship between a museum and society is not automatically created; it is not certain that each museum is or continues to be an identification object for all its life only because it exists.

I believe that each museum has its own threshold, that could be called "identification threshold," below which the museum is not representative anymore, its contents and activity do not correspond to society's aspirations anymore, so that it loses every value as an identification object and is erased from the collective memory. Well, I believe that the museum performs its social role only if its activity and contents are within the identification threshold, that is if it represents society not only in its historical structure, but also and foremost in its cultural aspirations. Now, since each society's culture evolves exponentially, that is the faster it evolves the higher its historical evolution degree, the maintenance of the threshold, that is of the museum's social role, is possible only if culture advances faster than the society to which it belongs. This can happen only if the museum is a primary culture producer, that is if it has the capability to ascribe a meaning to those objects that are part of its collections.

It is in fact through cultural production, that is through research on those objects constituting the museum's essence, that the museum itself gives objects their symbolic and evocative value, that metaphorical value that Stephen Greenblatt (1995) called the object's resonance, meaning *"the power of the exhibited object to overcome its own formal boundaries in order to take on a wider importance, thus evoking in the observer the complex and dynamic cultural forces it arose from and of which the observer can consider it a representative sample."*

Even though there are people who state that objects have a metaphorical value only because they belong to a museum's collections or because they are exhibited in a museum's hall, by means of what has been called the "museum effect," I believe that objects do not originally bear any symbolic value. In order for objects or collections to take on a metaphorical value, that is to become objects of identification for the society, by turning into a set of goods able to act as intermediaries between a community and its history and its culture usually called cultural heritage they must be absorbed by society, society must make them its own. To this aim it is necessary that objects and collections are subject to a re-elaboration attributing them, together with a material value, an immaterial or ideological value. This means that such objects must be placed in a precise location within an interpretation of history, of political, of cultural or of scientific development of the society producing them (or having taken possession of them), which can be carried out by the museum only if it operates culturally and scientifically on these objects.

Yet, the process of attribution of meanings that bestow a collective value upon the objects and to the collection is not easy. A society is not, in fact, a static reality, but it is an evolving reality; such evolution, which can take place through the most different factors such as technological progress, growth of economic welfare, or size of immigration flows, leads to a continuous modification of the relationship between society itself and its cultural heritage and to the creation of ever new cultural patterns. In order for a museum to keep its social role of society's identification place, its cultural heritage that is objects or collections needs to evolve over time, not just by increasing in number, because in this case its metaphorical value would be static, but by changing and enriching its meaning. This can be carried out only if the museum's scientific activity is a true cultural production creating new meanings and new cultural patterns able to be part of the society's cultural heritage.

As far as the relationship between a society and its own heritage is concerned, the role of creation of meanings is delicate, because, if cultural patterns are useful for the society's progress, the museum must precede society in the creation of meanings. This can take place if the museum is able to interpret not simply society's momentary shape, but its aspirations.

The relationship between the museum as an operating structure and its own collections is, therefore, different from the relationship between society and its own cultural heritage and precedes it in time. Whereas, in fact, the relationship between museum and objects is a symbolic- and cultural-pattern construction process, that is a scientific relationship for the creation of meanings, the relationship between society and heritage is a non-creative process of meaning absorption. All this must be borne in mind in the recovery and preservation process of the heritage and in the cultural spreading carried out by the museum.

As far as heritage recovery is concerned, basically two actions are carried out by the museum. It recovers from public propriety collections bearing an historical value and recovers new materials for, or thanks to, scientific research. The two kinds of collections deriving from these actions are not fundamentally different in their social, scientific, and cultural aims. In the natural sciences, old and new collections can have an almost identical scientific value, whereas from the social and cultural point of view, both historical collections and new collections resulting from scientific research bear a meaning of identification objects; the former because their history makes them symbols *de facto*, the latter because scientific research itself fills them with meanings, and, therefore, they are, potentially, future symbols. This means that each collection entering a museum sooner or later becomes part of society's historical and cultural heritage.

But the scientific ascription of meanings to collections is not sufficient to turn a museum into an object aimed at representing and identifying society, thus fulfilling its social function. In order to do this, the museum must spread the meanings it attributes to the objects belonging to its own heritage by the means at its disposal, that is especially through its own exhibits. From this standpoint, museums' exhibits take on a meaning that is significantly different from the mere display of materials; they become exhibits of physical objects and meanings at the same time. Thus, because it is the museum itself that attributes meanings to the objects, by means of a specific scientific processing of the objects themselves, it is clear that museums each will have to exhibit the meanings and ideas it drew up, that is, each museum will have to exhibit its own culture.

From what has been said up to now, we can draw an important general conclusion, one that I partly anticipated at the beginning of my presentation. If we want museums to play their social role of society-identification-object, each museum must take a step back and own and widespread its culture, its individuality, its "sense." Hence each museum once again will have to be different from every other museum in its contents, actions, and exhibits and will, therefore, have to set aside many if not all of the museum-universal-pattern homogeneities that have emerged over the past few decades.

REFERENCES

GREENBLATT, S. 1995. Risonanza e meraviglia. Pages 27–45 *in* I. Karp and S. D. Lavine, eds., *Culture in mostra. Poetiche e politiche dell'allestimento museale*. Clueb, Bologna (Italy).
LENIAUD, J.-M. 1992. *L'utopie Française. Essai sur le patrimoine*. Editions Mengès, Paris (France).
POMIAN, K. 1987. *Collectioneurs, amateurs et curieux. Paris, Venise: XVI–XVIII siècle*. Gallimard, Paris (France).

The Ranks and the Names of Species and Higher Taxa, or A Dangerous Inertia of the Language of Natural History

ALESSANDRO MINELLI
Dipartimento di Biologia
Università di Padova, Via Trieste 75
I 35121 Padova, Italy
E-mail: almin@civ.bio.unipd.it

Despite widespread contrary belief, biological nomenclature is not independent from taxonomy. An uncritical use of the Linnaean hierarchy and of the binomial nomenclature has made strong disservice to biological systematics. Uniformity of nomenclatural treatment has often concealed fundamental problems both in grouping less inclusive taxa together and in assigning ranks to taxa. For example, not all living beings belong to biological species and within the provisions of the International Code of Zoological Nomenclature there is no place for them. The ranks credited to supraspecific taxa are unjustified, despite recent efforts to overcome subjectivity in ranking. Indeed, the existence of categorial ranks stimulates spurious comparisons between entities assigned to the same rank but not otherwise comparable. Comparisons are made, e.g., in stratigraphy, ecology and biogeography, among simple lists of taxa whose comparability is taken for granted. Much of statistics involving numbers of species (or, still worse, higher taxa) must be looked at very cautiously. The advent of phylogenetic systematics is increasingly asking for a phylogenetic system of biological nomenclature. I believe that time is ripe for the development of a new phylogenetic nomenclature, but I do not think that it should and could fully replace the current Linnaean nomenclature, that will always appeal to many users. The main problem to solve will be, how to arrange the future relationships between the names to be used for the phylogenetic system and those surviving for the Linnaean classification.

Key words: biological nomenclature, arbitrariness of taxa, phylogeny, species, taxonomic ranks

Adanson and Linnaeus

En admetant des Espèces, il faudra nécessairement admettre, que ce qui constitue l'Espèce dans un regne, ne la constitue pas dans un autre; & que ce qui sufit pour la décider dans le Regne minéral, ne sufit pas pour cela dans les 2 autres Regnes; car l'Espèce est un terme abstrait, dont la chose n'existe qu'en considérant dans certains êtres, la durée ou la succession des tems; dans d'autres, la constance dans la géneration; dans d'autres, le nombre ou la collection, la ressemblance &tc. des individus: c'est ainsi que la succession dans la multiplication constituera l'Espèce dans les animaux constants qui ont les deux sexes tandis qu'ele deviendra inutile dans ceux dont l'Espèce chanje, ou dans les Afrodites qui n'ont pas de sexe, & dans lesquels elle est décodée

---

[1] If one recognizes species, one is forced to admit that what is a species in one kingdom is not necessarily the same thing in another; and what is enough to distinguish species in the mineral kingdom is not enough in the remaining two; because species is an abstract term: the corresponding object, in some instances, is recognizable with regard to duration or succession of times, in other cases with regard to the constancy in generation; in still others, to the number of relationships or similarity etc. among individuals. In this way, continuity through multiplication will determine species in those animals which breed true through the two sexes, but it will become useless in those where species is changing, or among the sex-less Aphrodites, where species is only determined by number or similarity of habitus; these same qualities, together with constancy, determine species among stones, where there is no succession of generation.

par le nombre ou la ressemblance de figure, come ces 2 qualités les décident, avec la durée, dans les pieres où la succession n'a pas lieu. (Adanson, 1763, I: clxvii).[1]

Michel Adanson, one of the most sensible theorists of systematic biology in pre-evolutionary times, was perfectly aware of the heterogeneous nature of the objects called species by naturalists although these were all uniformly christened by Linnaean binomens. No wonder, especially if we remark that in the times of Linnaeus and Adanson the binomial nomenclature, and the species concept under its umbrella, were commonly applied not just to living beings but also to the representatives of the third kingdom, the minerals. What is more astonishing, and positively worrying, instead, is the fact that what was quite clear two centuries ago is currently disregarded today.

Adanson was also well aware of the arbitrary nature of higher taxa. Deliberate target of his sharp attacks was of course Linnaeus, who, in his *Philosophia Botanica*, had stated that "Omnia genera & species naturales esse, confirmant revelata, inventa, observata. Genus omne est naturale, in primordio tale creatum, hinc pro lubito & secundum cujusdem theoriam non protervè discindendum aut conglutinandum."[2] (Linnaeus, 1751:100)

Adanson sadly remarked that Linnaeus's stance had been supported by several botanists, but on what foundations? "Je ne sai coments ni ceux ni aucun Botaniste poura soutenir une Tèse aussi générale; ce qu'il i a de certain, c'est que jusqu'à présent persone n'a pu le prouver, ni doner une définition juste du Genre naturel, mais suelement de l'artificiel."[3] (Adanson, 1763, I:cv)

To be sure, Adanson was all but alone in his views. Buffon, for example, had very clearly stated that "il n'existe réelemant dans la nature, que des Individus & les Genres, les Ordres & les Classes n'existent que dans notre imagination."[4] (Buffon, 1753:38)

More than two centuries later, we can only observe that the current uncritical use of the Linnaean hierarchy and of the binomial nomenclature have made, in the long run, a strong disservice to biological systematics. Uniformity of nomenclatural treatment has all too often concealed our fundamental problems both in grouping less inclusive taxa together and in assigning ranks to taxa. These problems were emerging in the scientific literature of the late XVIII and early XIX century but still too often remain outside the understanding and, especially, the practice of researchers.

Is Nomenclature Truly Independent from Taxonomy?

Stevens (1994:488) has recently remarked that "Biological nomenclature is supposed to deal with names alone, not with concepts, but historical examples show how wrong this idea can be." Purely nomenclatural arguments, indeed, are much less common than we think, "but the concepts brought to bear in such arguments are diverse. Species concepts are only one set of them, and possibly not even the most important. The whole systematic discipline, what systematists should do, and how the discipline should be organised, may also be at issue." (Stevens, 1991:166).

In the Preamble of the International Code of Zoological Nomenclature, the statement that "The objects of the Code are to promote stability and universality in the scientific names of animals and to ensure that the name of each taxon is unique and distinct" is immediately followed by the bold assertion that "All its provisions and recommendations are subservient to those ends and none restrict

---

[2] Revelation, observation and thought confirm that all genera and species are natural. All genera are natural, and have been created as such since the beginning of time, therefore one shall neither split or lump them arbitrarily or follow personal theory.

[3] I cannot imagine how those botanists, or any other, will be able to subscribe to such a general proposition. What is certain is, that nobody until now has been able to demonstrate it, or to provide a satisfactory definition of the natural genus, but only of the artificial one.

[4] In nature there is nothing but individuals: genera, orders and classes exist in our imagination only.

the freedom of taxonomic thought or action." (International Commission on Zoological Nomenclature, 1999:2). In this respect, the International Code of Botanical Nomenclature is less explicit. In its Preamble we read, indeed, that "the purpose of giving a name to a taxonomic group is not to indicate its characters or history, but to supply a means of referring to it." However, the final words of the same sentence acknowledge a link of taxonomy and nomenclature, in so far as names are also given to indicate the taxonomic rank of the groups (Greuter et al., 1994:1).

The mutual independence of taxonomy and nomenclature is a certainly desirable goal, but it is probably unattainable (Minelli, 1995).

Let us start with the species.

Species

Within the provisions of the International Code of Zoological Nomenclature, there is no place for animals not obviously belonging to species. On this topic I published the following remarks in the *Bulletin of Zoological Nomenclature*, the official journal of the International Commission on Zoological Nomenclature:

> Take, for instance, hybrids. Until recently, natural hybrids were regarded as a peculiarity of the plant world, their very rare occurrence among animals being so exceptional, as to be better ignored from the viewpoint of nomenclature. As for artificial hybrids, these could always be described as such, by listing together the names of the parental species, thus obtaining a more definitive nomenclatural treatment than the still uncertain names we use for some domestic animals (Groves, 1995). However, our traditional view of natural animal hybrids has changed as a consequence of the progress of cytogenetics, more recently complemented by biochemical and molecular studies. There are, naturally occurring, many hybrid forms which are at least as stable and well-circumscribed as many conventional species. In terms of nomenclature, these forms are often denoted by formulae, rather than by Linnean names, but there is no universality of attitude towards them. Echelle (1990a, b), for instance, argues that the 'non-Mendelian species' of hybridogenetic fishes and reptiles should be treated, from the point of view of nomenclature, as the usual 'Mendelian' species.
>
> Beside hybridogens, there are several other classes of uniparentally reproducing animals (and plants) which are usually given conventional species names. They are quietly listed in catalogues, or keyed out in monographs, in a way not different from that for the other named 'species'. The potential dangers of this uniform taxonomic treatment (Minelli, 1993) is hardly lessened by the fact that these uniparental 'species' are sometimes called — in some groups at least — agamospecies or microspecies, rather than species. According to several authorities (e.g. Dobzhansky, 1937; Mayr, 1969; Hull, 1980; Ghiselin, 1987), however, these organisms *do not form species*. If we agree with this view, how can we accept that they are named as if they *are* species? (Minelli, 1995:304).

Examples of unease with these 'microspecies' are not rare in the literature, botanical in particular. For example, Harper & Hawksworth (1995) remarked that the 242 species of *Hieracium* and 234 species of *Taraxacum* listed in Lid's (1952) flora of Norway are indicators of taxonomic traditions rather than descriptors of biological diversity.

There is also the other face of the coin, namely, big differences in the subjective taxonomic treatment, hence in nomenclature, of one and the same object. These differences are clearly perceived by the so-called users of nomenclature. According to Heywood (1991:54),

> What does provoke strong reaction from conservation workers is when there is great diversity of treatment in the literature, both taxonomic and nomenclatural, for the same plant or animal

group. This has been particularly acute in Europe where for historical reasons different countries may often treat the same plant at different ranks — form, variety, race, subspecies, species, species aggregate, or even hybrid between two species — and with an array of different nomenclature at each rank. The usage of the categories [. . .] varies so greatly from author to author as to render them meaningless for the purposes of comparison or generalization. In Europe, the varieties of Fiori may even equate with the species of Coste. And even politics come into the matter: the reason for the absence of infraspecific categories in the Flora USSR is as much due to the adoption of dialectical materialism as a philosophy as to any scientific judgement.

When Vernon Heywood presented these views before a lively group of botanists and zoologists in Kew, he elicited the immediate reaction of Peter Stevens, who remarked that "we must either develop a coherent theory of systematics at the species level and obtain agreement that way, or if that is impossible there needs to be a consensus agreement that species-level taxa in many cases do not mean much" (Stevens 1991:57).

A perusal of the scientific literature gives ample evidence that the taxonomic identity and status of the organisms we deal with are not always adequately conveyed by Linnaean binomens: "Formulae where a generic name is followed by an accession number or a locality name are not at all rare in papers dealing with molecular systematics or cytogenetics of some critical species groups. In many cases, the use of formulae rather than formal species names is not an expression of contempt towards traditional systematics and nomenclature, but the confessed perception that not everything in the living world does fit into our traditional taxonomic schemes." (Minelli, 1995:305)

Problems are particularly acute with fossils. Smith's (1994:17ff) "firm conviction is that fossil species are established on incomplete information and represent groups whose boundaries arise because of the practical limitation faced by systematists, not because of any inherent phylogenetic indivisibility of such units. [. . .] Minimal morphologically diagnosable groups in the fossil record therefore comprise a mixture of basal monophyletic taxa (species) and plesiomorphic grades awaiting additional information or higher resolution studies (metaspecies). [. . .] [C]ladistic analysis is required to establish which phena are monophyletic taxa (species) and which are grades (metaspecies). Although all phena should be named, there should be some convention by which species taxa are differentiated from metaspecies grades in the Linnaean hierarchy. [. . .] The widely held conflation of taxonomists' phena with biological species and thus 'individuals' has led to species duration being perceived as having particular importance. However, since phena in the fossil record belong to one of three distinct kind of groups (single populations, monophyletic taxa, and metataxa) they cannot be considered commensurate entities. Furthermore, the term 'species' is simply a tag of taxonomic convention for a level of inclusiveness that is determined by the systematist's ability (or preferences) and the resolution allowed by available morphological data." In spite of that, speculations and even calculations based on estimating the "duration of life" of fossil species continue to fill the literature."

Another problem with the uniform nomenclature applied to "species" of Recent and fossil organisms has been raised by Sheldon (1993:20): "The main descriptive biases [in] the perception of evolutionary patterns [derives from] the requirement to apply binomial taxonomy (sic) to fossils as well as living organisms. Linnaean names, particularly when plotted as vertical bars in stratigraphic range charts, cannot but give an impression of abrupt transition between discrete, static species."

With the time passing, the simple and convenient practice of naming species and genera seems to have gained such an importance, that concepts have to be looked for, in order to justify the nomenclatural practice. Literally, we witness sometimes, rather than an effort to establish a convenient nomenclature to convey theoretically sound concepts, a deliberate effort to establish concepts to justify continuing use of a traditional nomenclature (see below).

Higher Taxa and Their Rank

It is matter of taste to decide whether the opinions of contemporary systematists are more diverse as far as the nature and concept(s) of species, or the nature and concept(s) of supraspecific taxa; and the two problems might be not so different as tradition would suggest, if even they are not simply one and the same problem (e.g., Nelson, 1989, 1994; Cracraft, 1992).

Quite often, these basic problems of biological systematics have been a cause of schizophrenia in the minds of good researchers, their theoretical sensitivity inviting them to challenge tradition, their day-after-day practice, on the contrary, running towards an uncritical levelling of taxa traditionally treated in a nomenclaturally uniform way.

Alphonse de Candolle, for instance, commenting on species limits in *Quercus* adopted the position that all taxa were conceptually equivalent (de Candolle, 1862:231–233; cf. La Vergata, 1987). However, in a later letter to Bentham recently referred to by Stevens (1991) de Candolle seems to have agreed that species, genus and family rank are real, being somehow recognisable through "physiological" tests: good species do not interbreed and members of different families cannot be effectively grafted.

Let's briefly look at some modern efforts to find ontological justification to supraspecific taxa.

Some authors equated higher taxa with clusters of species sharing a more or less extensive set of adaptations to a specific environment. Inger (1958), for instance, defined the genus as a collection of strictly related species occupying the same adaptive zone. This view has been most vigorously championed by Simpson (1961:222):

> Most higher taxa involve some basic adaptation that evolves coevally with the taxon itself, that is, at the base of what later becomes a higher taxon, or with more or less parallelism among its early lineages. [. . .] Such origins of higher taxa by basic adaptation usually occur when there is a shift from one fairly distinct adaptive zone to another. The eventual rank of the taxon thus initiated is usually proportional to the degree of distinction of the [adaptive] zone entered, hence the amount of basic divergence involved, and to its scope or number of subzones and niches, hence the opportunities for diversification within it. Among the vertebrates the shift from the aquatic to the terrestrial zones involved great basic divergence and also entrance into a very broad, extremely varied zone. Several classes, dozens of orders, and many thousands of species eventuated. In the rodents, bats, and whales [. . .] an order eventuated in each case. The rank eventually achieved is not, however, a necessary function of the kind of adaptation involved. For example, gnawing adaptation similar to that of the rodents has occurred within several other orders (for example, marsupials, primates, various ungulates) but with less initial divergence and subsequent diversification so that in those groups it gave rise only to taxa around the rank of family or even genus.

Even within this Simpsonian concept of taxa, however, things were not so easy. Schaefer (1976:2), for instance, acknowledged that "it seems not likely that higher categories can be made equivalent even in related groups. I do not think the reasons are obscure. For there to be bases for establishing equivalence, there need to be some common criteria: either common adaptations to the same or different environments, or perhaps different adaptations to the same environment. Family-groups with the same adaptations to the same environment are ipso facto not different family-groups, if by 'same adaptations' we mean genetically the same."

There are several reasons, however, why a high rank has been given to a taxon. Smith (1988, 1994) identified the following five:

1. high categorial rank as a topological consequence of a group achieving considerable diversity;
2. high categorial rank as a topological consequence of perceived morphological distinctiveness;
3. high categorial rank as a result of sister-group relationships;
4. high taxonomic rank given to a paraphyletic ancestral group after abstraction of a number of well defined monophyletic groups;
5. high categorial rank given because of ignorance.

This last point is particularly interesting, especially as regards the highest taxa, namely, phyla, or kingdoms. The natural sciences inherited from folk taxonomy a basic split between the plant and the animal kingdom. Accordingly, there was no reason to look for homologous parts among representatives of these two worlds. Cuvier narrowed further the possible scope of comparative morphology, when he established his four *embranchements* (Vertebrates, Articulates, Molluscs and Radiates), each of them corresponding to a basically unique body plan, hardly comparable to those of the other *embranchements*. The higher taxa, called phyla in our current classifications, are simply the heirs of this Cuvierian tradition. Their number is increased to two or three dozen phyla, but these higher (or highest) taxa are implicitly perceived as so basically distinct from all other taxa of the same rank (whatever this expression may mean), as not to require any further effort to homologize their features with those of organisms classified in other phyla (Minelli, 1993). This feeling is still with us, despite the recent explosion of papers dealing with phylogenetic relationships between phyla and kingdoms.

The fact is, that most modern approaches avoid, or rather ignore, the traditional but everlasting problems of homology of organs and apparatuses, because of the reliance on molecular sequence data, rather than to morphology, and on algorithmical clustering techniques that circumvent the painstaking comparison of cell types, patterns of innervation, and the like. But, alas, there is always the chance of creating a new phylum, when it comes to fitting into the system of living beings something unconventional like *Nanalorycus mysticus*, the first-named of the Loricifera (Kristensen, 1983), or *Symbion pandora*, the first-named and to-date only representative of the Cycliophora, discovered five years ago (Funch & Kristensen, 1995). This point, that introducing a new phylum is, in a sense, a way of acknowledging our problems with identifying the affinities of a species, or a group of species, was stressed by Simon Conway Morris (1995) in the *Nature* Commentary that accompanied the description of the first cycliophoran. In the same vein we can explain why so many weird Cambrian creatures were accommodated in high taxa of their own, for example in distinct arthropod classes, before the morphological disparity of these taxa was reinterpreted in more sober terms (Briggs et al., 1992; Wills et al., 1994).

If supraspecific taxa are just the product of our arbitrary grouping and ranking procedures, most extraordinary appear the recent efforts of Dubois (1988). Looking for some *a posteriori* justification of the century long tradition of recognizing genera, he is faced with conflicting evidence from different groups of animals. Having established that two species must be placed in the same genus if they can be crossed to produce adult F₁ hybrids, irrespective of whether these hybrids are fertile or not, the French herpetologist goes on remarking that the vast majority of viable adult hybrids obtained in amphibians derive from pairs of species traditionally placed in the same genus, the only two known exceptions being one between a species in *Hyla* and one in *Pseudacris*, the other between species in *Pleurodeles* and *Tylototriton* respectively. In these two instances, he would therefore be inclined to regard *Hyla* and *Pseudacris* as subgenera (of *Hyla*) and similarly for *Pleurodeles* and *Tylototriton* (as subgenera of *Pleurodeles*). In his view, this taxonomic decision would help clarifying the phylogenetic relationships of these groups. He remarks, however, that things would be quite different in bony fishes, birds and mammals, where "intergeneric" hybrids are much more numerous. In these groups, uniting the "genera" involved in the production of hybrids would probably require uniting also families and other high-level taxa, to avoid suprageneric taxa remaining monogeneric, or nearly so!

The subjectivity of rank assignment, however, has been stressed over and over during these last two centuries. Interesting, in this context, is the reaction of Louis Agassiz to Strickland's recommendation to adopt an uniform ending *-idae* for all family names and, similarly, the ending *-inae* for all subfamilies. Agassiz (in Jardine, 1858:clxxxv; cf. La Vergata, 1987:197) pointed to the fact that "il n'y a pas deux naturalistes qui délimitent les familles de la même manière [. . .] vous voyez à chaque instant une division changer de rang aux yeux des naturalistes."[5]

Recent efforts to overcome the subjectivity in ranking higher taxa are those of Van Valen (1973), Hennig (1966) and Sibley and Ahlquist (1990). These efforts have failed, but are worthy of a little comment here. Van Valen (1973) discussed several possible standards of comparisons between, say, families of mammals and families of birds, including number of species or genera included, number of individuals, or biomass, or energy flow, represented at any one time by the members of each family, phenotypic diversity, genotypic diversity, ease of hybridisation among taxa, phylogenies (i.e. time of divergence, or average number of branching, or other measure of phylogenetic relationship), and 'adaptive diversity'. No wonder, Van Valen discarded in turn all these approaches, as unsuitable to offer a reasonable standard for absolute ranking. He developed instead what he called a 'metataxonomic' criterion, based on the structure of the classification itself. He argued that taxa ranked at intermediate levels between the species and the class should be proportionately spaced, so that their size (in terms of included species) would form a geometric series. By consequence, the average size of an order, a family, or a genus would depend on the size of the class to which the order, family, or genus belongs. The artificiality of this approach has been obviously criticised (Levinton, 1988; Minelli, 1993).

Hennig (1966) toyed for a while with the idea to correlate the rank of a monophyletic group with the age of its branching from the sister group, but this idea had little following until it was revived by Sibley (e.g., Sibley & Ahlquist, 1990). The new feature, in Sibley's work, is the vast amount of age estimates he has derived, for bird suprageneric taxa, from an extensive programme of DNA-DNA hybridization.

In a phylogenetic perspective, however, a taxon's formal rank is indicative of its relative level of inclusiveness only (Hennig, 1966; Smith, 1994). Absolute ranks are a myth. A dangerous myth, indeed.

The Taxic Approach

De Queiroz and Donoghue (1988:334) have aptly remarked that the existence of categorial ranks "encourages spurious comparisons between entities assigned to the same rank but that are not otherwise comparable." More drastic is Willmann (1988:901):

> Neontologists as well as palaeontologists have been trapped by one aspect of the current classification of organisms, namely the ranking of taxa. Following Linné, the neontologists used to deal with ranks such as orders, suborders, classes etc. Essential in ranking is the extent of the differences between the (recent members of) the groups. Fossils have often narrowed these gaps,

---

[5] No two naturalists circumscribe the families in the same way [. .] you steadily see groups changing their rank in the naturalists' eyes.

and according to the theory of evolution originally no such gap ever existed. The categorial ranks, however, remained. From this resulted the problem of the origin of 'classes' and 'orders'. There are however no 'orders' or 'classes', 'genera', 'families' or 'suborders' as real units of Nature, these are artificial mental constructs dating from pre-evolutionary times. They are of no use in modern biology, mere anachronisms, not even necessary for the systematization of life. [...] It thus seems medieval when Stanley wrote as late as 1978 (p. 36): "if genera typically arise by quantum speciation" [...] "then families, orders, and classes must arise in the same manner, normally by several discrete steps."

Indeed, the literature is replete with comparative studies relying on the so-called taxic approach. That means, that comparisons are made, either in stratigraphy, or in ecology, biogeography and other sciences, among simple lists of taxa whose comparability is taken for granted.

Much of statistics involving species numbers must be looked at very cautiously and even, sometimes, rejected outright as nonsense:

We are seldom ready to vigorously react, as we indeed should do, when somebody tells us that the named fossil species are, say, one in 10 000 of the cumulative number of species the Earth has generated since primeval past. This 1:10 000 ratio is just a ratio between the size of an actual list of names and the size of another, potential list. However, these two lists would deal with two different kinds of objects, not to say of the objections we could easily raise as to the nature, or the homogeneity, of the objects within each one of them.

In the face of such current examples of scientific nonsense, I do not need to develop much theoretical argument. There is, however, the need to stress, that such big slippings are made enormously easier by a less than critical attitude towards biological nomenclature. We cannot exceedingly blame the users of nomenclature for adding apples and cherries so far as we, the producers of taxonomy and taxonomic nomenclature, ruthlessly conceal this amazing and still problematic diversity of objects and concepts under the quiet veil of one and the same kind of names (Linnean binomina). (Minelli, 1995:305)

Higher taxa, too, are too often taken seriously, for statistical purposes:

an ideal index of biodiversity ought perhaps to be obtained [...] asking first the biggest question about diversity, "How many kingdoms are represented on a site?", then "How many phyla are represented per kingdom?", "How many orders per phylum?", and so on. There is sufficient logic in this suggestion to elicit a wringing of hands and even apoplexy from those who might have to apply it. (Harper and Hawksworth, 1995:9)

The basic problems with the taxic approach have been aptly summarised by Smith: "[The taxic approach] has to make two important assumptions about the taxa it uses. Firstly it assumes that the taxa used are real, not some arbitrary convention of taxonomists, and that their appearances and disappearances represent real biological events; secondly, it assumes that taxa of equal rank are approximately equivalent entities across diverse clades. Ultimately, therefore, the reliability of the taxic approach stands or falls on the validity of the taxa used as its primary data. [...] Traditional databases are riddled with nonmonophyletic groupings that arise solely because of *ad hoc* taxonomic practice and have no claim to biological reality, and taxonomic rank has always been assigned arbitrarily." (Smith, 1994:3) Again: "a number of taxic approaches rely on rank equivalence among taxa. Families, for example, are assumed to represent equivalent entities, and variation in the number of phena included is seen as having biological significance. But rank has meaning only within a single hierarchical scheme and can be only vaguely comparable among clades, due to the inconsistencies of taxonomic usage. The fact that families become richer in phena through time (Valentine, 1969;

Sepkoski, 1984; Flessa and Jablonski, 1985) is more a comment on how taxonomists, as a community, have gone about their business than about evolutionary process." (Smith, 1994:155)

In front of this basic problem of rank equivalence, the additional problems caused by the widespread nonmonophyletic nature of many taxa comprised in comparative papers following the taxic approach seems to be relatively minor. Nevertheless, this is also a severe bias damaging a lot of papers, including many recent ones. Convincing examples are those provided by Patterson and Smith. In Smith's (1994:79–80) summary, "The vast taxonomic database that we have inherited from the systematic endeavours of the past 200 years comprises a chaotic mixture of monophyletic, paraphyletic, polyphyletic, and monotypic taxa, and the work of transforming this into a consistent set of monophyletic taxa has hardly begun. [...] In a review of the taxonomic status of post-Palaeozoic echinoderm and fish families, Smith & Patterson (1988) found that only a third of families (33%) listed in the most up-to-date [at that time] summary of our taxonomic database (Sepkoski, 1982, plus updates) represented demonstrably monophyletic groups. Of the remainder, 14% were paraphyletic and 21% polyphyletic. A further 21% were monotypic and the rest (11%) were non-monophyletic taxa of uncertain status.[...] The frequency of monophyly in generic data was about the same (32%), but paraphyletic genera were more common (23%) and polyphyletic genera less common (7%). Monotypic genera accounted for 12.5% of records and non-monophyletic genera for 7%. The remainder (18%) could not be categorized because of a lack of recent revisionary work."

Are There Solutions to These Problems?

According to James (1991:64), "The way forward is to formally uncouple nomenclature from taxonomic theory" so that a name really becomes "merely a conventional symbol or cipher, which serves as a means of reference." I have already expressed my distrust of the practicality of this approach. I think, instead (see also Härlin, 1998; Härlin and Sundberg, 1998) that we should improve our awareness of the conceptual and linguistic requirements of modern biological systematics, irrespective of their compatibility with traditional nomenclature.

The most severe problems are perhaps those with the plurality of kinds of 'species' — I am not aware of any solution proposed and have none to offer today. Other problems, however, seem to be much more tractable.

The first knot of problems is the taxic approach to biological diversity. The obvious solution is to replace this approach, whenever possible, with a phylogenetic one: in Smith's (1994:190) words, "Since taxonomic rank is arbitrary, the only meaningful approach to taxic diversity is through comparisons of phenon diversity between sister groups (Cracraft, 1984; Novacek and Norell, 1982)." Moreover, we must seriously try to understand the reasons behind the now widespread dissatisfaction with the Linnaean hierarchy (see de Queiroz, 1997). This dissatisfaction is often coupled with the argument that classification, in the traditional sense, is a legitimate, but not necessarily the only, or even the primary, outcome of systematic research. To my knowledge, Griffiths (1974) was the first to argue that a consequential application of the Hennigian phylogenetic principles necessarily leads to the production of a *system* of hierarchically branching monophyletic units. The ontological status of the system is not the same as that of the traditional *classification* (cf. Griffiths, 1974, 1976; Hennig, 1975; Ax, 1984; de Queiroz, 1988; Minelli, 1991). A classification is a set of hierarchically nested subsets, or classes, whereas the system is a whole, of which the branches (from the major ones down to the finest terminal tips) are parts, or parts of parts.

De Queiroz and Gauthier (1990, 1992, 1994) have suggested how to start developing a 'phylogenetic system of biological nomenclature.' Their proposal implies a completely new approach to naming supraspecific taxa. These authors claim that the definition of supraspecific taxon names should follow new rules, without reference to Linnean categories and nomenclatural types (see also Bryant, 1994, 1996, 1997; Cantino et al. 1997; de Queiroz 1992, 1996,1997a, b; Härlin, 1998; Härlin and Sundberg, 1998; Kron, 1997; Lee 1996a, b; Rowe and Gauthier, 1992; Schander, 1998; Schander and Thollesson, 1995; Sundberg & Pleijel, 1994; but also, for contrary views, Brummitt, 1997; Lidén and Oxelman, 1996; Sosef, 1997).

Several people, including Haskell and Morgan (1988), Minelli (1991, 1993, 1995) and Bogan and Spamer (1995), see, either with approval or with anxiety, that current trends in nomenclature could (or should) lead to the development of a 'double nomenclature,' one side being for the phylogenetic system, the other side for the traditional, user-friendly classification.

There are several arguments, indeed, allowing us to hope that the system and the classification may actually enjoy a mutually compatible, if not completely identical, nomenclatural treatment (Minelli, 1991:186):

(1) a system of nested monophyletic units is topologically arranged as a hierarchy, in the same way as a classification;
(2) many monophyletic units within the system are likely to be coextensive with conventional taxa identified as classes, within a classification;
(3) a well-worked system leads to the recognition of a variety of branching levels, but these do not necessarily all need a formal name or even acknowledgement in terms of rank.

Therefore, I believe that system and classification should be developed side by side, in a strictly linked way and with the following provisos:

(1) that we carefully develop a nomenclature suitable to convey the wealth of concepts burgeoning in modern systematics;
(2) that we care, as far as possible, for a mutual compatibility between the names used for the system and those for the classification.

Let's hope that a more widespread awareness of these problems of language and representation will blow some fresh air into a dusty corner of the culture of natural history.

REFERENCES

ADANSON, M. 1763. *Familles des Plantes*. Vincent, Paris.

AX, P. 1984. *Das phylogenetische System*. Gustav Fischer Verlag, Stuttgart & New York.

BOGAN, A. E. and E. E. SPAMER. 1995. Comment on "Towards a harmonized bionomenclature for life on Earth" (Hawksworth et al., 1994). *Bulletin of Zoological Nomenclature* 52:126–136.

BRIGGS, D. E. G., R. A. FORTEY and M. A. WILLS. 1992. Morphological disparity in the Cambrian. *Science* 256:1670–1673.

BRUMMITT, R. K. 1997. Taxonomy vs. cladonomy, a fundamental controversy in biological systematics. *Taxon* 46:723–734.

BRYANT, N. H. 1994. Comments on the phylogenetic definitions of taxon names and conventions regarding the naming of crown clades. *Systematic Biology* 43:124–130.

BRYANT, N. H. 1996. Explicitness, stability, and universality in the phylogenetic definition and usage of taxon names: A case study of the phylogenetic taxonomy of the Carnivora (Mammalia). *Systematic Biology* 45:174–189.

BRYANT, N. H. 1997. Cladistic information in phylogenetic definitions and designated phylogenetic contexts for the use of taxon names. *Biological Journal of the Linnean Society* 62:495–503.

BUFFON, G. L. L. 1753. *Histoire naturelle générale et particulière, avec la description du cabinet du Roi*. Tome 4. Imprimerie royale, Paris.

Cantino, P. D., R. G. Olmstead, and S. J. Wagstaff. 1997. A comparison of phylogenetic nomenclature with the current system: a botanical case study. *Systematic Biology* 46:313–331.
Conway Morris, S. 1995. A new phylum from the lobster's lips. *Nature* 378:661–662.
Cracraft, J. 1984. Conceptual and methodological aspects of the study of evolutionary rates. Pages 95–104 *in* N. Eldredge and S. Stanley, eds., *Living Fossils*. Springer Verlag, New York.
Cracraft, J. 1992. The species of the birds-of-paradise (Paradisaeidae): Applying the phylogenetic species concept to a complex pattern of diversification. *Cladistics* 8:1–43.
De Candolle, A. P. 1862. Étude sur l'espèce à l'occasion d'une révision de la famille des Cupulifères. Suppl. à la Bibliothèque universelle et Revue suisse. *Archives des sciences physiques et naturelles* (2) 15:211–237, 326–365.
De Queiroz, K. 1988. Systematics and the Darwinian revolution. *Philosophy of Science* 55: 238–259.
De Queiroz, K. 1992. Phylogenetic definitions and taxonomic philosophy. *Biology and Philosophy* 7:295–313.
De Queiroz, K. 1996. A phylogenetic approach to biological nomenclature as an alternative to the Linnean systems in current use. *In* J. L. Reveal, ed., *Proceedings of a mini-symposium on Biological Nomenclature in the 21st Century*. University of Maryland, College Park, MD (http://www.life.umd.edu/bees/96sym.html).
De Queiroz, K. 1997a. The Linnean hierarchy and the evolutionization of taxonomy, with emphasis on the problem of nomenclature. *Aliso* 15:125–144.
De Queiroz, K. 1997b. Misunderstandings about the phylogenetic approach to biological nomenclature: a reply to Lidén and Oxelman. *Zoologica Scripta* 26:67–70.
De Queiroz, K., and M. J. Donoghue. 1988. Phylogenetic systematics and the species problem. *Cladistics* 4:317–338.
De Queiroz, K., and J. A. Gauthier. 1990. Phylogeny as a central principle in taxonomy: phylogenetic definitions of taxon names. *Systematic Zoology* 39:307–322.
De Queiroz, K., and J. Gauthier. 1992. Phylogenetic taxonomy. *Annual Review of Ecology and Systematics* 23:449–480.
De Queiroz, K., and J. A. Gauthier. 1994. Toward a phylogenetic system of biological nomenclature. *Trends in Ecology and Evolution* 9:27–31.
Dobzhansky, T. 1937. *Genetics and the origin of species*. Columbia University Press, New York.
Dubois, A., 1988. Le genre en zoologie: essai de systématique théorique. *Mémoires du Muséum national d'Histoire naturelle, Paris, Zoologie*, 139:1–130.
Echelle, A. A. 1990a. In defense of the phylogenetic species concept and the ontological status of hybridogenetic taxa. *Herpetologica* 46:109–113.
Echelle, A. A. 1990b. Nomenclature and non-Mendelian (clonal) vertebrates. *Systematic Zoology* 39:70–78.
Flessa, K. W., and D. Jablonski. 1985. Declining Phanerozoic background extinction rates: effects of taxonomic structure? *Nature* 313:216–218.
Funch, P., and R. M. Kristensen. 1995. Cycliophora is a new phylum with affinities to Entoprocta and Ectoprocta. *Nature* 378:711–714.
Ghiselin, M. T. 1987. Species concepts, individuality, and objectivity. *Biology and Philosophy* 2: 127–143.
Greuter, W., F. R. Barrie, H. M. Burdet, W. G. Chaloner, V. Demoulin, D. L. Hawksworth, P. M. Jørgensen, D. H. Nicolson, P. C. Silva, P. Trehane, and J. McNeill, eds. 1994. International Code of Botanical Nomenclature (Tokyo Code) adopted by the Fifteenth International Botanical Congress, Yokohama, August-September 1993. *Regnum Vegetabile*. 131 pp.
Griffiths, G. C. D. 1974. On the foundations of biological systematics. *Acta Biotheoretica* 23:85–131
Griffiths, G. C. D. 1976. The future of Linnaean nomenclature. *Systematic Zoology* 25:168–173.
Groves, C. P. 1995. On the nomenclature of domestic animals. *Bulletin of Zoological Nomenclature* 52:137–141.
Härlin, M. 1998. Taxonomic names and phylogenetic trees. *Zoologica Scripta* 17: 381–390.
Härlin, M., and P. Sundberg. 1998. Taxonomy and philosophy of names. *Biology and Philosophy* 13:233–244.
Harper, J. L., and D. L. Hawksworth. 1995. Preface. Pages 5–12 *in* D. L. Hawksworth, ed., *Biodiversity Measurement and Estimation*. Chapman & Hall, London.

HASKELL, P. T., and P. J. MORGAN. 1988. User needs in systematics and obstacles to their fullfillment. Pages 399–413 *in* D.L. Hawksworth, ed., *Prospects in Systematics.* Clarendon Press, Oxford.
HENNIG, W. 1966. *Phylogenetic Systematics.* University of Illinois Press, Urbana, Illinois.
HENNIG, W. 1975. "Cladistic analysis or cladistic classification?": a reply to Ernst Mayr. *Systematic Zoology* 25:244–256.
HEYWOOD, V. 1991. Needs for stability of nomenclature in conservation. Pages 53–58 *in* D. L. Hawksworth, ed., *Improving the Stability of Names: Needs and Options.* Koeltz Scientific Books, Königstein.
HULL, D. L. 1980. Individuality and selection. *Annual Review of Ecology and Systematics* 11:311–332.
INGER, R. F. 1958. Comments on the definition of genera. *Evolution* 12:370–384.
INTERNATIONAL COMMISSION ON ZOOLOGICAL NOMENCLATURE. 1999. *International Code of Zoological Nomenclature.* Fourth Edition. International Trust for Zoological Nomenclature, London.
JAMES, P. J. 1991. A view from a teacher. Pages 59–65 *in* D. L. Hawksworth, ed., *Improving the Stability of Names: Needs and Options.* Koeltz Scientific Books, Königstein.
JARDINE, W., ed. 1858. *Memoirs and papers of H. E. Strickland.* J. Van Voorst, London.
KRISTENSEN, R. M. 1983. Loricifera, a new phylum with Aschelminthes characters from the meiobenthos. *Zeitschrift für systematische Zoologie und Evolutionsforschung* 21:163–180.
KRON, K. A. 1997. Exploring alternative systems of classification. *Aliso* 15:105–112.
LA VERGATA, A. 1987. Au nom de l'espèce. Classification et nomenclature au XIX siècle. Pages 193–225 *in* S. Atran et al., eds., *Histoire du Concept d'Espèce dans les Sciences de la Vie.* Fondation Singer-Polignac Paris.
LEE, M. S. Y. 1996a. The phylogenetic approach to biological taxonomy: practical aspects. *Zoologica Scripta* 25:187–190.
LEE, M. S. Y. 1996b. Stability in meaning and content of taxon names: an evaluation of crown-clade definitions. *Proceedings of the Royal Society of London,* Series B, 263:1103–1109.
LEVINTON, J. 1988. *Genetics, Paleontology, and Macroevolution.* Cambridge University Press, Cambridge.
LID, J. 1952. *Norsk Flora.* Norske Samlaget, Oslo.
LIDÉN, M., and B. OXELMAN. 1996. Do we need "phylogenetic taxonomy"? *Zoologica Scripta* 15:183–185.
LINNAEUS, C. 1751. *Philosophia Botanica.* Stockholm, Amsterdam.
MAYR, E. 1969. *Principles of Systematic Zoology.* McGraw-Hill, New York.
MINELLI, A. 1991. Names for the system and names for the classification. Pages 183–189 *in* D. L. Hawksworth, ed., *Improving the Stability of Names: Needs and Options.* Koeltz Scientific Books, Königstein.
MINELLI, A. 1993. *Biological Systematics: The State of the Art.* Chapman & Hall, London.
MINELLI, A. 1995. The changing paradigms of biological systematics: new challenges to the principles and practice of biological nomenclature. *Bulletin of Zoological Nomenclature* 52:303–309.
NELSON, G. J. 1989. Species and taxa. Systematics and evolution. Pages 60–81 *in* D. Otte and J. A. Endler, eds., *Speciation and Its Consequences.* Sinauer Associates, Sunderland, Massachusetts.
NELSON, G. J. 1994. Homology and systematics. Pages 101–149 *in* B. K. Hall, ed., *Homology: The Hierarchical Basis of Comparative Biology.* Academic Press, San Diego–New York–Boston–London–Sydney–Tokyo–Toronto.
NOVACEK, M. J., and M. A. NORELL. 1982. Fossils, phylogenies and taxonomic rates of evolution. *Systematic Zoology* 31:366-375.
ROWE, T., and J. A. GAUTHIER. 1992. Ancestry, paleontology and definition of the name Mammalia. *Systematic Biology* 41:372–378.
SCHAEFER, C. W. 1976. The reality of the higher taxonomic categories. *Zeitschrift für systematische Zoologie und Evolutionsforschung* 14:1–10.
SCHANDER, C. 1998. Mandatory categories and impossible hierarchies — a reply to Sosef. *Taxon* 47:407–410.
SCHANDER, C., and M. THOLLESSON. 1995. Phylogenetic taxonomy — some comments. *Zool. Scripta* 24:263–268.
SEPKOSKI, J. J. 1982. A compendium of fossil marine families. *Milwaukee Public Museum Contribution to Biology and Geology* 4:1–125.

SEPKOSKI, J. J. 1984. A kinetic model of Phanerozoic taxonomic diversity. III. Post-Paleozoic families and mass extinctions. *Paleobiology* 10:246–267.
SHELDON, P. R. 1993. Making sense of microevolutionary pattern. Pages 19–31 *in* D. R. Lees and D. Edwards, eds., *Evolutionary Patterns and Processes*. Academic Press, London.
SIBLEY, Ch. G., and J. E. AHLQUIST. 1990. *Phylogeny and Classification of Birds*. Yale University Press, New Haven-London.
SIMPSON, G. G. 1961. *Principles of Animal Taxonomy*. Columbia University Press, New York.
SMITH, A. B. 1988. Patterns of diversification and extinction in early Palaeozoic echinoderms. *Palaeontology* 31:799–828.
SMITH, A. B. 1994. *Systematics and the Fossil Record*. Blackwell Scientific Publications, Oxford.
SMITH, A. B., and C. PATTERSON. 1988. The influence of taxonomic method on the perception of patterns of evolution. *Evolutionary Biology* 23:127–216.
SOSEF, M. S. M. 1997. Hierarchical models, reticulate evolution and the inevitability of paraphyletic supraspecific taxa. *Taxon* 46:75–85.
STANLEY, S. 1978. Chronospecies' longevities, the origin of genera, and the punctuational model of evolution. *Paleobiology* 4:26–40.
STEVENS, P. F. 1991. George Bentham and the "Kew Rule." Pages 157–168 *in* D. L. Hawksworth, ed., *Improving the stability of Names: Needs and Options*. Koeltz Scientific Books, Königstein.
STEVENS, P. F. 1994. *The Development of Biological Systematics: Antoine-Laurent de Jussieu, Nature, and the Natural System*. Columbia University Press, New York.
SUNDBERG, P., and F. PLEIJEL. 1994. Phylogenetic classifications and the definition of taxon names. *Zoologica Scripta* 23:19–25.
VALENTINE, J. M. 1969. Patterns of taxonomic and ecological structure of the shelf benthos during Phanerozoic times. *Palaeontology* 12:684–709.
VAN VALEN, L. 1973. Are categories in different phyla comparable? *Taxon* 22:333–373.
WILLMANN, R. 1988. Microevolution as the only evolutionary mode. *Eclogae geologicae Helvetiae* 81:895–903
WILLS, M. A., D. E. G. BRIGGS, and R. A. FORTEY. 1994. Disparity as an evolutionary index: a comparison of Cambrian and Recent arthropods. *Paleobiology* 20:93–130.

Index

A

Abrams, LeRoy 238, 244, 320
Academia Scientiarum Imperialis Petropolitana (Petersburg {St. Petersburg}, Russia) 28
Académie Royal des Sciences, Paris 27
Academy of Natural Sciences of Philadelphia 74, 80, 107, 183, 187–188, 191, 199–200, 204, 209, 212, 247
Academy of Science, Literature and Arts (Mantua {Mantova}, Italy); See Accademia di Scienze, Lettere e Arti (Mantua {Mantova}, Italy)
Academy of Useful Sciences; See Erfurt Akademie gemeinütziger Wissenschaften
Accademia del Cimento (Florence) 7
Accademia dell Scienze of Bologna 35
Accademia delle Scienze detta de' Fisiocritici 5–23
Accademia di Scienze, Lettere e Arti (Mantua {Mantova}, Italy) 28–29
Adams, John Quincy (U.S. President) 102–103, 123
Adanson, Michel 339–340
Adey, Walter 151
Agassiz, Alexander 250–254, 256–258, 260–261, 264–266, 301, 308, 313
Agassiz, Louis 87, 97, 99, 108, 112, 114, 124–125, 186, 188, 191, 214–215, 249–250, 252, 256–261, 263–265, 267, 345; Thayer Expedition 87; See also Museu Paraense Emílio Goeldi
Ajuda Museum (Lisbon, Portugal) 82
Alaska 115, 125, 131, 142, 148–150, 156, 201, 231; See also Western Union Telegraph Expedition (1865)
alchemy 39, 41–44, 46–47
Alemão, Francisco Freire 83
Alexander, Annie 244
algae 148, 151
Allen, Joel Asaph 78, 264, 299
American Academy of Arts and Sciences (Boston) 28
American Indian paintings; See Stanley, John Mix
American Museum of Natural History (New York) 92, 96, 123, 235, 301–309, 311, 313, 319, 330, 332, 334; Brazilian expedition 1956 307
American Philosophical Society (Philadelphia) 28, 124, 159, 284, 311, 313
ammonites 144, 306
AMNH; See American Museum of Natural History (New York)
Anancus arvernensis 11
Anderson, John 51, 60, 67, 69–73, 75, 78
Andrews, Roy Chapman 221, 304
anthropology 58, 81, 84–86, 88, 91, 94, 120–121, 125, 171, 181
Arago, Dominique François 103
Archivos do Museu Nacional (publication) 85, 98, 100
Arduino, Giovanni 14, 20
Arduino, Pietro 14
Argentina; See also Patagonia
Aristotelian teleology 41
Arthur, Chester A. (President) 117
Asiatic Society of Bengal (Calcutta, India); See Calcutta (India)

Astronomical Expedition to Chile; See United States Naval Surveys
Audubon, John James 107–108, 123
Axelrod, Daniel Isaac 320

B

Babcock, Ernest B. 200, 241, 246, 320–321
Bache, Alexander Dallas 103
Bacon, Francis 27, 29–30
Baer, Karl Ernst von 276, 284
Baird, Spencer Fullerton 73, 98, 101, 107–109, 112–126, 128–129, 159, 169, 181, 186–188, 190–194, 199–202, 209, 214
Baird, William M. 107–108
Baldacconi, Francesco 17
Baldassarri, Giuseppe 9–15, 18, 23–24
Ball, Valentine 65–66
Bansho-shirabesho; Tokugawa Shogunate center to translate foreign books 166
Bartalini, Biagio 14–15, 17, 21
Bartaloni, Domenico 14
Bassler, Ray Smith 138–139, 142, 144, 148–149
Bastiani, Annibale 13, 24
Bavarian Academy of Sciences; See Churbayeruische Akademie der Wissenschaften
Bay Area Biosystematists 2, 320; See also Biosystematists of the San Francisco Bay Area
Bean, Tarleton H. 118
Beddome, Richard Henry 70, 72
Behr, Hans Hermann 112, 155, 203, 206–207, 211, 220–222, 225–226, 229–231, 241, 245–246
Behrensmeyer, Anna Kay 155
Belém (Brazil) 81, 87, 98–100
bench fees 279; See also Tables
Benson, Richard Hall 151, 155
Benson, Seth Bertram 320, 322, 324
Berdan, Jean Milton 145
Bergquist, Harlan Richard 150
Berkeley, California; See University of California Berkeley
Bernardi, Francesco 18
Bertini, Pellegrino 18
Bessey, Charles E. 219
Beyer, H. G. 118
Bianchi, Giovanni 14
binomial nomenclature 340, 342; See also biological nomenclature
biological nomenclature 339–340, 346–347, 349–350; See also binomial nomenclature
biosystematics 241, 319–320
Biosystematists of the San Francisco Bay Area 2, 315–324, 327; gender barrier 322–323; its founding 318–319; officers 324–326; origin of the name 320
Blackwelder, Blake Winfield 150
Blanford, Henry Francis 65, 67–68
Blanford, William Thomas 65–70, 75; member Napier's Abyssian Expedition 1867 67, 76; travel in Persia (Iran) 1872 67
Bloomer, Hiram G. 221, 227, 247

353

Blyth, Edward 60, 62–63, 76–77, 79–80
Boardman, Richard Stanton 147, 149
Bodega Marine Laboratory 318
Bolander, Henry Nicholas 203, 209, 211, 214, 219, 221–222, 245–247
Boletim do Museum Paraense (publication) 88
Bombay (India); Grant Medical College 52; Victoria and Albert Museum 51
Bonnet, Charles 14
Born, Ignaz von 14
Bose, Pramatha Nath 69
Boston Society of Natural History 258, 261, 266
Botanic Gardens at Sharanpur (India); See Falconer, Hugh
Botanical Gardens 29, 34, 53, 58, 62, 74, 86, 88, 90, 246, 324; See also: Orto Botanico of Brera (Milan, Italy); Calcuttas (India), Royal Botanic Garden; Royal Botanic Garden at Sibpur (India)
Boucot, Arthur James 147–148
Boulenger, George Albert 69–71, 73
Bowsher, Arthur Leroy 149
Boyle, Robert 8, 22, 41, 49
Bradbury, Margaret 323
Brandegee Herbarium 239
Brandegee, Mary Katharine Layne Curran 194–196, 200, 202–203, 220, 224, 235–236, 239–241, 243, 246–247; See also Curran, Mary Katharine Layne
Brandegee, Townshend Stith 194, 196, 202–203, 225, 235, 239–240, 247
Branner, John 238
Brazilian Anthropological Exhibition of 1882 85
Brewer, William Henry 203, 208–213, 216, 218, 222, 237, 245–246
Bridge, Josiah 143, 146
British Association for the Advancement of Science 266, 279, 291
British Court of Chancery 102, 105
British Museum (Natural History) (London, UK) 53, 60, 62, 64, 67, 69–70, 73, 75, 86–87, 93, 166, 179, 251, 253, 258–259, 266–267, 293, 301, 312, 331
Brower, Elisabeth M. 151
Brown, Barnum 302–303
Brown, Roland Wilbur 144
Bryozoa 145, 147–148, 150–151
Buchanan, Francis; See Buchanan-Hamilton, Francis
Buchanan, James (U.S. President) 108, 166
Buchanan-Hamilton, Francis 58–60, 72, 76–78, 108, 166
Bureau of Ethnology 118, 120, 131, 134
Burgess Shale 140, 159
Burlamaque, Frederico Leopoldo Cesar 83
Burling, Lancaster Demorest 142
Burmannus, Johannes 55
Butt-Davy, Joseph 233, 241
Butterflies' Commission; See Comissao Cientificas de Exploraçao
Buzas, Martin Alexander 151–152, 155
Bybell, Laurel Mary 151

C

cabinets; See also naturalistic cabinets
Calcutta (India); Asiatic Society of Bengal 51, 59, 62, 74; Indian Museum 52, 60, 64, 67, 69–70, 72–74, 79; Presidency College 67, 69; Royal Botanic Gardens 55
Calhoun, John C. 101

California 1–2, 21, 25, 36–37, 39, 48–49, 51, 68, 71, 75–76, 80, 90, 100, 126, 144, 147–148, 151, 153, 156, 158–159, 173, 175, 182–202, 203–223, 225–248, 263, 265, 271, 273, 284–285, 288, 300–302, 311, 313, 315–317, 319–321, 324, 327, 332, 337, 351
California Academy of Natural Sciences 183, 187–188, 200, 204, 209, 212, 247; See also California Academy of Sciences
California Academy of Sciences 1, 25, 37, 39, 49, 51, 68, 71, 75–76, 80, 100, 126, 158–159, 182–184, 186–187, 189–191, 194–195, 197–200, 202–203, 215–216, 221–223, 226, 230–231, 237, 242–243, 246–248, 265, 271, 273, 285, 288, 300, 313, 316–317, 319–321, 327, 332, 337, 351; See also California Academy of Natural Sciences
California Botanical Club 235–236
California College of Pharmacy 220
California Institute of Technology (Pasadena, California) 144, 315
California State Agricultural Society 188, 212
California State Geological Survey 59–60, 64–67, 69, 73, 75–79, 86, 103, 112–113, 120, 127, 130–131, 133–140, 142–145, 147–154, 156–158, 166, 184, 188, 203, 208–218, 227, 237
Caluri, Francesco 12–15, 23
Cambrian Period 130, 140, 142, 144, 147, 151, 159, 255, 344, 348, 351
Camp, Charles 320
Campani, Giovanni 9, 16, 18–19, 21
Campbell, Douglas Houghton 237–238
Canada 64, 78, 80, 140, 142, 249, 265
Carboniferous Period 52, 67, 147
Cassin, John 107
Castle, William Ernest 321
Catholic University of Washington, D.C. 234
Cautley, Sir Proby Thomas 62, 64
Cayley, Sir George 103, 123
Cenozoic Era 131–133, 138–139, 142–144, 147–149, 151, 153, 156, 306
Cesar, Frederico Leopoldo 83
Ceylon (Sri Lanka) 55, 57, 70, 72, 77
Chambers, Robert 276, 285
Chamisso Botanical Club 233, 246
Chaney, Ralph Works 320
Chang, Chih Ye 321
Chapin, Steven 102
Charpentier, Wilhelm 14
Cheetham, Alan Herbert 151
Chicago Columbian Exposition 135
China 67, 80, 112, 162, 173
Choate, Rufus (U.S. Senator) 102, 124
Churbayerische Akademie der Wissenschaften (Munich Bavaria) 31
Churchill, Mary (Mrs. Spencer Fullerton Baird) 107–108
Churchill, Sylvester (U.S. Brigadier General) 112
Cifelli, Richard 149
Civil War (United States) 114, 130, 179, 210
Clarke, F. W. 118
Clausen, Jens 315, 319–320, 322
Clemens, William A. 324–325
Cloud, Preston Ercelle 145–149, 153
Cluss, Adolf (architect) 116
coal 35, 55, 60, 64–65, 69, 83, 112, 176
Cobban, William Aubry 146–147
Colbert, Edwin ("Ned") Harris 302–308, 311–313

INDEX

College of Agriculture (California) 218–219, 234–235
College of California 210, 212–213; See also University of California
Collins, O. Ray 326
colonial museums; See museums, colonial
Columbia University (New York) 22, 37, 302, 305–306, 309, 311–312, 319, 349, 351
Columbian College 102
Comissao Cientifica de Exploraçao (at Museu Nacional do Rio de Janeiro) 94
conodonts 146, 148, 150–151, 153
Constance, Lincoln 75, 210, 212, 214, 218–219, 232, 234–235, 241, 245, 317–323, 325
Cooke, Charles Wythe 143
Cooper, Gustav Arthur 144–145, 149–150, 155
Cooper, James Graham 187–188, 192, 209, 214
corals 147
Corcoran Gallery of Art (Washington, DC) 114
Cornell University (Ithaca, New York) 51, 63, 68, 71, 75, 137, 183, 238
Coromandel Coast (India) 55, 60, 79
Cosimo III, Granduke 8
Coues, Elliott 109
Court of Chancery; See British Court of Chancery
Couty, Louis 85
Creationism 262, 276, 283, 285
Cretaceous Period 67, 135, 143–144, 147, 149, 152, 155–156
Crocker, Charles 190, 192, 228
Cronin, Thomas Mark 153
Cuddalore (India); Fort St. David 55
Cummings, W. 321
Curran, Mary Katharine Layne 194–195, 202–205, 220–231, 235, 237, 245–247; See also Brandegee, Mary Katharine Layne Curran
Cushman, Joseph Augustine 147–148; Cushman collection of microfossils 148
Cusick, W. C. 236
Cuvier, Baron Georges 45, 62, 76–77, 258, 260–261, 264, 344
Cuvierian tradition 344
Cycliophora 344, 349

D

Daly, W. M. 70, 317, 324–325
Dana, James Dwight 108, 214, 265–266
Dangerfield, Frederick (East India Company, Captain) 64
Darwin, Charles 1, 39–41, 44–49, 52, 62, 108, 114, 123, 225, 256, 263, 274, 276–277, 284–285, 289–291, 293–296, 298–299; See also evolution
Darwinism 46, 262–263, 275, 282, 284, 289, 291, 293–294, 296, 299
Davidson, George 188, 190–192, 194, 201, 226–227, 231
Day, Francis 58, 72, 77, 80
de Candolle, Alphonse 343
De la Beche, Henry Thomas 65, 67
De-kaicho exhibitions 162–163, 165
Deccan volcanics (India) 67, 80
Deluge (Biblical) 11, 13
Denver, Colorado 135, 147–148, 151–154, 156, 304; See also: Simpson, George Gaylord; U.S. Geological Survey
Derby, Orville Adelbert 89, 91, 95, 99; São Paulo Geographical and Geological Commission 91
Devonian Period 137, 147–148, 151, 255

diatoms 144, 146
Dickinson College (Carlisle, Pennsylvania) 107–108, 123
DiMichele, William Anthony 155
Dobzhansky, Theodosius 315, 319, 322, 341
Dohrn, Anton 2, 48, 273–285, 292–293, 298
Dohrn, Reinhard 282, 284
Downey, John G. (Governor, California) 208–209
Dublin (Ireland); Science and Art Museum 64
Dudley, William Russel 203, 237–238, 244–247, 319
Duncan, Helen Margaret 145
Dunkle, David Hosbrook 148
Dunn, L. C. 319
Dutch East India Company 55
Duthiers, Henri de Lacaze 276, 285
Dutro, Jr., John Thomas 2, 148, 150, 154, 158, 199

E

Earl of Moira; See Lord Hastings
earthquakes 9, 16, 194, 196–199, 228, 240, 242–243; in Tuscany (1798) 16
East India Company 53, 55, 57–60, 62, 64, 72, 74, 79; Court of Directors 53, 57, 59–60, 79
Eastwood, Alice 194–196, 199, 202–203, 230, 236–237, 242–244, 247–248
echinoderms 142, 254, 347, 351
echinoids 143, 149, 152
Edo (= Tokyo, Japan) 161–163, 165, 173, 175, 180
Eigenmann, Rosa Smith; See Smith, Rosa
Elizabeth I 52
Ellenborough, Lord 62; See also Hodgson, Brian Houghton
embryonic recapitulation 276
Emry, Robert John 152
Eocene mammals 303
Erfurt Academy of Useful Sciences; See Erfurt Akademie gemeinnütziger Wissenschaften
Erfurt Akademie gemeinnütziger Wissenschaften 32–33
Ertter, Barbara 1, 317, 326
Erwin, Douglas Hamilton 155
Erythea 233, 245–247
Eschmeyer, William N. 325
ethnology (also ethnography) 59, 77, 86, 89–91, 93–94, 96, 99, 115
Ethnology, Bureau of; See Bureau of Ethnology
Euler, Leonhard 33
evolution 2, 35, 39–41, 43–48, 55, 59, 62, 75, 78, 118, 123, 157, 225, 234, 245, 247, 252–254, 256, 262, 275–276, 281–282, 284–285, 287–289, 291–294, 296, 298–299, 301, 304–305, 309, 311–312, 315–316, 319–323, 327, 330–332, 333–336, 340, 342, 346–347, 349–351; See also Darwinism
Ezo (= Hokkaido Id., Japan) 173–174

F

Falconer, Hugh 62, 64; Botanic Gardens at Sharanpur (India), superintendent of 62
Farragut, David (U.S. Naval Captain) 112
Fautin, Daphne 326
Fayrer, Joseph 72–73, 76–78
Fechner, Gustav Theodor 46
Fedden, Francis 66
Federal territorial surveys; See United States Territorial Surveys of the West

Feistmantel, Ottokar 65, 67
Ferber, Johann Jakob 10, 14, 23
Ferris, Gordon Floyd 320–321
Field, Stephen J. (Justice, California Supreme Court) 207
First Principles 287–288, 294
fishes 12, 45, 49, 52, 58–60, 64, 72–73, 75, 80, 93, 99, 109, 114, 119, 124, 148, 163, 171, 173, 175, 184, 186, 192–193, 200, 204, 224, 240, 249, 254, 262, 264, 275, 277, 292–293, 295, 302, 306, 341, 345, 347
Fleming, Andrew 52, 64, 75, 200
Fontana, Felice 14
Foote, Robert Bruce 66
foraminifers 146–149, 151–153, 155
Forester, Richard Monroe 151
Formey, Samuel 33
Forsyth, John (U.S. Secretary of State) 102
Foshag, William Frederick 149
fossils 5, 9–13, 15–20, 22, 62, 64–65, 86, 93, 108–109, 112, 127–128, 130–131, 133–134, 136–140, 142–144, 146–153, 155–157, 159, 163, 192, 208, 223, 254–256, 258, 262, 301–309, 311, 318, 329, 342, 346, 350; algae 148, 151; ammonites 144, 306; brachiopods 17, 137–138, 144, 147–149, 152–153; bryozoa 145, 147–148, 150–151; Cenozoic 138, 144; conodonts 146, 148, 150–151, 153; corals 147; diatoms 144, 146; echinoids 143, 149, 152; fusulinids 144, 147; gastropods 12, 147–148; insects 137, 155; invertebrates 133, 138, 302, 305–306; mammals 144, 152, 301–304; Mesozoic 131, 301–303; molluscs 13, 17, 93, 143–144; Paleozoic 136, 143; plants 147; reptiles 138, 149, 305–306; Tertiary 150; Triassic 151; trilobites 140, 144, 147, 151
France 7–8, 10, 12–14, 17–18, 23, 27, 29–30, 33, 35, 37, 51, 76, 78, 100, 268, 276, 287, 332, 335, 337
Francis of Lorraine 9
Franklin, Benjamin 28, 103, 106
Frederick I of Prussia 32–33; See also Frederick III of Brandenburg
Frederick III of Brandenburg 32–33
Friedich, Johann 14
Frisi, Paolo 14
Fritsch, Peter 326
Fukushima, Yoshikoto 167, 177, 180; See also Japanese Mission to U.S. (1860)
fusulinids 144, 147

G

Gabb, William More 7–8, 24, 209
Gabbrielli, Pirro Maria 7–8
Gaia hypothesis 46
Gallerani, Venturi 10, 19
Gardner, James Terry 143–144, 146, 148, 210, 265
Gardner, Julia Anna 143–144, 146, 148, 210, 265
Garfield, James (U.S. President) 117
Gaudry, Albert 330, 334
Gazin, Charles Lewis 144–146, 152
Geological Survey of Canada 64, 142
Geological Survey of Great Britain 65
Geological Survey of India 59–60, 64–66, 69, 75–78; See also: Ball, Valentine; Blanford, William Thomas; Bose, Pramatha Nath; Fedden, Francis; Feistmantel, Ottokar; Foote, Robert Bruce; Hacket, C. A.; Lal, Hira; Mallet, Frederic Richard; Medlicott, Henry Benedict; Medlicott, John G.; Museum of Economic Geology; Oldham, Thomas; Singh, Kishan; Singh, Ram; Stoliczka, Ferdinand; Theobald, William; Tween, Ambrose; Waagen, Wilhelm
geology (also geological) 1, 5–6, 10–11, 13, 15, 17–18, 20, 52, 58–60, 64–65, 67, 69, 75–76, 80–81, 83, 98, 100, 105, 113, 118, 128, 130–131, 133, 135, 138–139, 147, 157, 159, 168, 173, 184, 188, 207–208, 212–213, 256, 258, 303, 305–307, 309, 351
George Washington University (Washington, DC) 102
Germany 39, 41–42, 46, 93, 176, 239, 267, 282, 291–292
Ghiselin, Michael T. 1–2, 35, 39–40, 44, 46, 76, 80, 158, 245, 265, 273–274, 279, 283–284, 317, 326, 341
Gibbons, Henry 184, 186, 200
Gibbons, William Peters 186, 200, 205, 213, 216, 219, 231
Gibson, Thomas George 151
Gidley, James William 138, 144
Gilbert, Davies 103
Gilman, Daniel Coit 214–216, 218
Gilmore, Charles Whitney 137–138, 142
Girty, George Herbert 136, 139–140, 142–143, 149
Goeldi, Emílio August 81, 87–89, 93, 95, 97, 99; creating a scientific museum, the Museu Paraense 88; See also Museu Paraense Emílio Goeldi, director of
Goethe, Johann Wolfgang von 39, 41–42, 45–48, 275, 284
Goettingen (Germany); See Göttingen (Germany)
Goldschmidt, Richard Bennedict 315, 320–321, 327
Gondwana System in India 65
Gondwanaland 52, 65
Goode, George Brown 91, 99, 115, 117–118, 120, 123–125, 134
Goodrich, Edwin S. 282
Gordon, Jr., Mackenzie 145
Göttingen Royal Society Society 31; See also Königlich Societät der Wissenschaften (Göttingen, Germany)
Graham, Herbert William 187, 209, 321
Granger, Walter 302
Grant, Richard Evans 152
Gray Herbarium; See Harvard University, Gray Herbarium
Gray, Asa 108, 204, 206–207, 214, 216, 218, 246
Gray, John Edward 42, 58, 60, 69, 71, 73, 108, 204–207, 214, 216, 218, 222, 241, 246, 253–254, 257–260, 264–265
Great Trigonometrical Survey (India) 64–65
Greene, Edward Lee 203, 205, 219–227, 230–235, 237, 240–241, 243, 245, 247
Greenland and Smith's Sound; See Kane, Elisha Kent
Gregory, Joseph Tracy 317, 325
Gregory, William King 123, 146, 302, 317, 325
Grinnell, Joseph 263, 266, 320
Gross, M. Grant 155
Günther, Albert Carl Ludwig Gotthilf 48, 55, 69–70, 73

H

Hacket, C. A. 66
Haeckel, Ernst 39, 46, 48, 275–277, 284, 292
Hafernik, John 326
Hagen, Hermann 249–250, 257, 260–264, 267
Hall of Silent Men (in the U.S. National Museum) 144, 146–147
Hall, Harvey Monroe 241, 245
Hall, James 130

INDEX

Hamilton, Francis 58, 72, 77; See also Buchanan-Hamilton, Francis
Hapsburg (Austrian) government 29, 31, 34–35; attitudes toward science 30
Hardwicke, Thomas (East India Company, Major General) 59–61, 78
Harford, William 220, 231–232, 247
Harris, Anita Gertrude 150
Harvard University (Cambridge, Massachusetts) 98, 103, 108, 114, 123, 137, 188, 202, 204, 214–216, 218, 224, 234, 239, 243, 246, 249–252, 255, 260, 265, 267, 285, 301, 308–309, 331–332; Gray Herbarium 218, 241
Hass, Otto 304
Hass, Wilbert Henry 146
Hastings, Lord (Francis Rowdon) (Governor-General of India) 57, 59, 64, 216
Haupt, Theodor 18
Hawkins, Williams (British Naval Captain) 53
Hayden, Ferdinand Vandiveer 112–113, 131, 235
Hazel, Joseph Ernest 151
Hazel, Joseph Gregory 152
Henbest, Lloyd George 144
Henderson, L. H. 236
Henry, Joseph 48, 53, 65–68, 72, 75, 101, 103–106, 108–109, 112–118, 120, 123–124, 128–130, 137, 146, 152, 159, 166–169, 175–178, 180–181, 184–186, 188, 190, 194, 199–201, 203, 208–209, 214, 216, 221, 247, 274, 302, 311–312, 334; Captain Rodgers' suggestions on treatment of Japanese visitors 166, 180; demonstrations done for visiting Japanese Mission 175–176; invites Japanese Mission to visit Smithsonian Institution 166; wants to impress Japanese with American superiority in science and technology 178
Henshaw, Samuel 257
Herbert, James Dowling (East India Company, Captain) 2, 64, 136, 151, 287–288, 298, 319–320, 322
Hermann, Paul 55
Herre, Albert William Christian Theodore 221, 224–225
Hexaplex conglobatus 12
Hieracium 341
Hiesey, William McKinley 315, 318–320, 324
Hilgard, Eugene Woldemar 219, 232, 234
Hill, Robert Thomas 115, 133, 247, 350
Hitchcock, Romyn 118
Hittell, Theodore Henry 191, 196, 199–207, 209–212, 214–215, 218–219, 221–222, 227–232, 234, 236, 239, 242, 247
Hodgson, Brian Houghton 58, 62–63, 77–78; removed from office in Nepal by Lord Ellenborough 62; See also Nepal
Hoee Building (Washington, DC) 136, 139, 142
Hoffman, Charles F. 209
Holmes, William Henry 118
hologenesis 46
Hooke, Robert 8
Hooker, Sir Joseph Dalton 57, 204, 221, 274, 291, 296, 299
Hornblower, J. D. (architect) 121
Hotton III, Nicholas 149
Hough, Margaret Jean 103, 148
Hough, William Jervis (U.S. Congressman) 103, 148
Howe, Marshall Avery 232–234
Howell, Thomas 236, 317, 324–325
Huber, Brian Thomas 155
Hüber, Jakob 89
Huddle, John Warfield 148

Hueber, Francis Maurice 151
Hunter, John 258, 263
Hurd, Jr., Paul David 322, 324–325
Huxley, Thomas Henry 44, 274, 291–292, 320; See also Imperial School of Science and Technology
hybridogens 341
hybrids 225–226, 341–342, 344–345, 349
Hyla 344
Hylozoism 46

I

Ihering, Hermann von 91–93, 95–97, 99; Museu Paulista, director of 91; São Paulo Geographical and Geological Commission 91; theory on continental bridges 93, 99; views on museum organization and typology 93
Imlay, Ralph Willard 144, 146
Imperial School of Science and Technology 291
India Act 1784 58, 74
Indian Museum Act 1866 60, 69
Indian Museum, Calcutta (India); See Calcutta (India)
inheritance of acquired characters 290–291, 293–299
insects 93, 106, 109, 114, 117, 137, 155, 171, 175, 221, 254, 260–262, 264, 268–271, 276, 292
Institutos Históricos e Geográficos (Brazil) 81
International Code of Zoological Nomenclature 192, 339–341, 350
Iowa Geological Survey 131
Italian wars of independence 18
Italy 1–2, 5–6, 11, 14, 18, 20–21, 24, 27, 273, 275, 329, 332–333, 337, 339
Iwamoto, Tomio 317, 326

J

Jackson, Andrew (U.S. President) 101–102
Jacquemont, Victor 58, 75, 78
Japan 146, 161–163, 166, 173–175, 179–181; Meiji government 162, 179; See also Edo (Tokyo), Kyoto, Nagasaki, Nagoya, Osaka
Japan-U.S. Treaty of Amity and Commerce 161
Japanese Mission to Russia (1866) 179
Japanese Mission to U.S. (1860) 166–167, 173–175, 179, 181; American barbarity evidenced by displays 175; Henry demonstrates electrical devices 175–176; impact of visit to Smithsonian Institution 179–180; invited to visit Smithsonian Institution 166; reactions to Smithsonian's Art Gallery 177; reactions to visit to Smithsonian Institution 167–169, 171, 173–175, 177–178, 180–181, 213, 233, 235
Jefferson, Thomas (U.S. President) 106, 127
Jepson, Willis Linn 203–205, 209, 222–224, 227, 230, 232–233, 235–236, 238, 240–241, 243–245, 247
Jerdon, Thomas Claverhill 63–64, 70, 77–78
Jewett, Charles Coffin 113
John, Christopher Samuel 55
Johns Hopkins University 47, 200, 215
Johnson, Ned K. 323
Jones, J. R. 65
Jones, Marcus E. 59, 65, 122–124, 222–224, 235–236, 246, 266
Jones, Sir William 59, 122–124
Jordan, David Starr 159, 193, 227, 230, 238–239
Jurassic Period 144, 255

K

Karklins, Olgarts 150, 153
Kauffmann, Erle Galen 149
Kaunitz, Wenzel Anton (Austrian Chancellor) 31; See also Hapsburg (Austrian) government
Kavanaugh, David H. 326
Keck, David D. 315, 318–320
Kellogg, Albert 184, 200, 203, 205–206, 211, 214, 219–222, 230–232, 238, 245–246
Kennicott Club of Chicago 320
Kennicott, Robert 109, 112, 115, 320
Kerster, Harold W. 317, 326
Kier, Porter Martin 149
Kimura, Tetsuta 167–169, 173, 177, 180; See also Japanese Mission to U.S. (1860)
King, Clarence 131, 210, 216, 247
King, William 66, 302
Kingdom of Italy 18
Kirby, H. 199, 321
Kirk, Edwin 142
Klein, Jacob 55
Knight, James Brookes 149
Knowlton, Frank Hall 118, 133, 135, 139
Koenig (König), Johann Gerhard 55–56
Kongelige Danske Videnskabernes Selskab (Copenhagen, Denmark) 28
Königliche Preussische Akademie der Wissenschaften (Berlin, Prussia) 28, 33
Königlich Societät der Wissenschaften (Göttingen, Germany) 31
Kowalevsky, A. O. 275–276
Kumlein, Thure 222
Kyd, Robert (East India Company, Lieutenant Colonel) 53, 55–57
Kyoto (Japan) 163

L

La Plata River, U.S. Naval Survey of; See United States Naval Surveys
Labandiera, Conrad Columbus 155
Lacerda, João Batista de 82, 84–86, 96–97; Museu Nacional and his view of an ideal museum 86; Alipio Miranda Ribeiro challenges Lacerda on museum's future 86
Ladd, Harry Stephen 147
Lagrange, Joseph-Louis 33
Lal, Hira 69
Lancaster, Sir James 53, 142
Langley, Samuel Pierpont 120, 140
Lankester, Edwin Ray 287, 291–295, 298, 300
Layard, Edgard Leopold 87, 98
Lea, Isaac 107
LeConte, Joseph 218–219, 232, 238, 247
Leibniz, Gottfried Wilhelm 27, 32–33, 35–37; views on purposes of scientific investigation 32
Lemmon, John Gill 206–207
Leopold II, Granduke 17
Leopold, Granduke Peter 9
Lerner, I. Michael 315
Library of Congress (Washington, DC) 75, 102, 114, 192, 194
Lick, James 188–190, 201, 227
Lidicker, Jr., William Z. 2, 318, 324–327
Lindsay, George Edmund 66, 125, 323–325
Linnaean hierarchy 339–340, 342, 347
Linnaean nomenclature 339, 349; See also binomial nomenclature
Linnaeus, Carolus (Carl von Linné) 14, 47–48, 55, 73, 339–340
Linnean Society 291, 348
Lo Bianco, Salvatore 277–278
Loeblich, Jr., Alfred Richard 148
Lohman, Kenneth Elmo 144, 146, 151
London (UK) 21, 27, 29, 33, 36–37, 45, 48–49, 53, 55, 57–60, 62, 64, 69–73, 75–80, 86, 99, 101–103, 105, 119, 123, 125, 179, 200, 251, 253–254, 258–259, 266–267, 283, 288, 292, 295–296, 301–302, 308, 329, 334, 349–351; See also Royal Society of
Loomis, Leverett Mills 196, 200, 202–203, 243–244
Lori, Georg 31
Loricifera 344, 350
Low, Doris 147
Lowery, Dorothy 323
Lucas, Frederic Augustus 138
Lull, Richard Swann 301

M

Macaly, Nikolai Mikucho 277
Madras (India); Fort St. George 55; Madras Government Museum 51; Madras Literary Society 51
Mallet, Frederic Richard 65–66
Mamay, Sergius Harry 147, 154
mammals 12, 58, 62, 64, 67, 70, 72–73, 77, 85, 93, 107–108, 114, 117, 125, 138, 144, 151–152, 169, 171, 173–175, 249, 254, 262, 264–265, 301–305, 307, 329, 345; Cenozoic 144, 152
Man'en Gannen Mission (1860); See Japanese Mission to U.S. (1860)
Manaus (Brazil) 81, 90–91
Maratha Confederacy (India) 57
Marsh, George Perkins (U.S. Congressman) 102, 108, 116
Marsh, Othniel Charles 133
Mascagni, Paolo 15, 22–23
Mason, Herbert L. 319–321
Mason, Otis T. 118
Matthew, William Diller 112, 161, 181, 302, 311; leaves AMNH for University of California, Berkeley 302
Maupertuis, Pierre-Louis Moreau de 33
Maximilian II of Bavaria 31
Mayr, Ernst 40, 249–252, 255, 265–267, 307–310, 312–313, 315, 319, 341, 350
Mazzi, Gaspero 17
McClellan, George B. (U.S. General) 6–7, 33–34, 112
McClelland, John 58–59, 65, 75
McClintock, Elizabeth B. 245, 322–323
McIllriach, Effie A. 236
McKenna, Malcolm C. 309, 313
McMinn, Howard E. 320–321
MCZ; See Museum of Comparative Zoology, Harvard University
Medici, Cardinal Francesco Maria 8
Medlicott, Henry Benedict 65–66, 75
Medlicott, John G. 65
Meek, Fielding Bradford 113, 127, 130–132, 156–158, 200–201

INDEX

Megatherium Club 109, 112
Meigs, Montgomery C. (U.S. General) 116
Meiji government (Japan); Meiji Restoration 179; See Japan, Meiji government
Mello, James Francis 152
Menlo Park, California 147–148, 151, 153–154, 156
Merriam, Charles Warren 148
Merrill, George Perkins 118, 134, 137–138, 144
Mesozoic Era 67, 118, 131–133, 139, 142, 146, 148, 156, 301–303, 306; mammals 301–303; See also Cretaceous; See also Jurassic; See also Triassic
Mesozoic-Cenozoic boundary 139
Messina (Sicily) 275, 277
metaphysics 41, 43, 45; See also occult metaphysics
metaspecies 342; See also metataxa
metataxa 342, 345
metropolitan museums; See museums, metropolitan
Metschnikoff, Elias 46, 48, 275, 279, 284
Mexican Boundary Survey 112
Mexico 112, 139, 146, 204, 222, 236, 239–240, 246–247
Meyer, Adolf Bernhard 257–260, 265–266
microfossils 16–18, 21, 144, 148, 150, 152–153, 156–157
Milan (Italy) 1, 20–21, 28–30, 32, 34–37, 76, 265, 284, 329, 332–333; See also: Palatine Schools; St. Alexander's Mineralogical Museum; Società Patriotica per l'incremento dell'Agricoltura, delle Arti e delle Manifatture
military geology 146, 148
Military School of Engineering, Rio de Janeiro (Brazil) 84
Miller, Alden 315
Miller, Robert Cunningham 200, 319–321
Mills College (Oakland, California) 320
minerals 5, 9–10, 13–15, 17–21, 24, 34, 41, 65, 74, 80, 82–84, 101, 105–106, 108–109, 112, 114–115, 135, 149, 162–163, 171, 173, 175, 208, 212, 306, 339–340
Miocene 150
Mirov, N. 321
Mishler, Brent D. 317, 326
Mississippian Period 139, 147
Miyazaki, Ryugen 167, 174; See also Japanese Mission to U.S. (1860)
molluscs 13, 17, 67, 91–93, 131, 134, 143–144, 146, 148, 254, 262
Mongolia 304
monophyly 342, 344–348
Monti, Giuseppe 5–6, 22
Moore, Ellen James 148
Moore, John 309
Moore, Justin P. 221
Moore, Keith 154
Morita, Okataro 162, 167, 174, 177, 180; See also Japanese Mission to U.S. (1860)
Morrill Act (1862) 212
Morton, Samuel G. 107–108, 147
Müller, Fritz 46, 276, 284
Müller, Johannes 275
Münchhausen, Adolf von 31
Munich, Academy of Sciences; See Churbayerische Akademie der Wissenschaften
Muragaki, Norimasa (Japanese Vice Ambassador) 161–162, 167–168, 173–175, 177–181; See also Japanese Mission to U.S. (1860)
Murayama, Hakugen 167, 174, 180; See also Japanese Mission to U.S. (1860)
Murray, James 69–70, 72, 80, 123, 295
Museo di Storia Naturale, University of Pavia (Italy) 29

Museu Botânico do Amazonas (Manaus, Brazil) 81, 89–90, 95–96, 98, 100; founded by Barbosa Rodrigues 90
Museu de La Plata (Buenos Aires, Argentina) 86
Museu Nacional do Rio de Janeiro (Brazil) 81–86, 89–91, 93–98, 100; Comissao Científica de Exploraçao 94; institutionalization of natural science 94; Laboratory of Chemistry 84; metropolitan character 82–83, 86, 93, 96; public education 84; quarrel with director of Museu Paulista 95; Sociedade Vellosiana 94
Museu Paraense Emilio Goeldi (Belém, Brazil) 81, 87–90, 93, 95, 98–99; Emilio Goeldi director 87
Museu Paranaense (Curitiba, Brazil) 81
Museu Paulista (São Paulo, Brazil) 81, 91–93, 95, 99–100; collections go to Universidade de São Paulo 93, 99; Ihering becomes director 91; quarrel with director of Museu Nacional do Rio de Janeiro 95
Museum Diluvianum (Bologna, Italy) 5–6
Muséum National d'Histoire Naturelle de Paris 83–84, 86, 96, 98, 100, 258, 263, 266, 330, 333
Museum of Comparative Zoology, Harvard University (Cambridge, Massachusetts) 1, 98, 112, 249–261, 263, 265–267, 301, 308–310, 313
Museum of Economic Geology (Calcutta, India) 60, 69
Museum of Vertebrate Zoology (University of California, Berkeley) 244, 315, 320
museums (differing views about); colonial 97, 99; exhibits 2, 70, 83, 88, 92, 95–96, 104, 106–107, 115–120, 129, 134, 137, 142, 147, 150, 162–163, 166, 169, 171, 173–175, 177–178, 180, 190–191, 211–212, 243, 249–253, 256–262, 264–265, 267, 269–271, 304, 306, 308, 329–331, 333–334, 336–337; metropolitan 52, 74, 82–83, 86, 93, 96, 203, 230; See also: Goeldi, Emilio August; Ihering, Hermann von; Lacerda, João Batista de; museums and society (Pinna, this volume), and philosophy for (Pinna, this volume)
Myers, George Sprague 68, 71, 202, 246, 288, 320–321

N

Nagasaki (Japan) 173
Nagoya (Japan) 161, 163
Nagpur (India); Central Museum 51
Nanalorycus mysticus 344
Naples (Italy); Zoological Station 273, 284, 292–293
Napoleonic period (and wars) 16, 98
National Institute for the Promotion of the Arts and Sciences 103, 106–107, 113, 119, 123, 128, 169
National Museum in Rio de Janeiro (Brazil); See Museu Nacional do Rio de Janeiro
National Museum of Natural History (Washington, D.C.)(NMNH/USNM) 106, 108–109, 112–127, 133, 138–139, 141–142, 144–145, 149, 151, 153, 156, 158–159, 196, 311; See also United States National Museum
natural history 1–2, 5–6, 9, 11, 13, 16, 34, 41, 47, 51–52, 55, 57, 59, 62, 64, 67, 69–70, 72–73, 75–76, 81–82, 84, 92–93, 98, 100, 102, 104–105, 107–109, 112, 114–115, 119, 121, 123–124, 128, 134, 142, 151, 162–163, 167–169, 171, 173–174, 178–180, 188, 190–191, 196, 208, 213, 225, 228, 237, 242, 251–253, 255, 267, 291, 293, 301, 303, 329–331, 333–335, 348
natural products (natural history collections) 10, 13, 15, 29
Natural selection 40, 47, 62, 225, 289–291, 293–299; See also: Darwinism; evolution
naturalistic cabinets 14

naturalistic museum 5-6, 9-10, 14, 19
Naturphilosophie 39-40, 42, 46-49
neo-Darwinism 294, 299
Neoplatonism 43
Nepal 58, 62
Neri, Pompeo 9, 14, 20, 22
nested units (in classification) 347-348
Netherlands 162
Netto, Ladislau 83-86, 89, 97
Neuman, Robert Ballin 147, 154
New York Times (newspaper) 303, 311
Newell, Norman D. 302, 305-307, 309, 312-313
Newton, Sir Isaac 39, 41, 48
Nicol, David 149
numerology 39, 42
Nuttall, Thomas 107

O

occult metaphysics 41, 43
Oguri, Tadamasa (Japanese Counselor) 161-162, 167; See also Japanese Mission to U.S. (1860)
Oken, Lorenz 39, 42-49
Okinawa (Ryukyu Islands, Japan) 166
Oldham, Thomas 65-67, 69, 75
Oliver, Jr., William Albert 36, 67, 148, 154, 158, 216, 318, 327
Origin of Species 44-45, 48, 62, 108, 123, 256, 289-290, 295
Ormsby, M. H. 66
Ornduff, Robert 245, 317, 324-325
Orto Botanico (Botanical Gardens) of Brera (Milan, Italy) 29
Osaka (Japan) 163
Osborn, Henry Fairfield 302-303, 311-312, 334
Osterhout, W. J. V. 235
ostracods 145-146, 151, 153
Owen, David Dale 103, 129, 184
Owen, Richard 39, 44-46, 49, 103, 129, 184, 251-254, 267; Index Museum 254
Owen, Robert Dale 103, 129, 184

P

P&S; See United States Geological Survey, Paleontology & Stratigraphy Branch
Padian, Kevin 265, 326
Palatine Schools (Milan, Italy) 29
paleobotany 67, 131, 133-135, 138, 142, 144, 147-148, 151, 155
Paleocene mammals 303-304
paleontology (also paleontological) 1-2, 5-6, 10-13, 15-18, 62, 83, 86, 90, 94, 113, 127-128, 131-138, 140, 142, 144, 146, 148, 150-152, 154-158, 173, 209, 252-253, 256-257, 301-305, 307, 312, 330, 333, 350
Paleozoic Era 133-134, 136, 139-140, 142-149, 151-153, 155-156, 306, 351; See also: Bryozoa; Cambrian; Devonian; Mississippian; Pennsylvanian; Permian
Palmer, Allison Ralph 147-148
Pandolfi, John Michael 156
Panmixia 294-296, 298-299
Papenfuss, George A. 324-325
paraphyletic taxa 344, 347, 351
Parish, Samuel Bonsall 219-220, 230, 232, 236

Parker, Peter 116
Parr, Albert 304-308, 312-313
Parry, Charles Christopher 230-232
Patagonia, Argentina 303-304, 312
Patent Office Building (Washington, DC) 103, 106-107, 109, 128, 158, 168-171, 174, 180
Patriotic Society for the Development of Agriculture, Arts and Manufacture; See Società Patriotica per l'incremento dell'Agricoltura, delle Arti e dell Manifatture (Milan, Italy)
Peabody Museum, Yale University (New Haven, Connecticut) 137, 151, 301, 304
Peale, Albert Charles 138
Peale, Charles Willson 107, 171
Peale, Titian Ramsey 106-107
Pedro II, Emperor Don 85
Penna, Domingos Soares Ferreira 87, 96, 98-99; given credit for organizing Museu Paraense 87
Pennsylvanian Period 139, 152
Permian glaciation (India) 65
Perry, Matthew C. (U.S. Naval Commodore) 112, 161, 166, 174-175, 181, 324
Philadelphia Academy of Natural Sciences; See Academy of Natural Sciences of Philadelphia
Philadelphia, Pennsylvania 28, 74, 76, 78-80, 107, 115, 119, 123-124, 129, 134, 175, 181, 184, 191-192, 194, 199, 311, 313
philosopher's stone 41, 44
phylogenetic relationships 344-345
phylogenetic systematics 339, 349
Pierce, George James 154-156, 178, 216, 237-238
Pierce, Jack W. 154
Pini, Ermenegildo 35
plesiomorphic (characters) 342
Pleurodeles 344
Pliocene Epoch 11-12, 17
Poinsett, Joel (U.S. Secretary of War) 105-107, 121
Pojeta, Jr., John 150, 153-154
Polk, James K. (U.S. President) 103
polyphyletic taxa 347
Pondicherry (India) 55
Poore, Richard Z. 153
Powell, Jerry A. 317, 321-322, 324-325
Powell, John Wesley 112-113, 118, 131, 133-134, 137
Precambrian 148, 151
Principles of Sociology 287, 294
Pseudacris 344
pseudoscience 39-41
Punjab (India {now part of Pakistan}) 64, 69, 80
Purpus, Carl Albert 239, 246-247

Q

Quibell, Charles 326
Quinarianism 39-40

R

Rancho Santa Ana Botanical Garden (California) 244
Raniganj (Bengal, India) 60, 64-65; coal fields 60, 65
rank (in biological nomenclature) 72, 118, 131, 135, 139, 148, 193, 200, 202, 224, 327, 339, 341-348; rank equivalence 346-347; taxonomic rank 339, 341, 344, 346-347

INDEX 361

Rathbun, Richard 118, 126
Rau, Charles 118
Ray, Clayton Edward 151, 155
Read, Charles Brian 144
recapitulation, embryonic: See embryonic recapitulation
Reeside, Jr., John Bernard 143–145, 147
Regent Street Polytechnic Institute (London, UK) 103
Renwick, James 103, 121
reptiles 52, 58–59, 62, 64, 67, 70, 72–73, 77, 80, 93, 108–109, 125, 138, 149, 173–174, 249, 264, 302, 304–306, 341
Resser, Charles Elmer 142, 144, 146
Reston, Virginia (U.S. Geological Survey) 151–154, 156
Rezak, Richard 148
Ribeiro, Alipio Miranda 86; challenges Lacerda's view of an "ideal museum" 86
Ricasoli, Bettino (Baron) 18
Ricca, Massimiliano 7, 16–17, 22
Rick, Jr., Charles Madeira 324–326
Riley, Charles V. 118
Ringgold and Rodgers exploration of China Seas and Behring's Straits 112
Rio de Janeiro (Brazil) 81–84, 86–87, 89–91, 93–100, 330; See also Museu Nacional do Rio de Janeiro
Robertson, David 277
Robison, Richard Ashby 151
Rodgers, John (U.S. Naval Captain) 166; lands U.S. marines to enforce treaty 166
Rodolico, Francesco 7
Rodrigues, Barbosa 89–91, 95–96, 99; establishes Museu Botânico do Amazonas in Manaus 90; ethnographic publication on Krichanás causes problems 90–91
Roe, Anne (Mrs. George Gaylord Simpson) 301, 304, 309, 312
Romanes, George 168, 287, 291–293, 298, 300
Romer, Alfred Sherwood 308–309, 313
Roscoff (France) 276
Rovigo (Italy) 277
Roxburgh, William 55–57, 59
Royal Botanic Garden at Sibpur (India) 59
Royal Botanic Gardens in Calcutta (India); See Calcutta (India)
Royal College of Surgeons (London), Museum of 258, 263, 298
Royal Society of London 27, 29, 101, 308, 350
Rumphius, Georg Eberhard 55
Rupert, Earleen Atchison 323
Rush, Richard 102–103, 105, 183, 202–203, 207, 221, 245
Russell, Harry Luman 279
Russell, Patrick 60–61, 77–78, 279
Russia 46, 49, 51, 97, 112, 115, 179, 204, 275–277
Ruthven, Alexander 123, 304

S

São Paulo (Brazil) 81, 91, 93, 95, 98–100
Sacramento, California 188, 208, 210–212, 223, 228
Salt Ranges (Punjab, India {now Pakistan}) 64
Salvatore, Gaetano 283
samurai 161, 167, 174
San Casciano (Italy) 13, 20
San Diego Natural History Museum (San Diego, California) 244
San Francisco, California 1, 25, 37, 39, 49, 51, 80, 100, 126, 159, 161, 182–188, 190, 192–194, 196, 200, 202–204, 206, 208, 210–213, 218–221, 223, 226–229, 231, 233, 235–237, 242–248, 271, 273, 285, 300, 313, 315, 321, 327, 331–332, 337, 351
Sando, William Jasper 147, 154
Sano, Kanae 167, 173–175, 179, 181
São Paulo Geographical and Geological Commission; See Derby, Orville Adelbert; See also: Ihering, Hermann von; Museu Paulista
Sarich, Vincent M. 318
Sato, Hidenaga 167, 173–174, 179, 181
Sauer, C. O. 321
Scarritt, Horace 303, 312
Schaeffer, Bobb 302, 306–307, 309, 312
Schlinger, Evert I. 325
Schopf, James Morton 147
Schuchert, Charles 127, 137–139
scientific naturalism 94
Scientific societies in: Berlin (Germany) 33; Bologna (Italy) 5–7, 19–23, 35–37, 332, 337; Brunn (formerly part of Austria, now Czech Republic) 31, 34, 37; Copenhagen (Denmark) 28; Erfurt (Germany) 32–33; Göttingen (Germany) 31; Görz (also Gorizia) (Italy) 31, 34; Graz (Austria) 31, 34, 283; Innsbruck (Austria) 31, 34; Klagenfurt (Austria) 31, 36; Laibach (Ljubljana) (Slovenia) 31, 34; Linz (Austria) 31; London (England, UK) 27, 29, 101, 308, 350; Mantua (Italy) 28–29; Milan (Italy) 28–29, 34–37; Munich ({München} Germany) 31, 34; Paris (France) 27, 33–34; Pavia (Italy) 27, 29–30, 36; Petersburg ({now St. Petersburg} Russia) 28; Uppsala (Sweden) 27, 55, 267; Vienna ({Wien} Austria) 34
Sclater, William Lutley 73, 267
Scopoli, Giovanni Antonio 29–30
Scripps Institution of Oceanography (La Jolla, California) 143, 195, 199
Scudder, Samuel Hubbard 137, 270
Selvani, Emidio 9, 17–18
Senese (adj., referring to Siena) 7–15, 18, 20–21
Serini, Francesco Valenti 18
Serrão, Custódio Alves 84, 94
Setchell, William Albert 202, 218, 221–224, 226, 234–236, 238–241, 243–244
Seven Years' War, impact on scientific societies 33–34
Sherman, William Tecumseh (U.S. General) 116, 124, 184
Shimmi, Masaoki (Japanese Ambassador) 161–162, 167; See also Japanese Mission to U.S. (1860)
Siena (Tuscany, Italy) 5–25, 80
Silberling, Norman John 151
Simpson, George Gaylord 2, 301–313, 319, 343; Agassiz Professorship at Harvard University 308–309; begins Patagonian field work 303; Brazilian expedition 1956, suffers injury 307; Department of Geosciences, University of Arizona 310; employed by American Museum of Natural History 302; military service 305; moves to Tucson, Arizona 309
Simpson, Martha (sister of George Gaylord Simpson) 308
Singh, Kishan 69
Singh, Ram 69
Siwalik Hills 62
Sliter, William V. 153
Smedley, Jack Elwood 146
Smith, Rosa 194–195, 202
Smithson, Hugh 101

Smithson, James 101–106, 109, 113–114, 122–123, 128, 168, 190, 199
Smithsonian Institution 1, 61, 73, 75, 78, 89, 91, 98–99, 101–137, 140–141, 145, 151, 158–159, 161–162, 166–173, 175–176, 178–181, 183–194, 196, 199–200, 202, 208, 254, 267, 325; Castle building 112–116, 129–131, 134, 140–141, 168–169; Congressional appropriations 107, 114–115, 199; Exhibitions and Expositions 119; fire in 1865 114; Hirshhorn Gallery 121, 134, 138; See also United States National Museum
Snethlage, Maria Emilia 88–89, 95
Sociedade Philomática do Pará (Brazil) 87
Sociedade Vellosiana (at the Museu Nacional do Rio de Janeiro) 94
Società Patriotica per l'incremento dell'Agricoltura, delle Arti e dell Manifatture (Milan, Italy) 28–29, 34–37
Societas Regia Scientiarum (Berlin, Prussia) 32
Society for the Study of Evolution 305, 319
Society of Vertebrate Paleontology 305
Sohl, Norman F. 147, 149–150, 152–153, 156
Sohn, Israel Gregory 146, 285
Soldani, Ambrogio 14–18, 21–22
Sonnerat, Pierre 55
Southern California Biosystematists 320
Spallanzani, Lazzaro 29–30, 35–37
species; See geometric series; See also metaspecies
Spencer, Herbert 2, 73, 98, 101, 107–108, 119–120, 123–126, 128–129, 159, 169, 181, 186–188, 191, 199–201, 287–291, 293–299; See also *First Principles*
Spieth, Harman Theodore 323, 325
Springer, Frank 139, 284–285, 349
St. Alexander's Mineralogical Museum (Milan, Italy) 29
St. John, Oliver (British Army, Major) 67
Stanford University (Stanford, California) 203, 237–238, 240–241, 247, 317, 319, 323, 327
Stanford, Leland 190, 192, 214, 216, 237–239, 245–246
Stanley, Daniel Jean 155
Stanley, John Mix 113–114
Stanton, Timothy William 133, 135–136
state-supported institutions 6
Stearns, Robert Edwards Carter 118, 188–190, 193–194, 201–202
Stebbins, Jr., George Ledyard 315, 319–325, 327
Steele, Kelly 143, 326
Stejneger, Leonhard 118, 196, 202
Stephenson, Lloyd William 143–144
Stevens, Nettie 280
Stimpson, William 109, 112, 115
Stockwell, P. 321
Stoliczka, Ferdinand 65–70, 77, 80; Second Yarkand Mission to Kashgar 67, 69, 77
Suksdorf, W. N. 236
superspecific taxa 339, 343–344, 348, 351
Surat (India) 53
Symbion pandora 344
Symonds, John 14

T

Tables (Naples Zoological Station) 279; American Women's 279
Talchir coal fields (Orissa, India) 65, 69
Tamamushi, Sadayn 167–168, 171, 174–175, 179–181; See also Japanese Mission to U.S. (1860)

Taraxacum 341
Tarduzzi, G. 18
Taylor, Dwight Willard 148
Taylor, Michael E. 151, 201
Tertiary Period 62, 67, 150, 155, 255–256, 303
Thayer Expedition; See Agassiz, Louis; See also Museu Paraense Emilio Goeldi
Theobald, William 65–66, 68–70, 73
Theodore, Charles 34
Thomas, John Hunter 317, 323, 325
Thunberg, Carl Pehr 55
Tibet 62, 67
Todd, Ruth 147
Tokugawa Shogunate 161, 166
Toland Medical College (San Francisco, California) 220
Torrey, John 204–205, 215–216
Towe, Kenneth M. 151
Tozzetti, Giovanni Targioni 10, 14
Triassic Period 151
trilobites 140, 144, 147, 151
Trivandrum (India); Government (Napier) Museum 51
True, Frederick William 118, 124
Tuscan (Italy) naturalists 7, 10, 13
Tween, Ambrose 66
Tyrrhenian Sea 13

U

Ulrich, Edward Oscar 136, 139, 143
United Brothers (society) at Tranquebar (India) 55
United States Army Medical Museum 114
United States Coast Survey 103, 131, 227
United States Department of Agriculture 114, 196, 218
United States Exploring Expedition; scandal relating to its collections 129
United States Fish Commission 119–120, 126, 201
United States Geological Survey 59–60, 64–67, 69, 75–79, 86, 113, 120, 127, 131, 133–140, 142–158, 188, 203, 208, 210–213, 215, 217–218, 237; Alaskan Branch 150; Organic Act (founding of the Survey) 134, 213, 218–220; Paleontology & Stratigraphy Branch (P&S) 135, 143–157; See also Hall of Silent Men in the USNM
United States National Museum 98, 101, 105, 114–118, 120–127, 129–131, 133–139, 142–144, 146, 148–149, 151–153, 158, 254; See also National Museum of Natural History
United States Naval Surveys; Astronomical Expedition to Chile 112; survey of the La Plata River 112
United States Territorial Surveys of the West 127, 130–131, 135, 235
Universidade de São Paulo 93, 99
University Herbarium; See University of California, University Herbarium; See also Brandegee Herbarium
University of Arizona (Tucson) 310
University of California (Berkeley) 21, 36, 48, 75, 156, 159, 189, 194, 199, 201, 203, 205, 208, 212–213, 215–216, 218, 222–223, 232–241, 244–247, 284, 301–302, 311, 315, 321, 324; University Herbarium 208, 218, 222–223, 233–236, 239–241; See also Brandegee Herbarium
University of Michigan (Ann Arbor) 304
University of Notre Dame (South Bend, Indiana) 234
University of Pavia (Italy) 29–30
University of Siena (Italy) 6, 8–9, 12, 14, 17–19
University of Tübingen (Germany) 267, 303

Uppsala (Sweden) 27, 55, 267
Uroboros (symbol) 43–44
Urschleim 43, 46
Usinger, Robert L. 319–320, 322, 324–325, 327
USNM; See United States National Museum

V

Van Buren, Martin (U.S. President) 102
Vaughan, Thomas Wayland 143
Vellosia (publication) 90, 94, 98, 100
Vitman, Fulgenzio 29–30
Vivrette (Haller), Nancy 317, 323–325, 327
Vogt, Carl 276–277, 284
Volta, Alessandro 14, 35

W

Waagen, Wilhelm 66, 80
Wake, David B. 318
Wake, Marvalee 323
Walcott, Charles Doolittle 118, 131–133, 135–140, 142, 155, 159
Wall, Dennis 326
Wallace, Alfred Russell 251–257 261, 264–265, 293–294, 299
Waller, Thomas Richard 151
Wallich, Nathaniel 59, 61, 79
War of 1812 102
Ward, Lauke 150
Ward, Lester Frank 118; 131, 133–134, 150, 190
Washington, George (U.S. President) 102, 106, 113, 178
Watson, Sereno 40, 72, 216, 218, 222, 237, 246
Webb, William (East India Company, Captain) 64–65, 299
Weismann, August 287, 291–296, 298–300
Weltorganismus 43, 46
Werner, Abraham Gottlob 82
Western Union Telegraph Expedition (1865) 115
Wheeler, George Montague (U.S. Army Lieutenant) 112, 131
White, Charles Abiathar 118, 131–132
White, Charles David 133, 135, 142
Whitmore, Frank Clifford 148, 153–154
Whitney, Elizabeth 208
Whitney, Josiah Dwight 138, 188–189, 203, 208–216, 218, 232, 245
Wiggins, Ira Loren 318–325
Wilkes, Charles (U.S. Naval Lieutenant) 105, 124, 128–129, 168; See also U.S. Exploring Expedition
Wilkins, Sir Charles 60
Williams, David Hiram 65

Williams, Ernest 309
Williams, Henry Shaler 137
Williams, James Steele 143
Willson, Walter Lindsay 66, 107, 171, 203, 227
Wilson, Allan C. 318
Wing, Scott Lewis 155
Wojciechowski, Marty 326–327
Wolfe, Jack Albert 148
women in science; allowed access to higher education in Brazil in 1880s 85; American Women's Table, Naples Zoological Station 16, 59, 91, 109, 131, 171, 185, 215, 279; gender barrier, San Francisco area Biosystematists 322–323; See also: Behrensmeyer, Anna Kay; Berdan, Jean Milton; Bradbury, Margaret; Brandegee, Mary Katharine (Curran); Bybell, Laurel Mary; Curran (Brandegee), Mary Katharine Layne; Duncan, Helen Margaret; Eastwood, Alice; Eigenmann, Rosa Smith; Ertter, Barbara; Gardner, Julia Anna; Harris, Anita Gertrude; Hough, Margaret Jean; Low, Doris; McClintock, Elizabeth B.; Moore, Ellen James; Roe, Anne (Mrs. George G. Simpson); Smith (Eigenmann), Rosa; Snethlage, Maria Emilia; Stevens, Nettie; Todd, Ruth; Vivrette (Haller), Nancy
Woodring, Wendell Phillips 143–144
Woods Hole (Massachusetts) 119, 281, 285

X

X-club 291
Ximenes, Leonardo 14

Y

Yakuhin'e exhibitions 162–164, 171, 173, 175
Yale University (New Haven, Connecticut) 49, 78, 133, 137–138, 246, 267, 301, 305, 311, 351; See also Peabody Museum
Yanagawa, Masakiyo 167, 171, 175, 178, 181
Yatrow, Henry C. 118
Yeates, W. S. 118
Yochelson, Ellis Leon 147
Yosemite National Park (California) 211, 214, 236

Z

Zoe 200, 233, 235–237, 239–241, 245–246
Zoological Station at Naples (Italy); See Naples, Zoological Station
Zoological Survey of India 69, 73, 76